Russia, Ukraine, and the
Breakup of the Soviet Union

Pro-independence demonstration in Kyiv, October 1990

Russia, Ukraine, and the Breakup of the Soviet Union

Roman Szporluk

HOOVER INSTITUTION PRESS
Stanford University
Stanford, California

www.hoover.org

Hoover Institution Press Publication No. 446

First printing, 2000

Manufactured in the United States of America

05   04   03   02   01   00   9   8   7   6   5   4   3   2   1

The paper used in this publication meets the minimum requirements of American National Standard for Information Sciences—Permanence of Paper for Printed Library Materials, ANSI Z39.48-1984.

Front cover photo and frontispiece: © 1990 Victor Maruschenko. Used with permission.

Library of Congress Cataloging-in-Publication Data

Szporluk, Roman.
Russia, Ukraine, and the breakup of the Soviet Union / Roman Szporluk.
    p.   cm.
Includes bibliographical references and index.
ISBN 0-8179-9542-0
    1. Russia (Federation)—Relations—Ukraine.   2. Ukraine—Relations—Russia (Federation)   3. Nationalism—Russia (Federation)   4. Nationalism—Ukraine.   5. Ukraine—History—1944–1991.   6. Ukraine—History—1991–   7. Soviet Union—History—1953–1985.   8. Soviet Union—History—1985–1991.   9. Russia (Federation)—History—1991–   I. Title: Russia, Ukraine, and the break-up of the Soviet Union.   II. Title.
DK67.5.U38 S98   2000   99-050309

For my grandchildren,
Marco and Sofia

Contents

Foreword

The nationalities question in the former Soviet Union (FSU) bedeviled Soviet policymakers and continues to trouble post-Soviet authorities and scholars alike, even after the dissolution of the Soviet state. Russia, Ukraine, and other former Soviet republics remain multinational states, subject to interethnic tensions and secessionist tendencies. The recent situation in Chechnya shows that the FSU is still subject to fragmentation along national lines and underscores the urgent need to understand these incendiary issues.

Roman Szporluk, a well-known authority on Eastern Europe, Russia, and Ukraine, has grappled for years with the questions of Sovietization, Russification, and the rise of nationalism in the Soviet Union and the adjacent world. This volume, a selection of Professor Szporluk's essays published between 1972 and 1997, tells a story crucial to understanding the dissolution of the Soviet Union and the emergence of its fifteen successor states. Szporluk examines the historical relationship of Ukraine and Russia and the parallel processes of nation building before and during the Soviet period. These nascent nationalisms not only affected Ukrainian-Russian relations but ultimately played a pivotal role in the disintegration of the Soviet Union. Most challenging to conventional interpretations of the Soviet empire's demise, however, is Szporluk's emphasis on the role played by Eastern Europe and the "Soviet West" (Western Ukraine, Western Belarus, and the Baltics).

In order to understand the national question in the Soviet Union, one must recur to the tsarist era and imperial Russia's relations with both its minority populations and its "colonial" territories. According to Szporluk, precisely tsarist—and later, Soviet—Russia's successful imperial expansion undermined Russia's own attempts at nation building. The tsarist regime remained purblind to the difficulties of incorporating territories and peoples that were alien to Russian cultural traditions, and the Soviet regime inherited its obtuseness. Moreover, the Soviet regime, blinkered by internationalist ideology, never came to grips with the nationalities question that their successful territorial acquisitions posed. In fact, the new Bolshevik regime's division of the Soviet state into administrative units based on ethnicity (and with the constitutional right to secede!) was a time bomb implanted in the foundation of the Soviet state. As Szporluk observes, however, it was the Soviet Union's greatest triumph of legitimation—its World War II victory—that instigated its gradual decline. The postwar regime, like its predecessors, was ill-equipped to successfully integrate the newly annexed territories of West Ukraine, West Belarus, and the Baltics. Subsequently, these areas would become hotbeds of national dissent, susceptible to "ideological contagion" by their East European neighbors.

Szporluk addresses the challenges posed to Soviet ideological integrity by its incorporation of these western territories. Communist Party ideology held that the adoption of the Soviet system (Soviet vs. Western-style modernization) by national republics was the road to modernity and prosperity. Szporluk sees a dialectical relationship established between Russianness and communism in Stalin's Russification policy: The success of Russification would impel the success of the Soviet project, and successful economic and social modernization (Sovietization) would foster Russification.

The inclusion of the Baltics and West Ukraine in the Soviet Union in the wake of World War II, and the incorporation of Eastern Europe under the Warsaw Pact umbrella, allowed Soviet citizens to experience the disjuncture between ideological claims and reality. The legitimacy and stability of the Soviet Union required complete isolation, not only from the capitalist West, but from more advanced Eastern European nations that would provide Soviet citizens with a basis of comparison on which to judge the merits of their own system. In short order, the Baltics were acknowledged as Russia's "own abroad," and Balts evinced the greatest resistance to Sovietization and concomitant Russification. The Baltic republics strategically refrained from questioning the superiority of Soviet communism to capitalism and instead championed the preservation of their national distinctiveness. However, the implicit assertion that the road to modernity may be attained through nation building, rather than Soviet internationalism, paved the way for the emergence of explicit nationalisms and nationalist critiques of the Soviet system in Russia as well as in the other union republics.

Ultimately, peaceful dissolution of the Soviet Union would not have occurred if Russia had not embraced its own brand of nationalism. Suppressed in deference to Soviet and internationalist ideology, nationalist sentiments began to manifest themselves in anti-Soviet and anticommunist critiques by dissident intellectuals, as well as in the literary works known as "Village Prose" during the 1970s. Russian nationalism was already full blown when Boris Yeltsin played the national card in 1991. The great irony, as Szporluk and others have noted, is that Russification pursued with such vigor from the 1960s to the 1980s alienated non-Russians from the Soviet project without securing Russian devotion to the Soviet system or preempting the emergence of Russian nationalism.

In his early essays, Szporluk examines the tensions of Russification and Soviet internationalism with reference to Ukraine. Szporluk illuminates the way in which the Ukrainian question posed a unique challenge to Russians' self-definition. Before 1917, the Russians perceived the Ukrainians in terms of familial metaphors—as "little brothers," distinct but akin and, most important, subordinate. When the Bolsheviks assumed power, they sought to win Ukrainian allegiance by endowing the Ukrainian SSR with the trappings of administrative and ethnic sovereignty. Stalinist Russification policies and political purges, however, exposed these trappings as so much window dressing. After the postwar unification of West and East Ukraine, regional diversity added a further twist to the Ukrainian question. How would West Ukraine's different historical experience affect intra-Ukrainian intergration and, ultimately, Ukrainian-Russian relations? In the wake of the Soviet Union's precipitate collapse, would Ukraine split into West and East, as many augured? Would the Ukrainian language, long displaced by Russian, serve as the lingua franca and basis of national unity? Would the old Soviet elite foster or impede the transition to Ukrainian national statehood? And, finally, would national statehood become the basis of a reformed polity or a reactionary stronghold?

Roman Szporluk approaches the intriguing questions he poses in various ways. In order to assess the viability of the Russification of the vast and multiethnic Soviet state, he compares census data from 1959 and 1970. Would urban centers in the union republics have the critical mass of ethnic Russians and Russian speakers necessary to clinch Russification? Would Donetsk—the exemplar of Sovietization in the heart of Ukraine—become the primary urban center, the "future," as it were, of Ukraine? Szporluk also reviews the expressed attitudes of non-Russian speakers toward Russian-language usage. What positive effects ought exposure to and use of the Russian language have, according to the members of other Soviet ethnicities? Szporluk then considers the official stance: Did Soviet leaders act as if they believed that social and economic modernization would encourage assimilation? What administrative measures did the party adopt in order to effect linguistic assimilation?

This volume is the fruit of Szporluk's many years of assiduous research and expertise. He was particularly qualified to undertake this study. His intellectually formative years were spent in Poland, where he did his secondary and college education and began his graduate studies. He completed his graduate work at Oxford and Stanford. This accounts for the objectivity and insight with which he approaches the mixed Polish, Ukrainian, and Western political and intellectual milieu.

Between east and west, Ukraine has been frequently overlooked in studies of Eastern Europe and the Soviet Union. I concur with the author's contention that no national history should be studied in isolation from the larger historical context: Ukraine must be thoroughly integrated into the history of the Soviet Union and that of non-Soviet Eastern Europe, just as the history of the Soviet Union cannot be understood independently of Eastern—or Western—Europe. Professor Szporluk has substantially enriched Ukrainian and post-Soviet studies with his depth of analysis and historical and geographical breadth. Needless to say, the prescience of his conclusions is all the more striking in retrospect.

Wayne S. Vucinich
Mcdonnel Professor Emeritus
History Department
Stanford University

Acknowledgments

This book owes its existence first of all to my wife, Mary Ann Szporluk, whose idea it was in the first place, and who has worked on it at all stages of its preparation. Others to whom I owe thanks include my assistants, Kirsten Lodge Borovik, Albert Diversé, and Alina Motienko; their work was supported by the Ukrainian Research Institute, Harvard University. I am also grateful to Ksenya Kiebuzinski, librarian-archivist of the institute, for help with checking sources, and to my son, Ben Szporluk, for his considerable work on the preparation of the texts.

Patricia A. Baker, executive editor of Hoover Institution Press, has supported this project from the beginning. I am very grateful to her and to my editor at the Press, Ann Wood.

I am grateful to all the following publishers for giving me permission to reprint my articles in this volume. While working on this volume, I remembered vividly how much I owe, not only to the editors themselves, some of whom invited me to contribute to their journals and books, but also to my colleagues and students who commented on various drafts and discussed the ideas presented at conferences and seminars.

Chapter 1. "Nationalities and the Russian Problem in the USSR: A Historical Outline." First published in *Journal of International Affairs*

27, no. 1 (1973): 22–40. Reprinted by permission of the *Journal of International Affairs* and of the Trustees of Columbia University in the City of New York.

Chapter 2. "The Nations of the USSR in 1970." First published in *Survey* 17, no. 4 (1971): 67–100. Reprinted by permission of *Survey* and the London School of Economics and Political Science Publication Division.

Chapter 3. "Russians in Ukraine and Problems of Ukrainian Identity in the USSR." First published in *Ukraine in the Seventies*, ed. Peter J. Potichnyj (Oakville, Ont.: Mosaic Press, 1975), pp. 195–217.

Chapter 4. "West Ukraine and West Belorussia: Historical Tradition, Social Communication, and Linguistic Assimilation." First published in *Soviet Studies* 31, no. 1 (January 1979): 76–98. Reprinted by permission of *Soviet Studies* (now *Europe-Asia Studies*) and Carfax Publishing Ltd., PO Box 25, Abingdon, Oxfordshire OX143UE, UK.

Chapter 5. "Urbanization in Ukraine since the Second World War." First published in *Rethinking Ukrainian History*, ed. Ivan L. Rudnytsky (Edmonton, Alberta: Canadian Institute of Ukrainian Studies, 1981), pp. 180–202. Reprinted by permission.

Chapter 6. "History and Russian Nationalism." First published in *Survey* 24, no. 3 (108) (Summer 1979): 1–17. Reprinted by permission of *Survey* and the London School of Economics and Political Science Publication Division.

Chapter 7. "Dilemmas of Russian Nationalism." First published in *Problems of Communism* (July–August 1989): 15–35. Reprinted by permission of *Problems of Communism*.

Chapter 8. "The Imperial Legacy and the Soviet Nationalities Problem." Approximately 23 pages from *The Nationalities Factor in Soviet Politics and Society,* ed. Lubomyr Hajda and Mark Beissinger. Copyright © 1990 by Westview Press. Reprinted by permission of Westview Press.

Chapter 9. "The Soviet West—or Far Eastern Europe?" © 1991/90 by the American Council of Learned Societies. Reprinted from *East European Politics and Societies* 5, no. 3 (Fall 1991): 466–82, by permission.

Chapter 10. "The Press and Soviet Nationalities: The Party Resolution of 1975 and Its Implementation." First published in *Nationalities Papers* 14, nos. 1–2 (Spring–Fall 1986): 47–64. Reprinted by permission.

Chapter 11. "The Strange Politics of Lviv: An Essay in Search of an Explanation." First published in *The Politics of Nationality and the Erosion of the USSR*, Zvi Gitelman, ed. (New York: St. Martin's Press, 1992), pp. 215–31. Copyright © Zvi Gitelman, ed. From *The Politics of Nationality and the Erosion of the USSR*, Zvi Gitelman, ed. Reprinted with permission of St. Martin's Press, Inc. (North America only) and Macmillan Press Ltd.

Chapter 12. "Nation-Building in Ukraine: Problems and Prospects." First published in *The Successor States to the USSR*, John W. Blaney, ed. (Washington, D.C.: Congressional Quarterly, 1995), pp. 173–83. Reprinted with the permission of Congressional Quarterly Books.

Chapter 13. "Reflections on Ukraine after 1994: The Dilemmas of Nationhood." First published in *The Harriman Review* 7, nos. 7–9 (March–May 1994): 1–9. Reprinted by permission of *The Harriman Review*.

Chapter 14. "After Empire: What?" reprinted by permission of *Daedalus*, Journal of the American Academy of Arts and Sciences, from the issue entitled "After Communism: What?" 123, no. 3 (Summer 1994).

Chapter 15. "Ukraine: From an Imperial Periphery to a Sovereign State," reprinted by permission from *Daedalus*, Journal of the American Academy of Arts and Sciences, from the issue entitled "A New Europe for the Old?" 126, no. 3 (Summer 1997).

Chapter 16. "The Fall of the Tsarist Empire and the USSR: The Russian Question and Imperial Overextension." First published in *The End of Empire?* Karen Dawisha and Bruce Parrott, eds. (Armonk, N.Y., and London: M. E. Sharpe, 1997), pp. 65–93. Reprinted by permission of M. E. Sharpe.

A Note on Transliteration

In transliterating Russian and Ukrainian words and names in the notes, I have used the Library of Congress system. A modified form of names and places has been used in the text in order to facilitate readability or in cases where the name is commonly spelled that way in English. Thus, we find Mykhailo Hrushevsky in the text, but Hrushevs'kyi in the notes. The capital of Ukraine, Kyiv, has been consistently written in this new form except in quotations that use the older spelling, Kiev.

Introduction

The breakup of the Soviet Union in 1991 and the emergence of Russia and Ukraine and other independent states as its successors is the subject of many scholarly studies, as is the 1989 collapse of communist regimes in East Central Europe. With the passage of time, more and more facts become known and new explanations and interpretations of the events are proposed and debated. A new generation of specialists has emerged—the first post-Soviet one—to join those who were writing on Soviet and East European affairs before the 1989 and 1991 events.

Russia, Ukraine, and the Breakup of the Soviet Union is different from most other works on this subject in two respects. First, it has a special thematic focus. The common theme of this book is Ukraine and Russia and their relationship, which is treated as a potential and then actual threat to the Soviet state. It is not a comprehensive study of all or even the main causes or circumstances that brought about the fall of the Soviet Union. Instead, the book pursues several select problems, which in the author's opinion needed to be explored and elucidated but which by themselves, to repeat, do not provide a complete answer to the larger questions: "Why did the Soviet Union break up and why did an independent Russia and an independent Ukraine arise in its place?"

Second, this book has a unique history: Its chapters were written in succession over a period close to thirty years. Thus, in a way, this is a chronicle of, and running commentary on, the final two decades of the Soviet Union and the immediate post-Soviet years. These "commentaries" are mainly presented in the chronological order of publication, from the early 1970s to the late 1990s.[1] They have not been rewritten or updated for this publication—the only changes are minor stylistic ones. (In a few chapters, the statistical data, which were assembled by an amateur to begin with, are presented in a somewhat simplified but still not very scientific form.)

The book may thus be read as a record of one scholar's efforts, over a period of years, to understand the development of the Soviet Union which, as time went by, began to appear as its decline and then fall. In the early 1970s the author had not expected to live long enough to see the dissolution of the Soviet Union, let alone did he imagine how it would actually come about. In the end Russia and Ukraine played a crucial role.

Soviet Modernity versus Ethnicity

Even though they were written nearly thirty years ago, taken together chapters 1 and 2 may be read as an introduction to the main themes of this book. Chapter 1, "Nationalities and the Russian Problem in the USSR: A Historical Outline, " written in 1972, and first published in 1973, identifies the "problem areas"—areas of the Soviet state's vulnerability—that would become manifest only in the following years. It provides an outline of Soviet history, in particular of the nationalities policies, from the revolution of 1917 to the late 1960s and early 1970s as a background for a better understanding of the problems the Soviet Union was facing in the 1970s. I cite a long passage from *The Formation of the Soviet Union* in which Richard Pipes reflects on the potential long-term impact of the decision made in 1922 to subdivide what was supposed to be the prototype of a new international communist society into political and administrative units based on ethnicity. Pipes concluded:

> In view of the importance which language and territory have for the development of national consciousness—particularly for people who,

like the Russian minorities during the Revolution, have had some experience of self-rule—this purely formal feature of the Soviet Constitution
may well prove to have been historically one of the most consequential
aspects of the formation of the Soviet Union.[2]

Now, decades after Pipes wrote these words, one is tempted to add
that this formal feature of the Soviet constitution, because it granted the
Union republics the right freely to secede from the USSR, has also been
one of the most consequential aspects of the *dissolution* of the Soviet
Union. Moreover, we can see now, when the Soviet Union is history,
that the 1922 decision was fateful also because it related the communist
project and the Soviet state to the *Russian* nation by creating an arrangement that was to remain a source of tension and confusion until the very
end of the USSR.

Under this "internationalist" provision, Russia was theoretically
equal to Ukraine, Belarus, and the other Union republics. Then, during
the 1930s, without abrogating the formal provisions of the constitution,
Stalin decided that the new Soviet civilization was to have Russian as its
common language, and that Russian culture, even though it was carefully purged and supervised, was to enjoy a superior status within the
larger body of Soviet culture. (*Inside* the Soviet Union nobody called
the latter Russian—but abroad almost everybody treated "Soviet" as
a synonym, or a pseudonym, of "Russian," whether in politics or in
culture.)

In the West, during the 1960s, and for many years later, the Soviet
Union was generally perceived as a successful case of modernization.
Influential currents in Sovietology viewed the USSR as a modernizing,
indeed in many respects an already modern, country. Its social and economic and political system, while different from that in the West, was
viewed as another specimen of the same general phenomenon—modern
industrial society. (Some authors were even predicting the eventual
"convergence" of two systems, Western capitalist and Eastern socialist.)
In that "modernization" framework there was no room for serious consideration of the nationalities problem—and even less for reflection on
tensions between the Soviet system and the Russian nation.[3]

If the Soviet program of modernization, of building a powerful new
civilization, was so closely identified with Russia and its culture, what
were the implications of this for the sphere of inter-ethnic, in particular
Russian–non-Russian, relations within the USSR? The Soviet leadership

expected that progress in socialist construction would encourage the non-Russians to speak Russian and to adopt Russian culture as the culture of socialism, and that this assimilation to Russian in turn would further stimulate the building of socialism and communism. Khrushchev articulated this belief in 1959, when he said communism would come sooner if everybody spoke Russian. But there was another side to this communism/Russia nexus: If the communist project were to prove a failure at a time before everybody in the USSR had become Russified, the consequent disappointment of the non-Russians might take not only an anticommunist but also an anti-Russian form.

Was the Soviet system really a modernizing project, however? Was it successful? And, in any case, was modernity necessarily inseparable from Russianness, which was what Moscow wanted the citizens of the USSR to believe was the case? In a collective volume edited by Edward Allworth (1971), Zbigniew Brzezinski hypothesized that Russians prevailed among the "the engineers, technicians, scientists"—in other words "the modernizing elite"—while the "intellectuals, the humanists, the pseudo-intellectuals" tended to be spokesmen for the non-Russians. In a review of the Allworth volume, published in 1972, I referred to a new Soviet study's unexpected finding: Urbanization, that is, an aspect of modernization, did not make non-Russians give up their national identity for Russian. Non-Russian "ethnoses" were surviving, indeed thriving, in the city.[4]

Such an admission justified taking a look at the other side of the coin: Were the non-Russians willing to accept the Soviet system, in its Russian linguistic and cultural form, as their road to modernity? And was the Soviet formula—combining economic development with Russian linguistic dominance—sustainable demographically?

To answer the last question, chapter 2, "The Nations of the USSR in 1970," reviewed the returns of the 1970 census, region by region, republic by republic. The aim of this exercise was to see whether there was enough human mass to secure demographically the presence (and dominance) of a sufficient number of Russians or Russian-speaking non-Russians throughout the entire territory of the USSR. If Russians or Russian-speakers were the best specimen of the Soviet people, and if the march toward communism was measured by an increasing use of Russian in the public sphere, the census was an event of major ideological and political importance: It allowed scholars (and policymakers) to measure—to quantify—the progress to communism.

This article compares the 1970 data with those of 1959, the first post-war census. The 1959 census had been interpreted by the authorities and official academic circles as a demonstration of an accelerating assimilation of non-Russians to the Russian language and in the longer run also to Russian national identity. However, it appeared that as of 1970 the Russians and their assimilated allies were not growing fast enough to create a demographic basis for a Russian-speaking Soviet Union. There were signs at the time that the Soviet academic establishment was beginning to doubt that socio-economic factors alone would integrate the Soviet people without new active state measures to promote the Russian language. The article identified a researcher who claimed to have discovered that reading Soviet newspapers in Russian rather than in Ukrainian made one a better Soviet person. Some scholars and policymakers seemed to conclude, in a rather un-Marxian way, that the (Russian) medium was the (socialist) message.

Several years after chapters 1 and 2 were written, Moscow took additional measures in the area of language policy. They are discussed in chapter 10, "The Press and Soviet Nationalities: The Party Resolution of 1975 and Its Implementation." Since this article was published in 1986, its mention here may seem a digression from the argument, but this is not the case. The evidence collected shows the Soviet leadership's growing determination in the 1970s to promote Russian by administrative measures; in its view, being a good Soviet person was demonstrated by a preference for the Russian language over one's native tongue. (Little did the Soviet leaders expect in the 1970s and early 1980s that by the second half of the 1980s the Russian-language Moscow-based press might be more "subversive" than the press originating in the republics. This happened under Gorbachev, during the glasnost period, when the most anti-Soviet ideas were to be found in Moscow papers.)

It is now easy to see that those language-policy moves came too late (if they could ever have worked)—and were also misguided. They alienated the "ethnics" but did not win the gratitude of those anticommunist Russian nationalists who were not prepared to accept the Soviet regime as a Russian national institution in return for its promotion of Russification. In the early 1970s, though, these problems were not yet clearly discernible. At that time it was also possible to view Soviet domestic developments as a self-contained process. Little thought was given to any external influences on Soviet domestic processes, including the nationalities sphere.

The International Setting:
The Soviet System and
Territorial Expansion after 1939

The Soviet Union's territorial gains of 1939 to 1945 and the coming to power of Communists in East Central Europe were a partial realization of Lenin's grand hopes of 1919–20.[5] Twenty years later than originally planned, the first socialist state at last broke out from its capitalist confinement; there was no longer "socialism in one country." The official Soviet interpretation of what happened in Eastern Europe and the newly annexed Soviet regions was that newcomers to socialism were following the example of the more advanced Soviet society. But, paradoxically, this was not the case as far as the perceptions of the East Europeans were concerned—and in due course some people in the USSR arrived at the same conclusion. In the end, the situation after 1945 confirmed, in an ironic twist (because Russia had twenty years of socialism behind it), what Lenin had predicted in 1919: "After the victory of the proletarian revolution in at least one of the advanced nations . . . Russia will cease to be the model country and will again become (. . . in the socialist sense) a backward country."[6]

Stalin and his successors understood that Lenin's prediction was in fact confirmed after World War II, and they tried to keep Soviet citizens isolated from socialist countries of Eastern Europe. If it had been possible for Moscow to isolate the Soviet Union's domestic affairs, including its ethnic problems, within the borders of the USSR, there might have been a successful fusion of Sovietism and (communist-controlled) Russianness. To a population kept in isolation from the rest of the world, a Sovietized Russia might have looked like a model of modernity and progress. This, in turn, might have promoted the acculturation and assimilation of the non-Russians. But the events of 1939 to 1945 created conditions that were capable of subverting this model. The seeds of the Soviet Union's decline were thus planted at the moment of the Soviet Union's greatest triumph—in 1945. This was not so clear during the post-war decade, but matters changed in the post-Stalin years. The Soviet Union's new geopolitical environment began to exercise a subversive long-term effect on the country's domestic ethnopolitics, the Stalinist solution of the Soviet nationalities problem.

First, it proved impossible to keep the peoples of the USSR in total ignorance of life in the European countries of the Soviet Bloc. Once the originally tight iron curtain separating the USSR from the people's democracies was slightly lifted after Stalin's death, comparisons with Poland, Hungary and the GDR became inevitable—and were not in the Soviet Union's favor.[7] East Europe provided evidence challenging the official claim that the Soviet system was superior to what existed abroad.

Second, in an immediately less obvious way, the incorporation of the Baltic states and of West Ukraine into the Soviet Union had a comparable effect. At first few people reflected on the potential consequences of the fact that the USSR had become a country that was more than the "one country" it was in 1938, when it was admittedly multi-ethnic, but with one clearly recognized leading nationality. The Estonians, Latvians, and Lithuanians entered the USSR in 1940 as fully developed nations, with twenty years of state and nation-building behind them. They soon came to be universally perceived throughout the USSR as being more advanced, more modern, more *kul'turny*, than the rest of the USSR; life was better there. The Russians and other "old Soviets" recognized this by calling them, only half in jest, "Our Abroad" (*"Nasha zagranitsa"*). They were more advanced and less Russified at the same time. Moreover, while being more modern they were also the most "nationalistic" and anti-Soviet among the nationalities. Their denial of Soviet civilizational superiority took the form of national assertiveness. They did not argue that "capitalism" or democracy was better than communism, only that national independence was better than being a republic in the USSR.

There was also a third factor. In the 1970s and '80s, Moscow increasingly invoked the party's alleged role in "the Great Patriotic War" as it tried to build a Soviet national identity at a time when official promises of economic prosperity went unfulfilled and when the international prestige of the Soviet Union as a model of socialism was declining. This was a sure way to alienate even more the people in lands occupied by the USSR in accordance with the Molotov-Ribbentrop Pact of August 23, 1939. Indeed, in the period of glasnost, when heretofore suppressed historical facts became known to the people for the first time, the Soviet leadership's diplomatic and military blunders before and during the war were cited by Russians and others to question the regime's legitimacy.[8]

Like the East Europeans, the Balts in their resistance to Sovietization were in fact upholding Western values and institutions but they never admitted it openly, making their case instead under the guise of defending their national "specifics" or peculiarities. The result was to plant the thought in the minds of some people in the "old" USSR that Sovietism was not the only road to modernity; that national independence from Moscow might be a better setting in which to strive for this goal. Since national independence implied an opening to the world at large, in the Soviet setting "nationalism" seemed to promote a more universalist position than did Soviet "internationalism," which was in actuality increasingly functioning as a specimen of isolationism—an isolationism not only from the capitalist world but also from socialist Eastern Europe.[9]

In the 1960s and early '70s thoughts of this kind remained in the sphere of speculation mainly among the more independent-minded students and intellectuals, soon to be known as dissidents; a generation later they would mobilize popular movements. In the meantime, Soviet academics specializing in the discipline of Scientific Communism, as noted in chapter 1, felt they had better things to think about: Even after the Prague Spring of 1968, at least when writing for domestic Soviet consumption, they were speculating (daydreaming?) about Eastern Europe's coming integration into a new socialist commonwealth with the USSR as its central element, just as between 1917 and 1922 the Soviet republics gradually united around Russia to form a new entity, the USSR. Even at this late date the Soviets did not give up their earlier goal, supra-state economic structures for Eastern Europe, which the Romanians had already openly rejected in the early 1960s.[10]

Chapter 9, "The Soviet West—or Far Eastern Europe?," places West Ukraine together with the Baltic states and Moldova in a distinct region that, it argues, was not only "the Soviet West" but also "Far Eastern Europe." Thus, it reiterates the argument advanced some fifteen years earlier in *The Influence of East Europe and the Soviet West on the USSR* (see note 7) that "the Soviet West" was an alien and potentially disruptive element in the Soviet body politic. It was there that cultural, social, and political movements in the communist-ruled countries of East Central Europe found their most hospitable reception: In the 1950s this region was especially receptive to East Europe's national communism, and in the 1970s and '80s it was open to the democratic movements in Poland and Czechoslovakia. By 1989 the impact was not only intellectual but political. The Balts contributed to giving a *national* form to the anticommunist movement. They tended to stimulate those who had been raised as Soviet people to wonder about their own nationality. ("When did you begin to think of yourself as a Ukrainian?" I asked a young member of the Ukrainian parliament, a native of Donbas, in January 1992. "When I was doing my military service in Estonia," he answered.)

The Ukrainian Question

The nature of the Russian-Ukrainian relationship, including Russian perceptions of Ukraine, was one of the unresolved issues of the pre-Soviet period that the Soviets inherited. As we now know, the Soviet state had to deal with it until the end of the USSR. Ukraine and Russia resolved it by themselves, as independent states, and they did so without going to war. Moreover, Ukraine was spared a domestic ethnic or inter-regional war in the process.

When chapters 3, 4, and 5 were being written, such events were still far in the future. However, they do identify the Ukraine-Russia nexus as a fundamental problem, not the least because it bore directly on the Russians' definition of their *own* national identity. Before 1917 an over-whelming majority of Russians, of all political views, viewed Ukrainians as a subgroup of the larger Russian nation, which they took to consist of all East Slavs: the Great Russians, Little Russians (that is, Ukrainians), and Belorussians. As they saw it, Ukraine, or more precisely Ukrainian nationalism (or, as they preferred to call it, "separatism"), posed a chal-lenge not simply to the integrity of the Russian state as, say, Polish na-tionalism did, but also undermined the unity of the Russian nation. The Ukrainian challenge thus was qualitatively different from any Polish, Jewish, or Muslim "problem."

Lenin was the single major Russian figure, moreover, one destined soon to rule the state, who even before 1917 did not identify the Rus-sians with all East Slavs but viewed the Great Russians as a nation and the Ukrainians as another nation. In December 1914, Lenin published an article "On the National Pride of the Great Russians," the very title of which revealed his position on the national identity of the Russians. In it Lenin condemned those Great Russians who supported what he said were the tsarist state's war aims, including the plan "to throttle Poland and the Ukraine."[11]

But Lenin's position remained a minority one, and in 1917 even some of his closest associates denied that the Ukrainian national move-ment had a real social base. Against them, Lenin cited the great electoral

success of Ukrainian leftist parties in the election to the Constituent Assembly. It was in order to compete with these Ukrainian forces that the
Bolsheviks, in distinction from literally all other significant forces in
Russia, made such gestures as the formal recognition of the Ukrainian
state (in the form of the Soviet Ukrainian republic, of course), with "its
own" central state organs, its own party organization, and so forth.
These were tactical, pragmatic moves to promote the revolutionary
cause.[12]

Once they were securely in power, in the 1920s the Soviets recognized the Ukrainian language as a separate language—and decided, in
their internationalist mood of the time, to make it a tool of communist
education and propaganda. They certainly did not think that one became a better communist by reading Marx in Russian rather than by
reading Marx in Ukrainian. Whether this amounted to an admission
that the Ukrainians were a "nation" was of no importance to the Bolsheviks at a time when building an international socialist community was
their main goal. But in the 1930s the party changed its line on the
Ukraine-Russia relationship, including the place of Ukrainian versus
Russian language.

In a review of the ethnic scene published in 1968, John A. Armstrong offered a very insightful typology of Soviet nationalities. He classified Ukrainians and Belorussians as the "younger brothers" of the
dominant Russians, and placed the Balts in the category of "state nations."[13]

Armstrong's term for Ukrainians was well chosen. It brings to mind
not only younger brothers but also country cousins, members of the
family that you may employ in the family business, perhaps by letting
them run a branch office somewhere in the provinces. That's what the
Ukrainians were doing for the Russians while serving in the party apparatus in Kazakhstan or in Latvia, especially after Stalin's death. But the
younger-brother concept was also applicable to the conditions in
Ukraine. Chapter 3, "Russians in Ukraine and Problems of Ukrainian
Identity in the USSR," and chapter 5, "Urbanization in Ukraine since
the Second World War," ask how the Soviet conception of modernity
and ethnic integration was applied in the Ukrainian-Russian relationship within Ukraine. Their specific focus is on urbanization in relation
to ethnic identity and language loyalty. Indirectly, they also were an
attempt to see whether the ethno-demographic situation in Ukraine sup-

ported the Brzezinski hypothesis about scientific and technical Russians and "humanistic" ethnics, in this case the Ukrainians.

At first sight, the picture seemed clear: The part of Ukraine that by Soviet criteria of modernity was the most advanced in economic and social sphere was the Donbas region—the oblasts of Donetsk and Luhansk. That most highly urbanized and industrialized part of Ukraine, where the proletariat was clearly the most numerous social group, had the highest percentage of Russians in its population. The Ukrainians living there, moreover, were declaring Russian as their native language in much higher proportions than elsewhere. I rephrased for myself the question about the future of Ukraine versus Russia into a more narrow and manageable question: Was Donetsk the future of Ukraine?

Asking that question, one was immediately reminded that Ukraine was not only a big country but that its regions varied widely in social, economic, and ethno-linguistic indicators. The next question: Was post-1945 Ukraine becoming more diverse regionally, or was it becoming more unified and integrated? If the latter was the case, was Donetsk, or perhaps some other regional center in Ukraine, serving as the model for the whole?

One way to address the question was to look at urban hierarchy in Ukraine and the place of Ukraine's capital, Kyiv, in it. At the beginning of the twentieth century Kyiv was much smaller than Odessa, and at the end of the 1930s Kyiv was approximately the same size as Kharkiv, Soviet Ukraine's capital until 1934. It was reasonable to ask whether Kyiv's role as Ukraine's administrative and cultural center throughout the entire post-1945 period was accompanied by that city's numerical ascendancy over Kharkiv, Odessa, Dnipropetrovsk, and Donetsk. A review of Soviet census data revealed that indeed in the post-war years Kyiv's population was growing at much higher rates than that of its traditional rivals, and that Kyiv was indeed assuming the rank of the republic's "primate city." This could be seen as an indication that some kind of inter-regional integration was taking place within Ukraine. Moreover, since in 1959, for the first time in a hundred years, Ukraine's capital also registered a Ukrainian majority by nationality, and since by 1970 it had become larger, Kyiv also was becoming more Ukrainian.[14]

Kyiv was clearly not becoming like Donetsk. What about those western regions of Ukraine that became Soviet first in 1939–40 and then again, this time for good, in 1944–45? Were they starting to look like the rest of Ukraine or were they preserving their pre-Soviet identity?[15]

Chapter 4, "West Ukraine and West Belorussia," provides a partial answer. Its survey of demographic trends and of developments in the print media revealed that Soviet-style modernization was not making the region more Russian. The article sought an explanation of this in the fact that by 1939 the West Ukrainians had established a presence in the urban sector and their language served as a modern medium of communication for them before the Soviets arrived. Unlike the Balts, most of them had never before been under Russia; they lived under Austria from 1772 to 1918, followed by a brief experience of independence in 1918 to 1919, and under Polish rule between the two world wars. Consequently, Russian language and culture there did not acquire the status it had in the east, which meant that the West Ukrainians neither were nor were perceived by others as "younger brothers" of the Russians. Instead, they were an alien element in the Soviet body politic, similar in this respect to the Latvians, Estonians, and Lithuanians. Although an exposure to the Baltic peoples stimulated thinking in national terms among the natives of the "old-Soviet" regions, in the Ukrainian case the role of Galicia was much greater.[16]

Ever since the late 1950s West Ukraine had been the stronghold of the national movement that expressed itself among others in dissident religious, political, and cultural activities. In Gorbachev's time the former dissidents and their new followers pursued their cause openly. Chapter 11, "The Strange Politics of Lviv," updates the argument of chapter 4 to cover the final years of the USSR. It draws on demographic and media statistics as a background to a new Soviet feature— competitive elections. When it became possible for them to speak their mind, the West Ukrainians made it clear that their national goal was not only independence by leaving the Soviet Union (which the Balts aspired to)—but, because they considered themselves to be a part of a greater Ukraine, they also wanted to take the rest of Ukraine along with them. However much they loved Lviv, they wanted Kyiv to be their capital.

Concurrently with the national movements like those mentioned above, in the late 1980s the Soviet Union saw a wave of labor protests, most notably strikes of miners. Mass strikes and other forms of labor protest took place in the East Ukrainian regions of Donetsk and Luhansk. (There was also organized labor activity in the Lviv-Volhynia mine district.) For a while it seemed that a USSR-wide popular movement might form, representing, as it were, a united Soviet people, or at least Soviet labor, in opposition to the Soviet government. However, there was not going to be a Soviet version of Poland's Solidarity. The miners did not reach out to other sections of society the way the workers of Gdansk dockyards had done in 1980 to 1981, and they did not develop a broader political agenda for reform on the USSR scale. In the Ukrainian Donbas, miners turned toward a pro-Ukrainian independence position when they found that their interests collided with those of miners in Russia, considering that Moscow gave preferential treatment to Siberia and the Urals.[17] Miners of the Ukrainian Donbas and their comrades in the Russian part of Donbas and in other regions of Russia found themselves in two different countries, the former sharing a country with Lviv. Making workers Soviet, which the Communists had tried to do for seventy years, did not in the end produce the intended effect: The workers did not rise to defend the Soviet system or the territorial integrity of the USSR when these were in danger.

Just as no class-based social movement rose to save the USSR, so the Russian-speaking parts of Ukraine failed to produce a popular Russian nationalist movement to rival its Ukrainian counterpart in the western and even central regions. The concerns among the Russian-speaking people of Ukraine about the future position of the Russian language were real and serious enough. But the "Russophones" of the Donbas region did not form a Russian national bloc demanding separation of their region from Ukraine and the creation of an independent republic—or its union with Russia. Nor did they unite with analogous formations in Kharkiv, Odessa, Dnipropetrovsk, and, for that matter, Kyiv (there was no shortage of "Russophones" there), to fight within an all-Ukraine framework for recognition of their demands. In the end, during the breakup of the USSR—and in the immediate post-1991 years— nothing resembling the pre-1938 Sudeten-German movement in Czechoslovakia emerged among the Russians of Ukraine.

Chernobyl may be a part of the answer. The 1986 accident at the Chernobyl nuclear station—and Moscow's failure to react to it properly—gave birth to a civic or territorial national consensus that brought together people of diverse linguistic, ethnic, and religious backgrounds in Ukraine. No content-analysis study comparing the Russian- and Ukrainian-language media in the Ukrainian SSR during the Gorbachev era appears to exist, but one may surmise that it would reveal an identity of views, whether expressed in Russian or in Ukrainian, on the question of Chernobyl's significance for Ukraine.[18]

Chapter 11 provides some data supporting the view that the print media were not divided by language. While noting the significant decline in readership of Moscow newspapers and magazines in Ukraine in 1990–91, especially the losses of the Moscow-based *Komsomol'skaia pravda,* it cites figures revealing a sharp increase in the press run of *Komsomol'skoe znamia,* which was the Kyiv paper for young people published in Russian, like its Moscow competitor. However, this most popular Russian-language newspaper in Ukraine supported Ukraine's independence —in other words, it said in Russian what others were saying in Ukrainian. As one would have expected, the bulk of *Komsomol'-skoe znamia*'s readers lived in Russian-speaking parts of Ukraine—like Donetsk.

Some foreign experts in academia and government viewed the language question as a major threat to Ukraine's territorial integrity and indeed even survival after 1991. They interpreted the electoral success of the Communists in Ukraine's eastern and southern regions in the spring of 1994 and the victory of Leonid Kuchma over Leonid Kravchuk in the presidential election of July 1994 as signs of a deepening split between a Russian-speaking East and a Ukrainian-speaking West. Chapter 12, "Nation-Building in Ukraine: Problems and Prospects," and chapter 13, "Reflections on Ukraine after 1994: The Dilemmas of Nationhood," warned against this philological determinism or linguistic fatalism. They argued that there was more to Ukrainian national identity than language, that it did not depend exclusively on language, and that predictions of ethnic or language wars in Ukraine did not pay adequate attention to this fact. Moreover, the leaders and builders of the Ukrainian state were, and intended to remain, Russian speakers. Most of them had become, not linguistic, but political and economic "Ukrainians" after 1990–91.

Borrowing an expression from Italian political vocabulary, one might conclude that the emergence of an independent Ukraine, in the way and form in which it actually occurred, was the result of a "historic compromise." One party in that compromise were the party, state, economic, and military elites, including the regional bosses from the east, for whom Russian remained (with some exceptions) the preferred language of daily use after the fall of the Soviet Union. The leaders of the national movement formed the other party.[19] Their background had mainly been in literary and academic fields and their popular electoral support was concentrated in the western regions and in the capital city. With few exceptions, largely of a symbolic kind, they did not gain access to positions of power. Power remained in the hands of the old elite. If they thought about it, the leaders of the national movement likely reasoned that their de-facto renunciation of claims to power was not too large a price for persuading all of Ukraine to secede from the USSR. They probably understood that only a government consisting of members of the old apparatus could maintain the territorial unity of Ukraine and establish its authority over the regional bosses in Donetsk, Kharkiv, and Odessa. Could one imagine Soviet generals pledging allegiance to a Ukrainian state whose president was a native (or the preferred candidate) of Galicia? In December 1991, however, those generals were able to accept as their supreme commander a former secretary of the Central Committee, Communist Party of Ukraine.

To a historian, the Ukrainian declaration of independence of August 24, 1991, its ratification in the referendum of December 1, and the subsequent quick recognition of Ukraine first by both Poland the next day, and then by Russia a few days later, reflected something deeper than the designs and machinations of political operators. It was the conclusion of a continuous, "subterranean" process of nation-formation that had begun several generations earlier.

In January 1919, there were two Ukrainian states in existence, both fighting for survival. Facing a hopeless situation, they declared their unification. One was the Ukrainian People's Republic, whose government was about to be expelled by the Red Army from Kyiv; the other—the West Ukrainian People's Republic, engaged in a war with Poland that would soon end with Polish takeover of its entire territory (the former Austrian Galicia). Theirs was a paper declaration, a statement of intent, for the two governments and their two armies remained separate until the final suppression of both soon thereafter. In the meantime, the eastern parts of today's Ukraine were under the Ukrainian Soviet Socialist Republic, which was formally independent but under actual control of Lenin's government in Moscow. In the south, anarchist bands were active in the countryside, and remnants of the Russian White forces were holding on to Crimea, which by 1920 would become an autonomous republic within the RSFSR. And, finally, one region of what is now Ukraine was being transferred from Hungarian to Czechoslovak sovereignty, and another—from Austrian to Romanian. In 1944–45, for the first time in history, all these regions would find themselves, as the Ukrainian SSR, within one state. (Crimea was added in 1954.) By 1990, several generations of students had been taught that Kharkiv and Lviv,

Odessa and Chernivtsi, Ternopil and Donetsk, are all in the Ukrainian SSR; that Kyiv is Ukraine's capital; and that their republic is a member of the United Nations. These facts, too, helped to make it possible for both Donetsk and Lviv to accept Kyiv as their capital and Ukraine as their political home. There had been a monumental change since 1917–1921.[20] One can agree with those scholars who attribute to the Soviet constitutional arrangements a role in territorializing nations, and see independent Ukraine as a successor of the Ukrainian SSR.

The Russian Question

Three chapters in this book deal with the Russian question between 1973, when the present chapter 1 was written, and the Soviet breakup in 1991.

Chapter 6, "History and Russian Nationalism," was published in 1979. Its subject is Russian intellectual and political dissent at a time when the Soviet state was still strong and stable and when Russian nationalism was seen by many as "the principal force holding the USSR together."[21] Yet, before the end of the seventies specifically *Russian nationalist* critiques of the Soviet system emerged. These critiques, sometimes disguised thinly as literary criticism or historical analysis, appeared in the underground media but also found outlets in the official press. Some critics condemned the Bolshevik revolution of 1917 because they considered it, and the system it created, anti-Russian. This might appear surprising: By then, more than half a century after the revolution of 1917, and several decades after the triumphant Soviet victory in World War II, it was generally assumed that the Soviet system had established its legitimacy as a Russian national institution. However, as Yitzak M. Brudny demonstrates in his *Reinventing Russia,* a study published in 1998, soon after Stalin's death in 1953 a Russian nationalism distinct from, and even opposed to, the Soviet system began to form as a literary and more broadly a cultural movement. It had no trouble in finding issues on which to be critical of the Soviet record since 1917, and it gradually developed its own program in opposition to policies of the party.[22]

Thus, the "de-Sovietization of Russia," which chapter 8, "The Imperial Legacy and the Soviet Nationalities Problem," presents as an an important process taking place in Gorbachev's period, had begun much

earlier. That chapter, as well as chapter 7, "Dilemmas of Russian Nationalism," tries to describe a previously unimaginable situation when
the relations between "Russia" and the "Union" became a fundamental
political and constitutional issue. The creation of the Communist Party
of the Russian Federation, formally within the CPSU, in reality was an
expression of opposition to Gorbachev's leadership, and a sign of a
deepening split within the party itself. Even before this, some members
of the party demanded that the Soviet system and communist ideology
be openly and officially declared to be Russian. This was something the
party had never done explicitly, despite its pro-Russian bias, under Stalin or his successors. Later, in the '90s, the Communist Party of the
Russian Federation would openly adopt as its ideology this fusion of
communism with one current of Russian nationalism. By this time the
USSR no longer existed, and Russia's de-Sovietization had advanced far
enough for an independent Russia (or the Russian Federation) to emerge
as the successor of the Russian Soviet Federative Socialist Republic.[23]

How "Soviet" was Russia before its "de-Sovietization" began, before a new Russia was created or "re-invented"? This question is asked
in the final essay in the book, chapter 16, "The Fall of the Tsarist Empire
and the USSR: The Russian Question and Imperial Overextension,"
where the linkage between Russia and Marxism/Soviet Communism is
a major theme. This essay offers an interpretation of the making and
remaking (and, in 1917, of an attempted unmaking) of the Russian nation, including the impact of Marxism and the Soviet system on the ways
in which Russian national identity evolved in this century. There is not
much I would add to this account because I continue to believe that the
Soviet state tried to create a Soviet nation and in the course of several
decades claimed to have succeeded. In the end, the communist goal of
creating a Soviet nation and Soviet nationalism by combining communism with elements of Russian national identity failed, and it did not
prevent the emergence of what Brudny calls "nation-shaping Russian
nationalism," which he contrasts with the "official nationalism of the
Soviet state."[24] But their failure does not mean that the communists did
not try. Thus, I remain unpersuaded, by those scholars, the most influential of whom is Rogers Brubaker, that the Soviets, when they said
they were creating a Soviet people, were engaged in creating "a supranational, not national" entity, not a *Soviet* nation.[25]

Supra-nationalism in one country, just as socialism in one country,
is nationalism. One obvious case of what happens to supra-nationalism

in one country is the United States, where, according to Eric Hobsbawm, quoted in chapter 8, another universal ideology became the foundation of a *national* identity. In any case, the Soviet Union lost its claim even to the ideology of supra-nationality when it became clear, after the Second World War, that its territorial shape and ethnic composition were fixed, and that any new states embracing socialism would not be joining the USSR (the way the Balts were the last complete nations to do so in 1940). After 1945, the "Other," in distinction from whom the citizens of the USSR would define themselves as the *Soviet* people, included not only the world of capitalism but also *socialist* nation-states of Eastern Europe, and then also China, North Korea, and so forth.[26] Thus, being Soviet became analogous to being British, which identity embraced but did not obliterate the English, Scottish, Welsh, or Northern Irish territorial identities, or Spanish—which allows one to be Catalan or Basque and Spanish at the same time.

When Russia became an independent state in 1991, with Boris Yeltsin at its head, it defined itself territorially to be co-extensive with the RSFSR (according to the model I call "RSFSR nationalism" in chapter 7). (In Brudny's terminology, Yeltsin upholds "official Russian nationalism," which is different from "nation-shaping nationalism," the latter regarding the entire USSR to be the proper territory for the *Russian* state.)[27] This happened even though, in the virtually universal consensus of experts, the Russians had never considered the RSFSR to be a real entity, their real homeland.

Although the process of Soviet disintegration owed much to the Baltic states—for reasons we outlined above—and although Ukraine played an even more important role, it is impossible to imagine the peaceful and universally unanticipated breakup of the USSR without recognizing the role of the Russian Republic and its leadership. The decision to define Russia within the borders of the RSFSR may have been a major reason why the USSR did not follow the Yugoslav path, why Russia did not become another Serbia.

Soviet and Pre-Soviet Perspectives

While a new Ukraine and a new Russia were gradually establishing themselves as distinct entities in the consciousness of at least the mapmakers, it seemed right to move beyond the time frame of Soviet history in order to gain a better understanding of Russian-Ukrainian relations. The final three chapters of the book present this topic in a broader perspective.

Chapter 16 goes back in time to ask about the impact of the territorial expansion of the Russian Empire on the relations between the Russian people and their state. It argues that the course of Russian nation-formation was negatively affected first by the empire's and then the Soviet Union's westward expansion and the conquest of peoples who refused to become Russified.

Taking a cue from Sir Lewis Namier's thesis on 1848 as "Seed-plot of History," chapter 14, "After Empire: What?," argues that the history of Soviet communism can be better understood if it is placed in a time frame extending back to 1848 and in a geographical setting that, in addition to the Russian Empire and the USSR, includes the countries of Central Europe, the Habsburg monarchy, and its successor states. In this way, the article argues, it is possible to get a better grasp of the Ukrainian problem in tsarist Russia and the USSR. This discussion takes up certain themes that were put forward in chapters 4 and 9—the consequences of the Soviet Union's western expansion for the nationalities question, and especially for the Russian-Ukrainian relationship. When the Soviets invaded Poland in September 1939 and incorporated western Ukraine into the Soviet Union, they added a formerly Habsburg land with a political and cultural experience alien to that of tsarist Russia and the Soviet Union. As we now know, neither Stalin nor his successors quite imagined what effect this war prize would have at home.

A related and complementary historical argument is the subject of chapter 15, "Ukraine: From an Imperial Periphery to a Sovereign State." The article points out that the idea of a modern Ukrainian nationhood was first formulated not in the western regions, whether under Austria or Poland, but in those parts of present-day Ukraine that had been under the Russian Empire the longest. At the same time, however, the chapter insists that it is necessary to consider the Ukrainian confrontation and conflict with Poland in the nineteenth and first half of the twentieth centuries, and their reconciliation in recent decades, as a crucial factor in the emergence of modern Ukraine.[28]

Working on these broad topics I kept thinking of how mechanical and misleading it is to treat the "internal affairs" and "foreign relations" of any state in isolation, but particularly a large one. History is a process that transcends the boundaries of any single state—even a state as tightly isolated from the rest of the world as the Soviet Union was for many years. The "internal" or domestic history of both imperial Russia and the USSR has been intimately, indeed inseparably, tied to that of Eastern Europe.[29]

Ukraine and Russia Emergent and the Union Dissolved

On November 29, 1989, President George Bush's national security advisor, Brent Scowcroft, submitted his estimate of the likely Soviet position on the issues Bush and Gorbachev were to address at their summit in Malta several days later. According to Philip Zelikow and Condoleezza Rice's summary, in their *Germany Unified and Europe Transformed,*

> The Soviets were opposed to German reunification, which they thought "would rip the heart out of the Soviet security system." Their "worst nightmare" was a reunified Germany allied with NATO. "The Warsaw Pact, having lost its East German anchor, would quickly disintegrate and the Soviet line of defense would begin at the Ukrainian border." The gains of World War II, bought so dearly, would be gone.[30]

In 1989, more and more people in the USSR were questioning the suitability of the Soviet system for their respective nations. In Poland, 1989 began with the Round Table negotiations. By the spring the legalization of Solidarity took place, which was followed by a free parliamentary election in June, and by August that had produced Poland's first noncommunist government in over forty years. In the spring, in Ukraine, Russia, the Baltic states, and in other republics, independent deputies were elected to the Soviet Congress of People's Deputies, which was the name Gorbachev chose for the Soviet parliament. Leading party officials, in Moscow, Kyiv, and Leningrad, failed to get elected. Meanwhile, the unrest in Georgia, Armenia, and Azerbaijan was becoming an interethnic war.

In the Baltic states 1989 was the year of public commemorations and mass demonstrations in connection with the fiftieth anniversary of the Molotov-Ribbentrop pact under which Latvia, Lithuania, and Estonia became Soviet republics in 1940. The Balts used the anniversary to demand nullification of the pact and restoration of their independence.

The West Ukrainians also remembered the 1939 anniversary—but did not demand to leave the Union by themselves: They wanted to take the rest of Ukraine with them. In the east Ukrainian city of Poltava, in July, some young people demonstrated on the anniversary of Peter the Great's victory over the Swedes and their Ukrainian allies in 1709, a victory that had far-reaching repercussions not only for Ukraine but also Poland and the Baltic provinces. Some of those demonstrators (see chapter 7) honored the victors. Others honored the losers—and hoped for a reversal of the verdict of Poltava. Summer of 1989 was the time of mass strikes in the coal-mining industry in major centers of Russia and Ukraine. September saw the congress of Rukh in Kyiv—with a delegation of Polish Solidarity in attendance. Several weeks later came the dismissal of Volodymyr Shcherbytsky from the top party post in Ukraine—after seventeen years in office. There was a peaceful transition to democracy in Hungary. Outside the Soviet Bloc, 1989 was the year of the Tiananmen Square massacre and for Yugoslavia, the year when Kosovo lost its autonomous status within the Serbian Republic.

The Soviet leaders had reasons to be concerned as they prepared for the Malta summit. The year that was about to end was an eventful one for many of the socialist states, and especially so for the Soviet Union and its European allies. Shortly after the Malta summit, on December 25, Nicolae Ceausescu was overthrown in Romania, and a day or two later was executed.

Nineteen ninety was no less rich in events. For our focus the most significant among them were the March elections to the Supreme Soviets of both Russia and Ukraine, the Russian declaration of sovereignty in June, the Ukrainian declaration of sovereignty in July, and finally Boris Yeltsin's official visit to Kyiv, in November, and the signing of a Ukrainian-Russian treaty there. These events in turn provided the background to those of 1991—the creation of the institution of president in Russia and the election of Boris Yeltsin to that post, the August putsch, and its defeat. The Ukrainian declaration of independence came on August 24, 1991, and was quickly followed by the decision to form a Ukrainian army. The dissolution of the Soviet Union came exactly two years after the Malta summit. Today there is a general consensus that Russia, as represented by Yeltsin, together with Ukraine, and its first president, Kravchuk, played a crucial role in that dissolution.[31]

In their "Epilogue" to *Germany Unified and Europe Transformed,*

Zelikow and Rice look at the connection of events in different countries during those two years:

> We will never know precisely how to weigh the role of the unification of Germany in the collapse of the Soviet Union. Gorbachev's German policy undermined his political base at home and emboldened rebel nationalists throughout the USSR. The terms of unification ended the Soviet Union's reign as a dominant European power. With no East German anchor, the Warsaw Pact collapsed a few months later as Eastern European regimes rushed to negotiate the withdrawal of Soviet forces from their territory. Pushed back to the Ukraine, the socialist empire did not stop unraveling until it had receded to the approximate frontiers of Peter the Great's Russia.[32]

By December 1991, the Soviet leader's "worst nightmare" of 1989 proved to have been not bad enough. Having survived the demise of the German Democratic Republic by just over a year, the Soviet Union was gone. The collapse of the Soviet system coincided with the dissolution of the much older connection between Ukraine and Russia. The Russian line of defense mentioned in the Scowcroft memorandum did indeed begin "at the Ukrainian border." However, after 1991 that border was not the Ukrainian segment of the Soviet Union's border with East Central Europe but the border between the independent states of Russia and Ukraine.

These momentous events had many causes. It goes without saying that any serious treatment of what happened between 1989 and 1991 must address some, if not all, of the following fundamental themes: the defeat of the USSR in the Cold War, the Soviet Union's failure to adjust to and take advantage of the "scientific-technical revolution," and, more fundamentally, the defeat of the Soviet alternative to Western capitalist civilization and the Western version of modernity. When dealing with these issues one needs in turn to remember that the original Soviet design, never fully abandoned, had been inspired by Marx's vision of communism as abolition of private property, the withering away of the state, and, indeed, the transformation of human nature. Then there were more immediate "factors," such as Soviet policies and their consequences, including the war in Afghanistan, the ecological and health crisis, Chernobyl, corruption. Finally, it is impossible to avoid the role of leaders and other personalities in describing great events. The personality in question here is Gorbachev—his ideas and actions, and his character.

Those "causes" or circumstances or factors, taken together, constitute what the Polish historian and statesman, Leon Wasilewski, calls "conjuncture," or *konjunktura*. In 1934, in a book titled "The Ukrainian Question as an International Problem," Wasilewski reflected on why some nations managed to win their independence after World War I while others, most notably the Ukrainians, failed. He concluded that it was not enough for a people to want independence or to be prepared for it or even to fight for it. There was another indispensable requirement—a favorable constellation of circumstances which remained beyond any particular nation's control.[33]

This book does not claim that the collapse of communism and the breakup of the Soviet Union was "caused" by Russian and Ukrainian nationalisms, or by the failure of Russian nation-building before 1917, or the unresolved questions of Russian-Ukrainian relations, or the unification of Ukraine in 1939 to 1945, or, finally, by the existence, until 1989, of the Soviet bloc in Eastern and Central Europe. The collapse and breakup were made possible by a "conjuncture," global in its dimensions, in which all of these factors were only some of the components. However, an account that failed to include our story would provide an incomplete and flawed explanation of how what was unimaginable in November 1989 became a reality in December 1991.

Notes

1. Chapters 2–11 were written when their author was on the faculty of the University of Michigan, Ann Arbor; chapters 12–16, at Harvard University. Chapter 1 was written in 1972–73, while on a sabbatical leave from Michigan and on a Research Fellowship in Ukrainian Studies at Harvard.

2. Richard Pipes, *The Formation of the Soviet Union: Communism and Nationalism, 1917–1923*, revised edition (Cambridge, Mass.: Harvard University Press, 1964), p. 297.

3. See Tim McDaniel, *The Agony of the Russian Idea* (Princeton: Princeton University Press, 1996), pp. 87–88 and 119, for a critique of the influential works by Theodore Von Laue, *Why Lenin? Why Stalin?* (New York: Lippincott, 1971) and George Fischer, *The Soviet System and Modern Society* (New York: Atherton Press, 1968), which argued at that time that the Soviet system represented a form of modernity. A decade earlier, Isaac Deutscher's *The Great Contest: Russia and the West* (Oxford: Oxford University Press, 1960; revised edition, New York: Ballantine Books, 1961), predicted not only that the USSR

would soon surpass Western Europe and the United States economically, but that it would achieve a higher degree of political freedom than that attained in the West. Deutscher's predictions were an extreme case, but many others shared his overall optimism, even if they did not think that public ownership of the means of production by its very nature created more favorable conditions for scientific and technical innovation than did capitalism.

Needless to say, Deutscher paid no attention to the nationalities question (the words "Russia" and "USSR" were used interchangeably) and he did assume that "the Chinese-Soviet Bloc" would establish a huge common economic space under a single planning authority. In their neglect of nationalism even those who were less enthusiastic about Soviet economic performance or prospects agreed with Deutscher. Indeed, inter-ethnic relations was an area where the judgment on Soviet performance was generally positive—when the problem was acknowledged at all. See Harrison E. Salisbury, ed., *The Soviet Union: The Fifty Years* (New York: Harcourt, Brace and World, 1967), and a critical review by Hugh Seton-Watson, "Anniversary Report," *The New York Times Book Review,* Nov. 5, 1967, pp. 3 and 48.

There were exceptions, of course. Precisely in 1967, *Problems of Communism* devoted an entire issue to the Nationalities Question. In France there was Hélène Carrère d'Encausse, and in Britain Hugh Seton-Watson. In the United States, John A. Armstrong, Edward Allworth, Zbigniew Brzezinski, Frederick C. Barghoorn, Robert Conquest, and Richard Pipes were the best known.

For more recent examples of how Sovietology treated the nationalities, see Crawford Young, "The Dialectics of Cultural Pluralism: Concept and Reality," and Mark R. Beissinger, "Demise of an Empire-State: Identity, Legitimacy, and the Deconstruction of Soviet Politics," in Crawford Young, ed., *The Rising Tide of Cultural Pluralism: The Nation-State at Bay?* (Madison and London: University of Wisconsin Press, 1993), pp. 12–13, and 93–95, respectively.

4. Roman Szporluk, "The Plight of the Minorities," *Problems of Communism,* no. 5 (1972): 79–84. See Zev Katz, "Sociology in the Soviet Union," *Problems of Communism* 20, no. 3 (May–June 1971): 38, and Soviet works cited in chap. 2, note 10 (p. 68 below).

5. R. C. Raack, *Stalin's Drive to the West, 1938–1945: The Origins of the Cold War* (Stanford: Stanford University Press, 1995). Martin E. Malia, *Russia under Western Eyes: From the Bronze Horseman to the Lenin Mausoleum* (Cambridge, Mass., and London, England: Harvard University Press, 1999), p. 4, says that Soviet victory in World War II "in truth, marked one of the most profound changes of the world equilibrium in modern history."

6. Lenin's prediction, in "Left-Wing Communism, Infantile Disorder," quoted by Hans Kohn, "Soviet Communism and Nationalism: Three Stages of a Historical Development," in Edward Allworth, ed., *Soviet Nationality Prob-*

lems (New York and London: Columbia University Press, 1971), p. 49. After 1945, Kohn pointed out, "Soviet Communism had to face not only the problem of the national movements within its frontiers, but also that of survival and assertion in a world of nations, many of them better organized and economically more advanced than Russia." (Kohn, p. 43.) After World War II, and after the victory of the Chinese revolution in 1949, the USSR "did not expand as a further step toward a world union. It was no longer even regarded as its center or nucleus." (Kohn, p. 63.)

7. If I may be allowed a personal reminiscence, this is what I saw happening in Poland, where I lived until 1958, and during my three visits to Ukraine in 1956 and 1957. My conclusion, then formed, that these newly annexed Soviet territories, and the states that were socialist but were not part of the Soviet Union, would eventually prove to be important in the future domestic evolution of the USSR was reinforced by my later studies—and by views of scholars, including those who contributed to a volume titled *The Influence of East Europe and the Soviet West on the USSR* (New York, Washington, London: Praeger, 1976), of which I was the editor. That volume grew out a conference sponsored by the Center for Russian and East European Studies at the University of Michigan.

8. Nina Tumarkin, *The Living and the Dead: The Rise and Fall of the Cult of World War II in Russia* (New York: Basic Books, 1994), pp. 174–75: "Much of the struggle that, by the beginning of the 1990s, began to pull the Soviet Union apart was about memory as a source of power. Many of the non-Russian nationalities . . . were even more quickly swept away than the Russians by the desire to become heirs to their own histories and thereby masters of their own fates. The Baltic states' struggle for independence—which began the breakup of the Union of Soviet Socialist Republics—was inextricably bound up with the desacralization of the Great Patriotic War."

9. More on this in Roman Szporluk, "Nationalism after Communism: Reflections on Russia, Ukraine, Belarus and Poland," *Nations and Nationalism* 4, no. 3 (July 1998): 301–20, esp. pp. 313–15.

10. Ghita Ionescu, *The Break-up of the Soviet Empire in Eastern Europe* (Baltimore, Maryland: Penguin Books, 1965), was an early realistic assessment. It took another two or three decades before the title of this book was validated by actual events, but Ionescu had correctly seen the failure of the Soviet design for Eastern Europe.

11. "On the National Pride of the Great Russians," in V. I. Lenin, *Selected Works*, in three volumes (New York: International Publishers, 1967), vol. I, pp. 664–67.

12. Lenin's political moves were always determined by practical considerations. "Under these circumstances, to ignore the importance of the national

question in the Ukraine—a sin of which Great Russians are often guilty (and of which Jews are guilty perhaps only a little less often than the Great Russians)—is a great and dangerous mistake. The division between the Russian and Ukrainian Socialist Revolutionaries as early as 1917 could not have been accidental." Quoted by Steven L. Guthier, "The Popular Base of Ukrainian Nationalism in 1917," *Slavic Review* 38, no. 1 (March 1979), p. 46. On other occasions, when it suited him, Lenin argued that the Ukrainian movement had been destroyed by the German occupation of 1918, and had never had deep roots anyway. See Andrea Graziosi, *Bol'sheviki i krestiane na Ukraine, 1918–1919 gody* (Moscow: "Airo-XX," 1997), p. 100.

13. John A. Armstrong, "The Ethnic Scene in the Soviet Union: The View of the Dictatorship," Erich Goldhagen, ed., *Ethnic Minorities in the Soviet Union* (New York, Washington, London: Praeger, 1968), pp. 3–49. See also Yaroslav Bilinsky, "Assimilation and Ethnic Assertiveness among Ukrainians of the Soviet Union," Goldhagen, ed., *Ethnic Minorities*, pp. 147–84.

14. See "Kiev as Ukraine's Primate City," *Harvard Ukrainian Studies*, 3–4 (1979–80): 843–49, for details of this rise of Kyiv. It is clear to me now that when writing those chapters I took the Ukrainian identity to be in its essence linguistic, which meant that I measured the progress or decline of the Ukrainian nationality with such indicators as the percentage of Ukrainians, especially Ukrainian speakers, in the major cities. However, there are signs that I was beginning to recognize the historical and political elements of Ukrainian identity, when, as in chapter 5, I wondered whether it was possible to be a Russian-speaking person and yet to support a political or civic Ukrainian national identity. I was intrigued by the argument of Walker Connor, "Nation-Building or Nation-Destroying?," *World Politics*, 24, no. 3 (April 1972): 319–55, that language was not the real issue but a symbol in Ukrainian national dissent, and referred to his work in "The Ukraine and the Ukrainians," my contribution to Zev Katz, Rosemarie Rogers, and Frederick Harned, eds., *Handbook of Major Soviet Nationalities* (New York: The Free Press, and London: Collier Macmillan Publishers, 1975), p. 43. At that time it was common to treat those Russian-speaking Ukrainians as a group in transition to Russian national identity. But as I see it now, the matter was not so simple: Those people were saying, in Russian, that they were *not Russian*, and also perhaps revealing something scholars had ignored, that is, the formation of a territorial and civic Ukrainian identity. See Roman Szporluk, "The Ukraine and Russia," in Robert Conquest, ed., *The Last Empire: Nationality and the Soviet Future* (Stanford: Hoover Institution Press, 1986), pp. 151–82, for an acknowledgment of the historical as distinct from linguistic roots of the difference between Ukraine and Russia. My thinking along those lines was influenced by the writings of Ivan L. Rudnytsky. See his *Essays in Modern Ukrainian History*, edited by Peter L. Rudnytsky, Cambridge: Ukrainian Research Institute, distributed by Harvard University

Press, 1987. The great Russian scientist who was the first president of the Ukrainian Academy of Sciences founded in 1918, Vladimir I. Vernadsky, in an essay written during World War I but first published in 1988, saw the origins of the Ukrainian problem in the time when Ukrainians first found themselves under the state of Muscovy and he recognized among the factors producing the Ukrainian national identity the historic links with the West. In chapter 7, I refer to this essay's publication in Ukraine. Later, two journals in Moscow published it as well; see V. I. Vernadskii, "Ukrainskii vopros i russkoe obshchestvo," *Druzhba narodov*, no. 3 (1990): 247–54, and Vladimir Vernadskii, "Eti golosa ne byli uslyshany," *Rodina*, no. 1 (1990): 91–95. I am grateful to Professor Valery Tishkov for these references.

15. William Henry Chamberlin, *The Ukraine: A Submerged Nation* (New York: Macmillan, 1944), pp. 83–84, wondered long ago: "The reunion of the Ukrainians in Eastern Galicia, Bukovina, and Bessarabia with their racial kinsmen who have lived under the Soviet regime for a quarter of a century will present some interesting and perhaps difficult problems of assimilation. While there are strong sentimental and cultural ties between these two branches of the Ukrainian people, centuries of partition have subjected them to different influences. . . . It remains to be seen whether, in the future, the masses of Ukrainians in Eastern Galicia, Bukovina, and Bessarabia will prove to be clay in the hands of Soviet molders, or whether their stubborn adherence to nationalist and religious ideals will cause embarrassment to the Soviet rulers and perhaps affect their blood brothers, the Soviet Ukrainians."

16. This is the place to correct something I wrote on Belarus. According to Oleg Bukhovets and Dmitrii Furman, "Elektoral'noe povedenie belorusskikh regionov," in D. E. Furman, ed., *Belorussiia i Rossiia: obshchestva i gosudarstva* (Moscow: Izdatel'stvo "Prava cheloveka," 1998), pp. 184–225, in post-Soviet elections the western regions of Belarus have shown a definitely stronger "pro-Western" orientation than the eastern regions. (Also Minsk is more pro-Western than is the rest of the country.) I had argued that the western regions of Belarus, under Poland between 1919 and 1939, were more Russified and more Sovietized than its eastern regions. While this could not be seen clearly twenty years ago, western regions of Belarus also belonged to what I called "Far Eastern Europe."

17. Andreas Wittkowsky, "Nationalstaatsbildung in der Ukraine: Die politische Ökonomie eines 'historischen Kompromisses,' " *Osteuropa* 38, no. 6 (1998): 578–79, and idem, *Fünf Jahre ohne Plan. Die Ukraine 1991–1996. Nationalstaatsbildung, Wirtschaft und Elite* (Hamburg: Lit, 1998). There exists a Russian translation of the Wittkowsky book: *Piatiletka bez plana. Ukraina 1991–1996. Formirovanie natsional'nogo gosudarstva, ekonomika, elity* (Kyiv: Sfera, 1998). See also Heiko Pleines, "Die Regionen der Ukraine," *Osteuropa* 38, no. 4 (1998): 365–72. Among Ukrainian authors on this topic see Anatolii

Rusnachenko, *Probudzhennia: Robitnychyi rukh na Ukraïni v 1989–1993 rr.*, 2 vols. (Kyiv: KM Academia, 1995), and Oleksii Haran', *Ubyty Drakona: Z istorii Rukhu ta novykh partii Ukraïny* (Kyiv: Lybid', 1993). For a discussion of some of the complexities in Russian and Ukrainian identity, see Anatol Lieven, *Ukraine and Russia: Fraternal Rivalry* (Washington, D.C.: United States Institute of Peace Press, 1999). M. I. Beletskii and A. K. Tolpygo, "Natsional'no-kul'turnye i ideologicheskie orientatsii naseleniia Ukrainy," *Politicheskie issledovaniia*, no. 4, 1998, pp. 74–89, argue that many people in eastern and southern regions of Ukraine are neither Russians nor Ukrainians but "Ukrainorussians" (*ukrainorussy*).

18. On the critical importance of Chernobyl in the transition from an intellectual to a popular or mass character of the Ukrainian movement between 1986 and 1989, see my article, "National Reawakening: Ukraine and Belorussia," in Uri Ra'anan, ed., *The Soviet Empire: The Challenge of National and Democratic Movements* (Lexington, Mass., and Toronto: D.C. Heath and Company, 1990), pp. 75–93. According to the more recent assessment by Catherine Wanner, *Burden of Dreams: History and Identity in Post-Soviet Ukraine* (University Park: Pennsylvania State University Press, 1998), p. 33: "During the aftermath of Chernobyl, many Russians and russified Ukrainians . . . saw their republic as a colony for the first time. For many, Chernobyl was the most significant and traumatic event in their lifetime. The failure of political leaders to take responsible steps to mitigate the negative consequences of the accident served more than anything else for russified populations to discredit the Soviet regime and generate support for an independent state."

19. Wittkowsky, "Nationalstaatsbildung in der Ukraine," and *Fünf Jahre ohne Plan*, sees three parties in the Ukrainian "historic compromise," the third being the workers' movement in the Donbas region.

20. For a different view, see Andrew Wilson, *Ukrainian nationalism in the 1990s: A minority faith* (Cambridge, Eng.: Cambridge University Press, 1997), passim, but especially p. 194: "Regional cleavages remained remarkably stable throughout the period 1989–94 and are still the most salient influence on contemporary politics. The most striking fact about modern Ukrainian politics in general, and support for Ukrainian nationalism in particular, is the continuing importance of past historical divides. . . . The main theme of this work has been the lack of an established tradition of Ukrainian statehood and the consequent sharp historical differences between and within the Ukrainian regions. *Regional divisions helped determine the fate of the national movement in both 1917–20 and 1941–4, and have shown no sign of diminishing in importance in the 1990s.*" (Italics mine.) According to Orest Subtelny, *Ukraine: A History*, second edition (Toronto: University of Toronto Press, 1994), p. 359: "In 1919 total chaos engulfed Ukraine. Indeed, in the modern history of Europe no country experienced such complete anarchy, bitter civil strife, and total collapse of

authority as did Ukraine at this time. Six different armies—those of the Ukrainians [as we pointed out, there were at least *two* different Ukrainian armies then], the Bolsheviks, the Whites, the Entente, the Poles, and the anarchists—operated on its territory. Kiev changed hands five times in less than a year."

21. Alain Besançon, "Nationalism and Bolshevism in the USSR," in Conquest, ed., *The Last Empire,* p. 13.

22. Yitzhak M. Brudny, *Reinventing Russia: Russian Nationalism and the Soviet State, 1953–1991* (Cambridge, Mass., and London: Harvard University Press, 1998).

23. "Dilemmas of Russian Nationalism" presents not only varieties of Russian nationalism—from empire-savers to nation-builders—but also takes note of some non-Russian responses to Russian nationalism. Thus, we find the name of a Ukrainian party official, Leonid Kravchuk, joining in a controversy between Russians and Ukrainians, ostensibly about the anniversary of the battle of Poltava, 1709, on the side of the latter. This was just one small sign of how elements of party leadership in Kyiv were developing a common language with the Ukrainian intelligentsia on certain issues. As early as the summer of 1989 a national current (later known as *suveren-komunisty*) was emerging within the leadership of the Communist Party in Ukraine. This process must have been stimulated not only by the situation in Ukraine, but also by their growing awareness that Russian nationalists in Moscow wanted to transform the USSR into an openly Russian state.

24. Brudny, *Reinventing Russia,* p. 7. The official Soviet nationalism, Brudny says, even though it "had a strong Russian nationalist component, including such repressive policies as the russification of non-Russian nationalities," nonetheless promoted "the civic-ideological concept of the Soviet nation . . . [and] extended membership in the nation to all ethnic groups living on USSR territory." It came to be opposed by a "nation-shaping Russian nationalism" that "rejected two of its three primary components: the officially defined object of ultimate loyalty and the proper political, social, economic, and cultural arrangements that would best suit the Russian nation. Thus, nation-shaping Russian nationalism in effect challenged the legitimacy of the Soviet state itself." (The "component" on which both nationalisms agreed was the territorial question.)

25. Rogers Brubaker, *Nationalism Reframed: Nationhood and the National Question in the New Europe* (Cambridge, Eng.: Cambridge University Press, 1996), p. 28. On the other hand, Frederick C. Barghoorn, writing forty years earlier, had no doubt that although "Stalin never admitted that the Soviet Union was a nation, he and his collaborators attempted to mold a Soviet national consciousness." Barghoorn cited, from Soviet official sources, expressions like "Soviet national pride," "Soviet patriotism and national pride," "Soviet music," "Soviet science," and so forth, and quoted the Soviet Encyclopedia,

attributing the creation of "a single Soviet people" (which, it said, already existed) to "the Lenin-Stalin nationality policy." The expression "Soviet people," according to Barghoorn, "seems to have come into common use by about 1939." See Frederick C. Barghoorn, *Soviet Russian Nationalism* (New York: Oxford University Press, 1956), pp. 5–6 and 21–22.

26. Iver B. Neumann, *Uses of the Other: "The East" in European Identity Formation* (Minneapolis: University of Minnesota Press, 1999), critically reviews some of the political and cultural issues contained in debates about "Europe," "Central Europe," and "Eastern Europe," and the place assigned to Russia in them, but his work could be expanded into a study of how Soviet identity was being promoted within the USSR. One way was by emphasizing the Soviet Union's role as a mentor of those nations that "entered the path of socialism" after the Soviet people and were learning from the Soviet experience.

27. Brudny, *Reinventing Russia*, p. 8.

28. Ilya Prizel, *National Identity and Foreign Policy: Nationalism and Leadership in Poland, Russia, and Ukraine* (Cambridge: Cambridge University Press, 1998), recognizes Poland's place in Ukrainian history and politics, and Ukraine's in Polish, and does this without downplaying the importance of Russia for both.

29. In conformity with an academic (unwritten) rule that was strictly enforced not only in undergraduate textbooks and syllabi but also in works aimed at more advanced students, the Russian Empire/USSR had to be treated in strict isolation from "Eastern Europe"—and vice versa. See for example, Peter F. Sugar and Ivo Lederer, eds., *Nationalism in Eastern Europe* (Seattle and London: University of Washington Press, 1969), which projects the post-1918 status quo into the past and accordingly has chapters titled "Nationalism in Czechoslovakia" and "Nationalism and the Yugoslavs," but excludes from its purview not only Russia and Ukraine, but also the Estonians, Latvians, and Lithuanians (presumably because they stopped being "Eastern European" in virtue of their annexation by the USSR in 1940). It is not hard to guess that more than pure scholarship was involved in the creation of this mental iron curtain.

30. Philip Zelikow and Condoleezza Rice, *Germany Unified and Europe Transformed: A Study in Statecraft* (Cambridge, Mass., and London: Harvard University Press, 1997), pp. 125–26.

31. Valerie Bunce, *Subversive Institutions: The Design and the Destruction of Socialism and the State* (Cambridge, Eng., and New York: Cambridge University Press, 1999), p. 151, is more convincing when she says that the Ukrainian leadership's actions in December 1991 "proved decisive for the end of the Soviet state" than when she notes "Ukraine's sudden entrance into the Soviet game in early December, 1991."

32. Zelikow and Rice, *Germany Unified and Europe Transformed*, p. 369.

33. "Who knows," Wasilewski asked, "whether somewhere in the world

forces are not being born whose confrontation will create a wholly new, different conjuncture . . . . Who knows, maybe also the . . . Ukrainian nation in the not too distant future will find a conjuncture of which it will be able to avail itself successfully for its better, bright future, by drawing on the experiences of the past period." See Leon Wasilewski, *Kwestja Ukraińska jako zagadnienie międzynarodowe* (Warsaw: Ukraiński Instytut Naukowy, 1934), p. 20. A reading list of someone who wanted to follow Wasilewski's approach in trying to understand Ukraine's—or Russia's—road to 1991 would include Charles S. Maier, *Dissolution: The Crisis of Communism and the End of East Germany* (Princeton: Princeton University Press, 1997), Gale Stokes, *The Walls Came Tumbling Down: The Collapse of Communism in Eastern Europe* (New York and Oxford: Oxford University Press, 1993), Valery Tishkov, *Ethnicity, Nationalism and Conflict in and after the Soviet Union: The Mind Aflame* (London, Thousand Oaks, and New Delhi: Sage Publications, 1997), Jacques Lévesque, *The Enigma of 1989: The USSR and the Liberation of Eastern Europe* (Berkeley, Los Angeles, and London: University of California Press, 1997), Reneo Lukic and Allen Lynch, *Europe from the Balkans to the Urals: The Disintegration of Yugoslavia and the Soviet Union* (Oxford: Oxford University Press, 1996), and Andrzej Walicki, *Marxism and the Leap to the Kingdom of Freedom: The Rise and Fall of the Communist Utopia* (Stanford: Stanford University Press, 1995), to name just a few.

1 Nationalities and the Russian Problem in the USSR: A Historical Outline

I

The first All-Union Congress of Soviets met in Moscow on December 30, 1922, and adopted a declaration establishing the Union of Soviet Socialist Republics. It was a federal state, not restricted to any nation or area.[1] The new government was formed during 1923 and the Union's constitution was adopted in 1924. Many felt at the time that not only had a solution finally been found to the nationalities problem of the Russian Empire, but that the USSR would become the prototype of the future organization of mankind. In the communist doctrine of the following years, the Soviet Union was seen as the model for a world proletarian state. Even the establishment of other communist-ruled states in Eastern Europe after World War II did not immediately lead to the abandonment of this idea.

Only after Stalin's death did the Soviet model lose its initial universal significance. The doctrine of "different roads to socialism" implied that other communist states did not have to follow the Soviet model and had the right to build socialism and communism independently from the

First published in *Journal of International Affairs*, 1973.

USSR. According to this view, prominent in Eastern Europe between 1956 and 1968, the Soviet Union was a multinational state that had resolved the nationality problems of the nations of the former Russian Empire but was not necessarily a suitable model for others, not even in Eastern Europe.

Nineteen sixty-eight, the year when the USSR and its four allies intervened in Czechoslovakia, marked a change. According to the "Brezhnev doctrine" (the theoretical justification given for this act), the nations of Eastern Europe were now said to be a permanent part of a larger unity—the Socialist Community—of which the USSR was both the strongest and the most advanced component. What followed was a doctrinal reassessment of the Soviet experience, which was again elevated to the rank of universal (*obshchee*) as opposed to specific or particular (*chastnoe*) importance. This new stress on the Soviet experience as the model for the solution of the nationalities question throughout the world was particularly evident in publications honoring the fiftieth anniversary of the USSR.

Strangely enough, none of the other twelve communist-ruled states has so far adopted the Soviet formula of national relations in its internal organization. Most have retained the old ethnic designation of their states. Romania, for example, despite its large minorities, remains a Romanian national state. China likewise considers itself a national state first of all, though it formally recognized the local autonomy of its minorities. At one time, before they won power, the Chinese Communists had considered adopting the Soviet concept of national self-determination and a federal structure for China, but instead they chose a unitary structure similar to that which Stalin unsuccessfully proposed for Russia in 1922.[2] Two socialist states, Yugoslavia and Czechoslovakia, have adopted supranationalism and thus their "idea" resembles the theory on which the USSR was founded. Their actual organization, however, departs from the Soviet model in a fundamental respect. In the Soviet Union, the Russian nation functions as "the leading nation," with Russian as the privileged language, and the other nations and languages are in a subordinate position. The Serbs and Czechs do not enjoy a position analogous to that of the Russians in the USSR.

The departure from the internationalism that the Bolsheviks proclaimed in 1917 and practiced until the early 1930s was, in large measure, predetermined by the actual balance of forces between the Russians and non-Russians in the post-1917 decade. The actual revolution that transformed the nations of the USSR into subnations in relation to the Russians (or prevented the emergence of some peoples to full nation-hood) took place in the 1930s when the elites of the non-Russians were physically decimated and Russian language and culture firmly assumed a privileged position.

II

It was within the framework of the pre-socialist society of the Russian Empire that Lenin advanced the slogan of the self-determination of nations. Before 1914, Lenin treated nationality as a problem to be handled in the course of, or after, a democratic revolution that had yet to be completed in Russia.[3] Independence for the nationalities (along with the abolition of monarchy, land reform, and secularization) was viewed as one of the tasks to be accomplished by this bourgeois revolu-tion in Russia and Eastern Europe. Like other Marxists, Lenin felt that the nationalities question in the advanced capitalist countries was no longer an important issue, though Ireland was considered an exception.

Some of Lenin's fellow Marxists thought that his ideas contradicted the class approach expected of a proletarian leader. Lenin, however, held that so long as remnants of feudalism survived, the program of independ-ence for the nationalities (which he never considered a *proletarian* de-mand) was a progressive one, within the limits of bourgeois society. If in a future revolution some peoples of Russia opposed tsarism from a nationalist position, they would still be fighting tsarism and aiding progressive forces. Lenin did not advocate this attitude for workers, however. He only asked the Russian workers to support the right of non-Russian nationalities to separate themselves from Russia, thereby breaking with those Russian nationalists who wished forcibly to pre-serve the unity of the Empire. Non-Russian workers, on the other hand, were to demonstrate their renunciation of nationalism by not advocating separation from Russia and by working instead for *socialism*, side by side with Russian workers. Since socialism was by nature international, it was self-evident to Lenin that separation into independent national states would not take place under socialism.

Lenin felt that federalism, as a solution to the national question in the pre-socialist, democratic stage, would maintain divisions within the working class along ethnic lines. He did not exclude granting broad language rights to different regions of the state, but opposed making nationality the basis of political organization. Total political separation or complete political unity within the state would free the proletariat from nationalist influences. In this respect, he was essentially in accord with Engels, who argued that national independence for those nations that desired it would strengthen the socialist forces within them.[4]

What happened after the October Revolution was another matter, the Bolsheviks argued. Since various peoples of the former empire had established their national states in 1917–18, federalism under a Soviet regime and with Russia as the leading force was clearly a step *toward* unity. More importantly, the new Soviet federalism was as different from federalism as it was understood in the bourgeois world as the Soviet conceptions of free elections, democracy, and rights of the individual were different from those of the capitalist world. Besides, the Bolsheviks refused to introduce *any* form of federalism (that is, decentralization of decision-making power) into the party, the "driving force" of the Soviet state. Similarly, the army and the political police remained strictly centralized. To accept this kind of federalism required no serious revision of Lenin's original position favoring centralism.

Once the Bolsheviks had replaced the government of the capitalists with a government of workers and peasants, separation from Soviet Russia became clearly reactionary because it prevented the introduction of socialism into the "borderlands." Having dispersed the popularly elected Constituent Assembly, because it represented a political institution over which they did not have absolute control, the Bolsheviks likewise refused to respect the desire of Armenia or Georgia for independence.

Since, in Russia, it was the Communist party and not the Constituent Assembly that determined the course the country should adopt, the question arose as to who was entitled to determine the proletarian will of the various Soviet nationalities. Would national Communist parties be allowed to act on behalf of their nations? This was the hope of some Communists, but Lenin refused to allow the formation of independent Communist parties in the national republics. The only concession made was in response to the separation of Ukraine and other provinces of European Russia from the new Bolshevik state, a situation imposed on Moscow by the peace of Brest-Litovsk. This development led to the renaming of local organizations in non-Russian areas as "Communist parties." However, they were not given any autonomy from the center. This change of label was also a concession to the mood of the popular masses among whom formal symbols of national independence had won a certain popularity during the revolutionary period. Evidence that this autonomy was only nominal can be found in the Bolshevik refusal to allow the Ukrainian Communists to join the Communist International independently of the Russian party. They were reminded that their party was a regional branch of the Russian Communist party. In the final analysis, the Central Committee in Moscow was the sole spokesman for the national sovereignty of all nations of the Soviet state.

This does not mean that Lenin desired to maintain inequality among the nationalities. Rather, he desired the party to remain above all nationalities and wanted to prevent, in particular, the reassertion of Russian nationalism. But how could the party overcome a Russian national orientation when, in its composition, it was mainly Russian and those of its members who were not Russian by origin were more often than not thoroughly Russified? The Bolsheviks had their main strength in the Russian areas, since they were proletarian and urban-oriented. Furthermore, the historical and political traditions of Russia identified political power with Russian nationality. On the other hand, those parts of the former empire that in many ways had been more developed economically and politically, such as Finland, Poland, Latvia, and Estonia, did not emerge from the war and revolution as part of the Soviet world.

The hopes that the revolution would extend to Germany, Hungary, and other countries were soon disappointed. The identification of Russia with communism, which Stalin completed in the 1930s, began as early as the peace of Brest-Litovsk (which for a short time reduced Russia to its ethnic borders in Europe) and the march on Warsaw in 1920. "The International will pass . . . but the boundaries will remain," wrote V. Shulgin, an anticommunist Russian nationalist, in 1922.[5] His sentiments were shared by thousands of the ex-tsarist officers and officials who joined the Soviet cause because they considered the Bolsheviks the only force capable of saving the territorial unity of what they considered Russian lands.

Since so many of the former tsarist officials had entered the Soviet apparatus, Lenin feared that this element, which remained chauvinist in its attitude toward the non-Russians, might also make itself felt in the party. His notes, dictated on December 30–31, 1922 (precisely when the Congress of Soviets was proclaiming the establishment of the USSR), articulated those fears in unequivocal terms.[6] Still, Lenin failed to devise an effective method of curbing Russian nationalism. He believed that communism destroyed the conditions that give rise to nationalism and therefore he treated nationalism as a survival of the past. In the words of Richard Pipes, Lenin failed to recognize that nationalism "reflected also specific interests and strivings that could not be satisfied merely by tact but required real political and other concessions."[7]

If Lenin underestimated its seriousness under Bolshevik rule, he understood that nationalism was potentially a great force in Asia, Africa, and Eastern Europe, and for this reason he warned the party against a revival of a specifically Russian image of the Soviet state.[8]

III

Even after the Red Army, with the help of local Communists, had established Soviet regimes in Ukraine, Azerbaijan, Armenia, Georgia, and Belorussia, as well as in the Moslem areas of Central Asia, most of the republics (except those that were included in the Russian republic) formally constituted independent states and their relations with Moscow were regulated by treaties.[9] By virtue of these treaties, the Russian government gradually assumed the authority over military and economic matters, transportation, and communications that it had de facto enjoyed from the moment the Soviet regime was established in the area. The formerly separate republics preserved such formal attributes of sovereignty as the right to maintain diplomatic relations with foreign countries. Soviet Ukraine, for example, maintained diplomatic relations with Poland, Czechoslovakia, and Germany, and was a party to the treaty of Riga (1921), which established the eastern boundary of Poland.

In practice, the authorities of the Russian republic violated the agreements regulating their relations with the other Soviet republics and treated them as mere subdivisions of Russia like Bashkiria or Daghestan, which had been formed as autonomous, not independent, socialist republics within the Russian Soviet Federated Socialist Republic (RSFSR). In 1922, Stalin, then Commissar of Nationalities in the RSFSR government, proposed to transform Ukraine, Belorussia, Armenia, Georgia, and Azerbaijan into autonomous republics of the RSFSR.[10] The implications of the Stalin proposal were far-reaching. Both domestically and internationally they amounted to the restoration of a single Russian state on the entire territory ruled by the Communists. The communist state would bear the name of Russia (*Rossiia*) and combine the areas inhabited by ethnic Russians (*russkie* or *velikorossy*) and those inhabited primarily by non-Russians, who would be granted a national minority status *within* Russia.

Stalin's plan was accepted by a special commission dealing with the problem of relations between the republics, but it was firmly rejected by Lenin, who immediately saw that it amounted to a formal restoration of the Russians to a privileged position that would be opposed and resented within the Soviet state. It would also weaken the appeal of communism as a friend of national liberation movements in the outside world. Lenin's counterproposal, which was formally accepted, envisaged the formation of a new federal structure above the RSFSR and the other independent Soviet republics. The new formation was to be devoid of any ethnic connotation in its name, since it constituted a supranational state. Russia would join the new state as one of its component parts, an equal of Ukraine, said Lenin.[11]

When the constitution was actually adopted, the federal government was granted broader powers than Lenin had envisaged in his December 1922 notes and the Russian republic secured a majority of seats in both chambers of the federal legislature.[12] This was made possible, in part, by the failure to elevate such advanced nationalities as the Tatars to the status of a Union republic (Tataria, to this day, remains a part of the RSFSR) and the refusal to adopt a proposal that would have restricted the representation of a single republic in the second chamber to not more than two-fifths of the total membership. Yet, despite its restrictions, the new federal system recognized the principle of national equality and independence (that is, the Union republics reserved the right to secede from the Union). It granted the national republics a constitutional recognition as permanent elements of the Soviet state organization and thus contributed to the rise and strengthening of the national consciousness of the Soviet peoples. Pipes argues that the Soviet Union was a "compromise between doctrine and reality," between the communist ideal of a centralized organization and the empirical fact of nationalism. It was a temporary solution only, a transitional stage to a completely centralized and supranational worldwide Soviet state. He further contends that

> . . . from the point of view of self-rule the Communist government was even less generous to the minorities than its tsarist predecessor had been: it destroyed independent parties, tribal self-rule, religious and

cultural institutions. It was a unitary, centralized, totalitarian state such as the tsarist state had never been. On the other hand, by granting the minorities extensive linguistic autonomy and by placing the national-territorial principle at the base of the state's political administration, the Communists gave constitutional recognition to the multinational structure of the Soviet population. In view of the importance which language and territory have for the development of national consciousness—particularly for people who, like the Russian minorities during the Revolution, have had some experience of self-rule—this purely formal feature of the Soviet Constitution may well prove to have been historically one of the most consequential aspects of the formation of the Soviet Union.[13]

This fact, and the mass expansion of education, publishing, and the press, which in the 1920s and early 1930s was carried out in the national languages of the republics, unquestionably helped to strengthen the non-Russian elements in the USSR. The advantages to the communist cause were immediate. Internationalist nationality policy facilitated the acceptance of communism and the Soviet form of government in the non-Russian areas, making it possible to reach the peasantry and win the collaboration of the national intelligentsia with the Soviets. Abroad, the Soviets could present an image of a system that combined socialism with national equality and autonomy. Communism in these years represented a particularly attractive ideology for the dissatisfied national minorities of non-Soviet Eastern Europe.

IV

The adoption of political unity, in the form of the USSR, did not at first weaken the official status of non-Russian languages. The Soviet authorities treated language as a medium and were only concerned that the content be socialist in all languages. Linguistic pluralism did not seem to threaten socialism in the USSR. The view that Stalin expressed in a speech at the Tenth Party Congress (1921) was considered to be the party line on "language construction." Having stated that he had received a note contending that the Communists were "artificially cultivating a Byelorussian nationality," Stalin proclaimed that the Belorussian nationality existed and had its own language, different from Russian. "You cannot go against history," he declared. Furthermore, even though Russian elements still predominated in the Ukrainian towns, these towns would, he felt, inevitably become Ukrainian, exactly as Riga had ceased to be a German city and had become Latvian. Towns grow at the expense of the countryside, Stalin explained, which is the "guardian of nationality," and the towns of Belorussia would likewise become Belorussian.[14]

Later, in the 1920s, Stalin grew fearful of the direction the rise of formerly oppressed nationalities was taking. In particular, he was highly suspicious of the pressure developing in Ukraine for "de-Russification" of the towns, even though he claimed to oppose only the "excessive haste," not the goal itself. He was apprehensive of the demands made by Ukrainian Communists to have Ukrainians appointed to top party and government posts in the Ukraine and of the slogans, current in the circles of even the communist Ukrainian intelligentsia, which advocated a cultural orientation "toward Europe" and "away from Moscow."[15]

Since analogous processes and tendencies were discernible in other Soviet republics, Stalin may have decided that the policy of encouraging the broadest use of non-Russian languages in education, culture, government, and public organizations would have to be reversed, lest the national movements get out of hand and eventually pose a threat to the principle of party centralism and centralized management of the economy. The liberal linguistic policies rested on the premise that the party would serve as the leading and integrating political force, and that the class interests and solidarity of the proletariat would prevail over and counteract any centrifugal tendencies that might arise from cultural differences among the peoples of the USSR. There was, of course, a social class, the peasantry, especially the village "capitalist," the *kulak*, to whom the dissident nationalist intelligentsia might appeal for support (and conversely, that class might find its spokesmen and leaders in the urban intelligentsia). Stalin feared this alliance, and his behavior in the 1930s should possibly be interpreted as an endeavor to achieve what, in 1921, he had said could not be done (that is, he wished to "go against history"). As a Marxist, Stalin should have been satisfied with the social transformation of the countryside. His practice in that decade and later indicates that he was not prepared to let history take care of nationalism by eliminating its social causes. Even more paradoxically, Stalin rehabilitated one nationalism (Russian) precisely at the moment when, according to Marxism-Leninism, the whole socioeconomic base of nationalism had been eliminated.

Certain prerequisites for the operation he directed in the 1930s had already been established in the 1920s. Even though Stalin had at first to accept formally Lenin's idea of a supranational state, his later policies clearly suggest that he pursued his own line. Instead of blatantly incorporating the Union republics into the RSFSR, Stalin gradually deprived them of major prerogatives they had retained under the first federal constitution. Simultaneously, the RSFSR gradually lost much of its separate identity and the all-Union organs came to combine their functions with those of the Russian republic. There was, however, a limited departure from this system after Stalin's death and a number of separate RSFSR agencies were restored (certain ministries, the Writers' Union, and the Red Cross Society, for example).

As the struggle for power after Lenin was resolved in his favor, Stalin became free to concentrate on the problem of the nationally minded Communists, many of whom had earlier sided with him against Trotsky. The introduction of the first five-year plan resulted in further concentration of power, as did collectivization. For example, collectivization and the problem of what the Ukrainian Communists considered excessive quotas for grain deliveries actually led to Moscow's direct appointment of new leaders in Ukraine.

None of these political, administrative, and economic changes logically required a revision of the policy on language rights of the nationalities, even though such events as the mass famine in Ukraine and Kazakhstan had a direct effect on the demographic potential of the non-Russians.[16] The decade of the 1930s, however, saw not only collectivization, industrialization, and urbanization, but also mass arrests, deportations, and killings. The victims of the terror also included political, military, industrial, and cultural cadres of Russian nationality, but the long-range effect of these mass arrests and killings was particularly devastating to the non-Russian nationalities. In Ukraine and Belorussia, the removal of the prepurge elites (first the noncommunist cultural and technical intelligentsia, then the non-Stalinist Communists, and finally even the Stalinists) resulted in the replacement of non-Russian cadres by Russian or Russified elements. For example, of the 102 members and candidate members of the Ukrainian Central Committee, only three survived the purge of 1937. In addition, all members of the Ukrainian government and all provincial party secretaries were removed, as were uncounted numbers of lower functionaries.[17] The terror in the formerly Muslim republics of Central Asia was no less harsh. Between 1930 and 1938, seven successive purges eliminated almost all the native Party personnel. The scope of the purge can be seen in the following figures: (1) in Tadjikistan, two presidents and two prime ministers of the republic were liquidated; (2) Kirgizia's premier was purged; and (3) Uzbekistan lost its premier, Faizulla Khodzaev, who had occupied that post from 1924 to 1937, and, within one year, three of his successors were likewise purged.[18]

The terror was equally severe for the cultural and scientific cadres, journalists, writers, and teachers. As a result, both the national intelligentsia, which had survived the war and revolution, and the new Soviet intelligentsia were physically removed from the scene and the cities, which Stalin expected to become inevitably Belorussian or Ukrainian, regained their prerevolutionary Russian appearance. The policy of relying on Russian personnel was also pursued in Central Asia. The break between the pre- and postpurge periods was not only in personnel but also in outlook and the cultural and ethnic identity of the leading stratum.

Stalinism did not eliminate the non-Russian languages from public use entirely; their function was restricted to serving the rural population. Russian-language schools became common in Ukrainian and Belorussian cities, but the small towns and villages retained Ukrainian and Belorussian as the languages of instruction. This emphasized their social and historical inferiority in relation to Russian which, by virtue of the elimination of the non-Russian elites, would now enjoy the status of being the only medium of high culture, science and industry, and urban civilization in the non-Russian republics. This generalization does not apply, however, to Georgia and Armenia, where the local cultures retained a position in the cities.

Simultaneously, traditional Russian values and historical, military, and political traditions were "rehabilitated." The tsars were discovered to have been progressive historical figures, and the various peoples of Russia, previously described as victims of colonial conquest, were now said to have been saved by the Russians from their own as well as from Western oppressors.[19] In Russia itself, this ideological change was accompanied by a purge of Marxist ideological and academic cadres—for example, the historians who had been active in the 1920s and early 1930s.

The non-Russian languages were reformed "from within" when the party called for a wider use of Russian terminology in the other Soviet languages and ordered that foreign words be admitted into the other languages in the same form in which they were used in Russian.[20] This was not done solely with Slavic languages. In Bashkir and Yakut, for example, technical/scientific and political terminology is based on Russian words. Special lists of "forbidden words" were issued for the instruction of editors and publishers. This newspeak was presumably intended to weaken the capacity of languages for independent development and to facilitate the assimilation to Russian. Stalin seems to have considered linguistic unity a major factor in determining the chances of large empires to survive. In this respect, he thought class solidarity and economic factors to be less effective in integrating the peoples of the USSR than a common language or common historical memories (even if these had to be manufactured).[21]

V

The Stalinist solution of the nationalities problem might have been successful in the long run had later events not radically changed the domestic setup and international environment of the Soviet Union. World War II resulted in the inclusion of several European nationalities (Latvians, Estonians, Lithuanians, Western Ukrainians, and Western Belorussians) into the USSR and weakened the biological potential of the Russians and Slavs in general. Furthermore, the establishment of communist-ruled states in Eastern Europe had a subverting effect on the Soviet identity, which found itself between the national identity of individual Soviet nations (among which Russian nationalism enjoyed official approval) and the international socialist system of which the USSR was a part.

The war years and the immediate postwar period were characterized in domestic Soviet life by an intensified glorification of the Russian nation (note the famous Stalin toast in honor of the Russian nation at the victory reception in the Kremlin in May 1945) and by the continuation of the terrorist methods of the thirties. The Volga Germans, Kalmyks, Balkars, Kabardians, Chechens, Crimean Tatars, and Meskhetians were deported from their homelands en masse, including Communist party members, war veterans, and other seemingly nonseditious elements.[22] These peoples were deprived of all cultural and educational facilities in their native languages. As Khrushchev revealed at the Twentieth Party Congress (1956), Stalin did not similarly deport all Ukrainians only because there were too many of them. He did, however, deport some, as well as unreliable elements from the Baltic states. In addition, Stalin's treatment of the Jews clearly shows that he planned to obliterate a separate Jewish nationality in the USSR. In 1948, for instance, all Jewish cultural activities were put to an end and, in 1952, many leading writers, artists, and politicians were killed.[23]

The relations of the USSR with Eastern Europe, meanwhile, were very one-sided. Although an effort was made to popularize Soviet achievements in countries such as Poland and Czechoslovakia, the peoples of the Soviet Union were isolated from contacts with the cultures of those states. It is reasonable to suspect that the authorities feared that direct contacts between the Union republics of the USSR and the newly established "people's democracies" might tend to disrupt their efforts to promote integration of the Soviet population around the Russian language and to develop a distinct Soviet culture.

The very retention of separate communist nation-states required a doctrinal explanation. Earlier views that had interpreted the "people's democracies" as an alternative path to socialism were rejected. The official interpretation established in the late 1940s held that the "people's democracies" were at a lower stage in relation to the Soviet Union, not a parallel one. Their progress toward socialism was to be measured by the degree to which they approximated the Soviet example. It was not excluded that at some unspecified stage the "people's democracies" might reach a sufficiently high level to qualify for admission to the USSR. Even the Yugoslavs at first considered themselves potential candidates for inclusion in the USSR. It does not matter whether they really desired to surrender their independence; so long as they remained in ideological communion with Moscow, they lacked a theory to explain the permanence of national independence under communism. The defection (or rather expulsion) of Yugoslavia from the Soviet bloc, in 1948, was tantamount to denying it the character of a socialist state, since no socialist state could exist independent from the influence of, if not within, the USSR. The admission by the Soviets, in 1955, that Yugoslavia *was* a socialist state had a profoundly revolutionary effect in communist Eastern Europe, and the spread of Titoism to Eastern Europe was a natural consequence. If the Yugoslavs and then the Poles were to be allowed to search for and develop the best ways of building socialism in their respective countries, then the Soviet Union no longer presented *the* image of their future. The USSR was thus downgraded to the rank of the earliest—and somewhat obsolete—model of socialist construction. Moreover, since the Soviet Union was a multinational state, its legitimacy in a world of independent national states was open to doubt. Instead of appearing, in terms of the doctrine, to be ahead of the Poles or Bulgarians, the Ukrainians and Latvians were bound to look underdeveloped and less-than-independent if national independence, so successfully vindicated by Yugoslavia, was a prerogative of a socialist nation.[24]

VI

The intervention in Czechoslovakia restored the self-confidence of the Soviet leaders. Not only did their doctrine of the right of intervention prove successful in the first attempt to enforce it—their right to police the area was tacitly recognized by the world—but they also reasserted their dormant claim to represent the most powerful socialist state, one whose political organization was of a higher order than an ordinary national state.

From the point of view of the Soviet leaders, one of the most disturbing aspects of the Czechoslovak reform movement of 1968 may have been that the Czechoslovaks were developing an institutional mechanism to guarantee national equality to the Czechs and Slovaks, thus challenging both the Soviet doctrine and practice under which one nation occupied a superior and privileged position. The pre-1968 system, although it gave the Slovaks broad linguistic autonomy, placed Slovakia in a subordinate role in the Czech–Slovak partnership. The reform proposals of 1968, some of which were formally enacted only after August, corrected the balance. However, the Czechoslovaks were not allowed to reorganize their Communist party by establishing a separate regional organization within it for the Czech lands. That would have been an adoption of the Yugoslav practice, which has a Serbian Communist party, along with those of Croatia, Macedonia, and others. In the Soviet Union, there is no separate party organization for the RSFSR; the Central Committee of the CPSU acts also as the central party organization for Russia.

The celebration of the fiftieth anniversary of the USSR was not just an internal Soviet affair. It served to highlight the new image of the Soviet Union as a state that had solved its complicated nationalities problem in an exemplary manner. If the Soviet Union was on the defen-

sive in the post-1953 era of different roads to socialism, national communism, socialism with a human face, and the rest, after 1968 the roles
were reversed again, as clearly seen in the anniversary enunciations. Integration has now become the order of the day for the socialist states of
Eastern Europe, and the republics of the USSR, having passed through
the stage of isolated national existence, have already become members
of an international socialist structure.

It is no accident that a recent highly authoritative Soviet work on
"Leninism and the Nationality Question under the Present Conditions"
finds similarities between Soviet Russia's relations with the other Soviet
republics and Bela Kun's Soviet government of Hungary immediately
after the October Revolution, on one hand, and the present-day situation in the socialist camp (in particular, the states friendly to the Soviet
Union) on the other. For example, the book compares the military union
of the first Soviet republics with the present Warsaw Pact organization;
it also draws analogies between the economic cooperation of the early
socialist states ("Soviet Hungary" and "Soviet Russia," we are told, discussed supplying fuel and exchange of personnel as possible forms of
cooperation) and the contemporary COMECON.[25] Would it be against
the intentions of the authors if the reader concluded that a Socialist
Community might emerge in a not too distant future, much as the Soviet
Union had emerged from the variety of agreements between the formally
independent socialist states of fifty years ago? In fact, the Community is
already a reality, as exemplified by COMECON, the Warsaw Pact, and
the Political Consultative Committee. Other indicators of a presumed
unity are: (1) Its members share the same ideology, Marxism-Leninism;
(2) their socioeconomic systems are getting closer to each other; and (3)
they even have a language of interstate communication.[26] Furthermore,
as 1968 showed, the defense of socialism in each is a matter of common
concern, though the USSR may perhaps display its concern more force-
fully than others.

If the new line revives an old Soviet conception, it does so with a
difference. In the past, socialist states were expected to join the USSR at
an appropriate moment. Now the Soviet Union itself is joining, as it
were, a new, higher structure, the Socialist Community. There is no indication that the Soviet leaders are preparing to join the Community in a
multiple capacity through the Union republics. Ukraine and Belorussia,
though members of the UN, do not belong to any intra-bloc organizations (with the exception of Radio-TV associations). It might be argued

that if each Soviet republic joined the Community directly, the members of the Community would be more equal in population, power, and resources, but, on the other hand, the "leading role" which the Russian nation is enjoying now would certainly be undercut. For this reason it is unlikely to appeal to the Soviet leaders.

VII

Despite Soviet claims to the contrary, the problem of nationalities within the USSR has not been resolved to the satisfaction of the party. In the twenty years since Stalin died, the party has taken several different approaches.[27] From 1953 to about 1958, some of the excesses of Stalinism were corrected. Except for the Tatars, Meskhetians, and Germans, the deported nationalities were permitted to return to their former homelands, more non-Russians occupied important party and government posts in their republics and the central administration, and educational and cultural concessions were made.

The liberal line came to a halt, in 1958–59, when Khrushchev decided that Soviet school children spent too much time studying languages and proposed to make the teaching of the second Soviet language voluntary. The school debate that followed Khrushchev's "Theses," apparently against his intention, uncovered a great deal of ethnic feeling.[28] At the same time, party ideologists, having misread the 1959 census returns, began to write that a "fusion" of peoples was taking place in the USSR. The number of non-Russians who declared Russian as their native tongue was constantly cited as the harbinger of things to come, and legal journals argued that the Soviet federation had fulfilled its historic role and might soon be replaced by a unitary state.[29] These developments caused more resentment among non-Russians, however.

The fall of Khrushchev brought a change in the propaganda line. Since 1964, Soviet officials have been more careful not to offend the national sensitivities of non-Russians. The Soviet Union is to remain a federal state. Non-Russian languages have a future, and, according to the party, the nationalities of the USSR are not a single nation in the making, but a qualitatively new grouping of peoples who retain their ethnic characteristics while forming, at the same time, "the Soviet people." National cultures of all Soviet nationalities are said to be flourishing (*rastsvet*) and drawing together (*sblizhenie*). The latter, the party explains, does not mean that national cultures are to be eliminated, as was implied under Khrushchev.[30]

This more moderate, conciliatory language has been accompanied by an intensification of educational assimilation. Even Stalin abstained from an overt restriction of the formal rights of the republics in the area of education. However, in 1966, a decree of the Supreme Soviet's Presidium established a federal Ministry of Education to which the secondary and elementary school network was subordinated. Republic Ministries of Education were placed under the Moscow body, and such matters as school curricula in the non-Russian schools, the hours of Russian language to be taught, the length of the school term, choice of examination requirements, and the like were placed under central regulation. This gave them the same status as colleges and specialized secondary schools, which, with some exceptions, had been put under central government control in the 1930s. In 1972, in one of its enactments, the Ministry of Education critically reviewed the teaching of Russian in Estonia and Turkmenia and instructed all non-Russian schools in the Soviet Union to broaden the use of Russian in schoolwork and in extracurricular activities.[31] Simultaneously, preparatory classes for six-year-olds have been set up with the explicit goal of teaching Russian.[32] Thus, the Stalinist policy of changing languages from within has been continued by the educational authorities. The textbooks for most school subjects in the USSR are uniform throughout the country and the non-Russian schools use texts translated from Russian. Furthermore, a writer in the Ukrainian literary newspaper complained recently that the language used in those Ukrainian translations departs from the rules of present literary Ukrainian (which had already been made closer to Russian).[33]

The Soviet authorities, ever since Stalin, have, in practice, believed that the safest way to integrate the peoples of the USSR into a single community is through linguistic assimilation rather than through ideology or class solidarity. Since the mid-1930s, vast numbers of Soviet citizens of non-Russian nationality have been receiving advanced education in Russian and have functioned professionally in a Russian-language environment. Despite this, many have refused to consider themselves Russian by nationality, even when they declare Russian as their "native" language. The Soviet experience suggests that, despite the pressure for assimilation, urbanization and industrialization have produced unassimilated, though modernized, non-Russian cadres. Even in those cases where they have adopted Russian, linguistic assimilation has not necessarily resulted in a change in identity. Sometimes in non-Russian republics it may even be accompanied by anti-Russian attitudes and resentment of the "leading role" of the Russians and the Russian language.[34] Even a group as Russified as the Jews underwent a national reawakening in the late 1960s and began asserting the right of Jews to emigrate. The problem is further aggravated by recent demographic trends. The returns of the 1970 census showed that the non-Russians were increasing faster than the Russians and that the Muslim peoples, who are the least assimilated, also had the highest rates of growth. The hopes placed on the effectiveness of mixing populations also appear to have been exaggerated.[35] In the face of such problems, some of the Soviet social scientists have recommended that the linguistic assimilation of non-Russians should be attempted at a very early age, or, as one author put it, at a "pre-competitive" stage of personality formation.[36] The present system of teaching Russian at a preschool level seems to be an application of this recommendation.

It is reasonable to assume that the present policy toward nationalities does not reflect the point of view of all elements in the Soviet party and government apparatus. There may well be those who would prefer the system to respond to the demographic growth and rising ethnic assertiveness of Soviet peoples with concessions in the spirit of Leninism rather than with assimilation and its corollary, forceful suppression of those who resist assimilation.

Whether the party will choose to continue its present policies or decide to revise them, only the future can tell. If it opts for the latter course, there should be no shortage of ideas as to what should be done to bring about equal and free relations among the Soviet nations. In addition to the ideas expressed in the legal press, the Soviet Union has, in the past few years, had an underground literature or samizdat.[37] There are at least three standpoints on nationalities discernible in the samizdat literature. First, there is the "civil rights" or "general democratic" platform, which discloses the cases of national persecution as part of its general concern with the rights of man, including religious and national rights, freedom of speech, association, and the like. A second group is represented by the various nationality programs or demands that express particular grievances and aspirations of their respective peoples (such as Jewish demands for emigration, Tatar assertion of the right to return to Crimea, and Ukrainian and Baltic opposition to Russification efforts and the planned importation of Russian cadres). It is noteworthy, however, that no cases of inter-ethnic prejudice or hostility have emerged so far from this group. The ethnic dissenters are not intrinsically anti-Russian; rather, they oppose the uses made by the regime of the Russians and the Russian language for subduing the nationalities. Finally, there exists a Russian nationalistic, anti-Semitic, and chauvinist samizdat, which may be simply summed up as demanding open recognition of the entire Soviet Union as *Russia*, the Russian national state.

The existence of a Russian nationalist samizdat does not mean that genuine Russian nationalism, as distinct from the regime's manipulation of Russian national symbols, has not had outlets in the legally published journals. On the contrary, over the period of the past three or four years, Russian nationalism, expressed primarily in the form of historical, literary, and philosophical reflections, has been a regular fare offered to the readers of journals like the Komsomol monthly *Molodaia gvardiia* [Young Guard]. Some of the enthusiasts for the Russian past have gone so far as to condemn the radicals and revolutionaries of the nineteenth century for having allegedly been bad Russian patriots and for having slandered Russian customs and institutions. The Russian Communists consider the Decembrists, Herzen, and Chernyshevsky as Russia's progressive figures and themselves, in a sense, as their heirs. Rehabilitation of the Slavophiles, Panslavs, monarchists, and religious thinkers of the past—the other side of the writings of those who criticize the radicals— has had to be stopped and the party has officially condemned the more extreme expressions of the "nonhistorical," solidarist (as opposed to class) approach to the past.[38]

Considering the incidence of Russian nationalist pronouncements both in the official and unofficial press, it appears that the party is under pressure to bring about an even closer identification of the USSR with the "eternal Russia" and to show even less patience with the existing national identities of Soviet peoples than it is now doing. In any consideration of the Soviet record in achieving the integration of its ethnic groups around a common political identity, one should note not only that this identity is already loaded with Russian ethnic content, but also that some Russians consider it going too far toward accommodating the nationalities. While ruthlessly controlling the nationalities, the party seems to be realizing that it can no longer afford to view the extreme Russian nationalist outpourings with relative tolerance, since they are bound to stir the national emotions of non-Russians.

What can the party do to promote a genuine *Soviet* (as opposed to a Russian, Ukrainian, or Uzbek) political identity? The first step would seem to be a demonstration that the Soviet state organization constitutes a mechanism for articulation and resolution of all problems that are of concern to its citizens, including the issues of national rights, self-government, the use of language, and cultural freedom. This can only be done by bringing the masses to participate meaningfully in the Soviet political process and requires freedom of the press, discussion, and open airing of all topical questions. Are the Soviet institutions, from the local councils to the Supreme Soviet, ready to serve as a forum for free discussion? The same question, for example, can be asked of the party congresses, the press, and voluntary social organizations.

In the absence of an open, legal avenue for public debate, some form of samizdat press is bound to exist, despite the most severe repression. Soviet samizdat publications have concerned themselves with a broad variety of issues: religious, artistic, cultural, literary, political, legal, social, and economic. It is a matter of speculation whether the dissent they represent will coalesce "horizontally" in an all-Union movement concentrating on social, cultural, and economic issues across ethnic or regional divisions or, alternatively, whether the various strands of disaffection will unite "vertically," as components of separate but internally unified nationalist movements of respective Soviet nationalities. Among these nationalist trends, Russian nationalism is the most dangerous because it has powerful supporters within the official hierarchy. If the Soviet Union is to achieve a genuine political integration without eliminating ethnic distinctions, repudiation of Russian nationalism should be the most urgent task of the Soviet leaders. If they do not separate Russian national accretions from what (over the years) has come to be considered the Soviet identity, the regime is bound to go on mistaking Russification for the promotion of a new internationalist socialist civilization.[39]

Notes

1. For a history and analysis of the establishment of the Soviet Union and a summary presentation of the nationalities question in the Russian Empire, see Richard Pipes, *The Formation of the Soviet Union*, rev. ed. (New York: Atheneum, 1968). Among numerous other works dealing with various aspects of socialism, nationalism, and Russia, see Alfred C. Meyer, *Leninism*, rev. ed.

(Cambridge, Mass.: Harvard University Press, 1971), Stanley W. Page, *Lenin and World Revolution* (New York: New York University Press, 1959), Alfred D. Low, *Lenin and the Question of Nationality* (New York: Bookman Associates, 1958), and Elliot R. Goodman, *The Soviet Design for a World State* (New York: Columbia University Press, 1960). All these books, and many others, are criticized by a Soviet scholar, I. S. Zenushkina, *Sovetskaia natsional'naia politika burzhuaznye istoriki* (Moscow: Mysl', 1971). A historical background is provided in Hugh Seton-Watson, *The Decline of Imperial Russia, 1855–1914* (New York: Praeger, 1952), and his *The Russian Empire, 1801–1917* (London: Oxford University Press, 1967).

2. See Goodman, *The Soviet Design*, pp. 358–59, for references (in the 1930s) to a future Chinese Federation and its joining a "World-wide Soviet Republic."

3. The paragraphs in this section represent the briefest of summaries of Lenin's thoughts on nationality in the pre-1917 period and are meant to serve as a background for and an introduction to the Soviet treatment of the nationalities question. For more in-depth analyses and specific references to Lenin's writings, consult the works cited in note 1, particularly Pipes, *Formation of the Soviet Union*, pp. 34–49. Lenin's writings on this subject are conveniently assembled in an English translation, *V. I. Lenin, Selected Works*, 3 vols. (New York: International Publishers, 1967). Volumes 1 and 2 contain the pre-1917 writings.

4. As Marx and Engels pointed out: "It is in the direct and absolute interest of the English working class to get rid of their present connection with Ireland." Karl Marx and Friedrich Engels, *Selected Correspondence* (London, 1943), pp. 279–80, cited in Ivan Dziuba, *Internationalism or Russification? A Study of the Soviet Nationalities Problem*, 2d ed. (London: Weidenfield & Nicolson, 1968), p. 78. Furthermore, Engels wrote that "[a]s long as it lacks national independence, a . . . people is historically unable even simply to discuss in earnest any domestic questions." K. Kautsky, *Aus der Frühzeit des Marxismus. Engels' Briefwechsel mit Kautsky* (Prague: Orbis-Verlag, 1935), p. 67, cited in Dziuba, *Internationalism*, p. 77.

5. Cited in Dziuba, *Internationalism*, p. 66.

6. Lenin's notes, dictated to his secretary, were first published in V. I. Lenin, *Sochineniia*, 4th ed., vol. 33 (Moscow, Izdatel'stvo politicheskoi literatury, 1957), pp. 553–59, and are cited (in English) in Pipes, *Formation of the Soviet Union*, pp. 282–87.

7. Ibid., p. 277. [What I meant to say was that Lenin did not follow through on the implications of his statement that nationalism was not just a matter of inherited prejudices but was a response to real conditions and these real conditions would give rise to problems under socialism, too—*note added, 1999.*]

8. Lenin wrote: "It would be unforgivable opportunism if, on the eve of this

emergence of the East and at the beginning of its awakening, we should under-mine our prestige there with even the slightest rudeness or injustice to our own minorities." Cited in ibid., p. 286.

9. The texts of these treaties can be found in S. S. Studenikin, ed., *Istoriia sovetskoi konstitutsii (v dokumentakh), 1917–1956* (Moscow: Gosudarstven-noe izdatel'stvo iuridicheskoi literatury, 1957).

10. Stalin's proposal of 1922 has never been published in full, but for a re-construction on the basis of partial citations in Soviet literature, see Pipes, *For-mation of the Soviet Union*, pp. 270–71. Its existence had not been known until 1956, which explains why Isaac Deutscher, in his *Stalin: A Political Biography*, 2d ed. (New York: Oxford University Press, 1966), p. 244, called Stalin "the chief architect of the reform" and attributed Lenin's ideas to Stalin. Deutscher's book was first published in 1949 and the author did not correct this matter in the second edition.

11. Lenin's memorandum, "Ob obrazovanii SSSR," was published in V. I. Lenin, *Polnoe sobranie sochinenii*, vol. 45 (Moscow: Izdatel'stvo politicheskoi literatury, 1970), pp. 211–13. Lenin proclaimed: "We recognize ourselves as equals of the Ukrainian S.S.R. and others, and together with them, and as their equals, we enter a new union, a new federation, the 'Union of Soviet Socialist Republics of Europe and Asia'"(p. 211) [my translation]. For a summary and brief citations, see Pipes, *Formation of the Soviet Union*, pp. 272–73.

12. The text of this constitution can be found in Studenikin, *Istoriia sovet-skoi konstitutsii*, pp. 458–73, and (in English) in Jan F. Triska, ed., *Constitu-tions of the Communist Party-States* (Stanford: Hoover Institution Press, 1968), pp. 17–36.

13. Pipes, *Formation of the Soviet Union*, pp. 296–97.

14. J. V. Stalin, *Works*, vol. 5 (Moscow: Foreign Languages Publishing House, 1953), pp. 48–49.

15. Stalin's position was stated in his letter of April 26, 1926, addressed to Lazar Kaganovich, at that time first secretary of the Communist party of Ukraine, and was published for the first time only in 1948. For an English trans-lation, see ibid., vol. 18, pp. 157–63. See also George S. N. Luckyj, *Literary Politics in the Soviet Ukraine, 1917–1934* (New York: Columbia University Press, 1956), pp. 66–68, and Robert S. Sullivant, *Soviet Politics and the Ukraine, 1917–1957* (New York: Columbia University Press, 1962), pp. 126–34, for more information on this problem. By 1926, according to Sullivant, Stalin "was beginning to identify Russia and Russian institutions with Marxism and Bolshevik rule" (p. 132). For analogous problems, see Edward Allworth, *Central Asian Publishing and the Rise of Nationalism* (New York: New York Public library, 1965) and his *Uzbek Literary Politics* (The Hague: Mouton, 1964).

16. For further information about the famine of 1932–33, see *Ukraine: A Concise Encyclopedia*, vol. I (Toronto: Toronto University Press, 1963), pp. 200–201 and 820–22. For a literary account of the collectivization and famine in Ukraine, see the novel of a Soviet Russian writer, Vasily Grossman, *Forever Flowing*, trans. Thomas P. Whitney (New York: Harper & Row, 1972).

17. Robert Conquest, *The Great Terror: Stalin's Purge of the Thirties* (London: Macmillan & Co., 1968), Nicholas P. Vakar, *Belorussia: The Making of a Nation* (Cambridge, Mass.: Harvard University Press, 1956), especially pp. 145–54, and Hryhory Kostiuk, *Stalinist Rule in the Ukraine: A Study of the Decade of Mass Terror, 1929–1939* (New York: Praeger, 1961). For a Soviet historical review of the same period, see M. P. Bazhan et al., eds., *Soviet Ukraine* (Kyiv: Academy of Sciences of the Ukrainian SSR, 1970). For the purposes of this discussion it is relevant to note that in the period of their difficulties with Stalin in the 1940s Yugoslavs were fully aware of the real story of the purges. See Vladimir Dedijer, *The Battle Stalin Lost: Memoirs of Yugoslavia 1948–1953* (New York: Viking, 1971), especially pp. 99–100, 260–61, and 316–19. There are also references to the purge in the writings of Milovan Djilas.

18. Michael Rywkin, *Russia in Central Asia* (New York: Collier Books, 1963), pp. 103–4. He also notes that: "All were liquidated as enemies of the people, while at the same time thousands of their followers were purged. The potential or imaginary danger of national Communism was thus eliminated, but the cost for the Party was a heavy one: native Party cadres . . . became weaker and less efficient than ever and, consequently, more dependent upon outside (Russian) guardianship."

Another author, Hélène Carrère d'Encausse, spoke about "the elimination of most educated national cadres" following the purge of Uzbekistan's political leadership. See her chapter, "The National Republics Lose Their Independence," in *Central Asia: A Century of Russian Rule*, ed. Edward Allworth (New York: Columbia University Press, 1967), pp. 254–65.

19. The radical turn in the Soviet treatment of the tsarist past first became evident in Stalin's speech to industrial managers, made in February 1931. See Deutscher, *Stalin*, pp. 328–29. The open break with the previous internationalist conception of history, associated with the name of the famous Russian Marxist historian, M. N. Pokrovskii (1868–1932), took place in 1934. See Konstantin Shteppa, *Russian Historians and the Soviet State* (New Brunswick, N.J.: Rutgers University Press, 1962), and Roman Szporluk, ed., *Russia in World History: Selected Essays by M. N. Pokrovskii* (Ann Arbor: University of Michigan Press, 1970), especially pp. 35–42.

20. This party policy was never enunciated in a single, generally applicable decree; the measures to bring individual languages into closer conformity with Russian were taken at various times during the course of the 1930s and included changes both in script and in vocabulary. Retroactively, this treatment of the

non-Russian languages has been legitimized in the "principle of minimum discrepancies" (*printsip minimal'nykh raskhozhdenii*), which provides that new terms introduced into Soviet languages should be identical with, or very close to, those in Russian. For details about this "principle" see Iu. D. Desheriev and I. F. Protchenko, *Razvitie iazykov narodov SSSR v sovetskuiu epokhu* (Moscow: Prosveshchenie, 1968), pp. 82–87.

21. Frederick C. Barghoorn, *Soviet Russian Nationalism* (New York: Oxford University Press, 1956) is a very complete study of the Russian problem in Stalin's time. See also Klaus Mehnert, *Stalin Versus Marx* (London: George Allen & Unwin, 1952); Cyril Black, ed., *Rewriting Russian History* (New York: Random House, 1962); and Shteppa, *Russian Historians*.

22. For further information on these mass deportations, see Robert Conquest, *The Nation Killers: The Soviet Deportation of Nationalities* (New York: Macmillan, 1970).

23. Joseph Brumberg and Abraham Brumberg, "Sovyetish Heymland—An Analysis," in *Ethnic Minorities in the Soviet Union*, ed. Erich Goldhagen (New York: Praeger, 1968), pp. 274–76 and 313.

24. Vernon V. Aspaturian, *The Soviet Union in the World Communist System* (Stanford: Hoover Institution Press, 1966), especially pp. 11–12, 26–27, and passim; see also Zbigniew Brzezinski, *The Soviet Bloc: Unity and Conflict*, rev. ed. (Cambridge, Mass: Harvard University Press, 1967) for an area-wide treatment.

25. P. N. Fedoseev et al., eds., *Leninizm i natsional'nyi vopros v sovremennykh usloviiakh* (Moscow, Politizdat, 1972), especially pp. 285–99. See also *Sovetskii Soiuz i sovremennyi mir* (Prague, 1972), a collective work, published in Russian, which contains representative statements by Soviet, East European, and other pro-Soviet communist ideologists.

26. Soviet publications for domestic use in the non-Russian republics claim that the Russian language has already become not only the language of communication in relations between the East European countries and the USSR but also among these countries. The purpose of such statements is probably to promote the acceptance of the Russian language as not merely one of inter-republic communication in the USSR—a perfectly reasonable idea—but also as the language in which the non-Russians in their own republics are supposed to communicate with their Russian fellow-citizens; the latter are apparently neither required nor expected to feel a need to use the local language. For further explanation of these "intra-bloc" and "intra-republic" roles of the Russian language, see the article by H. P. Yizhakevych, "Mova mizhnatsional'noho spilkuvannia narodiv SRSR," *Ukraïns'ka mova i literatura v shkoli*, no. 11 (1972): 1–9, especially pp. 4 and 8–9. This journal is published by the Ministry of Education, Ukrainian SSR.

27. Goldhagen, *Ethnic Minorities*, is the standard work on the nationalities

question for the post-1953 period and contains much useful material on the earlier years.

28. Language policy was dealt with in Khrushchev's "Thesis 19." For details of Khrushchev's proposal and the subsequent discussion and legislation, see Yaroslav Bilinsky, "The Soviet Education Laws of 1958–9 and Soviet Nationality Policy," *Soviet Studies* 14, no. 2 (October 1962): 138–57. For a review in a historical perspective, see Jacob Ornstein, "Soviet Language Policy: Continuity and Change," in Goldhagen, *Ethnic Minorities*, pp. 121–46.

29. See Grey Hodnett, "The Debate over Soviet Federalism," *Soviet Studies* 18, no. 4 (April 1967): 458–81, and "What's in a Nation," *Problems of Communism* 16, no. 5 (September-October 1967): 2–15, for a detailed review of Soviet writings dealing with the problems of defining "nation" and the nature of Soviet federalism. The expectation of an imminent fusion of Soviet nations was also expressed publicly by some post-Khrushchev writers, such as M. Fazylov, *V druzhnoi sem'e tselinnikov* (Alma Ata, Kazakhstan: Izdatel'stvo Kazakhstan, 1966), pp. 115 and 122; see also P. G. Semenov, "Programma KPSS o razvitii sovetskikh natsional'no-gosudarstvennykh otnoshenii," *Sovetskoe gosudarstvo i pravo*, no. 12 (1961): 25. Views of this kind, including the idea that the Soviet federal system "has fulfilled its tasks and should make room for a unitary" system, have been criticized in a variety of authoritative Soviet statements, some of which are cited in V. P. Sherstobitov, "Obrazovanie SSSR i istoricheskie sud'by narodov nashei strany," *Istoriia SSSR*, no. 3 (1972): 36–38.

30. The most authoritative statement of the current Soviet line is to be found in L. I. Brezhnev's address of December 21, 1972, published in an English translation, "The Fiftieth Anniversary of the Union of Soviet Socialist Republics, Address by L. I. Brezhnev . . . ," *New Times* (Moscow), no. 1 (1973), pp. 4–23. See also the *Current Digest of the Soviet Press* (CDSP) 24, no. 25 (July 17, 1972): 10–11, and *CDSP* 24, no. 46 (December 13, 1972): 1–5, for statements by E. Bagramov, a leading ideologist, and P. Masherov, the party leader of the Belorussian republic, respectively.

31. For the ministerial order, see *Narodnoe obrazovanie*, no. 6 (1972): 114–15; see also the editorial article, "Vsemerno uluchshat' prepodavanie russkogo iazyka v shkolakh," in the same issue (pp. 2–4) of this organ of the Soviet Ministry of Education.

32. "Problemy obucheniia russkomu iazyku v podgotovitel'nykh klassakh natsional'nykh shkol," *Sovetskaia pedagogika*, no. 6 (1972): 148–50.

33. Petro Sevierov, "Uchen' viryt' pidruchnykovi . . . idut' korabli," *Literaturna Ukraïna*, November 14, 1972, pp. 1, 4.

34. Iu. V. Arutiunian, "Konkretno-sotsiologicheskoe issledovanie natsional'nykh otnoshenii," *Voprosy filosofii*, no. 12 (1969): 129–39. In this connection, see the comments by Professor V. V. Pokshishevsky in his "Urbanization and Ethnogeographic Processes," *Soviet Geography: Review and Translation*, 13,

no. 2 (February 1972): 114–15. Particularly relevant is his statement that "the traditional view among geographers and ethnographers that it is the village that tends to preserve distinctive ethnic features (while cities with their standardized material culture and a mixing of ethnic components are viewed as something "anti-ethnographic") . . . [has] now lost [its] validity, at least in the USSR, particularly in the case of the principal ethnic groups that are constituted as union republics and autonomous republics."

35. For a review of the nationality aspects of the 1970 census returns, see Roman Szporluk, "The Nations of the USSR in 1970," *Survey* 17, no. 4 (Autumn 1971): 67–100. Reprinted as Chapter 2 of this volume.

36. Arutiunian, "Konkretno-sotsiologicheskoe issledovanie," p. 139.

37. The main source of information on all factions of dissent in the USSR is *Khronika tekushchikh sobytii* [Chronicle of Current Events], which has been reprinted in the West as special supplements to the monthly Russian-language journal, *Posev*, published in Frankfurt. For further information about Russian national dissenters, see special discussions in *Survey* 17, no. 1 (Winter 1971) and *Survey* 17, no. 3 (Summer 1971); also see Dimitri Pospielovsky, "The Resurgence of Russian Nationalism in Samizdat," *Survey* 19, no. 1 (Winter 1973): 51–74; articles by Michael Glenny and Bohdan R. Bociurkiw in *Studies in Comparative Communism* 3, no. 2 (April 1970); and Peter R. Potichnyj, ed., *Dissent in the Soviet Union* (Hamilton, Ont.: McMaster University and Canada Council, 1971).

38. The long article by A. Yakovlev, "Protiv antiistorizma," *Literaturnaia gazeta*, November 15, 1972, represents the most comprehensive critique of a variety of contemporary Russian unorthodox views in literature, history, and ideology. An earlier broad criticism from the party standpoint is found in V. Ivanov, "Sotsializm ï kul'turnoe nasledie," *Kommunist*, no. 17 (1970): 89–100. The publication of some nineteenth-century Russian chauvinist poems in a popular edition (90,000 copies), without any editorial critical notes, was attacked in a letter to *Sovetskaia Rossiia*, June 26, 1972, p. 3 by four prominent Russian scholars.

39. From this point of view, it is the Russians who have been the pioneers in producing "national communism." According to Mark G. Field, in his "Soviet Society and Communist Party Controls: A Case of 'Constricted' Development," in *Soviet and Chinese Communism: Similarities and Differences*, ed. Donald W. Treadgold (Seattle: University of Washington Press, 1967), p. 196, national communism "may be described as the search, on the part of a nation that has recently emerged as a major world power on the world scene, for a national and cultural identity and rests on the fusion of the doctrinal bases of the Communist movement and identification of the interests of that movement (which is, in essence, supranational) with the interests of the Russian nation. This fusion was born primarily out of the recognition, on the part of the Soviet leadership

by the end of the twenties, that no proletarian revolution . . . was in sight and the resulting decision (primarily Stalin's) to build 'socialism in one country.' From that point on, according to Stalin, Russia was to be considered as the bastion of the Communist movement and, as a corollary, anything that added to the strength of Russia as a nation (industrialization, for example) was good for that movement."

One might comment here that from the point of view of long-range Russian national interest, it was disadvantageous to extend communism to other countries before the Soviet peoples were fully Russified. The possibility that this might happen, though he considered it unlikely, was discussed by N. V. Ustrialov (a Russian nationalist émigré who considered the Bolsheviks to be builders of a new communist Russian nation) in his article "O sovetskoi natsii" in *Nashe vremia* (Shanghai, 1934), pp. 38–39.

2 The Nations of the USSR in 1970

Ten years ago, when they read the results of the 1959 Soviet census, few people seemed to doubt that by 1970 the Soviet Union would be more of a Russian state, in the language and national identity of its citizens, than it was in 1959. In fact, the percentage of Soviet citizens who declared themselves to be of Russian nationality (or who declared Russian as their native language) was lower in 1970. Some observers even thought that before 1980 (when a new census was due), the Russians might become a minority in the Soviet Union. It would be wise to abstain from making forecasts of this sort when one is presented with the failure of many earlier forecasts. It does seem reasonable, however, to conclude that the relative decline of the Russian element is a sign that the nationalities question, including the Russian question, will remain important in the life of the USSR throughout the 1970s.

Shortly after the 1959 census the Central Statistical Office of the USSR worked out a population prognosis for 1970 and 1980. This prognosis was an important element in the preparation of the long-term plan, adopted in 1961 at the Twenty-Second Party Congress, for the "construction of Communism" in the Soviet Union. According to the prognosis, the population of the USSR, which numbered about 209 million in 1959, would rise to 250 million by 1970 and to 280 million by 1980. It

First published in *Survey*, 1971.

soon transpired that the statisticians had taken for granted something the demographers could have warned them against, had the former wished to listen. The birthrates of the late 1950s to early 1960s, which the Statistical Office assumed would remain constant in subsequent years, began to decline rapidly. In 1968 the projection for 1980 was "made more precise," that is, it was lowered by eight million. V. Pere-vedentsev, one of the fiercest demographer-critics of the Statistical Of-fice, wrote in 1967 that instead of the estimated 250 million, the Soviet Union would have 244 million people, and perhaps fewer, in 1970.[1] The next census confirmed his pessimism: In 1970 the Soviet population numbered 241,720,000 men and women, more than eight million under the projection (on which, let it be mentioned in passing, the economic plans for that year had presumably been based). The more recent and still "more precise" prognosis for 1980, worked out by the Institute of Economics, USSR Academy of Sciences, considered two variants, 270 or 265 million, both lower than the recently corrected projection of the Statistical Office. A high official of the Statistical Office recently pointed out with ill-concealed satisfaction that while his office had cut down its estimate for 1980 by eight million (to 272 million), the Institute of Economics associates, who had initially anticipated a population of 289.5 million in 1980, made an even greater correction in their esti-mates.[2] [The actual population of the Soviet Union in 1979 was 262.1 million and in 1989, the last Soviet census, 285.7 million.]

If some of the recent Soviet writers are correct, even the revised projections for 1980 (whether 270 or 265 million) may prove to be too high. The present population of Ukraine, the Baltic states, and consider-able parts of the Russian republic, according to the contributors to the collective work, *Voprosy demografii* (Moscow, 1970), is no longer capa-ble of increasing on its own and these areas are facing the prospect of depopulation. The "coefficient of reproduction" (net reproduction rate) in these areas is less than 1, which roughly means that without immigra-tion the next generation—the population 30 years later—will be smaller in size than the current one. The coefficient of reproduction in the USSR as a whole still remains slightly above 1, which means that the present generation will be succeeded by a slightly more numerous one, but this will be due only to the higher growth rates in Soviet Central Asia and Azerbaijan. The coefficient of reproduction there equals 2, which means that the population of those areas will double in the course of 30 years (while in the European areas with the coefficient lower than 1, it will decrease absolutely).[3] A more recent Soviet source lists the RSFSR, along with Ukraine and the Baltic states, among those parts of the Soviet Union where the coefficient is lower than 1.[4]

In most countries it would be no cause for particular alarm if a low population growth in some regions were sufficiently balanced by a higher growth in others, thus securing the whole country's population gains (assuming such gains are desired). However, under Soviet conditions the disparity between the European parts of the country and the Asian ones is not just a matter of geography. It has political significance because it means a weakening of the Slavic element (in which the Russians are the principal ethnic group) and a strengthening of the non-Slavic, chiefly Turkic, groups. If the Soviet scholars writing on this subject were truly "internationalist," that is, if they were disposed equally well to all Soviet people (without regard to race or language), they would have applauded the Central Asians for their contributions at a time when the Europeans are failing to increase. But such is not the case: Concern over the unfavorable demographic situation in Soviet Eastern Europe is sometimes accompanied by expressions of alarm over the seemingly *good* situation in Soviet Asia. Thus, a distinguished Soviet authority, D. I. Valentei, has proposed a policy of birth control for the Asian parts of the Soviet Union and a policy encouraging population growth in the European areas.[5] It is difficult to avoid the impression that the Soviet scholar regards the positive (from an impartial point of view) demographic situation in Asia as a threat rather than a blessing. It will not be surprising if the Uzbeks or Azerbaijanis conclude that the Moscow professor regards them as less valuable Soviet citizens than natives of Vologda or Smolensk. Thus, besides the disappointment that over eight million Soviet citizens caused the Central Statistical Office by failing to be born before 1970, many of those citizens who *were* born apparently were born in the wrong places and to parents who spoke the wrong languages.

Another demographic phenomenon in the 1960s also ran directly counter to plans made at the start of the decade. Millions of Soviet citizens had been expected to leave highly populated areas of the country, such as Ukraine, Moldavia, and North Caucasus, and move to Siberia, the north, or to the Far Eastern provinces of the Soviet Union.[6] Just the reverse happened: More people moved west or south than east or north, and some of those who did move east or north returned after a short time. Even the natives of Siberia and the Urals were said to be following the returning Europeans or moving to already well-populated Central Asian republics. (According to Soviet sources, immigrants from the outside, including Russia's eastern regions, constituted a majority of the population increase in the cities and towns of Kirghizia.[7])

The results of the 1970 census confirmed what some Soviet scholars had been pointing out earlier. The share of both the east of the Soviet Union (Siberia and the Far East) and of the west (the Urals and the European USSR) *declined* in the total of the Soviet population while the southeast (Central Asia, including Kazakhstan) gained. If one divides "the west" into a northern and a southern part, it becomes clear that in the west it was chiefly the southern part that increased rapidly: Transcaucasia, Southern Ukraine, Moldavia, and the North-Caucasus Region of the Russian Republic.[8]

All three of these negative phenomena—the lower than planned-for total population growth, the uneven levels of population growth, and the unexpected direction of migrations—have a direct effect on the nationalities question in the Soviet Union and the relations between Russians and the other nationalities. It is Russians (and to some extent other Slavs) in the European areas who had been projected to be born there. Had these eight million people been added to the Soviet total, the direction of the migrations would have been at least partially different. This study concentrates on one aspect of the demographic change between the censuses—ethnic relations in the Soviet Union, and more specifically on the changes in the distribution of the Russians in separate areas of the Soviet Union and changes in the numerical relationship in those areas between the Russians and the other major peoples of the USSR.

Before beginning a more detailed region-by-region survey, let us look at the statistics on the growth of the largest (one million and above) Soviet nationalities, first of all, the Russians. (See table 2.1 at the end of this chapter.) In the 11 years between the censuses, the population of the Soviet Union increased by 32,893,000—from 208,827,000 in 1959 to 241,720,000 in 1970, which equaled a 15.7 percent growth. The Russians increased by 13 percent (from 114,114,000 to 129,015,000), and thus their share in the country's total population dropped from 54.6 to 53.4 percent. Eleven of the 15 major Soviet nationalities possessing their own "Union republics" increased at a higher rate than the Russians; only the Ukrainians (increase of 9.4 percent), Latvians (2.1 percent), and Estonians (1.8 percent) had slower growth. The Russians ranked 17th among the 23 Soviet nationalities numbering more than a million people each (these include all 15 with Union republic status). Besides the 11 nationalities with their own Union republics, the Daghestanians (44.4 percent), Bashkirs (25.4 percent), Tatars (19.4 percent), Chuvashes (15.2 percent), and Germans (13.9 percent) also increased faster than the Russians. Three among the larger Soviet nationalities decreased in absolute numbers, the Mordovians (loss of 2.01 percent), Jews (loss of 5.16 percent), and Poles (loss of 15.4 percent), and thus ranked behind the Russians (as did the Ukrainians, Latvians, and Estonians who increased more slowly than the Russians).

These figures will no doubt be closely analyzed by specialists on the different peoples, as were the results of the 1959 census and the other nationality statistics published in the Soviet Union in the past.[9] Each of the studies should help to explain what appears to be the census's most important revelation: that in the Soviet Union the major non-Russian nationalities, and the non-Russians as a whole, were increasing faster than the Russians, and that consequently in 1970 the USSR was less Russian than in 1959. Although assimilation no doubt contributed to the net gain recorded by the Russians, Russian gains were too low to presuppose widespread assimilation; most of the major nationalities seem to have been relatively immune to its pressures. Even the Belorussians, who are linguistically close to the Russians and are generally thought to lack an intense feeling of separateness, and the Germans, who lack a republic of their own, increased faster than the Russians. When they adopted Russian as their principal language (as many Belorussians and Germans, and also Ukrainians, did), they still did not declare themselves as Russians.

The census also reveals the highly uneven growth of the Russian population throughout the USSR. The Russian ethnic group grew faster in the USSR at large than in the Russian republic, and faster in the (at least nominally) non-Russian parts of the RSFSR than in "ethnic Russia" or Russia proper. But most rapid of all was the growth of Russians in those parts of the USSR that are formally recognized as being non-Russian: the 14 Union republics other than the RSFSR. While in the USSR the Russians gained slightly over 13 percent and in the RSFSR as a whole slightly over 10 percent, their increase in the USSR minus the RSFSR exceeded 30 percent.

The population of the RSFSR, the national republic of the Russians, increased by almost 11 percent (10.67 percent), well behind the all-Union rate. The ethnic Russians in it gained even less (10.1 percent) and

Russians in	1939	1970	Gain (percent)
	(thousands)		
USSR	114,114	129,015	13.038
RSFSR	97,864	107,748	10.099
"Ethnic Russia"	90,666	99,718	9.983
ASSRs	7,198	8,030	11.559
Non-Russian Union Republics	16,250	21,267	30.874

Source: *Izvestiia*, 17 April 1971, and *Sovetskaia Rossiia*, 20 May 1971.

in consequence the Russians dropped from 83.3 to 82.5 percent in the population total. This change was due to the faster growth of the other peoples of the RSFSR, and the emigration of ethnic Russians from Russia. If these processes continue, the RSFSR may cease to have a majority of the Soviet Union's population and the Russian share will decline further. Between the censuses, the RSFSR's share in the Soviet Union's population dropped from 56.3 percent to 53.8 percent, and stood at 130,079,000 in 1970 (1959: 117,534,000). Even now a majority of the youngest citizens no longer live in the RSFSR; among those less than 10 years of age in 1970 (of whom the Soviet Union had 44,986,000—a decline of 2.97 percent from the 1959 total), only 21,286,000, or 47.3 percent, lived in the Russian republic. In 1959, before those 45 million Soviet citizens were even born, the Soviet Union's children under age 10 numbered 46,363,000, and the Russian republic still held a majority of 55.6 percent among them (25,768,000 in absolute figures). In this category of population the RSFSR has declined by over 9 percentage points, compared with a 2.5 percentage point loss in the total population.

Within the RSFSR itself, besides the regular predominantly Russian regions (oblasts), there exist 16 major subdivisions in the rank of "autonomous republics." Unlike the Union republics—which technically enjoy equal status with the Russian republic, have a constitutional right to enter diplomatic relations with foreign countries, to establish their own armed forces, and even to secede from the Soviet Union—the autonomous republics do not even formally constitute "sovereign states." In practice, an autonomous republic of the RSFSR differs from a "regular" Russian province in that a non-Russian language enjoys an official status there (particularly in education, the press, and broadcasting) along with Russian, which is the main language.

Some of the autonomous republics within the RSFSR, such as the

Tatar ASSR, are larger in population than many Union republics. They have been denied the latter status by a rather ingenious argument: Since they are surrounded on all sides by the territory of the RSFSR, Stalin declared in 1936 that they would be unable in practice to make use of their right to secede. Therefore, rather than being granted some rights they would be unable to exercise, they were simply denied this status and remained in the "non-sovereign" category. Autonomous republics are the only territorial subdivisions of the RSFSR whose ethnic composition has so far been disclosed.

These autonomous republics do not form a geographic or ethnic unity, although some of them may be grouped together on the basis of geography or language and culture (North Caucasus, the Volga area, and others). However, their ethnic identity and political and administrative status are distinct enough from the rest of Russia to allow some general observations about them. First, their combined population increased between the censuses from 15,903,000 to 18,592,000, or by 16.9 percent, which is significantly higher than the increase of population for the RSFSR as a whole (10.67 percent), and even exceeds the USSR's population increase (15.7 percent). Secondly, the Russians in those areas of the Russian republic increased faster than in the RSFSR as a whole. There were 7,198,000 Russians in the autonomous republics in 1959, and 8,030,000 in 1970, an increase of 11.6 percent, while in the RSFSR as a whole there was a 10.1 percent Russian increase. Nevertheless the Russian gains were surpassed by those of the non-Russians and as a result in 11 out of 15 autonomous republics there were relatively *fewer* Russians in 1970 than in 1959. In the combined population of the ASSRs the Russian ratio decreased from 45.3 to 43.2 percent.

"Ethnic Russia"

The separation, somewhat arbitrary, of the ASSRs from the Russian republic's totals allows us to take a look at the Russian republic without its non-Russian autonomous subunits. This "purer" Russia had a population of 101,631,000 in 1959, which rose to 111,487,000 in 1970. This gain of 9.7 percent was lower than the RSFSR average and much lower than that recorded by the combined ASSRs. The Russian population in this "Russia proper" grew faster than the population at large, however, though still more slowly than that of the Russians outside Russia. The Russians in this smaller RSFSR gained 9,052,000 people (from 90,666.000 to 99,718,000), which virtually equals an increase of 10 percent. Their share in the population was high (89.2 percent) in 1959 and increased slightly by 1970 (89.4 percent).

Unlike the autonomous republics, only population totals are available for the provinces of the RSFSR. Since these oblasts were overwhelmingly Russian in 1959, however, it may be correct to assume that changes in their population after the 1959 census closely reflected the changes in their Russian population. The figures published in *Sovetskaia Rossiia* (May 20, 1971) show that the growth of population in a majority of the "purely Russian" regions of the European RSFSR stood far below the republic's average. Thus, in the Central Economic region, whose importance is conveyed by its name, population grew from 25,718,000 to 27,658,000; that is, by 7.52 percent in an 11-year period. If one subtracts from these totals the figures for Moscow and Moscow oblast where growth was higher, we are left with 11 oblasts and a growth from 14,768,000 to 14,822,000, which equals 0.36 percent. None of these oblasts grew by more than 8 percent, most achieved less, while four (Kalinin, Kostroma, Riazan, and Smolensk) actually *lost* population. The population of Orel oblast gained 0.21, and that of Yaroslavl gained 0.28 percent over 11 years. Three of the provinces in the Northwestern region, Vologda, Novgorod, and Pskov, also lost population. (Leningrad, on the other hand, gained considerably.) The region of Volga-Viatka grew by just above 1 percent (this figure includes higher growth in the Mari, Mordovian, and Chuvash ASSRs), but the Kirov oblast in it fell considerably below its 1959 total. The Central Black Earth region, comprising five oblasts located to the south of the Central region, gained less than 3 percent, and two of its oblasts, Kursk and Tambov, recorded an absolute decline. The economic regions of the Urals and West Siberia were under the RSFSR levels of growth and so were two of the oblasts of the Volga (Povolzhskii) region. On the whole. however, the last-named region grew fast, especially its provinces of Volgograd and Astrakhan. The East Siberian region had a growth above the RSFSR average (15.3 percent) though not equal to the USSR average, and the Far Eastern increased even more (19.5 percent). However, the Far Eastern region's population was low in absolute terms (4,834,000 in 1959, and 5,780,000 in 1970), and it decreased on the island of Sakhalin (loss of 34,000 from the 1959 figure of 649,000). In the late 1950s the two Siberian regions and the Far East had been expected to grow especially rapidly in the next decades, while North Caucasus had been thought of as one of the sources of migrants to the east. Just the reverse happened in the 1960s: In the light of the Soviet 1970 census (and in accordance with the earlier admissions in the Soviet press) the Far East and the Urals were providing population to Ukraine, North Caucasus, and the Baltic states. Migration from European Russia that had been anticipated to go to the east assumed unexpectedly large dimensions—and turned in unexpected directions, to the south and west. Scholars began to write about the depopulation of central Russian provinces brought about by emigration and (since the migrants were mostly young) by a continuing decrease in the birth rate.

The Autonomous Republics of the RSFSR

The 11.5 percent increase of Russians in their republic's non-Russian subdivisions (and the decline in their percentage of the combined population) obscures considerable variations among the autonomous republics. (See table 2.2.) Thus, in five autonomous republics, Karelia, Komi, Udmurt, Chuvash, and Yakut ASSRs, the ratio of Russians in the total population rose. Karelia and Komi are located in the northwestern and northern parts of the RSFSR respectively. The Russians now constitute 68.1 percent in the population of Karelia (1959: 63.4 percent) and 53.1 percent in that of Komi ASSR (1959: 48.6 percent). In Far Eastern Yakutia the Russian population reached 47.3 percent by 1970, an increase from 44.2 percent in 1959. In the Ural-area Udmurt ASSR Russians increased from 56.8 to 57.1 percent, and in the Chuvash ASSR in the upper Volga from 24.0 to 24.5 percent of the total population.

Except for the Udmurt republic (where Russians and the population at large increased at a slower rate than in the RSFSR as a whole), the increase of the Russian population in these five autonomous republics was very considerable. Between 1959 and 1970 Russians increased by 13.26 percent in Chuvash ASSR, by 17.67 percent in Karelia, 29.3 percent in Komi, and 36 percent in Yakutia. This increase and the resultant strengthening of the Russians were likely achieved more by immigration than by natural means.

There was also a high Russian immigration rate to some of the 11 autonomous republics, in which their ratio in the population fell between 1959 and 1970. In others the Russians were increasing very slowly, and in the autonomous republic of Daghestan ASSR in North Caucasus, their number actually went down from 214,000 to 210,000 (a decrease of 1.87 percent), and their percentage in the population fell from 20.1 to 14.7 of the total. In two republics, Mari ASSR and Mordovian ASSR, the overall population increase was relatively small but the Russian increase lagged behind that of the natives, and though Russians still constitute a dominant element in these upper-Volga areas their percentage went down (in Mari from 47.8 to 46.9 percent, in Mordovia from 59.1 to 58.9 percent).

More interesting and more important seem to be the changes in the well-populated middle-Volga republics of Bashkiria and Tataria. In Bashkiria Russians decreased from 42.4 to 40.5 percent while Bashkirs rose from 22.1 to 23.4 percent, and Tatars (the second largest ethnic group in that republic) rose from 23.0 to 24.7 percent. In the Tatar ASSR Russians decreased from 43.9 to 42.4 percent of the total while Tatars came close to regaining a majority (47.2 in 1959 to 49.1 percent in 1970). There was no important Russian immigration to these areas; if there was any, it must have been counterbalanced by emigration. The Russian increase amounted to 9.1 percent in Bashkiria and 6.15 percent in Tataria.[10]

In the two Siberian republics, Buryat ASSR and Tuvinian ASSR (the latter once known to stamp collectors as the mysterious state of Tannu-Tuva), even as large an increase of the Russian population as 18.7 percent in Buryat and 27.5 percent in Tuva was not enough to prevent a relative decline (from 74.6 to 73.5 percent in the former, and from 40.1 to 38.3 percent in the latter). The "natives" were obviously increasing even faster than the Russians.

Keeping up with the natives in the North Caucasus area of the RSFSR proved even more difficult for the Russians. In the Kalmykian ASSR, whose population had been deported under Stalin and then rehabilitated, Kalmyks increased from 35.1 to 41.1 percent of the population (they numbered 110,000, an increase of 45,000 over 1959). Russians, although they still outnumbered Kalmyks by 13,000 in 1970, fell from 55.9 to 45.8 percent in the Kalmyk republic's population. Quite mysteriously, Ukrainians more than *doubled* in Kalmykia between the two censuses (the increase was 106.25 percent), from 1,600 to 3,300, although their share in the population remains small (1.8 percent).

An apparent Russian emigration from Daghestan (decline of 1.87 percent) caused their share in the population to fall from 20.1 to 14.7

percent. Population as a whole rose far above the Soviet average in Daghestan, and it also rose in Kabardino-Balkaria, North Ossetia, and the Chechen-Ingush ASSRs. In consequence, despite a 34.35 percent increase, Russians declined from 38.7 to 37.2 percent in Kabardino-Balkaria's population. A slower (but still above the RSFSR average) Russian increase in North Ossetia 12.85 percent) produced a Russian drop from 39.6 to 36.6 percent in the total population, which as a whole rose twice as fast as the Russians in it. The low—less than the RSFSR average—gain of 5.46 percent reduced the Russians from almost a half to just above a third of the population of the Chechen-Ingush ASSR (from 49.0 to 34.5 percent). That republic's population increased by a half between the censuses, when Chechens and Ingushes, another collective victim of Soviet deportations, seem to have returned from their exile. Chechens increased from 244,000 to 509,000 (from 34.3 percent to 47.8 percent) and Ingushes from 48,000 to 114,000 (6.8 to 10.7 percent).[11]

Beyond Russia

The Russian population grew most rapidly in the non-Russian Union republics, where it increased by over 30 percent, more than twice the rate of the Russian gains in the USSR as a whole, and three times as fast as in the RSFSR. In 1959, 14.24 percent of Soviet Russians lived outside the RSFSR, but 11 years later their ratio increased to 16.5 percent. How were those Russians distributed "in diaspora"?

It seems best to arrange the non-Russian Union republics into three geographic groups or regions, especially since the pattern of Russian population increase varies significantly and there are also variations in the general population growth among the regions. The three regions are: Transcaucasia, Central Asia (including Kazakhstan, which Soviet sources usually place in a separate category from Central Asia), and Soviet Eastern Europe.

Of the total of 5,017,000 Russians added to the population of the non-Russian Union republics between 1959 and 1970, the share of Transcaucasia equaled a mere 8,000, or 0.16 percent of the total gain of Russians outside the RSFSR. Soviet Eastern Europe received 2,714,000, more than half of the gain (54.1 percent), and Central Asia, including Kazakhstan, received 2,295,000, or 45.7 percent. By 1970, the Russian population in Central Asia reached 8,509,000 (1959: 6,214.000), in

Transcaucasia 973,000 (1959: 965,000), and in Eastern Europe 11,785,000 (1959: 9,071,000). There was a slight percentage shift in the total distribution of Russians over this period: Transcaucasia's share of the total number of Russians living outside the RSFSR dropped from 5.9 to 4.57 percent, Eastern Europe's declined from 55.8 to 55.4 percent, and Central Asia's gained from 38.24 to 40 percent.

Transcaucasia

In each of the three Transcaucasian republics the growth of titular nationalities was far higher than the growth of Russians and it also exceeded the growth of the population (in particular in Azerbaijan where the Azerbaijanis grew by over 50 percent while the total population grew by less than 40 percent). (See table 2.3.) The Russians declined most significantly in Georgia, where their number in 1970 (397,000) was 11,000 less than in 1959 (408,000). This was a decline of 2.7 percent and Russians now constitute 8.5 percent of Georgia's total population (1959: 10.1). In Azerbaijan the Russian population increased slightly (from 501,000 to 510,000, or by 1.8 percent) and the rapid growth of the principal nationality caused a serious drop in their share of the republic's population (1970: 10 percent; 1959: 13.6).

In Armenia Russians increased at a rate higher than their all-Union average (17.85 percent) but since their number had been low (56,000, or 3.2 percent in 1959) the net gain of 10,000 Russians in Armenia by 1970 merely meant that their relative drop in total population was smaller than it would have been otherwise. By 1970 Russians constituted 2.7 percent of Armenia's population—the lowest percentage in any of the 15 Soviet republics.

If one treats Transcaucasia as a single geographico-cultural area, which one is justified in doing despite the historic animosities between the Christian Georgians and Armenians and the Moslem Azerbaijanis, the relative decline of the Russian element there will become even more evident.

In 1959, the Russians in Transcaucasia constituted slightly over 10 percent of the population (10.15), or 965,000 in a population of 9,505,000. Eleven years later their number rose 8,000 (to 973,000), a rise of less than 1 percent (0.83), and their percentage in Transcaucasia's population dropped to 7.91. By contrast, both Armenians (who constitute a sizable minority in Georgia and Azerbaijan) and the Azerbaijanis (who likewise live in Armenia and Georgia besides their own country) gained significantly in the whole area. The Armenians in Transcaucasia as a whole increased by over 700,000 (from 2,437,000 to 3,146,000) or by 29.1 percent, while Azerbaijanis did even better. Their increase in Transcaucasia equaled 50.3 percent, slightly under the increase in their own republic. In Transcaucasia there were 2,756,000 Azerbaijanis in 1959 and 4,143,000 in 1970. The figures for the Georgian population in Armenia and Azerbaijan were not included in the release of the Central Statistical Board of the USSR, presumably because of their small size. A vast majority (3,131,000 out of 3,245,000) of Georgians live in Georgia, and the RSFSR has a majority of those not in Georgia (69,000 out of the total of 114,000 in 1970).

There are reasons for thinking that the factors which have tended to keep Russians out of Transcaucasia or at least to slow down their immigration will continue to operate in the foreseeable future. While the rural population in the USSR as a whole declined slightly (by about 3 percent) over the 11-year period and constituted about 44 percent of the Soviet population (105,749,000) in 1970, there was an absolute growth of rural population in all three Transcaucasian republics, from a small increase in Georgia (4.9 percent) and somewhat higher growth in Armenia (14.75 percent) to a quite substantial one in Azerbaijan (32.1 percent). Since the rural population still constitutes a majority in Georgia and about a half in Azerbaijan (about 41 percent in Armenia) there will no doubt be pressure for jobs in industry and towns. Since the natives of Transcaucasia are reluctant to go farming in Kazakhstan or Siberia, jobs will have to be found for them at home.

The task of providing work for the natives of Transcaucasia may not only require the creation of new jobs but may also mean a pressure on the "outsiders," especially Russians and other Slavs, to leave. Since the Russian population in that area increased by less than 1 percent over a period of 11 years, the Russians were either becoming Georgian, Armenian or Azerbaijani, or—more likely—were already leaving.[12]

Soviet Central Asia

The demographic situation in Central Asia shows that a high increase in the number of local nationalities (including the rural population) is not necessarily accompanied by a low growth of the Russian population. Four of the five principal nationalities of Central Asia (those with their own Union republics) grew faster than any other of the major Soviet nations. The Tadzhiks in the USSR as a whole grew by 52.9 percent, the Uzbeks by 52.87 percent, the Turkmens by 52.2 percent, and the Kirghiz by 49.8 percent. Kazakhs grew by 46.3 percent, a rate lower than that of Azerbaijanis, whose growth equaled 49 percent. If one considers the growth rates of the principal 15 nations in their respective republics, all five Central Asian nations took the top five positions; they were among the six nations to increase by more than half in their own republics (Azerbaijanis took sixth position). Their rates of growth at home were faster than on the all-Union scale, which means that in 1970 they were more concentrated in their own republics than in 1959. (See table 2.4.)

All five Central Asian republics had a high proportion of rural population in 1959, which continued to grow in the following 11 years. Although in the European republics (except Moldavia) rural population was declining relatively and absolutely, and especially rapidly in the RSFSR, including most of its Asian provinces, Central Asia recorded the highest growth rates for rural population as well. Uzbekistan (rural population up by 41.3 percent), Turkmenia (37.6 percent), Tadzhikistan (36.65 percent), and Kirghizia (33.9 percent) produce a striking contrast with the RSFSR (European and Asian parts combined), whose rural population, already relatively much smaller in 1959, *decreased* during the same period by slightly over 12 percent. Kazakhstan, too, had a high rate of growth of rural population (21.1 percent) though again behind that of Azerbaijan (32.1 percent). Kazakhstan was the only one of the five Central Asian republics to achieve a slight majority in its urban population by 1970, Turkmenia had a rural population of about 52 percent, and the other three each had a rural population of more than 60 percent. Russia's rural population had in the meantime dropped to about 38 percent of the republic's population.

Admittedly, the percentage growth of the urban population of Central Asia was even faster. Its effect, however, was very small; except for Kazakhstan where approximately twice as many people were added to the urban population as to the growing rural population, the net effect of urbanization in the Central Asian republics was to shift the urban-rural ratio by just 2 or 3 percentage points.

Among the reasons why the growth in urban population did not cause any significant slowing down in the growth of the rural population, one of the most important seems to have been the vast Russian immigration, which, except in Kazakhstan, was directed primarily to cities and towns. As Soviet scholars have pointed out many times (and without any visible effect), the population leaving the villages of the RSFSR has provided the major contingent of new urban residents for the cities of Central Asia. The construction of new industrial enterprises, roads, and the like in those republics as a rule means the importing of personnel from outside, not only at the managerial level but also as regular workers. When a textile factory is being built in an Uzbek or Turkmen city, for example, not only the equipment but also the workers are brought in from the central Russian regions of Moscow or Vladimir. The natives of Soviet Central Asia have apparently not yet reached the point of demanding that a share of jobs in construction projects be guaranteed to local residents (as well as provision for the training of skilled labor).

In Central Asia as a whole (see table 2.5), Russians increased by almost 37 percent (36.9); in individual republics their growth varied from a "low" of 19 percent in Turkmenia to a high of 39.2 percent in Kazakhstan. The rate of the Russian increase in Kazakhstan was almost equal to that of the total population (40.4 percent), but still significantly below the growth of Kazakhs themselves (52.3 percent), who even managed to regain some of the lost ground. They are still a minority in their own country, but their percentage has gone up from 29.8 to 32.4, while the Russians dropped from 43.2 to 42.8 percent. Whether the Kazakhs will go on improving their position or the Russians resume their upward trend of the pre-1959 years will depend on which process now at work will slow down first and more: Russian immigration or Kazakh birthrates. In Uzbekistan, the Russian increase of more than a third (34.3 percent) brought the number of Russians there up to almost one and a half million—but was not enough to improve or even maintain their relative standing in the country's population. The Russian share declined by one percentage point (down to 12.5 percent) while Uzbeks increased to 64.7, a gain of 4.6 percentage points. Russians were also relatively worse off in the remaining republics, and the principal nations correspondingly improved their position. Although the data for ethnic composition of urban and rural population are not yet available, individual republics in some cases published a breakdown in ethnic terms of the population of the republic's capital city. Thus, according to *Pravda*

Vostoka (April 28, 1971), Tashkent, Uzbekistan's capital, whose population grew by almost half between the censuses and reached 1,385,000 in 1970 (1959: 927,000), had 513,000 Uzbeks in 1970, an increase of 202,000 over the 1959 figure of 311,000. Uzbeks are still only the second largest nationality in their capital (37.1 percent; in 1959: 33.6 percent), but Russians have dropped from 44.1 to 40.8 percent, and in absolute numbers are no longer so much above the Uzbeks: 565,000 in 1970, merely 54,000 more Russians than Uzbeks. (There were 409,000 Russians in Tashkent in 1959.) It seems that what the German scholar K.-E. Wädekin foresaw seven years ago as the possible "Returkicization" of Tashkent is in fact taking place. The high ratio of young people among the Uzbeks (relatively low among the Slavs), their high birthrate, and the likelihood of an Uzbek immigration from the surrounding countryside were factors that Wädekin considered to favor such an outcome. However, it could be countered, he noted, by a strong Slavic immigration from other parts of the USSR and by cultural Russification in the city. (He thought that neither of these factors would be strong enough to prevent the "Returkicization" from happening.[13])

What has been said here about Kazakhstan (which in its northern provinces does in fact have large Slavic rural populations to draw upon) and Uzbekistan applies also to Kirghizia, Turkmenia, and Tadzhikistan, where the Russian position has been considerably weaker from the start. Only large Russian immigration (or an immediate and significant decrease in the birthrate of the non-Russians) can prevent a further relative decline of Russian human potential in Central Asia. Can the Russians, with their responsibilities on the all-Union scale, biologically, economically, and politically afford to maintain these necessary levels of immigration? And, whether or not the Russians keep on coming in big numbers, will the native peoples of Central Asia, in whose opinion there may possibly *already* be too many Russians (and Slavs in general) in Central Asia, continue to tolerate the present situation?[14]

The Baltic States

The Russian population growth in Central Asia, despite its large size, failed to change the ethnic balance of that region in favor of the Russians. All it achieved was to slow down the relative decline of the Slavic element there. What appeared at one time like a Russian offensive has proved to have been a defensive, holding-off action. In Eastern Europe Russians have done much better.

In Latvia and Estonia, where the local population grew very slowly, Russian immigration was most successful in changing the Russian-to-native ratio in favor of the Russians. The number of Russians in Estonia between the censuses increased by 39.6 percent and that of Estonians by 3.6 percent; the Russian growth was about 11 times higher than the Estonian. In absolute numbers, there were 95,000 more Russians in Estonia in 1970 than in 1959 (total in 1970: 335,000), but only 32,000 more Estonians (total in 1970: 925,000).[15]

In Latvia the Latvians added another 44,000 to their number of 1,298,000 in 1959; that is, they grew by 3.4 percent, while dropping from 62 percent in their republic's population to 56.8 percent. (In Estonia the Estonians fell from 74.6 to 68.2 percent.) The Russians, who increased in Latvia from 556,000 to 705,000 (26.8 percent), now constitute a sizable minority of 29.8 percent (1959: 26.6 percent).

The third Baltic republic, Lithuania, is often mentioned together with Latvia and Estonia, but the population changes in it followed another pattern. First of all, the Lithuanians themselves increased at a quite different pace: There were 2,507,000 Lithuanians in Lithuania in 1970, which was a gain of 16.5 percent over the 1959 figure of 2,151,000. They even managed to *improve* their majority in the country's total population from 79.3 to 80.1 percent. Secondly, Russians also increased (16 percent), but at a rate considerably lower than anywhere else in Soviet Eastern Europe and even slightly lower than that of Lithuanians themselves. There were 231,000 Russians in 1959, and 268,000 in 1970 in Lithuania. Their relative position improved only slightly, from 8.5 to 8.6 percent of the total population.

When one discusses the Baltic-Russian relationship it is also necessary to consider the Belorussian and Ukrainian presence in and immigration to these areas. In view of the total lack of cultural or educational facilities for Ukrainians and Belorussians outside Ukraine and Belorussia respectively, and their linguistic closeness to the Russians, members of these nationalities outside their own republic function in practice as a Russifying element. The importance of this in the Baltic states should not be underestimated. Ukrainians increased in the Baltic area by more than two-thirds (from 63,000 in 1959 to 106,000 in 1970) and Belorussians by more than half (from 103,000 to 159,000). Since in Estonia the Estonians gained by only 32,000, an increase of the Ukrainian population in that republic from 16,000 to 28,000, and of the Belorussian from 11,000 to 19,000, produced a weighty addition of 20,000 East Slavs to reinforce the Russian gain of 95,000. In Latvia the joint gain of Ukrainians and Belorussians was in fact higher than that of the Latvians. The Belorussians increased from 62,000 to 95,000 and the Ukrainians from 29,000 to 53,000; jointly they gained 57,000 in Latvia, 13,000 more than their host, the Latvian nation. Since there was also a gain of 149,000 Russians, these figures mean that in absolute numbers, for every new Latvian, Latvia was simultaneously getting five new inhabitants who were Russian, Belorussian, or Ukrainian. How is one to interpret the fact that the growth of the Ukrainian population in Latvia exceeded 82 percent, reached 75 percent in Estonia, and came close to 40 percent in Lithuania when, as will be shown below, in Ukraine itself the growth of the Ukrainian population was less than 10 percent (while that of the Russians was nearly three times as large), and the Ukrainian share in the total population there declined considerably?

A review of the Baltic situation should not consist only of information on the weakening of the Baltic nations. One of them, the Lithuanian, has in fact won a major achievement in the period under consideration. Vilnius, the ancient capital of Lithuania, seems to have become more of a Lithuanian city than it has ever been during the past three or four hundred years. In consequence of a series of Polish–Lithuanian agreements that were finalized in the act of Polish–Lithuanian union at Lublin (1569), Vilnius and other cities of Lithuania became gradually Polonized, so that throughout the nineteenth and the first half of the twentieth centuries Lithuanians in Vilnius numbered about 2 percent of the population. After the Second World War a majority of the Poles moved west to Poland, but even as late as 1959 the Poles constituted a 20 percent minority in the city. The places of those Poles who went west, and of the Yiddish-speaking Jews (in the past the second largest group in Vilnius) who perished under the Nazis, were taken by Lithuanians moving in from the countryside and by Russians coming in from the east. (The Russian element in Vilnius before the Second World War was insignificant.) The table at the top of the facing page shows the ethnic distribution of population of Vilnius in 1959 and 1970.

Although Russians in Vilnius still remain numerically far out of proportion to their share in Lithuania's population as a whole—and the Lithuanians far below theirs—the improved position of Lithuanians in

Vilnius in 1959 and 1970

	1959 231,100 (100 percent)	1970 372,100 (100 percent)
Total		
Lithuanians	33.6 percent	42.5 percent
Russians	29.4	24.5
Poles	20.0	18.3
Belorussians	6.2	6.5
Jews	6.9	4.4
Others	3.9	3.5

Source: *Sovetskaia Litva,* 6 May 1971.

their capital is comparable to the Uzbeks' partial recovery of their own capital of Tashkent and promises to make local resistance to Russification more effective.[16]

Belorussia and Moldavia

Belorussia and Moldavia became part of the Russian Empire (1772–1795 and 1812) later than Latvia and Estonia (1721) but for various historical, cultural, and religious reasons their identity was never as distinct as that of the two Protestant nations in the Baltic area. Although Russians form a relatively small minority in Belorussia (1959: 8.2 percent; 1970: 10.4 percent) and Moldavia (1959: 10.2 percent; 1970: 11.6 percent), these republics give the impression of being more Russified than either Latvia or Estonia. In fact the Russians are relatively much stronger in the latter. There are at least two reasons why Belorussia looks Russian or Russified. First, linguistically Belorussians are very close to the Russians and their language was not used in schools, the periodical press, or book publishing until after the Civil War. (The first modest use of Belorussian in print occurred after the 1905 revolution.) The period when the use of Belorussian was encouraged ended abruptly in the Stalinist purges of the early 1930s and thus lasted just about ten years. The other reason why Russian prevails in Belorussia is that, until quite recently, the Belorussians remained primarily country people—the towns have traditionally been more Russian, Jewish, or Polish than Belorussian. More than in the case of other nationalities the city has appeared to a Belorussian immigrating from the village as a foreign, non-Belorussian, world—and at the same time one not sufficiently alien to provoke in him a nationalist reaction instead of the more common desire to adjust by assimilation.

Among the nationalities with their own Union republics, the Belorussians have the largest proportion of those individuals who regard Russian, not their own nation's language, as their "native" tongue. Almost one out of five Belorussians in the USSR is Russian linguistically, although many of those Russian-speaking Belorussians know Belorussian and declare it to be their second language. In Belorussia itself, the proportion of Russian-speaking Belorussians was lower than in the USSR as a whole; 719,000, or 9.9 percent of the Belorussians in 1970, as compared with 442,000 or 6.9 percent in 1959, declared Russian to be their first language. However, according to *Sovetskaia Belorussiia* (May 19, 1971), 321,000 of those 719,000 Belorussians declared that they also had a good command of Belorussian. (The question about second language was not asked in 1959.) According to the same source, 285,000 members of other nationalities also claimed a good knowledge of Belorussian, thus raising to 83.4 percent the total number of Belorussia's inhabitants familiar with that language.

It is worth noting that high linguistic assimilation even among a people as close to the Russians as the Belorussians does not seem to lead to a change in national identity. The Belorussians continue to declare themselves as such (is Belorussianness becoming to some extent a territorial or political concept?) and their numerical increase in Belorussia has virtually kept pace with the increase of the republic's total population.[17] (See table 2.6.) The Russian gain there was higher than in any East European republic, indeed, the highest recorded in any Union republic (42.1 percent), and their share in the population grew significantly. However, the Belorussians maintained their position virtually without change (a drop of one-tenth of 1 percent, from 81.1 to 81 percent), while the Poles lost heavily (a drop from 539,000 to 383,000), and it is possible that some Poles declared themselves as Belorussians in the 1970 census. (A majority of the Poles had declared Belorussian as their language in 1959.)

High mobility was another distinguishing feature of the Belorussians and it was no doubt connected with the first, that is, their high assimilation to the Russian language. Heavy Belorussian immigration to the Baltic states has already been noted, but Belorussians were also moving to the RSFSR, the Ukraine, Kazakhstan, and Kirghizia. Discounting the Georgians (who increased in the USSR by a fraction of a percent faster than in Georgia), no other Union republic nationality except the Belorussians was growing faster in the USSR than at home. While gaining 11.6 percent in their republic, Belorussians increased by 14.4 percent in the USSR as a whole and by 27.6 percent in the USSR excluding Belorussia. Even more puzzling is the disparity between the increase of Belorussian-speaking Belorussians "at home" and "abroad": In the former situation they increased by 7.9 percent (the assimilated ones by 62.7 percent), while outside the borders of Belorussia the number of Belorussian speakers increased by 25.6 percent and of Russian-speaking Belorussians by 29 percent. One can only speculate about the causes of this emigration of the natives from a republic that was attracting at the same time vast numbers of Russians and Ukrainians from the outside.

What has been said here about the traditionally agrarian character of Belorussia can be said with even greater force about Moldavia. In 1959 that republic had the dubious distinction of being the least urbanized of all 15 republics of the USSR. It retained this position 11 years later when the census showed that 68 percent of Moldavia's population still lived in the villages (the figure for 1959 was 78 percent). Moldavia's rural population *increased* by almost 9 percent, from 2,242,200 to 2,438,800, while in all other East European republics there was a decrease in the absolute number of rural residents. Compared with Moldavia even Belorussia was doing much better in this respect; rural population there fell by 8.6 percent and constituted 57 percent of the population in 1970.

In 1959, the Moldavians were a predominantly rural people (they constituted a minority of about one-third in their own capital) and they presumably remained so in 1970 despite the impressive growth of their urban population in the intervening years (from 642,300 to 1,130,000). The move of Moldavians to cities could not but have been obstructed by the vast Russian inflow to Moldavia. (The Moldavian press release on the 1970 census does not give an ethnic breakdown of the population of Kishinev, Moldavia's capital.) While Moldavians increased (22.1 percent) at a high pace, not much below that of the total population growth (23.7 percent), Russians increased nearly twice as fast (41.3 percent). In addition, Ukrainians seem to have found Moldavia preferable to virtually all parts of Ukraine (a 20.4 percent increase between 1959 and 1970). In Ukraine itself, only the city of Kyiv and the provinces of Kherson and Crimea recorded a higher growth of the Ukrainian population than did the agrarian and already overpopulated Moldavia. (In the nearby Odessa province in Ukraine, on the other hand, Russians increased twice as fast as Ukrainians.) What was it that was making so many Russians and Ukrainians go to Moldavia, a small republic located next to Romania, whose native population is linguistically close to if not identical with Romanians? (The Soviet official line regards Moldavian as a Romance language but one distinct from Romanian; this view is not generally shared outside the borders of the Soviet Union, where the Moldavians are regarded as Romanians.[18])

The relative weakness of modern, urban Moldavian culture, Moldavia's isolation from Romania, and finally the demographic, political, and cultural invasion from the east have all combined to aid Russifying pressures. Between the censuses there was a downward shift among the Moldavian-speaking Moldavians (from 98.2 to 97.7 percent); this shift was not as large as that noted in Belorussia (or in Ukraine), but still a dangerous sign for Moldavian identity.

The Three Regions of Ukraine

Because of the large size of the population of the Ukrainian republic one must be cautious about making generalizations with regard to Russian–Ukrainian relations there or in drawing comparisons with the other republics. The first fact one notices about the census in Ukraine is the extraordinary numerical power of the Russian element—over 9 million in 1970—and a growth exceeding 2 million since 1959. When one translates the absolute figures into percentages and compares the latter with ethnic relationships in other Union republics, however, the apparent power of the Russians no longer appears to be so unusual or overwhelming. Taking only Eastern European republics for this comparison, one notes, first, that in 1970 there were relatively more Russians in Estonia or Latvia than in Ukraine and, second, that the Russian increase between censuses in Belorussia, Moldavia, and Estonia proceeded faster than in Ukraine. (In addition, Russians increased faster in Kazakhstan, Uzbekistan, Kirghizia, and Tadzhikistan.) Finally, the relative strength of the republic's principal nationality, Ukrainians, was and remained higher than that of the principal nationalities in a majority of the Soviet republics (in East Europe Ukrainians ranked above Estonians, Latvians, and Moldavians but were behind Lithuanians and Belorussians).[19]

The preceding are precisely those generalizations and comparisons that, however correct they may be in themselves, do not probe much below the surface. A republic whose size is about equal to that of France (with a smaller population than France), Ukraine is a composite of regions with different historical experiences in modern times and with different population, especially ethnic, patterns. Although it takes little account of these dissimilarities, a division of the 47 million strong republic into three areas, corresponding to the so-called "Large Economic Regions of the Gosplan," is nonetheless a minimum step for a better understanding of the Russo–Ukrainian relationship in Ukraine and its evolution between 1959 and 1970. (See table 2.7.) [For a map of oblasts of Ukraine, see chapter 3.]

East Ukraine

The Donetsk-Dnieper region comprises the main industrial centers of Ukraine, including the coal-mining area of Donbas (Donetsk and Voroshylovhrad [now Luhansk]), the manufacturing and transportation center of Kharkiv, and the Dnipropetrovsk-Zaporizhia industrial region on the Dnieper River. Although it also includes the traditionally agrarian areas of Poltava, Sumy, and Kirovohrad, the overwhelmingly urban character of the whole region is best represented by such cities as Kharkiv, Donetsk, and Dnipropetrovsk. This is the region, especially its most industrialized and urbanized parts, that in modern times has been most Russianized. Even though the inclusion of the provinces of Poltava, Sumy, and Kirovohrad in the totals for the Donetsk-Dnieper region tends to lower Russian strength where it matters most, the gains achieved by Russians between the two censuses are impressive enough. Their share in the total population rose by 26.7 percent (more than 3 percentage points) and in absolute figures their gain there exceeded one million people (1,177,000). This was about 58 percent of the net Russian increase in the Ukrainian SSR. The number of Ukrainians added to the population of this region was lower (1,053,000), though in Ukraine as a whole Ukrainians gained over a million more people than did the Russians. In relative terms, only one-third of the net Ukrainian growth (33.7 percent) went to the Donetsk-Dnieper region, and Ukrainians there grew by 8.4 percent. Even more striking was the disparity between Russian and Ukrainian population growth in the most urban subregion of this most urban region of Ukraine. In Donbas (the oblasts of Donetsk and Voroshylovhrad combined), Russians increased by 584,000 (28.7 percent of their net gain in Ukraine) and Ukrainians by 318,000 (10.2 percent of Ukrainian gain in the whole republic). Ukrainians in Donbas dropped from 56.4 to 53.7 percent of the population, while Russians went up from 38 to 41 percent. Since in 1959 this area also included the relatively greatest number of Ukrainians whose native language was Russian, one may assume that a majority of the population in Donbas spoke Russian in 1970.

Kyiv and the West

The Southwestern region comprises 13 provinces (oblasts) of the Ukrainian SSR and has the largest population (20,689,000 in 1970). Its population was growing much more slowly than in the Donetsk-Dnieper or the Southern region and its relative proportion fell between 1959 (when 44.4 percent of Ukraine's population lived there) and 1970 (43.9 percent). The Donetsk-Dnieper region recorded a slight increase for the same period (from 42.4 to 42.5 percent) while the South gained considerably (from 12.1 to 13.5 percent). There are only two major cities in the region: Ukraine's capital, Kyiv, and the West Ukrainian city of Lviv, which was the capital of the Crownland of Galicia under the Habsburgs (1772–1918) and then a provincial center in Poland (1918–1939). Historically, this is the area of greatest Western influence in Ukraine—major parts of this region never belonged to the Russian Empire and became Soviet only during or after the Second World War (Galicia, 1939; Bukovina or Chernivtsi oblast, 1940; Transcarpathia, 1945). Even those parts under Russia before 1914 were mostly relatively recent acquisitions, dating back to the second and third partitions of Poland (1793–1795). Only in Kyiv and its immediate vicinity and in Chernihiv did Russians appear as early as the second half of the seventeenth century.

Since much of the area was outside Russian control until about 30 years ago, and as a whole was densely populated and predominantly agrarian in character, there has been relatively little Russian immigration to it. The only exception in this regard was the Russian immigration wave to the "new" Soviet provinces, where there had been no Russians previously, after the Second World War. There Russians partially replaced in the urban population the Poles and Jews who were either killed or expelled during and after the war. In 1959, the Southwestern region's population was 87.82 percent Ukrainian; by 1970 Ukrainians had dropped by a fraction of 1 percent to 87.81. The increase in the Ukrainian population was slightly lower than the total population growth. The Russians grew by 22.86 percent (below their average republic growth of 28.7 percent) and their share in the region's population rose from 5.84 to 6.6 percent. In absolute terms, however, the number of Russians involved was much lower than in the Donetsk-Dnieper region. Their net gain there (254,000) equaled one-eighth of the total Russian gain in Ukraine, less than their gain in Donbas alone. In 1959, 15.7 percent of Ukraine's Russians lived in the Southwestern region; in 1970 the percentage had fallen to 14.9.

The growth of the Russian population in separate provinces of the Southwest varied extensively. It was highest in the city of Kyiv and in the provinces of Kyiv, Ivano-Frankivsk, and Cherkasy (ranging from 23.7 percent in Ivano-Frankivsk to 46.5 percent in Kyiv City). In most cases it was higher than that of Ukrainians and in only one did the actual number of Russians decline (Ternopil oblast, a drop from 27,000 to 26,000, or from 2.5 to 2.3 percent of the oblast's population). Ukrainians recorded their highest gain in the city of Kyiv, where in 1970 they constituted 64.8 percent of the population. This was a considerable gain from the 60.2 percent recorded in 1959, and seems to mean that Kyiv has been a center of particular attraction to Ukrainians (a growth from 668,000 to 1,057,000, or of 58.2 percent).[20] In two oblasts of Ukraine the absolute number of Ukrainians declined between the censuses, and one of these was located in the southwestern region. In Chernihiv province Ukrainians declined by 1.5 percent and Russians increased by 17.7 percent. The other oblast was Kirovohrad in the Donetsk-Dnieper region, where the Ukrainian decrease of 0.1 percent was accompanied by a Russian gain of 12.6 percent.

Odessa and Crimea

The Southern region's population grew by over 25 percent (25.7), an increase almost double Ukraine's growth and almost three times faster than that of the Southwestern region. The region comprises four oblasts: Crimea (the population of which increased by 1970 by more than half of the 1959 total), Kherson, Odessa, and Mykolaiv. This was one of the areas of greatest population growth for the Russians (a change of 38.5 percent, far above the republic average of 28.7 percent), who improved their position in three of the four oblasts: Odessa, Kherson, and Mykolaiv. Russians were also growing very fast in Crimea (a change of 42.1 percent), where in 1959 they already constituted a strong majority of the population (71.4 percent). However, after 1959 the Ukrainian immigration to Crimea seems to have been on an even larger scale, as indicated by the increase of Ukrainians there by something like 79.5 percent (from 268,000 to 481,000) and their gain in the total population from 22.3 to 26.5 percent (and a Russian decline to 67.3 percent). The Ukrainian population gains in the other provinces were above the Ukrainian republic average but still lower than the Russian ones and could not therefore prevent the relative decline of Ukrainians in the region's population (from 57 to 55 percent). Ukrainians may even lose their slim majority in the region as a whole (Russians have gone up from 30.85 to 34 percent) unless Russian immigration, which seems to be flowing mainly from the RSFSR, is slowed down by exhaustion or otherwise, and/or Ukrainian immigration rises. The Southwestern region remains the principal Ukrainian reservoir of human resources and much will depend on whether the people leaving villages and small towns of the Southwest in search of better living conditions will go to the Ukrainian provinces on the Black Sea rather than to the Baltic states, Central Asia, or Siberia, as so many have been doing in the recent past.

The population growth in the South of Ukraine appears to be part of the wider process of southward migration in the USSR, which includes Moldavia, the North-Caucasus region of the RSFSR (Krasnodar and Rostov), and Central Asia. This is largely an unplanned development, contrary to the centrally designed and publicly announced directives, which call for an eastward migration.

The Southern region, unlike the other two, seems to be still in the process of acquiring its ethnic shape: Both Russians and Ukrainians there have been increasing fast, although at an uneven pace. From 1959 to 1970, the South's share in Ukraine's population went up from 12.1 to 13.5 percent. Although in 1959 only 22.1 percent of Ukraine's Russians and 8.9 percent of Ukraine's Ukrainians lived in the Southern region, by 1970 these percentages rose to 23.7 and 9.9, respectively. In 1970, there were in the South 616,000 more Ukrainians (an increase of 20.3 percent) and 604,000 more Russians (an increase of 38.5 percent)

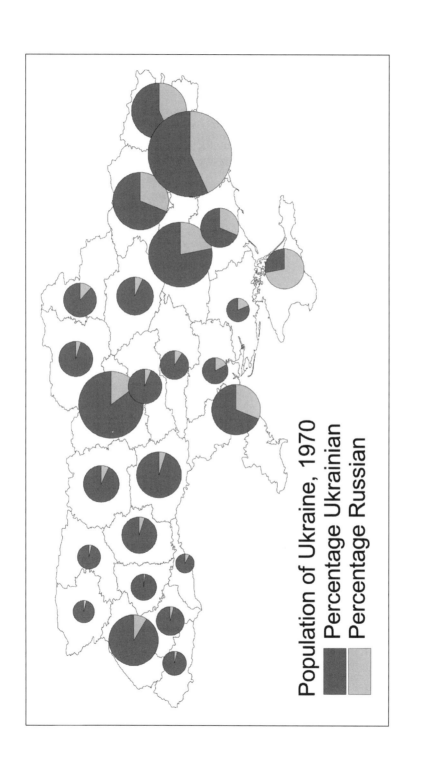

Population of Ukraine, 1970

Percentage Ukrainian

Percentage Russian

than in 1959. In Ukraine, the South accounted for 19.7 percent of the increase in Ukrainians and for 29.7 percent of the Russian gain.

This brief survey of the ethnic situation in the major regions of Ukraine warrants some cautious conclusions. While the Russians gained throughout Ukraine, they are particularly strong in the Donetsk-Dnieper region or, to be more precise, in the easternmost and most urbanized part of it, Donbas. Their increase was fastest in the South and their relative position there improved, but that area was also the primary center of attraction to Ukrainians (at least on the territory of the Ukrainian SSR), who were doing better in Crimea than the Russians. Finally, Russian overall gains in the Southwestern region, relatively high though they were, were far too low to change the ethnic balance in any serious way. Despite their relatively high percentage gains in individual provinces of the Southwest, Russians remain in a minority of less than 10 percent in all of them except the city of Kyiv (which enjoys the status of an oblast in its own right), where they have been traditionally strong (in 1959 Russians constituted 23 percent of Kyiv's population, and in 1970, 22.9 percent).

The overall numerical increase of Russians in Ukraine was serious, and when one adds to this the considerable increase in the number of Ukrainians declaring Russian as their first language (Ukrainian-speaking Ukrainians in Ukraine dropped from 93.5 to 91.4 percent of all Ukrainians between the censuses), the Russian presence in Ukraine will become even more conspicuous. Russian gains in Ukraine were distributed very unevenly, however, and in some areas there were counter-processes at work leading to an absolute or relative strengthening of the Ukrainian element. It does not seem that Ukraine and Ukrainians are about to disappear or dissolve into an all-Russian or Soviet nationality.

Conclusion

Dissolution or disappearance does not seem to be a prospect facing any of the nations of Soviet East Europe, not to mention those of Central Asia or Transcaucasia. Should the Russians ever win a majority in Latvia or Estonia (or in a number of Ukrainian provinces),[21] this will not by itself eliminate the non-Russians, although it will perhaps make them more dissatisfied with their fate in the USSR. After all, the Kazakhs and the Kirghiz have survived their transformation into minority nations in their own country, but may now be reversing the trend.

The policy of promoting and encouraging an "inter-republic exchange of cadres," which was much extolled in Khrushchev's time, still remains in force and was quite recently reasserted in an authoritative article in *Pravda* by E. Bagramov.[22] In practice it means that the Russians and the non-Russians, *provided they have become fully proficient in Russian*, should be employed anywhere in the USSR without the necessity of learning the local language. The natives, at the same time, are being refused employment in their own country because they do not know Russian well enough and they see the jobs being given to recent arrivals from Russia who have frequently been transferred to Uzbekistan or Tadzhikistan by the administration. These transfers involve not only highly skilled specialists but also truck drivers, janitors, and the like.[23] To remedy this situation (which is said to exist in other areas as well), V. Perevedentsev has proposed an improvement of Russian teaching in village schools and possibly the reservation of some jobs for local residents.

There are other indications in Soviet scholarly and political journals that the intensification of Russian-language instruction (in some republics it has now been extended to pre-school children) is seen by some at least as the way to maintain the privileged position of the Russian language, which is being threatened by the numerical increase of Central Asians and the nations of the Caucasus. Though not put in these words, it is presumably hoped that an increased assimilation to the Russian language will weaken resistance to Russification and nullify the effect of higher birthrates among the non-Russians, thus removing the pressure for a change in linguistic policies. If assimilation proves effective, enough Russians will be found to make Riga, Vilnius, and Kishinev more Russian than they are now; it will be possible to maintain and even improve the present Russian level in the population of Central Asia; and, finally, there will be sufficient cadres to repopulate the Central Russian provinces and to go east, as far as the Chinese-Soviet border. Although it is no longer held (as had been the case in the early years after 1959) that the non-Russian peoples of the Soviet Union are abandoning their languages in favor of Russian (the survival of other Soviet languages into a distant future is recognized now), assimilation to Russian is still being upheld as a "progressive" phenomenon. One Soviet author, L. M. Drobizheva, has discovered, for example, that among the unspecified number of Belorussians and Ukrainians who read newspapers and books both in their own language and in Russian, respectively 99.3 and 90.9 percent approve of the "joint work of people of different nationalities"; among those who read only Belorussian or Ukrainian publications, the corresponding figures are 90.5 and 80.7 percent. In face of such overwhelming evidence, the conclusion that the Moscow newspapers should be circulated even more widely was axiomatic; among other measures to promote internationalism, Drobizheva recommended "the extension of the network of clubs and libraries" in the rural localities of Central Asia.[24]

Linguistic assimilation is not the only means for "the drawing of Soviet peoples together." This aim is also being pursued through an "interchange of cadres," which presupposes in the present setup the adoption of the Russian language by non-Russian migrants. (In most cases, the non-Russians outside their own republics have no cultural or educational facilities in their own language.) Despite economic and social arguments against such practices, the policy of sending people to places where they would not normally go voluntarily is continued: In the spring of 1971 one could find in a Kyiv youth newspaper an appeal addressed to young Ukrainians to go to work and study in a Central Asian republic noted for its rural overpopulation.[25] (Needless to say, other, more widespread measures, such as the assignment of graduates to work in other republics and the organized resettlement of peasants in Siberia and the Far East, are also being followed.)

Contrary to their declarations, the Soviet leaders still seem to think that not being Russian linguistically makes a Soviet citizen less reliable and less valuable (or less "progressive"). They still seem to be pursuing the long-range aim of making all Soviet citizens Russian in language and spirit. If they accepted the proposition that the Soviet Union should remain a multilingual and multicultural society, however, they would no longer have to think (as they seem to be doing now) that the interests of the Soviet state require a constant intermixing of Soviet peoples and that a high percentage of Russians in an area's population is an index of its progress. For example, an industrialization of Kirghizia or Uzbekistan that provided work to the natives might prove economically and politically preferable to the present practice of sending Russians and Ukrainians there and telling the natives in the villages that they should brush up their Russian before they can ask for a job in town. Further, industrialization, rather than the policy of birth control advocated by Professor Valentei, might be a sounder way to reduce the present excessively high birthrates in Central Asia. Next, all Soviet citizens, whether in or out of their republic (and, indeed, those without a republic of their own), might be granted an opportunity to cultivate their own traditions and language. If Yugoslavia can publish a special newspaper for its 30,000 Ukrainians, would it be too hard for the RSFSR to maintain one for its three million Ukrainians? (One could compile a long list of examples contrasting Soviet and East European practices in the treatment of minorities.)

The results of the 1970 census make the success of the assimilationist drive at best problematic in the long run. More immediately, this drive is likely to be met with increased resentment and possibly resistance, and it also entails economic and social drawbacks for the Soviet state. One of these is the demographic draining (and economic neglect) of Central Russia for the sake of maintaining the Russian presence on appropriate levels in Kzyl-Orda, Uzhhorod, and Tartu (among numerous other places). Another is related to the population problems of Siberia and the east. Various sources confirm that the Russians make the best immigrants to those areas; they adjust much better to climate, for example, and generally are more likely to stay there because they regard these areas as their own country.[26]

The time may come when both the non-Russian peoples of the USSR and the Russians conclude that the interests of communism in the Soviet Union do not require the ubiquitous Russian presence, if it is going to act (and be perceived) as a political constraint on the non-Russian groups and even an instrument for their eventual elimination, while at the same time impeding economic and social progress in the Russian areas, such as Siberia. A Siberian worker-correspondent of the Moscow *Literary Gazette*, N. Shchitov, suggested several years ago that in order to improve the economic management of the areas east of the Urals something like a ministry for Siberia should be set up in Novosibirsk.[27] This seems to be an excellent idea—which can be improved on, though, by giving consideration to ethnic factors as well. Why not move the capital and whole government of the Russian republic from Moscow to the east, thus visibly separating the "Soviet Union" from "Russia," and making it clear that the former name is not a temporary pseudonym for the latter and that all nations of the USSR are truly equal? The transfer of the Russian capital, not just setting up one agency, would make itself immediately felt in the east in many beneficial ways; for example, its new site would attract (and retain) immigrants from the west. Moscow would continue as the capital of the Soviet Union, of course, though perhaps after being separated with its immediate region from the RSFSR and constituted into a federal district, a common property of all Soviet nations.

Table 2.1
Largest Nationalities of the USSR (in thousands)

	1959		1970		Percentage Change, 1959–1970
USSR total	208,827	100.0%	241,720	100.0%	15.8%
Russians	114,114	54.6	129,015	53.4	13.1
Ukrainians	37,253	17.8	40,753	16.9	9.4
Uzbeks	6,015	2.9	9,195	3.8	52.9
Belorussians	7,913	3.8	9,052	3.7	14.4
Tatars	4,968	2.4	5,931	2.5	19.4
Kazakhs	3,622	1.7	5,299	2.2	46.3
Azerbaidzhanis	2,940	1.4	4,380	1.8	49.0
Armenians	2,787	1.3	3,559	1.5	27.7
Georgians	2,692	1.3	3,245	1.3	20.5
Moldavians	2.214	1.1	2,698	1.1	21.9
Lithuanians	2,326	1.1	2,665	1.1	14.6
Jews	2,268	1.1	2,151	0.9	−5.2
Tadzhiks	1,397	0.7	2,136	0.9	52.9
Germans	1,620	0.8	1,846	0.8	14.0
Chuvash	1,470	0.7	1,694	0.7	15.2
Turkmens	1,002	0.5	1,525	0.6	52.2
Kirghiz	969	0.5	1,452	0.6	49.8
Latvians	1,400	0.7	1,430	0.6	2.1
Daghestanis	945	0.5	1,365	0.6	44.4
Mordovians	1,285	0.6	1,263	0.5	−1.7
Bashkirs	989	0.5	1,240	0.5	25.4
Poles	1,380	0.7	1,167	0.5	−15.4
Estonians	989	0.5	1,007	0.4	1.8

Source: *Izvestiia*, 17 April 1971. Percentages calculated by author.

Table 2.2
Population Characteristics of the Autonomous Republics of the RSFSR (in thousands)

Name of ASSR	Total Population			Russians					Titular Nation(s)				
	1959	1970	Change from 1959 to 1970 (%)	1959	%	1970	%	Change from 1959 to 1970 (%)	1959	%	1970	%	Change from 1959 to 1970 (%)
Bashkir	3,340	3,818	14.3	1,417	42.4	1,546	40.5	9.1	738	22.1	892	23.4	20.9
Tatar	2,850	3,131	9.9	1,252	43.9	1,329	42.4	6.2	1,345	47.2	1,536	49.1	14.2
Daghestan	1,063	1,429	34.4	214	20.1	210	14.7	-1.9	736	69.2	1,061	74.2	44.2
Udmurt	1,338	1,418	6.0	760	56.8	810	57.1	6.6	476	35.6	484	34.1	1.7
Chuvash	1,098	1,224	11.5	264	24.0	299	24.4	13.3	770	70.1	856	69.9	11.2
Chechen-Ingush	710	1,065	50.0	348	49.0	367	34.5	5.5	244	34.4	509	47.8	108.6 Chechens
									48	6.8	114	10.7	137.5 Ingushes
Mordovian	1,002	1,029	2.7	592	59.1	607	59.0	2.5	358	35.7	365	35.5	2.0
Komi	815	965	18.4	396	48.6	512	53.1	29.3	245	30.1	276	28.6	12.7
Buryat	673	812	20.7	503	74.7	597	73.5	18.7	136	20.2	179	22.0	31.6
Karelian	651	713	9.5	413	63.4	486	68.2	17.7	85	13.1	84	11.8	-1.2
Mari	648	685	5.7	310	47.8	321	46.9	3.5	279	43.1	299	43.6	7.2
Yakut	487	664	36.3	215	44.1	314	47.3	46.0	226	46.4	286	43.1	26.5
Kabardine-Balkar	420	588	40.0	163	38.8	219	37.2	34.4	190	45.2	265	45.1	39.5 Karbardines
									34	8.1	51	8.7	50.0 Balkars
North-Ossetian	451	552	22.4	179	39.7	202	36.6	12.8	215	47.7	269	48.7	25.1
Kalmyk	185	268	44.9	103	55.7	123	45.9	19.4	65	35.1	110	41.0	69.2
Tuvinian	172	231	34.3	69	40.1	88	38.1	27.5	98	57.0	135	58.4	37.8

Source: *Sovetskaia Rossiia*, 20 May 1971. Percentages of population growth calculated by the author.

Table 2.3
Ethnic Composition of the Transcaucasian Republics

	Total Population (in thousands)			Titular Nationality					Russians				
	1959	1970	Change (%)	1959	%	1970	%	Change (%)	1959	%	1970	%	Change (%)
Azerbaidzhan	3,698	5,117	38.4	2,494	67.4	3,777	73.8	51.4	501	13.5	510	10.0	1.8
Georgia	4,044	4,686	15.9	2,601	64.3	3,131	66.8	20.4	408	10.1	397	8.5	-2.7
Armenia	1,763	2,492	41.3	1,552	88.0	2,208	88.6	42.3	56	3.2	66	2.6	17.9

Table 2.4
Ethnic Composition of Soviet Central Asia Republics (in thousands)

Republic	Total Population			Russians					Titular nation(s)				
	1959	1970	Change from 1959 to 1970 (%)	1959	%	1970	%	Change from 1959 to 1970 (%)	1959	%	1970	%	Change from 1959 to 1970 (%)
Kazakhstan	9,153	12,849	40.4	3,950	43.2	5,500	42.8	39.2	2,723	29.7	4,161	32.4	52.8
Uzbekistan	8,261	11,960	44.8	1,114	13.5	1,496	12.5	34.3	5,044	61.1	7,734	64.7	53.3
Kirghizia	2,066	2,933	42.0	624	30.2	856	29.2	37.2	837	40.5	1,285	43.8	53.5
Tadzhikistan	1,981	2,900	46.4	263	13.3	344	11.9	30.8	1,051	53.1	1,630	56.2	55.1
Turkmenia	1,516	2,159	42.4	263	17.3	313	14.5	19.0	924	60.9	1,417	65.6	53.4
Areawide	22,977	32,801	42.8	6,214	27.0	8,509	25.9	36.9					

Source: *Izvestiia*, 17 April 1971. Percentages of change calculated by author.

Table 2.5
Major Nations in Soviet Central Asia Republics (in thousands)

Population	Central Asia Including Kazakhstan					Central Asia Excluding Kazakhstan				
	1959	%	1970	%	Change from 1959 to 1970 (%)	1959	%	1970	%	Change from 1959 to 1970 (%)
Total	22,977		32,801		42.8	13,824		19,452		40.7
Uzbeks	5,973	26.0	9,120	27.8	52.7	5,843	42.3	8,912	45.8	52.5
Kazakhs	3,233	14.1	4,809	14.7	48.7	510	3.7	648	3.3	27.1
Kirghiz	956	4.2	1,431	4.4	49.7	956	6.9	1,431	7.4	49.7
Tadzhiks	1,380	6.0	2,109	6.4	52.8	1,380	10.0	2,109	10.8	52.8
Turkmen	979	4.3	1,488	4.5	52.0	979	7.1	1,488	7.6	52.0
Tatars	780	3.4	1,038	3.2	33.1	591	4.3	754	3.9	27.6
Russians	6,214	27.0	8,509	25.9	36.9	2,264	16.4	3,009	15.5	32.9

Source: *Izvestiia*, 17 April 1971. Percentages of change calculated by author.

Table 2.6

Ethnic Composition of Soviet Republics in Eastern Europe (in thousands)

Republic	Total Population			Russians				Titular Nation(s)			
	1959	1970	Change from 1959 to 1970 (%)	1959	%	1970	%	Change from 1959 to 1970 (%)	1959	%	1970	%	Change from 1959 to 1970 (%)
Estonia	1,197	1,356	13.3	240	20.1	335	24.7	39.6	893	74.6	925	68.2	3.6
Latvia	2,093	2,364	12.9	556	26.6	705	29.8	26.8	1,298	62.0	1,342	56.8	3.4
Lithuania	2,711	3,128	15.4	231	8.5	268	8.6	16.0	2,151	79.3	2,507	80.1	16.6
Belorussia	8,056	9,002	11.7	660	8.2	938	10.4	42.1	6,532	81.1	7,290	81.0	11.6
Moldavia	2,885	3,569	23.7	293	10.2	414	11.6	41.3	1,887	65.4	2,304	64.6	22.1
Ukraine	41,869	47,126	12.6	7,091	16.9	9,126	19.4	28.7	32,158	76.8	35,284	74.9	9.7

Source: *Izvestiia*, 17 April 1971. Percentages of change calculated by author.

Table 2.7

Ethnic Composition of the Economic Regions of Ukraine (in thousands)

Region	Total Population			Ukrainians					Russians				
	1959	1970	Change from 1959 to 1970 (%)	1959	%	1970	%	Change from 1959 to 1970 (%)	1959	%	1970	%	Change from 1959 to 1970 (%)
Ukraine	41,869	47,126	12.6	32,158	76.8	35,284	74.9	9.7	7,091	16.9	9,126	19.4	28.7
Donetsk-Dnieper Region	17,766	20,057	12.9	12,555	70.7	13,608	67.8	8.4	4,414	24.8	5,591	27.9	26.7
Southwest Region	19,028	20,689	8.7	16,711	87.8	18,168	87.8	8.7	1,111	5.8	1,365	6.6	22.9
Southern Region	5,075	6,380	25.7	2,892	57.0	3,508	55.0	21.3	1,566	30.9	2,170	34.0	38.6

Source: *Radianska Ukraina*, 25 April 1971. Percentages calculated by author.

Notes

1. V. Perevedentsev, "Spor o perepisi," *Literaturnaia Gazeta*, January 11, 1967, p. 13. For earlier, optimistic views see S. G. Strumilin, *Nash mir cherez 20 let* (Moscow: Sovetskaia Rossiia, 1964), and I. Iu. Pisarev, *Naselenie i trud v SSSR* (Moscow: Ekonomika, 1966).

2. " 'Piat' milliardov otvetov," *Literaturnaia Gazeta*, January 21, 1970, pp. 1, 3. (Interview with P. G. Podiachikh, the official in charge of the 1970 census.) The Institute of Economics was expecting a population of 270 or 265 million in 1980. (Ibid.)

3. A. G. Volkov, L. E. Darskii, A. Ia. Kvasha (eds.), *Voprosy demografii (Issledovaniia, problemy, metody)* (Moscow: Statistika, 1970), especially the papers by B. Ia. Smulevich and A. Ia. Kvasha. See also a review of this book by V. Perevedentsev, "Problemy nauki o naselenii," *Druzhba narodov*, no. 1 (1971): 278–80.

4. V. Guseinov, V. Korchagin, "Voprosy trudovykh resursov," *Voprosy ekonomiki*, no. 2 (1971): 45–51, esp. p. 50.

5. D. I. Valentei, *Teoriia i politika narodonaseleniia* (Moscow: Vysshaia shkola, 1967), pp. 163–65.

6. For an estimate of the anticipated railway passenger traffic from the west to the east see O. A. Kibal'chich, "Opyt razrabotki gipotezy mezhraionnykh passazhirskikh potokov na perspektivu," *Voprosy geografii* 57 (1962): 180–93, esp. pp. 186–87.

7. See *Regional'nye osobennosti ekonomicheskogo razvitiia raionov strany (Na primere Sibiri)* (Moscow: Mysl', 1966), p. 165. According to this source, immigration from the outside, especially immigration of the Russians, was one of the reasons why native rural populations were unable to move to the cities in their own republics. According to P. P. Litviakov, ed., *Demograficheskie problemy zaniatosti* (Moscow: Ekonomika, 1969), p. 184, among every 100 former *rural* residents who migrated to the cities of Uzbekistan, Kirghizia, Tadzhikistan, Turkmenia, and Kazakhstan, those coming from the other republics equaled, respectively, 49, 45, 50, 52, and 50. (There were, of course, also *urban* migrants from the other republics.)

8. For an analysis of the changes in the regional distribution of the Soviet population between 1959 and 1970, see S. A. Kovalev, "Noveishie izmeneniia v razmeshchenii naseleniia SSSR (K momentu perepisi 1970 g.)," *Vestnik Moskovskogo Universiteta, Seriia V geografiia*, no. 6 (1970): 42–48, and ibid., "Izmeneniia v chislennosti i razmeshchenii naseleniia SSSR za period mezhdu perepisiami 1959 i 1970 gg.," *Geografiia v shkole*, no. 6 (1970): 13–20.

9. For a comprehensive overview, see Erich Goldhagen, ed., *Ethnic Minorities in the Soviet Union* (New York, Washington, London: Praeger, 1968).

10. Ethnic relations in the Tatar ASSR have been the subject of several recent Soviet studies. See Iu. V. Arutiunian, "Konkretno-sotsiologicheskoe issledovanie natsionalnykh otnoshenii," *Voprosy filosofii*, no. 12 (1969): 129–39; O. I. Shkaratan, "Etno-sotsial'naia struktura gorodskogo naseleniia Tatarskoi ASSR," *Sovetskaia ètnografiia*, no. 3 (1970): 3–16; and S. S. Savoskul, "Sotsialnoetnicheskie aspekty dukhovnoi kultury sel'skogo naseleniia Tatarskoi ASSR," *Sovetskaia ètnografiia*, no. 1 (1971): 3–13.

11. See Robert Conquest, *The Nation Killers: The Soviet Deportation of Nationalities* (London: Macmillan, 1970) and "An Unreported Incident of National Unrest," *Radio Liberty Dispatch* (June 26, 1969).

12. This writer knows no Soviet source confirming Russian emigration from Transcaucasia. However, V. Sh. Dzhaoshvili, "Rozselennia ukraïntsiv na terytoriï Hruzyns'koï RSR," *Ukraïns'kyi istorychnyi zhurnal*, no. 1 (1970): 104–8, claims that since 1956 more people have been going from Georgia to Ukraine than vice versa, and he thinks that Ukrainians constitute a major segment of those migrants to Ukraine.

13. Karl-Eugen Wädekin, "Nationalitätenpolitik and Lebenskraft der Völker in der Sowjet-Union heute und morgen," *Osteuropa*, no. 11 (1964): 837–50.

14. Several years ago a Polish reporter was told by an Uzbek in Tashkent: "The cadres of our own intelligentsia are growing, including the professional (*specjalistyczna*) intelligentsia. . . . They are looking for a place for themselves." A Russian official, on the other hand, complained that "the Uzbeks, of course, support each other, whether it is justified or not. And secondly, they prefer to shift the more difficult work, and, first of all, the difficult and unpopular decisions, off to that deputy, to that *evropeyets* [i.e., a Russian] . . ." Jerzy Lovell, "Podróż na Wschód," *Życie Literackie* (Kraków), December 19, 1965, pp. 7, 9. The Arutiunian study (referred to in note 10) confirms a relatively higher incidence of nationalist attitudes among the Tatar intelligentsia. Zev Katz, "Sociology in the Soviet Union," *Problems of Communism* 20, no. 3 (May-June 1971): 38, attributes a "revolutionary character" to Arutiunian's findings confirming the existence of both a traditional nationalism and a "nationalism of a new type."

15. It may be worthwhile to note here that the percentage growth of Estonians, Latvians, and Lithuanians (as of almost all other Soviet nationalities with their own Union republics) was higher in their respective republics than in the USSR as a whole, which seems to confirm the assertion of those Soviet authors who argue that non-Russians are generally disinclined to leave their own areas. For the Balts, see Iu. G. Saushkin, T. M. Kalashnikova, "Gipoteza perspektivnogo razvitiia sistemy raionnykh territorial'no-proizvodstvennykh kompleksov SSSR," *Voprosy geografii* 57 (1962): 121–46, esp. p. 128, and for the Ukraini-

ans, see V. V. Pokshishevskii, "Migratsii naseleniia v SSSR," *Priroda*, no. 9 (1969): 67–75, esp. p. 72. V. I. Perevedentsev, "O vliianii etnicheskikh faktorov na territorial'noe pereraspredelenie naseleniia," *Izvestiia Akademii Nauk SSSR, Seriia geograficheskaia*, no. 4 (1965): 31–39, considers ethnic distinctions to be a major factor influencing interrepublic migrations.

16. For the role of capital cities in national development in the USSR, see V. V. Pokshishevskii, "Etnicheskie protsessy v gorodakh SSSR i nekotorye problemy ikh izucheniia," *Sovetskaia ètnografiia*, no. 5 (1969): 3–15. Cf. the classic article by Mark Jefferson, "The Law of the Primate City," *Geographical Review* 29, no. 2 (April 1939): 226–32.

17. On the language problem in Belorussia, see Nicholas P. Vakar, "The Belorussian People between Nationhood and Extinction," in Goldhagen, op. cit., pp. 218–28.

18. International political considerations cannot be discounted because the "Bessarabian Question" may be coming up again. See Alexander Suga, "Bessarabien—noch immer umstritten?," *Osteuropa*, no. 5 (1971): 316–23.

19. For an analysis of the population in Ukraine between 1926 and 1959, see Volodymyr Kubijovyč, ed., *Ukraine: A Concise Encyclopedia* (Toronto: University of Toronto Press, 1963), vol. I.

20. The drawing power of Kyiv for migrants from all over Ukraine was noted by V. I. Tovkun, "Osoblyvosti mihratsii naselennia Ukraïns'koi RSR u 1959–1963 rr.," *Ukraïns'kyi istorychnyi zhurnal*, no. 4 (1966): 49–56, esp. pp. 55–56. Kyiv's "zone of gravitation" in railroad passenger traffic was compared with that of Kharkiv (and found superior) by O. A. Kibal'chich, "Nekotorye osobennosti passazhirskikh sviazei krupnykh gorodov SSSR," *Voprosy geografii 66* (1965): 141–52, esp. pp. 146–49.

21. The volume of migratory movements tending to weaken titular nationalities in their republics should not be underestimated. Immigrants accounted for 43.4 percent of Latvia's population growth between 1950 and 1965, reaching 52.7 percent in 1961–1965 and 60.6 percent in 1965 alone (*Voprosy demografii*: 232). Moldavia's and Belorussia's urban population increased through immigration from Russia and Ukraine; Ukraine's, through immigration from the RSFSR, Kazakhstan, Belorussia, and Georgia (L. Denisova, T. Faddeeva, "Nekotorye dannye o migratsii naseleniia v SSSR," *Vestnik statistiki*, no. 7 [1965]: 16–21).

22. E. Bagramov, "Razvitie i sblizhenie sotsialisticheskikh natsii," *Pravda*, 16 July 1971, pp. 3–4.

23. V. Perevedentsev, "Chto chelovek ishchet?," *Zhurnalist*, no. 4 (1968): 72–75, and "O vliianii ètnicheskikh faktorov, . . ." *Izvestiia Akademii Nauk*, no. 4 (1965): 34–37.

24. L. M. Drobizheva, "O sblizhenii urovnei kul'turnogo razvitiia soiuznykh respublik," *Istoriia SSSR*, no. 3 (1969): 61–79, esp. pp. 77–79. See also M. N.

Guboglo, "Vzaimodeistvie iazykov i mezhnatsionalnye otnosheniia v sovet-skom obshchestve," *Istoriia SSSR*, no. 6 (1970): 22–41.

25. See an advertisement in *Molod' Ukraïny* (Kyiv), 20 April 1971, p. 4, offering scholarships and room and board to young men and women willing to learn a job at a textile plant in Leninabad, Tadzhikstan. Cf. note 23.

26. Dora Fischer, "Arbeitskräfte-Fragen in der regionalen Wirtschaftspla-nung der Sowjet-Union," *Osteuropa Wirtschaft* 12, no. 1 (1967): 71, concluded that the success of Soviet plans for the industrialization, settlement, and security of Siberia and the Far East would depend on the initiative of the *Russians* and their readiness to employ their own forces for that purpose.

27. N. Shchitov, "Otkrovenno o sokrovennom," *Literaturnaia gazeta*, 17 April 1968, p. 10.

3 Russians in Ukraine and Problems of Ukrainian Identity in the USSR

It is only in the most literal, arithmetical sense that Russians in Ukraine are a national minority. Over three million strong in 1926, over seven million in 1959, and more than nine million in 1970, they are not an ordinary minority. Perhaps they could be considered so if Ukraine were independent, but it is not, and the main areas of Russian concentration—Donbas and Kharkiv—are contiguous to the boundaries of the RSFSR.

It is hardly useful to present here the usual statistics, which would show the status and role of the real minority nationalities. Although full data are lacking, we know that Russians have more than their share of the republic's total population in the Communist party, in the party elite, and among academic, managerial, and other leading groups. (We may presume that they are vastly "overrepresented" in the police.) They are concentrated in the cities, where they constitute over 30 percent of the population, unlike the Ukrainians whose share in urban population—over 60 percent—is far below their share in the total population (ca. 75 percent).

It is even less necessary to dwell upon the obvious facts of Soviet political life: that the Russian nation is the leading Soviet nationality and that Russians, helped by Russified "nationals," run the Soviet

First published in *Ukraine in the Seventies*, 1975.

Union. Certain small facts, such as that all secretaries of the Central Committee of the CPSU are ethnic Russians, are well known and need not be recalled here.

Although these considerations are applicable to other Soviet peoples, there is one issue specific to the Russo-Ukrainian relationship that is absent in the relations of Russians with Georgians, Latvians, or Uzbeks: Russians and Ukrainians have a long history of shared experience from the period of Kyivan Rus' and throughout the past three centuries. This sharing of experience was so close at times that it gave rise to a view that Russians and Ukrainians either had been, or continue to be, members of a common, single nation. Of the other Soviet peoples, only Belorussians—perhaps even more so than Ukrainians—have had this problem with their national identity. Rather than being a minority, an external, as it were, body or element within the distinct social and cultural organism of the Ukrainian nation, the Russians of Ukraine, or a significant part of them, have lived there for centuries and most of them have felt it to be their own homeland. It is fair to argue that only in the twentieth century have the broad masses of people and not just the intelligentsia realized and accepted the differentiation of the two nations.

For these reasons—and there may be other, no less valid ones—we propose to discuss the Russians in Ukraine from a broad, comprehensive point of view and to use their situation and position in Ukraine to answer certain questions concerning the national identity of Ukrainians, both in the Ukrainian SSR and in the Soviet Union at large. There should be no objection: It hardly seems possible to consider Russians in Ukraine without keeping in mind that while they are a minority in a land primarily inhabited by Ukrainians, they are a part of a larger polity called the USSR, which to many has been and remains best described as Russia. In similar fashion Ukrainians could be discussed as "Ukrainians in the USSR," or "Ukrainians in Russia." Thus, this chapter has a double title: Russians in Ukraine and Problems of Ukrainian Identity in the Soviet Union.

It is common knowledge that Ukrainians are seen in the other non-Russian republics as Russians, and even those who know that in principle Ukrainians are a different nationality quite rightly perceive their function in the national republics as identical to that of the Russians. A recent document of the Estonian samizdat, complaining of massive Russian immigration to that country, counts Ukrainians and Belorussians as

Russians.[1] This is justified insofar as the function of these two East Slavic peoples in the Baltic areas is concerned.

V. V. Pokshishevsky, a specialist in nationality problems and urbanization, has usefully classified various ethnic groups from the point of view of their role in relation to the Russians outside of their proper ethnic area and has concluded that in Central Asia and the Caucasus Ukrainians have traditionally functioned as the Russians' "fellow-travellers" or "satellites" (*sputniki russikh*), and are considered Russian by the indigenous population.[2]

The concept of *sputniki russkikh* corresponds to a concept introduced by John A. Armstrong, the view that Ukrainians function as the Russians' "younger brothers"—"younger" because their level of social mobilization is still relatively low, and "brothers" because they are similar to Russians in major cultural respects. Armstrong expected the Soviet regime to make particularly intensive efforts to integrate Ukrainians. The success of the regime, Armstrong thought, would depend on its improving the position of "submerged social strata, particularly the peasantry."[3] He evidently took the view that the peasantry is the principal group maintaining a separate Ukrainian identity and that improvement of its economic and social position would promote this Ukrainian-Russian "fraternal" relationship.

It is a thesis here that the Ukrainians' role as the Russians' helpers in Russifying Estonia, Latvia, or Uzbekistan is related to the respective position of Russians and Ukrainians inside Ukraine; to wit, the identification of the city with Russia and the countryside with Ukraine. When Ukrainians move upward, by becoming technicians, scientists, or the like, they become (at least linguistically) Russified and mobile in the entire USSR. Once they leave Ukraine, regardless of their subjective attitudes, they function as Russians. The party seems to understand that in order to retain the connection of Ukrainian culture and Ukrainian nationality with the rural world, as opposed to Russian as a synonym of urban and modern, those Ukrainians who no longer fit this "village" description should be moved outside Ukraine. For how is one to interpret the fact that almost sixty years after the establishment of Soviet power, Ukrainians form just barely more than 50 percent of the scientific cadre in Ukraine, whereas more than one-third of the scientists of Ukrainian nationality in the USSR work in the other republics?

How are these considerations related to the question of Ukrainian identity in the USSR?

It is our thesis that the status of Russians, and of Russian culture, in Ukraine has its counterpart in the status of Ukrainians outside Ukraine. In Ukraine Russians and the Russian language enjoy superior positions, and Russians are expected to, and do, use the Russian language as the means of communication, but Ukrainians outside Ukraine are totally deprived of any nationality rights. Moreover, since the world of modern culture in Ukraine—science and technology particularly—is the world of the Russian language, a Ukrainian functioning in this world is denationalized; Ukrainian culture is limited to literature and the humanities.

A comparison between the Russian and Ukrainian literary newspapers, *Literaturnaia gazeta* and *Literaturna Ukraïna,* distinctly illustrates the difference. The Ukrainian paper writes only about books and problems relating to *belles lettres*, poetry, and *publitsystyka*, and does so on an elementary level. Occasionally other topics are treated that may be of professional interest to librarians, elementary, and possibly high school, teachers. The Russian paper writes for the entire intelligentsia, not only the humanistic cadre. Psychology, philosophy, urban life, family matters, demography, the scientific revolution, and the organization of science are regularly covered. The paper clearly addresses itself to the intelligent, educated urban reader. International affairs (political perhaps more than literary) receive broad coverage. It is a safe bet that *Literaturnaia gazeta* has several times more readers in Ukraine than does *Literaturna Ukraïna.*

I would like to treat the Russians in Ukraine both in a broad historical perspective—the emergence of the modern Ukraine as a political, national, and geographic concept and reality, and from a special angle—the role of the Russians as a modernizing force in relation to the Ukrainian population. Accordingly, our discussion will develop the following questions. First, what is Ukraine and what are the origins of what we know today as the Ukrainian Soviet Socialist Republic? Second, to what extent is it possible to view the Russians in Ukraine as the sole modernizing force and the Ukrainians as a people to be brought to modernity by becoming like the Russians? Or are the Ukrainians a distinct nation capable of developing its own form of modernity? Should one continue to identify Ukrainians with the countryside and the village way of life and outlook, and Russians as the representatives of modern, urban culture? Or perhaps there exists evidence suggesting that this simple dichotomy is no longer descriptive of the Russo–Ukrainian relationship in Ukraine?

What is Ukraine, then?

The Soviet Ukrainian republic as we know it today has been in existence for about thirty years. It was only in 1944–45 that its present western oblasts were incorporated into the USSR (Lviv, Ternopil, Ivano-Frankivsk, Volyn, Rivne, Chernivtsi, Transcarpathia). Crimea was added about ten years later, in 1954. The Ukrainian SSR in its earlier shape, before 1939, was about twenty years old when its western expansion began. Its pre-1939 boundary was basically established only after the Soviet-Polish war of 1920 (except that in 1923 it lost the Taganrog and Shakhty regions to the RSFSR).

Ukraine as it existed before the establishment of Soviet power and after the March 1917 revolution did not have firm boundaries for any significant length of time. The area under Hetman Skoropadsky was perhaps the most stable: It survived under German occupation from the spring of 1918 to December 1918. After the fall of the Hetman, throughout 1919, Ukraine was under a variety of competing forces: Ukrainian, Communist, White Russian, local partisan forces such as those of Makhno and Hryhoriiv, and the Allied forces in the Black Sea region.

The predecessor of the Hetmanate was the Ukrainian People's Republic, at first autonomous, but after the fall of the Provisional Government in Petrograd, de facto independent; it formally proclaimed its independence in January 1918. However, the area under effective control of the Kyiv government was not clear: The authority of the Central Rada did not extend to the southeastern and southern parts of the present Ukrainian SSR—that is, to Donbas, and to such cities as Odessa, Kherson, Dnipropetrovsk, Kryvyi Rih, or Zaporizhia. Before that, the autonomous Ukraine, as recognized by the Provisional Government in the summer of 1917, consisted of the following five gubernii: Kyiv, Volyn, Podillia, Poltava, and Chernihiv (excluding the latter's northern counties). Such centers as Kharkiv, Odessa, and Dnipropetrovsk were thus excluded.[4] It was not obvious even to nationally conscious Ukrainians, let alone others, exactly what should be considered as Ukrainian territory. In principle the answer was simple and easy: The Ukrainian "ethnographic" territory at that time was understood to mean the territory where the peasant population was predominantly Ukrainian. But where should the cities—obviously not Ukrainian "ethnographically"—be assigned? Was Odessa a part of Ukraine, a city where Ukrainians represented something like one-tenth of the inhabitants? Small wonder that not only many of its inhabitants but also some Ukrainians felt that "Odessa is not Ukraine."

One of the indications that what we have now come to know and accept as Ukraine was not a single unit—whether administratively, politically, or economically or, ideally, in the perceptions of the population—is the fact that no single city enjoyed a clear position of superiority in the area. Kyiv was, of course, the most famous and historically the "prime city," but neither Odessa (which was a larger city in population until after 1917) nor Kharkiv nor the cities of the Donbas-Kryvyi Rih area were accustomed to consider Kyiv as their capital in any meaningful way. The story of the split in the Bolshevik camp between the Kyivans and Katerynoslavians and the attempt to establish a separate Soviet republic of Donets-Kryvyi Rih and an "Odessan Soviet republic" by means of secession from the Soviet Ukrainian republic is well known. These cases are directly relevant to this discussion: When we are speaking about Russians in Ukraine, we have to know what kind of Ukraine it is.

What about earlier times, before the confusing events of 1917–1945? The area of an autonomous Ukraine in the eighteenth century, the Hetmanshchyna and the region of the Zaporizhian Cossacks, roughly corresponded to the present administrative oblast of Dnipropetrovsk, Zaporizhia, Poltava, Chernihiv, and (partially) Kyiv. To the west of this area, until 1793–1795, was Poland. To the east were lands under the direct rule of the tsar, which were being (or had been) colonized by Ukrainians alone or jointly with Russians. These areas included what we now know as the oblasts of Kharkiv and Sumy. Such was the territorial status quo of the eighteenth century. (In the seventeenth century, before the partition of Ukraine in 1667, the independent Ukraine that was established de facto in 1648 extended to the west of the Dnieper and thus included the present-day oblasts of Cherkasy, Vynnytsia, Zhytomyr, and Kyiv. It did not include the west Ukrainian areas.)[5]

None of these old territorial-political structures (nor any of their predecessors, we should add) extended to the coast of the Black or the Azov Seas, and none included what we now call Donbas. It is worth remembering that Ukrainians began to settle in those areas only in the late eighteenth and in the nineteenth and twentieth centuries, when many others, including Russians, Greeks, Serbs, Jews, and Germans, were moving there as well, and when the political or administrative status of those areas was different from that of the older Ukrainian territories. Until the tsarist state collapsed, Ukraine was divided into a number of gubernii belonging to three governships-general, Kyiv, Odessa, and Kharkiv, which were all directly under St. Petersburg's administration.

Although it is true that by and large Ukrainians proved to be the most numerous of all those peoples in the newly settled area, interestingly enough they settled in the country, not in towns, and worked primarily in agriculture. Ukrainians did not show an equal readiness or desire to enter the cities of this area or indeed the cities of other areas of Ukraine. The Ukrainian peasant appears to have preferred to move to places where he could get enough land to engage in farming.

In a study of migrations in Ukraine in the light of the 1897 and 1926 censuses, A. Hirshfeld pointed out that while migrants from the Ukraine to other parts of the Russian Empire or Soviet Union had been overwhelmingly employed in agriculture and continued that work after their move (although there was also a white collar element), migrants to Ukraine from the provinces of Russia were employed in Ukraine as industrial workers in a similarly overwhelming proportion. He cited figures relating to the place of origin of migrants to Donbas in order to demonstrate that a vast majority of those born outside the region had been born outside Ukraine (151,130), but those born in Ukraine in areas other than Donbas numbered much less (49,098).[6] Why did migrants from the predominantly agrarian and ethnically Ukrainian areas of the Right Bank Ukraine settle beyond the Urals, in Kazakhstan, and similar places, rather than in southeast Ukraine?

> It appears we are dealing here with the historic inertia of the peasant population of the Right Bank and Polissia, which has no desire to change its profession and prefers in its move to the East to go beyond the Urals in search of free land.[7]

These patterns of migration, discernible through an analysis of the 1926 census, had also been in force before the revolution, as demonstrated by the census of 1897. Hirshfeld hoped that Ukrainian migration from Ukraine would cease in the future (his book was published in 1930), and that Ukrainian agricultural surplus labor would seek employment in industry in Ukraine instead.[8] In the meantime, ethnic Russians were migrating from the north to the rapidly growing cities in Ukraine and the urban jobs being created there, to which Ukrainians were not attracted.

Because of these diverse migratory patterns (in addition to obvious and self-explanatory factors, such as that Ukraine was a part of Russia and Ukrainians were considered the "Little Russian" branch of the Russian nation), the towns, located mainly in the east, and the country in Ukraine differed ethnically and linguistically up to the time of the revolutionary events of 1917 to 1921. The prevalence of Russians and corresponding scarcity of Ukrainians in the cities in those years was a decisive factor, according to some scholars, in bringing about the failure of the Ukrainian struggle for independence.[9]

It had seemed that the Ukrainization policies inaugurated in the 1920s would result in the linguistic integration of the urban east and the rural west of the Ukrainian SSR. These policies were abandoned in the thirties, however, and as Robert S. Sullivant has observed, "the old division of the Ukraine into an urban area which was distinctly Russian and a rural area which was distinctly Ukrainian remained basically unchanged." According to Sullivant, the "striking dichotomy" established in prerevolutionary years of an urban-Russian east versus a rural-Ukrainian west was not affected by Soviet rule. "Stalin and his successors alike agreed that, whatever the language program for the cities, the Ukrainian character of the countryside was to be maintained."[10]

We do not have to agree with Sullivant that once Ukrainization of the cities was rejected as a policy, Russification proceeded naturally as a product of sociological pressures and a consequence of the advantage enjoyed by the Russian language. We might respond by suggesting that the role of force, including terror and deportations, was no less instrumental in producing Russification. Sullivant's statement that the "extent of Russification was more a measure of the Ukraine's urbanization trend and of the growing mobility of the USSR's population than of influence exerted by official Russifying policies"[11] seems to ignore the extraordinary intensity of terror and other administrative measures used under Stalin to undo the achievements of the Ukrainian element in Ukraine's cities. However we may distribute the responsibility for what happened, Sullivant appears to be right in stating that the old dichotomy survived Stalin and was in evidence during the immediate post-1953 years. The question may be raised whether this generalization is equally valid today.

It is customary to review ethnic conditions in Ukraine by treating that republic as a homogeneous unit, and then to compare the ratio of Russians to the republican nationality in Ukraine to that same ratio in Lithuania, Latvia, or other Soviet republics. Even on purely statistical grounds this method appears to be questionable. More importantly, we believe, it is faulty for historical reasons, in view of the fact that what is present-day Ukraine until 1945, indeed 1954, had never formed a single political or administrative unit. However, let us begin with some general all-Ukraine comparisons with other European Soviet republics according to data from 1970.

Among the European republics of the USSR, in the percentage of Russians in the total population Ukraine (19.4 percent) ranks behind Latvia (29.8 percent) and Estonia (24.7). In Moldavia (11.6 percent), Belorussia (10.4 percent), and Lithuania (8.6 percent) the percentage of Russians is lower. Russians were increasing in Ukraine, between the censuses of 1959 and 1970, at a rate lower than that in Belorussia, Moldavia, and Estonia. The intercensal percentage increase of Russians in Ukraine and these three republics was 28.7 percent, 42.1 percent, 41.3 percent, and 36.9 percent, respectively. In Latvia the increase of Russians was 26.8 percent and in Lithuania, 16.0 percent. The Russians increased at a rate higher than that of their respective titular nations in all republics except Lithuania, where Lithuanians grew by 16.6 percent compared to the Russians' 16 percent. In Estonia the Russian rate exceeded the native by a full 11 times, in Latvia by close to 8, in Belorussia by 3.6, in Ukraine by close to 3 times, and in Moldavia by close to 2 (Moldavians increasing by 22.1 percent against the Russians' 41.3 percent).[12] As we said, these comparisons suffer from a major limitation in that in terms of its population Ukraine is in a different class: Its population more than twice exceeds the combined total of the rest. Even if one were to divide Ukraine into the three major economic regions, the South (6.4 million) would in terms of population be larger than all the other European republics except Belorussia; the other two regions are over 20 million each, thus exceeding the population of Belorussia by more than twice.

For this reason, and also considering the historical differences in the pattern of Russian settlement in Ukraine, we have subdivided the entire territory of the Ukrainian SSR into six units (see table 3.1, Ethnic Composition of Major Regions). [In chapter 2, we reviewed three regions of Ukraine as defined by central authorities in Moscow (Large Economic Regions of the Gosplan). Those three regions correspond in the following way to the six regions discussed here: Odessa and Crimea or "The South" in chapter 2 is identical with the South as defined here (including the oblasts of Odessa, Crimea, Kherson, and Mykolaiv); East Ukraine

Table 3.1

Ethnic Composition of Major Regions of Ukraine

Region	Total Population			Ukrainians					Russians				
	1959	1970	Percentage Change	1959	Percent	1970	Percent	Percentage Change	1959	Percent	1970	Percent	Percentage Change
Donbas	6,714,220	7,642,545	13.83	3,784,427	56.36	4,103,479	53.69	8.43	2,551,284	33.38	3,135,551	41.03	22.90
South	5,066,132	6,380,614	25.95	2,883,000	56.91	3,506,931	54.96	21.64	1,566,070	24.54	2,170,150	34.01	38.57
Dnieper	5,386,561	6,377,109	18.39	4,182,207	77.64	4,766,924	74.75	13.98	947,376	14.86	1,327,005	20.81	40.07
Northeast	5,665,553	6,037,018	6.56	4,589,545	81.01	4,739,075	78.50	3.26	916,333	15.18	1,129,214	18.70	23.23
Central West	11,238,688	11,932,950	6.18	9,921,534	88.28	10,445,550	87.54	5.28	706,782	5.92	918,761	7.70	29.99
West	7,799,058	8,754,552	12.25	6,797,780	87.16	7,721,898	88.20	13.59	402,938	4.60	445,650	5.09	10.60
Ukraine (total)	41,870,212	47,124,788	12.55	32,158,493	76.81	35,283,857	74.87	9.72	7,090,783	15.05	9,126,331	19.37	28.71

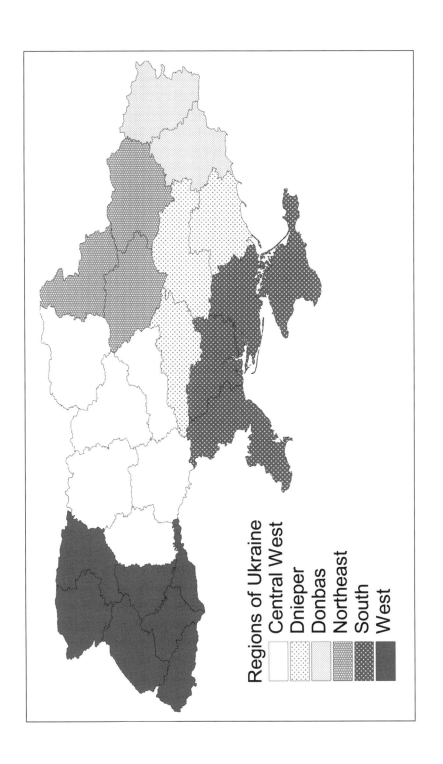

Regions of Ukraine

Central West

Dnieper

Donbas

Northeast

South

West

or the "Donetsk-Dnieper" region corresponds to what are here Donbas (Donetsk and Luhansk), Dnieper (Dnipropetrovsk, Zaporizhia and Kirovohrad), and Northeast (Kharkiv, Poltava, Sumy) regions; and Kyiv and the West or "The Southwest" is subdivided into Central West (oblasts of Kyiv, Chernihiv, Cherkasy, Khmelnytsky, Vinnytsia, and Zhytomyr) and West (Lviv, Chernivtsi, Ivano-Frankivsk, Rivne, Ternopil, Transcarpathia, and Volynia).] The six regions have been ranked in decreasing order of the proportion of Russians in the population. The Donbas is clearly the most Russian part of Ukraine, followed by the South, Dnieper, Northeast (Kharkiv), Central West (Kyiv), and West (Lviv). In Donbas Russians constitute 41.03 percent, and in the West, 5.09 percent of the total population. Donbas and the South surpass Latvia and Estonia in the share of Russian population. The Northeast and Dnieper trail these two republics, and the Central West and the West have fewer Russians than any European republic of the USSR.

The growth rates of the Russian element in the respective regions of Ukraine also display wide diversity, ranging from 40 percent in Dnipropetrovsk and just under 40 percent in the South to a low of 10.6 percent in the West. The higher figures resemble the growth rates of the Russian population in Belorussia, Moldavia, and Estonia, but the low figure in the West is lower than the Lithuanian one of 16 percent.

Considering that most of these regions are large, comparable in size to certain Union republics, we propose to analyze some of the demographic data in a regional breakdown, concentrating our attention especially on demographic and ethnic trends in the urban sector of the population. The concentration on urban population is warranted by various reasons, not only the fact that the USSR is undergoing a process of urbanization that is likely to continue, but also in view of the peculiar nature of the Russo–Ukrainian relationship. We have in mind, of course, the coincidence of the dichotomy urban–rural with that of Russian–Ukrainian, both historically and in the present.

What is happening in the cities of Donbas from the ethnic point of view?[13]

While the share of Ukrainians in the total population of Donetsk oblast declined from 55.56 percent to 53.08 percent during 11 intercensal years, the percentage of the population that considered Ukrainian its native language dropped from 44.42 to 31.89 percent. In the cities that decline was even more marked: The number of native speakers of Ukrainian declined from 39.39 percent in 1959 to 30.55 percent in 1970.

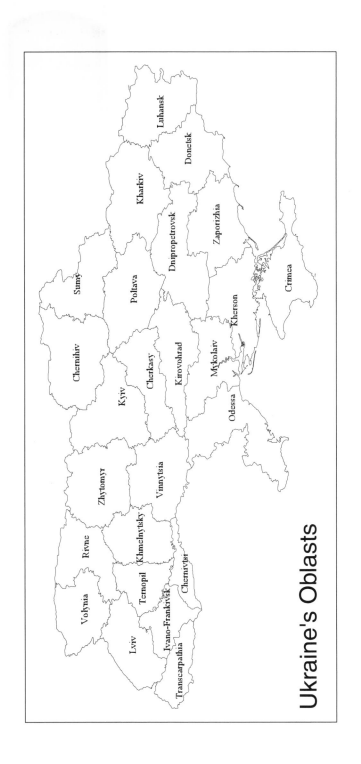

Ukraine's Oblasts

Those speaking Russian as their native language, including Ukrainians, Greeks, and others, increased from 58.67 percent to 65.38 percent. Not only percentagewise but also in absolute figures, the number of persons declaring Ukrainian as their native language declined in Donetsk, both in the towns and in the country, while the numbers of Russian-speakers rose in both categories. In the cities, Ukrainian-speakers declined by 1.86 percent and Russian-speakers increased by 30.31 percent. In the Ukrainian ethnic group alone, the total population increase was 12.32 percent (compared with a 23.77 percent increase of Russians), of which those speaking Ukrainian declined by 1.89 percent and those Ukrainians declaring Russian as their language rose by 54.81 percent.

The significance of these figures is hardly challenged by the data, available for 1970 only, on knowledge of Ukrainian as a second language. According to the census, 488,049—that is, 26.11 percent of the Russians (1,869,071)—know Ukrainian; also 347,696 Ukrainians—or 47.10 percent of the total of Ukrainians speaking Russian as their first language—know Ukrainian. In 1959, Russian was the native language to 25.06 percent of urban Ukrainians in Donetsk oblast, but by 1970 the figure was 34.54 percent, an increase of almost 10 percentage points. (To be precise, among Donetsk Ukrainians there was a 0.86 percent annual increase in the change from Ukrainian to Russian. At this rate, by the year 2056 all urban Ukrainians in Donetsk oblast will consider Russian their first language.) Those who either consider Ukrainian their first language or declare knowledge of it as a second language constitute 56.74 percent of the total population and 53.55 percent of the urban population. Conversely, Russian is a language native to, or known by, 83.64 percent of Donetsk oblast, and 87.77 percent of Donetsk oblast's urban population. Thus, there exists a considerable reciprocally bilingual population, and an absolute majority of Ukrainians who speak Ukrainian also know Russian. Only in the villages do a majority of Ukrainians not speak Russian. (The rural population of the oblast, 613,383, was only 12.60 percent of the total oblast population.) In the cities, besides those 738,182 Ukrainians whose native language was Russian in 1970, an additional 891,879 declared familiarity with it. This leaves only 506,772—that is, 23.71 percent of all urban Ukrainians—not speaking Russian. The case of Donetsk (and Donbas as a whole) seems to indicate that an increasing number of people speak Russian there. The share of those who consider themselves Russian is also on the rise. Is Donbas today what Ukraine will become in the coming years? To make any analyses along these lines one must compare these data with data on the other principal urban centers of Ukraine and also consider the historic, political, and cultural factors that may have influenced the linguistic situation in these centers.

Before moving on to a review of the ethnic composition of other regions, let us briefly pause to note two Soviet sources relating to the Russian element in eastern Ukraine and its interaction with Ukrainians.

Speaking about the pre-Soviet period, Kurman and Lebedinsky, two recent Soviet authors of a book on Kharkiv, admitted that the immigration of Russians to Ukraine was not only a demographic or social process but also one directly involving the use of force and application of discriminatory practices. Ukrainians were forced to make room for Russians in Kharkiv. The tsarist government pursued a deliberate policy of increasing the ratio of Russians in the population of Kharkiv, according to these writers, and had been sending various administrators to the city ever since pre-Petrine times. This process continued after the abolition of serfdom, when railroad construction and industrialization were accompanied by the immigration of Russian officials and workers. Another relevant aspect was the Russification policy, including the prohibition of Ukrainian-language schools. It was this factor, Kurman and Lebedinsky suggest, that must be considered in explaining why, in the 1897 census, only 25 percent of Kharkiv's population declared Ukrainian as their native language—even though over two-thirds of the city's inhabitants had been born in Ukraine.[14]

According to Kurman and Lebedinsky, the "flowering of national culture" in the USSR after the revolution and the rise in the national consciousness of Soviet citizens lie behind the increase of self-declared Ukrainians in Kharkiv: In 1926, over 38 percent, and in 1939, 48.6 percent of the Kharkiv residents were Ukrainian by nationality. By 1959, however, the share of Ukrainians in the city had decreased slightly (to 48.4 percent), while that of Russians rose from 32.9 percent in 1939 to 40.4 percent in 1959. Considering that virtually all Russians declared Russian to be their native language, while 35.9 percent of Ukrainians declared Russian as their language, the population of Kharkiv in 1959 was divided linguistically in the following way:[15]

Russian	628,000	67.2 percent
Ukrainian	291,600	31.2 percent
Other	14,500	1.6 percent
TOTAL	934,000	

Although these figures suggest that Russian was clearly the dominant language in Ukraine's second largest city, however, the authors argue that in fact both languages were widely known in the city. One of the reasons for this is that Russian was taught in Ukrainian schools, and Ukrainian was a "required" subject in Russian schools.[16] Since the book was published about eight years after the Khrushchevian educational reform abolished the teaching of non-Russian languages in Russian schools as a required subject, one wonders whether the authors are misinformed or the reform proved to be something different from what it was thought to be.

Additional material on ethnic relations in eastern Ukraine may may be found in a study published in 1968 in *Sovetskaia etnografiia*. As we noted earlier, Russians had been living in the eastern regions of Ukraine, especially the oblasts of Kharkiv and Sumy, both in towns and the countryside, ever since the seventeenth century. According to the findings of an expedition sent in 1966 by the Institute of Ethnography of the Academy of Sciences of the USSR, the bulk of Russians and Ukrainians living there had retained their national consciousness, but there were also cases of changes of national self-consciousness among Russians who lived in mixed Russo-Ukrainian villages. Such changes among Ukrainians were reportedly rarer. In one village, Aleshnia, which had been settled by Russians in the second half of the seventeenth century (previously it had been a Ukrainian village), two village soviets were established after the revolution, in view of the mixed ethnic composition of the village. "At the end of the 1950s, considering that a majority of the population of that village came to consider themselves Ukrainian, the two village soviets were combined into one and one secondary school, with Ukrainian as the language of instruction, was formed."[17] This change in national consciousness apparently occurred in the 1950s and 1960s. According to local records, in 1950 to 1952, Ukrainians and Russians in the village constituted 46.4 percent and 53.6 percent, respectively; by 1964 to 1966 the corresponding figures were 91.2 percent and 8.4 percent. In the 1959 all-Union census the entire population of the village was recorded as Ukrainian. L. N. Chizhikova, from whose study all these data are cited, gives various examples of how persons with names such as Orekhov, Maksakov, Kriukov, Kozmin, Lukianov, Machulin, and Pushkariev declared themselves as Ukrainians, even though 12 or 15 years earlier they had given their nationality as Russian. Sometimes children of Russian parents declare their nationality as Ukrainian. Russian names at times become Ukrainianized: Krivoguzov becomes Kryvohuz, Maksakov—Maksak, Slinkov—Slynko.[18]

> Asked about the reasons for changes in national self-definition, they usually answer that they live in Ukraine and among the Ukrainian people; moreover, many emphasize along with this that it is not of great importance to them what they call themselves—Russian or Ukrainian. Some local residents find it difficult to answer to which nationality they belong, which unquestionably is to be explained by the occurrence in those regions of active processes of ethnic change in the population.[19]

Needless to say the expedition also recorded cases when nationality was changed from Ukrainian to Russian, especially in locations where the population was mixed with a predominance of Russians. The language of the school appears to exert an influence on national self-identification. It is interesting, however, that the terms "Ukrainian" and "Russian" were not commonly used as late as this century: Even the participants of the 1968 expedition encountered villagers who called themselves "khokhol" or "pereverten" and referred to others as "moskali." These terms were not considered derogatory but descriptive.[20]

Since similar changes from Ukrainian to Russian, much more significant in terms of numbers, have occurred in the predominantly Ukrainian-inhabited districts of Kuban and other areas outside the Ukrainian SSR, it may be worth noting that Ukrainians there often were at a stage of premodern national consciousness. Without denying that the policies pursued by the Stalinist regime in the 1930s were very effective (terror, prohibition of education and the press in Ukrainian, and the like), one should add that these objects of Russification switched from a "Little Russian," "khokhol," or similar ethnic consciousness to Russian without ever having consciously accepted the national Ukrainian identity, including its literary language, political symbols, and so forth. There is no doubt that a similar transfer to Russian nationality occurred in Ukraine, considering that the period of relatively pro-Ukrainian policies in Soviet Ukraine was very brief and even then was more likely declared in official statements rather than actually implemented in the work of the local administration.[21]

How do these statements of Kurman and Lebedinsky and of Chizhikova look in the light of the 1970 census returns?

According to the 1970 census, Russians represented 34.15 percent of the urban population in Kharkiv oblast (in 1959 the ratio was 31.97 percent); of those, 30.14 percent declared that they spoke Ukrainian fluently and another 0.97 percent considered Ukrainian to be their native language. The percentage of Ukrainians in Kharkiv oblast's urban population was 59.78 percent (compared with 60.77 percent in 1959). Of those Ukrainians (considered as 100 percent), 24.27 percent regarded Russian as their native language (in 1959, the figure was 19.21 percent), and 44.62 percent said they knew Russian. However, out of the 284,170 Ukrainians who chose Russian as their first language, 162,795, or 51.29 percent, declared a command of Ukrainian as well; this figure represents 13.91 percent of the total of urban Ukrainians, which means that about 10 percent of all urban Ukrainians in Kharkiv oblast neither consider Ukrainian as their first language nor claim to know it as their second language.[22]

It is not certain to what extent the census declarations accurately reflect the real language situation, in particular knowledge of a second language, among Ukrainians and Russians. It may well be that the census understates the extent of reciprocal bilingualism.[23] In practice, it seems that the Russians, or rather those who use Russian as their first language in the urban centers of Ukraine, do have a command of Ukrainian sufficient to allow them to read Ukrainian newspapers and journals, listen to radio broadcasts, and so forth. In 1969 an evening newspaper, *Vechirnii Kharkiv,* was established in the Ukrainian language in Kharkiv. According to a Soviet journalist, prior to its appearance some publishing people argued that the paper would not sell well if it were published in Ukrainian. However, the paper proved to be quite successful despite the "handicap" of appearing in Ukrainian. The initial circulation of *Vechirnii Kharkiv* was 100,000 copies daily, and by 1974 it had risen to 150,000.[24]

Limitations of space allow only the briefest reference to nationality processes in the south of Ukraine, Crimea and Odessa, or the area of lower Dnieper with the major urban and industrial centers of Dnipropetrovsk, Zaporizhia, and Kryvyi Rih. Table 3.2 has data on the ethnic composition of the urban population of select oblasts of Ukraine, namely those containing the metropolitan centers of the republic: Kharkiv, Donetsk, Dnipropetrovsk, Kyiv, and Lviv. As table 3.2 shows, the urban Russian population in Dnipropetrovsk rose very rapidly between the censuses of 1956 and 1970 (54 percent) and was also high in Odessa (39 percent). However, Ukrainians were also increasing relatively

Table 3.2
Selected Oblasts of Ukraine

Region	Total Urban Population			Urban Ukrainians					Urban Russians				
	1959	1970	Percentage Change	1959	Percent	1970	Percent	Percentage Change	1959	Percent	1970	Percent	Percentage Change
Donetsk	3,656,240	4,275,596	16.94	1,902,583	52.04	2,137,010	49.98	12.32	1,517,860	41.51	1,878,618	43.94	23.77
Odessa	956,694	1,334,381	39.48	421,126	44.02	633,658	47.49	50.47	341,720	35.72	474,622	35.57	38.89
Kharkiv	1,573,738	1,958,194	24.43	956,369	60.77	1,170,648	59.78	22.41	503,074	31.97	668,708	34.15	32.92
Dnipropetrovsk	1,898,765	2,548,964	34.24	1,358,025	71.52	1,765,675	69.27	30.02	417,388	21.98	642,951	25.22	54.04
Kyiv (city and oblast combined)	1,547,907	2,286,725	47.73	1,024,029	66.16	1,595,675	69.78	55.82	312,904	20.21	463,526	20.27	48.14
Lviv	821,338	1,148,649	39.85	575,377	70.05	878,998	76.52	52.77	168,937	20.57	193,042	16.81	14.27
Ukraine (total)	19,147,419	25,688,560	34.16	11,781,750	61.53	16,164,254	62.92	37.20	5,726,476	29.91	7,712,277	30.02	34.68

quickly, especially in Odessa, and somewhat more slowly in Dnipropetrovsk, but even there more quickly than in Donetsk or Kharkiv oblasts. One may speculate that ethnic tensions will accelerate in the south, including the lower Dnieper, since it is an area in which both nationalities remain in a stage of rapid growth. Let us note that it was in Dnipropetrovsk that students and young intellectuals and artists protested against Russification in 1969 and were put on trial in 1970,[25] and that samizdat materials contain information on the prevalence of the Russian element and subordinate position of Ukrainians in Odessa and Crimea. Thus *Ukrainskyi visnyk,* no. 6, refers to restrictions on the Ukrainian language in Crimea's schools and colleges and the virtual absence of Ukrainian in common use. A recent work, published in the West in 1974, describes an Odessa that recalls Mykola Skrypnyk's statement that during the revolution neither Russians nor Ukrainians felt that Odessa was in Ukraine. Skrypnyk would have been surprised, one imagines, to learn that as late as the 1970s some inhabitants of Odessa remained convinced that their city was not located in Ukraine. Danylo Shumuk, the author of *Beyond the Eastern Horizon,* came to Odessa in 1970 after his release from a labor camp and found that unlike in Kyiv, where Ukrainian could still occasionally be heard, nobody spoke Ukrainian in Odessa. When he spoke Ukrainian, he was met with insults and hostility. One woman commented:

> "Young man, you're well dressed and seem to have an intelligent face, but you speak like a savage. You really don't know Russian?"

Another woman added:

> "You know, even here in Odessa these *khokhly* have become so impudent that they asked me to fill out a form in their Ukrainian language. And I answered, 'I'm not from the collective farm, I'm from Odessa.' So I ignored them and filled out the form in Russian."

When Shumuk replied that in Moscow or Leningrad he would speak Russian but in Ukraine he always spoke in Ukrainian, a man joined in with this observation (the discussion took place in a streetcar): "I see we've got a Banderite here—he even thinks Odessa is Ukraine."[26]

Later, the author ran into someone he had known in the camps who had been employed in construction work in Odessa for the past fourteen years. The friend was totally resigned about the prospects of Ukraine.

He argued that intellectuals in Kyiv—such as Ivan Svitlychnyi and Ivan Dziuba, whose names he knew—were completely isolated from the Ukrainian masses, and besides, "What can some group of intellectuals do when the entire working class blabbers in Russian and doesn't even want to hear about any independence. . . . We're not a nation, Danylo, not a nation but just a Little Russian nationality [*narodnist'*] which is only proud of its varenyky, halushky and borshch, and nothing else."[27]

This issue has also been addressed in the Russian samizdat. A document entitled *Slovo Natsii* ("A Word to the Nation") admits that "a strong nationalist movement" exists in Ukraine, but considers its aims "utterly unreal." "The present-day frontiers of Ukraine . . . do not correspond with its ethnographical [boundaries]." On ethnic grounds, the document says, Ukraine should lose its eastern and southern provinces, especially those like Crimea where Ukrainians do not constitute a majority. If the Russian and Russified areas of Ukraine are ceded to Russia, the remaining part will find itself without an outlet to the sea and without the basic industrial areas; the Ukrainians will have no choice—faced as they will be by Polish claims to Ukraine's western regions—but to ask to be accepted back by Russia, the return of the "prodigal son." (The author(s) do not seem to be very well aware of conditions in West Ukraine inasmuch as they attribute a "pro-Polish disposition to the population of Ukraine's western provinces."[28])

It is also significant that Alexander Solzhenitsyn, who in his celebrated letter to the leaders of the Soviet Union (1973) expressed readiness to accept the secession of various borderland nationalities from a state common with the Russians, thought that in the case of Ukraine only some "parts of Ukraine" might secede; presumably, he considered the other parts of the Ukrainian Soviet Republic to be more Russian than Ukrainian.

This view seems to be in accord with the position traditionally taken by Russians of various orientations that Odessa and Donbas are not Ukrainian.

There is evidence that Russians and Ukrainians view the West and Central West differently. The Central West (see table 3.1) is characterized by a low population growth (the lowest in the republic) and a relatively low rate of growth of the Ukrainian population. However, to understand the demographic processes at work there, one should consider its center, the city of Kyiv, separately from the rest of the region (possibly together with Kyiv oblast, considering the large number of commuters from Kyiv's satellite towns to the capital). Splitting the Central West region along these lines we see two rather different trends. Our initial impression of a rather slow demographic growth is reinforced if we subtract the figures for Kyiv from the totals. Even if we add the data for Kyiv oblast to the city data to avoid distortion, we see that the population of the Central West minus the Kyiv metropolitan area was stagnant during the intercensal period; it rose by only 0.80 percent. Ukrainians grew by even less (0.76 percent) but Russians, interestingly enough, rose by as much as 16.98 percent.

Developments in Kyiv were notably different. The city and oblast combined rose by 22.60 percent, Ukrainians by 20.97 percent, and Russians by 43.92 percent. Since Russians represented only 11.92 percent of the population in 1959, their rise by such a high percentage resulted in their gain of 2 percentage points by 1970 (to 13.99 percent). In the capital itself, the increase of Ukrainians was higher than that of Russians, resulting in an increase in the Ukrainian population in the city from 60.0 to 61.76 percent. The total population rose by 47 percent, Russians by 46.5 percent, and Ukrainians by 58.2 percent. Only in Crimea was the Ukrainian increase higher (79.5 percent). Kyiv thus proved to be the only one of the five largest cities in Ukraine in which the Ukrainian element increased faster than the Russian. (Lviv, where the Ukrainians also grew faster, is not one of those largest cities.)

In order to make the situation in Kyiv comparable with that in the other major urban centers, we assembled data on Kyiv and the urban population of the rest of Kyiv oblast in table 3.2. In Kyiv and Lviv Ukrainians increased faster than Russians, and while in Kyiv the Russian proportion remained virtually the same, in Lviv the Russians actually declined from 21 to 14 percent of the urban population. We shall return to Lviv shortly, but let us note some comments by the Soviet demographer and geographer, V. V. Pokshishevsky, that seem to apply directly to Kyiv. Pokshishevsky argues that the "ethnically-oriented state structure" of the USSR and the industrialization of non-Russian areas gave rise to urban centers in those non-Russian areas that became "the centers of national culture and ethnic consciousness." They became centers of education, publishing, and broadcasting, and they developed a need for ethnic personnel in administration and in training indigenous workers for industry. For these reasons, these cities "began to attract ethnic contingents from rural areas, in some cases from other union republics and even from cities in those republics. This suggests that in the USSR it is now the city, perhaps more than the countryside, that has become the 'carrier of the ethnos.' " According to Pokshishevsky, the Ukrainian element has been on the rise in Kyiv because Kyiv has attracted Ukrainians from the entire territory of Ukraine and because of the "further consolidation of the Ukrainian nation and a strengthening of ethnic consciousness . . . it may be supposed that some Kievans, after some hesitation whether to consider themselves Ukrainian, later did so with absolute conviction; more children of mixed marriages have also declared themselves Ukrainians."[29]

In table 3.3 we assembled information about the capitals of the non-Russian republics in the USSR, ranking them in order of the proportion of Russians who declared in 1970 that they spoke fluently the language of the respective Union republic. In all the capitals of the Central Asian republics, where the Russians constituted either an absolute majority or exceeded 40 percent, Russians speaking the native language ranged from 0.72 percent to 2.47 percent. In Baku 5.14 percent of Russians knew Azeri; their share in the capital's population was 27.74 percent. The percentage of Russians speaking the local language elsewhere in the Caucasus reached 17.86 percent in Tbilisi and as high as 30.95 percent in Erevan. However, in Erevan the Russians constituted only 2.81 percent of the population in 1970, a drop from 4.4 percent in 1959. It is reasonable to imagine that those few Russians were under some pressure to learn Armenian. It is rather strange that less than a third said they had actually done so. All the more interesting, therefore, is the case of Russians in Kyiv, of whom 41.05 percent declared knowledge of Ukrainian. This, compared with just above 20 percent in Vilnius, 18 percent in Minsk, and 12 percent in Tallin, suggests, in our view, a high degree of reciprocal bilingualism in the Ukrainian capital, indirectly testifying to a relatively high status for Ukrainian language and culture. In Minsk (Belorussia seems to be the most suitable for comparison in view of the close resemblance of both Belorussian and Ukrainian to Russian), where Russians were almost exactly as numerous percentagewise as in Kyiv, Russians knew Belorussian less than half as often as their compatriots in Kyiv knew Ukrainian. We may add that the popular daily evening paper *Vechirnii Kyiv,* with a circulation of over 300,000 copies, appears in Ukrainian and is read by Russians too, while in Minsk a comparable paper has a Russian and a Belorussian edition, the former printing about 150,000 copies, the latter under 2,000.

Capitals, as is well known, influence the country of which they are

Table 3.3

Russians in Republic Capitals

Capital City	Total Population (1970)	Russians (1970)	Russians in Republic who Know Republican Language (%)	Russians in Capital who Know Republican Language (%)	Russians as Percent of Capital's Population (1959)	Russians as Percent of Capital's Population (1970)	Population of Capital as Percent of Republican Population
Frunze (Kirghizia)	430,618	284,676	1.5	0.72	71.8	66.11	14.68
Alma-Ata (Kazakhstan)	729,633	512,900	0.99	0.73	73.2	70.29	5.61
Ashkhabad (Turkmenia)	253,118	108,144	2.08	1.23	50.3	42.72	11.72
Dushanbe (Tadjikistan)	373,885	157,083	2.36	1.25	47.7	42.01	12.89
Tashkent (Uzbekistan)	1,384,509	564,584	3.77	2.47	43.8	40.78	11.73
Baku (Azerbaidjan)	1,265,515	351,090	7.56	5.14	34.2	27.74	24.73
Kishinev (Moldavia)	356,382	109,313	13.34	11.84	32.1	30.67	9.99
Tallin (Estonia)	362,706	127,103	12.57	12.23	32	35.04	26.75
Riga (Latvia)	731,831	312,857	17.08	15.15	39.4	42.75	30.95
Tbilisi (Georgia)	889,020	124,316	10.51	17.86	18.2	13.98	18.97
Minsk (Belorussia)	916,949	214,208	20.6	17.88	22.9	23.36	10.19
Vilnius (Lithuania)	372,100	91,004	30.76	20.45	29.7	24.46	11.89
Erevan (Armenia)	766,705	21,519	18.95	30.95	4.4	2.81	30.77
Kyiv (Ukraine)	1,631,908	373,569	25.95	41.05	22.7	22.89	3.46

Sources: *Itogi 1970*, Vol. IV, Tables 7–29, and *Sovetskaia etnografiia*, No. 5, 1969, p. 8.

the center. In the case of Ukraine we may ask: Does Kyiv function as the capital of the entire Ukraine (we do not question that it functions as the administrative capital of the republic)? Is it the primate city, enjoying a superior position in relation to such giants as Kharkiv, Odessa, or Donetsk? Employing the concepts of urban geography concerning the rank-size order of cities, Professor Chauncy D. Harris has suggested that Kyiv's population in 1959 was about one-third as large as would be expected from the network of 301 cities and towns in Ukraine with a population of more than 10,000. "The rank-size analysis suggests that the Ukraine, established on ethnic principles, may not be a single urban economic unit but rather that it may be composed of as many as five urban network regions."[30] (According to Harris, these were Kyiv, Kharkiv, Odessa, Donetsk, and Dnipropetrovsk.) Another American scholar, David Hooson, has taken a somewhat more affirmative view of the relative role of Kyiv among the cities of Ukraine, saying that "Kharkov may conceivably grow larger, but cannot now challenge Kiev's pre-eminent position, anymore than Milan can supplant Rome as capital of the Italian State."[31]

Without disputing Hooson, I feel that Harris is right in arguing that for Kharkiv, Odessa or Donetsk, Kyiv does not exercise, as yet, the role of the capital city. If it actually establishes its position as the primate city of Ukraine by gaining a population far above the population of cities such as Odessa or Kharkiv, this will be an indication that the present-day Ukraine has gained economic and social cohesion within its present territorial limits of a Soviet republic. This in turn might promote the growth of a Ukrainian territorial identity as a real factor, independently from any linguistic assimilation. Some scholars have argued in recent years that there exist objective economic conditions for the rise of such a nonlinguistic, territorial, and economy-concerned community of interest.

Thus, for example, Professor Hooson believes that although the Moscow region has "poor and transitional natural endowments," for which it compensates by its political role of a national metropolis, the Greater Ukraine (an area including Moldavia, the lower Don and Kuban lowland) is "physically homogeneous—almost all black earth (*chernozem*)—and rich in a variety of industrial resources and productive activities. It is clearly the region most nearly indispensable to the Soviet Union and conversely the only one comparable in population and potential to the great nation-states of Western Europe."[32] According to Hooson, despite the growth of population, industry, and agriculture in the east, north, and south,

> . . . most of the economic and other indicators of rationality point to an optimum area for future development and growth in south European Russia. Its core may be broadly encompassed within a radius of six hundred miles from Kharkov, taking in the whole of the Greater Ukraine region . . . stretching to Kuibyshev on the Volga, and beyond Moscow and Minsk. Within this circle is contained over half the Soviet population and agricultural and industrial production, as well as a considerable range of natural resources and potential for further development. The area's middle lies at the center of gravity of the population of the whole Soviet bloc, and it contains the densest transport network in the Soviet Union. Not only is labor plentiful but its productivity per capita is in general markedly higher than in the regions to the east and south. The population is overwhelmingly Slavic in ethnic composition, which is of considerable—though unacknowledged—significance. The potential resurgence of Ukrainian nationalism is a significant unanswered question. Incidentally, many people in this region, particularly the Ukrainians and Belorussians, are becoming increasingly dissatisfied with the prolonged disproportionate allocation of scarce investment capital to eastern regions, where the return tends to be lower, and with the comparative underestimation of the natural resources of their own regions.[33]

Whether or not a territorial Ukrainian identity will develop, including those who consider themselves ethnic Russians and those Ukrainians who speak Russian as their first language, Kyiv has clearly been gaining in importance as the largest city in Ukraine and the third largest in the USSR. Simultaneously it is becoming more of a Ukrainian city. If it appears to be a thoroughly Russian city now, it is worth remembering that it is also less Russian now than it was ten, twenty, or fifty years ago. As a result, Kyiv, and to a much smaller degree Lviv, are the testing ground for the capacity of the Ukrainian people to establish a Ukrainian presence in the metropolitan framework on the basis of the Ukrainian language. If the attempt succeeds, at least Western and Central Ukraine will become modern while remaining Ukrainian. More broadly, such an achievement will reinforce the Ukrainian ethnic element elsewhere, not only in Eastern Ukraine but also beyond its boundaries, thus making it possible to redefine the Russo–Ukrainian relationship on a basis different from the present "younger brother" or "country cousin" pattern.

A priori, Lviv could play an even greater modernizing role in

Ukraine on the basis of Ukrainian, not Russian, identity. Demographic data cited in tables 3.1 and 3.2 show that Western Ukraine as a whole is large in terms of total population (were it a republic of its own it would be among the most populous ones) and the urban population of the main oblast, that of Lviv. It is here more than anywhere else in Ukraine that the Russians fit the description of a national minority. They are new, having come only thirty or so years ago; and they are relatively few even though they are in control of the "commanding heights"—the Communist party apparatus, the police, and managerial cadres. Here the Russian language and culture have not been traditionally identified with modernity in the popular perception. Historically, it was Polish, German, and Hungarian rather than Russian culture that represented the city, and before the Soviets came Ukrainian society, culture, and politics had won a firm position in the city to a degree not later achieved. If Lviv does not influence Ukraine today as much as it could, however, the reason lies in deliberate efforts to limit its possible impact. It only has one monthly periodical, for example, compared with the dozens of weeklies and monthlies in Ukrainian published there before 1939; and it lacks the status symbol of a big city—an evening paper—although many smaller Soviet cities do enjoy this privilege. Thus, its capacity to influence Ukrainian developments is much smaller than that of Kyiv.

It is reasonable to speculate that the local population would perceive the presence and role of the Russians in this western area quite differently from the local population in the older, formerly tsarist Russian parts of Ukraine that had been Soviet from 1919 or so. There exist certain documentary samizdat materials on Russians in the West, mainly limited to issues involving persecution of dissenters by police and judiciary personnel of Russian nationality. Officially approved accounts, documentary or fictional, dealing with Russo–Ukrainian relations in West Ukraine in everyday conditions are less frequent. Soviet Ukrainian writers, for example, avoid dealing with inter-ethnic relations in fiction. The more remarkable, therefore, are the few works that directly address those themes and thus provide some information about the nationality aspects of daily life in the Soviet Ukrainian cities.

The author Iakiv Stetsiuk, born in 1922 in the Zhytomyr region, has been living in Western Ukraine since 1944, first in Ivano-Frankivsk, and subsequently in Lviv. In 1969 the Kyiv Komsomol literary journal *Dnipro* published a long story by Stetsiuk entitled "A Mother's Namesday."[34] The story is set in Lviv in the 1960s, although there are flashbacks to the immediate postwar years. The characters include teachers, government officials, and students, both Ukrainian and Russian. Let us briefly note those passages dealing with our subject, the Russians in Ukraine, remembering of course that this is a nonliterary approach; we are interested in the work's sociological inferences.

Stetsiuk draws a distinction between the two Russian migrations to Western Ukraine. The first migratory wave, during and immediately after the war, is represented in his story by Oleksii, who decides to stay in the city where he was wounded while fighting the Germans, and where he feels he will be needed more than in his homeland, Russia.

It is commonly known that the towns and cities of Western Ukraine were mainly Polish and Jewish before 1939 and that they lost most of that population through the Nazi genocide and population transfers. Moreover, many of the Ukrainians who lived in the cities before 1939 were arrested and deported by the Soviets, or left with the Germans. For these reasons, after the war managerial, economic, technical, engineering, and administrative personnel were brought into the area from outside. Given the political unreliability (from the Soviet point of view) of the local population, it was also necessary to bring into the area numerous administrative, party, police, and ideological cadres from the east. In Stetsiuk's story, then, Oleksii, as a Russian immigrant of the 1940s vintage, stands for all of these. Oleksii decides to identify his life and work with the people of Ukraine. He learns and uses the Ukrainian language in professional and public work; he also marries a local Ukrainian.

At first, Oleksii is not sure whether his decision to remain is right: He does not know Ukrainian, and most schools in the area had been Ukrainian (and of course Polish). He becomes a teacher in a Russian school in which Ukrainian is also taught. A new colleague, the Ukrainian teacher, Maria Ivanivna, "in order to please him," attempts to speak Russian but does so very poorly. (Let us note that she is supposed to be teaching Ukrainian in a school where Russian is the language of instruction. It is highly improbable that someone not fluent in Russian would hold such a post.) Oleksii suggests that she should speak her own language, and when she expresses a fear that he will not understand, he responds: "I will try. Besides, to be frank, it is not you who should be getting used to me, but the reverse. You are the host here." Maria teaches Oleksii Ukrainian, he reciprocates by teaching her Russian, and she develops an admiration for the "richness and power" of that language. As one might guess, they eventually get married.

Oleksii not only learns Ukrainian but also speaks it at various conferences and meetings. A former army acquaintance chances to attend one such conference and later visits Oleksii and Maria in their apartment. In a conversation with Oleksii he refers to Maria as "your *baba*." This is enough to offend Oleksii, but then the aquaintance remarks:

> "You're really good at blabbing like them. Where did you learn, I wonder? You can even do it with that very . . . local accent. Come on, don't get excited. I know—politics. But why, really? Why play? In any case, everything is moving toward unity. One language on the whole planet—that's convenient and simple."
>
> "Chinese?" Oleksii responded at last.
>
> "Don't be silly! Ours!" the offended guest said. "This game is good for nothing. I'm a descendant of the Zaporozhians. My ancestors used to be Cossacks. But if it has to be done . . . so what?"
>
> "So you don't give a damn about your soul?"

Oleksii asks his former friend to leave even though he knows very well that the latter will report on him.[35]

Later, Oleksii dies, and Maria and their child, Yaroslav, become the principal positive characters in the story. Maria is now forty-five and Yaroslav a first-year journalism student. Maria remarries. Her second husband is Ruslan Hlibovych Nosarsky, who becomes Yaroslav's stepfather, and also the main negative character.

When we meet him, Ruslan Hlibovych holds a high post in the city administration. His previous career merits a brief recounting because it contrasts sharply with the story of Oleksii and symbolizes the second (one is tempted to call it "parasitical") wave of Russian immigration in Western Ukraine. Before coming to Western Ukraine, Nosarsky was a career officer in the Soviet Army and the author presents him as a typical careerist. Internal evidence suggests that he was one of those officers who were released from a full-time military career during the celebrated Khrushchevian reduction of the armed forces (1959–60); the author remarks that many other officers left the service at the same time. He was then just over forty, with the rank of lieutenant colonel, and his civilian pension was 150 rubles a month. (The author explains that this was relatively low pay for an ex-officer.) Ruslan's first civilian job is "deputy director for economic matters" in the high school in which Maria is a language teacher. Ruslan has an apartment larger than that of Maria and her son, and after Ruslan and Maria marry, they exchange both apartments for a single four-room apartment in a "luxury" house built in "Polish times." Subsequently he is moved to a higher post, and we learn that he is trying to get an even higher promotion. He is a totally despicable character and cheats on his wife, but we will only look at him here from our special angle. Owing to his official position, he is able to arrange a residence permit in Lviv (even though this is a city of restricted residence) for Maya, the third Russian in the story, also a negative character.

Unlike Ruslan, who is about fifty and had come a decade or so earlier, Maya is quite young and has just arrived in Lviv. She lacks any good qualities; the author characterizes her as a morally dissolute person. She dislikes Lviv, commenting, "In general, the climate here is just good for nothing. Damp and unpleasant. It smells rotten. I don't understand why people get so attached to this town. Take Novosibirsk or Omsk . . . there's a real climate. . . ."[36]

Despite Lviv's clear inferiority to Omsk and Novosibirsk—which Maya seems to know from personal experience—she is determined to get a residence permit for Lviv and gets Ruslan to help her. She comes to see Ruslan with Yaroslav's friend, Bohdan, a local Ukrainian, who is a de facto professional athlete but officially an employee of some factory. Bohdan sees a book open on Yaroslav's desk and says:

> "What are you reading, old man? Oh, you've made so many marks.
> . . . Something interesting?" He began to read the passage marked with
> a red pencil: "In 1516 the Polish king Stefan Batory in a letter written
> in Polish invited some Ukrainian lords to come to see him. The lords
> became angry, and wrote back: 'Your Majesty, our liberties and rights
> are violated because the letters sent to us from Your Majesty's chancel-
> lery are written in Polish. Therefore, we humbly beg Your Majesty to
> maintain our privileges in the future, and instruct that letters from
> Your Royal Chancellery be written in the Rus' language.' " He read
> this in a mockingly solemn voice and added, "There's nothing strange
> about that."
> Maya said, "It appears that in those times there were those . . .
> what do you call them?"

Those present became rather embarrassed, because Maya was clearly groping for the expression "Ukrainian bourgeois nationalists" but she is undeterred: "What's the matter? Am I not right?"[37]

As far as I know this story has met with no critical response in the Soviet Union and has passed unnoticed abroad despite its unusual content. Its principal significance, it seems to me, is in presenting the second wave of Russian immigrants to West Ukraine as socially parasitical and spiritually alien to the people among whom they have settled.

In concluding, let us consider what kind of future the Ukrainians might have in the Soviet Union and, accordingly, what the prospects are for the Russian population of Ukraine.

The prospect that the Ukrainians will disappear from their historic area, the southwest region, is very small indeed. Nor is it likely that this area will acquire a Russian majority or a large minority as appears to be happening in Estonia and Latvia. Rather, somewhat in the pattern of Lithuania and Moldavia, West and Central-West Ukraine appears to be maintaining an internal cohesion and developing ways to make itself immune to the corroding influence of Russification. On the other hand, it seems to be equally clear—barring unforeseen developments—that the Donbas and the South are either becoming increasingly more Russian and correspondingly less Ukrainian linguistically, or that at least certain parts of that area are on the way to becoming almost exclusively Russian in language (Donbas); others may remain bilingual, such as the Dnipropetrovsk-Zaporizhia area and Crimea (the latter due to exceptionally large Ukrainian immigration). At any rate, the entire territory beyond the historical Ukrainian lands is unlikely to switch to using Ukrainian as a main language so long as Ukraine is part of the USSR. It seems doubtful that even the secession of Ukraine would necessarily be followed by de-Russification (assuming that no major transfers of population would occur). What bearing, then, do these demographic facts and trends have on the status of the Russians in Ukraine, and on the status of Ukraine in a Russian-dominated USSR?

There seem to be two major alternatives for the survival of Ukraine and the Ukrainians within the USSR and for resolving the problem of the Russian element in Ukraine within a Ukrainian context. The first alternative would be to partition the Ukrainian SSR along ethnic-nationality lines: Donbas and possibly several other oblasts would be separated from Ukraine and the size of the Russian-language element in that smaller Ukraine would be decreased. To become acceptable to Ukrainians the Russian population in that smaller Ukraine would probably have to be reduced to a truly national minority and not a dominant and privileged element. There would have to be a clear understanding, supported by practical guarantees, that Russification would stop at a certain point and that the status of the Ukrainian language and culture would be institutionally secure. Some Ukrainians might find this a gain worth paying for with a territorial redefinition of Ukraine. Such a reduced Ukraine would enjoy national rights somewhat comparable to, if not exceeding, those of Armenia or Georgia.

The second alternative would maintain the present territorial integrity of the Ukrainian SSR but would redefine the Ukrainian nationality in a territorial sense: The population of the republic might have the option of considering itself Ukrainian regardless of whether its language of communication is Ukrainian or Russian. We have even now many persons who declare themselves to be Ukrainian by nationality but Russian by native language. Both Soviet and non-Soviet commentators consider this phenomenon of Russian-speaking Ukrainians to be an anomaly of sorts, a transitory state in the movement toward Russian ethnic identity. This may be the case, but the matter should be investigated statistically, among other things, before any firm conclusions can be reached. Do those who declare Russian as their native language actually switch to Russian nationality after some time? Do their children do so? Or is there some retention of this dual identity from generation to generation? Indeed, at least hypothetically, it may be asked whether some of those who start as Russian by both language and nationality do not switch to a Ukrainian identity while retaining their Russian language. We know it is possible to regard oneself as Ukrainian while speaking Russian. The question is whether this phenomenon is considered an inherently transitory and unstable one (leading to either complete Russification or a return to full Ukrainian identity) or whether Ukrainian identity can be so redefined as to allow the combination of Ukrainian nationality with Russian language.

We may only suggest here, in passing, that one of the several ways in which this identity option might be tested empirically would be to study the Russian-language press in Ukraine: Is it mainly a Russian press by Russians and for Russians who happen to live in Ukraine, or is it in some significant way different from the Russian-language press in, say, the RSFSR, or Kazakhstan, or Latvia? Might one view it as a Russian-medium Ukrainian press?

To admit that Ukrainians may have two languages and still remain "good" Ukrainians would mean to base the Ukrainian identity on territory and community of interests derived from a commonly shared territory rather than a common language. It is impossible to envision this development as a practical prospect. Its acceptance would require not only formal declarations on the part of the regime but also a variety of practical measures, such as the use of Russian language for transmission of Ukrainian national messages. No declaration could by itself transform the millions of declared Russians (by language and nationality) into Ukrainians in the territorial–political sense. However, a policy shift might facilitate the political assimilation or "naturalization" of some of them and also slow down or reverse the process of a national identity shift from Ukrainian to Russian along with and through linguistic assimilation. I would like to know more in this connection about the nationality processes currently under way in Belorussia, because although the linguistic assimilation of the Belorussians appears to be progressing, it also appears that the Belorussian national identity, based on a political–territorial identity, is not weakening. Will Belorussians remain a separate nation even when they are Russian-speaking? Are there any Belorussians who speak Russian but have a Belorussian national consciousness politically? And how important are they?

There are no Soviet precedents for this type of national identity, and the only successful case in Eastern Europe seems to be that of Finland where Swedish and Finnish are both considered national languages. (Needless to say, Sweden does not pose anywhere near the threat to the survival of a Finnish-speaking Finland that Russia does in relation to Ukraine.) On the other hand, the cases of Ireland and, more recently, Scotland, where it has been possible to be not only Irish and Scottish but also anti-English via the medium of the English language, suggest that the emergence of Ukrainian nationalism among Russian-speakers may not be a figment of the imagination.

The adoption of either of these "options" would not resolve the problem of Ukrainian identity in the USSR. Whether or not the Ukrainian republic is made smaller or whether or not the definition of Ukrainian nationality is based on the community of territory, there will remain persons considering themselves Ukrainian all over the USSR. If the Soviet state seriously treats its claims to be a truly multinational structure, it is hard to understand its policy of denying to the Ukrainians a minimum of national–cultural rights beyond the boundaries of the

Ukrainian SSR. How is one to justify such a treatment of the close to two hundred thousand Ukrainians who live in the city of Moscow or over half a million Ukrainians in Moldavia? Long before 1914, Thomas Masaryk argued in the Austrian Reichsrat that if the Czechs were to accept the Austrian Monarchy as their state, they would have to be given an opportunity to feel equally at home in Vienna as in Prague. To deny them the right to live as Czechs outside their own Czech homeland was tantamount to treating them as less than equal citizens of the state.[38]

The possibility of disentangling the bond between nationality and territory (which makes the nationality right dependent on one's place of residence) should be prima facie attractive to the leaders of the USSR. To accept it, however, would require them to renounce their present goal of Russification of non-Russians living outside their national territories. It is impossible to foresee whether a refusal to reform their system along the lines suggested by Masaryk will cause any political difficulties. At any rate, it seems reasonable to suppose that it makes it difficult for Ukrainians to view the USSR as a country in which they are at home everywhere, even though their numbers in the Ukrainian republic and their relatively wide dispersion through the USSR would make it quite practicable to grant them the status of an "all-Union" nationality, which now only Russians possess everywhere—and notably in Ukraine.

Notes

1. See "Two Estonian Memoranda to the United Nations," *Baltic News*, no. 5 (1974): 2.

2. V. V. Pokshishevskii, "Etnicheskie protsessy v gorodakh SSR i nekotorye problemy ikh izucheniia," *Sovetskaia etnografiia*, no. 5 (1969): 6.

3. John A. Armstrong, "The Ethnic Scene in the Soviet Union: The View of the Dictatorship," *Ethnic Minorities in the Soviet Union*, ed. Erich Goldhagen (New York: Praeger, 1968), pp. 14–21, 32.

4. For the problem of the territorial delimitation of Ukraine during 1917–21, see *Ukraine: A Concise Encyclopaedia*, ed., V. Kubijovyc, vol. I (Toronto: University of Toronto Press, 1963), pp. 735 and 797. See ibid., p. 811, for figures indicating the percentage of Ukrainians in the population of major cities of Ukraine in 1923 and 1933. The ratio of Ukrainians in those cities during the revolution may be presumed to have been lower.

5. The boundaries of Ukraine in the seventeenth and eighteenth centuries

are presented on the maps on pp. 642–43 and p. 653 of *Ukraine: A Concise Encyclopaedia*, vol. I.

6. A. Hirshfel'd, *Migratsiini protsesy na Ukraini (v svitli perepysu 1926 g.)*, (Kharkiv: Derzhvydav "Hospodarstvo Ukraïny," 1930), pp. 73–74, 81, 86.

7. Ibid., p. 82. According to Hirshfeld's calculations, the number of migrants from the Right Bank region and Polissia to areas outside Ukraine was 587,849; to other parts of Ukraine, 311,777, but of these only 26,671 migrated to Donbas.

8. Ibid., pp. 83, 87.

9. See, for example, Richard Pipes, *The Formation of the Soviet Union: Nationalism and Communism, 1917–1923* (New York: Atheneum, 1968), p. 149.

10. Robert S. Sullivant, *Soviet Politics and the Ukraine, 1917–1957* (New York: Columbia University Press, 1963), pp. 296–97.

11. Ibid., pp. 299–300.

12. These calculations are based on table 6 in Roman Szporluk, "The Nations of the USSR in 1910," *Survey* 81, no. 4 (1971): 99. [Reprinted as chapter 2 of this volume.] The full data are available in *Itogi Vsesoiuznoi perepisi naseleniia 1970 goda,* vol. 4 (Moscow: Statistika, 1973).

13. All calculations relating to the population of Donetsk oblast are based on *Itogi Vsesoiuznoi perepisi naseleniia 1959 goda, Ukrainskaia SSR* (Moscow: Gostatizdat, 1963), table 54, pp. 174, 180, and *Itogi 1970*, vol. IV, table 8, p. 173.

14. M. V. Kurman, I. V. Lebedinskii, *Naselenie bol'shogo sotsialisticheskogo goroda* (Moscow: Statistika, 1968), pp. 121–22.

15. Ibid., pp. 122–25.

16. Ibid., p. 125.

17. L. N. Chizhikova, "Ob etnicheskikh protsessakh v vostochnykh raionakh Ukrainy (po materialam ekspeditsionnogo obsledovaniia 1966 g.)," *Sovetskaia etnografiia*, no. 1 (1968): 22.

18. Ibid., p. 23.

19. Ibid.

20. Ibid., pp. 23–24.

21. It is enough to consult any contemporary document, for example the articles and speeches of Mykola Skrypnyk, to learn how common the opposition to Ukrainianization was not only in the predominantly Ukrainian regions of the RSFSR, such as the provinces of Kursk, Voronezh, and Stalingrad, or in the Kuban region, but also in the eastern districts of the Ukrainian SSR. See Mykola Skrypnyk, *Statti i promovy z natsional'noho pytannia*, ed. Iwan Koszeliwec (Munich: Suchasnist', 1974).

22. All these calculations are based on *Itogi 1959 goda, Ukrainskaia SSR,*

table 51, p. 180, and *Itogi 1970 goda*, vol. IV, table 8, p. 187. The following are figures for the urban population of Kharkiv oblast in 1959 and 1970 and its Ukrainian and Russian components:

	1959	Native Language Ukrainian	Russian	1970	Native Language Ukrainian	Russian
Total	1,573,738			1,958,194		
Ukrainian	956,369	772,622	183,699	1,170,648	886,441	284,170
Russian	503,074	5,734	497,317	668,708	6,546	662,122

Of those Russians and Ukrainians whose native language was Russian and Ukrainian respectively in 1970, 522,346 Ukrainians knew Russian and 201,563 Russians knew Ukrainian.

23. Two Soviet scholars have argued recently that the knowledge of Russian among Moldavians is much wider than indicated by the census. See S. I. Bruk and M. N. Guboglo, "Razvitie i vzaimodeistvie etnodemograficheskikh i etnolingvisticheskikh protsessov v sovetskom obshchestve na sovremennom etape," *Istoriia SSSR*, no. 4 (1974): 44.

24. Personal information obtained by the author. Information contained in issues of *Vechirnii Kharkiv* in possession of the author.

25. See *Molod' Dnipropetrovs'koho proty rusyfikatsiï* (Munich, Suchasnist', 1970); *Ukraïns'kyi visnyk,* no. 6 (1972) (Baltimore: Smoloskyp, 1972); Skrypnyk, *Statti i promovy.*

26. Danylo Shumuk, *Za skhidnim obriiem* (Baltimore: Smoloskyp, 1974), pp. 440–41. An English translation was published after this article: *Life Sentence: Memoirs of a Ukrainian Political Prisoner,* eds. Ivan Jaworsky and Halya Kowalska (Edmonton: Canadian Institute of Ukrainian Studies, 1984).

The original reads: "Vy, molodoi chelovek, i odety khorosho, i vashe litso kak-budto intelligentoe, a razgavarivaete kak-to ne po-chelovecheski. Neuzheli vy ne znaete russkogo iazyka?" . . . "A vy znaete, eti khokhly dazhe zdes' v Odesse do togo obnagleli chto predlagali mne biulleten' zapolniat' na ikh khokhlatskom iazyke. A ia im otvetila: 'Ia vam ne kolkhoznitsa, ia odessitka.' I ne obrashchaia vnimaniia, zapolnila biulleten' po russki . . . O, vidish, i zdes' kakoi-to bandera poiavilsia, on dazhe Odessu schitaet Ukrainoi."

"Banderite" is a derogatory reference to a member of the organization of Ukrainian Nationalists under Stepan Bandera.

27. Shumuk, *Za skhidnim obriiem,* p. 445.

28. "A Word to the Nation," *Survey* 17, no. 3 (1971): 196–97. See also Dimitry Pospielovsky, "The Resurgence of Russian Nationalism in *Samizdat,*" *Survey* 19, no. 1 (1973): 51–74.

29. V. V. Pokshishevsky, "Urbanization and Ethnodemographic Processes," *Soviet Geography: Review and Translation* 13, no. 2 (February, 1972): 116, 118.

30. Chauncy D. Harris, *Cities of the Soviet Union, Studies in Their Functions, Size, Density and Growth* (Chicago: Rand McNally, 1970), pp. 134–35.

31. David J. M. Hooson, *The Soviet Union: People and Regions* (Belmont, Calif.: Wadsworth, 1966), p. 163.

32. David J. M. Hooson, "The Outlook for Regional Development in the Soviet Union," *Slavic Review* 31, no. 3 (September, 1972): 540.

33. Hooson, "The Outlook," p. 552. Hooson refers in this connection to Leslie Dienes, "Issues in Soviet Energy Policy and Conflicts over Fuel Costs in Regional Development," *Soviet Studies* 23, no. 1 (July 1971): 26–58.

34. Iakiv Stetsiuk, "Imenyny materi," *Dnipro*, no. 8 (1969): 80–123. For a brief biographical account of the writer, see *Literaturna Ukraïna*, December 15, 1972, p. 2, which contains an article by S. Trofymuk in honor of Stetsiuk's fiftieth birthday.

35. Stetsiuk, "Imenyny," pp. 90–93.

36. Ibid., p. 95.

37. Ibid.

38. One wonders if granting such a status to the Jews, by dissociating the availability of national rights from any particular area, would not have made their dissatisfaction less intense and induced some of them at least from seeking to emigrate from the USSR.

4   West Ukraine and West Belorussia: Historical Tradition, Social Communication, and Linguistic Assimilation

The first postwar Soviet census, held in 1959, revealed that West Belorussians were much more assimilated to the Russian language than were West Ukrainians. By 1970 this differential had widened. Assimilation (adoption of Russian as the "native tongue") was especially marked among urban West Belorussians. Yet it was low in the cities of West Ukraine.[1] It was clear that population change, including urbanization, was producing strikingly different results in language maintenance among the West Ukrainians and West Belorussians. How is one to account for this divergence, considering that both regions had been under the same regime ever since 1944?

This article suggests that linguistic assimilation and population change (urbanization) should be viewed in connection with another process, the development of the press. The evidence assembled in this study shows that throughout the entire period after the war the local press in West Ukraine was overwhelmingly Ukrainian in language; however, in West Belorussia the provincial press from the very outset was published in both Belorussian and Russian. Clearly, a high-level political decision had been made sometime after the expulsion of the Germans to promote a Russian-language press in West Belorussia but not in West

First published in *Soviet Studies*, 1979.

Ukraine.[2] Why was there one policy in West Ukraine but another in West Belorussia?

It would be revealing to consult the relevant archives. Even though this cannot be done, we do have at our disposal published evidence linking the initial decisions to the official perception of the pre-Soviet history of those regions and their political problems after the expulsion of the Germans in 1944. A resolution of the Central Committee of the CPSU, adopted on September 27, 1944 (but first published in 1971), was specifically concerned with the problems of "the ideological–political struggle against nationalism in the western oblasts of the Ukraine where the populace and the intelligentsia were for decades educated in the spirit of bourgeois ideology and have lived under Soviet power for only a year and a half" (that is, from September 1939 to June 1941). The resolution singled out the necessity of ideological work among the intelligentsia, "a significant part of which was educated in German, Austro-Hungarian, Polish, and Romanian schools in the spirit of bourgeois ideology." It declared that the local party organizations "commit a major error in underestimating the role of the newspaper as an important centre of political work among the masses," and it made specific recommendations on how the local press, especially the Ukrainian-language Lviv daily paper, should be improved. The resolution clearly set the tasks of political work in the context of the region's past experience and its current difficulties by naming such factors as armed resistance by the Ukrainian nationalist partisans and the latter's activities "in distributing significant numbers of anti-Soviet newspapers, brochures, and leaflets, and in spreading provocational rumours."[3]

However, a resolution of the Central Committee dealing with political and educational work in Belorussia (West Belorussia was not singled out), adopted on August 9, 1944, lacked any reference to organized anti-Soviet resistance or to the tenacity of pre-Soviet values and traditions as something that the party had to consider in ideological work. Moscow's recommendations for Belorussia included, rather significantly, an authorization to set up a Russian-language youth newspaper and a weekly for children that was to come out in Belorussian and Russian (in an equal number of copies).[4]

This limited but important documentary evidence suggests that the post-1944 treatment of West Ukraine and West Belorussia in the press reflected a political assessment of their diverse past and problems. In the long run it appears that the initial political decision to Russify (partially) the press in West Belorussia but to keep it Ukrainian in West Ukraine may have facilitated linguistic assimilation in the former but maintenance of the local language in the latter during subsequent urbanization of those areas—an outcome that may have been neither intended nor anticipated by those who made the decisions about the press in 1944 or 1945.

This chapter has the following structure: The first part reviews briefly the pre-Soviet experience of West Ukraine and West Belorussia, especially that relating to the use of the local languages in social communication. The second part presents a brief history of the press there after 1945, and pays particular attention to the language aspect of the press. Part three, finally, presents a demographic analysis of linguistic assimilation, especially among urban populations. This part uses the materials of the censuses of 1959 and 1970 as a source.

Pre-Soviet History

Western Ukraine, a name given to those parts of the Ukrainian SSR that were annexed from 1939 to 1945, consists of four historically distinct regions. Two of these regions, Galicia (the present oblasts of Lviv, Ivano-Frankivsk, and Ternopil) and Volhynia (oblasts of Volhynia and Rivne), were under Poland until 1939. Romania held the province of Bukovina (Chernivtsi oblast) until 1940 and again from 1941 to 1944, and Czechoslovakia formally ceded Ruthenia (Transcarpathia) in 1945.[5]

It is virtually impossible to establish the exact demographic data for West Ukraine prior to its Sovietization. The Ukrainian geographer and demographer, V. Kubijovyč, has estimated that in 1933 the combined population of Galicia and Volhynia was about 66 percent Ukrainian, less than 1 percent Russian, and the bulk of the remaining 33 percent was Polish and Jewish. In Bukovina and Bessarabia the Ukrainian share was 52.4 percent, and in Transcarpathia it was slightly over 60 percent. There were few Russians in these two regions; Hungarians, Jews, Romanians, and smaller numbers of Czechs, Poles, and Germans made up the remaining portion.[6]

The absence of Russians was one common trait of those areas; another was the low level of social and economic development of the Ukrainian inhabitants. The overwhelming majority of Ukrainians lived in the countryside and were employed in agriculture. They represented a minority among inhabitants of towns and cities and were also in a minority among those employed in industry, commerce, transport, and government service. Politically, the situation of the Ukrainian population varied considerably between the three states and, indeed, within Poland the Ukrainians of Galicia were treated somewhat differently from the Ukrainians of Volhynia.

The Ukrainians of the Austrian province of Galicia were recognized as one of the nationalities of the Empire after the revolution of 1848–49. Ukrainian was used in schools and to a limited extent also in the courts of justice and in public administration. It was the working language of the many and diverse social, cultural, economic, and political associations maintained by the Ukrainians under Austria. Most importantly, the Uniate Church (an eastern rite of the Catholic Church) became firmly associated with Ukrainian nationalism and it used Ukrainian in its pastoral work. From the 1860s to 1918 Ukrainians in Galicia lived under a constitutional regime. They enjoyed a brief period of independence in 1918–19. From 1919 to 1939 the area was ruled by Poland. Although Polish rule was harsher than the old Austrian regime, the Ukrainian language continued to be used in the press and in voluntary societies of various kinds, including consumers' and producers' cooperatives.

The Ukrainians of Bukovina essentially paralleled in their development the experience of their co-nationals in Galicia: Until 1918 they lived under Austria, and from 1918 to 1940 under Romania. Transcarpathia, a part of Hungary until 1919, had been subject to strong assimilationist policies by the Budapest government. By 1919, when it was assigned to Czechoslovakia, its ethnically Ukrainian population had not yet determined which nationality it considered itself to be. During the Czechoslovak period, however, Ukrainian appeared to have won out over Ruthenian or Russian as the chosen nationality. In Czechoslovak times Ukrainian was widely used, and in 1938–39 it was the region's official language. During the Second World War Transcarpathia was reoccupied by Hungary; in 1945 it became Soviet.

The only West Ukrainian region to have been under Russia before 1914 was Volhynia. As everywhere in the Russian Empire, the Ukrainian language was banned in that province from 1876 to 1906. In 1917, Volhynia was included in the autonomous Ukrainian state then organized in Kyiv, and in 1919 it was occupied by Poland. Under Poland the

Ukrainians of Volhynia enjoyed more limited rights than those in Galicia; but despite Polish efforts to keep them isolated from the highly nationalistic Galicians, by the late 1930s they had become basically assimilated in outlook to the Galicians.

West Belorussia in this discussion stands for the present oblasts of Brest and Grodno.[7] Historically, the term "West Belorussia" came into use after the treaty of Riga (1921), which divided the ethnic Belorussian territory between Poland and the USSR. Before 1914, all Belorussian lands were under Russia. The Russian government considered Belorussia to be a branch of the Russian nation and the language a Russian dialect. From 1859 to 1906 publication in Belorussian was prohibited in Russia. After 1906, the first Belorussian-language periodicals were founded, and Vilnius became the principal center of Belorussian activities. The Belorussians used both Cyrillic and Latin script, a sign of the competing pressures—Russian and Orthodox versus Polish and Catholic. There were no schools with Belorussian as the language of instruction. During World War I and the Russian revolution, the Belorussians made some progress in the area of education and culture, but they were unable to establish an independent state. In 1921 Belorussia was partitioned.

At first, the Poles supported cultural Belorussianization, but this tolerant policy was soon replaced by Polonization. Belorussian schools were gradually Polonized or closed down altogether. Periodicals and societies also were forced to cease operation. By 1938, no Belorussian publication appeared regularly in Poland. The masses of the peasantry were illiterate and poor, and West Belorussia was the most backward part of Poland economically.

In September 1939 West Belorussia was occupied by Soviet troops and within a short time was formally incorporated into the USSR. (This Soviet West Belorussia included Bialystok, which would be retroceded to Poland in 1945, but not Vilnius, transferred to Lithuania in October 1939.) Initially, the Belorussians seem to have been rather well disposed toward Soviet rule, but later they became disillusioned as mass arrests and deportations began. Under the Nazis life became worse, and the Belorussian language was even denied recognition as the main language of the country. Belorussia was the scene of an active partisan movement, but this was a Soviet, not a nationalist Belorussian force. (The Polish underground was also active.)

In this last regard West Belorussia was very different from West

Ukraine where a strong nationalist underground had operated through-out the war years and continued to resist the Soviet authorities until about 1950. The USSR clearly faced much tougher and better-organized opposition in West Ukraine. This opposition included the Uniate Church, whereas in Belorussia the Catholics belonged to a Polish-dominated church and the Orthodox to a church that was Russian in cultural and national orientation. Finally, despite large-scale emigration to the west, there remained a Ukrainian intelligentsia in West Ukraine, including the main city, Lviv. Vilnius, West Belorussia's traditional center, which had also been a major center of Polish and Jewish culture, was not included in Belorussia. Most importantly, perhaps, the West Belorussians found themselves in the USSR with little prior experience of using their language in social communication, whereas the Ukrainians of Galicia and Bukovina could look back at almost a century of such use of their language. Transcarpathia and Volhynia had also had their own schools and press during the interwar period—something West Belorussians had failed to achieve except for a brief period in the 1920s.

Yet, even though Belorussian nationalism was weak before 1944, the people of West Belorussia, who were overwhelmingly rural, spoke Belorussian. Therefore, the Soviet government would have been justified in establishing a predominantly Belorussian-language local press for them. If it decided to do otherwise—that is, to operate a Russian-language press along with papers in Belorussian—this decision reflected its estimate of the strength of nationalism in Belorussia, not purely linguistic considerations. Once the decision had been made to introduce Russian into social communication in the region, however, not only was the rise of a future Belorussian nationalism made more difficult, but also a linguistic assimilation of the Belorussians began.

The Press, 1945–1970

This part of our study will present the basic structure of the press in West Ukraine and West Belorussia in the period from 1945 to 1970, with an emphasis on the language aspect. To what extent were Ukrainian and Belorussian used? What facilities were available to the minorities, such as Poles and Hungarians? What role did the Russian press play?

The Soviet press is organized hierarchically; corresponding to the administrative structure of the country (all-Union papers, republic, oblast, raion, town).[8] We will follow this order in our discussion.[9]

Republic-Rank Papers for the Western Regions

In 1945, a republic-rank newspaper specifically designed for distribution in the western regions of the Ukraine was founded in Kyiv.[10] Its name was *Radians'kyi selianyn* (*Soviet Peasant*). The Ukrainian SSR had two other newspapers specifically designated for rural readers, but it cannot be ascertained whether they too were sold in the west. In 1949 *Radians'kyi selianyn* was merged with these two papers into a new paper called *Kolhospne selo* (*Kolkhoz Village*). Under a new name, adopted in 1964, *Sil's'ki visti* (*Village News*), it continues to be published to this day. In 1975, *Sil's'ki visti* was the second-largest daily newspaper in the Ukraine (press run of 649,000, compared with 781,000 for *Molod' Ukraïny*).[11] Except for 1950 to 1963, when a parallel Russian-language edition was also printed, the republic-level press for the countryside has been Ukrainian.

No other Kyiv-based paper has been published for the western regions at any time since 1945, but the principal Ukrainian-language daily of the UkSSR, *Radians'ka Ukraïna* (*Soviet Ukraine*), printed a special "western" page in its editions sold in the western oblasts.[12] The magazine of humor and satire, *Perets'* (*Pepper*) also maintained a separate western edition from 1945 to 1950. It printed 20,000 copies per issue, compared with the 50,000 press run of the main version.

It is impossible to ascertain whether these Kyiv-based "western" publications were in any way subordinated to the special party and government agencies formed in Kyiv to deal with West Ukraine. One of these agencies was the Council for Assistance to the Western Regions, headed by a deputy prime minister of Ukraine; the other was the western department in the Central Committee of the CP of Ukraine. These agencies ceased to function in 1950, when, presumably, the authorities decided that the integration of West Ukraine had been achieved.[13]

Like Ukraine, Belorussia founded its own republic newspaper for the western regions in 1945.[14] Even its name was the same; it was called *Savetskii salianin*, or *Soviet Peasant*. The language was Belorussian. Oddly enough, Belorussia did not have a general newspaper for the countryside, that is, one that was also circulated in the east. Only in 1950 was its initially "western" paper transformed into a general republic-wide daily for the country readers. Earlier, in December 1947, *Savetskii salianin*, although still only a West Belorussian paper, began to publish a Russian-language edition, too. Someone must have decided that the peasants of West Belorussia should be reached by means of a Russian paper.

In the mid-1950s—we lack precise figures for those years—the Russian and the Belorussian editions were about even in circulation. In later years the Belorussian version gradually declined and was altogether closed down in 1962, when its printing was 2,233 copies per issue. The Russian paper had by then risen to 108,628 copies per issue.

No journal was founded specifically for West Belorussia, but a party publication for grass-roots agitators, called *Blaknot ahitatora* (*Agitator's Notebook*), appeared in two separate (western and eastern) editions in the immediate postwar years. At first, its language was Belorussian; then in 1948 a Russian version was added to both the eastern and the western editions. By 1950 the Russian version was the larger of the two in both west and east. That year the regional editions were merged into a single Belorussian SSR publication, with the Russian version taking the larger share of the total printing. In 1962 the Belorussian edition was discontinued.[15]

Unlike West Belorussia, which lacked any significant publishing center when it was a part of Poland, West Ukraine's principal city, Lviv, functioned as one of the most important press and book publishing centers in Poland and was the main center of the West Ukrainian press until 1939.[16] What role did it play in this regard in Soviet times?

In 1945 a literary-cultural monthly, organ of the Writers' Union, Lviv branch, was founded under the name of *Radians'kyi L'viv* (*Soviet Lviv*), with a printing of 5,000 copies (1946–47). The establishment of a literary journal in Lviv, at a time when such major cities as Kharkiv and Odessa lacked them, was a recognition of the fact that the West Ukrainian intelligentsia had a rich cultural tradition and that the area's individuality had somehow to be acknowledged. In 1951 *Zhovten'* (*October*) became the name of this journal, and it was transformed into a republic-rank publication. Its press run was raised then to 15,000 (it was also at that level in 1978, although at various times in the past it had reached 20,000 copies).

The other journal operating in Lviv after the war was a religious monthly, *Eparkhial'nyi visnyk* (*Diocesan Herald*), in 1946 and 1947, subtitled "the organ of the Lviv-Ternopil diocesan administration." In 1948 and 1949, renamed *Pravoslavnyi visnyk* (*Orthodox Herald*), it served as a joint organ of the West Ukraine's Orthodox bishops, and in 1950 became a publication of the Metropolitanate of Kyiv. (Lviv remained, however, the headquarters of its editors.) This had been the clergy's—not the rank and file's—publication. The appearance of a religious journal in the USSR was unusual in those days. (Only the Moscow patriarchate and the Armenian church had similar publications.) However, if one considers the fact that the Ukrainians of Galicia had been Catholic until their coerced conversion to Orthodoxy in 1946, one can appreciate the regime's desire to smooth the transition somehow. (During Khrushchev's antireligious campaign the *Herald* was closed down in 1962, but it was revived in 1968 and transferred to Kyiv in 1969.)

Oblast-Rank Newspapers

In West Ukraine, the first papers to reappear after the expulsion of the Nazis were oblast (or regional) party-Soviet dailies. In all regional capitals—Lviv, Ternopil, Stanislav, Rivne, Drohobych, Lutsk (capital of Volhynia), and Uzhhorod (Transcarpathia)—a Ukrainian-language daily was established. Transcarpathia, in addition, had a semiweekly youth paper in Ukrainian. In 1946, the combined circulation of these Ukrainian papers (excluding Drohobych and Lutsk, whose figures are not available), was 136,000 copies. The Lviv daily *Vil'na Ukraïna* (*Free Ukraine*), with a circulation of 45,000, was the largest.

The national minorities—ruling nations in pre-Soviet times—were provided with oblast papers in Lviv, Uzhhorod, and Chernivtsi. In Lviv there was a Polish-language daily, *Czerwony Sztandar*, which printed 5,000 copies. (Until June 1941 its circulation was 60,000.) Uzhhorod had a Hungarian paper (7,000 daily), and Chernivsti a Romanian one (4,000 copies daily). These papers served the needs of that part of the population that presumably could not be reached in Ukrainian.

Transcarpathia was the first West Ukrainian region to publish a Russian-language daily. It was called *Zakarpatskaia Ukraina* and it printed 10,000 copies. Its founding in 1945 seems to have reflected the local traditions (we recall that under Hungary and Czechoslovakia a segment of the indigenous population was Russian in national orientation) rather than some massive immigration. Quite certainly Russian immigration was responsible, however, for the founding of a Russian daily in Lviv in March 1946. Its name was *L'vovskaia pravda* and its press run was 20,000. (It may be proper to add that Soviet press circulations until 1956 were determined by plan from above and this figure represented an allocated quota, not popular demand. The same applies to other papers.)

West Belorussia was organized after the war into five oblasts: Brest, Grodno, Baranovichi, Molodechno, and Pinsk. In Brest and Grodno (which happened to be the largest cities in West Belorussia), the oblast paper at first was printed in Russian only, and in the latter three, in Belorussian only. By 1948 all oblasts in the west had a double edition, one Russian, one Belorussian. (See table 4.1 at the end of this chapter.) Their combined press runs were equal, although in Brest the Russian paper printed more copies, while in Baranovichi the Belorussian one was the larger. (In East Belorussia, at the same time, only Belorussian-language oblast papers were published, with the single exception of Polotsk region, which had both a Russian and a Belorussian edition.)

The subsequent developments in West Belorussia's oblast press can be summarized very easily. In 1954 the oblasts of Pinsk and Baranovichi were absorbed by Brest and Grodno, respectively. In place of its old daily, Pinsk now received a city paper in Belorussian, with a lower frequency and circulation. In 1956, when cultural concessions were won by many Soviet nationalities, the Pinsk paper became Russian. In 1963 the same fate befell the Baranovichi paper.

Three East Belorussian oblasts were also abolished in 1954. The Belorussian language was retained as the language of their city papers. East Belorussia, it appears, was being treated differently insofar as the language of the press was concerned. Finally, in 1960 Molodechno ceased to be an oblast center when its oblast was divided between Minsk and Grodno. Molodechno itself was attached to the Minsk oblast— which may explain why it is the only West Belorussian former oblast center to retain a Belorussian-language newspaper.

The final and most serious blow to the Belorussian-language oblast press in the west came in 1962. In December 1962 the Belorussian-language editions of Brest and Grodno oblast papers were discontinued. This means that, ever since, West Belorussia's oblast-rank press has been available only in Russian. While in 1948 the share of the Russian-language press of oblast rank, with a press run of 51,000, was 50 percent, in 1970 the two oblast papers printed a total of 167,398 copies daily, and the Russian share was 100 percent.

There were no changes in the West Ukrainian press on the oblast level until 1950, when the Polish paper in Lviv was liquidated. Thus ended the history of the Polish press in that city. Immediately thereafter a Ukrainian-language Komsomol paper was started, so the number of Lviv papers did not change. Its name was *Lenins'ka molod'* (15,000 copies per issue).

When the Drohobych oblast was merged with Lviv in 1959, its paper was downgraded to the rank of a city paper and the circulations of the Lviv papers were raised (*Vil'na Ukraïna* to 88,000, *L'vovskaia pravda* to 40,000). The Drohobych city paper was published in Ukrainian.

One of the major developments in the Soviet Ukrainian press after 1956 was the gradual establishment of oblast Komsomol papers in all those places that did not have them. (There were only four such papers before 1955: Donetsk and Crimea had them in Russian; Lviv and Transcarpathia in Ukrainian.) All the new papers were published in Ukrainian, with the only exception being Transcarpathia, where a Hungarian paper was added to the already existing Ukrainian youth paper. This has made two-paper cities of all the oblast centers of West Ukraine, except for Lviv, Uzhhorod and Chernivtsi, which have more than two.

In one of Khrushchev's reorganizations, the party and state provincial apparatus in the USSR was split in most oblasts into "industrial" and "agricultural" obkoms and soviets (1963 to 1965). This particular reorganization wrought havoc in the structure of the Soviet press. Suffice it to mention that several thousand raion papers were replaced by "territorial administrations" organs, and that all transport papers were closed. In Ukraine in nine oblasts the oblast press was also split into "industrial" and "rural" papers. Lviv was the only western oblast to reorganize its papers, with *L'vovskaia pravda* becoming an industrial paper and *Vil'na Ukraïna* a rural one. However, a parallel Ukrainian-language edition of the former was also organized, with an initial printing of each in 40,000 copies. By 1964, the Russian version had declined to 32,000. In 1965, this system was abolished and *L'vovskaia pravda* and *Vil'na Ukraïna* returned to their previous status. (Their post-reform circulations in 1965 were 60,000 and 115,000, respectively.)

Quantitative changes in the west Ukrainian press—included are oblast party-soviet and youth papers—are summarized in table 4.2.

When these data are translated into percentages, we discover that over a 20-year period (1950 to 1970) the share of the Ukrainian and Russian oblast papers, calculated as a percentage of the total pre-issue press run, has changed in the following way:

	1950	1960	1970
Ukrainian papers as percent of total press run	77.8	80.7	85.0
Russian papers as percent of total press run	14.8	13.1	10.5

Although this does not reveal the full picture of press conditions in West Ukraine (there was without doubt an increase in the number of Moscow-originating papers sold in the area),[17] it is clear that the Ukrainian-language press originating locally has remained a vital presence.

Raion or Local Newspapers

The raion or district is the lowest administrative unit in the USSR to have a newspaper of its own.

West Ukraine had a total of 212 raion newspapers in 1946, ranging from 37 in Ternopil oblast to 11 in Transcarpathia. Of this total, 210 were in Ukrainian, and one each in Hungarian and Romanian. Thus, only two counties in West Ukraine did not receive their local paper in Ukrainian. There were also three town newspapers in West Ukraine; their language was Ukrainian. By 1970 the total of raion papers was reduced to 109. Of these, 103 papers were printed in Ukrainian, and three each in Hungarian (Transcarpathia) and Moldavian (Chernivtsi). The six raions where a non-Ukrainian paper appeared also maintained a Ukrainian-language edition of the same paper. (In conformity with Soviet practice we have counted them as separate papers.)[18]

From the outset of the Soviet regime there, Russian was introduced into the local (raion) press of West Belorussia. Perhaps it could be argued that West Belorussia's urban population had been more accustomed to Russian than Belorussian, and that this justified publishing oblast papers in Russian along with Belorussian. It is harder to understand on what grounds the decision was made to address the village population of many districts of West Belorussia in Russian. This population was ethnically Belorussian or Polish, not Russian. And yet, as early as 1946, only 36 raions of West Belorussia had a Belorussian paper, as against 32 that had exclusively a Russian one. In percentage terms, 53 percent of the raions were served by the Belorussian press and 47 percent by Russian. (The Belorussian papers had a combined circulation of 41,000 copies or 55 percent of the total; the Russian papers, 34,000 or 45 percent.) In contrast, only three raions of East Belorussia maintained Russian papers; the remaining 102 published their newspapers in Belorussian.[19] Whereas a Ukrainian-language paper was published in all raions of West Ukraine (including those that also had a Hungarian or Moldavian paper), about half of the West Belorussian rural population was receiving its local paper only in Russian.

In 1970 the number of raions in West Belorussia was reduced in comparison with 1946. Of a total of 33 raions, 23 had a Belorussian paper, and the other 10 a Russian one. Thus, the Belorussian share of titles had risen to 69.7 percent, and the Russian was reduced to 30.3 percent. The combined press run of the Belorussian papers was 139,244 copies, which represented 59.4 percent of the total, and that of the Russian papers was 95,096 (40.6 percent). On average, however, a Russian paper printed 9,510 copies against the average figure of 6,054 achieved by the Belorussian papers.[20] Considering that since 1962 there has been no Belorussian-language oblast press in the west, we have to conclude that the overall position of the Belorussian language in the press was weaker in 1970 than it had been in 1946 or 1948. (At that time the Belorussian share of the oblast circulations was 50 percent.)

As this brief review has shown, the Soviet regime has not been over-generous in providing for the press in West Ukraine or West Belorussia. Especially striking is the weakness (or, in West Belorussia, absence) of the journal and magazine press: A region of over eight million people, which West Ukraine is, has one literary monthly and no magazines of any kind. The daily press, on the other hand, is in a much better position both in numbers and in circulation. From the language point of view, the press in West Ukraine has developed in a direction strikingly different from that followed in West Belorussia. We surmise that this happened because of certain political decisions made immediately after the war. It is conceivable, however, that over the years West Belorussians have formed a habit of reading their local press in Russian even though this practice had been imposed on them, initially, by an arbitrary action from the outside. This practice—reinforced, we suppose, by a similar promotion of Russian in the educational system (data on this are lacking)—may have resulted in a general increase of the number of those Belorussians who consider Russian to be their first, or "native," language. We would tend to suppose that in West Ukraine the effect of the press was different. However limited its thematic range was—one literary monthly for the intelligentsia, a journal for the clergy—the press in West Ukraine was generally published in Ukrainian. By analogy, we would judge that there was relatively less pressure to adopt Russian.

Population Change and Assimilation

This study first discussed the functions of Ukrainian and Belorussian in pre-Soviet West Ukraine and West Belorussia and then reviewed Soviet language practices in the press of those regions. The language preferences of local Ukrainian and Belorussian populations remain to be examined.[21] Our findings relating to West Ukraine will be compared with those relating to West Belorussia, as well as with the data on the eastern parts of the UkSSR and BSSR.[22]

When one looks at Ukraine and Belorussia as a whole, both republics appear to have been very similar in 1959 and 1970 in the extent to which their titular nationalities had adopted Russian as their principal language. In 1959, 6.45 percent of all Ukrainians in the UkSSR and 6.77 percent of all Belorussians in the BSSR declared Russian as their "native language." By 1970, those percentages grew to 8.55 in Ukraine and to 9.84 in Belorussia. Even more similar were the figures for the eastern portions of the UkSSR and BSSR alone, those portions of the two republics that were Soviet before 1939:

	1959	1970
Assimilated Belorussians as % of all Belorussians	7.27	10.46
Assimilated Ukrainians as % of all Ukrainians	7.94	10.71

The degree of assimilation did not seem to be clearly related to the proportion of Russians in the population: In East Belorussia the Russians constituted 8.62 percent in 1959, and 11.32 percent in 1970; in East Ukraine the corresponding percentages were 19.63 and 22.62. If assimilation of non-Russians is a function of the strength of the Russians, the Ukrainians should have been much more assimilated in comparison with the Belorussians. The data for urban assimilation show even more clearly that this was not the case. The Russians were much stronger in the cities of Ukraine (29.10 percent in 1959, 30.02 percent in 1970) than in Belorussia (19.37 percent in 1959; 19.67 percent in 1970), but urban Belorussians were more assimilated than urban Ukrainians.

	Whole republic		*Eastern parts only*	
	1959	*1970*	*1959*	*1970*
Assimilated urban Belorussians (%)	22.42	24.52	22.35	24.22
Assimilated urban Ukrainians (%)	15.30	17.14	16.97	19.58

Since Ukraine had both a higher percentage of Russians and was also more urbanized than Belorussia, the explanation of the greater resilience of the Ukrainian language must lie in some factors other than the number of Russians. In 1959 the Russian minority constituted 5.17 percent of West Ukraine's and 7.67 percent of West Belorussia's population. And yet there was a striking disparity between the extent of assimilation of West Belorussians and West Ukrainians.

	1959	*1970*
Assimilated West Belorussians (%)	5.31	8.01
Assimilated West Ukrainians (%)	0.92	0.85

West Belorussian indicators were quite close to republic averages; those for West Ukraine were sharply out of line with the situation in the UkSSR and, especially, in the east.

Among the urban population in the west, Russians were predictably stronger than they were in the general population. In 1959 they made up 15.53 percent and 22.99 percent in the towns of West Ukraine and West Belorussia, respectively. If they influenced the speech preference of their fellow Ukrainian and Belorussian residents, their impact was uneven: Fewer than 4 percent of urban Ukrainians but almost 23 percent of urban Belorussians in the west declared Russian as their native language in 1959. West Belorussians were slightly more assimilated than were East Belorussians, but West Ukraine was quite unlike East Ukraine. By 1970 the discrepancy between urbanization and assimilation in West and East Ukraine, and between West Ukraine and West Belorussia, became more pronounced:

	1959	1970
Assimilated urban West Belorussians (%)	22.73	25.75
Assimilated urban West Ukrainians (%)	3.83	2.68

If we remember that from 1959 to 1970 the number of assimilated urban East Ukrainians rose from 16.97 percent to 19.58 percent, the suspicion is almost inescapable that West Ukraine may have found some way to achieve "urbanization without Russification."

We have shown that between 1959 and 1970 assimilation to Russian was proceeding apace in Belorussia, including West Belorussia, and in East Ukraine—but not in West Ukraine. What was the impact of these processes on the population at large?

To determine precisely the changing relationship between different components of population, we will compare the rates of growth of the total population and its ethnic components—assimilated followed by unassimilated Belorussians/Ukrainians, and the Russians; we will repeat the same for the urban population.

First, the republic-wide processes are summarized in table 4.3, which shows that, while the population of both republics was increasing at a very similar rate, individual groups within those overall figures varied considerably. In Belorussia, the Belorussians were growing at virtually the same rate as the total population, but within the Belorussian ethnic group assimilated Belorussians were increasing the most rapidly. Assimilated Ukrainians in Ukraine also were increasing rapidly, although their rate of growth, in relation to the rate of growth of the whole population, was slower (an index of 3.61 versus 5.29 in Belorussia).

In general, table 4.3 reveals a basic similarity of ethno-demographic processes in the two republics: an accelerated growth of assimilated members of titular nationalities and of Russians. A look at the eastern regions of these two republics reinforces the impression of the basic similarity between Ukraine and Belorussia in assimilation processes (see table 4.4).

In the Belorussian case, the growth of the assimilated segment of the Belorussians was especially striking; in the Ukrainian case assimilated Ukrainians were likewise growing very rapidly, while the unassimilated portion of Ukrainians grew at a rate less than half that of general population growth. East Ukraine was rapidly becoming less Ukrainian in both language and nationality.

The population of West Belorussia in the intercensal period grew half as fast as that of East Belorussia; West Ukraine maintained a rate slightly lower than average in the same period (12.25 for West Ukraine, versus 12.63 for East Ukraine and 12.56 for the UkSSR). But this was not the only significant difference between West Ukraine and West Belorussia (see table 4.5).

The pattern we discerned in the east was reversed in the west insofar as the Ukrainians are concerned. Even more revealing is the divergence of ethnic processes in the two "wests": in West Belorussia assimilated Belorussians registered a growth rate exceeding the rate of growth of the total population by a factor of 10; assimilated Ukrainians, on the other hand, increased by a mere 2 percent, less than half the rate of population increase in the area. Further, the Russians failed to keep up with the general population growth (although they did twice as well as assimilated Ukrainians), while in West Belorussia they increased three times faster than the population at large.

Trends in the urban sector of the population of the UkSSR and BSSR and their western and eastern parts are in the long run even more important. The cities represent modernity, and if Belorussian and Ukrainian are to survive in a modern urban environment it is vitally important that those Ukrainians and Belorussians who live there maintain their language identity.

The picture on republic-wide scale is presented in table 4.6. It shows both in Ukraine and in Belorussia that assimilated titular nationals have been growing far ahead of the other components of the population, while the unassimilated ones barely kept pace with the general growth. (This was by no means a reason for optimism from a non-Russian's point of view: Since a major part of urban growth was due to migration from the countryside, the proportion of the unassimilated should have been higher.)

The urban population in East Ukraine grew more slowly than the republic average; in East Belorussia it grew faster than the BSSR as a whole. Ethnic processes presented by means of a weighted index, however, reveal that individual population components grew in both regions at closely comparable rates in relation to the rate of growth of urban population as a whole (index of 1.00).

The usefulness of a weighted index is demonstrated in table 4.7. We realize, for example, that while the rate of growth of assimilated urban Belorussians was higher than that of comparable Ukrainians by 20 percentage points, the impact of that growth in East Ukraine was greater—because total population also grew in Ukraine more slowly, and thus the relative strength of the assimilated titular nationality became greater in Ukraine. Since in East Belorussia assimilated Belorussians increased slightly more slowly than the republic average, and in East Ukraine assimilated Ukrainians grew more quickly than the Ukrainian average, these relationships had to be reversed in the west.

Table 4.8 shows that indeed assimilated Belorussians increased at a much faster rate—36 percentage points—than the entire urban population (also 28 percentage points faster than the unassimilated Belorussians), and significantly faster than assimilated Belorussians in the east. In West Ukraine, unassimilated Ukrainians grew well ahead of the general population (14.5 points, index of 1.34), and overwhelmingly exceeded the growth rates of assimilated Ukrainians. The latter grew by 8.8 percent, or at one-fifth of the rate of growth of the urban population as a whole. The Russians also increased more slowly in West Ukraine than in West Belorussia.

This survey makes it possible to advance certain generalizations on ethno-demographic developments in West Ukraine and West Belorussia in light of the 1959 and 1970 censuses.

First, we note that in 1959 West Belorussia was approximately as assimilated linguistically as was East Belorussia, and that urban Belorussians in the west were in fact slightly more Russified linguistically than were their co-nationals in the east. By 1970 this feature of West Belorussia was confirmed: It continued to be the more Russified part of the BSSR.

Our second conclusion is that in 1959 West Ukraine was very unlike East Ukraine in the language loyalty of its Ukrainian population. This difference was very pronounced in the general population and in its urban segment. By 1970 East Ukraine had become more Russified, especially in the cities, but West Ukraine remained loyal to Ukrainian. Moreover, there was a relative decline in the number of assimilated urban West Ukrainians. This decline was so large that it suggests some "reassimilation" back to the Ukrainian language.

Finally, we note that West Belorussia was very different from West Ukraine in 1959, and that they became even more unlike by 1970. Although this cannot be fully argued here, we are skeptical of the thesis that the size of the Russian minority, or the degree of a region's urbanization, is invariably a predictor of the degree of assimilation of non-

Russians in the USSR. Those disparities between ethno-demographic processes in West Ukraine and West Belorussia ought to be explained by a complex group of factors, including Soviet language policies and the pre-Soviet experience of these regions.

Conclusions

We have concluded that linguistic assimilation in West Belorussia was being promoted by the Belorussians' exposure to Russian in the press. Having been in contact with Russian ever since 1944–45, when an overwhelming majority of them still lived in the countryside, the West Belorussians gradually acquired not only a knowledge of that language, but became ready to consider it their "native" tongue. This switch to Russian as a native tongue, which was especially common in the cities, was facilitated by social communication.[23] On the other hand, in West Ukraine the media, insofar as they had any effect on language maintenance, encouraged loyalty to Ukrainian. Language assimilation, we then conclude, is not an inevitable consequence of population change, including urbanization per se, but depends rather on several factors, one of which is language policy.

Although this was not our explicit concern, this study provides evidence, in our view, to support the argument of those scholars who have claimed that the annexation of West Ukraine has strengthened Ukrainian national distinctiveness in the USSR;[24] conversely, we would tend to conclude that West Belorussia's contribution to the maintenance of a separate Belorussian linguistic or cultural identity has been minimal.

Developing an argument of John A. Armstrong, who has classified both the Ukrainians and Belorussians as "younger brothers" of the Russians in the context of inter-ethnic relations in the Soviet Union,[25] we might suggest that the inclusion of West Ukrainians—who tend to become urbanized without being assimilated to Russian (unlike East Ukrainians)—represents a departure from this traditional Ukrainian role in both tsarist Russia and the USSR. If this is indeed the case, and if Armstrong is right in arguing that "the major thrust of Soviet nationality policy . . . will be toward drawing the younger brothers (especially the Ukrainians) into indissoluble junior partnership with the Russians as the dominant ethnic group,"[26] then West Ukraine must be seen as the critical area of the Ukrainian nationality problem as well as one of the most sensitive zones of inter-ethnic relations in the USSR.

Table 4.1

Oblast Newspapers in West Belorussia in 1948

	Press Run	
Oblast	Belorussian	Russian
Baranovichi	10,000	5,000
Brest	5,000	10,000
Grodno	15,300	15,300
Molodechno	15,000	15,000
Pinsk	6,000	6,000
West Belorussia combined	51,300	51,300
	50%	50%

Source: *Letopis' periodicheskikh izdanii SSSR 1948* (Moscow, 1949), cols. 542, 545, 551, 555.

Table 4.2
Regional (Oblast) Newspapers in West Ukraine, 1950 to 1970

	1950		1960			1970		
	Number	Press Run	Number	Press Run	Increase over 1950	Number	Press Run	Increase over 1960
Ukrainian*	10	252,000	10	400,700	59.0%	14	1,104,700	175.7%
Russian	2	48,000	2	65,000	35.4%	2	137,000	110.8%
Hungarian	1	15,000	2	20,950	39.7%	2	35,300	68.5%
Moldavian**	1	4,000	1	10,000	150.0%	1	22,265	122.7%
Polish	1	5,000						
Total	15	324,000	15	496,650	53.3%	19	1,299,265	161.6%

*1950 figure includes the 1949 circulation of the Chernivtsi Ukrainian paper (1950 not available); 1960 figure includes the 1961 circulation of the Chernivtsi Ukrainian paper (1960 not available).

**Figure represents 1949 circulation of Moldavian paper.

Sources: *Presa Ukrains'koi RSR, 1918–1975* (Kharkiv, 1976), pp. 188–94, 199; *Letopis' periodicheskikh izdanii SSSR 1950–1954* (M., 1955), pp. 350, 359; *Letopis' periodicheskickh izdanii SSSR 1961–1965*, *Gazety* (M., 1967), p. 641; *Letopis' periodicheskikh izdanii SSSR 1966–1970*, *Gazety* (M., 1975), p. 358.

Table 4.3

Population Change, Belorussia and Ukraine, 1959 to 1970

| | Increase (%) | | Weighted Index | |
	Belorussia	Ukraine	Belorussia	Ukraine
Total population	11.77	12.56	1.00	1.00
Titular nationality	11.6	9.72	0.99	0.77
Unassimilated titular nationality	7.97	7.27	0.68	0.58
Assimilated titular nationality	62.31	45.4	5.29	3.61
Russians	42.34	28.71	3.60	2.29

Table 4.4

Population Change, East Belorussia and East Ukraine, 1959 to 1970

| | Increase (%) | | Weighted Index | |
	East Belorussia	East Ukraine	East Belorussia	East Ukraine
Total population	13.84	12.63	1.00	1.00
Titular nationality	12.05	8.63	0.87	0.68
Unassimilated titular nationality	8.2	5.41	0.59	0.43
Assimilated titular nationality	61.29	46.66	4.43	3.69
Russians	49.54	29.8	3.58	2.36

Table 4.5

Population Change, West Belorussia and West Ukraine, 1959 to 1970

| | Increase (%) | | Weighted Index | |
	West Belorussia	West Ukraine	West Belorussia	West Ukraine
Total population	6.47	12.25	1.00	1.00
Titular nationality	10.29	13.59	1.59	1.11
Unassimilated titular nationality	7.32	13.71	1.13	1.12
Assimilated titular nationality	66.39	5.00	10.26	0.41
Russians	19.93	10.6	3.08	0.87

Table 4.6

Urban Population Growth, Belorussia and Ukraine, 1959 to 1970

| | Increase (%) | | Weighted Index | |
	Belorussia	Ukraine	Belorussia	Ukraine
Total population	57.54	34.16	1.00	1.00
Titular nationality	62.79	37.18	1.09	1.09
Unassimilated titular nationality	58.46	34.24	1.02	1.00
Assimilated titular nationality	78.00	53.73	1.36	1.57
Russians	59.99	34.68	1.04	1.02

Table 4.7

Population Change, East Belorussia and East Ukraine, 1959 to 1970

| | Increase (%) | | Weighted Index | |
	East Belorussia	East Ukraine	East Belorussia	East Ukraine
Total population	58.72	33.09	1.00	1.00
Titular nationality	61.8	34.56	1.05	1.04
Unassimilated titular nationality	57.91	30.35	0.99	0.92
Assimilated titular nationality	75.35	55.21	1.28	1.67
Russians	69.6	35.75	1.19	1.08

Table 4.8

Population Change, West Belorussia and West Ukraine, 1959 to 1970

| | Increase (%) | | Weighted Index | |
	West Belorussia	West Ukraine	West Belorussia	West Ukraine
Total population	53.26	42.81	1.00	1.00
Titular nationality	67.01	55.28	1.26	1.29
Unassimilated titular nationality	60.83	57.31	1.14	1.34
Assimilated titular nationality	89.16	8.8	1.67	0.21
Russians	32.1	18.07	0.60	0.42

Table 4.9

Population of the Ukrainian SSR, East Ukraine, and
West Ukraine, 1959 to 1970

	Total		Urban	
	1959	*1970*	*1959*	*1970*
Ukrainian SSR	41,869,046	47,126,517	19,147,419	25,688,560
Ukrainians	32,158,493	35,283,857	11,781,750	16,164,254
of which unassimilated	30,072,651	32,257,360	9,973,430	13,388,207
assimilated	2,075,527	3,017,823	1,802,510	2,771,002
Russians	7,090,813	9,126,331	5,726,476	7,712,277
East Ukraine	34,069,988	38,371,965	17,040,275	22,679,286
Ukrainians	25,360,713	27,561,959	10,281,648	13,834,904
of which unassimilated	23,345,641	27,608,103	8,535,577	11,126,320
assimilated	2,012,665	2,951,821	1,745,063	2,708,502
Russians	6,687,875	8,680,681	5,378,266	7,301,158
West Ukraine	7,799,058	8,754,552	2,107,144	3,009,274
Ukrainians	6,797,780	7,721,898	1,500,102	2,329,350
of which unassimilated	6,726,710	7,649,257	1,437,853	2,261,887
assimilated	62,862	66,002	57,447	62,500
Russians	402,938	445,650	348,210	411,119

Table 4.10

Population of the Belorussian SSR, East Belorussia, and
West Belorussia, 1959 to 1970

	Total		Urban	
	1959	1970	1959	1970
Belorussian SSR	8,054,648	9,002,338	2,480,505	30,907,783
Belorussians	6,532,035	7,289,610	1,662,654	2,706,595
of which unassimilated	6,086,302	6,571,489	1,288,924	2,042,470
assimilated	441,925	717,296	372,828	663,638
Russians	659,093	938,161	480,396	768,610
East Belorussia	5,786,554	6,587,393	1,945,568	3,087,936
Belorussians	4,860,076	5,445,523	1,347,302	2,179,921
of which unassimilated	4,506,006	4,875,530	1,045,902	1,651,616
assimilated	653,150	569,585	301,140	528,036
Russians	498,835	745,969	301,140	528,036
West Belorussia	2,268,094	2,414,945	534,937	819,847
Belorussians	1,671,959	1,844,087	315,350	526,674
of which unassimilated	1,580,296	1,695,959	243,022	390,854
assimilated	88,775	147,711	71,688	135,602
Russians	160,258	192,192	122,998	162,475

Notes

1. West Ukraine, that is, the oblasts of Lviv, Ivano-Frankivsk, Ternopil, Volhynia, Rivne, Transcarpathia, and Chernivtsi, had 7.8 million population in 1959 and 8.6 million in 1970. West Belorussia, that is, the oblasts of Brest and Grodno, had 2.3 million people in 1959 and 2.4 in 1970. (See tables 4.9 and 4.10 for full details.) In 1959 West Ukraine was larger than the Baltic republics combined; West Belorussia had more people than Latvia and was twice as large as Estonia.

2. From 1937 to 1953, and in most important respects until 1956, all matters relating to newspaper publishing were reserved to the exclusive control of the Central Committee of the CPSU. See *Bol'shevistskaia pechat'*, no. 1 (1937): 34, and ibid., no. 7 (1938), 36; *O partiinoi i sovetskoi pechati, radioveshchanii i televidenii. Sbornik dokumentov i materialov* (Moscow, Mysl', 1972), p. 292; and *Spravochnik partiinogo rabotnika*, no. 1 (Moscow, 1957): 320, 441–42.

3. "On Deficiencies in Political Work among the Populace of the Western Oblasts of the Ukrainian Soviet Socialist Republic," in Robert H. McNeal, ed., *Resolutions and Decisions of the Communist Party of the Soviet Union*, vol. 3, *The Stalin Years, 1929–1953* (Toronto: University of Toronto Press, 1974), pp. 226–32. (All quotations in the text are from p. 229.) The Russian text of this document is in *Kommunisticheskaia partiia Sovetskogo Soiuza v rezoliutsiiakh i resheniiakh s"ezdov, konferentsii i plenumov TsK*, vol. 6, 1941–1954 (Moscow: Izdatel'stvo politicheskoi literatury, 1971), pp. 124–29. (See pp. 125–26 for passages quoted in the text.)

4. *Kommunisticheskaia partiia Sovetskogo Soiuza*, vol. 6, pp. 106–12.

5. West Ukraine's history is presented succinctly in V. Kubijovyč, ed., *Ukraine: A Concise Encyclopedia*, vol. I (Toronto: University of Toronto Press, 1963), pp. 697–725, 770–89, 833–59. See also Ivan L. Rudnytsky, "The Ukrainians in Galicia under Austrian Rule," *Austrian History Yearbook* 3, pt. 2 (1967): 394–429, and Jerzy Holzer, *Mozaika polityczna Drugiej Rzeczypospolitej* (Warsaw: Książka i Wiedza, 1974), *passim*. Antony Polonsky, *Politics in Independent Poland, 1921–1939* (Oxford: Clarendon, 1972), deals with the national minorities, including Ukrainians and Belorussians.

6. Kubijovyč, ed., *Ukraine*, p. 212. World War II fundamentally changed the ethno-demographic structure of West Ukraine and West Belorussia—a subject that cannot be treated here adequately. First, in 1939 to 1941, the USSR deported about 1.2 to 1.6 million people to the east. In 1941 to 1944, the Nazis exterminated the Jewish population. After 1944, an overwhelming majority of the Poles from West Ukraine, and a smaller proportion from West Belorussia, moved to Poland. Some Romanians and Hungarians, and most Czechs, mi-

grated to their respective countries, Ukrainians and Belorussians migrated from Poland, and from the east came successive waves of Russian officials, managers, educators, and workers. The scope of those Russian migrations is reflected in the returns of the 1959 census. For some of these population changes, see Kubijovyč, *Ukraine*; Krystyna Kersten, *Repatriacja ludności polskiej po II wojnie światowej* (Wrocław: Wydawnictwo Polskiej Akademii Nauk, 1974); I. F. Evseev, *Sotrudnichestvo Ukrainskoi SSR i Pol'skoi Narodnoi Respubliki* (Kyiv: Izdatel'stvo Akademii Nauk Ukrainskoi SSR, 1962), pp. 125–28; V. Malanchuk, *Torzhestvo lenins'koï natsional'noï polityky* (Lviv: Knyzhkovo-zhurnalne Vydavnytstvo, 1963), p. 492; and Yaroslav Bilinsky, "The Incorporation of Western Ukraine," in Roman Szporluk, ed., *The Influence of East Europe and the Soviet West on the USSR* (New York: Praeger, 1976), p. 207.

7. See Nicholas P. Vakar, *Belorussia: The Making of a Nation* (Cambridge, Mass: Harvard University Press, 1956) and Ivan S. Lubachko, *Belorussia under Soviet Rule, 1917–1957* (Lexington: University Press of Kentucky, 1972) for basic facts. On Belorussian lands under Poland, see also Holzer, *Mozaika polityczna*; Jerzy Tomaszewski, *Z dziejów Polesia 1921–1939. Zarys stosunków społeczno-ekonomicznych* (Warsaw: Państwowe Wydawnictwo Naukowe, 1963); and Zbigniew Landau and Jerzy Tomaszewski, *Druga Rzeczpospolita: Gospodarka, Społeczeństwo, Miejsce w Świecie* (Warsaw: Książka i Wiedza, 1977), pp. 217–40.

8. See Mark W. Hopkins, *Mass Media in the Soviet Union* (New York: Pegasus, 1970), and Gayle Durham Hollander, *Soviet Political Indoctrination: Developments in Mass Media and Propaganda since Stalin* (New York: Praeger, 1972). The fullest Soviet reference work is I. V. Kuznetsov and E. M. Fingerit, *Gazetnyi mir Sovetskogo Soiuza*, 2 vols. (Moscow: Izdatel'stvo Moskovskogo universiteta, 1972 and 1976). Vol. 1 deals with "central" papers, vol. 2 is devoted to "republican, krai, oblast and okrug" papers.

9. The research for this part of the study is based on official publications of the All-Union Book Chamber of the USSR, published in Moscow regularly since 1947. To avoid excessive citation, the reader is referred to those works now. For all references to events of 1946 to 1949, see the annual publications of the Vsesoiuznaia knizhnaia palata entitled *Letopis' periodicheskikh izdanii SSSR 1946, Letopis'. . . 1947, Letopis'. . . 1948,* and *Letopis'. . . 1949* (Moscow: Kniga, 1947, 1948, 1949, 1950). All references to years 1950 to 1954 are based on *Letopis' periodicheskikh izdanii SSSR 1950–1954* (Moscow: Kniga, 1955). The important (because of a vast expansion of the Soviet press) period of 1955 to 1960 is covered in two volumes: *Letopis' periodicheskikh izdanii SSSR 1955–1960. Chast' I. Zhurnaly, trudy, biulleteni* (Moscow: Kniga, 1963) *and Letopis' periodicheskikh izdanii SSSR 1955–1960. Chast' II. Gazety* (Moscow: Kniga, 1962 [sic]). The period of 1961 to 1965, which is important in the history of

136   Russia, Ukraine, and the Breakup of the Soviet Union

the Belorussian press for a series of liquidations of Belorussian-language publications, and in the history of the Ukrainian press during the age of the Khrushchevian reorganization, is fully documented in *Letopis' periodicheskikh izdanii SSSR 1961–1965. Chast' II. Gazety* (Moscow: Kniga, 1967) and *Letopis' periodicheskikh izdanii SSSR. Chast' I. Zhurnaly, trudy, biulleteni* (Moscow: Kniga, 1973). (Part I was published in two volumes.) Finally, the five years between January 1966 and December 1970 are covered in *Letopis' periodicheskikh izdanii SSSR 1966–1970. Chast' I. Zhurnaly* (Moscow: Kniga, 1972), and the same for *Gazety* (M., 1975). This time "trudy, biulleteni" were not included in a joint volume with "zhurnaly" but were registered in separate annual issues. The entire period from 1917 to 1960 is covered in a work now in progress entitled *Gazety SSSR 1917–1960. Bibliograficheskii spravochnik* (Moscow: Kniga, 1970–1984). By 1977, only two volumes of this work had appeared. Unlike all the others listed above, this reference work does not provide press-run figures.

10. For the press in the Ukrainian SSR, in addition to sources listed in note 9, the following publications of the Ukrainian Book Chamber may be usefully consulted: *Periodychni vydannia URSR 1918–1950. Zhurnaly. Bibliohrafichnyi dovidnyk* (Kharkiv: Knyzhkova palata URSR, 1956), and *Periodychni vydannia URSR 1917–1960. Hazety. Bibliohrafichnyi dovidnyk* (Kharkiv: Knyzhkova palata URSR, 1965). For a brief profile of the Ukrainian press, see Roman Szporluk "The Ukraine and the Ukrainians" in Zev Katz, ed., *Handbook of Major Soviet Nationalities* (New York: Free Press, 1975), pp. 31–34.

11. *Presa Ukrains'koi RSR 1918–1975. Naukovo-statystychnyi dovidnyk* (Kharkiv: Knyzhkova palata URSR, 1976), pp. 186, 204. (This is a very useful source of information on the Ukrainian press since 1970.)

12. Malanchuk, *Torzhestvo lenins'koï natsional'noï polityky*, p. 374.

13. I. F. Ievseichyk, "Vidnovlennia i zmitsnennia partiinykh orhanizatsii zakhidnykh oblastei Ukraïny v 1944–1945 rr.," *Ukraïns'kyi istorychnyi zhurnal*, 1974, no. 2, p. 43, and Malanchuk, *Torzhestvo*, pp. 366, 452. Posts of deputy ministers for the western regions were created in Ukrainian ministries (ibid., p. 676). These facts confirm the supposition of John A. Armstrong that West Ukraine "very probably . . . was treated as a regional unit of the apparatus." See *The Soviet Bureaucratic Elite* (New York: Praeger, 1963), p. 114.

14. S. V. Martselev, *Pechat' Sovetskoi Belorussii (Istoricheskii ocherk)* (Minsk: Belarus', 1967) contains much useful information. See also Jan Zaprudnik, "Belorussia and the Belorussians," in Katz, ed., *Major Soviet Nationalities*, pp. 55–61. The Belorussian Book Chamber publishes a full account of the BSSR press in *Letapis druku BSSR* (Minsk: Palata), in a special section entitled "Letapis periadychnykh vydanniau." (Only the issues for 1972 and after were available to me.)

15. For some of those developments, see Roman Szporluk, "The Press in Belorussia, 1955–1965," *Soviet Studies* 18, no. 4 (April 1967): 487–90.

16. The fullest account in English is in *Ukraine: A Concise Encyclopaedia*, vol. II (Toronto: University of Toronto Press, 1971), pp. 476–505. It was written by A. Zhyvotko and B. Krawciw. Michał Derenicz, "Prasa na Ziemiach Wschodnich," *Rocznik Ziem Wschodnich*, 1938, vol. IV (Warsaw: Wydawnictwo Zarządu Głównego Towarzystwa Rozwoju Ziem Wschodnich, n.d.), p. 162, cites seven Polish dailies and over fifty periodicals and serials as appearing in Lviv in the late 1930s, when it was still in Poland. According to him, there were also four Ukrainian-language daily papers and one Yiddish daily paper in the city.

17. In 1970, in Lviv, 1,665,000 copies of Moscow (exclusively Russian-language) papers were printed daily from printing plates delivered by plane or transmitted by cable. (This can be compared with the total of 392,000 copies of Lviv oblast papers then printed daily.) *Pravda* printed 160,000 copies and *Komsomol'skaia pravda*, 140,000 copies. (See M. N. Yablokov, *Gazeta i rasstoianie* (Moscow, 1971), pp. 19, 122.) Those papers were also distributed outside Lviv oblast, however.

18. Calculated by the author from *Letopis' periodicheskikh izdanii SSSR 1966–1970. Gazety* (Moscow, 1975), pp. 345–47, 358–60, 362–64, 371–73, 381–82, 384–86, 398–99.

19. Calculated by the author from *Letopis' periodicheskikh izdanii SSSR 1946* (Moscow, 1947), cols. 439–56.

20. Calculated by the author from *Letopis' periodicheskikh izdanii SSSR 1966–1970. Gazety*, pp. 232–34, 238–40.

21. This part of our study is based on the returns of the 1959 and 1970 Soviet censuses. See tables 4.9 and 4.10 for the actual figures on which all our calculations in the text are based. See *Itogi Vsesoiuznoi perepisi naseleniia 1959 goda, Ukrainskaia SSR* (Moscow, 1963), tables 53–54; *Itogi . . . 1959 goda, Belorusskaia SSR* (Moscow, 1963), tables 53–54; and *Itogi Vsesoiuznoi perepisi naseleniia 1970 goda* (Moscow, 1973), vol. 4, tables 9 and 10.

22. See Steven L. Guthier, "The Belorussians: National Identification and Assimilation, 1897–1970," *Soviet Studies* 29, no. 1 (January 1977): 37–61, and no. 2 (April 1977): 270–83, for a full-scale review of Belorussia. This writer has examined some of the demographic problems discussed in this article in Roman Szporluk, "The Press in Belorussia, 1955–65," pp. 482–93, and in "Russians in Ukraine and Problems of Ukrainian Identity in the USSR," in Peter J. Potichnyj, ed., *Ukraine in the Seventies* (Oakville, Ontario, 1975), pp. 195–217, reprinted as chapter 3 of this volume.

23. See Szporluk, "The Press in Belorussia . . . ," p. 491, for a suggestion that this might be the case in West Belorussia. The example of Belorussia appears to support the argument of Karl W. Deutsch on conditions favoring linguistic assimilation. See Karl W. Deutsch, *Nationalism and Social Communication: An Inquiry into the Foundations of Nationality* (Cambridge, Mass: Technology

Press of the Massachusetts Institute of Technology and John Wiley & Sons, 1953), p. 99: "assimilation to a new language is progressing if the number of persons who are learning it during a given period . . . is larger than the number of persons who are as yet ignorant but who are entering into intensive economic, social, or political contact with its speakers—that is to say, who are added to the 'mobilized population' . . . assimilation is gaining ground if . . . community is growing faster than society." "The need for communication does not immediately produce the proportionate ability to communicate. Assimilation occurs if this ability grows faster than this need; differentiation is sharply felt if the need outruns the ability." As this study shows, West Belorussians read Russian when they still lived in the countryside, that is, before they needed to know it at work. They spoke it and accepted it as their own after moving to the city.

24. See Ivan L. Rudnytsky, "The Soviet Ukraine in Historical Perspective," *Canadian Slavonic Papers* 14, no. 2 (Summer 1972): 244–48; Y. Bilinsky, "The Incorporation of Western Ukraine," p. 215; and John A. Armstrong, *Ukrainian Nationalism*, 2d ed. (New York: Columbia University Press, 1963), pp. 309–10.

25. For the concept of "younger brothers," see John A. Armstrong, "The Ethnic Scene in the Soviet Union," in Erich Goldhagen, ed., *Ethnic Minorities in the Soviet Union* (New York: Praeger, 1968), esp. pp. 14–15.

26. Ibid., p. 32.

5 Urbanization in Ukraine since the Second World War

The Second World War marked a significant change not only in the history of the urbanization of Ukraine but in the history of the Ukrainian people as well. For the first time since the middle of the seventeenth century, all Ukrainian ethnic lands were united under a single political authority; Kyiv and Lviv were no longer separated by an international boundary. The only period comparable in this regard was the period from 1569 to 1648, when most Ukrainian lands found themselves within the confines of the *Korona*, the Polish-dominated part of the *Rzeczpospolita*.

The Second World War also witnessed a profound ethno-demographic transformation in Ukraine. This subject is too complex to discuss here; suffice it to say that some five to seven million persons lost their lives in the war, including no less than four million civilians. Proportionately, the most extensive were the losses suffered by the Jewish population, but in terms of absolute numbers they were equaled and even surpassed by the deaths of Ukrainian civilians and military personnel. The war and its aftermath also witnessed mass population losses due to migration. The overall, long-term effect was a drastic cut in the number of Poles, Jews, Tatars, Germans, Czechs, and other smaller groups living within the present boundaries of Ukraine, which estab-

First published in *Rethinking Ukrainian History*, 1981.

lished conditions for the immigration of vast numbers of Russians into Ukraine.[1]

Perhaps the following very general data will convey something of the vastness of the population change brought about by the war and its aftermath. Since Ukraine did not exist in its present shape before 1939, let us first cite data for the Ukrainian SSR in its boundaries prior to September 17, 1939, and then compare these with the postwar figures. In 1939 the population of the Ukrainian SSR was 31,785,000, of which 73.5 percent (or 23,362,000) was Ukrainian by nationality and 12.9 percent Russian (or 4,100,000).[2] The remaining 13.6 percent consisted primarily of Jews, Poles and Germans. (There had also been a great change in population between 1926 and 1939: While the total population of Ukraine in those intercensal years rose by about 12 percent, its Ukrainian component registered a growth of only 1.9 percent, as compared to the Russian element's 56.7 percent.[3])

In 1959, the year of the first postwar census, "Eastern Ukraine" had a population of 34,069,988. Ukrainians numbered 25,360,713 or 74.44 percent, Russians 6,687,875 or 19.63 percent and the remaining 5.93 percent consisted of Jews, Bulgarians, Greeks, and other minorities. Proportionately, non-Ukrainians and non-Russians were reduced to less than half their prewar share. The number of Ukrainians increased by about 1 percentage point; and the Russian population increased by 6.7 points. Between 1939 and 1959 the number of Russians in Eastern Ukraine rose by over 60 percent; the number of Ukrainians, by about 9 percent.

The change in "Western Ukraine" was no less dramatic. On January 1, 1933, the Ukrainians formed about 66 percent of the population of "Polish Ukraine" (Galicia and Volhynia), 52.4 percent in Bukovyna and Bessarabia, and 61.2 per cent in Transcarpathia.[4] (In Western Ukraine, Poles, Jews, Czechs, Romanians, and Hungarians were more numerous than Russians, who basically consisted of émigrés from the Soviet state.) In 1959 the demographic scene in Western Ukraine bore little resemblance to the prewar situation. The Ukrainians increased their share of the population in all parts of the historical region and constituted 87.2 percent of Western Ukraine's population (6,797,780 Ukrainians out of a total population of 7,799,058). The "historic" nationalities of the region had been greatly reduced in size, and the Russians now made up the second largest group; numbering 402,938, they constituted over 5 percent of the population.[5]

Before the Second World War Ukrainians were in a minority in the cities and towns of Ukraine. According to the 1926 Soviet census, they constituted 41.3 percent of Ukraine's urban population. In the urban areas of Western Ukraine, they were similarly outnumbered by other nationalities, and the population of the unofficial capital of the region, Lviv, was only 16.2 percent Ukrainian in 1931. To put the matter in another way, only one in ten Ukrainians lived in cities or towns in 1926; the proportion was about the same in Western Ukraine.[6] By 1959 the situation had changed: For the first time in their modern history, Ukrainians made up the majority of the population in their own cities. In the republic as a whole, their share was 61.53 percent; in Eastern Ukraine it fell slightly to 60.34 percent; in Western Ukraine it was much higher at 71.19 percent. (However, Western Ukraine was much less urbanized than the East, and it had little influence on the republic average. Eastern Ukraine was 50 percent urban in 1959, while the West was 27 percent urban. The republic average was 46 percent.)[7]

As an urban system, prewar Ukraine was characterized by the lack of a primate city. In 1897 Odessa was the largest city but also the least Ukrainian of the major cities located in Ukrainian territory. By 1939 Kyiv was the largest city in Ukraine with a population of 847,000, followed by Kharkiv with 833,000 and Odessa with 602,000. The other principal cities were Dnipropetrovsk (527,000), Donetsk (466,000) and, across the Polish border, Lviv (340,000).[8] If one defines a primate city as one that is at least twice the size of the second largest, in accordance with what Mark Jefferson has called "the law of the primate city" ("A country's leading city is always disproportionately large and exceptionally expressive of national capacity and feeling"),[9] Ukraine clearly was not an integrated entity as late as 1939. If one scales the population of Kyiv in 1939 as 100, the population of Kharkiv was 99 and that of Odessa, 70. This would place Ukraine at the bottom of a list of fifty-one cases illustrating the position of primate cities in relation to the second and third cities of their respective countries. (Italy in 1936 had a ranking of 100–96–75, and Spain in 1934 a slightly higher one of 100–91–31.)[10]

In 1939 Ukraine was still a predominantly rural country (only 34 percent of the population in the present boundaries of the Ukrainian SSR, and 37 percent in the former boundaries, lived in urban locations; the urbanization level of Western Ukraine was even lower).[11] Large-scale urbanization in Soviet Ukraine commenced only after 1945. Because the Ukrainians had historically been so closely identified with the village, their relationship with the Russians and Poles, the two nationalities most closely linked with Ukrainian history, had been reflected in terms of an urban–rural dichotomy. In popular perception—and in sociological fact—Ukrainian ethnicity came to be identified with village ways of life, values, and styles, and Poles and Russians in Ukraine became associated with the city and the world of high social, cultural, and economic life. It was therefore of critical importance for the Ukrainian national movement in modern times to establish a Ukrainian presence in urban areas. To a considerable extent, the Ukrainians accomplished this goal in the Austrian part of their land, in that Ukrainians who were employed in the cities or who were otherwise occupied outside agriculture, forestry, or fishing defined themselves politically and culturally as members of the Ukrainian nation. Under Austria and Poland the Ukrainians succeeded in establishing socially mobilized but culturally differentiated (from the Poles and to a lesser extent from the Romanians, Czechs, and Hungarians) strata to provide leadership for the masses. By their example, these strata demonstrated that one could be urban, educated, high on the occupational ladder, in short, "modern"—*and* Ukrainian.

The development of analogous processes in Russian Ukraine proceeded more slowly and faced virtually insurmountable obstacles until 1917. The policy of Ukrainianization, which was proclaimed in the 1920s, aimed at the establishment of a Ukrainian presence (if not Ukrainian hegemony) in the modern urban environment. As is well known, this policy was not carried out as thoroughly as is portrayed in official decrees. Moreover, the whole concept was abandoned before the mid-1930s and the Russian language and culture were restored to their previous position of superiority in the cities of Ukraine. The Ukrainians were relegated to the role they had played in tsarist Russia—that of the ruling nation's "younger brothers," to use the term popularized by John A. Armstrong. Armstrong stresses cultural proximity to the ruling nation as one of the characteristics of a "younger-brother" nation, the other being the latter's low level of social and economic development—in short, a predominantly rural habitat.[12] In such a relationship, as Armstrong has noted, the cities in the younger-brother area were relatively small before the onset of mass industrialization, and they were also dominated linguistically by the ruling nation. (This included assimilated members of the dominated nationality.) In such a context:

> The cities are . . . fortresses from which dominant ethnic forces sally
> forth to control the countryside economically and politically, and

(through control of rural socialization and communication processes) to effect a measure of assimilation even there.[13]

When rapid industrialization (and thus urbanization) begins, large numbers of the younger-brother group enter the city and one of two possible results emerges: Either this influx "swamps" the hitherto dominant group or the dominant group maintains its position by means of continuing in-migration from the outside.

Armstrong's scenario, which is inspired by the work of Karl Deutsch on nationalism and social communication, has to be amended in application to Ukraine. Stalin's treatment of Ukraine in the 1930s shows, in our opinion, that political violence on a mass scale can be used to regulate ethno-demographic processes in a period of rapid social change, urbanization, and industrialization. It became quite clear in the late thirties that Ukraine was to become a modern region, but in the process the cities, industry, high culture, and the world of science were to be Russified rather than Ukrainianized.

Stalin, however, did not as yet control the western portions of Ukraine, in which, as we have already observed, the Ukrainians had succeeded, however modestly, in establishing a presence in the city. Moreover, their struggle for a place in the urban sun had been fought not against the Russians but against their western neighbors. The West Ukrainians were free, accordingly, of an inferiority complex toward Russia, and in general associated modernity with centers such as Warsaw, Vienna, Prague, perhaps Berlin or Paris, even New York, but certainly not tsarist or Stalinist Moscow or Leningrad.

This preliminary discussion may now be concluded and the principal concerns of this essay laid out. Urbanization being a complex, multifaceted process, with wide ramifications, connections, and consequences,[14] this article will limit itself to a discussion of two themes. First, we would like to examine the processes of population growth in postwar Ukraine with regard to ethnic change. Is urbanization accompanied by a change in the ethnic composition of the urban population? Are urban Ukrainians becoming assimilated to the Russian culture, or do they maintain their ethnic identity as city residents? Our examination of this problem will be conducted along with, and we hope illuminated by, a review of urbanization processes pertaining to the question of the primate city in Ukraine. Ukraine before 1939, we remember, lacked a really dominant urban center. What changes have occurred since 1945? In the conclusion, we will attempt to tie the theme of assimilation and urbanization together with that of the rise of the primate city. What is the position of Ukrainians in the primate city (or its closest equivalent) of their homeland?

First of all, let us briefly characterize general population trends in Ukraine as revealed in the data assembled in table 5.1. Two southern regions of Ukraine, the South (proper) and the Dnieper, registered a significantly higher population growth between 1959 and 1970. This trend (southward migration) was continued in 1970 to 1977, when these two regions, especially the South, grew much faster than the republic as a whole. The Northeast and Central West, on the other hand, were increasing at a below-average rate. The growth rate of the Central West was about half the republican average, whereas the Northeast region grew slightly faster in 1959 to 1970 but dropped behind the Central West in 1970 to 1977. As will be seen later, both these regions owed their gains to the two main cities of their respective areas, Kyiv and Kharkiv. Some oblasts located in these areas of Ukraine were actually declining in population. The West, on the other hand, appears to have stayed close to the republic average: It was very slightly behind it in 1959 to 1970, but virtually level in 1970 to 1977.

In the post-1959 period, urban population (table 5.2) has grown relatively slowly in the Donbas basin, but one should take into account this region's already high degree of urbanization. The Northeast has also been relatively high on urbanization indices due to the location in this area of the major city of Kharkiv. Moreover, there appears to have been a continual growth of urban population also in Poltava and Sumy oblasts. The urban population of the Dnieper region showed only a slight increase, but this region, which includes Dnipropetrovsk, Zaporizhia, and Kryvyi Rih, remains the second most highly urbanized part of Ukraine.

The South has increased its urban population considerably throughout the postwar period, improving its share of Ukraine's urban population from 12.9 percent in 1959 to 14.7 percent in 1977. There has also been an above-average increase of urban population in the Central West (Kyiv, Vinnytsia, Cherkasy, and Chernihiv being among the fastest growing cities), and in the West, where the population of such oblast capitals as Rivne, Ternopil, Ivano-Frankivsk, and Lutsk increased especially rapidly.[15] On the whole, however, Western Ukraine has remained a rural region and as late as 1977 less than 40 percent of its population

Table 5.1
Population of Ukraine and Regions, 1939–77 (thousands)

	1939	%	1959	%	1970	%	1977	%	Change (%)	
									1959–70	1970–77
Ukraine	40,469	100.0	41,869	100.0	47,127	100.0	49,300	100.0	12.6	4.6
Donbas Basin	4,940	12.2	6,715	16.0	7,643	16.2	7,997	16.2	13.8	4.6
South	4,852	12.0	5,066	12.1	6,381	13.5	7,006	14.2	26.0	9.8
Dnieper	4,847	12.0	5,387	12.9	6,377	13.5	6,766	13.7	18.4	6.1
Northeast	6,159	15.2	5,632	13.5	6,037	12.8	6,154	12.5	7.2	1.9
Central West	11,622	28.7	11,228	26.8	11,935	25.3	12,221	24.8	6.3	2.4
West	8,049	19.9	7,800	18.6	8,754	18.6	9,156	18.6	12.2	4.6

Table 5.2
Urban Population of Ukraine and Regions, 1939–77

	1939	%	1959	%	1970	%	1977	%	Change (%) 1959–70	Change (%) 1970–77
Ukraine	13,569	100.0	19,147	100.0	25,689	100.0	29,844	100.0	34.2	16.2
Donbas Basin	3,631	26.8	5,601	29.3	6,546	25.5	7,010	23.5	16.9	7.1
South	1,785	13.2	2,465	12.9	3,641	14.2	4,389	14.7	47.7	20.5
Dnieper	1,972	14.5	3,108	16.2	4,268	16.6	4,902	16.4	37.3	14.9
Northeast	2,044	15.1	2,539	13.3	3,293	12.8	3,792	12.7	29.7	15.2
Central West	2,386	17.6	3,327	17.4	4,932	19.2	6,119	20.5	48.2	24.1
West	1,751	12.9	2,107	11.0	3,009	11.7	3,632	12.2	42.8	20.7

lived in the cities (table 5.3). The figures for the Central West region were higher—50 percent—due to the presence of Kyiv in the region.

In the intercensal period of 1959 to 1970, the Ukrainian share in the population of the Ukrainian SSR declined from 76.8 to 74.9 percent. In the republic as a whole, the Ukrainians increased by 9.7 percent while the overall population increased by 12.6 percent; with a gain of 28.7 percent Russians were maintaining a rate of growth three times higher than Ukrainians. In the component regions, the rates of growth of Ukrainians and Russians varied, but the general trend was toward a decline of the Ukrainian majority (table 5.4).

In view of these figures, brief comments on the ethnic scene may be in order. First, we note that in only one major region, the West, did Ukrainians improve their relative strength; conversely, the Russian population declined, albeit very slightly. Secondly, Ukrainians seem to be facing the prospect of becoming a minority in two important areas—the Donbas and the South (particularly the former). In relative terms the Ukrainian population was growing in the South and in the Dnieper region but the Russian population was increasing at an even faster rate. This illustrates our earlier comment about the southern migration of population. One should not exclude the possibility that the census of 1979 may reveal an improved Ukrainian standing in the Crimea or Kherson oblast, if not in the South as a whole; such an outcome will depend on the intensity of Russification and the volume of Russian in-migration from other areas of Ukraine and the USSR. Finally, Ukrainian strength has declined in traditional centers of Ukrainian life—the

Table 5.3
Urban Population as Percentage of Total Population of
Ukraine and Regions, 1939–77

	1939	1959	1970	1977
Ukraine	33.5	45.7	54.5	60.5
Donbas Basin	73.5	83.4	85.6	87.7
South	36.8	48.7	57.1	62.6
Dnieper	40.7	57.7	66.9	72.5
Northeast	33.2	45.1	54.5	61.6
Central West	20.5	29.6	41.3	50.1
West	21.8	27.0	34.4	39.7

Table 5.4

Ethnic Composition of Ukraine and Major Regions
(Percentages)

	Ukrainians			Russians		
Region	1959	1970	Percentage Change, 1959–1970	1959	1970	Percentage Change, 1959–1970
Ukraine	76.8	74.9	9.7	15.1	19.4	28.7
Donbas	56.4	53.7	8.4	33.4	41.0	22.9
South	56.9	55.0	21.6	24.5	34.0	38.6
Dnieper	77.6	74.8	14.0	14.9	20.8	40.1
Northeast	81.0	78.5	3.3	15.2	18.7	23.2
Central West	88.3	87.5	5.3	5.9	7.7	30.0
West	87.2	88.2	13.6	4.6	5.1	10.6

Northeast, which includes Poltava and Sumy oblasts (this may be due to Russian immigration to Kharkiv, Poltava, and other cities of the region), and the Central West. The latter had a 30 percent increase in Russian population from 1959 to 1970 due mainly to in-migration.

The 1959 census revealed that the cities and towns of Ukraine possessed Ukrainian majorities (table 5.5). The overall majority was only 61.53 percent, but significant nonetheless. The Russian population was virtually half the size of the Ukrainian (29.9 percent), and the number of Russian speakers was much higher. Other nationalities traditionally present in Ukrainian urban life were much reduced in size by 1959.

The distribution of Ukrainians in the cities was uneven. They were strongest in the West (a remarkable change from the pre-1939 era) and had a clear lead also in the Central West, where they constituted a majority in Kyiv, but were much weaker in the cities of the East and South, traditionally more urban and more Russian. The regions of the South, Donbas, Dnieper, and Northeast together registered a Ukrainian majority of 57.9 percent. Donetsk oblast had a Ukrainian majority of 52 percent in 1959, Voroshylovhrad (Luhansk) one of 53 percent. In Odessa oblast Ukrainians had a plurality of 44 percent. In Crimea, a new Ukrainian region (added to the Ukrainian SSR in 1954), 18 percent of the urban population were Ukrainians. Ukrainians were particularly weak in the principal cities: Odessa (42 percent), Kharkiv (47 percent), Donetsk (51 percent), and Dnipropetrovsk (59 percent); they were better

Table 5.5

Ethnic Composition of Urban Population: Ukraine, West, Central West, East, and South, 1959 and 1970

	1959	%	1970	%	Percentage Change, 1959–1970
Ukraine	19,147,419	100.0	25,688,560	100.0	34.2
Ukrainians	11,781,750	61.5	16,164,254	62.9	37.2
unassimilated	9,973,430	84.7	13,388,207	82.8	34.2
assimilated	1,802,510	15.3	2,771,002	17.1	53.7
Russians	5,726,476	29.9	7,712,277	30.0	34.7
West	2,107,144	100.0	3,009,274	100.0	42.8
Ukrainians	1,500,102	71.2	2,329,350	77.4	55.3
unassimilated	1,437,853	95.9	2,261,887	97.1	57.3
assimilated	57,447	3.8	62,500	2.7	8.8
Russians	348,210	16.5	411,119	13.7	18.1
Central West	3,328,307	100.0	4,931,518	100.0	48.2
Ukrainians	2,340,673	70.3	3,668,765	74.4	56.7
unassimilated	2,049,511	87.6	3,304,330	90.1	61.2
assimilated	290,928	12.4	364,214	9.9	25.2
Russians	559,929	16.8	812,484	16.5	45.1
East and South	13,711,968	100.0	17,747,768	100.0	29.4
Ukrainians	7,940,975	57.9	10,166,139	57.3	28.0
unassimilated	6,486,066	81.7	7,821,990	76.9	20.6
assimilated	1,454,135	18.3	2,344,288	23.1	61.2
Russians	4,818,337	35.1	6,488,674	36.6	34.7

represented in the smaller towns, hence their regional totals were higher than those in the centers.[16] The population of the Central West had a Ukrainian share of 71.2 percent; Kyiv itself reported 60.1 percent (an impressive gain over the 1926 figure). In the West, there was a Ukrainian majority in Lviv (60 percent); and an even higher one in the cities of Ternopil, Lutsk, Rivne, and Ivano-Frankivsk, a plurality in Chernivtsi, and in Uzhhorod Ukrainians accounted for 50 percent of the population.[17]

By 1970, the year of the next census, Ukrainians had slightly increased their 1959 majority from 61.5 to 62.9 percent. Considering that the urban population grew by more than one-third, mostly through migration, one has to conclude that there was either an inordinately large inflow of Russians into Ukraine or widespread assimilation of Ukrainians into the Russian nationality. At any rate, the Ukrainian component of the urban population increased at a rate barely above the average and in the East and South fell somewhat below the average. (See table 5.5.)

Focusing on the oblasts where regional centers are located, we note that Ukrainians suffered a relative decline in the cities of Donetsk, Kharkiv, and Dnipropetrovsk; they improved their position in the oblast of Odessa without, however, achieving a majority there; and they registered substantial growth in Kyiv (city and oblast combined) and Lviv (table 5.6). [At the time this article was written the national composition of individual cities for 1970 had not been disclosed, except for Kyiv.]

Perhaps more important and in the long run more threatening to Ukrainian survival in the cities was the disclosure that among Ukrainians, the number of Russian-speakers was increasing more rapidly than the number of those declaring Ukrainian as their mother tongue. (Again, this suggests a high degree of linguistic assimilation, which some scholars consider a transitional stage toward a change in ethnic self-identification.) From 1959 to 1970 the former increased by 53.4 percent, the latter by 34.2 percent. In the West (especially) and Central West, the proportions were reversed. In the eastern and southern regions, however, it was clear that urban Ukrainians were becoming Russified linguistically on a mass scale: Those assimilated increased at a rate three times higher than those who retained the Ukrainian language. In the oblasts of Donetsk and Voroshylovhrad (Donbas) there was actually an

Table 5.6

Ukrainians and Russians in Urban Population of Six Oblasts (in percentages)

	Ukrainians			Russians		
Oblast	1959	1970	Percentage Change, 1959–1970	1959	1970	Percentage Change, 1959–1970
Donetsk	52.0	50.0	12.3	41.5	43.9	23.8
Odessa	44.0	47.5	50.5	35.7	35.6	38.9
Kharkiv	60.8	59.8	22.4	32.0	34.2	32.9
Dnipropetrovsk	71.5	69.3	30.0	22.0	25.2	54.0
Kyiv (city, oblast)	66.2	69.8	55.8	20.2	20.3	48.1
Lviv	70.1	76.5	52.8	20.6	16.8	14.3
Ukraine	61.5	62.9	37.2	29.9	30.0	34.7

absolute, not merely a relative, decline in the number of Ukrainians who considered Ukrainian as their native language; simultaneously the total urban population of the region increased by almost 17 percent (table 5.7).

A question arises: Since the Donbas basin is also the most highly urbanized region of Ukraine (see table 5.3), will urbanization elsewhere in the republic be accompanied by a similarly intensive linguistic assimilation of Ukrainians? The answer, it seems, depends on which parts of Ukraine are involved. The rates registered for the oblasts of Kharkiv, Dnipropetrovsk, and Odessa from 1959 to 1970 are presented in table 5.8.

In Kharkiv, from 1959 to 1970, assimilated Ukrainians grew 3.7

Table 5.7

Urban Ukrainians in the Donbas Basin (by native language), 1959–1970

	1959	%	1970	%	Percentage Change, 1959–1970
Donetsk	3,656,240	100.0	4,275,596	100.0	16.9
Ukrainians	1,902,583	52.0	2,137,010	50.0	12.3
unassimilated	1,425,590	74.9	1,398,651	65.4	−1.9
assimilated	476,817	25.1	738,182	34.5	54.8
Voroshylovhrad	1,944,633	100.0	2,270,884	100.0	16.8
Ukrainians	1,031,116	53.0	1,159,020	51.0	12.4
unassimilated	862,994	83.7	843,179	72.7	−2.3
assimilated	168,036	16.3	315,748	27.2	87.9

Table 5.8

Ukrainian Urban Population in the Oblasts of Kharkiv, Odessa, and Dnipropetrovsk: Percentage Rates of Change, 1959–1970

	Kharkiv	*Odessa*	*Dnipropetrovsk*
Urban Ukrainians	22.4	50.5	30.0
unassimilated	14.7	47.2	25.7
assimilated	54.7	58.0	66.1

times faster than those who considered Ukrainian their native language. In Dnipropetrovsk, the former increased 2.5 times as fast, but in Odessa the rate was much slower, at 1.3, perhaps because of the rapid growth of the Ukrainian urban population in that oblast (50.5 percent), compared with a 30 percent increase in Dnipropetrovsk, 22.4 percent in Kharkiv and even lower rates in the Donbas basin. One may further surmise that the migrants in Odessa were coming from less assimilated areas of Ukraine, such as the Central West or West. These figures confirm the strong assimilationist currents in the South and East, but they also suggest that the Donbas basin represents an extreme case.

We have yet, however, to find data that would positively disprove the example of the Donbas basin as a trendsetter in the urban development of the Ukrainians. The case of Lviv may provide such evidence (table 5.9). In Lviv the situation was dramatically reversed: The increase in the numbers of nonassimilated urban Ukrainians exceeded that of Russified Ukrainians by twenty times. If official statistics are to be believed, the cities of Lviv oblast were less Russified linguistically in 1970 than they had been in 1959.

To forecast the likely course of linguistic assimilation in those parts of Ukraine lying outside the zone that we designated as "South and East," one should turn to Kyiv. Let us look at the urban population of Kyiv oblast together with that of the city itself. (As Kyiv is the capital of the republic, information about the city is more readily available than is the case with other cities of Ukraine.) We note that Ukrainians increased in Kyiv and in the urban population of Kyiv oblast at a higher rate than the total average; also, that those Ukrainians who declared Ukrainian as their native language increased twice as fast as those who preferred

Table 5.9

Urban Ukrainians in Lviv Oblast (by native language), 1959–1970

	1959	%	1970	%	Percentage Change, 1959–1970
Lviv	821,338	100.0	1,148,649	100.0	39.9
Ukrainians	575,377	70.1	878,998	76.5	52.8
unassimilated	545,128	94.7	848,228	96.5	55.6
assimilated	29,742	5.2	30,505	3.5	2.6

Russian. In consequence, by 1970, the proportion of Ukrainians, and among them those who declared Ukrainian as their mother tongue, was higher than in 1959. By disaggregating the data on Kyiv oblast from the combined figures in table 5.10, we discover that in the towns of the oblast the total population increased by 47.6 percent, Ukrainians by 49.6, including Ukrainian-speakers by 50.0 and Russian-speakers by 38.3 percent. (The Russian urban population outside Kyiv increased by 53.4 percent, which exceeded the Ukrainian total.) Table 5.11 presents data for the city of Kyiv itself. This summary also includes data on the Russian segment of Kyiv's population in order to compare the position of both principal nationalities in the Ukrainian capital.

In the city of Kyiv, the Ukrainians were more Russified linguistically in 1959 than the "provincials." This is not surprising: We saw in the South and East that the larger a city is, the greater is its Russian population and the higher the proportion of assimilated Ukrainians. But by

Table 5.10

Urban Ukrainians in Kyiv Oblast (including the city of Kyiv), 1959–1970

	1959	%	1970	%	Percentage Change, 1959–1970
Kyiv	1,547,907	100.0	2,286,725	100.0	47.7
Ukrainians	1,023,925	66.1	1,595,564	69.8	55.8
unassimilated	826,350	80.7	1,341,429	84.1	62.3
assimilated	197,575	19.3	254,135	15.9	28.6

Table 5.11

Ukrainians and Russians in the City of Kyiv, 1959–1970

	1959	%	1970	%	Percentage Change, 1959–1970
Kyiv	1,104,334	100.0	1,631,908	100.0	47.8
Ukrainians	663,851	60.1	1,056,905	64.8	59.2
unassimilated	477,492	71.9	818,315	77.4	71.4
assimilated	186,276	28.1	238,507	22.6	28.0
Russians	254,269	23.0	373,569	22.9	46.9

1970 something rather unexpected had happened in Kyiv: Ukrainian speakers emerged as the fastest growing segment of the city's population in the intercensal period. Those assimilated Ukrainians maintained a rate of growth somewhere near 40 percent of that of the nonassimilated. Moreover, Ukrainians increased faster than did Russians and by 1970 Kyiv had not only a Ukrainian majority—it had acquired this by 1959— but also a Ukrainian-speaking majority or, to be more precise, a majority that had declared to the census takers that they considered Ukrainian to be their first language. (Besides 77.4 percent of the Ukrainians, self-declared Ukrainian-speakers included 9,000 non-Ukrainians, mostly Russians, Poles, and Jews.)

How is one to explain this development, which differs so significantly from the tendency prevailing in the East and South? Of the several explanations that come to mind, two appear most sound. One is that both Kyiv and Lviv had experienced especially marked population displacement during the war and thus their population underwent a more fundamental change than the rates of growth would indicate (see table 5.12). Lviv lost its Jewish and Polish citizens and although it had a Russian in-migration after 1944, this was not large enough to prevent the city from adopting a definitely Ukrainian—new Ukrainian—appearance. Kyiv also suffered heavy population losses in the war and seems to have drawn heavily on the Ukrainian countryside for its post-1945 growth. In this respect the situation after 1945, including the intercensal period of 1959 to 1970, was very different from that before 1939, when the fastest-growing cities were located in the East and when the population growth could not draw on migration from the western regions of Ukraine (at that time located in Poland, Romania, and Czechoslovakia). Iu. I. Pitiurenko has compiled a statistical table estimating the volume of migration to the cities, cited in table 5.12.[18] We have adapted his data to produce table 5.13.

Since 1945, in contrast to the prewar period when its growth rates were rivaled and even surpassed by Kharkiv and Donetsk, Kyiv has maintained a migration-based growth rate larger by far than any of its competitors for the status of the primate city in Ukraine. This may in turn have been due to such geopolitical factors as the westward expansion of the Ukrainian SSR, which opened up a densely populated hinterland, to the improved security after the establishment of socialist states in East-Central Europe, and, last but not least, to Kyiv's role as the Ukrainian capital. (We remember that Kyiv did not become the capital

Table 5.12
Population of Supraregional (Inter-oblast) Centers in Ukraine, 1939–77

Rank in 1939	City	1939 (000)	As percentage of largest	1959 (000)	As percentage of largest	1970	As percentage of largest	1977	As percentage of largest	Percentage Change			
										1939–1959	1959–1970	1970–1977	1939–1977
1	Kyiv	851	100.0	1,110	100.0	1,632	100.0	2,079	100.0	30.4	47.0	27.4	144.3
2	Kharkiv	840	98.7	953	85.9	1,223	74.9	1,405	67.6	13.5	28.3	14.9	67.3
3	Odessa	599	70.4	664	59.8	892	54.7	1,039	50.0	10.9	34.3	16.5	73.5
4	Dnipropetrovsk	528	62.0	661	59.5	862	52.8	995	47.9	25.2	30.4	15.4	88.4
5	Donetsk	474	55.7	708	63.8	- 879	53.9	984	47.3	49.4	24.2	11.9	107.6
6	Lviv	340	40.0	411	37.0	553	33.9	642	30.9	20.9	34.5	16.1	88.8
7	Zaporizhia	289	34.0	449	40.5	658	40.3	772	37.1	55.4	46.5	17.3	167.1
11	Kryvyi Rih	192	22.6	401	36.1	573	35.1	641	30.8	108.9	42.9	11.9	233.9

Table 5.13

Population Increase Due to In-Migration in Selected
Ukrainian Cities, 1926–1939 and 1959–1970 (in thousands)

	1926–1939	Annual Increase	1959–1970	Annual Increase
Dnipropetrovsk	294	22.6	203	18.4
Donetsk	360	27.7	180	14.5
Kharkiv	416	32.0	289	26.3
Kyiv	333	25.6	528	48.0
Lviv	—	—	142	12.9
Odessa	181	13.9	225	20.5

of the Ukrainian SSR until 1934. Had all those bureaucrats, apparat-chiks, media people, and so on, who customarily live and work in the capitals, not moved from Kharkiv to Kyiv between 1934 and 1939, Kharkiv would have been the largest city of Ukraine in 1939.)

Besides the administrative aspect of city-building, one might distinguish a more clearly national contributory element in the rise of Kyiv. V. V. Pokshishevsky has noted that certain cities of the Soviet Union have become "the centers of national culture and ethnic consciousness."[19] For Ukrainians, Kyiv has been such a city: It houses the most important research institutes, publishing houses, libraries, editorial boards of journals, and theater companies. Such institutions are to be found also in Lviv (although on a smaller scale, especially insofar as the press and publishing are concerned), but much less so in Donetsk or even Kharkiv. The cities in the East and South are mainly industrial and transportation centers, as well as seats of research and teaching in technology and science. For political reasons, work in the latter fields is carried out in the Russian language. Thus in contemporary Ukraine only two cities are both large and (relatively) Ukrainian—Kyiv and Lviv. Of these two the more important is Kyiv, since Lviv cannot aspire to national leadership. (In 1569, when Kyiv and Lviv found themselves within one polity, Lviv appears to have been the more important; but it was also the larger then.) To what degree is Kyiv the primate city of Ukraine in terms of urban hierarchy, not just as an administrative center?

Table 5.14 applies Mark Jefferson's index of primacy—a ratio of

Table 5.14

Primacy Index for Ukraine

	1939	1959	1970	1977
Kyiv	100	100	100	100
Kharkiv and Odessa	169	150	130	118

population of the largest city to the combined population of the second and third cities in a given country or region—to Ukraine. The results suggest, first, that Kyiv still does not possess a commanding lead over its immediate rivals and, second, that its relative position has nonetheless been improving throughout the entire period under discussion. (In 1939 four cities of Ukraine were more than half Kyiv's size; in 1977 only Kharkiv remained so, and Odessa was only half the size of Kyiv.)

Some scholars believe that Kyiv is too small to be the central city of Ukraine. Chauncy Harris believes that in 1959 Kyiv was "only about a third as large as would be expected from the network of 301 cities and towns of more than 10,000 population in the Ukraine."[20] Peter Woroby, on different grounds, also concludes that Kyiv is undersized.[21] Russell B. Adams, in his classification of the Soviet Union's regions, divides Ukraine into two major regions: one centered in Kyiv (including Odessa and Lviv), the other based in Kharkiv and consisting of the industrial eastern and southern parts of Ukraine.[22] On the basis of the 1959 census, Harris divided Ukraine into five urban-network regions (Kyiv, Kharkiv, Donetsk, Odessa, and Dnipropetrovsk).[23] David J. M. Hooson seems to have taken the most affirmative view of Kyiv's rise to preeminence in Ukraine:

> The regaining of Kiev's capital function in 1934 has ensured a steady growth, in spite of its destruction during the War. It is a minor edition of Moscow in some ways. . . . Its industrial structure is well balanced. . . . Its historical significance in the Russian nationality, State and Church make it something more than a politico-regional center for the Ukraine. Kharkov may conceivably grow larger, but cannot now challenge Kiev's pre-eminent position, anymore than Milan can supplant Rome as capital of the Italian state.[24]

Conclusions

This writer does not consider himself competent to evaluate the processes of urbanization in postwar Ukraine from the point of view of demography, geography, economics, or urban studies. As a political historian he is interested to discover that after 1945 the Ukrainians appeared in the cities of Ukraine in numbers large enough to make it possible to modify that old distinction between "Ukrainian/village/West" and "Russian/urban/East." The East has clearly remained Russian, but the West, including the "Central West," has become more urban and more Ukrainian in its urban component. This outcome has to be connected with the territorial unification of the Ukrainian nation during the Second World War. Secondly, a historian notes the rise of Kyiv to a position of primacy (even if precise definitions of what constitutes primacy may be lacking) and he connects this with the westward shift of the Ukrainian SSR. He observes with interest the reemergence of the Lviv-Kyiv axis in Ukrainian life—after a 300-year break. Finally, the example of Kyiv and Lviv suggests that it may be possible even under the political conditions now prevailing in the USSR to emancipate the Ukrainians from the status of "younger brother" to the Russians: Certain parts of Ukraine are both urbanized and remain loyal to the Ukrainian language. It might be argued that the contemporary phenomenon of dissent in Ukraine is a result of this fact. Our discussion suggests that behind the individual figures representing that phenomenon there may well exist a sizable constituency of socially mobilized (urbanized) but linguistically nonassimilated people.

Notes

1. See *Ukraine: A Concise Encyclopaedia*, ed., Volodymyr Kubijovyč, 2 vols. (Toronto: University of Toronto Press, 1963–71), 1: 200–207; V. Kubiiovych [Kubijovyč], "Natsional'nyi sklad naselennia Radianskoï Ukraïny v svitli sovetskykh perepysiv naselennia z 17.12.1926 i 15.1.1959," offprint from *Zbirnyk prysviachenyi pamiati Z. Kuzeli* (Paris, 1962) (*Zapysky NTSh* 169); and S. G. Prociuk, "Human Losses in the Ukraine in World War I and II," *The Annals of the Ukrainian Academy of Arts and Sciences in the United States* 13, no. 35–36 (1973–77): 23–50.

2. V. I. Kozlov, *Natsional'nosti SSSR (Etnodemograficheskii obzor)* (Moscow, 1975), p. 109. I am grateful to Bohdan Krawchenko, Canadian Institute of Ukrainian Studies, for drawing my attention to this item of information in Kozlov's book. According to Professor Krawchenko, this is the first published disclosure of the ethnic composition of the Ukrainian SSR in 1939.

3. *Itogi vsesoiuznoi perepisi naseleniia 1959 goda. Ukrainskaia SSR* (Moscow: Gosstatizdat, 1963), Table 53; Kozlov, *Natsional'nosti*, p. 109; and Kubiiovych, "Natsionalnyi sklad," p. 6.

4. *Ukraine: Encyclopaedia*, 1: 212.

5. Calculated by this writer from *Itogi 1959*, Table 54; for a breakdown by historic regions (such as Volhynia and Galicia), see *Ukraine: Encyclopedia*, 1: 219. The ethnic composition of Western Ukraine by oblasts (in 1930 and 1970) is given by Yaroslav Bilinsky, "The Incorporation of Western Ukraine and its Impact on Politics and Society in Soviet Ukraine," in Roman Szporluk, ed., *The Influence of East Europe and the Soviet West on the USSR* (New York, Praeger 1976), p. 204.

6. Kubiiovych, "Natsional'nyi sklad," p. 6, and *Ukraine: Encyclopaedia*, 1: 216. For the occupational breakdown of the Ukrainians, Russians, Jews, and Poles in prewar Ukraine (Soviet and Western), see *Ukraine*, 1: 174–75.

7. Calculated by this writer from *Itogi 1959*.

8. *Itogi 1959*, Table 6; see also *Narodnoe khoziaistvo SSSR za 60 let. Iubileinyi statisticheskii sbornik* (Moscow: Statistika, 1977), pp. 59–68, for a listing of all Soviet cities with a population of 50,000 and above in 1939, 1959, 1970, and 1977. All figures given here are rounded off to the nearest thousand. (This source will be cited later as *Nar. khoz. 1977.)*

9. Mark Jefferson, "The Law of the Primate City," *Geographical Review* 29 (1939): 227 and 231.

10. Ibid., p. 228.

11. *Itogi 1959*, Table 1.

12. John A. Armstrong, "The Ethnic Scene in the Soviet Union," in Erich Goldhagen, ed., *Ethnic Minorities in the Soviet Union* (New York: Praeger, 1968), pp. 14–15. See also my own discussion of Ukrainian-Russian relations in "Russians in Ukraine," in Peter J. Potichnyj, ed., *Ukraine in the Seventies* (Oakville, Ont.: Mosaic Press, 1975), pp. 195–217. (Included as chapter 3 of this book.)

13. Armstrong, "Ethnic Scene," p. 15.

14. For a comprehensive treatment of urbanization in Ukraine, see Peter Woroby, "Effects of Urbanization in the Ukraine," *The Annals of the Ukrainian Academy of Arts and Sciences in the United States* 13, no. 35–36 (1973–77): 51–115.

15. *Nar. khoz. 1977*, pp. 59–68.

16. V. I. Naulko, *Karta suchasnoho etnichnoho skladu naselennia Ukrainskoi RSR* (Kyiv: Naukovo dumka, 1966).

17. Figures in Bilinsky, "Incorporation," p. 207.

18. Pitiurenko has an interesting classification of Ukrainian cities in terms of their functions. He places Kyiv in a special category and then in the class of oblast centers, which he terms "multifunctional cities," he distinguishes a group of multifunctional centers of supraregional importance. These supraregional centers are Kharkiv, Dnipropetrovsk, Odessa, Donetsk, and Lviv. See Iu. I. Pitiurenko, *Rozvytok mist i mis'ke rozselennia v Ukrainskiï RSR* (Kyiv, 1972), pp. 80–81.

19. V. V. Pokshishevsky, "Urbanization and Ethnodemographic Processes," *Soviet Geography* 13, no. 2 (February 1972): 116. More recently Pokshishevsky has written on the role of ethnic composition as a factor in the rise of the service sector in the cities. See "Differences in the Geography of Services and the Characteristics of Political Structure," *Soviet Geography* 16, no. 6 (June 1975): esp. 359–64.

20. Chauncy D. Harris, *Cities of the Soviet Union: Studies in Their Functions, Size, Density, and Growth* (Chicago: Rand McNally, 1970), pp. 134–35.

21. Woroby, "Effects of Urbanization," p. 113. He notes, however, an improvement in the rank of Kyiv between 1959 and 1970 (p. 114).

22. Russell B. Adams, "The Soviet Metropolitan Hierarchy: Regionalization and Comparison with the United States," *Soviet Geography* 18, no. 5 (May 1977): 314–15 and ff.

23. Harris, *Cities*, p. 135.

24. David J. M. Hooson, *The Soviet Union: People and Regions* (Belmont, Calif.: Wadsworth, 1966), p. 163. This was confirmed by the preliminary results of the 1979 census, which were published when this work was in press. Kyiv further strengthened its leading position among Ukrainian cities (it had 2.144 million inhabitants compared with Kharkiv's 1.444 million and Dnipropetrovsk's 1.066 million), and the Ukrainian share in its population rose to 68.7 percent even though in Ukraine as a whole the number of Ukrainians dropped from 74.9 percent in 1970 to 73.6 in 1979. See Roman Solchanyk's analyses: "The Ukraine and Ukrainians in the USSR: Nationality and Language Aspects of the Census of 1979," *Radio Liberty Research*, no. 100/80, March 11, 1980, and "The Ukrainization of Kiev Continues: Partial Results of the 1979 Census," *Radio Liberty Research*, no. 68/80, February 15, 1980.

6   History and Russian Nationalism

The Soviet Union is a multinational state and of all its nationality problems that of the Russians is the most important, as they are the largest and most powerful national group. The resurgent interest in Russian history, which is characteristic of Russian nationalism today, has import for the Soviet political and ethnic situation corresponding to the role Russia plays in the USSR. Russian nationalism is concerned with two basic issues: First, the relationship between the Russian nation and the Soviet regime and, second, the position of the Russians among the nations of the USSR. On both these issues Russian nationalist thinking has been developing its point of view by reference to history.

Although such distinctions involve an oversimplification of individual positions, this article argues that Russian nationalist opinion, insofar as it is concerned with historical problems, divides into two currents. One current conceives of Russian nationality as basically cultural or spiritual in nature. It attaches fundamental importance to the language, literature, ancestral homelands (soil) and religion, as markers of Russian identity, and it tends to judge politics—the state—in terms of its conformity to these nonpolitical dimensions of Russian nationhood. We will try to show that some, but by no means all, conceptions of Russian history inspired by this position result in a political challenge to the

First published in *Survey*, 1979.

Soviet system, or even in a denial of its legitimacy. To some, the Soviet regime, because it is based on Marxism-Leninism, is "un-Russian."

The second current in Russian nationalist thought sees Russian history as an essentially political process, as the history of the Russian state, which it views as the most genuine expression of the Russian nation.[1] On the whole, those who share this position treat the Soviet regime as a continuation of the old Russian state, including its immediate predecessor, the Romanov empire, and they believe that the uniquely Russian genius has created a political form of government that is opposed to western, liberal and democratic, political systems. They are less interested in ideologies *per se*, which they judge from the point of view of their usefulness to the state. Since their approval of the Soviet regime is based on their recognition of it as a Russian institution, the challenge which this current of nationalism now poses is directed against the federal structure of the USSR, the principle of equality of the nations of the USSR, and not against the party in power. The former, or "culturalist," current attacks the regime as un-Russian, but this one, which we might call "statist," directs its attack against the non-Russian nationalities by advocating the transformation of the USSR into a centralized Russian nation-state which would officially be called Russia.

To understand these two challenges to official ideology it is necessary to place them in historical perspective, against the background of Soviet history since 1917. So viewed, they appear to be critiques of the Stalinist historical ideology that was consolidated in the 1930s and has essentially been retained up to the present time.

First let us ask ourselves whether historical ideas really are politically important. This is a big topic which cannot be discussed here in a way that would do it justice.[2] Instead, we shall dispose of the issue by means of quotations from two very prominent, but also very different, authorities. One, Karl Deutsch, writes:

> . . . autonomy in the long run depends on memory. Where all memory is lost, where all past information and preferences have ceased to be effective, we are no longer dealing with a self-determining individual or social group, but with a self-steering automaton. . . . There is no will, no conation, without some operating memory.[3]

The other, Alexander Solzhenitsyn, speaks about literature but it is clear that his words also apply to historical writing:

There is one . . . invaluable direction in which literature transmits incontrovertible condensed experience: from generation to generation. In this way literature becomes the living memory of a nation. . . . woe to that nation whose literature is cut short by the intrusion of force. This is not merely interference with "freedom of the press" but the sealing up of a nation's heart, the excision of its memory. A nation can no longer remember itself, it loses its spiritual unity, and despite their seemingly common language, countrymen cease to understand one another.[4]

The emergence of unorthodox historical ideas in the post-Stalinist USSR is one aspect of the broader process of the rise of social and political thought, the formation of ideas expressing the points of view of diverse social, including ethnic, groups. According to Deutsch, "The development of separate memories and memory facilities [for this is what the emergence of uncontrolled historical views is—RS] . . . may represent . . . aspects of the process of secession."[5] In our case, we are dealing with "secession" from Stalinism.

The Stalinist historical conception was imposed on historians in the Soviet Union after a period that may be described as "internationalist" or, perhaps more accurately, "antinationalist." Although Marxism considers class, not nation, the primary form of social tie, its followers did not develop a conception of history as a history of classes and class struggles; such a history, one would have thought, would treat nations and states as important but subordinate phenomena in a class history; naturally, it would be a history transcending narrow geographic, not to mention ethnic, boundaries. Since the Bolsheviks took power in Russia in the name of the world proletariat, claiming to be only its advance guard, it would have made sense from their point of view to develop an appropriate large-scale view of history. In such a history, the "precursors" of modern socialism, especially its Bolshevik incarnation, would be Spartacus, Wat Tyler, Jan Hus, Thomas Münzer, various radical religious reformers, peasant rebels, and so on. They would also be Russian revolutionaries, of course, but the history that the first Socialist state on earth would regard as its own would not be any one nation's history.[6]

Indeed, immediately after 1917 universalisn was in vogue, and Spartacus and the Communards, not to mention Rosa Luxemburg or Karl Liebknecht, became household (or perhaps communal apartment) names. No new history was formed, however; in place of "Russian history" a "history of the peoples of the USSR" was introduced.[7] In practice, in the largest and most powerful of the republics, the RSFSR, a new name covered the same old subject, a history of Russia. (In the other republics, but not in Russia, in addition to a common history of the peoples, national histories were also written.) It became, however, "anti-history" in relation to what it replaced: The heroes of tsarist text-books—tsars, generals, saints—were its villains; the outcasts of the old (the Pugachevs, the Razins, the Shamils) were now transformed into heroes. This "anti-history" pictured the tsarist state as a class exploiter and as a conqueror and oppressor of the non-Russian nationalities. Implicit in the conception of a "history of the peoples of the USSR" was the idea that before 1917 they were united by common oppression; no positive value was attached to any nationality's inclusion under tsarist rule. The Soviet Union as a multinational state was seen as a product of the 1917 Revolution and its aftermath, not as in any way a continuation of a "unity" that had been formed earlier, in however rudimentary a form. October represented a new opening, an initial step toward a wider international community, a transformed Russian Empire that had become the USSR.

This historical formula provided a framework for the study of pre-revolutionary history at a time when the USSR was still seen as a way station toward a wider international community that would emerge as the revolution spread to other countries of Europe and Asia. Its emphasis on the negative aspects of the prerevolutionary association of the non-Russian peoples with Russia was useful to the Soviet regime because it provided such a contrast to the liberal linguistic and cultural policies of the 1920s.

As the hopes of a world revolution began to recede, however, and Soviet domestic policies turned toward centralization, with a corresponding decrease in cultural and administrative autonomy for the nationalities, attacks on prerevolutionary Russian history ceased to be useful (we hardly need to mention that these changes took place against the background of the first five-year plan, with rapid industrialization and collectivization). It was now accepted that the Soviet Union as a state with a predominant Russian element was there to stay, and its continuity with the Russian Empire became clearer. As the nationalities began to suffer under the new Soviet policy, a new historical interpretation was developed to show that under tsarism things had not been so bad after all. "Soviet patriotism" became the legitimizing device for this postponement of the coming of a world Soviet state; "friendship of the peoples" was a retroactive application of this formula to the period of tsarist Russia.[8] As the USSR under Stalin was building "socialism in one country," so its new history was constructed as a history of peoples who allegedly had a common country in the past.

This new historical view re-examined the record of tsarist Russia and discovered that besides being an exploiter of the toiling masses the Russian state (the word "tsarist" was avoided here) had also played a "progressive" role: It had defended the Russian people and the other peoples of Russia from foreign invaders. In most cases, therefore, its wars had been "just." Gradually, the official historians stopped referring to Russian tsarist conquests and explained the rise of the Russian Empire as a product of a series of voluntary "unions," "reunions" and "extensions." Even if tsarism was not exactly the best conceivable form of government, the non-Russian peoples were better off under it than they would have been had they come under Polish, Turkish, Persian, or British rule. In the case of the Estonians, for instance, the idea was clearly being promoted that Russian rule was somehow less foreign than the Swedish or German rule of former times. The "rehabilitation" of the Russian state meant the restoration to national glory of the various tsars, generals, and diplomats who had previously been condemned as oppressors. The peoples of the Caucasus were told to admire their conqueror, General Yermolov, and in Stalin's time even the Poles were required to celebrate the anniversaries of General Suvorov, whom they remembered from their pre-Stalinist history as the commander whose troops had massacred the population of Warsaw and suppressed a Polish national uprising in 1794.

Old Russian culture was also re-evaluated. Even those prominent artists of the pre-Soviet period who had displayed no "progressive" inclinations, had belonged to the ruling classes, and served the tsars, were now accepted as Russian figures and were extolled as the teachers and inspirers of their junior colleagues among the non-Russians.

Although this return to Russian preeminence only took place in the 1930s, some anticommunist Russians, at home and abroad, detected signs of what they called the "Nationalization of October," to cite the title of an article by N. V. Ustrialov written in the 1920s. They were prepared to support the Soviet Union because it was a Russian state, even though they disapproved of its political and economic policies and goals. What they valued most was the Soviet government's success in basically preserving the territorial unity of old Russia. Ustrialov did not care about the name of the state—he thought it was a camouflage—and welcomed the emergence of what he called the new "Soviet state nation." He understood by this term a multiethnic community of the peoples of the USSR who were politically integrated in the USSR "in a Russian national form." He was not concerned with the rights of the nationalities in education or culture; what mattered was the Russian character of the state.[9]

An overwhelming majority of Russian émigrés did not accept Ustrialov's argument. They objected to Soviet communism for political, cultural, and religious reasons. Many correctly perceived that Stalinism did not mark the return to an unqualified Russian orientation. Indeed, Soviet nationalism, as Frederick C. Barghoorn noted over twenty years ago, never was "a purely 'Russian' product." It was more an ideology that manipulated both Russian symbols and those of Marxism. This combination of a national Russian culture with the universalist ideology of Marxism contained an element of contradiction. Besides, the commitment on the part of the regime to Russian nationalism was not fully "sincere": It did not accept such elements of traditional Russian culture as the Orthodox religion. Barghoorn argued that tension between government and people would exist as long as the Soviet system remained totalitarian and that the Soviet population felt that "the government and the people do not really speak the same language." Soviet patriotism helped to conceal the internal contradictions of Soviet society under "familiar, vague and emotionally moving" words. In 1956, Barghoorn speculated that "non-official thought" existed in Russia, although one could only guess at its context.[10]

Even though Stalin gave a privileged position to the Russian nation, history, language, and culture in the USSR, he preserved the formal structure of the state as a multinational federation in which Russia, under the name of the RSFSR, was simply one constituent republic, formally an equal of Ukraine, Georgia, and others. Ideologically, the Soviet regime claimed to derive its legitimacy from its allegiance to Marxism-Leninism. It was known abroad, and wanted to be so known, as the first socialist state, the fatherland of the workers of all countries. Its use of Russian symbols was manipulative and selective, and Russian culture was subjected to strict ideological and political controls. Stalin promoted Russification but he did not publicly affirm a Russian character for the Soviet Union, and he virtually obliterated a separate identity of the RSFSR within a broader concept of the Soviet Union (Soviet people, Soviet patriotism).

It was therefore natural that the first concessions to specifically Russian national feeling after Stalin's death found their expression in a revitalization of the Russian Republic, which recovered its separate governmental and public institutions, previously submerged under or blended with "all-Union" entities. There appeared specifically Russian (RSFSR) ministries, societies, publishing houses, and newspapers. In 1956, a newspaper called *Sovetskaia Rossiia* was founded as an organ of the CC Bureau for the RSFSR—itself a post-Stalinist innovation. This was the first newspaper in the Soviet Union for several decades to use the word "Russia" in its title.

Such "concessions" to Russian national feeling did not prevent the rise of Russian dissent any more than concessions in the non-Russian republics satisfied the aspirations of the Ukrainians, Lithuanians, or Armenians. This is not the place to trace the history of dissent and opposition in the Soviet Union after Stalin. For our purposes it is enough to note that in the general consensus of scholars there exists, among the various currents of dissent, a Russian nationalist current.[11]

As we suggested earlier, for the purposes of this particular investigation, Russian nationalist thought may be seen to be concerned with two issues. Needless to say, Russian nationalism is not a homogeneous movement and, moreover, Russian dissident opinion also includes explicitly nonnationalistic elements.[12]

One broad current, within which further subdivisions could be made, is concerned with Russian history as the history of the Russian nation that it defines in cultural terms. The history of Russia is the history of its art, architecture, literature, ideas, church, and religious thought. Its territorial core is located where the Great Russian nationality was formed. Relatively less importance is attached to the political organization of society, although such institutions as monarchy are recognized by at least some "culturalists" as part of the Russian heritage. (The monarchy itself is seen as a religious institution, to some extent: "the Orthodox tsar.") From a conception of history like this, a variety of political conclusions may be drawn that are of import today. Some people express concern about the preservation of Russian historical monuments. Some others believe that the works of Russian Orthodox theology should be made available, and that the Church should enjoy greater freedom. Yet others view the peasants of the central Russian provinces as the most authentic representatives of Russian nationality and demand that various social, economic, and cultural measures be taken to help them and the region in which they live. Still others—and we are entering now more dangerous political ground—question the ideological foundations of the Soviet state by arguing that Marxism-Leninism is a foreign, thus non-Russian, body, and should be replaced by an ideology that is "truly Russian." Finally, there are those who are prepared to go one step farther and advocate a violent overthrow of the Soviet regime and its replacement by a national regime.[13]

The "culturalist "position in its most extreme political form may be found in Solzhenitsyn. Among his many statements to this effect, the following might be considered representative:

> . . . the transition from pre-1917 Russia to the USSR is not a continuation but a mortal fracture of the spine, which almost destroyed Russia as a nation. The Soviet development is not a continuation of the Russian one but a distortion of it in a completely new, unnatural direction, inimical to the Russian people. . . . The terms "Russian" and "Soviet," "Russia" and "USSR," are not only not interchangeable, not equivalent, not part of the same order of ideas: They are irreconcilable opposites, they completely exclude each other, and to confuse them or use them wrongly is a gross error and a mark of slipshod thinking.[14]

While Solzhenitsyn was engaged in intellectual struggle with the Soviet regime and its ideology, there existed in Russia from 1964 to 1967 a secret organization that sought, as its ultimate goal, to overthrow communist rule and replace it by a system based on "Social-Christian" ideology. This organization called itself the All-Russian Social-Christian Union for the Liberation of the People.[15]

The conception of Russian identity upheld by the Union was cultural and ideological, not political or ethnic in the linguistic sense. It conceived of Russia as an Orthodox Christian nation, and it viewed this spiritual or cultural identity of the Russian nation as something taking precedence over its political organization. The legitimacy of the government, in its view, depended on the government's conformity to the spiritual character of the nation. Although the program of the Union promised that in a future Russia other religions would be allowed to preach and worship without hindrance, the Russia it hoped to establish was not going to be a secular state by any means. It would be a country with an official ideology and the leaders of the Orthodox Church would enjoy a political function within the state. (See articles 50 and 51 of their program, but compare them with articles 31 and 33, which declare the independence of the Church from the state and the rights of other "known" religions.)[16]

Indeed, at least some of the ideologues of the Union appear to think that a real Russian cannot but be a religious person. Evgeny Vagin is reported to have said over Radio Liberty:

> In relation to this quotation which you cited, whether a Russian can be an atheist, and to what extent the Russian nature is compatible with this: Yes, in this sense I share Dostoevsky's belief that to be Russian is to be Orthodox, and that religion is certainly the profound nature of the Russian person.[17]

One may further infer that the Union intended to follow its ideologically determined political conception in relations between Russia and other nations. Thus, article 83 offered Russian help to those nations where Soviet troops are now stationed "to initiate their own national self-determination on the basis of Social-Christianity." Is one to conclude that if those nations chose to determine their fate in some *other* form, they would not be helped? Insofar as Soviet internal nationality problems were concerned, the Union claimed to speak for all the nationalities of the USSR when it declared it was "a patriotic organization consisting of selfless representatives of all the nationalities of Great Russia" (article 73). The Union rejected the right to independence for Ukraine, Belorussia, and the smaller nationalities of the USSR, and one of its publicists maintains that Russia is by nature a multinational state.[18] Russian Social Christians seem to care very little about the status of the Catholic Lithuanians, Buddhist Kalmyks, or Moslem Uzbeks in a new Orthodox Russia they hope to see one day.

Although the All-Russian Social-Christian Union was suppressed by the authorities, John B. Dunlop considers that its ideas present the most serious challenge to the regime. He believes they will gain in influence in the future. Among the reasons for the appeal of the Union's ideology, according to him, are the comprehensiveness of its program as an alternative to the Soviet system, its preference for a "maximally bloodless revolutionary coup" as a means of winning power, and, finally, the personal heroism of its leader, Igor Ogurtsov.[19]

Indeed, ideas close to those of the Union have been presented in such samizdat publications as *Veche* (*Assembly*), *Zemlia* (*Land*), and *Moskovskii sbornik* (*Moscow Symposium*). These publications are not as uncompromisingly hostile to the government, but they base their conception of Russian nationhood on cultural (religious and spiritual) features and judge political problems through an ideological, "culturalist" prism.[20]

The other major grouping within Russian dissent may be given the name of "statism." While "culturalism" in any form contains an element of ideological dissent (its concern with Russian historical identity implies that the Marxist-Leninist doctrine is an inadequate tool for the comprehension of the richness of Russian culture), "statism" views ideology, Marxist or any other, instrumentally. Its classic spokesman in the 1920s, Ustrialov, was not in the least disturbed by Moscow's being the seat of the world communist movement. On the contrary, he regarded this internationalist, universal ideology and movement as an instrument in the policies of the Russian state. An identical sentiment was expressed by another anticommunist Russian in the 1920s: "The International will pass, but the boundaries will remain," wrote the émigré Vasily Shulgin in 1922, and he expressed essentially the same view in the 1950s and 1960s, when he was in the Soviet Union.[21]

Just like the "culturalists," the "statists" do not form a single current. One point of view within the "statist" orientation is represented by the authors of a document known as *Slovo natsii* ("A Word to the Nation"). According to Professor Pospielovsky, the authors of that manifesto

> . . . may be much more interested in a revitalized national centralized dictatorship, a sort of national Bolshevism of the Ustryalov type, than in Christianity *per se*. Their attitude to the Church may be purely instrumental, their view of it as an institution being of the Pobedonostsev type.[22]

Pospielovsky further argues:

> . . . they show themselves as opponents of the October Revolution, i.e., of Bolshevism-Communism, from beginning to end. But at the same time their insistence on the necessity of a strong centralized government, their acceptance of dictatorship as a system of government, their elitism, are such that it becomes difficult to see in what essentials they oppose the Soviet system. . . . What the group may be heading for is a

type of neo-Bolshevism, without Marx and Lenin, but with the Church as a moral instrument in the hands of a nationalist state.[23]

The document is racist and antisemitic (egalitarianism and cosmopolitanism are called "an ideology of the Jewish diaspora") and demands that Russians should play the dominant role in the multinational state in which they live. It definitely rejects federalism.[24] The "statist" school, then, sees the essence of Russian nationhood in the state as it developed in the course of Russian history: that is, a centralized, absolutist, multinational empire, opposed to western-style liberal and democratic societies, and dominated by the Great Russians.

Who are the contemporary "statists" in the USSR? What do they criticize, and what do they want to achieve?

The monthly journal *Molodaia gvardiia* (*Young Guard*), organ of the youth organization Komsomol, served as a vehicle of "statist" historical ideas in the years 1968–1970. Alexander Yanov has devoted a special chapter in his book on the Russian New Right to the ideology of "Young Guardism." He concludes that the journal, through the contributions of its leading authors (Lobanov, Chalmaev, Semanov), replaced the Marxist analysis of modern problems of the world in terms of classes and class conflicts with an approach based on a juxtaposition of "Russia" and "Russianness" to "Americanism." Lobanov's program, says Yanov, was to give the regime and its policies a more pronounced Russian character. For Chalmaev, "there is no gulf between Soviet and tsarist Russia." "From his point of view the October Revolution was only another stage in the maturing of the 'Russian spirit,' and by no means the epochal date of the birth of socialism . . . the actions of Ivan the Terrible . . . are just as important as those of Lenin—all of them alike led the 'national spirit' to feats on behalf of the state."[25]

Yanov believes that the ideologists of *Molodaia gvardiia* enjoyed considerable official support until the publication of the article by S. S. Semanov entitled "On Relative and Eternal Values." In that article Semanov not only described the October Revolution as the "Great Russian Revolution" and called it "our national achievement" but he unconditionally praised the Stalinist constitution of 1936, which, according to Semanov, introduced complete unity and equality among the people. The period of the late 1930s, moreover, was especially favorable to the development of culture, according to the same writer. In Yanov's view, this was such an open refutation of the line of the 20th Party

Congress that the regime had to intervene: The editor of *Molodaia gvardiia* was transferred to another post and the theoretical journal of the party, *Kommunist*, published a critique of the youth magazine's errors.[26]

Among the most significant articles published in *Molodaia gvardiia*, in addition to those by Lobanov, Chalmaev, and Semanov, one might include M. Alpatov's "Letter by a Historian to a Writer." One of its themes is the idea of Russia's superiority over the West, and its position as the "No. 1 country" (strana No. 1) in "the world camp of socialism"; another—the argument that Russia's particular claim to greatness lies in its having skipped the historical stage of "bourgeois democracy" and in its immunity to democratic socialism (*sotsial-demokratism*), the latter vice afflicting such countries as Czechoslovakia.[27] Thus, it is not any one state that the writers of *Molodaia gvardiia* approved of: The Stalinist regime of the 1930s (Semanov) was to their liking, they had good things to say about Ivan the Terrible, Peter I, even Nicholas I, but they were uniformly proud that Russia had managed to avoid the experience of western-style constitutional government.

To their credit, one has to note that both A. N. Sakharov and Semanov quite explicitly stated that they viewed critiques of the tsars, of Russia's past persecutions of the individual, absolutist abuse, and terror as indirect criticism of the Soviet system. (They diligently registered camouflaged critiques that had been published in *Novyi mir* and other less nationalistic periodicals.) They were thus providing independent confirmation of the argument that interest in Russian history has import for the Soviet political and ethnic situation.[28]

"Statist" ideas produced critical reaction not only in official circles, but also among non-nationalist dissidents, one of whom, R. B. Lert, published a scathing attack on Semanov. Her article, entitled "Traktat o prelestiakh knuta" ("A Treatise on the Charms of the Knout"), first appeared in the samizdat journal *Politicheskii dnevnik*, and was then reprinted in the West. Lert pointed out, very correctly, that Semanov, despite his words on the Russian people and Russian culture, did not care about either. What he did care for, however, was the idea of Russian Great Power (*velikoderzhavnost'*), and he praised Stalin because Stalin, while pretending to glorify the Russian people, had in fact rehabilitated Russian tsarism. Classifying the ideas of Semanov as chauvinism, Lert warned that great-power chauvinism provokes among smaller nations a negative reaction toward that nation on whose behalf "the Semanovs" presume to speak.[29] A similar warning, more camouflaged in form, appeared in the legal press in an article by Igor Kon, the learned Soviet philosopher and sociologist of liberal persuasion.[30] Semanov's, and other Young Guardist, ideas, interestingly enough, were noted in at least one communist country in Eastern Europe.[31]

In his stimulating work on the New Right in Russia, Yanov has devoted a chapter to the thought of Gennady Shimanov. From the vantage point of our discussion, Shimanov is another representative of "statist" nationalism. Shimanov argues that Russians are God's chosen people: It was for this reason that God sent great calamities on the Russian nation (Peter's reforms, the October 1917 revolution, the Gulag), but this was done in order to preserve and purify Russia.[32] In his political program, Shimanov advocates an "ideocratic state" (the ideology being a mixture of Russian Orthodoxy with Lenin), but the accent is on the state, not the specific content of ideas. He attacks Solzhenitsyn for his support of "the free flowering of ideas" in the future Russia. He is opposed in principle to freedom of thought and creative freedom.[33] Consistently, he condemns democracy. In Yanov's summary of Shimanov's conception of the good state

> . . . a state which is "not absolute," "not autocratic," which does not possess "a highly developed nervous system in the form of a Party which embraces the entire organism of society almost down to its smallest cell"—such a state is for Shimanov not a state at all! . . . The Soviet regime is good because it contains the potential of totalitarianism and is able to provide such control. . . . The state takes the place of God in this totalitarian utopia. . . .[34]

Although Shimanov considers Russia God's chosen nation, and although he advocates national isolationism—nations must not "have communion with foreigners when there is no need"—he upholds the idea of a Russian multinational empire. In Shimanov's words:

> The Soviet Union is not a mechanical conglomeration of nations of different kinds . . . but a MYSTICAL ORGANISM, composed of nations mutually supplementing each other and making up, under the leadership of the Russian people, a LITTLE MANKIND—the beginning and the spiritual detonator for the great mankind.[35]

Yanov concludes that in terms of practical politics "the Russian people is the only one which is permitted to have an *empire*." This empire would be closed and isolated from other nations until they in turn were ready to "speak with it in its own language."[36]

It is clear that it is "culturalism" in its extreme political form, whether as an ideological current represented by Solzhenitsyn or as an incipient political movement represented by the All-Russian Social-Christian Union, that poses the most serious danger to the regime because it denies its legitimacy and aims at its overthrow. It is another question, and one that cannot be discussed here, what degree of support this current enjoys among the Russian population.

On the other hand, "statism" as such is not dangerous to the regime's security, even though some of its implications may be disturbing to those elements in the establishment that have retained faith in the universal meaning of Marxism-Leninism. Thus, some found it offensive that "statists" have reduced the meaning of the October 1917 Revolution to the status of a Russian—albeit Great-National—revolution.[37] (But this "ranking," on the other hand, legitimizes Bolshevism in Russian nationalist terms: It thus helps to support the Soviet regime, whereas "culturalist" nationalism, viewing 1917 as an anti-Russian event, opposes Lenin and the revolution.) What "statism" proposes is to de-ideologize the system by making it less internationalist in outlook, and more firmly committed to Russian national goals. In this aspect the thrust of "statism" is directed against the non-Russian nationalities of the USSR, rather than against the regime in Moscow, the principal target of "culturalism." (At least some "culturalists" can face the prospect of secession by the non-Russians; not so the "statists," who believe in a Russian *empire*.)

One may surmise that the idea that the entire USSR, not just the RSFSR, is a country in which the Russians play a special role, is likely to win a sympathetic response among the Russian masses, who seem to be offended by the idea that they should learn the local languages when they decide to live outside Russia proper, and who feel threatened by the prospect of becoming a minority in consequence of the demographic growth of Central Asian peoples.[38] When Dunlop comments that it is "startling but true that many Russians today have the psychology of an oppressed minority,"[39] one is reminded of those English nationalists today, such as Enoch Powell, who complain of the takeover of their old country by "coloured" immigrants.[40] One should never underestimate the popular potential of a racially tinged nationalism.[41]

On a more elevated level, this "statism," drawing its support for

Russian hegemony from the argument that the USSR is but a continuation of the old Russian state, can count on support in the military establishment, whose many prominent figures have proudly declared that they see a continuity between tsarist Russia's and the Soviet Union's military and territorial foreign-policy goals. One such prominent figure is Admiral Isakov, whom Ivan Dziuba criticized in his exposé of Russification.[42] A recent Soviet work on the history of Russian-Finnish relations since 1713 presents in a consistently favorable light tsarism's foreign and military policies and its treatment of Finland, denies that tsarism attempted to Russify that nation, and condemns Finnish nationalism for its anti-Russian position before 1914.[43]

It is understandable, then, that both Yanov and Dunlop see the possibility of a rapprochement between the regime and Russian nationalism. "There is evidence," says Dunlop, "that elements in the Communist Party are attempting to direct Russian nationalist fervour into a neo-national-socialist direction. (As Mussolini's biography suggests, a journey from Communism to Fascism has a certain logic.)"[44] Yanov is even more explicit on this prospect.[45]

In this situation, the regime may have found an issue to link it firmly with the Russian masses—the maintenance of the dominant position of the Russians in the USSR. It would go beyond the theme of this discussion to explore in the light of this hypothesis the meaning of the purges that took place in 1972–73 in Ukraine, Georgia, Armenia, and elsewhere. Their consequence everywhere has been increased emphasis on the use of the Russian language and on limiting the social functions of the non-Russian languages correspondingly, and it is possible that this antinationality thrust has been the regime's response to an intensification of "unofficial" Russian nationalism.[46] Another such concession to Russian ethnic feeling, and simultaneously an admission that Marxism-Leninism is no longer an operative guide to its policies, seems to be the return to an idealization of tsarist Russia, including its conquests, in grass-roots propaganda. Thus, Nekrich points out that after nationalist demonstrations by the Ingush in the north Caucasus area in 1973, local propaganda work came to emphasize "the progressive significance of the unification [read: conquest] of Checheno-Ingushetia with Russia," and public praise was given to "the exploits of General Yermolov, the strangler of the Caucasian peoples." Nekrich speaks of "intensified Great Russian chauvinism in Checheno-Ingushetia" but it may be worth exploring whether this symptom is not noticeable elsewhere in the USSR as well.[47]

It appears that having staved off the challenge from Russian "culturalists" such as Solzhenitsyn, the regime has chosen to seek the support of the Russian masses by adopting a "pro-Russian" stand in the question of language in the non-Russian republics, thus letting the average Russian know that he is equally at home everywhere in the USSR. However, the regime has thought it imprudent to eliminate the Union republics, or to deprive them of their right to secede from the USSR, or to proclaim the emergence of a "Soviet nation." Such proposals were in fact advanced during the "nationwide discussion" of the draft of the new Soviet Constitution, but they were rejected, as L. I. Brezhnev disclosed, as "erroneous." The Soviet peoples, he said, were in fact drawing ever closer together, but it would be dangerous to "step up this objective process of national integration . . . artificially."[48] Simultaneously, a renewed stress on the historical continuity of Soviet and pre-1917 policies brings home to Russians and non-Russians alike that the Russian nation is the leading force in today's USSR. Although they were suppressed, the "culturalists" may indeed have inspired some official policies. Solzhenitsyn's "Letter to the Soviet Leaders," with its passionate concern for the fate of the Russian northeast, that historic "core area" of the Russian nation, may have inspired the program for the development of the Non-Black Earth Zone or at least have given that program a nationalistic legitimation, and the *Veche* circles have been known to believe in the necessity of developing Siberia as the "second" Russia—another goal sympathetic to the Kremlin.[49]

Notes

1. This is an ironic development because before the Revolution, to quote Hans Rogger, Russian nationalism "could only with difficulty, if at all, view the tsarist state as the embodiment of the national purpose, as the necessary instrument and expression of national goals and values, while the state, for its part, looked upon every autonomous expression of nationalism with fear and suspicion." Hans Rogger, "Nationalism and the State: A Russian Dilemma," *Comparative Studies in Society and History* 4, no. 3 (1962): 253.

"In the years after 1905, attempts at a liberal nationalism (Struve) as well as at a national socialism (the Union of the Russian People) failed equally to find a wide public resonance because of the stumbling block of the state and the diversity in interests and outlook between the various sectors of society. It is conceivable, though it must remain a matter of speculation, that the Soviet regime, by reducing this diversity and by its ruthless policy of industrialization and modernization, has gone further in bridging the gulf between itself and the nation than the more easy-going autocracy of tsarist days." Ibid., pp. 263–64.

2. Some works dealing with this problem may be listed here. This writer's thinking about the subject owes a good deal to two seminal Polish works: Nina Assorodobraj, " 'Żywa historia.' Świadomość historyczna: symptomy i propozycje badawcze," *Studia Socjologiczne* (Wroclaw), no. 2 (9) (1963), and Roman Zimand, "Uwagi o teorii narodu na marginesie analizy nacjonalistycznej teorii narodu," *Studia Filozoficzne*, no. 4 (51) (1967). Relevant works in English include David C. Gordon, *Self-Determination and History in the Third World* (Princeton: Princeton University Press, 1971); Stanley Mellon, *The Political Uses of History: A Study of Historians in the French Revolution* (Stanford: Stanford University Press, 1958); Donald Denoon and Adam Kuper, "Nationalist Historians in Search of a Nation: The 'New Historiography' in Dar Es Salaam," *African Affairs* 69, no. 277 (October 1970); Frank Hearn, "Remembrance and Critique: The Uses of the Past for Discrediting the Present and Anticipating the Future," *Politics and Society* 5, no. 2 (1975), and David Thomson, "Must History Stay Nationalist?" *Encounter*, June 1968. Needless to say the role of history in nationalism is discussed in most standard works on nationalism.

3. Karl W. Deutsch, *The Nerves of Government* (New York and London: Free Press and Collier-Macmillan, 1966), pp. 128–29. (See also pp. 206–7.)

4. Alexander Solzhenitsyn, *The Nobel Lecture*, trans. Alexis Klimoff (New York: Ad Hoc Committee for Intellectual Freedom, 1973), pp. 14–15.

5. Deutsch, *The Nerves of Government*, p. 207.

6. The problem of the antecedents of socialism interested Marx and Engels; Karl Kautsky wrote a number of works on this question, including one entitled "The Predecessors of Modern Socialism." See Assorodobraj, " 'Żywa historia'," p. 19.

7. Historiography after 1917 is reviewed in Anatole G. Mazour, *Modern Russian Historiography* (Princeton: Van Nostrand, 1958) and in his *The Writing of History in the Soviet Union* (Stanford: Hoover Institution Press, 1971); in Konstantin F. Shteppa, *Russian Historians and the Soviet State* (New Brunswick, N.J.: Rutgers University Press, 1962); in Cyril E. Black, ed., *Rewriting Russian History* (New York: Vintage Books, 1962); in Lowell Tillett, *The Great Friendship: Soviet Historians on the Non-Russian Nationalities* (Chapel Hill: University of North Carolina Press, 1969); in Walter Kolarz, *Stalin and Eternal Russia* (London: Lindsay Drummond, 1944); and in Klaus Mehnert, *Stalin ver-*

sus Marx (London: George Allen and Unwin, 1952). Historical problems in a wider context of Soviet ideological development are examined by Frederick C. Barghoorn, *Soviet Russian Nationalism* (New York: Oxford University Press, 1956) and in Elliot R. Goodman, *The Soviet Design for a World State* (New York: Columbia University Press, 1960).

8. For the ideology of Stalinism in relation to Russian nationalism, see Barghoorn, *Soviet Russian Nationalism, passim.* See also Richard Pipes, *The Formation of the Soviet Union* (New York: Atheneum, 1968), and Richard V. Burks, *The Dynamics of Communism in Eastern Europe* (Princeton: Princeton University Press, 1961).

9. N. V. Ustrialov, "Natsionalizatsiia Oktiabria," *Novosti zhizni,* November 7, 1925, reprinted in *Pod znakom revoliutsii* (Kharbin, 1927), pp. 212–18.

10. Frederick C. Barghoorn, *Soviet Russian Nationalism,* pp. 25, 148–52, 182, 233–37, and 260.

11. For a scholarly treatment of dissent, including Russian dissent, see Rudolf L. Tökes, ed., *Dissent in the USSR: Politics, Ideology, and People* (Baltimore and London: Johns Hopkins University Press, 1975); Peter Reddaway, "The Development of Dissent and Opposition," in Archie Brown and Michael Kaser, eds., *The Soviet Union since the Fall of Khrushchev* (New York: Free Press, 1975), pp. 121–56; F. M. Feldbrugge, *Samizdat and Political Dissent in the Soviet Union* (Leyden: A. W. Sijhoff, 1975); and Frederick C. Barghoorn, *Detente and the Democratic Movement in the USSR* (New York: Free Press, 1976). These are only some of the more recent works. The subject of Russian nationalism is dealt with by Dimitri Pospielovsky, "The Resurgence of Russian Nationalism in *Samizdat," Survey,* no. 86 (Winter 1973): 51–74, and in Roman Szporluk, "Nationalities and the Russian Problem in the U.S.S.R.: A historical outline," *Journal of International Affairs* 27, no. 1 (1973), included as chapter 1 in this book.

12. Of course, there are other useful ways of classifying this current. Thus, Andrei Amalrik distinguishes within the broad concept of nationalism (which he sees to be one of three major currents, the others being Marxism and liberalism): neo-Stalinist nationalism, chauvinism, neo-Slavophilism, and messianism; cf. "Ideologies in Soviet Society," *Survey,* no. 99 (Spring 1976): 1–11. There are several subcategories in Alexander Yanov, *The Russian New Right: Right-Wing Ideologies in the Contemporary USSR* (Berkeley: Institute of International Studies, 1978). See also works on dissent cited above. A representative selection of Russian dissident writings is to be found in Michael Meerson-Aksenov and Boris Shragin, eds., *The Political, Social and Religious Thought of Russian "Samizdat": An Anthology* (Belmont, Mass.: Nordland, 1977). This is a massive volume of over 700 pages.

13. See, for the less anti-Soviet trends, for example, Deming Brown, "Na-

tionalism and Ruralism in Recent Soviet Russian Literature," *Review of National Literatures* 3, no. 1 (1972), and the symposium on "The Revival of Interest in the Russian Past in the Soviet Union," with an article under the same title by Jack V. Haney (from whom we have borrowed the term "culturalism"), and comments by Thomas E. Bird and George I. Kline in *Slavic Review* 32, no. 1 (March 1973): 1–44.

14. Solzhenitsyn's speech at Stanford University, Russian text in *Vestnik RKhD*, no. 118: 170, here quoted from Boris Shragin, *The Challenge of the Spirit* (New York: Knopf, 1978), p. xiii. The representative text of political "culturalist" position is *From Under the Rubble* (New York: Bantam Books, 1976), especially the contributions of Solzhenitsyn, Igor Shafarevich, and Vadim Borisov.

15. See John B. Dunlop, *The New Russian Revolutionaries* (Belmont, Mass: Nordland, 1976), a study of the origins, ideas, and suppression of the Union.

16. Ibid., pp. 287 and 290.

17. Yanov, *The Russian New Right*, p. 34. This principle was reflected in the Union's program: Article 84 granted the Russians now in exile "after their return normal rights and opportunities in the Social-Christian Union of the entire populace." (Dunlop, *The New Russian Revolutionaries*, p. 293.)

18. Dunlop, *The New Russian Revolutionaries*, pp. 214–17. The quotes from articles 82 and 73 are in ibid., pp. 292–93. See also Vladimir Osipov, *Tri otnosheniia k rodine* (Frankfurt: Posev, 1978), pp. 119–20, who seems to adhere to a rather idealized view of Russian history when he claims that tsarist Orthodox Russia did not oppress Muslims, Catholics, Jews, or Buddhists. Rather than by oppression, the Russian Empire "was supported by a moral authority of the great Russian culture and its carrier, the Russian people." Osipov favors the maintenance of a Russian-led multinational state in the future, and in this sense his position resembles that of the "statists," but he seems also to believe that in such a state the non-Russians would be allowed freedom of national life. The "statist" position denies such rights to the non-Russians. (It may be worth noting, though, that in accord with an old tsarist position, Osipov considers Ukrainians and Belorussians to be Russian. See *Tri otnosheniia*, p. 205.)

19. Dunlop, *The New Russian Revolutionaries*, pp. 224–27.

20. Ibid., and Yanov, *The Russian New Right*, pp. 62–84.

21. See Ivan Dziuba, *Internationalism or Russification?* (New York: Monad Press, 1974), p. 66. Dziuba complained that "today even the enemy of communism V. Shul'gin is welcomed among us, because he has expressed his great-Power sympathies for the existing boundaries" (a typical "statist" position that cares about power, not ideology). See ibid., p. 57.

22. D. Pospielovsky, "The Resurgence," *Survey*, no. 86 (1973): 56. "Slovo natsii" is translated as "A Word to the Nation" in *Survey*, but Pospielovsky argues it would be better translated as "A Nation Speaks."

23. Ibid., p. 62.

24. Ibid., pp. 60–61.

25. Alexander Yanov, *The Russian New Right*, p. 45.

26. Ibid., pp. 52–55.

27. M. Alpatov, "Pis'mo istorika pisateliu," *Molodaia gvardiia*, no. 9 (1969): 306, 310–11, 314–15.

28. Ibid., p. 318, A. N. Sakharov, "Istoriia istinnaia i mnimaia," *Molodaia gvardiia*, no. 3 (1970): 320, and S. N. Semanov, "O tsennostiakh otnositel'nykh i vechnykh," ibid., no. 8 (1970): 312–13.

29. See "Trakat o prelestiakh knuta," *Novyi kolokol* (London: New Bell, 1972): 62, 68–69, and 71. See also *Politicheskii dnevnik 1965–1970*, II (Amsterdam: Fond imeni Gertsena, 1975), pp. 711–12 and ff.

30. I. Kon, "Dialektika razvitiia natsii," *Novyi mir*, no. 3 (1970): 141.

31. W. (sic), "Polemiki literackie," *Polityka* (September 27, 1969), pp. 8–9.

32. Alexander Yanov, *The Russian New Right*, p. 117.

33. Ibid., p. 120.

34. Ibid., p. 122.

35. Ibid., p. 123. Shimanov's work is entitled "Kak ponimat' nashu istoriiu," a samizdat text.

36. Ibid.

37. A. N. Iakovlev, "Protiv anti-istorizma," *Literaturnaia gazeta* (November 15, 1972), pp. 4–5. Yakovlev's article received a reply in the samizdat journal *Veche*, in an editorial entitled "Bor'ba s tak nazyvaemym rusofil'stvom, ili put' gosudarstvennogo samoubiistva" ["The Struggle Against the So-Called Russophilism, or the Road to Suicide for the State"]. Its author was Vladimir Osipov. (See *Tri otnosheniia*, pp. 112–47). *Veche* pointed out that if he were consistent, Yakovlev should allow the non-Russian nations of the USSR the freedom to secede; otherwise he had no right to condemn old Russian conquests of Ukraine or Central Asia. (See Yanov, *The New Russian Right*, p. 59.) Soon thereafter, Yakovlev lost his post in the Central Committee, CPSU, apparatus and was sent to Canada as ambassador, so that he could see, one imagines, what toleration in ethnic matters can lead to.

38. Several authors have argued that the Russians are greatly, and increasingly, concerned about the potential dangers of population growth among the Muslim peoples. See, e.g., George L. Kline, "Religion, National Character, and the 'Rediscovery of Russian Roots,'" *Slavic Review* 32, no. 1 (March 1973): 39: "There is the 'demographic trauma' experienced by Great Russians when the latest Soviet census was published. . . . For the first time the Great Russians face the prospect of being reduced to a minority of the total Soviet population. . . . It is not surprising that Great Russians should be retreating into 'the greatness of their past.' " An official response to the population explosion in Soviet Central Asia is an intensified pressure to make the "ethnics" speak Russian from

the earliest possible age. See Roman Solchanyk, "Russian, Russian Everywhere," *The New York Times*, October 11, 1979, p. A27.

39. Dunlop, *The New Russian Revolutionaries*, p. 226.

40. It would be interesting to compare the malaise which at about the same time seems to have afflicted two historically imperial nations, the Russians, whose "coloureds" live along with them in the same state, and the English, who seem never to have minded going themselves to India, Africa, or the West Indies, but find it more difficult to welcome the return visits of the latter's natives to England. See the stimulating discussion by Tom Nairn, "English Nationalism: The Case of Enoch Powell," in his *The Break-Up of Britain: Crisis and Neo-Nationalism* (London: NL Books, 1977), pp. 256–90.

41. Alexander M. Nekrich, *The Punished Peoples*, trans. George Saunders (New York: Norton, 1978), provides telling examples of popular hostility to non-Russian victims of Stalinist deportations in the post-1956 period.

42. Dziuba, *Internationalism or Russification*, pp. 67–69.

43. V. V. Pokhlebkin, *SSSR-Finliandiia. 260 let otnoshenii 1713–1973* (Moscow: Mezhdunarodnye otnosheniia, 1975). A Polish reviewer has noted such statements and the fact that Pokhlebkin often quotes approvingly the works of "the reactionary tsarist general, one of the theorists of the Russification policy," Mikhail Borodkin, and has observed that those patriotic actions of the Finns that Pokhlebkin condemns were supported in their time by Lenin, Social-Democrats, Lev Tolstoy, Maxim Gorky, and other progressive Russians. See Bernard Piotrowski's (untitled) review in *Kwartalnik Historyczny* (Warsaw), 85, no. 2 (1978): 456–60.

44. John B. Dunlop, "The Eleventh Hour," *Frontier* 18, no. 2 (Summer 1975): 81.

45. Yanov, *The New Russian Right*, p. 127: "The Shimonovites . . . are practical politicians offering the 'leaders' more flexible and effective tactics, a deeper social base, a broader field of operations for political manuevre in case of crisis." (See also ibid., pp. 130–31 and 141 ff.)

46. For authoritative scholarly and political statements reaffirming the role of the Russian language, and justifying corresponding limitations on the use of the non-Russian languages in the 1970s, see, for example, I. P. Tsamerian, *Teoreticheskie problemy obrazovaniia i razvitiia sovetskogo mnogonatsional'nogo gosudartsva* (Moscow: Nauka, 1973), pp. 243–44, 269, 273–74; Iu. D. Desheriev, *Razvitie obshchestvennykh funktsii literaturnykh iazykov* (Moscow: Nauka, 1976), p. 86, and E. A. Bagramov, *Leninskaia natsional'naia politika: dostizheniia i perspektivy* (Moscow: Mysl', 1977), p. 128. It is noteworthy that these official arguments had been advanced earlier by such a dissident Marxist figure as Roy Medvedev. In his *On Socialist Democracy* (New York: Alfred A. Knopf, 1975), p. 359, written in 1970–71, Medvedev criticized the publication of original scientific research in Georgia, Armenia, Ukraine, and Estonia in the

182 Russia, Ukraine, and the Breakup of the Soviet Union

native languages, and thought that to publish scientific journals in the local languages was "rather ludicrous." It is strange that a freedom fighter like Roy Medvedev would support such a position but then, as F.J.M. Feldbrugge (*Samzidat and Political Dissent*, p. 189) has noted, "The general tenor of Medvedev's treatment of the national question suggests that on this count the majority of the authors of political samizdat is not too much out of step with the regime's policy which . . . promotes Russification in the guise of a gradual rapprochement between the nations of the Soviet Union. . . ."

47. Nekrich, *Punished Peoples*, pp. 163–64.

48. L. I. Brezhnev, *On the Draft Constitution (Fundamental Law) of the Union of Soviet Socialist Republics* (Moscow: Novosti, 1977), p. 21.

49. A. Solzhenitsyn, *Pis'mo vozhdiam Sovetskogo Soiuza* (Paris: YMCA Press, 1974), pp. 23–33. For the nationalists' thinking on Serbia, see Yanov, *The New Russian Right*, pp. 73–75. It would take a special study to explore the "historical geography" of contemporary Russian nationalists, a study on the lines of Ladis K. D. Kristof's "The Russian Image of Russia: An Applied Study in Geopolitical Methodology," in C. A. Fischer, ed., *Essays in Political Geography* (London: Methuen, 1968).

7   Dilemmas of Russian
       Nationalism

The present state of ethnic relations in the Soviet Union results from the literal collapse of the "command-administrative system," writes Alexander Zharnikov in the June 1989 issue of *Kommunist*. That system had consistently undermined the principle of self-determination of nations, replacing it with the concept of the Russians as "elder brother" of the other Soviet peoples. Recent expressions of anti-Russian sentiments can be understood as a response to this change. It is not surprising, argues Zharnikov, that the sins of the compromised command-administrative system tend to be partly attributed to the "elder brother," that is, to the Russian people. Unfortunately, there are people who deliberately "speculate" on the problems of their nations—"and what nation has no problems?"—and try to make the "elder brother" responsible for all their troubles.[1]

Zharnikov's is only one of many recent voices that have explicitly or implicitly argued that the relationship between the Russian nation and the Soviet state—let us call it the Russian national problem—is the central ethnic problem in the Soviet Union today, not least because it also defines the nature of the other nationality problems in the USSR. For the non-Russians tend to formulate their own agendas in light of

First published in *Problems of Communism*, 1989.

their perception of the status and role of the Russian nation in the Soviet state.

If that is the case, then the roots of the Russian problem go deeper than the bankrupt command-administrative system or Stalinism. After all, it is commonplace to view Stalinism, and by extension the present Soviet system, as a continuation of the tsarist, imperial pattern of inter-nationality relations. Thus, the search for solutions to current national-ity problems must go back to the relationship established in tsarist times between the state and the Russian nation. Moreover, a genuine normal-ization or "regularization" of the Soviet nationality situation requires above all that the Russian national problem be properly defined—and resolved.

There is a large and growing body of writing on Russian nationalism in particular, and on Russian political thought in general. The most re-cent addition to it is a collection of insightful essays by John Dunlop, Darrell Hammer, Ronald Suny, Andrei Siniavsky, and Alexander Yanov in a special edition of the *Radio Liberty Research Bulletin* entitled "Rus-sian Nationalism Today."[2] These and other scholars have also produced studies of diverse currents in the broad phenomenon of past and present Russian nationalism. Under the Romanov empire, there were Slavo-philes, Westernizers, and adherents of "Official Nationality," as well as *pochvenniki*, Pan-Slavs, liberal nationalists, and integral nationalists. In the contemporary Soviet Union, Dunlop discerns liberal nationalists, centrists, a nationalist Right, including the National Bolsheviks, and so forth. For his part, Yanov carefully distinguishes between nationalism, chauvinism, and patriotism:

> Patriotism, chauvinism, and nationalism have one thing in common: they are all manifestations of love of one's country. Yet, distinctions are evident—at least in the Russian context.
>   A patriot loves his country, but this does not prevent him from loving humanity.
>   A chauvinist loves his country but dislikes humanity, especially if it is of Jewish origin.
>   A nationalist loves his country but sees humanity as an invading force ready to conquer it—with the Jews in the vanguard.[3]

Although the conceptual distinctions of Yanov, Dunlop, and other scholars help to clarify intellectual currents in contemporary Russian nationalism, this essay proposes to focus on a question they do not consider—namely, what do Russian nationalists, patriots, or chauvinists mean by the country they claim to love? Is one Russian patriot's "Russia" the same as the "Russia" of another patriot (chauvinist, nationalist)? Moreover, this "geographic" question will be linked to a political theme developed by Siniavsky in his discussion of the acuteness of the nationality problems facing the Soviet government. Siniavsky writes:

> The main reason for this can be summed up in a single word—empire: first, the Russian empire, shaped in the course of centuries and inherited by the new order; then, the Soviet empire, built on the ruins of the old order, consolidated and extended as a world power. Today, it is the only empire in the world and unique as a country in terms of the sheer extent of its territory and number of its constituent peoples. Of necessity, being an empire complicates the nationality problem to an unusual degree.[4]

Siniavsky also notes that "Soviet ideology has collapsed in ruins, and whatever attempts are made to revivify it, it will never imbue life with higher meaning. Soviet society today . . . is without ideals."[5]

It is worth noting that in his speech before the Congress of People's Deputies in Moscow on June 5, 1989, Andrei Sakharov characterized the Soviet situation in exactly the same way. Even as the country finds itself "in the throes of spreading economic catastrophe and a tragic worsening of interethnic relations," Sakharov said, "one aspect of the powerful and dangerous processes at work has been a general crisis of confidence in the nation's leadership . . . accumulating tensions . . . could explode, with dire consequences for our society." With regard to nationality problems, Sakharov said: "We have inherited from Stalinism a constitutional structure that bears the stamp of imperial thinking and the imperial policy of 'divide and rule.' " Among the victims of the imperial system Sakharov counts not only the non-Russian nations but also the Russian nation, which "had to bear the main burden of imperial ambitions and the consequences of adventurism and dogmatism in foreign and domestic policy."[6]

Such opinions on the present condition of the USSR are heard with increasing frequency and intensity, both inside and outside the USSR. In a much discussed article in *Literaturnaia Rossiia* published in 1988, Yuri Afanasiev claimed to see an "ideological vacuum" in the Soviet Union resulting in what he called an "identity crisis" of society. He attributed the crisis and the "vacuum" to the "systematic destruction of collective memory" perpetrated under Stalin and Brezhnev. Yet, historical memory is the pivotal formative component of social group identity. Afanasiev directly attributed the rise of what he called "chauvinist, anti-Semitic groups, like the extremists from Pamiat'," to that destruction of historical memory.[7]

Alain Besançon has concluded that, with the bankruptcy of Marxism-Leninism, the only alternative source of legitimacy is the empire, regardless of how anachronistic it may be:

> Once the ideological magic has been destroyed, there would only be one source of magic left—the imperial or colonial legitimacy of the Russian people in a world that today is entirely decolonized.[8]

Is Besançon necessarily right? Are the Russians incapable of defining themselves as other than an imperial nation?

Empire or Nation-State

The Bolshevik victory in the Civil War stopped what in 1917 to 1919 looked like the natural process of disintegration of the Russian Empire into a number of independent nation-states following the February (March) Revolution of 1917. As we can now see, this victory also prevented Russia's evolution into a "normal" nation and state.[9] At first the Bolsheviks attempted to transcend altogether the dialectic of nation and nationalism by establishing class as the basic referent and class solidarity as the principle of new legitimacy and identity. This policy failed, however. Instead, the imperial model was restored in a communist guise and the Russian nation was elevated to the rank of "elder brother," though it was itself manipulated by Stalin and the system he created. The establishment of communist regimes in Asia and Eastern Europe after World War II extended the power and influence of the Soviet state beyond anything the tsars had ever achieved. But the establishment of the "socialist bloc" did not end the Soviet Union's reliance on and promotion of Russia. It was not until *after* 1945 that the "Russia First" slogan became paramount in philosophy, culture, science, and so on, first in the Soviet Union and then in Eastern and Central Europe. Domestically, the annexation of the Baltic states, Western Belorussia, and Western Ukraine further complicated the already existing nationality problem—as became especially evident under glasnost. The extension of communism beyond the borders of the USSR, and the territorial expansion of the Soviet state in turn tied the Russians more closely to the problems of both the "inner" and the "outer" empires, thereby additionally inhibiting their search for national self-definition.

This legacy makes the question "What is Russia?" even more complex. But the present map of Soviet and Russian politics will become clearer if one distinguishes between two basic responses from the Russian people to that question—the response of "empire-savers" and that of "nation-builders."

"Empire-savers" regard the present Soviet Union in its current boundaries as the proper and legitimate national "space" of the Russian nation. Indeed, some of them may extend it to the Soviet bloc. They may and indeed do differ profoundly about how they would like to see that country governed, how non-Russians should be treated in it, and so forth. But they all share the conviction that the USSR is in essence a synonym for Russia and consider the preservation of its political unity as a Russian (or Russian-dominated) state to be their primary political goal. That they may include extreme right-wingers and no less extreme left-wingers is not as important as the fact that they all agree on this fundamental point.

On the other side are those Russians who think of Russia as something very different from the USSR—as a geographical, historical, and cultural entity that does not encompass what they themselves recognize to be non-Russian lands and nations, even if these are part of the USSR. The geographical extent of Russia is not identical for all "nation-builders." Unlike the empire-savers, some nation-builders exclude the Baltic states from Russia but include the Caucasus; others exclude both of these but include Ukraine and Belorussia, and so on. What unifies them is a basically national position and the political goal of establishing a Russia that is a *nation-state*. Their goal is not to save, reform, transform, or modernize the empire but to establish in its place a Russian and a number of non-Russian nation-states. Insofar as nation-builders envisage close ties between Russia and some or all of the other "successors"— and some Russian nation-builders are in favor of such ties—they want Russia, and not the imperial center, to be a party to such arrangements.

It is impossible to determine how many Russians prefer empire-saving to nation-building or vice versa. But it is remarkable that in a recent article called "Preservation of the Empire or Self-Preservation by Way of National Sovereignty—The Main National Problem of the Russian People," Vladimir Balakhonov formulates the Russian national dilemma in these same terms,[10] which suggests that the issue is entering the political agenda.

"Empire-Savers"

It is essential to keep in mind that the broad designation of "empire-savers" encompasses ideas and programs, individuals and organizations that in most other respects have little in common and may disagree and oppose one another on some fundamental matters. But this fact does not make "empire-saving" a meaningless concept. When the chips are down, all empire-savers (it would be much simpler to call them "imperialists," but this term has now become one of abuse) agree that the preservation of the territorial integrity of the state is more important than anything else.

The classical expression of this approach is to be seen in the post-1917 phenomenon of "National Bolshevism," a designation describing those Russian anticommunists in the Civil War who opted for the Bolsheviks because they saw the latter as the only force capable of saving the empire. Private property, independent courts, freedom of religion, representative government—all these could be given up in exchange for "Russia's" retention of Ukraine, the Caucasus, or Central Asia. For the National Bolsheviks, a smaller but democratic Russia was no consolation for the loss of the empire.

Among today's most obvious empire-savers are the military and the police, the state and party bureaucracies, and members of other "all-Union" structures and apparatuses, such as foreign ministry or cultural officials, engaged in foreign relations. Imperial nationalism offers an ideological justification for the dominant position of the central bureaucracy (and its departments and territorial subdivisions). For the Moscow bureaucracy, the whole of the USSR—be it Estonia or Armenia, Russia "proper" or Moldavia, Ukraine or Uzbekistan—represents the canvas for its "creative" undertakings. The ministries of nuclear power stations and of water irrigation, not to mention the State Planning Committee, embody this imperial perspective and vision. A song that was popularized by the official media during the era of "stagnation" (and is now criticized for its wrong attitude) "artistically" reflects the same imperial outlook, especially in this much-quoted refrain: "Not some house, not some street—my address is the Soviet Union."

Some of today's empire-savers may continue to believe that the political system established by Lenin and Stalin is the best for the Soviet Union. As a matter of principle, they may question whether political freedom is a desirable goal in any circumstances, and they are certain to oppose political freedoms when these threaten the unity, and thus indirectly the territorial integrity, of the Soviet state. Indeed, some may go even further and favor some kind of military or fascist-style dictatorship that would openly and completely abandon the Marxist-Leninist ideology. For our purposes, they are empire-savers, because they consider the USSR to be a Russian state. But right-wing extremism is not the only "empire-saving" outlook today. It may even be the least important, although it is very vocal.

Other empire-savers seem to favor Western, liberal-democratic, and constitutional institutions for the Soviet Union. Indeed, when some of those "liberals" think of their ideal Russia, they envisage a polity closely resembling what they imagine the United States to be. That their empire would be a liberal one, have independent courts, and accept the equality of all citizens before the law (without regard to ethnic origins, national background, religion, and so forth), is praiseworthy, of course. But what is fundamental in this outlook is that it treats the non-Russian peoples—and the Russians too—as subject to decisions made in Moscow, not by those peoples themselves. Some of these "imperial" admirers of the United States are prepared to allow local and regional autonomy in their state, and they even discuss the possibility of basing such autonomy on what they see as the most significant aspect of the U.S. model: dissociation of ethnicity from territory.

Some of the "Westernizers" go even farther. They openly proclaim their own desire for a total separation of ethnicity from politics and the state, for making nationality, as it were, a private matter of concern only to individuals, rather than having it be a factor affecting the state structure. Again, some Soviet scholars seem to think that this idea is realized in the United States.[11]

There are grounds to surmise that in the face of rising ethnic nationalism the current line of the center is to defuse the threat coming from the larger nations by having Moscow assume the role of defender of smaller nations, and especially of scattered national and religious groups living among the non-Russian peoples. This policy would serve two purposes. It would weaken the union republics by granting their citizens the right to go to Moscow for justice, and it would create a new mission for the old apparat as the protector of ethnic and human rights all over the USSR, in the same old centralized way to which it has become accustomed. The newly elected head of the Ethnography Institute of the USSR Academy of Sciences, Valery Tishkov, for one, is on record against "absolutizing" the rights of the Union republics over the rights of other entities such as autonomous republics or national districts.[12] Indeed, the center seems to be advocating, in self-defense, the granting of broader rights to the subdivisions of the Union republics, presumably in order to give Moscow more things to do, and not because the Moscow bureaucracy now consists of converts to libertarianism and individualism.

Whether empire-savers are fascist or liberal, extremist or moderate, atheist or Orthodox, their "geography" is the same—it is an imperial geography, and their Russia is coextensive with the empire. But why should the hoped-for liberal empire be called Russian? Why should it not have the "Soviet" or some other nonethnic designation? Recent Soviet discussions help answer this question.

The historic failure of the Soviet system is openly conceded today. The declaration of the Congress of People's Deputies issued in June 1989 speaks about the present "crisis" of the Soviet Union. It is admitted that the Soviet system has failed to defeat capitalism in their historic "great contest." This failure has called into question the concept of a "Soviet people." If a new Soviet civilization has not been created, as is also being admitted, then in what sense are the peoples living in the USSR a *Soviet* people?[13]

The empire-savers are noticeably concerned to preserve the concept of a "Soviet people." But when one examines their arguments closely, one discovers that the "Soviet people" they defend is a form of the Russian nation. Academician Iulian Bromlei (until 1989 director of the Ethnography Institute) defined the "Soviet people" as a real community that is held together by common socialist features. He called it a "meta-ethnic community."[14] In an article in *Voprosy istorii* (January 1989), Bromlei recognized that demands for greater use of "national"—which in the Soviet usage means subnational or local or regional—languages in the non-Russian republics of the Soviet Union are legitimate. But he stressed the necessity of a continuing and expanding use of Russian throughout the USSR. Revealingly, Bromlei referred to the publication of fiction and poetry in the non-Russian languages as indicating the growth of the "nationally specific" as opposed to the "general," which means that he considers the publication of fiction and poetry in Russian to represent "the general," that is, the integrating or internationalizing tendency.[15]

Bromlei attributes "international" qualities to the Russian language, and by extension to the Russian ethnos, even though to an outsider there would appear to be no more internationalism in the Russian language than there is in Georgian or Abkhazian. One may well ask whether a poem praising Lenin in Armenian would be "nationally specific" while one written in Russian praising Nicholas II would be "general and integrating" just because it was written in Russian. Absurd as this may be, such categorizations lay at the root of imperial thinking in Stalin's time—and seem to be still alive today. The Estonian scholar Jaan K. Rebane has recently made the point that in this view, the "internationalist" (Soviet) or "general" means one ethnically specific aspect—the Russian.[16]

Bromlei's reference to the non-Russian languages as expressing "the specific" and his assumption that Russian stands for "the general" reflects quintessential Russian imperial thinking and shows why it is Russian, and not Soviet, imperial thinking. It is based on the assumption that Russian ethnicity is not in the same category as all the other ethnicities in the USSR: It is above them, and it is a distinguishing feature of the "universality" of Sovietism. This approach holds that the unity of the USSR is based on the non-Russians' submergence in—not their integration as equals with—Russia.

What some other prominent figures understood by "internationalization" became clear from Yevgeny M. Primakov's speech to the Nineteenth Party Conference in June 1988. Primakov proposed the establishment of "international structures" by means of a "rotation of cadres along horizontal lines in the whole country," a move made imperative by "the lessons from recent events in Azerbaijan and Armenia." Primakov argued:

> Only through such a horizontal transfer of party and economic personnel will it be possible to create a single international fusion in the Soviet Union, one that will be more monolithic than the sum of national [that is, ethnic] formations that gravitate toward seclusion.[17]

Academician Primakov did not explain who would implement such a transfer of cadres. The new political reforms in the USSR seem to make the decision as to who shall head a given party or economic organization subject to elections. This would mean that Moscow could no longer appoint or transfer leading cadres from one republic or region to another. It is obvious that Primakov's plan would require that the center retain the power of appointment.

Exchange of cadres between republics was a standard theme in the times of Brezhnev and Andropov, and Mikhail Gorbachev also used to endorse it, at least until the January 1987 plenum of the Central Committee, after which this topic seems to have disappeared from his public pronouncements. But in April 1989, Abdul-Rakhman Bezirov, first secretary of the Azerbaijan Central Committee, spoke strongly in favor of an exchange of party officials between republics and the center, although from a different perspective than Primakov's. His complaint was that for years no party officials from his republic had been called to serve in Moscow.[18]

Academician S. L. Tikhvinsky, an influential historian, insisted at an academic conference in 1987 that it was necessary to develop new forms of interrepublic cooperation in the scholarly sphere. Tikhvinsky stressed the need to "resolutely overcome the harmful tendency to divide science (*nauka*) into Ukrainian or Azerbaijani, central or peripheral." According to him, only one, Soviet, historical science existed, and it was "firmly grounded" in Marxism–Leninism and socialist internationalism.[19] It is worth noting that Tikhvinsky spoke about Soviet scholarship and about internationalism, but did not deny the existence of a Russian historical science. One suspects that he identified Russian with Soviet or "internationalist" scholarship, even though it was hard in 1987, and impossible in 1989, to ignore the fact that Russian historical writing is not firmly grounded in either Marxism–Leninism or in socialist internationalism.

Some scholars do not have Tikhvinsky's or Primakov's inhibitions about explicitly identifying "Soviet" with "Russian." Examples of uninhibited Russian imperial thinking may be found in the symposium "Democracy Is Conflict" published in the monthly magazine *Vek XX i Mir*. Doctor of Philosophical Sciences A. Prigozhin was refreshingly open in characterizing the Russian nation as the "patron-nation" (*narod-patron*) of all the Soviet peoples. Prigozhin thought it quite self-evident and normal that the Russians should form the highest leadership of the country (that is, of the USSR), and should predominate among the heads of the state's central agencies, in the USSR Academy of Sciences, the Central Committee of the CPSU, and so forth. He even thought that in the non-Russian national republics, Russian leaders should "also occupy a special position."[20] Clearly, for Prigozhin, being "Russian" means embodying and personifying the general or universal, the "Soviet" in the Soviet Union. By the same token, the other ethnic elements in Prigozhin's scheme of things represented the "specific," or particular—in other words, something local, subordinate, and inessential.

"Nation-Builders"

One of the consequences of the Soviet Union's identity crisis is the current rise of ethnic assertiveness in many regions of the country. Dissatisfaction with the Soviet system, general disillusionment with the empty promises of a better "Soviet way of life," and the search for alternative explanations of the current problems and alternative ways of solving them lie behind the present processes in which ethnic communities "construct" and "reconstruct" themselves.

Among the nations in search of an identity and purpose are the Russians. They are increasingly asserting themselves—and defining themselves—as a Russian nation and, especially important, as a nation that exists independently of the state, which in this case means the empire. Some of the emerging Russian nationalists take pains to dissociate the Russian nation from the Soviet state's record, not only in the 1930s but also in the 1920s. Indeed, some are repudiating even the immediate postrevolutionary years. The process of reevaluation of history has assumed sufficiently large proportions to raise the possibility of a "divorce" or secession of Russian nationalism from the Soviet state and Marxist–Leninist ideology. If the trend continues and gains in scope, it may lead to the dissolution, "ungluing," or coming apart of what has been called by some Russia's "national communism."

More than twenty years ago, Mark G. Field defined national communism as "the search, on the part of a nation that has recently emerged as a major world power on the world scene, for a national and cultural identity." National communism, he wrote, rested on "the fusion of the doctrinal bases of the Communist movement and identification of the interests of that movement (which is, in essence, supra-national) with the interests of the Russian nation." Field saw the sources of that "fusion" in the Soviet leaders' recognition that "no proletarian revolution . . . was in sight and the resulting decision (primarily Stalin's) to build 'socialism in one country.' " Stalin considered Russia the bastion of the communist movement and held that "anything that added to the strength of Russia as a nation (industrialization, for example) was good for that movement."[21]

It is a separate question whether Stalin ultimately proved to be "good" for the world communist movement; what is relevant here is that more and more people say openly now that Stalin's regime was very bad for Russia. Bad not just for the Russian "landlords and bourgeoisie," for kulaks or even peasants in general, but also bad for Russia in the sense of the entire people and country. This theme has long been heard from declared anticommunists, for example, Alexander Solzhenitsyn, who in the early 1970s, when he was still in the USSR, used to be the most prominent spokesman for this assessment of communism's relationship to Russia. While Solzhenitsyn criticized communism on behalf of the old, Orthodox Russia, certain extremist chauvinist elements among the dissidents criticized the Soviet past and present from another vantage point. They blamed the Soviet state's negative aspects on the Jews, Zionists, Freemasons, and so on, but professed their profound loyalty to "genuine" Soviet socialism (under which term they also understood Stalinism).[22]

Today, many people are convinced that Russia is hopelessly behind when compared with the other Soviet republics (not to mention foreign countries), and it is frequently said or implied that the ruling party, the state, and the ideology are to blame. Many examples can be cited to illustrate this pervasive mood, but a few will have to suffice. The well-known "village" writer Vasily Belov, speaking as a candidate for the USSR Congress of People's Deputies, said: "The ill-considered collectivization of the '30's inflicted great losses not only on the peasantry but also on the whole Russian people [narod]. According to my information, Russians now constitute less than one half of the country's [population]." Belov complained that despite this fact, some scholars claimed that the Russians were characterized "by some special kind of aggressiveness." Those unnamed scholars even "dare to say that there exist special medical means to treat this aggressiveness. I was deeply angered to hear such a statement at one very representative conference."

Belov was no less critical of the government's conduct of foreign trade under the terms of which, he said, the Soviet Union exports its best goods, which are not accessible to the Soviet population, and buys industrial machinery from abroad, thus perpetuating the country's traditional role as a backward nation dependent on foreign "technology of yesterday." (Belov assumed that foreigners do not sell their most up-to-date products.) If such practices continue, the country risks becoming "a colony."[23]

In an article in a series remarkably called "Who Is to Blame or What Is to Be Done?" Iurii Chernichenko referred to Russia (meaning the RSFSR, not the USSR as a whole) as the dirtiest country in all of the USSR and in all of Europe, even dirtier in the Soviet era than in the early nineteenth century when the poet Mikhail Lermontov had called Russia "*nemytaia Rossiia*" (unwashed Russia). Chernichenko said it was time to "wash up" Russia, and he drew a direct connection between the sorry state of Russia and the rule by party bureaucrats who headed a "purely totalitarian regime, an administrative regime."[24]

It is not unusual to identify Russian nationalism with the most extreme, fascist, or racist ideas and groups. This point of view is erroneous. Fascism, racism, and extremism are not the only Russian-proposed alternatives to the ideology of communism and the present Soviet political system. There are many diverse currents in Russia and it would be an impossible task to classify them without crude oversimplification. For the purposes of this discussion, however, let us rather consider several different models envisaged for Russia, each of which has at its source its proponents' sense of alienation from the present system.

First, there are those Russians who reject communism and sovietism and who look for an alternative in a nationalism rooted in culture, especially in religion. A second model for Russia proposes a democratic, liberal, Western-style, modern nation-state. A third model is advanced by those who are critical of the Soviet Union's imperial structure and expect a change for the better if the RSFSR were to become a full-fledged republic. Their opposition to "Moscow"—read the Stalinist bureaucratic and centralized machine—leads these Russians to call for a basic change in the status of the Russian Soviet Federated Socialist Republic within the Soviet Union. They think that the national needs of Russia might be addressed and met if the RSFSR acquired an identity that was separate from the USSR and its governmental, party, and other organizations.

RSFSR Nationalism

Let us begin with the third model, which is anti-empire but not anti-socialist or anti-Soviet in principle. It calls for an institutional rearrange-

ment for the RSFSR that would amount to the removal of the Russian
nation from its position as the imperial nation in the USSR. An interview
given recently by the secretary of the Moscow Writers' Union, Anatoly
Zhukov, to *Literaturnaia Rossiia* well conveys the mood of the "RSFSR-
Russians." Zhukov cited some of the ethnic problems arising in Central
Asia, the Baltic states, Armenia, and Azerbaijan, as well the rise of "Rus-
sophobia" in Kazakhstan and elsewhere, and attributed them to neglect
of specific conditions in those particular regions. These republics could
not deal with their problems adequately because they lacked the freedom
to run their own affairs. When asked if this was also true of the Russian
Federation, Zhukov responded:

> Of course. Why should we be an exception? But we are an exception.
> In Russian schools, for example, Russian history is not being taught,
> there is only the history of the USSR. We do not have our own republic
> academy of sciences, we do not have our own republic party or Komso-
> mol central committee, there are no [republic-rank] trade union or-
> gans, and no congresses are held. The Russians are last in the number
> of specialists with college education and in the number of scientists per
> 1000 of population, our countryside has been ruined, our birth rates
> have fallen, our national culture has been almost destroyed. What is
> this if not an exception? We do not even have a capital of our own—we
> "share" one with the whole country.[25]

It goes without saying that Zhukov's statements are not always accurate.
For example, he seems not to know that Ukrainian schools do not teach
a subject called "Ukrainian history." What is more interesting is that
Zhukov—and other Russian critics who complain that Russian history
is not taught in Russian schools—do not think that what is being presented as the "history of the USSR" is a history of Russia. What is called
"history of the USSR" in Soviet textbooks is principally the history of
the tsarist state. When critics of this kind of history say they want a
history of the Russian people, the Russian nation, they are revealing a
belief that the story of the grand princes and tsars is not real Russian
history. Indeed, some dispute the propriety of calling the pre-1917 history a history of the "USSR" (which is what Soviet historians do, and
not only in textbooks but also in scholarly works). Thus, in a letter to
the journal *Nash sovremennik*, Colonel (Ret.) I. A. Zaichkin and Major-
General of the Air Force I. N. Pochkaev called it absurd to have book
titles such as "History of the USSR: Feudal Epoch." On the pre-1917
era, they said, there should be histories of Russia and of other nations.[26]

Admittedly, there is nothing politically subversive in such proposals. However, Russian demands of this kind are frequently presented by individuals who combine them with chauvinistic, including anti-Semitic, views. Thus, a letter to the Nineteenth Party Conference signed by a group of Russian cultural figures contained a demand for ethnic quotas in those RSFSR institutions that the letter signers wanted to have established.[27] (Incidentally, like Zhukov, the authors of this letter seem convinced that in the non-Russian republics the histories of the respective nations are taught. This, as mentioned above, is certainly not the case now in Ukraine, and it seems most unlikely to be the case in Belorussia and a number of other republics.) The Russian "cultural figures" charge that the absence of RSFSR structures (they also included in their list the KGB and academies of sciences and arts) perpetuates a "Zionist Trotskyist program," which they describe as follows: "A federation for the 'nationalities' with separate centers for them, but without one for the Russians." They state that Lenin had protested this program—evidently without success. "And so the Russians have now proved to be without rights in their own country!"[28]

The support for some of the Russian national desiderata by professed anti-Semites and reactionaries should not obscure the fact that not all of these desiderata are objectionable. Although it would obviously be wrong to restrict employment in a Russian academy of sciences by ethnic quotas, the idea of establishing such a new academy is not discriminatory per se. Indeed, if realized, it might help to develop Russia and at the same time help to dissociate "Sovietism" from the Russian people as the Soviet Union's allegedly dominant master nation, or "patron-nation" in Prigozhin's phrase. Indeed, some years ago similar Russian demands circulated in samizdat and were then supported by leftists.[29]

One such idea that constantly reappears and seems to bother Russians of all political persuasions is the dual role of Moscow as capital of the USSR and the RSFSR. Many Russians also complain that Leningrad has fallen from the rank of an imperial capital to that of a regional center. The question of the status of Leningrad was again raised quite recently in *Literaturnaia gazeta* and *Literatunaia Rossiia*. Writing in the latter, the Leningrad writer Feliks Dymov recalled that one of Stalin's charges against the Leningrad party leaders in 1949–50 was their proposal to move the capital of the RSFSR to that city. (Stalin regarded this as separatism.) Although Dymov did not take a definite stand in favor of such a move, he deplored the low ranking of the former capital, which, he said, in population, scientific potential, and industrial output, was far ahead of the fourteen union republic capitals.[30]

Nation as Culture

No current of contemporary Russian opinion, whether unofficial or "legal," has attracted Western scholars more than the complexities of Russian national-religious and "culturalist" thought. Indeed, there are Russian thinkers who want to explore and affirm the importance of the Orthodox religion and the Orthodox Church in the history of Russia, and who consider this spiritual aspect a formative influence on modern Russian identity. These thinkers disagree profoundly among themselves in their specific assessments of individuals and events in Russia's spiritual history, and even more profoundly on the implications of Russia's past for its present spiritual and political problems. Their ideas deserve attention.

Until very recently, most of those cultural and national debates were conducted among the intelligentsia on the pages of "thick" journals. In the past year or two, however, formal organizations have emerged seeking to promote their respective visions of a culturally defined Russia among the general public. One might see in these emerging structures initial attempts to give an institutional shape to the different ideas of Russia. It is evident that these organizations are characterized by diverse approaches to the questions of Russian national identity, the territorial shape of "Russia," and the empire.

Remembering that such distinctions lack precision, especially because a certain overlap is evident in the positions of the groups in question, let us first mention those that concentrate their attention on Russian culture broadly defined but make it clear that they do not claim for Russia any special position in relation to the other nationalities in the Soviet Union.

One such organization was founded in June 1989 under the name of "National [or People's] Home of Russia" (*Narodnyi dom Rossii*). The "National Home" expressly limits its sphere of operation to the RSFSR, and its program aims at "the revival of the spiritual, social, cultural, and socio-economic life of the Russian Federation." It wants to achieve this goal by freeing the energies of a society that had long lived under "the oppression of a totally prohibitive system."[31]

Another Russian national initiative that emphasizes its autonomy from the state is the "Russian Encyclopedia Cultural Center." The projected Russian encyclopedia is to be devoted to all aspects of Russian history, culture, and civilization, and will not attempt to be a universal encyclopedia of the kind represented by the *Great Soviet Encyclopedia* or the comprehensive encyclopedias published in the Union republics. The Russian encyclopedia planners insist on their independence from the state.[32]

John B. Dunlop draws attention to two other recent nationalist initiatives in the cultural area. Both are remarkably political—not to say "imperial"—in their "cultural" concerns. One of these is called "Foundation for Slavic Literature and Slavic Cultures" (*Fond slavianskoi pis'-mennosti i slavianskikh kul'tur*) and includes among its founders individuals whom Dunlop calls "conservative Russian nationalists." As he puts it, the Foundation is "pan-Slavic in orientation."[33] Dunlop notes that the Foundation, launched in March 1989, has among its more than eighty sponsoring organizations the Writers' Union of the RSFSR as well as those of Ukraine and Belorussia, the academies of sciences of Ukraine and Belorussia, and numerous Russian and general Soviet organizations. He thinks that the "de facto goal of the new organization" is "to cement relations among Russians, Ukrainians, and Belorussians." Only secondarily, according to Dunlop, is the Foundation concerned with Slavic and/ or Orthodox nations abroad.

Dunlop quotes from a statement by Dmitri Balashov, "the well-known Russian nationalist historical writer," who expresses this view: "The question of the day . . . is whether the 'supra-ethnic' state created by ethnic Russians can be preserved." It would be lamentable, according to Balashov, "if the miracle of Russian statehood should be consumed by 'chaos.' " This and similar statements led Dunlop to the following general observation: "Conservative Russian nationalists are concerned about the future political fragmentation of the Soviet empire. They are attempting to shore up the Eastern Slav nucleus of the USSR."[34]

The other organization discussed by Dunlop is the "Association of Russian Artists," also organized in early 1989. Dunlop notes that one of the association's primary aims is to "combat separatist minority nationalist tendencies that are seen as threatening the unity of the Soviet Union," and he quotes from a declaration of the Association to support his assessment:

> The once-powerful union of the peoples of Russia, joined together by the idea of steadfast unity, is experiencing a difficult period, during which, under the guise of demagogic slogans, nationalist groups . . . are seeking to break up and destroy the unity of peoples.[35]

Recently, Boris Tsarev, the Association's business manager, declared that the organization supported the free development of all nationalities even though its own focus was on Russian culture. The Association firmly defends the unity of the USSR, which it views as a product of historical development that has produced a "brotherhood" of all peoples living in a common state. Tsarev warned the non-Russian nationalities against (unnamed) elements who work for the destruction of the USSR and aspire to establish their domination "over all nations."[36]

At least two other Russian nationalist organizations also began their existence in the spring of 1989. The Union for Spiritual Rebirth of the Fatherland (*Soiuz dukhovnogo vozrozhdeniia Otechestva*) was officially organized in Moscow on March 16–17, 1989. According to *Moskovskii literator*, the organizing session was attended by some 200 delegates from "patriotic associations and organizations" of Moscow, Leningrad, the Volga region, the Urals, Siberia, Belorussia, Ukraine, and Kazakhstan, as well as by representatives of the Russian Orthodox Church. The organization's listed "founders" included the *Sovetskaia Rossiia* Publishing House, the Lenin Library, the Scientific Council for Problems of Russian Literature in the USSR Academy of Sciences, a kolkhoz in Chuvashia, and "eight patriotic associations from regions of the Urals and Siberia."[37]

One week after the initial announcement, M. Antonov, president of the Union for Spiritual Rebirth, publicly explained the Union's goals. The Union expects resolution of the country's crisis "only on the condition that there is a moral rebirth of every nation of our great Fatherland." Only those patriotic organizations that have actually shown by deeds that they support socialism and the preservation of the country's independence, and that support the party in its perestroika policies, may join the Union. The manifesto of the Union, which was published next to Antonov's article, was directed to "our compatriots, fellow Russian (*rossiiane*) brothers and sisters, all nations that have flourished in our Fatherland."[38]

Judging by the text of the manifesto and Antonov's article, the Union is a strongly nationalistic, anti-Western, and anti-liberal body that appeals simultaneously to communist and Russian nationalist slogans. It would not be unfair to call the Union a national-socialist organization, envisioning the "Fatherland" as a multinational country led by the Russians. As if one such Union were not enough, many of the same organizations that sponsored the Union for Spiritual Rebirth were behind the establishment of yet another body, also in March 1989 and also in Moscow, namely, the "Moscow Russian Patriotic Society 'Fatherland' " (*Moskovskoe russkoe patrioticheskoe obshchestvo "Otechestvo"*). The Moscow Society clearly sees itself as an ethnic organization, as shown by its use of the adjective *russkoe*, not *rossiiskoe*, the former being an ethnic or personal designation, the latter a territorial one in which non-Russian citizens of the Russian Republic can also be included. Its program advocates the establishment of a Russian (meaning RSFSR) television network and a Russian academy of sciences, and several other causes. It stresses "military-patriotic education" and includes on its board at least one military officer.[39] In its stronger emphasis on Russian ethnicity, the association differs from the Union for Spiritual Rebirth, which is clearly interested in extending its activities throughout the entire Soviet Union.

This brief and necessarily superficial review of recent Russian initiatives nevertheless reveals a rise in nationalist sentiment and concerns, and testifies at the same time to the continuing confusion about what kind of country it is that the Russians are envisaging. Some of the positions mentioned here closely parallel those of empire-savers, although the empire-savers prefer to call themselves Soviet rather than Russian, even when they really mean Russian. Other positions are more clearly concerned with Russia proper, the RSFSR. But those "culturalist" nationalists who stress the Orthodox religious factor and who emphasize the Russians' ties to their fellow Slavs appear to be rather oblivious to the fact that the Russian Republic is the homeland of several Muslim nations, including the Volga Tatars, who form a large nation not only by RSFSR but also by all-Union standards. The culturalists' neglect of the non-Slavs within Russia, and their accenting of Ukrainian and Belorussian affinity with the Russians—some of them imply that the three nations are really one—seem to betray an "empire-saving" rather than a "nation-building" orientation.

Russia as a Democratic Nation-State

The third model of Russia is that which is beginning to take shape in the thinking of the activists and theorists of the national democratic movement of Russia. As of the summer of 1989, the Russian democratic movement has not created all-Russia structures comparable to those already existing in the Baltic states or even those emerging in Ukraine and Belorussia. But "popular" or "national" fronts have already been created in the Urals, Yaroslavl, Leningrad and, most recently, Moscow. It is only a matter of time, one imagines, before they coalesce into a Russian popular front.

It is also conceivable that these fronts will unite to proclaim the establishment of an "all-Union"—rather than a Russian—popular front, thus setting up the Russians in a position of leadership once again. If this happens, Russian democrats will be following in the footsteps of the Bolsheviks as well as of their democratic predecessors in pre-1917 Russia, who until the very last declined to identify themselves simply as "Great Russians." On this subject, the recollections of Paul Miliukov, written in the 1920s, are very revealing. He recalled how before the 1917 revolution non-Russian nationalists asked the Russian democratic intelligentsia to redefine its national identity as a precondition for cooperation. In asking the Russians to become "Great Russian," to define themselves in ethnic terms rather than as a group representing the whole empire, the non-Russians argued that this redefinition would make it possible for all parties to act as equals. But by defining themselves as "Russian" in an imperial rather than a national sense, in the view of the non-Russians, Russian democrats were making a claim to superiority and leadership (*pervenstvo*) over the other nationalities. In Miliukov's retrospective view, the Russian intelligentsia could not have acted other than it did, since yielding to those demands required "undoing" Russian history.[40] In other words, it required denying legitimacy to that product of Russian history that Miliukov and his fellow intellectuals really valued—the empire.

Will the Russian intelligentsia in the 1990s agree to do what its predecessors refused to do in the 1900s? The article by Balakhonov mentioned earlier is remarkable for addressing, in the most explicit manner possible, the necessity to dissociate the Russian nation from imperial ambitions, thereby possibly giving the answer that Miliukov was unable to give.[41] If Balakhonov's proposal for the solution of the "Russian question" were implemented, it would not only allow the non-Russian peoples of the USSR to become free but, in the words of Milovan Djilas, would also mean "the emancipation of the Russian nation from the present (and often unwillingly borne) burdens of empire." In a conversation with George Urban, Djilas put his view of the Soviet-imperial versus Russian-national problem in the following way:

> We are talking about the natural expiry of an unnatural tyrannical régime which is bound to come, as surely as the British and French Empires had to face their demise when the time was ripe. The Russian people would benefit the most. They would gain a free and more prosperous life and yet remain, undoubtedly, a great nation.
>
> You see, the Communist system has forced the Russian people into a state of sulking introspection which seeks outlets in xenophobia, petulant demonstrations of national superiority—or, at the opposite end, maudlin admissions of national inferiority. I firmly believe that a reduced but self-confident, opened-up democratic Russian state would induce much less brooding in the Russian people and make them a happier race, to the extent that Russians can be happy. Imagine what it would mean for free men and women everywhere to see this last bastion of universal unfreedom go the way of all tyrannies![42]

Let me summarize the most important points of the Balakhonov proposal—bearing in mind that at least some of his ideas are also being debated and presumably shared by the Democratic Union, which may well be the first major Russian political force that is both national (or "nationalist") and liberal, pro-Western, and democratic. For complex and deep historical reasons, Balakhonov argues, Russian national consciousness has become tied to the idea of empire (which also happens to be an autocratic, centralized state). In these deep historical recesses he sees the source of the most recent expressions of "imperial ideology." Balakhonov also thinks that the extremist positions of the organization Pamiat' are rooted in an imperial-statist outlook.

The primary task of the Russian nation, Balakhonov writes, should be to reshape its national consciousness. The Russians need to fathom the value of democracy and to see that Russia's "voluntary withdrawal from the 'large empire' of the USSR" will be beneficial to the Russian people. The Russians ought to understand, too, that the "'small empire'—the RSFSR," which he says forms the core of the "large empire," should also be dismantled.

Specifically, Balakhonov proposes the formation of three or four Russian-speaking states out of those parts of the RSFSR where Russians predominate. Those democratic and sovereign states would include: (1) Russia proper, embracing Moscow and historic Russian lands to the west of the Urals where the Great Russians and the Russian state were originally formed; (2) West Siberia; (3) East Siberia (although he takes into account the possibility that there would be a single Siberian state); (4) the Russian Far East. Balakhonov thinks that the creation of independent states in Siberia and the Far East would enable the Russian nation to participate in, and benefit from, the development of the "Pacific Community" in the twenty-first century. In any case, he believes that the dismantling of the empire would benefit both the non-Russians and the Russians themselves. Indeed, he thinks that some Russians already acknowledge this possibility: "Both in Russian Siberia and in the Far East, voices are already heard in favor of their economic, state-political, and cultural autonomy, in favor of reducing their dependence on the supercentralized administration."[43]

Balakhonov recognizes that his plans are not likely to win mass support in the foreseeable future. Therefore, he thinks that the most urgent task is to advance a restructuring of the Russian people's consciousness, because most Russians still remain under the influence of an imperial mentality: "The imperial instinct of the Russians is exceptionally strong, and as yet we simply do not imagine a form of existence other than the framework of the present empire from Brest to Vladivostok." Because the Russians have not been under foreign rule for many centuries, they do not understand what national oppression means and accordingly do not sympathize with the national-liberation movements of dependent nations. Nevertheless, the Russians will have to accept the fall of the empire as a result of which they will become free themselves—or they can try to preserve the empire but in doing so they will deprive themselves of freedom. The latter course might ultimately lead to the rise of a "great-power Russian Nazism."[44]

Balakhonov's is not a lone voice. *Atmoda*, the newspaper of the National Front of Latvia, recently published a speech before the Baltic Assembly by Boris Rakitsky, vice-president of the Soviet Sociological Association. As quoted in *Literaturnaia Rossiia*, Rakitsky said:

> The Russian democratic movement, I assure you, is concerned now precisely with its inability to penetrate into the thicket of popular consciousness in order to try to root out its imperial component. This consciousness is great-power consciousness in form, but slavish in content. But we are working, we are trying on our part to support your efforts.[45]

In his article "To Russian Society on Russian Problems," Alexander Kazakov called upon his compatriots to stop identifying their fatherland with the state and "the authority." The Russian people have to learn, Kazakov said, not to mistake their love for their native land with love of the state and its political, military, and economic might. The Russians should work above all for "the revival of a national Russia" (*natsional'-naia Rossiia*).[46]

It is impossible to determine at this stage how widely ideas like Balakhonov's, Rakitsky's, or Kazakov's are supported. Balakhonov himself began to speak out in the 1970s in favor of dismantling the Soviet empire and replacing it by a Russian democratic nation-state as one of the empire's successors—and was punished for it at the time. Irrespective of how widely his ideas are shared, he is certainly right in paying attention to the political prospects of regional movements within the Russian Republic, including those in the ethnically Russian core of the RSFSR.

If the Russian nation ever frees itself of its "imperial mentality," by which Balakhonov and his fellow-thinkers claim it is dominated, this will not happen as a consequence of some kind of massive intellectual revolution originating in Moscow or Leningrad. It is more realistic to suppose that the change will begin along the path that many are apparently taking in "the provinces," where regional "popular fronts," like those already formed in the Urals, various Siberian centers, and in European Russian provincial capitals, are being established.

Some signs point to a democratic Russian nationalism—a democratic Russian national consciousness—taking shape in organized form. The Democratic Union appears to be a Russian, not an "all-Union," organization. On March 12, 1989, it held a demonstration in honor of the first Revolution of 1917, and the participants, according to *The New York Times,* carried Russian flags of a pre-Soviet vintage. Just as the Balts and Ukrainians celebrate various dates in 1918 as their national independence days, so democratic Russians seem to have adopted the March 1917 anniversary as a Russian national holiday to mark their nation's emancipation from tsarism.[47]

March 1917 is not a date Russian nationalists in the RSFSR Writers' Union (not to mention the Pamiat' Society or its fellow travelers) would choose for a Russian national holiday. Some of them are more critical of those who overthrew the tsar in March 1917 than they are of those who seized power in November 1917.[48] It is easy to understand why this should be so: The liberals, radicals, and democrats inaugurated the disintegration of the empire; the Bolsheviks restored it.

Non-Russian Responses

The debate about Russia's identity is not an internal Russian national affair. The questions that the Russians ask themselves also evoke reactions from their fellow citizens of other nationalities on such matters as the status of the RSFSR and Russian ideas about relations between the Russian nation and the two other East Slavic nations. Most important of all is the question of Russian versus Soviet identity. It is under this last rubric that Russian-Jewish relations are being debated.

Those Russian nation-builders who think of the Russian republic solely as the national homeland of the Russians seem to pay scant attention to the fact that the RSFSR includes about 20 autonomous republics, including the Tatar, Bashkir, Daghestan, and Yakut ASSR's. Those Russian culturalists who are preoccupied with the question of Slavic unity, especially East Slavic unity, and stress the religious, Orthodox contribution to Russian identity, seem oblivious to the fact that even if the Russian nation as they define it is Slavic and Orthodox-Christian (the latter at least in tradition), many millions of citizens of Russia (the RSFSR) are neither Slavic nor Orthodox.

It is commonly known that the coterie of ethnic Russian nationalists grouped around *Nash sovremennik* is anti-Semitic. *Nash sovremennik* was also involved in conflicts with Georgian writers. But, as Julia Wishnevsky has noted, the non-Russian members of the RSFSR Writers' Union, especially Tatars and members of the nationalities of the Soviet North, have made it clear that they have "no time for Russian nationalism." At the 1988 RSFSR Writers' Union plenum they protested about the discrimination in wages, occupations, and cultural matters in favor of Russians and against their nations in their ethnic homelands. They also objected to discrimination within the RSFSR Writers' Union itself, pointing out that *Nash sovremennik*, the journal of the Union, did not have a single non-Russian on its editorial board.[49]

Some non-Russians propose that the RSFSR should become a real federation, which it is in name but not even in its formal constitutional structure. The so-called autonomous republics do not enjoy any autonomy, and most of the Republic, considered as ethnic Russian territory, does not have any even formally autonomous organs. To correct this problem, a deputy from the Evenki autonomous district to the Congress of People's Deputies proposed the establishment in the Russian Republic parliament of two chambers—a chamber of the Republic and a chamber of Nationalities.[50]

The Tatars, Russia's largest non-Russian nation, wish to go further in trying to improve their position. In late 1988, the journal of the Tatar party committee, *Slovo agitatora*, published a draft of the program of the "Tatar Civic Center," which is the Tatar counterpart to the national fronts familiar from the Baltic republics. The draft demanded that the sovereign rights "of the people of the Tatar ASSR" be realized, that the people of "Tatarstan" be equitably represented in the government of the USSR and RSFSR, and that the rights of the Tatar ASSR be gradually widened, eventually making Tatarstan a Union republic.[51] In May 1989, the congress of the Tatar ASSR Writers' Union unanimously voted to ask an upcoming plenum of the CPSU Central Committee to grant the Tatar ASSR the status of Union republic. It was noted at the congress that only 12 percent of Tatar children in Tataria study Tatar in school, and only 7 percent of Tatar children in the entire RSFSR do so. The Tatars clearly hope that this situation will change for the better if their republic is raised in status. Among other issues discussed were matters of history: Speakers called for a reassessment of an official condemnation of the "Sultan-Galievist" national deviation and for the repudiation of the 1944 CPSU resolution that branded Tatar history of the medieval period (the period of the "Mongol Yoke" in Russia) as "reactionary."[52]

Acknowledging the validity of many complaints of the non-Russian nationalities (of which those cited above are only examples), a group of Russian writers, including M. Alekseev, V. Belov, Iu. Bondarev, and V. Rasputin, published an appeal entitled "We Have a Common Fate." The writers thanked various Bashkir, Tatar, Chuvash, and Mari writers by name for not blaming the Russian nation for their own plight. The Russian authors also issued a call for the restoration of national and cultural rights, including language rights, to all nations living in Russia. They specifically endorsed a prompt establishment of a Tatar newspaper in Moscow, "where hundreds of thousands of Tatars live." They called on regional Russian-language literary journals as well as local radio and television to cover the life of "fraternal nations."[53]

However welcome these declarations may be to the non-Russians of the RSFSR, it is doubtful that they address their most important concerns. And, in any case, statements in defense of the Tatars or the Peoples of the North need to be weighed against those that emphasize the Slavic and Orthodox character of "Russia." This in itself would tend to promote a sense of second-class citizenship among non-Russians. There is no evidence suggesting that many influential Russians are prepared to accept today the ideas of Eurasianism, a current in Russian cultural and political thought in the 1920s and 1930s that proposed to redefine Russian identity in a fundamental manner by establishing a new entity of "Eurasia." In it, the Russians were to be fully equal with the peoples of the former empire's Asian possessions, such as the Volga Tatars. The only well-known figure who speaks in favor of Eurasian ideas today, but without calling himself a Eurasian, is Lev Gumilev.[54]

As might be expected, the resurgence of Russian nationalism, which expressed itself in the publication on a mass scale of such Russian nineteenth-century historians as Nikolai Karamzin (1766–1826), Sergei Soloviev (1820–79), and Vasily Kliuchevsky (1841–1911), was watched with great attention by the Ukrainian intelligentsia. However gratifying the works of these and other historians might be to Russian national feeling, they are bound to displease the Ukrainians, who think of themselves as a separate nation from the Russians. The Russian history presented by these pre-1917 scholars assumes that all Eastern Slavs are, and have been throughout their history, one Russian nation—albeit with regional differences and characteristics—which found its authentic expression in the tsarist state. In other words, these Russian histories of the pre-1917 period, which are now becoming accessible to the general public, are helping those who favor an imperial model of Russia. Karamzin believed that the tsarist state was the most perfect expression of the national character of Russia, and even the title of his magnum opus, *History of the Russian State*, conveys this idea. In the words of Anatole G. Mazour, Karamzin's work "is not even a history of the state—it is a rhetorical, panegyrical narrative that endeavors to prove that autocracy alone has bestowed all the blessings that the Russian Empire ever enjoyed." Mazour quotes the famous Pushkin epigram on Karamzin to illustrate how the contemporaries of the historian understood the political message of his work:

> In his history, beauty and simplicity
> Prove without bias
> The necessity of Autocracy
> And the charm of the Whip.[55]

Bearing some of these things in mind, one can appreciate why members of the Ukrainian intelligentsia responded to the revival of interest in Russian history by asking questions similar to that of Pavlo Zahrebelny, an establishment figure par excellence:

> There is much talk these days about Russian patriotism. . . . But has anyone ever said anything about Ukrainian patriotism? Now, when the histories written by Kliuchevsky, Soloviev, and Karamzin are being republished, perhaps we should raise the matter of republishing *The History of Ukraine-Rus'* by Mykhailo Hrushevsky, on the pages of which issues of Ukrainian patriotism are elucidated.[56]

Mykhailo Hrushevsky (1866–1934), unlike Karamzin and the latter's Russian successors, Soloviev and Kliuchevsky, was not a "statist" but a "populist" and a "federalist." While working as professor of Ukrainian history at the University of Lviv (then in Austria's province of Galicia), where he was appointed in 1894, Hrushevsky became active in many scholarly projects, the most important of which was a multivolume history of Ukraine. Hrushevsky's life was dedicated to demonstrating that the Ukrainian people—who, he thought, constituted a society distinct from the state—have had a history of their own, even when they lacked a state. That history should not be subsumed under some artificial formula of a broader "all-Russian" or imperial history. (Hrushevsky thought that the history of the Russian people also should not be reduced to the history of the Muscovite and imperial *state,* and his position on this subject had sympathizers among Russian historians.)

Hrushevsky was also a political activist. In March 1917, he became the head of the Ukrainian Central Rada and held that post until the overthrow of the Rada in the Skoropadsky coup of May 1918. During Hrushevsky's tenure, Ukraine proclaimed its independence from Russia in January 1918 and then signed a peace treaty with Germany and Austria-Hungary at Brest-Litovsk in February 1918. (The Soviets signed "their" Brest treaty in March.) In 1924, with Moscow's consent, Hrushevsky returned to Kyiv from his Vienna exile. As was to be expected, he again played a highly visible public role. But as Stalin launched his attack on Ukraine, Hrushevsky was exiled in 1931 to Moscow. He died under somewhat mysterious circumstances in 1934.

Hrushevsky had been attacked even in his lifetime, but after his death he became a symbol of Ukrainian "bourgeois nationalism" and "fascism." After 1937, no work by Hrushevsky was published in the USSR and the historian's name gradually disappeared from books and journals. A modest attempt to bring Hrushevsky into the realm of scholarly and public discussion was made in the 1960s, but it ended soon and in any case never resulted in the republication of his writings. In the 1970s, Ukrainian scholars were forbidden even to mention his name.[57] This background information allows one to appreciate the significance of Zahrebelny's "raising the matter" of Hrushevsky in 1988. Zahrebelny's question has since been answered in the affirmative in his homeland. The most important work of Hrushevsky, his ten-volume history of "Ukraine-Rus'," has not been republished, but some of his other writings have been serialized in literary journals.[58] [Hrushevsky's history was finally published in Ukraine in the 1990s.]

Literary journals have become the forum for what amounts to a Ukrainian-Russian debate on a number of questions, including the legacy of Kyivan Rus'. The debate on Kyivan Rus' began when a corresponding member of the USSR Academy of Sciences, O. Trubachev, declared that it should be called a Russian, and not an "East Slavic" state, and that its culture, including its language, should be called Russian.[59]

One might add that the Russian-Ukrainian dispute about Kyiv is not limited to the question of its identity in the Middle Ages. A leading Moscow journal, *Novyi mir*, in its April 1989 issue, published a selection of essays by the prominent Russian historian and philosopher G. P. Fedotov (1886–1951), including the previously unpublished "Three Capitals." That essay contains the following passage about the third of the three capitals in question and touches on the very essence of the Ukrainian-Russian relationship:

> It seems strange to speak about Kiev in our times. Until very recently, it was easy for us to renounce Kiev's glory and infamy and trace our descent from [the banks of] the Oka and the Volga [rivers]. We ourselves gave Ukraine away to Hrushevsky and paved the way for Ukrainian separatists. Did Kiev ever occupy the center of our thought, of our love? A striking fact: Modern Russian literature has completely left Kiev out.[60]

As for the debate inaugurated by Trubachev, it has since moved to a literary journal published in Moscow, *Druzhba narodov*.[61] The debate has expanded in scope to examine traditional Russian attitudes toward the Ukrainian language, culture, and history. A young Ukrainian critic, Mykola Ryabchuk, listed no less a figure than Vissarion Belinsky among those Russians of the past who had denied the Ukrainians the right to consider themselves a nation.[62] Another literary critic, Serhii Hrechaniuk, linked Trubachev's ideas with those of a pre-1917 enemy of the Ukrainians, N. S. Shchegolev, the author of a notorious anti-Ukrainian tract, "The Ukrainian Movement as a Contemporary Stage of South-Russian Separatism," described by some as a "textbook for policemen."[63]

The feeling among the nationally conscious Ukrainian intelligentsia that the basic problems of the Ukrainians in the USSR today have less to do with Marxism or even Marxism–Leninism and more with traditional Russian conceptions about Ukraine was considerably reinforced when a Kyiv Komsomol daily, *Moloda hvardiia*, published an essay by Vladimir I. Vernadsky, "The Ukrainian Question and Russian Public Opinion." Vernadsky, known to the world primarily as a Russian scientist, was also a Ukrainian patriot. In 1918 he became the first president of the Ukrainian Academy of Sciences established under Hetman Skoropadsky. The article in question was apparently written in 1915 but not published previously. In it, Vernadsky reviewed the history of the Ukrainian–Russian relationship from the Union of Pereiaslav until the outbreak of World War I. His leitmotif was that both the Russian state and Russian liberal society had consistently sought to diminish and eventually to obliterate a separate Ukrainian national identity. The Vernadsky text created something of a sensation when it was published in 1988, and it has been reprinted in the chief literary monthly, *Vitchyzna*, and in several regional newspapers.[64]

All these themes were synthesized by Ivan Dziuba in an article called "Do We Conceive of National Culture as a Totality?" which appeared in the cultural weekly, *Kul'tura i zhyttia*, in early 1989.[65] (Dziuba was jailed in the early 1970s for arguing in his book *Internationalism or Russification?* that Ukrainian culture should be allowed to develop into a full-fledged, complete, and modern national culture, and not treated as an ethnographic, provincial version of a higher "all-Russian" culture, and for asserting that there was continuity between the tsarist and the Soviet treatment of Ukraine.) Even more surprising, the Kyiv article was reprinted, at the end of 1988, in *Kommunist*, the CPSU's main theoretical journal.[66] The publication of Dziuba's article in *Kommunist* would support the view that some influential circles in Moscow favor a reconsideration of traditional Russian notions on Ukrainian nationality.

The view that Stalinism, Khrushchevism, and Brezhnevism-Suslovism (these designations are used in the Ukrainian press) continued tsarist policies toward Ukraine is expressed with increasing openness. Borys

Kharchuk, for example, claimed to see a direct and uninterrupted line from Peter the Great's ban on Ukrainian printing in 1720, to Alexander II's decrees of 1863 and 1876 (which respectively restricted and banned the use of Ukrainian in publishing), to Stalinist and Brezhnevian anti-Ukrainian measures.[67]

Borys Oliinyk, a poet in good standing with the authorities, who was elected deputy to the USSR People's Congress from the Communist Party list, stressed wryly in a speech commemorating Taras Shevchenko, the great nineteenth-century Ukrainian poet, that the same poems of Shevchenko were banned under the tsars and under Stalin and Brezhnev, and had become available to the Ukrainian public only under glasnost. "Isn't this a striking coincidence?" he asked.[68]

Those Shevchenko poems (or parts of poems) that were not published until quite recently dealt with the relations of Russia and Ukraine from the times of Bohdan Khmelnytsky in the mid-seventeenth century, through the era of Ivan Mazepa and Peter the Great in the early eighteenth century, to the reign of Catherine II at the end of that century. Shevchenko condemned Khmelnytsky for entering into what Soviet historiography likes to call the "re-union of Ukraine with Russia" (1654), and had harsh words for Peter I and Catherine II. Thus, Peter "crucified Ukraine," and Catherine "finished off" her victim. Even before the "rehabilitation" of Shevchenko's banned poems, some Ukrainian literary figures—not official historians—undertook a reappraisal of the heretofore totally negative assessment of Ivan Mazepa. Mazepa's alliance with Sweden's Charles XII in order to free Ukraine from its Russian connection, as is well known, ended at the Battle of Poltava (July 1709) with the rout of the combined Swedish-Cossack forces and was followed by Mazepa's exile and Peter's brutal suppression of Ukrainian autonomy. Ever since the mid-1930s, the official Soviet line has condemned Mazepa's "treason"—thus holding exactly the same view of the unlucky Hetman as apologists for tsarist Russia. (In tsarist Russia, Ukrainian nationalists, even mild autonomists, were called "Mazepists," which was a derogatory term denoting separatist and traitor.) However, in December 1988, two periodicals presented a new view of Mazepa. *Kultura i zhyttia* published a poem by the late Volodymyr Sosiura originally written in the 1920s. (A fragment of the poem had been published in 1929.) The Ukrainian poet, who continued to work on this poem as late as 1960, was aware that his approach to Mazepa went against not only the party line but also Alexander Pushkin's famous narrative poem *Poltava*.

Sosiura wrote, "O Pushkin, I love you but I love truth even more." He compared Mazepa with George Washington as a leader who fought for his country. The publication of the poem was accompanied by articles that took a somewhat more cautious line but in the end agreed that even if Mazepa betrayed Peter his actions did not necessarily mean that he also committed treason against Ukraine.[69]

This cautious attempt to explain Mazepa's action was subsequently challenged by a historian who argued that the designation of "traitor" did not at all apply to Mazepa. Mazepa owed loyalty to Ukraine, not to Russia or Peter, and was required to follow a policy he considered best for the Ukrainian people. If anyone, Peter was the traitor, for he violated the agreements Moscow had made with the Ukrainians in 1654.[70]

It is quite clear that these "historical" controversies and celebrations are really about the present status of Ukraine in the Soviet Union. Some commentators do not even pretend otherwise. Thus a Kharkiv writer, Radii Polonsky, in an article written in late 1988, quotes from notes he made in 1974–1977, which, he said, contained the following passage: "What used to be considered chauvinism and Ukrainophobia now is called internationalism. People whom Lenin used to call 'great-power bullies' now call themselves Leninist-internationalists."[71] Such people, Polonsky went on, continue to be active in the period of glasnost and perestroika. Polonsky described Yevgeny Primakov's project to develop "international structures" via a "rotation of cadres along horizontal lines" as a plan "to artificially mix nations." It is clear to Polonsky that "national nihilism" has supporters in high places.

In Polonsky's opinion, such a position derives from two different sources. One is the tsarist idea of "one and indivisible Russia" and comes from the past. The other source of inspiration to the "Brezhnev-ite-Suslovist" policy comes "from outside": the United States of America. The Brezhnevites were impressed by the American model because the American nation is based on a non-national—"extra-na-tional"—principle, and because the American nation represents a con-glomerate of peoples who are united by a common English language. But "our pseudo-ideologists" have forgotten, Polonsky says, that "the great American nation" has behind it "powerful historico-geographic and socio-economic factors of long duration, and not armchair fantasies of power-hungry individuals." Second, and more important, the Brezh-nevites "have ignored" the will of the Soviet peoples, including the un-flinching will of Russia itself to remain Russia, and not to dissolve itself in a conglomerate. "As we now see," Polonsky observed, "they have not succeeded."[72]

Precisely because they fear for their own survival as a nation, the Ukrainians are among the most vocal supporters of the restoration of Russia as a full-fledged republic in the form of the RSFSR. The already quoted poet-politician Oliinyk, for example, went so far in defending Russia's rights as to complain that Russia did not have a separate seat in the United Nations, which it obviously much deserved. He also said that Russia needs its own Central Committee, its own academy, and all the rest.[73]

The theme of Russia as a republic like the others emerged especially strongly in the speeches of some Baltic deputies to the USSR Congress of People's Deputies. Janis Peters from Latvia, for example, pointed out that central agencies such as Gosplan also "violate the sovereignty" of Russia, and he wondered why the Russians themselves were not speaking up more in behalf of their republic. "Why is Russia afraid to become independent of the all-Union diktat?" Peters asked.[74]

In what was unquestionably the most remarkable analysis of the entire complex issue of the nationalities under the Soviet system presented at the Congress, the Estonian Deputy Klara Hallik argued that the interests of Russia, the Russian nation, also suffer under the "unnatural" and "antidemocratic" socialism that preserves "habits of imperial thinking."[75] Russian national consciousness suffers because of its "truncated" state structure, whose powers have been taken over by the organs of the USSR. Moscow rules Russia not as a country but as a conglomerate of regions, and Russian identity becomes diluted in an all-Union identity. This impedes Russia's national revival. The struggle against bureaucratic centralism that other republics are waging is, in consequence, mistaken for a struggle against Russia. If a full-fledged institutional structure were created in Russia, the majority of existing all-Union agencies and organizations would no longer be necessary.

Hallik also warned against the tendency to confuse integration with centralization and subordination. Only free nations can join the process of integration—and so the centralization being practiced in the USSR runs counter to natural tendencies toward integration. "Russia, let alone Moscow, cannot be considered a center even for Slavic languages, let alone Turkic, Baltic, or Finno-Ugric ones." Similarly, religion and the church are gaining in importance in the contemporary world, but Moscow, the state's capital, is the center for the Russian Orthodox Church alone. For the adherents of Islam, their centers are outside the borders of the state, as they are for Catholics and some other Christians. For Latvians and Estonians, the cultural attraction is to the Scandinavian countries in the Baltic. All Soviet nations should be free to contribute in their unique ways to world culture. Hallik questioned the meaning of various slogans applied to internationality relations in the USSR, including "a strong center and strong republics." What is that "strong center of ours?" Hallik asked. Has some previously unknown "sixteenth republic" been formed in the USSR?[76]

Conclusions

There is no question that the Russian intelligentsia is giving much thought to the problems of Russian national identity, including the political issues involved in those problems. It is also clear that the non-Russians are pressing for a solution of the Russian problem by means of an institutional separation of Russia from the USSR as a prerequisite for overcoming "imperial thinking" and imperial practices in the Soviet Union.

What do "ordinary" Russians—the *russkii narod*—think about the matter? Sergei Grigoriants started his recent article on "The Russian National Movement" in the following way: "As yet, a Russian national movement that could become the support of a future democratic state does not exist in our country."[77] Although democratic organizations do exist among the Russians, they are relatively weak and often lack a clearly defined national outlook. Grigoriants, who thinks that Pamiat' represents the statist or imperial version of Russian national consciousness taken from the tsarist past, concedes that no counterweight to it has yet emerged that would be both democratic and national. In his view, the political spectrum lacks a force that would promote the cause of a democratic Russia and focus on the fact that Russians too are one of the nationalities of the Soviet Union and that their national needs should be met as well. Grigoriants's analysis cannot help but make a historian wonder if those democrats of his acquaintance are not behaving in the same way as did the prerevolutionary Russian democrats in Miliukov's recollections.[78]

Other historical analogies come to mind as well. Especially suggestive are the parallels between the problem of "Russia" versus the Soviet state and the problem of German nationalism in the nineteenth-century Habsburg monarchy up to its fall in 1918. Allan Janik and Stephen Toulmin drew such parallels in their book, *Wittgenstein's Vienna*, which was first published in 1973. As in the present-day Soviet Union, in the Habsburg monarchy of the late nineteenth and early twentieth centuries, all problems were conceptualized as "national" problems. Moreover, the Germans in the Habsburg monarchy—just as the Russians today— did not have certain political options available to other nations precisely because of their identification with the ruling center.[79]

A somewhat different parallel suggests itself from the experience of the Ottoman Empire, whose fall did result in the rise of a Turkish na- tion-state in the old territorial and political core of the empire. More- over, much of its periphery had gradually "peeled away" even before the Ottoman Empire disintegrated. Whether "Ottomanization" is in fact a prospect for the Soviet Union in its "inner" empire is another matter, but Timothy Garton Ash believes it is already under way in the East European "outer" empire.[80]

The Soviet Union and Yugoslavia are heirs of the old Habsburg, Ottoman, and tsarist Russian monarchies, and according to John A. Armstrong both are facing a fundamental problem of reconciling within their borders nations with Christian and Islamic traditions and their profoundly contrasting ways of life and value systems. Armstrong ex- pects the Christian–Muslim conflict to become a major issue in the com- ing years not only in Yugoslavia, where it has already been visible for some time, but also in the USSR.[81]

The above observations may be of use in studying the Soviet nation- alities problem, but they do not tell us which ideas are supported by ethnic Russians today. It may be useful to keep in mind the Germans in Bohemia, Slovenia, and other regions of the Habsburg empire before 1918, where indigenous nationalist movements were a threat to the Ger- mans, not simply as Germans—as one of many ethnic groups—but also as representatives of imperial authority. If this analogy is followed up, then Grigoriants's comments on the Russian reactions in the Baltic area are worth noting. The rise of the "interfronts," or "international fronts," consisting mainly of Russians and other Russian-speaking im- migrants, says Grigoriants, should be seen as an expression not of Rus- sian national sentiment but of an "unquestionably Soviet" sentiment."[82] In other words, most Russians in Latvia or Estonia view themselves as representatives of the state, of the Soviet-imperial principle, and feel they are living in a potentially rebellious province. They do not view themselves as a (Russian) national minority living in a country that is different from Russia.

It would seem, therefore, that a democratic, "normal" Russian national consciousness has a better chance of emerging in Russia proper, perhaps by developing from some regional autonomist grass roots. There may be reason to see the workers' movement in Siberia in the summer of 1989 in this light. It is evident that the striking miners objected not only to intolerable material conditions but equally strongly to the entire way of life to which they were condemned. They spoke up against bureaucracy, "colonialism," "domination by Moscow," and similar enemies. This would suggest that at stake there are relations between an imperial center and its dependent province.

What role did the intelligentsia have in this conflict? It so happens that in April 1989 the establishment in Novosibirsk of a "Siberian Independent Information Agency" was announced. (That announcement was not printed in the official Soviet media.) The inaugural meeting of that "Agency" was attended by representatives of independent journals from Novosibirsk (three publications) and Omsk, as well as by "independent journalists" from Irkutsk, Krasnoyarsk, Novokuznetsk, Kemerovo, and Yakutsk. The declaration adopted at the meeting contains phrases that reveal a sense of a distinct Siberian identity and suggest that it may be assuming a political form. Thus, the declaration protests that Siberia, "which finds itself in a colonial dependence on Moscow authorities," has no mass media of its own and is subject to an "information diktat" by the all-Union publications. Siberia has to make do with regional media, but lacks media covering Siberia as a whole. It was in order to correct this lack of specifically Siberian media that the Siberian information agency was founded. The agency's organizers said they would be willing to cooperate professionally with international and national news services interested in covering Siberian affairs. They also hoped that the new agency would be supported by the "Siberian people" (*Sibirskii narod*) as well as the authorities.[83]

Speeches at the April 1989 plenum of the CPSU Central Committee supplied another kind of evidence that social and economic problems are being perceived in Siberia as in essence problems of *regional* dependence on the center, which is viewed as the embodiment of the bureaucratic, command-administrative system. The plenum agenda was devoted to assessing the results of the March elections to the Congress of

People's Deputies. The elections resulted in defeats of numerous party officials and regional bosses, notably in Leningrad, Moscow, and Kyiv, the three largest cities of the Soviet Union. But as one of the losers, the Kemerovo oblast first secretary, noted, the biggest defeats of party officials happened in Siberia and the Far East, "from the Urals to the ocean." The secretary, A. G. Melnikov, noted that the whole area—with 30 million inhabitants—suffered from profound social tensions, that "people have come to live much worse," and that the problems were "critical." Melnikov cited coal and oil output figures on Siberia's contribution to the economy and complained that despite its importance Siberia was not treated as a single unit but that its regions were separately managed by central agencies from Moscow, all employing administrative-command methods "because we still do not know of any other way" to manage. The only way out of the critical situation was to give Siberia its own rights, its economic and administrative autonomy, and to treat it as an economic partner—and so assure its contribution to the national economy.[84] The appropriateness of these warnings was confirmed by the Siberian strikes.

The key issues for Russian democratic nationalism are also key for all currents of Russian national consciousness. The one to which most attention has been devoted in this study is the attitude toward the state. The second issue, whose urgency and potential destructiveness is daily becoming more apparent, is the social and economic question broadly defined. This somewhat general and academic term covers the most serious and pressing matters of daily life for millions of people: health, ecology, food supplies (or rather food shortages), education, wages, housing, work safety—the list goes on. The realization that in all these respects the Soviet Union lags behind most of the developed world, even certain parts of the Third World, is universal in the Soviet Union. Among Russians, this awareness is increasingly assuming the form of injured national feelings: "We, the Russians, who have suffered most, we who helped the others in the USSR, in Eastern Europe, Asia, Cuba, Africa, we are now poor and backward."

The resulting anger is directed against many targets. One obvious target is the state and party bureaucracy—"Moscow"; another—the nationalities, such as the Balts and the peoples of the Caucasus. Some elements are explaining the plight of Russia by accusing "the Jews, the internationalist Zionist conspiracy," or "the Masons." These extremists do not blame the state for the present crisis—and for the most part also not the communist ideology per se. Rather, they attribute the sins of the Soviet regime to the Jews who at one time or another occupied important posts in it and, by extension—to Jews as a people.

In such a situation it would seem imperative for the liberal and democratic Russian intelligentsia to make sure that the specifically national or nationalist Russian concerns and issues are not left to extremists of the Pamiat' kind. Against the right-wing models of Russia, which so prominently feature anti-Semitism and other forms of prejudice, the democrats and liberals need to propose their own democratic, tolerant, and progressive model of Russia. They cannot afford to ignore the specific Russian problem as they concern themselves with general social, economic, or political issues in somewhat abstract terms. In this regard, the Russian intelligentsia would do well to ponder the circumstances that in the 1920s had allowed the Fascists in Italy and the Nazis in Germany to capture considerable popular support by appealing to national sentiments and traditions.[85]

Clearly, the situation is very critical; and the intellectual and political confusion, overwhelming. The second question, therefore, that Russian nationalists, and everybody else in the Soviet Union, have to ask is: Which ideology and program currently "on the market" will the masses accept as their own? As so many thinking Russians are doing these days, Balakhonov quotes in his article the famous Pushkin lines expressing the poet's dread of "Russian mutiny, senseless and merciless." To prevent such a "mutiny," the intelligentsia will have to find a common language with the workers, the likes of whom struck the mines in Siberia. Will the Russian intelligentsia prove capable of accomplishing what Polish intellectuals accomplished in the 1970s? As the world knows, the Polish strikes of 1980 produced Solidarity, not a "senseless and merciless mutiny."[86]

One of the most insightful analyses of the Solidarity phenomenon was provided by Alain Touraine, the French sociologist. As Stanley Aronowitz puts it, Touraine sees the historical meaning of Solidarity, whose rise he believes to signal the end of communist society, in setting an alternative agenda of historical action, thereby challenging a major prerogative that the communist regime had reserved for itself.[87] To follow Solidarity in this respect will require that the Russian nationalist intelligentsia put aside its more abstract debates about Orthodox tradition and forget about Zionist plotters. Instead, the intellectuals in Russia (and in other republics) will have to think of ways in which they can help construct a new agenda, an alternative vision of the future. How they perform this task will help determine the shape of any new national identity or identities that are likely to emerge in the USSR. Touraine also offers some instructive thoughts on identity:

> To the sociologist, identity is . . . no longer an appeal to a mode of being but the claim to a capacity for action and for change. It is defined in terms of choice and not in terms of substance, essence, or tradition . . . if identity is opposed to the organization of social life, it will be marginalized or manipulated by those who direct it. On the other hand, the appeal to identity can be considered a labor of democracy, an awareness of the effort by which the actors of a social system that exerts a great deal of power upon itself and that is engaged in ceaseless change attempt to determine for themselves the conditions within which their collective and personal life is produced.[88]

As we have tried to show, any effort in this area will require the Russians to understand that the political entity many of them now accept as an empire is the same state they reject as an oppressive bureaucratic machine.

Notes

1. Aleksandr Zharnikov, "Natsional'noe samoopredelenie v zamysle i realizatsii," *Kommunist* (Moscow), no. 9 (June 1989): 62. Zharnikov is the scientific secretary of the Scientific Communism Section in the Institute of Marxism-Leninism in Moscow.

2. Radio Free Europe-Radio Liberty (hereafter RFE-RL), "Russian Nationalism Today," *Radio Liberty Research Bulletin* (Munich), Special Edition, December 19, 1988.

3. Ibid., p. 49.

4. Ibid., p. 25.

5. Ibid., p. 33.

6. *Izvestiia* (Moscow), June 11, 1969. Sakharov's address has been translated by Edward Kline; see *The New York Review of Books*, August 17, 1989, pp. 25–26. The quotation here is from p. 25.

7. Iurii Afanas'ev, "Perestroika i istoricheskoe znanie," *Literaturnaia Rossiia* (Moscow), June 17, 1988, pp. 2–3 and 8–9.

8. Alain Besançon, "Nationalism and Bolshevism in the USSR," in Robert

Conquest, ed., *The Last Empire: Nationality and the Soviet Future* (Stanford: Hoover Institution Press, 1986), p. 11.

9. Ibid., pp. 12–13.

10. Vladimir Balakhonov, "Sokhranenie imperii ili samosokhranenie na puti natsional'nogo suvereniteta—glavnaia natsional'naia problema russkogo naroda segodnia," *Russkaia mysl'* (Paris), June 23, 1989, pp. 6–7. Balakhonov's article was originally published in issue no. 13 of *Svobodnoe slovo*, the independent publication of the Democratic Union.

11. See the various "liberal" views expressed in the round-table discussion entitled "Demokratiia est' konflikt: poisk pravogo resheniia natsional'nykh problem v SSSR," *Vek XX i mir* (Moscow), no. 12 (1988): 8–17.

12. Valerii Tishkov, "Narody i gosudarstvo," *Kommunist*, no. 1 (January 1989): 49–59. In the original publication I erroneously called Tishkov the newly *appointed* head.

13. For a fuller discussion of this problem, see Roman Szporluk, "The Imperial Legacy and the Soviet Nationalities Problem," in Lubomyr Hajda and Mark Beissinger, eds., *The Nationalities Factor in Soviet Politics and Society* (Boulder, Colo.: Westview Press, 1990). Included as chapter 8 of this book.

14. Iu. V. Bromlei, "Byt' tsementiruiushchei siloi," *Sovetskaia kul'tura* (Moscow), June 25, 1988, p. 8.

15. Iu. V. Bromlei, "Natsional'nye problemy v usloviiakh perestroiki," *Voprosy istorii* (Moscow), no. 1 (1989): 40.

16. J. K. Rebane, "Stroit' vmeste razumnye otnosheniia," *Kommunist*, no. 4 (March 1989): 85. This argument is not new, of course, as the title of Ivan Dziuba's book written a quarter of a century ago—*Internationalism or Russification?*—reminds us. [The Ukrainian title of Dziuba's book is *Internatsionalizm chy rusyfikatsiia?*]

17. *Pravda* (Moscow), July 2, 1988, p. 8.

18. Ibid., April 27, 1989, p. 6.

19. S. L. Tikhvinskii, "Zadachi koordinatsii v oblasti istoricheskoi nauki," *Istoriia SSSR* (Moscow), no. 1 (1988): 119.

20. "Demokratiia est' konflikt," p. 10.

21. Mark G. Field, "Soviet Society and Communist Party Controls: A Case of Constricted Development," in Donald W. Treadgold, ed., *Soviet and Chinese Communism: Similarities and Differences* (Seattle: University of Washington Press, 1967), p. 196.

22. Alexander Yanov's and John B. Dunlop's many publications provide full documentation and analysis of those currents.

23. G. Sazonov, "Vasilii Belov: Ne boites' glasnosti!," *Pravda*, March 5, 1989. p. 1

24. Iurii Chernichenko, "Otmyt' Rossiiu," *Znamia* (Moscow), no. 2 (1989): 168–69.

25. Interview in *Literaturnaia Rossiia*, June 2, 1989, pp. 6–7.

26. "Za ob'ektivnost' v otechestvennoi istorii," *Nash sovremennik* (Moscow), no. 5 (1988): 186–88.

27. "Letter to the Soviet Government," *Literaturnyi Irkutsk*, December 1988, pp. 4 and 7.

28. Ibid. The authors refer to Lenin's *Polnoe sobranie sochinenii* (*Complete Collected Works*), vol. 22, pp. 229–30, to support their assertion. The Soviet scholar G. I. Kunitsyn, in "Samoopredelenie natsii—istoriia voprosa i sovremennost'," *Voprosy filosofii* (Moscow), no. 5 (1989): 66–86, argues that the Stalinist conception of the role of the Russian nation as the ruling nation of the Soviet state was put into practice after 1917, and that this was done in direct violation of Lenin's view. By depriving the RSFSR of the normal state structure of Soviet republics, and by placing Russia directly under central authorities, Stalin restored the prerevolutionary great-power, imperialist concept, but he disguised it under revolutionary terminology. (See especially pp. 76–78.) There is not a word about "Zionists" or "Trotskyists" in Kunitsyn's balanced and well-documented account.

29. Roy Medvedev wrote more than ten years ago: "It is a fact that the national life of Russians is hampered to a far greater degree than that of say, Armenians, Georgians, and the Uzbek peoples.

"Thus, for example, the villages and hamlets of basically Russian districts are in an immeasurably more neglected condition than the villages of Ukraine, Moldavia, the Transcaucasus, and the Baltic. Furthermore, Russians are basically deprived of their capital. As the capital of a multinational Union, Moscow has almost lost its traits of a national Russian city, a capital of Russian lands such as it was prior to the revolution. The more European, industrial, and bureaucratic Petersburg was the capital of the Empire. This transformation of Moscow into an international center devoid of clear national lines is by no means a positive consequence for the whole Russian nation.

"At present, the weakening of the national foundations of Russian life is neither legal [*zakonomernyi*—i.e., a natural process], nor progressive.

"How could not only the preservation but also the development of the distinctive originality of the Russian people be furthered? This is a question that demands social analysis. Let us note, first of all, that the old proposal of separating the capitals of the U.S.S.R. and the R.S.F.S.R., for which many people were condemned under Stalin, is not so fruitless. Similarly, it is necessary to undertake wide ranging and urgent measures for upgrading agriculture and culture in the basically Russian districts, especially in the center and the north of the European area of the R.S.F.S.R."

See "What Awaits Us in the Future? (Regarding A. I. Solzhenitsyn's Letter)," in Michael Meerson-Aksenov and Boris Shragin, eds. *The Political, Social, and Religious Thought of Russian "Samizdat"—An Anthology* (Belmont, Mass.: Nordland, 1977), pp. 77–78.

30. Feliks Dymov, "Chto ne zapreshcheno—razresheno," *Literaturnaia Rossiia*, no. 24, June 17, 1988, pp. 2–3. See also a report on the symposium (whose participants included D. S. Likhachev and N. A. Tolstoy), "Velikii gorod s oblastnoi sud'boi?" *Literaturnaia gazeta* (Moscow), March 2, 1988, p. 10.

31. S. Galaeva, "Narodnyi dom Rossii," *Literaturnaia Rossiia*, no. 25, June 23, 1989, p. 18.

32. See the interview with the chairman of the board, corresponding member of the USSR Academy of Sciences Oleg Trubachev, entitled "Russkaia èntsiklopediia," in *Literaturnaia gazeta*, March 22, 1989, p. 5; and the report entitled "Plany 'Russkoi èntsiklopedii'," *Literaturnaia Rossiia*, April 14, 1989, p. 3.

33. John B. Dunlop, "Two Noteworthy Russian Nationalist Initiatives," RFE-RL, *Report on the USSR* (Munich), no. 21 (May 26, 1989): 3.

34. Ibid., pp. 3–4.

35. *Moskovskii literator*, December 16, 1988, p. 3, as quoted by Dunlop, "Two Noteworthy Russian Nationalist Initiatives," p. 2.

36. Boris Ivanovich Tsarev, "Siloi rossiiskogo bratstva," *Literaturnaia Rossiia*, June 16, 1989, p. 11.

37. "Sozdan Soiuz dukhovnogo vozrozhdeniia otechestva," *Moskovskii Literator*, March 24, 1989, p. 1; and *Literaturnaia Rossiia*, March 31, 1989, p. 10.

38. M. Antonov, "S pozitsii sotsializma," *Moskovskii literator*, March 31, 1989; and "Vozzvanie Soiuza dukhovnogo vozrozhdeniia otechestva," ibid.

39. "S dumoi o rodine, o Rossii," *Literaturnaia Rossiia*, March 31, 1989, p. 10; and "Otechestvo—glavnaia tsennost'," ibid., June 23, 1989, p. 14. The former source calls the organization a "movement" (*dvizhenie*); the latter, a "society" (*obshchestvo*).

40. P. N. Miliukov, *Natsional'nyi vopros—Proiskhozhdenie natsional'nosti i natsional'nye voprosy v Rossii* (No place of publication, Biblioteka izdatel'stva "Svobodnaia Rossiia," 1925), pp. 116–17.

41. Balakhanov, "Sokhranenie imperii," pp. 6–7.

42. "Djilas on Gorbachev (II): Milovan Djilas and George Urban in Conversation," *Encounter* (London), November 1988, p. 30.

43. Balakhonov, "Sokhranenie imperii," p. 6. Suggestions about subdividing the RSFSR have appeared in an official Moscow weekly, *Literaturnaia gazeta*. See Vladimir Sokolov, "Demokratiia i granitsy: kontseptsiia," August 2, 1989, p. 10.

44. Ibid., pp. 6–7.

45. *Literaturnaia Rossiia*, June 30, 1989, p. 14.

46. Ibid.

47. *The New York Times*, March 13, 1989, p. A9.

48. Julia Wishnevsky, "*Nash Sovremennik* Provides Focus for 'Opposition Party,'" *Report on the USSR*, January 20, 1989, p. 3.

49. Ibid., pp. 5–6.

50. M. I. Mongo, *Pravda*, June 7, 1989, p. 3.

51. "Tezisy k podgotovke platformy Tatarskogo obshchestvennogo tsentra," *Slovo Agitatora* (Kazan), nos. 23 and 24, December 1988, pp. 34–35.

52. Kamilla Iunusova, "Kak nikogda—otvetstvennost'," *Literaturnaia Rossiia*, June 2, 1989, p. 10.

53. "Sud'ba u nas obshchaia," ibid., May 26, 1989, p. 5.

54. For a discussion of Eurasianism see Roman Szporluk, "The Search for Identity in Russia and Eastern Europe," *Cross-Currents: A Yearbook of Central European Culture* (Ann Arbor, Mich.), no. 9 (1990).

55. Anatole G. Mazour, *Modern Russian Historiography* (Westport, Conn.: Greenwood Press, 1975), pp. 81 and 85.

56. "Spravi perebudovy—tvorchu initiatyvu," *Literaturna Ukraïna* (Kyiv), July 28, 1988, p. 1. Whether he knew it or not, Zahrebelny rephrased the famous question asked by the Ukrainian Communist writer Mykola Khvylovyi in the 1920s: "Is Russia independent?—It is? Well, then Ukraine is independent too."

57. For Hrushevsky's life, times, and writings, see Thomas M. Prymak, *Mykhailo Hrushevsky: The Politics of National Culture* (Toronto, Buffalo, and London: University of Toronto Press, 1987), and his "Hrushevsky and the Ukraine's 'Lost' History," *History Today* (London), (January 1989): 42–46. On the prohibition to mention Hrushevsky's name in Ukraine (but not in Russia, where scholars were free to cite his writings), see Vasyl' Skurativs'kyi, "Zakhysnyi imunitet—narodoznavstvo," *Literaturna Ukraïna*, July 21, 1988, pp. 3 and 5. Without saying so directly, Skurativsky implies that the ban on Hrushevsky's name went into effect when Petro Shelest was replaced by V. V. Shcherbytsky as Ukrainian Communist Party first secretary. Two contrasting stands on the Ukrainian historian and politician are revealed in Serhii Bilokin', "Mikhailo Hrushevs'kyi," ibid., p. 7; and V. Sarbei, "Iak nam stavytysia do M. Hrushevs'koho?" *Radians'ka Ukraïna* (Kyiv), August 27, 1988, p. 2. Sarbei views the historian primarily as a dangerous enemy of the Soviet state, although he, too, recognizes the scholarly value of Hrushevsky's work.

58. See Mykhailo Hrushevs'kyi, "Spomyny," *Kyiv* (Kyiv), no. 9 (1988): 115–49, and subsequent issues; and idem, "Kul'turno-natsional'nyi rukh," *Zhovten'* (Lviv), no. 1 (1989), pp. 98–108 (and subsequent issues). *Vitchyzna* (Kyiv) began the publication of Hrushevsky's work dealing with the Cossack period in its January 1989 issue. [Hrushersky's *History of Ukraine-Rus'* is currently being published in English by the Canadian Institute of Ukrainian Studies, Edmonton and Toronto.]

59. O. N. Trubachev, "Slaviane. Iazyk i istoriia," *Pravda*, March 28, 1987, p. 3.

60. G. P. Fedotov, "Tri stolitsy," *Novyi mir*, no. 4 (1989): 215.

61. O. N. Trubachev, "Slaviane: iazyk i istoriia," in *Druzhba narodov* (Moscow), no. 5 (1988), pp. 243–49, and his response in "O iazykovom soiuze i eshche koe o chem," ibid., no. 9 (1988), pp. 261–64. The same issue contained several critical letters from readers, including one by Bohdan Senkiv, who argued that Trubachev's stand implies the subordinate position of the Ukrainian and Belorussian languages vis-à-vis the Russian language in the Ukrainian and Belorussian republics. *Druzhba narodov*'s opening of its pages to Ukrainian contributors is important because Ukrainian journals are printed in incomparably fewer copies and, in any case, are not read by the Russian public.

62. Mykola Riabchuk, "Ukrainskaia literatura i malorossiiskii 'imidzh'," ibid., no. 5 (1988): 250–54. On Belinsky's view of the Ukrainians, see Victor Svoboda, "Shevchenko and Belinsky," in George Luckyj, ed., *Shevchenko and the Critics* (Toronto: Toronto University Press, 1980), pp. 303–23, and Svoboda and Richard Martin, "Shevchenko and Belinsky Revisited," *Slavonic and East European Review* (London) 56, no. 4 (1978): 546–62. (I would like to thank Dr. David Saunders for bringing these references to my attention and for his comments on an earlier draft of this chapter.)

63. Serhii Hrechaniuk, "Trubachov ide na 'my', abo mifichna babtsia i trubadury modernizovanoï shchoholevshchyny," *Vitchyzna*, no. 12 (1988): 196–200.

64. V. I. Vernads'kyi (Vernadsky), "Ukraïns'ke pytannia i rosiis'ka hromads'kist'," *Moloda hvardiia* (Kyiv), March 12, 1988. For an English translation, see *Soviet Ukrainian Affairs* (London), no. 2 (1988). *Vitchyzna* published the whole Vernadsky text in its June 1988 issue, pp. 172–77. Since 1988, the Ukrainian press has published a number of Vernadsky texts from the period 1917–18, when he was engaged in the organization of the Ukrainian Academy of Sciences. This Vernadsky revival has led in turn to the admission that the Academy was founded when Ukraine was a non-Soviet, independent state. See M. Dobrov et al., "Novyi pohliad na istoriiu zasnuvannia Akademiï nauk Ukraïny," *Visnyk Akademiï Nauk URSR* (Kyiv), no. 4 (1989): 58–74.

65. *Kul'tura i zhyttia* (Kyiv), January 24, 1988. The Ukrainian text was republished in *Nauka i kul'tura: Ukraïna* (Kyiv), no. 22 (1988): 309–25.

66. I. Dziuba, "Osoznaem li my natsional'nuiu kul'turu kak tselostnost'?" *Kommunist*, no. 18 (December 1988): 51–60.

67. Borys Kharchuk, "Slovo i narod," *Prapor* (Kharkiv), no. 10 (1988): 147–63, reprinted in *Suchasnist'* (Munich), no. 3 (1989): 113–26.

68. "Umyty svit zhyvoiu vodoiu pravdy," speech by Borys Oliinyk, in *Literaturna Ukraïna*, March 16, 1989, p. 4.

69. Volodymyr Sosiura, "Mazepa: Fragment z poemy," *Kul'tura i zhyttia*, December 18, 1988, p. 5, and idem, "Mazepa," *Kyiv*, no. 12 (1988): 77–107. See also the articles by S. Hal'chenko and V. Serhiichuk in *Kul'tura i zhyttia*, December 18, 1988, and Iurii Barabash, "Ivan Mazepa—shche odna literaturna versiia," ibid., pp. 140–49.

70. Vasyl' Marochkin, "Hirka chasha Ivana Mazepy," *Ukraïna* (Kyiv), no. 25 (1989): 14–15. The Battle of Poltava polemic was not restricted to literary journals. The youth branch of the Pamiat' society, "Rossiia Molodaia" or "Young Russia" (its name is taken from a Pushkin poem, where he speaks of "young Russia reaching manhood with the genius of Peter") announced it would commemorate the battle in Poltava in July 1989. According to press accounts, about 300 activists of Young Russia arrived by train from Moscow. Before this happened, the July 9 event was discussed at a July 1 conference of the Kyiv regional branch of the Popular Movement for Restructuring in Ukraine—*Rukh*. The head of the ideological department of the Central Committee of the Communist Party of Ukraine, L. M. Kravchuk, reported at that meeting that the Ukrainian authorities had asked appropriate authorities in Moscow not to allow in Ukraine the celebration of the Poltava anniversary according to the scenario of "Rossiia Molodaia," which Kravchuk called the youth branch of the "ill-reputed Pamiat'." Indeed, the police sent the Pamiat' group back to Moscow after their arrival in Poltava. They also removed from Poltava people from several Ukrainian cities who had come to protest. See *Literaturna Ukraïna*, July 6, 1989, p. 1; ibid., July 13, 1989, pp. 6–7; and *Svoboda* (Jersey City, N.J.), July 20, 1989, p. 1.

71. Radii Polons'kyi, "Iakshcho v serdtsi zhyve revoliutsiia," *Prapor*, no. 1, (1989): 146.

72. Ibid., p. 152.

73. Quoted in Pavel Emelin, "Energiia slova: govoriat narodnye deputaty SSSR," *Literaturnaia Rossiia*, June 16, 1989, p. 2.

74. *Izvestiia*, June 4, 1989, p. 4.

75. *Pravda*, June 7, 1989. Her speech is on pp. 2–3.

76. Ibid. Hallik did not say so, but the slogan "a strong center and strong republics" was coined by Gorbachev.

77. Sergei Grigoriants, "Russkoe natsional'noe dvizhenie," *Russkaia mysl'*, no. 3775, May 12, 1989, p. 6.

78. But this assessment may be too pessimistic. At least one contemporary critic, and moreover one who is not a friend of the democratic option, speaks of public opinion becoming split into two extremes, one being Pamiat', the other the Democratic Union. See Sergei Kurginian, "O mekhanizme soskal'zyvaniia," *Literaturnaia Rossiia*, July 7, 1989, pp. 8–9, and July 14, 1989, p. 2.

79. See Allan Janik and Stephen Toulmin, *Wittgenstein's Vienna* (New York: Simon and Schuster, 1973), pp. 271–72. I discuss their thesis in my article, "Defining 'Central Europe': Power, Politics, and Culture," *Cross-Currents: A Yearbook of Central European Culture*, no. 1 (1982): 30–38. For reflections on the German problem under the Habsburgs, see Benedict Anderson, *Imagined Communities: Reflections on the Origin and Spread of Nationalism* (London: Verso and NLB, 1983), p. 81.

80. Timothy Garton Ash, "The Empire in Decay," *New York Review of Books*, September 29, 1988, p. 56.

81. John A. Armstrong, "Toward a Framework for Considering Nationalism in East Europe," *Eastern European Politics and Societies* (Berkeley, Calif.) (Spring 1988): 301–2.

82. Grigoriants, "Russkoe natsional'noe dvizhenie," p. 6.

83. "Sozdano Sibirskoe nezavisimoe informatsionnoe agenstvo," *Russkaia mysl'*, April 14, 1989, p. 2.

84. *Pravda*, April 27, 1989, pp. 3–7.

85. See Geoff Eley's chapter "What Produces Fascism: Preindustrial Traditions or a Crisis of the Capitalist State?" in his book *From Unification to Nazism: Reinterpreting the German Past* (Boston, London, and Sydney: Allen and Unwin, 1986), pp. 245–82; see also Roman Szporluk, *Communism and Nationalism: Karl Marx versus Friedrich List* (New York and Oxford: Oxford University Press, 1988), pp. 189–90.

86. According to Bill Keller, writing from Moscow on the strikes in the Ukrainian SSR, "miners who walked out today in the western Ukrainian city of Chervonograd included in their demands the creation of an independent national coal union explicitly modeled on the Polish union Solidarity." ("Soviet Strikers Hinting at Independent Union," *New York Times*, July 21, 1989.) Future events will show whether these demands will acquire substance and whether the workers of Siberia and Donbas will organize unions modeled on Solidarity.

The original Solidarity in Poland had many dimensions—religious and national as well as social and economic. Just as it is too early to tell whether the workers of Siberia feel any definite regional Siberian or national Russian identity, so it is impossible to detect any specific regional or national Ukrainian identity in the workers' consciousness in Donbas or Western Ukraine. This brings to mind Ukrainian writer Yuri Shcherbak's recent remark that unlike elsewhere in the USSR, in Ukraine there have emerged not inter-ethnic conflicts but rather a conflict between Ukrainians and those whom Shcherbak calls "Little Russians." (Interview with Yuri Shcherbak, interview in *Literaturnaia Gazeta*, January 18, 1989, p. 3.) The latter term would describe those ethnic Ukrainians who prefer to consider themselves members of a larger Russian nation while preserving some specific regional Ukrainian features. Thus, the "Little Russians" represent Ukrainian supporters of an "all-Russian" national identity discussed earlier. It would seem, therefore, that in contemporary Ukraine, especially in such heavily Russified areas as Donbas, at least three identities are competing for popular support: Russian, Ukrainian, and "Little Russian." Conceivably, there is a fourth one, too—some form of *Soviet* identity. The possibility of such an identity actually taking place should not be dismissed a priori, even though the concept itself was originally "manufactured upstairs." For ample evidence on how national traditions and national identities were being "invented," that is, consciously produced (not to say manufactured) in nineteenth-century Europe and elsewhere, see Eric Hobsbawm and Terence Ranger, eds., *The Invention of Tradition* (Cambridge, England: Cambridge University Press, 1988).

87. Stanley Aronowitz in his foreword to Alain Touraine, *Return of the Actor: Social Theory in Postindustrial Society*, trans. by Myrna Godzich (Minneapolis: University of Minnesota Press, 1988), p. xix.

88. Ibid., pp. 81–82.

8 The Imperial Legacy and the Soviet Nationalities Problem

What is meant when one speaks about the legacy of Imperial Russia and the nationalities problem of the contemporary Soviet Union?[1]

The most visible legacy of Imperial Russia is the territorial configuration and ethnic composition of the USSR. The resemblance becomes even more striking when one compares the world map of 1913 with that of 1990 and notes the absence from the latter of the colonial empires of Britain, France, Germany, Belgium, the Netherlands, and Portugal, with their vast possessions in Asia and Africa. The contours of Russia then and the USSR now, in the meantime, have hardly changed. Admittedly, neither Helsinki nor Warsaw lies within the USSR, but their loss has been compensated by the gain of areas that in 1913 had been known as Galicia, Bukovina, and the Ruthenian counties of Hungary. Then they belonged to the Austro-Hungarian Empire—of which no trace remains today.

That the Soviet Union is a multinational state, territorially largely coterminous with the former Russian Empire, does not in itself prove the existence of an "imperial legacy" in Soviet politics, however. More important is the question of whether the Soviet Union is just "another name" for the Russian Empire or a fundamentally new kind of polity. To attempt an answer to this question it is essential to identify the spe-

First published in *The Nationalities Factor in Soviet Politics and Society*, 1990.

cifically political points of similarity and contrast between the two states.

The first and perhaps most important issue concerns the relationship between state and society in the pre- and post-1917 eras. It is the contention of this essay that the nationalities problem is defined by the nature of this fundamental relationship. Thus we need to examine the structure of state-society relations under the tsars and compare it with that in the Soviet period.

The nature of this relationship between state and civil society will emerge more fully in the course of our discussion. At this point suffice it to say that the autocratic tsarist state, which in its origins was based on a religious and dynastic legitimization, failed to adjust to the modern political principle of constitutionalism, let alone that of sovereignty of the nation. It also took the state in Russia much longer than elsewhere in Europe to accept the principle of private property and the related distinction between the tsar's authority as sovereign and as owner of property. In tsarist ideology and practice the tsar was the owner and master of his realm, not merely a ruler in the public sphere. Nonetheless, a civil society had emerged in Russia by the early twentieth century. In the Bolshevik revolution, however, not only the state, which had been a legacy of tsarism, but also that very civil society was destroyed, and the new rulers, the Bolsheviks, proclaimed an entirely new concept of social organization.[2]

The second question, in a sense the obverse of the first, concerns the status of Russians in the tsarist and the Soviet state. How does the Soviet Marxist-Leninist state relate to the Russians as a nation? And, vice versa, how do the Russians, in terms of their national aspirations, relate to the state? The tsarist Empire ultimately did not succeed in establishing a modus vivendi with the Russian nation as it was represented by the emerging civil society and failed to gain acceptance as a Russian national state. We shall try to determine whether the Soviet state is accepted as "Russian" in a sense in which its imperial predecessor was not.

At this stage, by way of establishing an agenda for discussion, it should be noted that the empire never became a Russian nation-state. Instead, in the words of Ladis K. D. Kristof, it promoted "Rossification," which meant "the development of an unswerving loyalty and direct attachment to the person of the tsar, by God's will the sole power-holder (*samoderzhets*) and head of *the* Church." The essence of "Rossification" lay in Orthodoxy, not in Russianism. "The Orthodox idea, not the Russian tongue or civilization, was the *spiritus movens* of the Tsardom. Russia was first of all Holy, not Russian."³ This explains, for example, why the tsarist authorities approved the publication of Orthodox texts in Tatar to promote the "Rossification" of the Muslims. In this respect "Rossification" resembles the postrevolutionary policy of Sovietization, with its principle of "national in form, socialist in content."

"Russification," on the other hand, aimed at making the non-Russian subjects of the state Russian in language and identity. This was the goal of Russian nationalists, whatever their other differences. Although, especially in its last decades, tsarism also promoted "Russification" policies, one may agree with Kristof's notion of a discrepancy or conflict between the "state idea" of the imperial regime and the "national idea" of the Russians. Kristof recognizes that in reality "the difference between the state and national idea is rather subtle, a matter of shades," but he believes that in Russia it became more acute than elsewhere and found reflection in the "dichotomy between *narod* and *gosudarstvo*—the aims and ideals of the 'people' and 'the state'." Even the language recognized "the distinction between *russkii* and *rossiiskii*, between what pertains to the (Great) Russian people and what to All-the-'Russias'." The German, French, and Spanish nations had "their" empires, Kristof continues, but the tsarist Empire was not officially "Russian." Its formal name was *Rossiiskaia Imperiia*, not *Russkaia Imperiia*, and the tsar likewise was not *russkii*, but *vserossiiskii imperator*. Admittedly, certain Russian statesmen supported the *russkaia* (national) idea, while others preferred the *rossiiskaia* (state or, rather, imperial) idea; "still others tried to fuse the two."⁴

Thus, we may conclude that before the Revolution, the Russians themselves were not of one mind about what kind of country they wished Russia to be. Their search involved not only a political debate, but also an important debate about the geographical shape of Russia, for it was understood that geography, culture, and politics were intertwined. Kristof distinguishes at least four different ideas or models of "Russia" in Russian political thought: "Kievan," "Muscovite," "St. Petersburg," and "Eurasian."⁵ (We shall return to the topic of models of "Russia" when we discuss the "Russian problem" in the USSR.)

The Russian problem, albeit unique in kind, was only one of the nationalities problems in the empire. The empire encompassed many other ethnic and national groups, and their treatment by the state, and by Russians of different persuasions, depended on a variety of factors. Among these were religion (the Jews were treated the worst), and attitudes toward Russian rule (the Poles were the least willing to accept Russian domination and suffered severe repressions, but as a nation with a long tradition of independent statehood, they also enjoyed certain privileges that others lacked). The Ukrainian problem posed a special challenge to the state and to Russian nationalists. For historic reasons—including religious, as the Russians interpreted them—the Ukrainians were viewed as a branch of the Russian nation. Precisely because they were thought to be closer to the Russians than any other group (save the Belorussians), expression of Ukrainian distinctness was especially subject to persecution. Still another category of ethnic groups was represented by the so-called diaspora peoples, including, besides the Jews, the Germans and Armenians. Only Finland was actually recognized as a political nation; but as Russian nationalism gained ascendancy at the imperial court, the tsarist government began curtailing Finland's autonomy, despite that nation's loyalty to the throne.

In the end, Russian nationalism failed to transform the tsarist Empire into a liberal, democratic Russian nation-state. Nor did the nationalists among the non-Russian nationalities, with several exceptions, succeed in establishing their own states by secession from Russia. (These important exceptions—Finland, Poland, and, for about twenty years, Latvia, Lithuania, and Estonia—need, however, to be kept in mind.) Those who won the Russian civil war advanced a program that claimed to transcend the nationalist way of thinking altogether. Since it is their ideological and political heirs who rule the Soviet Union today, it may be useful to cite Lenin's assessment of the nationalities problem prior to World War I:

> Throughout the world, the period of the final victory of capitalism over feudalism has been linked up with national movements. For the complete victory of commodity production, the bourgeoisie must capture the home market, and there must be politically united territories whose population speak a single language, with all obstacles to the development of that language and to its consolidation in literature eliminated. Therein is the economic foundation of national movements. Language is the most important means of human intercourse. Unity and unimpeded development of language are the most important conditions for genuinely free and extensive commerce on a scale commensurate with modern capitalism, for a free and broad grouping of the population in

all its various classes and, lastly, for the establishment of a close connection between the market and each and every proprietor, big or little, and between seller and buyer.

Especially important for our purpose is his conclusion:

> Therefore, the tendency of every national movement is toward the formation of national states, under which these requirements of modern capitalism are best satisfied. The most profound economic factors drive toward this goal, and, therefore, for the whole of Western Europe, nay, for the entire civilized world, the national state is typical and normal for the capitalist period.[6]

Lenin's assessment of the nature of nationality under the conditions of capitalism—no matter how one judges his analysis of capitalism—can serve us as a point of reference today. It prompts the question of whether under Soviet-style socialism, especially now, in the period of perestroika, the introduction of elements of market economy will tend to intensify ethnic identities. Is "the tendency of every national movement . . . toward the formation of *national states*" also operative under "socialism" of the Soviet kind? This critical question in the "state-nationalities" area at the present time is attended by a host of others. What will the non-Russians do now as they search for their own options, and as they consider, in this search, the behavior of the Russians? Will they view the Russians' national aspirations today as a legacy of the tsarist, imperial era? Will they define their own aims in a manner Lenin had considered in 1914 as normal, legitimate, and consistent with the historical process itself?

One final point that requires consideration is the tsarist empire's—and the Soviet Union's—standing in the world. As we shall argue later, the legitimacy of the tsarist regime within the state, whether among Russians or non-Russians, was determined among other factors by the state's performance abroad as a Great Power. Will the same apply to the Soviet Union, and will its peoples' perception of the Communist party and the Soviet state's legitimacy be influenced by how they judge the Soviet Union's status in the world at large?

By way of introducing all these questions as they arise today, let us consider the current Soviet political agenda, and then see where on this agenda the "nationality question" fits in.

Gorbachev's Revolution

According to Mikhail Gorbachev, there is a revolution under way in the USSR today. "We are talking about restructuring and related processes of the thoroughgoing democratization of society, having in mind truly revolutionary and comprehensive transformations in society." Gorbachev acknowledges that "this fundamental change of direction" is necessary because the Soviets "simply have no other way."[7]

On more than one occasion Gorbachev has admitted that unless the Soviet Union carries out the necessary revolutionary changes in its economy, political system, and culture, its standing as a great world power will be in danger as it slips further behind the advanced countries of the capitalist world. (There is no more talk of catching up with and surpassing "the West.") How serious is the condition of the Soviet Union was evident from the general secretary's June 28, 1988, address to the Nineteenth Party Conference. The greatest accomplishment of the new course over the past three years, said Gorbachev, consists in that "through the efforts of the Party and the working people, we have managed to halt the country's slide toward crisis in the economic, social and spiritual spheres."[8] But Gorbachev warned his audience and the Soviet public at large that much more remains to be done, because "the revolutionary transformations" have not yet become irreversible.[9]

Gorbachev and his supporters now admit that the economic improvement necessary for keeping up with the West is impossible without deep political and social, as well as cultural and intellectual, changes in the Soviet Union. This is the major difference between the present approach and the Soviet reform efforts of the 1950s and 1980s, which were limited to the economy. This recognition of the centrality of *political* reform was restated by Gorbachev at the Party Conference: The "crucial" question is that of reforming the political system.[10]

Thus, Gorbachev identifies the source of the Soviet Union's problems in the model of state-society relations established after the Revolution, although he prefers to speak about Lenin's death as the time when things took a wrong turn. That model is not effective and, indeed, it is now admitted, has never suited the Soviet Union. Gorbachev thus virtually repudiates the whole Soviet historical experience; albeit claiming to reject only its Stalinist distortions. The political system established in the USSR under Stalin and surviving to this day is now generally characterized as a "command-administrative" system. It is openly admitted that under Stalin—and under his successors before Gorbachev—there had taken place a virtual absorption of society within the all-powerful party-state. That absorption is now considered to have been a negative development, a development contradicting the "real meaning" of Leninism and Marxism.

For decades, however, the merger of society within the state, and consequently the abolition of the tension between the two, was represented as socialism's great achievement, socialism's special claim to superiority over capitalism. Although Stalin is now being condemned by Communists, he long expressed their view with exceptional clarity. Stalin quite openly and proudly used to define the "system of the dictatorship of the proletariat" as a "mechanism" or structure in which the party constitutes "the main guiding force." All the remaining organizations—the soviets, trade unions, women's and youth groups, and the like—were, according to Stalin, instruments to "link" the party with "the masses."[11] In essence, Stalin proclaimed the absorption of society by the state and the destruction of all intermediate associations between the state and the masses: "The Soviet state apparatus, in the profound meaning of the term," he wrote, "consists of the Soviets plus all the diverse non-Party and Party organisations, which embrace millions, which unite the Soviets with the 'rank and file.' " They "*merge* the state apparatus with the vast masses and, step by step, destroy everything that serves as a barrier between the state apparatus and the people."[12]

Thus, Gorbachev's policy of glasnost and perestroika constitutes a genuine revolution not only against Stalinist theory and practice—that is, in effect, against most of Soviet history—but also against the classic Marxist tradition, including the "statist" tradition of the Second International (1889–1914). It does not matter whether Gorbachev himself understands or accepts the implications of his course; his argument reintroduces into the political agenda concepts that Marxism, and not only Stalinism, has long regarded as out of place under the rule of the proletariat.[13]

In his struggle for reform Gorbachev is also dealing with a legacy of Imperial Russia—an issue the tsarist state never resolved. This was tsarism's stubborn refusal to accept the autonomy of society, and its insistence that the state is the sole creative force. Society, in this view, was merely an instrument, if not mindless material, at the state's disposal. Even though the tsarist regime was forced after 1905 to accept constitutional limitations on its powers, it never fully reconciled itself to a Western, liberal system for Russia.

State and Society

Intentionally or not, Gorbachev has unleashed, as we are witnessing today, the demand, indeed a movement, for the establishment of a civil society in the Soviet Union. Gorbachev has implicitly admitted—and the public, insofar as it is able to speak, heartily agrees with him—that the Soviet state controlled by the Communist party has failed in its self-appointed historic mission. Sooner or later the party will have to decide how its role as "the leading force" in every aspect of public life can be reconciled with autonomous expressions of opinion and autonomous actions necessary, as he admits, for the success of the economic and scientific transformation.

According to Ernest Barker, the distinguished British scholar and political theorist,

> a nation is simultaneously, and coextensively, two things in one. It is a social substance, or Society, constituted of and by a sum of voluntary associations, which have mainly grown of themselves—in the sense that they have been formed by voluntary and spontaneous combination—and which desire to act and to realize their purposes as far as possible by themselves. That is one side of the nation. The other side (which we may call either the reverse or the obverse, according to our preference) is that it is a political or, as it is perhaps better called, a legal substance; a single compulsory association including all, and competent, in all cases where it sees fit, to make and enforce rules for all.[14]

Barker's use of the term "nation" may seem to be singularly inappropriate in a Russian or Soviet context, where "nation" has a different meaning from that in which Barker employed it: The term "polity" would be more appropriate here. But despite this terminological infelicity, Barker's ideas can certainly be "retranslated" and applied in a discussion of the Russian and Soviet cases. According to Barker, "This double nature of the nation—this simultaneity and coextension of its social and its legal aspect—raises a threefold problem." Since they are applicable to our subject, we may quote Barker's questions verbatim, remembering that his understanding of "nation" is not ours:

1) What are the things which belong to the nation in its legal aspect, as an organized State?

2) What are the things which belong to the nation in its social aspect, as a sum of voluntary associations?

3) What control should the nation, as organized in a State (and therefore competent to deal with all persons and judge in all cases *in the legal sphere*), exercise over itself as organized in a society of voluntary associations acting *in the social sphere*?[15]

Although it would be very premature to say that Barker's language describes the Soviet reality, it certainly describes the issues currently being debated and fought over in the USSR. It is quite evident that Gorbachev's declarations and actions have resulted in the formation of a public opinion that demands the legalization of independent groups and the establishment of an independent press. In other words, calls are being heard for legal steps that would make "society" a meaningful concept in the Soviet polity and give it a place in the system.[16]

What does all this mean for specific Soviet nationalities? How will it affect the "nationalities problem" as a whole? It raises, first of all, the question regarding the meaning and tenability of the concept of the "Soviet people." That concept, as we shall see, is intrinsically related to the Soviet theory and practice of socialism, and specifically to the idea of the state. What does the rejection of the latter imply for the future of the "Soviet people"?

The "Soviet People"

If one took Stalin's point to its logical conclusion, the Soviet state apparatus—"in the profound meaning of the term"—encompassed the entire population of the Soviet Union. Although Stalin never admitted this explicitly, his view implied depriving individual Soviet nationalities of any autonomy, in the same manner as all associations and organizations were deprived of theirs. One spoke of "peoples of the USSR" (*narody SSSR*), of course, of their self-determination and even "sovereignty," but these were meaningless phrases if the party controlled everything. Gradually, a new term, the "Soviet people" (*sovetskii narod*), was introduced to designate all citizens of the Soviet Union, in order to emphasize their unity above differences of nationality. According to the official view, the peoples of the USSR formed an integrated whole, a single entity in that they all shared an allegiance to Marxism-Leninism as their world view and to the party and state that represented and realized that outlook in practice. In this sense, the "Soviet people" was another name for "the state apparatus" as defined by Stalin.

It was also argued that the shared historical experience of building socialism and communism forged the unity of the "Soviet people." (Their common historical experience also included the defense of "socialist achievements" against external enemies, notably Nazi Germany in World War II.) The promoters of the concept of a "Soviet people" thus tried to support an ideologically legitimized Soviet system with a historical argument that stressed the people's shared experience and hence a community of outlook and character.

In the early 1920s the leaders of the new Soviet state proclaimed the principle of national equality and self-determination, which meant the equality of the non-Russian peoples with the Russians. In the "Union of Soviet Socialist Republics," "Russia" was one of several constitutionally equal constituent parts. This constitutional arrangement recognized the power of nationalism among the non-Russians and, in the opinion of Lenin, was the only way to legitimate the linking of Russians and non-Russians in one political structure in the age of nationalist revolutions.[17] In a way, it was also a measure that "downgraded" Russians from their former superior position in tsarist Russia, though most Russians did not seem to take this implication too seriously. As Richard Pipes has noted, the Soviet Union was "a compromise between doctrine and reality: an attempt to reconcile the Bolshevik strivings for absolute unity and centralization of all power in the hands of the party, with the recognition of the empirical fact that nationalism did survive the collapse of the old order." The Bolsheviks viewed it as "a temporary solution only, as a transitional stage to a completely centralized and supra-national worldwide soviet state."[18]

Although the new Soviet state was unitary, centralized, and totalitarian, Pipes noted that "by granting the minorities extensive linguistic autonomy and by placing the national-territorial principle at the base of the state's political administration, the Communists gave constitutional recognition to the multinational structure of the Soviet population." And since language and territory are very important in the development of national consciousness—particularly for people who, like the non-Russian peoples, had had some experience of autonomy during the Revolution—"this purely formal feature of the Soviet Constitution may well prove to have been historically one of the most consequential aspects of the formation of the Soviet Union."[19]

The Great Contest Lost

As was suggested earlier, the concept of the "Soviet people" was meant to deprive the ethnic factor of any capacity to challenge the unitary Stalinist system. To have built socialism was an experience and a bond far superior to any ethnic ties or allegiances. To proceed further and build communism would complete the union and fusion of all Soviet peoples. Khrushchev certainly thought so when he announced, in 1961, that by 1980 the Soviet Union would become the first society to have built "communism."

There is no reason to assume a priori that the policy of creating a "Soviet people" by an ideological bond was doomed to fail. As Eric I. Hobsbawm has noted, "even where the common criteria of belonging to a state are constructed on entirely nontraditional lines (and even when they may actually be deliberately ecumenical in their ideological content), the very fact of their being the possession of one state among several others, is likely to infuse them with a 'national' or 'nationalist' element."[20] Hobsbawm illustrates his point by noting that "Americanism" ("whatever its present political connotation"), had been originally "a universal programme . . . an invitation to all men to become Americans if they so chose, as well as an ideal description of those who already were. This has not prevented it from turning into a strongly nationalist slogan."[21]

One might apply this argument to the Soviet case and say that "Sovietism" also originally had been a universal formula that subsequently might have become a "nationalist slogan." Has it indeed become one? Is there a "Soviet people" analogous to the "American people"? And if not, why not? Perhaps what was needed for the "Soviet people" to become a reality was for the "Soviet dream" to become a reality, at least to the extent that the "American dream" has. There was a time when even those who did not necessarily share Khrushchev's millennarian moods—"a millennium in twenty years"—had been prepared to recognize the Soviet achievement as an unprecedented feat. Foreign observers, whether Marxist or non-Marxist, were ready to recognize that whatever else they may have failed to do, the Bolsheviks had found a way previously unknown to raise Russia out of its historic backwardness. It had been generally recognized that the division of the globe into the advanced and the underdeveloped countries was "the most profound and the most lasting" of the consequences of the French Revolution and the industrial Revolution. The Bolsheviks' main claim to recognition, therefore, was that in the 1930s they "developed means of leaping this chasm between the 'backward' and the 'advanced.' "[22]

This Soviet achievement would have matched the American achievement—were it true. But it is now being denied by no less a person than the current Soviet leader: Contradicting Hobsbawm (and many other writers), Gorbachev now says that the Russians have *not* found a new way to overcome backwardness. What *did* happen in the 1930s, according to him, has made it even more difficult for the Soviet Union to advance. It is the legacy of the 1930s that the Soviets are now trying to overcome. In the process they are acknowledging that in relation to the West they continue to remain "backward" in science, technology, standard of living, and so forth. The most fundamental claim of the Revolution's historical legitimacy—the transformation of the Soviet Union into a modern society and the creation of a civilization that was to be an alternative to the West and free of its drawbacks—is thus denied. The Soviets now admit that they have not found a socialist way out of backwardness and toward modernity, one that would prove superior to what the West has produced. Indeed, the recently launched revolution is necessary to stop the USSR from falling further behind the West.

To make matters worse, what Hobsbawm thinks the (*communist*) Russians achieved in the 1930s has been, in fact, accomplished by the (*capitalist*) Japanese. This appeared as a shocking discovery to the Soviet people in the 1980s. Some members of the younger generation have been inspired by this discovery to ask awkward questions—for example, whether socialism is capable of competing with capitalism. *Komsomolskaia pravda*, the main youth daily, reported in the spring of 1988 that at a student discussion on the topic "Socialism: Collapse or Rise?" a question was raised whether it would have not been better for Russia to follow the capitalist way instead of the course adopted in 1917. When asked how they imagined their future, some young people replied: a well-paid job, comfortable living conditions, wonderful technology— "like in Japan."[23] Japan is clearly on many Soviet minds. Olzhas Suleimenov, the Kazakh writer, in a recent interview said, among other things: "And now our country is in twenty-fourth place in computerization. When I asked a Japanese specialist when we would be able to catch up with you, the response was: never, for we shall not stand still, either. . . ."[24]

We may better understand what "Japan" evokes in Soviet thinking when we consult a Western historian, a specialist in the history of science and technology in Russia, who draws apt parallels between the present situation and Russia's imperial past. The late Kendall E. Bailes wrote in 1986, when perestroika was only beginning:

> More rapid economic growth is essential if the Soviet leadership is to meet its goals of catching up with the West economically. In fact, one of the real dangers for the Soviet Union today is that Japan . . . will catch up with and surpass the Soviet Union in the next few years. If this happens, it would be a major humiliation for the Soviet Union, nearly as important, I think, as the defeat of Russia by Japan in 1905—a military defeat that sent shock waves through the Russian Empire. An economic defeat of the Soviet Union by Japan would probably send similar shock waves through the Soviet leadership, if not through the population as a whole . . . Since both nations began their emergence from a traditional economic and social system at approximately the same time—in the 1860s—a rapidly growing Japan that may surpass an increasingly sluggish Soviet Union in the near future would dramatize the failures of the Soviet system, much as the defeats at Port Arthur, Mukden, and Tsushima in 1904–1905 dramatized the failures of tsarist Russia.[25]

Mention of the Russo-Japanese War of 1904–1905 also recalls Stalin's famous 1945 speech in which he expressly treated the Soviet victory over Japan in World War II as Russia's revenge for the defeat it had sustained in the earlier war. To suffer a defeat by Japan in economic development forty years after that military revenge must bring to many Soviet minds truly ominous, if not apocalyptic, images.

The relationship between economic performance and political legitimacy and identity is well worth pondering as one analyzes the Soviet situation. It would seem that the cumulative effect of the revelations of Stalin's crimes and the admission that all those inhuman sufferings and exertions had failed in the economic sphere as well would have an impact on the popular perception of the Soviet system's legitimacy, and even on the viability of the "Soviet people" as an integrated political entity.

Legitimacy and Identity

The Russian Revolution of 1905, as is well known, was directly inspired by tsarism's defeat in the Japanese war. Tsarist Russia might not be democratic or liberal—so the argument in its favor ran—but at least it was a Great Power. To have lost a war with Japan, therefore, meant that tsarism was compromised and deprived of legitimacy in a critical area. The revolution, as Hugh Seton-Watson has noted, was not only a revolution of workers, peasants, and radical intellectuals against autocracy, but "a revolution of non-Russians against Russification." Seton-Watson further noted: "The two revolts were of course connected: the social revolution was in fact most bitter in non-Russian regions, with Polish workers, Latvian peasants, and Georgian peasants as protagonists."[26]

Now that Marxism-Leninism is no longer a guide to the future, and the state is forced to allow a measure of autonomous opinion and action, what will become of the "Soviet people"? What will hold all the peoples of the USSR together—other than the Soviet state and the Communist party, whose historical legitimacy and record are now openly proclaimed wanting? Will a lost economic competition with Japan—and with capitalism as a whole—accelerate the Gorbachev revolution of the late 1980s, just as a lost war contributed to the revolt of 1905? Will the revolution in process be primarily political and social, or ethnic and nationalist, or a combination of both, just as the revolution of 1905 was?

Turning to the first question, the very reality of a "Soviet people" is being openly questioned today, though important officials have spoken in its defense. One of them is Iulian Bromlei, Brezhnev's chief specialist in matters of nationality and long-time head of the Institute of Ethnography at the Academy of Sciences of the USSR (replaced only in April 1989 by Valery Tishkov). According to Bromlei, the "Soviet people" is a real community that is held together by common socialist features. It is a "meta-ethnic community."[27]

Another defense of the concept of the "Soviet people" comes from Genrikh Borovik, the prominent publicist-commentator and head of the Soviet Peace Committee. In his speech at the Nineteenth Party Conference, Borovik disagreed with those who claim that the "Soviet people" is an "invention" or "fiction" (vydumka). "But the Soviet people is not a fiction. It is, fortunately, a reality." Borovik continued: "We are talking about the rise of national self-consciousness. This is wonderful; but not at the expense of the Soviet national self-consciousness. [Or at the expense] of the self-consciousness of citizens of the Soviet Union and of Soviet patriotism."[28]

The fact that these two prominent defenders of the concept of the "Soviet people" understand quite different things by the term is additional proof of the present ideological confusion, if not crisis. Bromlei calls it a *meta-ethnic* entity, Borovik calls it *national*. This lack of clarity about what should be a basic concept supports the argument of another prominent figure, the historian Yuri Afanasiev, who speaks about an ideological "identity vacuum" in the USSR. According to Afanasiev, historical memory is the most important, indeed, a constitutive or formative element of social identity. However, a "systematic destruction of collective memory" was being carried out under Stalin and under Brezhnev, and this destruction has resulted in a "crisis of identity of our contemporary society." This in turn has created an ideological "identity vacuum" that made possible the rise of "such chauvinist, anti-Semitic groups like the extremists from Pamiat', who by flirting with irrational, easily excitable elements are capable of putting forward their own variant of identity: an antihistorical, mythical, racist one—anything you want. . . ."[29]

Afanasiev's reference to Pamiat', the extremist Russian nationalist organization, warrants a closer look at the situation prevailing in "Russia proper," among the Russians themselves. One of the strongest currents in the post-Brezhnev Soviet Union is Russian national assertiveness, Russian nationalism. Let us examine this phenomenon, bearing in mind the larger issue that underlies this discussion—the legacy of Imperial Russia in current Soviet politics. In what ways does contemporary Russian nationalism reopen the unsolved agenda of tsarist Russia? Are the Russians as a nation suing for divorce, as it were, from the Soviet state?

De-Sovietization of Russia

It is common knowledge that Stalin and his successors—Khrushchev, Brezhnev, Andropov, and Chernenko—manipulated the symbols of Russian nationhood and promoted Russification of the non-

Russians. But it is also well known that at the same time the Soviet leaders did not allow the Russian nation to express itself—indeed, to exist—independently of the party and the state: The Russian nation itself was dissolved in the Stalinist state. Official propaganda glorified the "great Russian people" and "Russia" in ways that were insulting to non-Russians and embarrassing to many Russians, but the Russian nation, culture, and history were manipulated to achieve specific political goals. The Soviet scholar, Gavriil Popov, has recently pointed out that the Russian nation's historical experiences and memories were selectively manipulated by Stalin in order to make the Russians a pliable instrument in his rule over the Soviet Union.[30] (This meant obliterating from collective memory libertarian traditions and ideas.) In other words, Stalin (and his successors) sought to create an image of a "Russia" that would serve the system.

It is understandable that the Russians should be the first to express themselves as a nation under Gorbachev's perestroika. Even though Russian identity had been managed by the party, the Russians have always had at their disposal the necessary infrastructure—the journals, research institutes, theaters, publishing houses, and the rest—to express themselves more easily in the cultural sphere than, say, the Ukrainians or Georgians. Precisely because of this rich infrastructure, and because they always enjoyed special privileges as the "leading nation" and the "elder brother," it proved easier for the Russians to emancipate themselves from "Sovietism." The fusion of state and civil society sought by Stalin had never been complete in the cultural sphere—and it is natural that artists, writers, and playwrights would be the first to assert their autonomy. If one were to describe their achievement in a single phrase, the most accurate would be "de-Sovietization of Russian culture." But since culture is a defining marker of a nation, the issue of "de-Sovietization of Russia" has become an important item on the political agenda as well.

Recent developments in Russian culture are well known. A number of major writers whose total oeuvre or most important works had been banned—for example, Anna Akhmatova, Mikhail Bulgakov, Evgenii Zamiatin, Boris Pasternak, and Vladimir Nabokov—have become available to a wide reading public for the first time. The same is true for many of Russia's pre-Soviet or non-Soviet historians, philosophers, and social thinkers, including Nikolai Karamzin, Petr Chaadaev, Sergei Soloviev, and Vasilii Kliuchevsky. Cumulatively, all these moves are leading to a gradual but comprehensive devaluation of the specifically Soviet cultural figures and their alleged accomplishments. (This tendency is reflected in attempts to "debunk" Gorky and Maiakovsky, for example.) Of the great men and women who wrote in the post-1917 era, those who were victims of the Soviet regime seem to be the most highly regarded now. It is in this sense that Russian culture is becoming "de-Sovietized."

Another element in the emerging de-Sovietized model of "Russia" has been the new treatment of the Russian Orthodox Church, highlighted during the celebrations of the millennium of the introduction of Christianity in Kyivan Rus'. The Orthodox Church is the only Russian institution in the USSR that represents a pre-Soviet Russia, one without the Communist party and without Lenin. "The Orthodox Church," says Edward L. Keenan, "is slowly recapturing a role in which it has often been cast by both well-wishers and enemies—that of the only authentically Russian national institution."[31]

The emergence of that complex phenomenon, Russian nationalism, has understandably attracted scholarly attention abroad, as the writings of Alexander Yanov, John B. Dunlop, and Dina Rome Spechler attest. It has also given rise to certain political hopes that seem at best premature. Thus, David A. Moro, who views "the emergence of a new national consciousness among ethnic Russians" as the most important of "internal Soviet developments in recent decades," expects that "Russianization" of the Soviet Union might prompt "Russia" to abandon its communist global goals. This, in turn, should shape a new American strategy, which "would be to induce the Soviet state to move from its present ideocratic, totalitarian structure toward a more traditional nation-state with a nationalist rather than a Communist orientation. This evolution, if it could be brought about, would remove the root causes of Soviet aggressiveness."[32]

Indeed, Moro continues, "Russians are in no meaningful sense a favored nationality under Soviet rule—since 1917 their people and culture have endured persecutions far greater than those inflicted on minority nationalities." Russian dominance is a "myth" that "is easy to feed, given Russia's imperial past and the Soviet state's outward physiognomy (a multinational empire controlled from the Russian capital, with Russian as the official language)." But Moro dismisses this "myth"; in his view, "[b]y giving Russian imperialist overtones to its domination of other peoples, the regime deflects the resentment of other nationalities from the Communist state entity onto the Russian national entity."[33]

Moro does not ask what the reaction of the non-Russian peoples would be if the Soviet Union became an openly Russian "nation-state," a prospect he would clearly welcome. It is far from self-evident that the adoption of "Russianism" as the state's official ideology would make the non-Russian nationalities less resentful of the Russians than they are now, when, purportedly, that resentment is misplaced and should be addressed instead to the nonnational regime.

Moro's view of the Soviet Union as Russia is hardly unique among Western writers. Mark Frankland, the author of *The Sixth Continent: Russia and Mikhail Gorbachev*, as one of his reviewers, Alastair McAuley, has noted, "could be mistaken for a Russian nationalist." He "has produced a marvellous evocation of Russia, rather than the Soviet Union as a whole." Frankland conveys the Russians' "almost mystical pride in the Russian language and its literature, their identification with the villages, fields and woods of the Russian countryside. He gives the impression that he shares in this pride." But, McAuley points out, Frankland "fails to convey any sense of the tensions that come from the fact that the Soviet Union is a multi-ethnic state and that the Russians about whom he writes so lovingly make up little more than half the total population."[34]

The Non-Russians

The other half of the Soviet population has responded to the revival of Russia by asking questions such as that posed by the Ukrainian writer, Pavlo Zahrebelny: "There is much talk these days about Russian patriotism. . . . But has anyone ever said anything about Ukrainian patriotism? And now, when the histories written by Klyuchevsky, Solovyov, and Karamzin are being republished, perhaps we should raise the question of republishing *The History of Ukraine-Rus'* by Hrushevsky, on whose pages the issues of Ukrainian patriotism are elucidated . . . ?"[35]

Thus, as the non-Russians witness the restoration of non-communist figures and institutions as part of the Russian ethnic and national heritage, they cannot help but notice that this heritage is not *theirs*. They have responded to the de-Sovietization of Russia by raising analogous demands for the rehabilitation of *their* respective cultural figures from both their pre-Soviet and Soviet histories, especially those who had been denigrated under Stalin. This movement has been stimulated, and certainly legitimized, by the developments in ethnic Russia, which are being carefully studied in the non-Russian republics. The phrase, "as our Russian brothers are showing us, it is necessary to love one's language, study one's history, rehabilitate suppressed historical figures," and so forth, is frequently met in non-Russian cultural periodicals and at cultural gatherings.

With specific reference to religion, it is obvious that an open incorporation of Orthodoxy into the Russian national identity not only further de-Sovietizes Russia but also further separates the Russians from other Soviet peoples. This is bound to complicate, especially, Russian-Ukrainian and Russian-Belorussian relations—for two reasons. First, the Soviet state, in full accord with the Russian Church, had banned separate Belorussian and Ukrainian Orthodox Churches, whereas the Russian Orthodox Church continues to treat these two East Slavic peoples as part of a "Russian" nation. Second, the state, in a dramatic demonstration of its direct engagement in religious matters, had also banned the Uniate Church. In the Soviet context, the rehabilitation of Russian Orthodoxy revives an old imperial legacy—the tsarist policy of denying the Ukrainians and Belorussians a distinct identity, including a separate identity in religious matters.[36]

The Russian-Ukrainian and Russian-Belorussian relationships concern peoples with a long common cultural and religious past; the Soviet nationality problem is much broader and more complex. This complexity, too, in all its aspects, is an inheritance, a legacy taken over from Imperial Russia. There are the Baltic peoples, with their Protestant and Catholic religious background, their German, Polish, and Swedish historical ties, and living memories of independent statehood between 1918 and 1940. Then there are the peoples whom John A. Armstrong calls "mobilized diasporas"—Jews, Armenians, Germans. These peoples played "key roles as innovators and managers" in the past, and the question now is whether the dominant nation will allow them to resume those roles as the Soviet Union tries to modernize itself again.[37]

The Armenians are, of course, not only a "diaspora" people, but also—like the neighboring Georgians—a nation with its own territorial homeland and republic. The recent upheavals in the Nagorno-Karabakh region have been largely viewed as an Azerbaijani-Armenian territorial dispute. Although this is correct, the ramifications are much broader, as Armstrong helps us to see in his essay. Armstrong analyzes Muslim-Christian relations in Yugoslavia and the Soviet Union and reminds us of some significant history:

> The three great empires—Austro-Hungarian, Ottoman, and tsarist Russian—which divided East Europe and its borderlands prior to World War One all arose during the struggle between Islam and Christianity. Since recent evidence indicates the strong, indeed almost incredible persistence of a distinctive Islamic culture, one may expect East Europe to present in the future, too, not *one* system of nations but *two* distinctive types: a "Christian" and an "Islamic."[38]

The latter, Armstrong explains, includes not only the Middle East but also "numerous nations" of Muslim background in Yugoslavia and the USSR. Speaking of these, Armstrong presents a broad historical assessment:

> In crucial respects these nations are linked more closely to the Middle Eastern northern tier (Afghanistan, Iran, Turkey) than to the historic Orthodox Christian centers (Moscow, Belgrade) which dominate their present state institutions. Today, of course, both these centers are formally Leninist. . . .
>   Persistent variation between nations of the Moslem type and those of Christian background reflect incompatible ways of life and historic symbols more than overt religious cleavage, although religious revival draws strength from distinctive traditions. Incompatibility of ways of life is indicated by objective social characteristics (notably demographic patterns) as well as by in-group attitudes. . . . Given the enduring force of these incompatibilities, any polity composed of nations of Islamic as well as of Christian background is likely to become fragile.[39]

One can only speculate on the likely impact of the "de-Sovietization of Russia"—or of Moscow's becoming less Leninist in order to maintain its Great Power standing—on the Muslim peoples of the Soviet Union. One would like to know, for instance, what natives of Tashkent, Samarkand, and Dushanbe—or, for that matter, people in Novosibirsk and Vladivostok—think of Mikhail Gorbachev's idea of the Soviet Union as belonging to a "Europe from the Atlantic to the Urals."[40] When Gorbachev calls Europe "our common home," do they not ask themselves if they are "at home" in that Europe too?[41]

On the other hand, one may well imagine such "European" talk evoking very positive feelings in Riga, Vilnius, Lviv, and Kyiv. The idea of a European unity is also likely to be received with understanding and support by *some* people in Moscow, and even more so in the city formerly known as St. Petersburg.

But the emphasis should be on *some*, for not all Russians necessarily agree that Russia's "home" is in Europe—or only, or mainly, in Europe. Just as they had before 1917, the Russians are still debating the question of their country's identity.

Conclusions

Historical evidence suggests that the unity of multiethnic polities depends largely on the willingness of the dominant element *not* to think of itself as an ethnic category. It is not enough for the state to seek to assimilate its diverse groups; the dominant element in the state has to dissolve itself within or identify itself with a broader territorial, political, and/or ideological concept as well. And so we have Americans, not "WASPS"; Ottomans, not Turks; British, not English; Spaniards, not Castilians.

The likelihood of the rise of a new, more authentically common Soviet political identity, therefore, will largely depend on the willingness of the Russians to submerge or dissolve themselves in a broader entity encompassing all the peoples of the state. The viability of the "Soviet people" remains problematic for reasons indicated earlier: How can there be a "Soviet people" as long as there is no "Soviet power" in the Soviet Union, as long as political power belongs to the Communist party, and not to the (popularly and freely elected) *soviets* (councils)?

There were moments in Imperial Russia's history when one could be a Russian in the political or, more precisely, dynastic sense (a *rossiianin*), without being an ethnic Russian (*russkii*). Today, as Russians seek to reconstitute their national memories and build a Russian national identity, they are in effect telling all others in the USSR what they think about the "Soviet people" (*sovetskii narod*): They show not the slightest inclination to call their country anything but "Russia," or themselves anything but "Russians." They are *russkie*, not *sovetskie*—Russian, not Soviet, people.

This does not mean that all Russians know what parts of the Soviet Union they understand "Russia" to include, or who they consider to be

Russian and who not. Many conflicting answers to these questions are being currently offered.[42] Thus, some Russians seem prepared to accept the "RSFSR" (the Russian Soviet Federated Socialist Republic) as their narrower homeland within the USSR. Others think of the entire USSR as Russia—although not all of them necessarily accept all Soviet citizens as their compatriots in that "Russia."

There is another current of Russian thought—or better, model or image of "Russia"—that finds adherents in the Soviet Union today. This is "Eurasianism," of which Kristof provides a succinct summary:

> . . . the Eurasian image of Russia identifies Russia with that vast stretch of continental land from the Carpathians to the Pacific, which was for centuries controlled by the nomads who roamed the grassy plains between Mongolia and the Pripet marshes. The Eurasiatic steppe, it is said, was the cradle of an imperial state-idea, and the Russians rule an empire which preceded them. There was a "Russia" (or rather, a *Rossiia*) prior to the Russian Russia. The Russians have inherited a cultural-political domain and with it a certain teleological impetus conditioned by history and geography. They are the non-nomadic heirs to the nomads; they have rebuilt the Mongol empire from its Western end. In other words, the concept of Russia as Eurasia unites two distinct historical realities and epochs, and it is both logically and historically a two-way street: Before there was a European Asia there was an Asiatic Europe.[43]

In the Eurasianist point of view, the peoples of the old empire possessed a common past that preceded both tsarism and Soviet communism. Those ties were forged during the Middle Ages, in the period of the so-called "Mongol Yoke." Russia, therefore, was an Asian as much as a European power—in brief, it was special, "Eurasian."

Although it was first formally developed over sixty years ago, Eurasianism has relevance to the present national debate. It has become clear, in the late 1980s, that what Pipes once called a "purely formal feature of the Soviet Constitution," has acquired—or recovered—a life of its own. Some Russians grasped as early as the 1920s the fundamental importance of this revolutionary transformation of the position of the non-Russian nations and therefore also of the Russian nation. Among them was Prince Nikolai Trubetskoi, one of the main proponents of Eurasianism. His interesting attempt to reconcile the doctrines of Eurasianism with the consequences of the Russian Revolution in the area of nationality affairs deserves attention today. Writing in 1927, Trubetskoi argued that the Russian nation had saved the unity of the state, which otherwise would have disintegrated into a number of independent units, by sacrificing its "previous status of the only master of the state." Thus, the non-Russian peoples acquired a position in the state they had never enjoyed before, and the Russians ceased to be the ruling nation. The Russian nation "is no longer the master of the household, but only the first among equals." The rights the non-Russians had won "cannot any more be taken away from them."[44]

Clearly, Eurasianism is a doctrine that supports with broad historical and cultural arguments the unity of the present USSR, a unity otherwise threatened by the failure of Marxism-Leninism. (It would let the Balts secede, however, which should win it mass support in Riga, Tallinn, and Vilnius.) One might also argue that Eurasianism represents an early attempt to forestall or preempt the rise of an anti-Russian Muslim separatism of whose potential Armstrong speaks. Whether Eurasianism is an influential political current in the USSR today is not clear. But it does have vocal intellectual spokesmen. Lev Gumilev is the chief proponent for the view that the USSR is neither a Russian nor a Slavic state, but one that is both Slavic and Turkic, European and Asian, Christian and Muslim. For understandable reasons the party does not encourage "Eurasianism," although the view finds its way into print.[45] Nor is this model of Russia likely to generate much enthusiasm among the Leningrad and Moscow intelligentsia, whose mental map of the world clearly includes Paris, New York, and Munich, but seldom Ulan-Ude and Karaganda.

The politically dominant trend in the Soviet Union today is "statism" or "imperial nationalism," although these names are not used except by its critics. This trend may be said to represent a communist version of the "Official Nationality" concept of the Russian nation from tsarist times, except that it inserts Marxism-Leninism in place of Orthodoxy, and party rule in place of autocracy. Although it is ostensibly a nonnational ideology, Marxism-Leninism became in Stalin's time a "neo-tsarist Marxism," or "imperial Bolshevism," as Robert C. Tucker has termed it.[46] Tucker also calls Stalinism "a nationalistically and imperialistically wayward form of Bolshevism, a Bolshevism of the radical right."[47] However, just as the apologists of tsarism were not altogether clear about what they understood by "nationality," so the Soviet ideologues, as we have seen, are having trouble with defining the nature of the "Soviet people." Statist or imperial nationalism does not believe that political freedom is a desirable goal for the Russians—especially not if it should threaten the territorial integrity of the state.

There are Russians who oppose the idea of an empire in principle, such as Alexander Zinoviev (although he is rather vague on details). In an interview several years ago, Zinoviev stated that his "sole concern is the future of the Russian people." Since he wanted "the Russian people to be educated, cultured, and self-confident so that they can share the treasures of world culture and contribute to them" and thus "lift the Russians out of their centuries-old backwardness and subjection," he understood that it "is impossible for the Russian people to attain any of these things within the Soviet empire."[48]

It is impossible to tell how numerous or influential are those Russians who share Zinoviev's view of the empire. Recently, however, the Soviet press has published criticisms of the outlook termed "imperial consciousness" (*imperskoe soznanie*). Thus, the Leningrad historian Evgeny Anisimov attributed the present sharpening (*obostrenie*) of national relations in Soviet society to various and serious shortcomings in the treatment of the history of Soviet nationalities, especially the "relapses into imperial consciousness" (*retsidivy imperskogo soznaniia*). Anisimov cites examples of "imperial" thinking on such topics as the conquest of the Caucasus and the "Shamil problem," and observes that "about the partitions of Poland, the suppression of Polish uprisings, or of the Hungarian uprising of 1849, one does not talk at all"—and if one does, it is in "Aesopian language."[49]

These practices denounced by Anisimov can only mean that the Soviet Union is indeed perceived as an heir of the tsarist Empire—or, rather, that the empire is viewed as a "Soviet Union before the name." Interestingly, the communist authorities in Poland had also treated criticism of tsarist Russia as attacks on the Soviet Union, thus assuming the continuity if not identity between the two states. Polish censors in Gierek's time (1970 to 1980) openly stated that the party treats any criticism of tsarism as a camouflaged criticism of the Soviet Union. Accordingly, certain works of Adam Mickiewicz (1798–1855) were not published for decades, and scholars were not allowed to write on such topics as the tsarist Russification of Poland or the tsarist deportations of Poles to Siberia.[50]

It is not surprising, therefore, that "imperial consciousness" or "imperial outlook," that legacy of tsarist Russia, is especially evident in the current Ukrainian-Russian relationship. An essay about the tsarist state's (and Russian "society's") treatment of the "Ukrainian Question," written before 1917 by Vladimir Vernadsky, the famous scientist, sounds quite topical and relevant today, and may be treated as a critique of the present Soviet treatment of Ukraine.[51]

The current leader of the Soviet Union is committed to a policy that, if it is to succeed, requires the restoration of civil society. But civil society under Soviet conditions means something quite different from what Ernest Barker envisaged when he differentiated between the State, or the legal sphere, and Society, the social sphere. In the Soviet Union, the restoration of the social sphere immediately produces a number of entities that want to perform the functions of the state, to exercise the prerogatives of sovereign nations. The conflict between Armenia and Azerbaijan is the first and most dramatic illustration of what is likely to happen when the party really abdicates its authority or simply chooses on occasion not to exercise it.

What will be the response of Moscow if the non-Russians again go "too far"? What will happen if the Russians press on with their nationalist goal to transform the Soviet Union into a Russian nation-state free of Marxism-Leninism and the Communist party?

Paul Goble, a U.S. analyst of Soviet nationality problems, says: ". . . Gorbachev may now be learning what many students of that part of the world have long suspected: that a liberalized Russia might be possible but that a significantly liberalized Soviet Union is probably a contradiction in terms."[52] A very similar view was stated by a Czech historian twenty years earlier. In 1969, shortly after the suppression of the Prague Spring, Milan Švankmajer published an article on Tsar Nicholas I and his struggles against the revolutionary movements in Europe in 1848–49. According to Švankmajer, the Russian Empire was "constantly exposed to the danger of disintegration, which can be prevented only by a strong central government." The very existence of multinational empires is threatened by "civil rights," and Russia intervened in 1849 because civil rights and national self-determination "threatened the very foundations of Russian autocracy."[53]

Will the reformer Gorbachev one day have to face the problem that the reactionary Nicholas I faced? If he does, will he respond differently? Paul Goble, as we see, doubts it. Should Goble prove wrong, should the Soviet Union become a liberal polity while remaining multinational, it will need to overcome more than "imperial consciousness"—that attitude some contemporary Soviet historians now discern in the USSR's treatment of non-Russians within its borders and in its dealings with such foreign countries as Poland. A way will have to be found to satisfy the national aspirations of the Soviet peoples, including the Russian people, to their own political autonomy and cultural self-expression, and at the same time it will be necessary to convince them of the benefits of maintaining a larger, supranational framework in which no one nation dominates the others. In the meantime, an "imperial consciousness" is alive in the USSR seventy years after the death of the empire. This means either that this consciousness is a "false consciousness" or that the empire is not dead after all and that therefore those conditions of equality are still lacking.

Notes

1. It is clearly superfluous in an essay of this kind to cite the standard literature, but it may be helpful to identify some of the works that the author found particularly important. For the treatment of the nationalities question as an essential aspect of Russian history, see especially two books by Hugh Seton-Watson, *The Decline of Imperial Russia, 1855–1914* (New York: Praeger, 1961), and *The Russian Empire, 1801–1917* (Oxford: Oxford University Press, Clarendon Press, 1967). The "Russian problem" in all its ramifications, including historical continuities and discontinuities, is treated by many scholars in two collective volumes: Robert Conquest, ed., *The Last Empire: Nationality and the Soviet Future* (Stanford: Hoover Institution Press, 1986), and Edward Allworth, ed., *Ethnic Russia in the USSR: The Dilemma of Dominance* (New York: Pergamon, 1980). For a thorough account of how the Bolsheviks dealt with nationalism, see Richard Pipes, *The Formation of the Soviet Union: Communism and Nationalism, 1917–1923,* rev. ed. (New York: Atheneum, 1968). The current Soviet agenda is presented in James Cracraft, ed., *The Soviet Union Today: An Interpretive Guide,* 2d ed. (Chicago: University of Chicago Press, 1988).

2. For a more detailed discussion by the author, see Roman Szporluk, "The Ukraine and Russia," in Conquest, *The Last Empire,* pp. 151–82, where references to the relevant literature may also be found, and *Communism and Nationalism: Karl Marx versus Friedrich List* (New York: Oxford University Press, 1988). Richard Pipes, *Russia under the Old Regime* (New York: Charles Scribner's Sons, 1974), presents a full-scale treatment of the Russian state as the "Patrimonial State" and of its ideology of "Patrimonialism."

3. Ladis K. D. Kristof, "The Russian Image of Russia: An Applied Study in Geopolitical Methodology," in Charles A. Fischer, ed., *Essays in Political Geography* (London: Methuen, 1968), p. 350.

4. Ibid., pp. 349–50.

5. Ibid., pp. 356–64. Those who saw in Kyivan Rus' the real core of Russia denied by definition that Ukrainians were a nation distinct from the Russians. This conclusion was not implicit in the "Muscovite" or "St. Petersburg" models of Russia, although their proponents, with few exceptions, also held the position.

6. "The Right of Nations to Self-Determination" (1914), in V. I. Lenin, *Collected Works*, vol. 20 (Moscow: Progress, 1964), pp. 396–97; trans. in A. W. Orridge, "Uneven Development and Nationalism: II," *Political Studies* 29, no. 2 (June 1981): 185–86.

7. Mikhail Gorbachev's report to the CPSU Central Committee, "O perestroike i kadrovoi politike partii," January 27, 1987, *Pravda*, January 28, 1987, pp. 1–5, as translated in *Current Digest of the Soviet Press* (henceforth *CDSP*) 39, no. 4 (February 25, 1987): 6.

8. "O khode realizatsii reshenii XXVII s'ezda KPSS i zadachakh po uglublenii perestroiki," Report by Mikhail Gorbachev, General Secretary of the CPSU Central Committee, at the Nineteenth All-Union CPSU Conference, June 28, 1988, *Pravda*, June 29, 1988, pp. 2–7, as translated in *CDSP* 40, no. 26 (July 27, 1988): 7.

9. Ibid.

10. Ibid., pp. 7, 11–22.

11. J. V. Stalin, *Works*, vol. 8 (Moscow: Foreign Language Publishing House, 1954), pp. 37–38; see also Szporluk, *Communism and Nationalism*, p. 221.

12. Stalin, *Works*, vol. 7 (1954), p. 6.

13. For an informative and stimulating guide to the current socialist attempts to free socialism from its historic attachment to statism and to establish the validity of the state versus civil society dualism in socialism, see John Keane, *Democracy and Civil Society: On the Predicaments of European Socialism, the Prospects for Democracy, and the Problem of Controlling Social and Political Power* (London: Verso, 1988), and idem, ed., *Civil Society and the State: New European Perspectives* (London: Verso, 1988).

14. Ernest Barker, *Principles of Social and Political Theory* (Oxford: Oxford University Press, Clarendon Press, 1956), p. 4.

15. Ibid.

16. Before any of these desiderata are realized, however, it will be more realistic to look for elements of an *independent society*, the term preferred by H. Gordon Skilling to describe those departures from Stalinism emerging in Eastern Europe and, more recently, in the Soviet Union. Skilling recognizes that an "independent society" is a significant phenomenon, a major modification of the old model, but he warns against viewing it as a development that can be described

in terms of the "civil society vs. the state" dichotomy. He points out, for example, that an "independent society" does not enjoy a legally recognized autonomy—and that the state is not a *Rechtsstaat*. See H. Gordon Skilling, *Samizdat and an Independent Society in Central and Eastern Europe* (Basingstoke: Macmillan, 1988). I am grateful to Professor Skilling for his comments on an earlier version of this chapter.

17. Pipes, *The Formation of the Soviet Union*, is the standard account and analysis of the events of 1917 to 1923. For briefer, capsule histories of the major Soviet nationalities, see Zev Katz, Rosemarie Rogers, and Frederic Harned, eds., *Handbook of Major Soviet Nationalities* (New York: Free Press, 1975). For a detailed development of my view of this problem in a broader context between Marxism-Leninism and nationalism, see Szporluk, *Communism and Nationalism*, pp. 229–33.

18. Pipes, *The Formation of the Soviet Union*, p. 296.

19. Ibid., pp. 296–97.

20. Eric J. Hobsbawm, "Some Reflections on Nationalism," in T. J. Nossiter, A. H. Hanson, and Stein Rokkan, eds., *Imagination and Precision in the Social Sciences: Essays in Memory of Peter Nettl* (London: Faber & Faber, 1972), p. 395.

21. Ibid.

22. Eric J. Hobsbawm, *The Age of Revolution, 1789–1848* (New York: New American Library, 1962), p. 217, quoted (and discussed) in Szporluk, *Communism and Nationalism*, p. 148.

23. *Komsomol'skaia pravda*, March 27, 1988, p. 1.

24. *Komsomol'skaia pravda*, June 3, 1988, p. 2.

25. Kendall E. Bailes, "Science and Technology in the Soviet Union: Historical Background and Contemporary Problems," in Alexander Dallin and Condoleezza Rice, eds., *The Gorbachev Era* (Stanford: Stanford Alumni Association, 1986), pp. 69–70.

26. Hugh Seton-Watson, *Nations and States. An Enquiry into the Origins of Nations and the Politics of Nationalism* (Boulder, Colo.: Westview Press, 1977), p. 87, quoted by Benedict Anderson, *Imagined Communities: Reflections on the Origin and Spread of Nationalism* (London: Verso, 1983), p. 84.

27. Iulian Bromlei, "Byt' tsementiruiushchei siloi," *Sovetskaia kul'tura*, June 25, 1988, p. 8.

28. Genrikh Borovik, speech at the Nineteenth Party Conference, *Pravda*, July 2, 1988, p. 3.

29. Iurii Afanas'ev, "Perestroika i istoricheskoe znanie," *Literaturnaia Rossiia*, June 17, 1988, pp. 2–3 and 8–9; reference to "identity crisis" is on p. 9.

30. G. Kh. Popov and Nikita Adzhubei, "Pamiat' i *Pamiat'*," *Znamia*, no. 1 (1988): 192–93.

31. Edward L. Keenan, "The Millenium of the Baptism of Rus' and Russian Self-Awareness," *Harriman Institute Forum* 1, no. 7 (July 1988): 3.

32. David A. Moro, "The National Rebirth of Russia: A U.S. Strategy for Lifting the Soviet Siege," *Policy Review*, no. 43 (Winter 1988): 2.

33. Ibid., p. 5.

34. Alastair McAuley, "Ready for Action," *Times Literary Supplement* (London), August 14, 1987, p. 883.

35. "Spravi perebudovy—tvorchu initsiatyvu," *Literaturna Ukraïna*, July 28, 1988, p. 1. Consciously or not, Zahrebelny was paraphrasing the famous question asked by Mykola Khvylovyi in the 1920s: "Is Russia independent?—It is? Well, then Ukraine is independent too."

36. See Szporluk, "Ukraine and Russia," in Conquest, *The Last Empire*, pp. 162–63 and p. 177, n. 27.

37. John A. Armstrong, "Toward a Framework for considering Nationalism in East Europe," *Eastern European Politics and Societies* 2, no. 2 (Spring 1988): 280–305, esp. pp. 296–97, 300–301, and 304. Also see idem, "Mobilized and Proletarian Diasporas," *American Political Science Review* 70, no. 2 (June 1976), especially pp. 403–4.

38. Armstrong, "Toward a Framework," p. 301.

39. Ibid., p. 302.

40. Gorbachev's speech in Prague (1987), quoted in Karen Dawisha, *Eastern Europe, Gorbachev and Reform: The Great Challenge* (Cambridge: Cambridge University Press, 1988), p. 192.

41. Ibid.

42. For a more detailed discussion of this problem, see Roman Szporluk, "Dilemmas of Russian Nationalism," *Problems of Communism* 38, no. 4 (July-August 1989): 15–35. Reprinted as chapter 7 of this book.

43. Kristof, "Russian Image," in Fischer, *Essays in Political Geography*, p. 363.

44. N. S. Trubetskoi, "Obshcheevraziiskii natsionalizm," *Evraziiskaia khronika* (Paris), no. 9 (1927): 24–25.

45. See Iu. Afanas'ev, "Proshloe i my," *Kommunist*, no. 14 (1985): 110, for a scornful reference to "Evraziistvo."

46. Robert C. Tucker, *Political Culture and Leadership in Soviet Russia: From Lenin to Gorbachev* (New York: Norton, 1987), pp. 67 and 97.

47. Ibid., p. 70.

48. George Urban, "Portrait of a Dissenter as a Soviet Man: A Conversation with Alexander Zinoviev," *Encounter* 62, no. 4 (April 1984): 23.

49. E. V. Anisimov, "U zhurnala dolzhna byt' svoia pozitsiia," in the symposium titled " 'Kruglyi Stol': istoricheskaia nauka v usloviiakh perestroiki," *Voprosy istorii*, no. 3 (1988): 17.

50. See the report titled " 'Belye piatna': Ot èmotsii k faktam," in *Literaturnaia gazeta*, May 11, 1988, p. 14.

51. V. I. Vernads'kyi, "Ukrains'ke pytannia i rosiis'ka hromads'kist'," *Mo-*

loda hvardiia (Kyiv), March 12, 1988, as translated in *Soviet Ukrainian Affairs* (London) 2, no. 2 (Summer 1988): 22–26. The main Ukrainian literary journal *Vitchyzna* (Kyiv) published the whole Vernadsky text in the June 1988 issue.

52. Paul Goble, "Gorbachev and the Soviet Nationality Problem," in Maurice Friedberg and Heyward Isham, eds., *Soviet Society under Gorbachev* (Armonk, N.Y.: M. E. Sharpe, 1987), p. 99.

53. Milan Švankmajer, "The Gendarme of Europe," *Dějiny a současnost* (Prague) 11, no. 4 (April 1969), quoted by Antonin J. Liehm, "East Central Europe and the Soviet Model," *Problems of Communism* 30, no. 5 (September-October 1981): 51–52.

9   The Soviet West— or Far Eastern Europe?

Geography Defined by History

What does the title of this chapter mean? There are various ways of defining the space it refers to, all of them historical in one way or another.[1] Might we view as "Far Eastern Europe" what has often been called "the Soviet West"? Each term includes territories that the USSR acquired between 1939 and 1945. These are, from north to south:

1. Areas annexed from Finland after the Finnish-Soviet War of 1939–40 and then reconfirmed in Soviet possession after 1944

2. The three Baltic states of Estonia, Latvia, and Lithuania, which "joined" the USSR in the summer of 1940

3. The former German city and province of Königsberg in East Prussia, now known as Kaliningrad

4. Areas of Poland that the USSR occupied in September 1939, after it had joined Germany in attacking Poland

5. The former Czechoslovak province of Sub-Carpathia or Ru-

First published in *East European Politics and Societies*, 1991.

thenia (also known as Carpatho-Ukraine), incorporated in the USSR in 1944–45
6. The northern part of the former Romanian province of Bukovina, now the oblast of Chernivtsi
7. "Moldavia," which now calls itself "Moldova"; it was known as Bessarabia before World War I, when it was under Russia, and between 1918 and 1940 it was Romanian

Those formerly Polish territories mentioned in item 4 now belong to three Soviet republics: (a) Vilnius and its vicinity is part of Lithuania; (b) the oblasts of Brest and Grodno are in Belorussia; (c) the former Polish provinces of Wołyń, Lwów, Tarnopol, and Stanisławów are now in the Ukrainian SSR. The last three form the eastern part of the pre-1918 Austrian province of Galicia. Its main city is Lviv in Ukrainian, known as Lwów in Polish, and as Lvov in Russian.

Even after this mechanical listing it is clear that we are dealing with a very diverse and geographically extensive region—from the Arctic to the Black Sea—if indeed one may call it a single region. What really matters is, first, that its only unity lies in its being a "new" Soviet territory, having been acquired more than twenty years after the revolutionary days of 1917, and, second, that it really consists of at least four distinct historical-cultural-national entities.

First, there are the Baltic states of Estonia and Latvia. These two states, unlike Lithuania, with which they are often grouped, first became associated with the Russian Empire during the reign of Peter the Great. Their previous historical experiences were connected with Sweden and before that with the German Order of the Knights of the Sword. By going farther back than 1939 to 1945, or even 1917, we begin to arrive at a more historical definition of "Far Eastern Europe." It is not simply the "Soviet West"—it is also the eastern fringe of what used to be a multinational space whose core had been located outside the present borders of the Soviet Union. One such larger multiethnic or multinational state was the kingdom of Sweden. There was a time when it extended to Finland, Latvia, and Estonia. Their cities belonged to the Hanseatic League, German was their language of culture until as late as World War I, and Protestantism was the dominant religion since the Reformation.[2]

The second multinational state to which some areas of "Far Eastern Europe" belonged for considerable periods of time was the Polish-Lithuanian Commonwealth. It is arguable that the formation of such modern nations as Lithuania, Belorussia, and Ukraine owes much to the historical linkages of those peoples to Poland from the fourteenth to the twentieth centuries. Historically Lithuania belongs to a cultural circle quite different from that in which the Latvians and Estonians lived for many centuries. Its emergence on the stage of European history was connected with Poland and has been profoundly shaped by Roman Catholicism. But unlike the other Balts, and unlike the Belorussians and Ukrainians, the Lithuanians were a state nation in the old Rzeczpospolita—always the constitutional equal of their Polish partner. Thus, they acquired a distinct cultural and political tradition that they share with Poland, especially during the fifteenth to seventeenth centuries, when Lithuania was a great power. Lithuanians eventually lost their distinct identity, and one might argue that modern Lithuanian nationalism, which emerged in the nineteenth century just as did its Ukrainian and Belorussian counterparts, developed in reaction to Polish national identity and Polish domination.[3]

The third multinational state whose historic core is located outside the USSR but certain of whose provinces are now in the USSR was the Austro-Hungarian Empire. Eastern Galicia, northern Bukovina, and Transcarpathia, all now in the Ukrainian SSR, belonged to that empire until 1918.[4] Fourthly and finally, the republic of Moldavia and certain adjacent regions of the present Ukrainian Republic belonged to the Ottoman Empire until 1812. Indeed, the Ukrainian Bukovina, before it became Austrian in 1775, had been under the Ottomans. The republic's immediate pre-Soviet experience was as a constituent part of Romania, and since 1944, Moldavia, or "Moldova," has been an extremely complex area of ethnic interaction and conflict.[5]

Although the distant historical experiences and the memories evoking them are important, it is more important for anyone concerned with understanding current Soviet politics, especially the revival of Far Eastern Europe in the post-Stalin years, to pay particular attention to the immediate pre-Soviet years as a background to the current situation. For the Baltic states, the most relevant pre-Soviet experience was their independence, their existence as sovereign nation-states between 1918 and 1940. It was then that the world began to think of Lithuania, Latvia, and Estonia as forming a single group, "the Baltic States." The year 1940, accordingly, is for all three a year of great national tragedy.

After enjoying full sovereignty for over twenty years, the Balts felt especially deprived under Soviet rule. Writing more than twenty years ago, V. Stanley Vardys noted that the Balts "are not admitted to the national [sic] apparatus of decision making. . . . Generally, Baltic-raised and educated cadres have not been accepted as junior partners in the governing of the Soviet Union . . . the Baltic party and government authorities do not act as coparticipants in the decision-making process but only as lobbyists trying to promote their own advantage." He further pointed out that "the Baltic republics play a negligible role in Soviet politics, a very special role in economics, and a rather important, for Soviet conditions, cultural-social role."[6]

The three Baltic republics, even after their annexation, were always treated by Moscow as something different, something special compared with the other nations of the USSR, and Armstrong attributes this to their status as "state nations."[7]

It is revealing that in the interwar period a number of Russian anti-Communist émigrés living in the West accepted the independence of the Baltic states from Russia. Thus, thinkers belonging to the so-called "Eurasian" school in the 1920s and 1930s, when they reflected on the future state that they expected would one day replace Russia and the USSR (it was to be called "Eurasia") recognized the separation of the Baltic states from Russia as final and did not expect them to join that "Eurasian" state. They agreed that the Balts belonged to a different civilization, that of Europe—to which Russia did not belong, in their opinion.[8]

The very Russians who reconciled themselves to the loss of the Baltics, however, always insisted on retaining not only the Soviet Ukraine in the future postcommunist state they hoped to create—they also demanded the inclusion of Galicia, which between the wars was under Poland and had never belonged to the tsarist state. Galicia belongs to the second very special area in the post-World War II USSR, a complex of quite diverse regions that is conveniently called "West Ukraine." Because of its special character as a bridge from the non-Soviet West to the "old-Soviet" (that is, Soviet before 1939) East Ukraine and less directly even Russia, we shall discuss West Ukraine's role in contemporary USSR later in a separate section. Those areas are now very much on the minds of many Poles. As contemporary Poland, newly emancipated from communism, is trying to reconstruct its national identity, it pays a special attention to history, properly recognizing that historical consciousness is an essential component of national identity. Although preoccupied with their relations with Germany and Western Europe, the Poles are also restoring their memories of the East, thus recovering the political and emotional and intellectual geography of their national imagination. By reviving their historical ties with their eastern neighbors, they will follow not only a political tactic, but will facilitate the restoration of their once intimate ties to their eastern "Borderlands." Anyone familiar with the post-Stalinist history of Lithuania, Belorussia, and Ukraine knows how significant a role Poland played in their national revivals. Oddly enough, the Poles themselves have been slow in realizing this.[9]

Geography as Ideology—or Is It the Other Way Around?

Our earlier divisions and subdivisions of "Far Eastern Europe" were based on certain facts of pre-Soviet history, and by themselves do not suggest any weighty dividing lines between the worlds of culture and ideology. But such divisions have often been suggested, by reference to history and geography, in the course of political battles and wars. One influential historical-cum-ethnic-cum-ideological definition of a larger geographic area that included what we now call the Soviet West was provided more than seventy years ago by Tomáš Garrigue Masaryk, the future first president of Czechoslovakia. In his arguments for a basic reconstruction of Eastern Europe that was to include the establishment of a Czechoslovak state, Masaryk spoke about a huge geographical area extending across Europe from the north to the south. Masaryk pointed out that a group of dependent peoples lived there. Those peoples tried to survive between Germany and its allies in the West and Russia to the East. Masaryk was interested in justifying the emancipation of those peoples who until World War I were ruled from Berlin or Vienna, but he himself admitted that nothing in principle denied the same status to those peoples who were under St. Petersburg. Masaryk acknowledged that some of those peoples in the western regions of the Russian Empire were more advanced culturally than the Russians.[10]

In an argument that in a sense applies Masaryk's way of treating East Europe to the present situation in the USSR, Ernest Gellner reminds us that the Soviet Union, as it emerged from the Russian Revolution, was a restored Russian Empire under a new ideological legitimation.

The Russian Empire survived under a new principle that wanted to abolish nationality by introducing Marxist-Leninist ideology as the integrating principle. The Austro-Hungarian Empire and the Ottoman Empire had disintegrated after World War I. In recent years, however, says Gellner, the processes of nation-building, or rather nation-formation that we know so well from the history of nineteenth- and twentieth-century Europe, have resumed in the USSR itself and thus the USSR today is dealing with issues that elsewhere in East Europe were faced and dealt with over seventy years ago.[11]

Gellner makes another important point: In such a traditional multinational state as the Habsburg monarchy before 1918, the principles of universalism, rationalism, and the rights of the individual were advanced by those powers who defended the unity of the state, and ethnic, regional, and parochial movements were concentrated among the nationalities, but in the USSR a reverse relationship has formed. As Gellner puts it, in the USSR it is the Baltic peoples who speak for economic liberalism: "The centrifugal nationalism, by opposition to the center, has come to embrace economic nationalism. You can now speak of national liberalism, especially in the Baltic region"—the political and cultural legacies of the Soviet West, that is, the European Far East, are richer, more democratic, and more pluralistic than those of the Soviet imperial center.

The difficult situation of Gorbachev and his "center" can be appreciated when one compares the current Soviet scene with a strikingly relevant case from another historical situation. Gellner draws illuminating parallels and contrasts between the Habsburg monarchy before 1914 and the Soviet Union today, pointing out that in the Habsburg monarchy, those people who were interested in retaining a cosmopolitan, united large society included "the high bourgeoisie [that] was cosmopolitan, individualistic and atomised, with an open culture and an economic interest in having a large society."[12] Gellner asserts that this bourgeoisie of Vienna found "its ideological reflection" in such superb thinkers as Popper, von Mises, and Hayek: "Their view of man, society and knowledge was atomistic, individualistic, open; it was hostile to cultural mysticism and holism." Gellner contrasts this "economic liberalism, cultural cosmopolitanism and universal humanitarianism" at the Vienna center with "socialist communalism or populism in the provinces and amongst the lower classes." With this picture of Austria before 1914, Gellner contrasts the contemporary Soviet Union. He finds that the classical Austrian "alignment" has been reversed in the USSR:

> The force at the centre which is interested in retaining unity is not, as in Austria-Hungary, an individualistic bourgeoisie, but the centralist construction in its nature. . . . . The partisans of a universalist humanism of a general citizenship, the people who say firmly their [*sic*—they are—*RS*] human being[s] first and ethnics much later, who wish to see ethnic mentality eliminated from the internal document or passport, who say that universal citizenship must prevail, and that ethnicity must become a private matter, are to be found at the centre, attracted to political centralism. . . . The Estonian nationalists are also partisans of economic liberalism. This situation is quite new. What kind of compromise may emerge from this, I don't know.[13]

The distinguished Polish author Ryszard Kapuściński has returned from a year traveling across the Soviet Union, and he notes, in an interview with a Warsaw newspaper correspondent, that the Soviet Union is becoming "Asianized." This is happening under the impact of the emancipation of East Europe and comparable processes in the European USSR, especially in the Baltic states, those regions that are becoming less communist. According to Kapuściński, it is in the eastern regions of the USSR, the Central Asian republics especially, that the old Stalinist ways are surviving even though they may sometimes adopt local national forms and thus give a misleading impression of change, and the forces of democracy are very weak there. Kapuściński sees the Soviet Union falling apart into a European and an Asian component. When asked what kind of key he had to interpret Russia itself, Kapuściński replied: "I think there exists no key to Russia." Russia is still searching for its own identity and continues to look for its own way. Kapuściński does not think that the conflict between Gorbachev and Yeltsin is the most important conflict dividing Russian society; rather, he sees the real conflict being between "the inertia of the Russian society" and the forces of change, whose embodiment is the intelligentsia.[14]

It would appear that the only forces supporting the Soviet Union are the army, the central bureaucracy, and the police. Are there no *other*, broader *societal* forces that are interested in saving a unitary Soviet state that would stand above the nationalities? In Austria, Gellner has reminded us, there was such a force—the cosmopolitan bourgeoisie and the intelligentsia, largely Jewish but also consisting of Germanized individuals from many non-German provinces of the monarchy. Those people did represent an all-Austrian force. On the right side of the spectrum, Austria had a unifying force in the Catholic church. As is well known, there was also a supranational imperial army, a dynastic army, not a German army, even though German was its language of command. In the Soviet Union, the potentially most *Soviet* cosmopolitan force, one would expect, should be the nonterritorial ethnic groups. For historic and cultural reasons, the most prominent of them should be the Jews, but they are emigrating in ever-increasing numbers, a kind of *secession*. Less important but also useful for the preservation of the Soviet state's unity might have been the ethnic Germans, whose ancestors came to Russia over two hundred years ago. Soviet Germans might have been a consolidating factor, especially as an element promoting closer relations with the West and one promoting economic modernization within the country. They, too, are leaving in ever-increasing numbers. Another nationality that might have played, and at one time indeed did play, a comparable role are the Armenians. They, too, are alienated from the central State.

This secession by emigration clearly weakens the relative strength of the reformist element within the Soviet population, but those who remain are breaking up not only ideologically but also geographically into two different blocs—into "European" and "Asian" worlds. John A. Armstrong draws on anthropology and history in foreseeing the breakup of both the USSR and Yugoslavia into Christian and Moslem nations. Armstrong offers pertinent observations on the role of nonterritorial minorities in any future economic liberalization of the USSR, and he arrives at conclusions very close to those of Gellner.[15]

The Making and Re-Making of Ukraine and Its Effect on Russia

The inclusion of West Ukraine into the Soviet body politic may have been one of Stalin's most fateful decisions during the years from 1939 to 1945. Stalin surely did not expect that fifty years after its annexation West Ukraine would spearhead the movement for a national liberation of Ukraine from Moscow. Could he have imagined that West

Ukraine would inspire and lead a national awakening in the east, in Kyiv and in cities farther east? And yet this is precisely what has happened.

West Ukraine is the least Soviet area in the USSR. It is also the least Russian and the least Russified, both in historic and demographic terms. (The Kaliningrad region has to be treated as a special case because all of its original inhabitants were expelled in 1945.) In West Ukraine the Soviets acquired not only a land, but also a people that were formerly subjects of Warsaw, Prague, Vienna, Bucharest, and Budapest. Their formative nation-building experiences in the modern era paralleled in many respects those of the other peoples of the Habsburg monarchy—the Czechs, Slovaks, Croats, Slovenes, and others.

The inclusion of the West Ukrainians into the USSR introduced new forces in the centuries-long Ukrainian-Russian relationship. The historical contest between "Great Russia" and "Little Russia" that has been going on since the middle of the seventeenth century was importantly affected by the annexation. For several centuries the inhabitants of Russian Ukraine, known as "Little Russia," had remained in a relationship of inferiority, functioned as "younger brothers"—or perhaps country cousins—of the Great Russians. But what has been often forgotten when viewing this relationship is the fact that only Ukraine east of the Dnieper (and Kyiv on the west bank) entered that relationship with Moscow in 1654. The part to the west of the Dnieper (the so-called "Right Bank Ukraine") was acquired by Russia in 1793 to 1795. In the meantime, the historic province of Galicia was already Austrian, since 1772. The other western parts of the Ukrainian ethnic territory were also outside Russian control, and thus not subject to the "Little Russian" status.

Writing in the 1920s in exile in Paris, the Russian philosopher Georgy Fedotov reflected on the nature of the Russian-Ukrainian relationship and its role in the preservation of Russia's identity as a great nation. He felt relatively confident that the smaller peoples of the then-USSR might remain under Russian cultural influence, but he worried that their emerging intelligentsias were looking toward Warsaw or Ankara for inspiration, rather than Moscow. Fedotov was concerned that "if the nations of Russia will study not in Moscow and in St. Petersburg but in Paris and in Berlin, then they will not stay with us."[16]

Fedotov was thinking of the traditionally Russian-ruled Ukraine when he analyzed the Russo-Ukrainian nexus. The West Ukrainians, who became Soviet subjects ten years after Fedotov wrote his piece, were a people who did not have the historic feeling of inferiority versus Russia that their eastern co-nationals had had—and had been taught to have—for so long. Russia did not impress the West Ukrainians as a higher civilization, and their spiritual leader resided in Rome, not in Moscow. They felt that one should look to the West when looking for models of a modern civilized way of life. Vienna, not Moscow, used to be the model of cultural and political modernity for their grandparents, and Vienna, not Moscow, was the place where they wanted to study. Now, their grandchildren think of New York and Toronto rather than Vienna as places one looks up to—and they still do not admire Moscow.

Fedotov thought of the Orthodox faith as a common bond of the two branches—the Great and Little Russians—of what was to him one Russian nation. But the inclusion of Galicia into the Soviet Ukrainian Republic, and the infusion of the West Ukrainians into the population of a larger Ukraine, created a new situation in both intra-Ukrainian affairs and in the traditional Russian-Ukrainian relationship because the Galicians had been (Uniate) Catholic for several centuries before 1939.

This is no place to discuss the powerfully complex religious situation in Ukraine and the other lands of the Soviet West, but let us limit ourselves to mention of a news item in *L'Osservatore Romano*, datelined the Vatican, January 17, 1991. It stated that on January 16, the Pope restored the Roman Catholic hierarchy in the regions of West Ukraine—both of the Uniate and the Latin rites—that had been removed from the region or had been forced to operate underground for almost half a century. This is a move that will unquestionably have profound impact on the religious and political situation in Ukraine, on Ukrainian-Russian relations, and also on Polish-Ukrainian relations. Simultaneously with this announcement, the Vatican restored the Ukrainian Uniate bishopric in Przemyśl, in Poland, which had been formally closed by the authorities since 1946.[17]

West Ukraine has now become an integral part of Ukraine as a whole, and one may surmise that the region's future will be determined together with that of the rest of Ukraine. In this respect West Ukraine's future is likely to be shaped in a quite different way from what may happen to the Baltic region. This does not mean, of course, that the process of spiritual and political integration of Ukraine has been completed. Early in the twentieth century, the great Ukrainian historian and nation-builder, Mykhailo Hrushevsky, who was educated in Russian

Kyiv and was teaching in Austrian and Polish Lviv, seriously considered that a single Ukrainian nation might break up into two:

> . . . up to the present, Galicia has gone forward and Dnieper Ukraine has either stood still or gone beyond Galicia. Now Ukraine will go along its own separate road and its distance from Galicia will grow with each step if care is not taken to shorten the distance between these roads. Should each go along its own road and rapprochement not be secured, in twenty or thirty years we will have before us two nationalities on one ethnographic base. This would be similar to the position of the Serbs and Croatians, two parts of one Serbian ethnic group divided in its political, cultural, and religious circumstances, resulting in complete alienation [*vidchuzhennia*].[18]

That Hrushevsky's fears had a strong foundation is shown by the current east-west tensions within Ukraine. One wonders if a more fundamental split would not have taken place had the western regions not been attached to the USSR fifty years ago.[19]

Demography behind Ideology

Brief as it is, this outline easily demonstrates that potentially disruptive elements were introduced into the Soviet body politic by Stalin's annexations of 1939 to 1945, particularly against the political order he created with such great effort in the 1930s, and against the Russian character of the Soviet state. The latter derived not only from Stalin's formidable Russifying measures but also reflected that the pre-1939 Soviet Union was more clearly a Russian country in its population than Russia had ever been since Peter the Great. Let us also remember that the most "western" parts of the Empire's west—Poland, Finland, and the Baltics—were not yet within Lenin's restored Empire.

Our discussion has focused on cultural and ideological incompatibility of the Soviet Union and the Soviet West. What kind of human mass and demographic potential does the Soviet West/Far Eastern Europe represent in the Soviet population?

First of all, especially in view of the recent newspaper headlines—and the gravity with which Moscow views the Baltic challenge—it is striking how small the Baltic nations are: In 1959 and then in 1989, when the total population of the USSR was 208,827,000 and 285,689,000 (rounded off to the nearest thousand) respectively, there were the following numbers of Russians and Balts in all of the USSR:

	1959	*1989*
USSR	208,827,000	285,689,000
Russians	114,114,000	145,072,000
Lithuanians	2,326,000	3,068,000
Latvians	1,400,000	1,459,000
Estonians	989,000	1,027,000

This means that over thirty years the number of Russians grew by almost 31 million, that of Lithuanians by 742,000, Latvians by 59,000, and Estonians by 38,000. In their own republics the figures were somewhat different, but the most telling was the gain of 350,000 Russians in Latvia—compared with the growth of the Latvian population by 90,000 over the same period—and in Estonia, where the Russians increased by 235,000 while the Estonians gained 70,000. As is well known, the proportion of the titular nationalities in these two republics has declined drastically since 1959, the first postwar census. Latvians fell from 62 to 52 percent in their country, and the Estonians from 75 to 62 percent. In 1959, of course, their share was already lower than before the war.

The demographic situation in Lithuania has been more favorable to the Lithuanians, who increased from 1959 to 1989 by 773,000, while the Russians gained by 113,000, and thus the titular nationality in Lithuania retained its share of the total (79.32 percent in 1959 versus 79.6 percent in 1989).[20]

The demographic situation of the Moldavians closely resembles that of the Lithuanians. There were 2,214,000 Moldavians registered in the 1959 census, and by 1989 their number rose to 3,355,000, with a net gain of 1,141,000. In their republic the Moldavians gained 304,000, and the Russians, 267,000. There was also a substantial increase in the Ukrainian population. Overall, the Moldavians virtually retained their share of the republic's population, having declined from 65.4 percent (1959) to 64.42 percent of the total.[21]

In the case of Ukraine and Belorussia, we have at our disposal only the republic totals, combining the western regions with the rest. These totals show a gain of 6,883,000 for Ukrainians and that of 2,117,000 for Belorussians in the USSR as a whole. These two nationalities declined, as a proportion of the Soviet Union population, from 17.84 percent to 15.45 percent for Ukrainians, and from 3.79 percent to 3.51

percent for the Belorussians, which indicated a much faster decrease of the relative strength of the Ukrainians. As for the Balts, the Lithuanians constituted just over 1 percent of the USSR population in 1989, and slightly over 1.1 percent in 1959; the Latvians numbered two-thirds of 1 percent in 1959 and fell to one-half of 1 percent by 1989; the Estonians dropped from .47 to .36 of 1 percent in the thirty years between 1959 and 1989.

In their own republics, Ukrainians gained 5,212,000 but Russians came close with 4,249,000, which increased their share of the republic population from 16.94 to 22.04 percent, and correspondingly reduced that of the Ukrainians from 76.81 to 72.64 percent, and in Belorussia the analogous figures are a 1,366,000 and 681,000 gain for the two largest nations, and the drop of the Belorussian component from 81.09 to 77.82 percent. Russians grew from 81.09 to 13.21 percent.[22]

In early 1991, the regional returns of the census were not yet available, with one very important exception—Lviv oblast and the city of Lviv. Those data indicate that while in Ukraine as a whole the number of Russians since 1959 has increased very significantly, and while the share of Ukrainians within the republic has correspondingly declined, in the Lviv region and city in the thirty intercensal years the Russians hardly increased at all, and reduced considerably their share of the total population. These figures are so significant that they can speak for themselves. In view of the past role of the Jewish and Polish components in the region's and city's population, we include also the figures for these two groups:

Lviv Oblast

	1959	*1989*	*Gain/loss*
Ukrainians	1,818	2,465	647
Russians	181	195	14
Jews	30	14	-16
Poles	59	27	-32
TOTAL	2,108	2,727	619

SOURCE: *Vilna Ukraïna*, April 10, 1990, p. 1, and *Itogi Vsesouiznoi perepisi naseleniia 1959. Ukrainskaia SSR*, Moscow, 1963. (All figures in thousands.)

Equally impressive are the figures for the city of Lviv, whose demographic growth in the post-1959 decades clearly runs in a direction opposite to that discernible in Riga and Tallinn, and even to some extent opposite to that of Vilnius. Between 1959 and 1989, Ukrainians raised their share in this city from 60 percent to 79.1 percent, while Russians declined from 27 percent to 16.1 percent. Jews and Poles also declined, not only relatively but also in absolute numbers.

It is reasonable to assume that ethnic relations in the other regions of West Ukraine have basically followed the Lviv region's model. This would imply that not only that region—whose population is larger than that of Latvia—but all of West Ukraine with a population of close to ten million in 1989—that is, about the population of Hungary—is becoming less Russian and more Ukrainian just when the rest of Ukraine (or most of the rest, for Kiev is also becoming more Ukrainian) is going in the direction of Russification.

Although we do not have any data for the regions of Belorussia, it may be hypothesized safely that Belorussia continues its previous ethno-demographic trends. While West Ukraine was becoming less Russian and more Ukrainian from 1959 to 1970, nothing comparable happened in the western regions of Belorussia. In fact, the processes of linguistic Russification proceeded in the western part of Belorussia faster than in the east. (I have tried to provide an explanation of this west-east anomaly in Belorussia and of Belorussia's divergence from the Ukrainian pattern elsewhere.[23]) This does not mean the Belorussian national movement does not have popular support or lacks issues around which to mobilize. Quite the contrary.[24] It means simply that language as a marker of national identity plays a clearly different role in Belorussia, which differentiates it from the West Ukrainian regions as well as from the Baltic nations.

The Return to History

The region of Far Eastern Europe deserves attention from anyone interested in Eastern Europe, traditionally so-called and also known as East-Central Europe, for several reasons at least. First, nation-building processes known in the nineteenth- and early twentieth-century Habsburg monarchy and the Balkans appear to be continuing—are resuming?—in the western fringes of the USSR. Some of these processes, especially the developments in Ukraine, and we may presume also in Belorussia, have significant repercussions in the pre-1939 areas of the

USSR, and indirectly affect even the relations between these two East Slavic nations and the Russians. Second, those processes deserve attention by the neighboring peoples in East Central Europe—Poles, Hungarians, Czechs, Slovaks, Romanians—because they are taking place in areas that formerly belonged to one or more of them, and hence are in a way a continuation of the history of those non-Soviet nations. And last but not least, by abandoning the rigid and mechanical separation of "East Europe" from "Russia/USSR," so strictly enforced in Western scholarship after 1945, teaching and research not only will stop honoring the territorial and political arrangements made in 1939 by Molotov and Ribbentrop and their masters, but may find it easier to bring Russia into a common framework of East European and European studies.

Notes

1. Particularly important recent works dealing with the region include: Roman Solchanyk, "Ukraine, Belorussia, and Moldavia: Imperial Integration, Russification, and the Struggle for National Survival," in Lubomyr Hajda and Mark Bessinger, eds., *The Nationalities Factor in Soviet Politics and Society* (Boulder, San Francisco, and Oxford: Westview Press, 1990), pp. 175–203, and Romuald J. Misiunas, "The Baltic Republics: Stagnation and Strivings for Sovereignty," in Hajda and Bessinger, eds., *The Nationalities Factor*, pp. 204–27. Although it appeared over fifteen years ago, *Handbook of Major Soviet Nationalities*, Zev Katz, Rosemarie Rogers, and Frederic Harned, eds. (New York and London: Free Press, 1975), contains chapters that are still worth consulting on Belorussia, Estonia, Latvia, Lithuania, Moldavia, and the Jews.

2. For the pre-Soviet background of the Baltic nations, see Joseph Rothschild, *East Central Europe Between the Two World Wars* (Seattle and London: University of Washington Press, 1974), and Hugh Seton-Watson, *The Russian Empire, 1801–1917* (Oxford: Clarendon, 1967). See also Taras Hunczak, ed., *Russian Imperialism from Ivan the Great to the Revolution* (New Brunswick, N.J.: Rutgers University Press, 1974), and Edward C. Thaden, with Marianna Foster Thaden, *Russia's Western Borderlands, 1710–1870* (Princeton: Princeton University Press, 1984).

3. Piotr S. Wandycz, *The Lands of Partitioned Poland, 1795–1918* (Seattle and London: University of Washington Press, 1974), besides the Poles and the Lithuanians, covers Belorussians and Ukrainians in their relation to Polish history.

4. For recent treatments, see Orest Subtelny, *Ukraine: A History* (Toronto:

University of Toronto Press, 1988); Paul Robert Magocsi, *Galicia: A Historical Survey and Bibliographic Guide* (Toronto: University of Toronto Press, 1983); and Andrei S. Markovits and Frank E. Sysyn, eds., *Nationbuilding and the Politics of Nationalism: Essays on Austrian Galicia* (Cambridge, Mass.: Harvard Ukrainian Research Institute, 1982).

5. Stephen Fischer-Galati, "The Moldavian Soviet Republic in Soviet Domestic and Foreign Policy," in Roman Szporluk, ed., *The Influence of East Europe and the Soviet West on Soviet Society* (New York, Washington, and London: Praeger, 1976), pp. 229–50.

6. V. Stanley Vardis, "The Role of the Baltic Republics in Soviet Society," in Szporluk, ed., *The Influence of East Europe*, pp. 172–73. See also Alexander Shtromas, "The Baltic States," in Robert Conquest, ed., *The Last Empire: Nationality and the Soviet Future* (Stanford: Hoover Institution Press, 1986), pp. 183–217.

7. For a review of the Balts, Ukrainians, Moldavians, and other "Western" nationalities within the larger Soviet context as it appeared in the early 1960s, see John A. Armstrong, "The Ethnic Scene in the Soviet Union: The View of the Dictatorship" (originally published in 1968 and reprinted in *Journal of Soviet Nationalities* 1, no. 1 [Spring 1990]: 14–65, accompanied by the author's comment, "The Soviet Ethnic Scene: A Quarter-Century Later," and followed by comments of S. Frederick Starr and Mark R. Bessinger, pp. 66–75, 76–90, and 91–100 respectively). Armstrong discusses "state nations" on pp. 37–40.

8. For relevant citations, see Roman Szporluk, "The Eurasia House," *Cross Currents* 9 (1990): 3–15.

9. Roman Solchanyk, "Poland and the Soviet West," in S. Enders Wimbush, ed., *Soviet Nationalities in Strategic Perspective* (London: Croon Helm, 1985), pp. 158–80.

10. For a discussion of Masaryk's view, see Roman Szporluk, "Defining 'Central Europe': Power, Politics, and Culture," *Cross Currents* (1982): 30–38. For recent "ideological" divisions of Europe, see Jenö Szücs, "The Three Historical Regions of Europe," and Mihály Vajda, "East Central European Perspectives," in John Keane, ed., *Civil Society and the State: New European Perspectives* (London and New York: Verso, 1988), pp. 291–332 and 333–60.

11. Ernest Gellner, "Ethnicity and Faith in Eastern Europe," *Daedalus* (special issue on "Eastern Europe . . . Central Europe . . . Europe"), *Proceedings of the American Academy of Arts and Sciences* 119: no. 1 (Winter 1990): 279–94.

12. Ernest Gellner and Igor Kon, "Nationalism Today: Its Origins and Nature," *Social Sciences* (Moscow) 20, no. 4 (1989): 191.

13. Gellner and Kon, "Nationalism Today," p. 191.

14. "Do Rosji nie ma klucza," Ryszard Kapuściński's interview with Sławomir Popowski, *Gazeta Wyborcza*, September 22, 1990, pp. 8–9.

15. John A. Armstrong, "Toward a Framework for Considering Nationalism in East Europe," *East European Politics and Societies* 2, no. 2 (Spring 1988): 280–305.

16. G. P. Fedotov, "Budet li sushchestvovat' Rossiia?," 1929, reprinted in *O Rossii i russkoi filosofskoi kul'ture, Filosofy russkogo posleoktiabrskogo zarubezh'ia* (Moscow: Nauka, 1990), p. 461. For a discussion of Russian-Ukrainian relations in terms of intellectual history and political ideologies, see Roman Szporluk, "The Ukraine and Russia," in Conquest, ed., *The Last Empire*, pp. 151–82, and Kristian Gerner, "An Alternative to Moscow: Ancient Rus', Modern Ukraine and Byelorussia," in Alexander Bon and Robert van Voren, eds., *Nationalism in the USSR: Problems of Nationalities* (Amsterdam, 1989), pp. 68–86.

17. See *The Ukrainian Weekly,* January 27, 1991, pp. 3 and 16 for the Vatican announcements.

18. "Halychyna i Ukraina," originally published in *Literaturno-naukovyi vistnyk* 36 (1906): 489–96, and *Dilo,* nos. 269–70 (1906), reprinted in *Z bizhuchoi khvyli, statti i zamitky na temu dnia,* 1905–1906 (Kyiv, 1906), pp. 117–26, cited in Thomas M. Prymak, *Mykhailo Hrushevsky: The Politics of National Culture* (Toronto, Buffalo, and London: University of Toronto Press, 1987), pp. 79n–80n.

19. Yaroslav Bilinsky, "The Incorporation of Western Ukraine and Its Impact on Politics and Society in Soviet Ukraine," in Szporluk, ed., *The Influence of East Europe and the Soviet West,* pp. 180–228.

20. All figures for the Baltics taken from Misiunas, "The Baltic Republics," pp. 216–17.

21. For Moldavia, see Solchanyk, "Ukraine, Belorussia, and Moldavia," p. 182.

22. All figures for Ukraine and Belorussia taken from Solchanyk, "Ukraine, Belorussia, and Moldavia," p. 182. Figures for the Baltic Republics are from Misiunas, "The Baltic Republics," pp. 216–17.

23. See Roman Szporluk, "West Ukraine and West Belorussia: Historical Tradition, Social Communication, and Linguistic Assimilation," *Soviet Studies* 31, no. 1 (January, 1979): 76–98 [reprinted as chapter 4 of this book], and "Urbanization in Ukraine since the Second World War," in Ivan L. Rudnytsky, *Rethinking Ukrainian History* (Edmonton, 1981), pp. 180–202 [reprinted as chapter 5 of this book]. For the Belorussian "anomaly" see Roman Szporluk, "The Press in Belorussia, 1955–1965," *Soviet Studies* 18, no. 4 (April 1967): 482–93.

24. Jan Zaprudnik, "Belorussian Reawakening," in *Problems of Communism* 38, no. 4 (July–August 1989): 36–52.

10 The Press and Soviet Nationalities: The Party Resolution of 1975 and Its Implementation

Many scholars have written on Soviet nationality policies, including language policies. This study does not aspire to add to the general literature on that subject.[1] Rather, it is concerned with one particular decision of the Soviet leadership regarding the periodical press. All information presented here is derived from Soviet sources. The sources include, first of all, a periodical that is not generally known in the West, which may explain why the decision in question was not noted by foreign observers when it was announced.

Sometime in 1975, Soviet leaders decided to impose restrictions on the circulation of the periodical press published in the non-Russian republics of the Soviet Union and, at the same time, to further the dissemination of the Russian-language press as widely as possible. The first confirmation that such a new policy was in effect appeared in the Ukrainian-language Komsomol newspaper, *Molod' Ukrainy*, in October 1975. The deputy chief of the Ukrainian Republic agency for the dissemination of periodicals (*Soiuzdruk*), M. Zdorenko, reported that the "subscription campaign" for 1976, then in progress, had a novel feature: "The circulations of all newspapers and journals in 1976 must not exceed the levels of 1975."[2] (As we shall see, this restriction applied to *Ukrainian* newspapers and journals, not "all" newspapers and jour-

First published in *Nationalities Papers*, 1986.

nals). In September 1976, an official source revealed that a new policy had been introduced in 1975, and that it applied to the entire Soviet Union, not just the Ukrainian SSR.

In order to understand the 1975 resolution and its subsequent implementation, it is necessary to begin with some background on how newspapers and magazines are distributed in the Soviet Union. The organization charged with accepting orders for newspapers and magazines is called Central Subscription Agency *Soiuzpechat'* *(Tsentral'noe podpisnoe Agentstvo Soiuzpechat')*. It operates within a larger structure headed by the Main Administration for the Dissemination of the Press (*Glavnoe upravlenie po rasprostraneniiu pechati,* or GURP). GURP itself is an entity under the USSR Ministry of Communication (*Ministerstvo sviazi SSSR*).[3] GURP publishes a monthly journal, *Rasprostranenie pechati,* which is the principal source of information here on the 1975 decision and its realization by the apparatus of the *Soiuzpechat'*.

Until 1975, Soviet newspapers and journals, both "central"—those published mainly in Moscow (and a few published in Leningrad and other cities but enjoying "all-Union" status and thus destined by their designation as "central" for distribution throughout the Soviet Union)— and a majority of those given a "Union-republic" or "autonomous-republic" rank were in principle available throughout the USSR to all those willing to subscribe to them. There was only one condition: The periodical in question had to be listed in the all-Union subscription catalog. By and large, all major non-Russian periodicals, both newspapers and journals, were included in this catalog along with the "central" journals and newspapers.

The latter were almost without exception published in Russian or in foreign languages, such as German or English, but not in the other languages of the USSR.

Those periodicals *not* included in the central catalog could be ordered only in the area corresponding to their territorial-administrative ranking. A Ukrainian republic-rank publication that did not make it to the all-Union catalog could still be obtained in Ukraine, and a Kyiv oblast-rank newspaper only in Kyiv oblast. Similarly, the Moscow city daily, *Vecherniaia Moskva,* was available only in Moscow, and so forth.

Certain periodicals enjoying an especially high demand that could not be filled were allocated quotas from year to year, and fractions of the overall quotas were then allocated to different regions and republics. On the whole, the Russian-language journals and newspapers seem to have been treated more generously in these allocations than the Ukrainian (or other non-Russian) periodicals were, but the authorities encouraged the growth of the press in all languages of the Soviet Union. The quotas (*limity*) were regarded as undesirable but necessary in order to allow the sharing of scarce newsprint among many competing claimants. Every year, during the customary "subscription campaign," branches of *Soiuzpechat'* and individual employees of the agency were praised on the pages of *Rasprostranenie pechati* for winning new subscribers or scorned for failures in their work, such as a loss or only a small gain in the number of subscribers. There is evidence that the performance of the agency was judged in particular by its success in selling "central"—that is, Russian-language—periodicals, but in principle the Moscow press was to be disseminated along with the other publications. Admittedly, the party strongly encouraged the widest possible distribution of certain publications (such as *Pravda*, *Politischeskoe samoobrazovanie*, and others), but even this did not prevent a rise in the circulation of other, less energetically promoted periodicals, if there was sufficient public demand for them.

In any case, the policies pursued until 1975 gave no explicit preference to central periodicals and they contained no hint that subscriptions for the other types of periodicals should be discouraged and maintained below levels imposed by an order from above. Such a course was adopted only in 1975 with regard to 1976 subscriptions.

The September 1976 issue of *Rasprostranenie pechati* reported on an all-Union conference of Union-republic and RSFSR regional chiefs of *Soiuzpechat'*, held in Moscow in August of that year. Those attending the conference included I. I. Simdiankin and V. I. Aristarkhov, CPSU Central Committee instructors; representatives of a number of Union-republic party central committees, as well as of party *kraikoms* and *obkoms* "in charge of problems of press dissemination"; leading officials of the Ministry of Communication and of the Central Committee of the Trade Union of Communication Workers. Deputy Minister of Communication D. I. Mangeldin and the head of a sector in the Propaganda Department of the Central Committee of the CPSU, M. N. Iablokov, addressed the meeting.[4]

The main speech was delivered by the chief of GURP, L. D. Barashenkov, who urged the heads of administrations and agencies of *Soiuzpechat'* "to fulfill the decisions of the directive organs and the requirements of the order of the Ministry of Communications, USSR, [and] not to repeat the errors of the previous year." "Directive organs" (*direktiv-nye organy*) usually refers to the Politburo or the Secretariat of the CC, CPSU.

There had been instances of "a lack of discipline" in 1975, Barashenkov said, because certain branches of *Soiuzpechat'* exceeded the circulation quotas set for some periodicals. He reported that the *kollegiia* of the ministry had adopted a resolution on this subject, warning the ministers of communications in the Union republics and their counterparts in the RSFSR "of their personal responsibility" in carrying out subscription work for newspapers and journals," and drawing their attention to the "inadmissibility" in the future of violations such as those that occurred in 1975.[5]

The same issue of *Rasprostranenie pechati* also published an abridged version of the speech by Mangeldin. According to the deputy minister, Order No. 375 of the USSR Ministry of Communications, dated August 17, 1976, and defining the rules of the subscription campaign for 1977, was based on "a decision of the directive organs." It was essential that the errors of the previous year would not be repeated: Although the circulations of 1976 were kept on the level of 1975 in the majority of the Union republics, there were also violators (those who had accepted more subscriptions than allowed). They included the *Soiuzpechat'* in Ukraine, Belorussia, Uzbekistan, and the Chuvash, Bashkir, and Tatar ASSRs, Krasnodar Krai, and the Smolensk, Omsk, and Kursk oblasts. The heads of *Soiuzpechat'* (named by Mangeldin) in these regions had thus shown "a lack of discipline in the realization of decisions of the directive organs."[6]

Before the Moscow meeting, a conference was held in Kyiv at which the Ukrainian distributors of the press heard themselves taken to task for pushing subscriptions for Ukrainian periodicals too energetically. "Circulation discipline" was the expression frequently used. Barashenkov, accompanied by some of his aides from GURP, attended the Kyiv meeting. Also represented was the propaganda department of the Ukrainian Party Central Committee. Besides *Soiuzpechat'* operatives, criticism was directed at editors of several oblast newspapers for their zeal in trying to win new readers.[7]

The new policy was also in effect in 1977, during the subscription campaign for 1978, when, according to Barashenkov, subscriptions for 1978 were to "remain on the level of 1977."[8] The same goal was also set in 1978, during the campaign for 1979. In a lead editorial entitled

"An Important Political Campaign," *Rasprostranenie pechati* referred to the ministry's Order No. 355 of August 18, 1978, and explained that in it "the terms and manner of conducting the subscription for central newspapers and journals (basically without restrictions, with one small exception) are specified and the order given that the circulations of local (republic, krai, oblast, city, and raion) publications should be retained at the levels of 1978.[9]

Subsequently, in its October 1978 issue, the journal *Rasprostranenie pechati* published an article by M. Shuvaeva entitled "We Shall Justify Trust!" in which a speech by USSR Minister of Communications N. V. Talyzin was quoted. In his speech, made at the pre-subscription-campaign meeting in Moscow, he focused on "shortcomings in the organization of subscription" during the three years the new policy had been in effect. He singled out Latvia, Lithuania, and Estonia as especially guilty of violating the rule that subscriptions must not exceed those of the previous year. By contrast, subscriptions for central periodicals were not to be restricted, with some exceptions.[10]

Another major theme stressed during the campaign of 1979 (but also mentioned during other years) was the need to reduce official subscriptions for offices, enterprises, libraries, and the like, which were paid for from those organizations' budgets. The editorial in *Rasprostranenie pechati* quoted above also stated that in 1979 the volume of this kind of official subscription was to be "no more than 70 percent of the level attained in 1978." (The editorial mentioned "literary-artistic journals" as those that should be eliminated.)[11] It is probably fair to surmise that periodicals in the non-Russian languages were high on the list of those to be discarded through this directive. For reasons of space, a complete survey of those non-Russian periodicals that suffered especially heavy losses after 1975 was omitted from the first part of this essay; however, an official order for a reduction of subscriptions for libraries, schools, and so forth may be an explanation for the decline in subscriptions.[12] There is evidence that Ukrainian scholarly journals in the social sciences and humanities have also suffered enormous losses in subscriptions in recent decades: These are publications typically ordered by libraries rather than by individual subscribers.

Despite the fact that there continued to be cases in which local "disseminators of the press" violated "subscription discipline" and were duly castigated in their official journal, *Rasprostranenie pechati*, by 1980 the directive organs had reason to feel satisfied with the effects of their orders. In that year, the circulation of an overwhelming majority of non-Russian newspapers and journals had either declined in absolute terms from the levels of 1975 or, if not, were growing at a slower rate than that of Russian-language newspapers and journals.

The conspicuous expansion of the Russian-language press was stimulated by a gradual abolition of *limity* in those few cases where it still applied. Barashenkov, who is a prolific author besides being the head of GURP (he published at least four major articles in *Rasprostranenie pechati* in 1979), happily reported that for 1979, in accordance with Order No. 355, subscriptions for "local" periodicals had been accepted "up to the level (*do urovnia*) of subscription circulations of 1978"; subscriptions for central periodicals were conducted without restriction, with very few exceptions (certain literary and popular-science titles).[13] Several months later, Barashenkov was even more specific: Out of 800 "central" newspapers and journals, 762 titles would be available without any limitations for 1980. At the same time, to avoid any misunderstanding about the real purpose of the formula that the non-Russian periodicals were "to remain at the level of the previous year," he left nothing to the imagination: This formula, he said, was *not* to be interpreted as a requirement "to attain the level of the preceding year." To put it simply: The less you got, the better you were.[14]

This message was not limited to tactful hints. A number of articles in *Rasprostranenie pechati* identified subscriptions violators. In one, characteristically entitled "First and Foremost—Problems of Improving the Quality of Subscription," an official of GURP, N. Kosivtsova, singled out the agencies of Ukraine, Belorussia, Kazakhstan, Uzbekistan, Georgia, the Tatar ASSR, and Krasnodar Krai for "serious violations of circulation discipline" (*serioznye narusheniia tirazhnoi distsipliny*) for "accepting subscriptions for literary-artistic journals above the level of 1979."[15] Barashenkov also mentioned employees of *Soiuzpechat'* in Belorussia, Ukraine, and Smolensk and Ryazan oblasts as being guilty of accepting subscriptions above the planned level.[16] A provincial official from Dnipropetrovsk (Ukrainian SSR) had a similar confession to make for his region, where the policy of not exceeding the previous year's level had been violated.[17]

There were a number of articles of this ilk, but one in particular deserves special attention because it sheds some light on the puzzling ups and downs in the statistics for the Tatar press. Summing up the results of the campaign of 1981 in the Russian Republic, L. Korotchenko, deputy head of the RSFSR GURP, focused on failures in the work of the Tatar ASSR *Soiuzpechat'*. Specifically, he pointed out that the Kazan comrades had accepted too many orders for *Chaian*, the Tatar journal of humor. (These orders had come from 66 regional agencies of *Soiuzpechat'*, including 22 in the RSFSR alone.) To be precise, they exceeded the level of 1980—which, as noted above, they were told not to attain—by 100,000 copies.

This excess was to be explained, said Korotchenko, "by the complete lack of control" over the course of subscription work on the part of the Tatar ASSR *Soiuzpechat'*.[18] Korotchenko also noted that in a number of cases, editorial offices of periodicals exercised pressure on *Soiuzpechat'*, and that publishers' representatives conducted *agitatsiia* in favor of their publications. For example, he said, *Kazan utlary*, no. 7, 1970, published an advertisement claiming that the publication was available without restrictions, whereas, in fact, "subscription for local publications beyond the boundaries of regions in which they are published should not exceed the level of 1980."[19]

Rasprostranenie pechati displayed no inhibition in celebrating subscription triumphs of the Russian press, however. The prolific Barashenkov proudly reported that "the demand of working people in our country has been fully met for a majority of mass circulation periodicals," including *Pravda, Izvestiia, Sel'skaia zhizn', Rabotnitsa, Zdorov'e, Krestianka, Partiinaia zhizn', Politicheskoe samoobrazovanie, Pioner, Ogonek, Murzilka,* and "many others."[20]

Kosivtsova, Barashenkov's subordinate as head of the Department of the Organization of Subscription at GURP, and herself an occasional contributor to *Rasprostranenie pechati*, thought that the subscription work of 1979 had been carried out in "an organized manner," as evidenced by an increase in the readership of children's and young people's publications, such as *Pioner, Iunyi tekhnik,* and *Iunyi naturalist.* She was especially happy that the magazine for preschoolers and children in the lower grades, *Veselye kartinki*, was being received by about 8 million "tots" [*malyshei*] and that *Murzilka*, another children's magazine (needless to say, like all the others she mentioned, published in Russian), had 5.8 million subscribers.[21] By 1981, the circulation of *Veselye kartinki*, no doubt owing to the organizational efforts of Kosivtsova, had reached 10 million copies per issue. Reporting this, its editor-in-chief noted that between 1956 and 1959, *Veselye kartinki* had printed 300,000 copies per issue.[22]

To gain a proper appreciation of the import of these figures—to which more examples of the extraordinary growth of Russian children's and youth magazines might easily be added—it is useful to bear in mind that the Russians have, of all the peoples of the USSR, the lowest birthrates, with one-child families a common occurrence, whereas the Muslim peoples are noted for having the highest birthrate, with families of five children not atypical. How did the magazines that are published for children in the languages of the Muslim peoples of Central Asia and the Caucasus fare between 1975 and 1980? As shown in table 10.1 (at the end of this chapter), it is clear that either the preferences of a rising number of Muslim children (or of their parents) suddenly shifted in the second half of the 1970s away from their native language, or that the Barashenkovs and Kosivtsovas had done a very good job in imposing "circulation discipline" on the Central Asians and the Azeris.

It should be possible to form an opinion of the meaning on the new course inaugurated with regard to the printed media in 1975 and its initial impact. After launching a policy of gradual restriction of the non-Russian press and all-out promotion of the Russian press, however, the authorities modified the rules of subscription in several ways. First, beginning in 1979, in the Far East and Siberia and in rural settlements of the Non-Black Earth Zone of the RSFSR, all Soviet periodicals were to be available to subscribers. This presumably included both those few Russian journals whose subscription volume still remained restricted, as well as all the non-Russian journals and newspapers that were restricted everywhere else.[23] (When Soviet sources speak about "all" periodicals, it must always be remembered that "all" means all those that are included in the all-Union subscription catalog.) Second, as of 1983, "the free subscription area" (so to speak) was broadened to include the rural settlements of the entire USSR, which, according to Deputy Minister Mangeldin, made it possible for 105 million Soviet citizens to subscribe to all Soviet periodicals without restrictions. Finally, in the same year it became possible for residents of the Union and autonomous republics to take out subscriptions for periodicals in languages of those republics for delivery to persons living outside those republics.[24]

Under this rule, it became possible for parents or friends to arrange delivery of periodicals from their ethnic homeland to, say, Uzbek or Belorussian servicemen in the Soviet army or to workers in the Non-Black Earth Zone of the RSFSR, who might find it hard to arrange this themselves. Such a practice is understandable, considering the lack of special catalogs throughout the USSR that contain descriptions of non-Russian periodicals. Catalogs of "central" periodicals are published annually, as are "republican" catalogs for use in their respective republics.[25]

The 1983 decision to liberalize subscription rules for non-Russian publications may have been taken in response to protests coming from the non-Russian republics. It may have also been related to an increase in the number of workers sent from the non-Russian republics to Russia proper and the need somehow to accommodate them in their new habitats. An article entitled "Internationalism in Action" disclosed that farm workers from Belorussia, Ukraine, Lithuania, Central Asia, and Transcaucasia were employed in the Smolensk region, and that for all these people newspapers, magazines, and journals in their native languages were available through subscription. The Belorussian women's magazine, for example, had about 3,000 subscribers in the Smolensk area in 1982. Publications from autonomous republics of the RSFSR were also being received in the Smolensk region—among them over 200 copies of the Tatar journal of humor, *Chaian*. The author of the article foresaw that there would be an increase in the number of such publications in 1983 since, beginning in that year, newspapers of republics in nationality languages could be sent "to any corner of the land."[26]

Thus, as of 1984, the non-Russian periodicals had again become accessible to subscribers living in rural areas, while they continued to be subject to the rule of "no more than last year" in the cities and towns. This meant that they were not accessible to the majority of the population, which, according to Soviet statistics, is urban.

For 1985 there was a further change in the rules. The newspaper circulation of republic, oblast, and city rank, as well as regional radio and TV program guides, remained subject to restrictions (their number in 1985 was not to exceed the 1984 levels). However, an exception was made for raion and city/raion newspapers, that is, papers of the lowest rank: They became available without restriction. According to *Rasprostranenie pechati*, "almost all local journals" also became available in subscription without restricted output. Finally, teachers, other pedagogical personnel of vocational schools, and sailors received the right to order their periodicals without limitations. Informing the personnel of the *Soiuzpechat'* of these new measures, Barashenkov did not fail to point out again that "permission to maintain circulation at the level of the preceding year must not be understood as an obligatory task for the new subscription."[27] In an earlier article, Barashenkov declared that unrestricted subscription circulation for all newspapers and magazines published in the USSR was a matter for "the long term."[28]

For 1986, the regulations established for the 1985 campaign appear to have remained basically unchanged. An unsigned editorial in the September 1985 issue of *Rasprostranenie pechati* announced that for 1986 the number of publications subjected to the quotas would be further reduced, and it specified several "central" magazines as well as a number of Russian-language literary journals published in the republics as ones that would become available without restriction. The editorial also stated that "all journals in the national languages" would likewise become available to subscribers without restriction.[29] From the context in which the latter point was made, it is impossible to determine whether "all" refers here to literary journals in languages other than Russian (which would appear to be one way to read this statement) or whether it applies to all journals in languages other than Russian.

It is possible that the authorities decided that the basic goal of their campaign launched in 1975 had been achieved; namely, that the growth of the press in the Union republics had been slowed or, at least, was kept at a rate that allowed the Russian-language periodicals to expand for about a decade without having to compete with the Ukrainian or Uzbek or Tatar press. Judging by the statistical data published in the yearbook of the All Union Book Chamber (*Pechat' SSSR*), the authorities have been especially successful not simply in halting the growth, but in decimating the circulation of the Ukrainian-language press (see tables 10.4 and 10.5). It is possible that they succeeded to a higher degree and faster than Moscow itself had at first intended. At any rate, L. Malakhova, a high executive of the Ukrainian SSR Administration for the Dissemination of the Press, in an article published in 1985, criticized, instead of praising, the fact that in 1984 the local retail-trade agencies in Ukraine ordered 14.9 percent fewer Ukrainian newspapers and 21.3 percent fewer magazines than they had done in 1983.[30]

Malakhova's article, however, should not be viewed as a sign of retreat from the generally anti-Ukrainian trend in the post-1985 period. In February 1986, in an authoritative survey of current subscription problems, *Pravda* singled out an incident in Kyiv in which an employee of the subscription agency allegedly "insistently recommended" a Ukrainian-language newspaper to a customer who claimed not to be fluent in Ukrainian.[31] It is highly unlikely that *Pravda* selected this case because it was the most typical example of abuse of the principle that readers should be free to choose periodicals they want. (Besides, *Pravda* might have used the incident to point out that reading a Ukrainian-language newspaper might be a good way to improve one's Ukrainian when one lives in Ukraine's capital.) There must be many more cases in the USSR of non-Russians being "firmly encouraged" to order Russian-language periodicals. It is likely that by using the case it did, *Pravda* was communicating a message to the *Soiuzpechat'* personnel that although the demand for newspapers and magazines was indeed rising in the USSR (*Pravda* itself cited several cases involving the Moscow-based periodicals to illustrate this recently increased interest in the printed media),[32] the Ukrainian-language press should not be allowed to benefit under this general trend.

What conclusions are to be drawn from this account? This essay deliberately avoids drawing any major conclusions or making broad generalizations regarding the subject discussed here.[33] It also abstains from analyzing the meaning of the statistical data assembled in tables 10.2 through 10.5. Such an analysis would require taking into account a number of special circumstances of each republic and language. It is hoped that this article will stimulate such an examination by other scholars.

One obvious conclusion seems to be warranted, however. The post-1975 course has clearly hurt the Ukrainian-language press severely. The Ukrainian press is the only one to have suffered a significant loss in the absolute number of titles of both newspapers and journals. Press runs of Ukrainian newspapers and journals were reduced on a large scale. As tables 10.4 and 10.5 show, Ukrainian-language newspapers declined between 1975 and 1984 more than newspapers of any other nationality save the Tadjiks. Except for the Azeri, the same can be said of Ukrainian journals. (Why Tadjik newspapers and Azeri journals declined so drastically, presumably only specialists on these two nationalities can say.)

The anti-Ukrainian course in the media appears to have begun before 1975—to be precise, immediately after the dismissal of Petro Y. Shelest from the post of First Secretary of the Central Committee, CP of Ukraine (1972).[34] This new course manifested itself in several ways. First, there was the closing of Ukrainian-language scholarly journals devoted to, among other disciplines, geology, chemistry, physiology, biochemistry, physics, and mathematics.[35] Second, the press runs of some, but not all, Ukrainian-language mass-circulation periodicals, most notably the weekly illustrated magazine, *Ukraïna*, were sharply reduced. Table 10.6 illustrates this decline.

Third, the authorities took a number of measures to reduce the use of Ukrainian in publications for urban readers. For example, in the Ukrainian capital the daily press run of the Ukrainian language *Vechirnii Kyiv* was reduced from 344,550 copies in 1975 to 200,000 in 1980. In 1983, a Russian version of the same paper, *Vechernii Kyiv*, was added, and by 1985, approximately 100,000 copies of both editions were printed daily.[36] In Kharkiv the circulation of the Ukrainian-language *Vechirnii Kyiv* was reduced from 158,000 to 84,000 between 1979 and 1980, and in Dnipropetrovsk, the Ukrainian daily was replaced by a Russian newspaper in 1973.[37] There is more evidence of a policy aimed at removing the Ukrainian language from the urban milieu.

There are different examples in evidence, however. In 1978, a new Ukrainian-language daily paper, an organ of the city party organization and the city administration, was founded in Kyiv (*Prapor komunizmu*), in an initial run of 100,000 copies (140,900 in 1986).[38] In addition, in 1983, Ukrainian writers began to publish a new monthly journal, *Kyiv*, as a joint organ of the writers' organizations of both the republic and Kyiv.[39]

This article has noted certain trends in the Ukrainian press during the past decade. A fuller study would be required to examine the Ukrainian press of this period in all its important aspects. Still other studies need to be done of the press in the other Union and autonomous republics of the USSR before an overall assessment of the impact of the 1975 decision can be made.

Table 10.1

Children's Magazines in Selected Languages of Muslim Nationalities

Title, Language	Circulation (in thousands)	
	1975	1980
Kejerchin, Azeri	206–215	152–156
Funcha, Uzbek	548–561	487–493
Gulkhan, Uzbek	604–614	504–512
Pioner, Turkmen	40–48	41
Pioner, Azeri	115–119	119–120
Baldyrgan, Kazakh	195–199	200–201
Mashial, Tajik	152–159	103–108
Zhash leninchi, Kirghiz	53–54	54–55

Source: *Letopis' periodicheskikh izdanii SSR, 1971–1975, Zhurnaly* (Moscow, 1977); and *Letopis' periodicheskikh izdanii SSSR, 1976–1980, Zhurnaly* (Moscow, 1983).

Note: Titles transcribed from Russian. Totals rounded to nearest thousand.

Table 10.2

Newspapers in Russian and Selected Non-Russian Languages, 1970 to 1984

Language	Number of Titles				Net Gain/Loss			
	1970	1975	1980	1984	1970–1975	1975–1980	1980–1984	1975–1984
Russian	4,956	4,944	5,216	5,390	−12	272	174	446
Ukrainian	936	1,573	1,278	1,275	637	−295	−3	−298
Uzbek	137	169	197	204	32	28	7	35
Belorussian	130	129	128	130	−1	−1	2	1
Kazakh	139	151	167	172	12	16	5	21
Tatar	77	85	85	88	8	0	3	3
Azeri	100	100	112	120	0	12	8	20
Armenian	82	83	90	93	1	7	3	10
Georgian	107	122	122	126	15	0	4	4
Moldavian	56	65	80	87	9	15	7	22
Tadjik	53	53	54	62	0	1	8	9
Lithuanian	74	86	98	103	12	12	5	17
Turkmen	33	14	45	56	−19	31	11	42
Kirghiz	42	57	61	63	15	4	2	6
Latvian	53	52	62	64	−1	10	2	12
Estonian	31	29	31	34	−2	2	3	5

Source: *Pechat' SSSR v 1970 godu. Staticheskie materialy* (Moscow, 1971) and the issues for 1975, 1980, and 1984 (Moscow, 1976, 1981, and 1985).

Table 10.3

Journals in Russian and Selected Non-Russian Languages,
1970 to 1984

Language	Number of Titles				Net Gain/Loss			
	1970	1975	1980	1984	1970– 1975	1975– 1980	1980– 1984	1975– 1984
Russian	822	929	981	1,030	107	52	49	101
Ukrainian	63	63	50	51	0	−13	1	−12
Uzbek	18	19	22	22	1	3	0	3
Belorussian	17	17	18	19	0	1	1	2
Kazakh	12	14	16	17	2	2	1	3
Tatar	6	6	6	7	0	0	1	1
Azeri	23	23	23	23	0	0	0	0
Armenian	29	21	21	21	−8	0	0	0
Georgian	18	22	27	27	4	5	0	5
Moldavian	11	12	12	12	1	0	0	0
Tadjik	7	8	9	9	1	1	0	1
Lithuanian	23	23	25	25	0	2	0	2
Turkmen	8	8	8	8	0	0	0	0
Kirghiz	7	9	10	10	2	1	0	1
Latvian	18	19	19	19	1	0	0	0
Estonian	18	18	18	18	0	0	0	0

Source: *Pechat' SSSR v 1970 godu. Staticheskie materialy* (Moscow, 1971) and the issues for 1975 and 1984 (Moscow, 1976 and 1985).

Table 10.4

Newspapers in Russian and Selected Non-Russian Languages, 1970 to 1984 Press Runs

	Copies (in thousands)				Rate of Change			
Language	1970	1975	1980	1984	1975 as % of 1970	1980 as % of 1975	1984 as % of 1980	1984 as % of 1975
Russian	105,646	127,618	135,281	144,571	120.8	106.0	106.9	113.3
Ukrainian	13,455	16,347	15,659	15,155	121.5	95.8	96.8	92.7
Uzbek	2,703	3,516	3,875	4,153	130.1	110.2	107.2	118.1
Belorussian	1,529	1,693	1,611	1,578	110.7	95.2	98.0	93.2
Kazakh	1,593	1,766	1,772	1,853	110.9	100.3	104.6	104.9
Tatar	703	778	812	786	110.7	104.4	96.8	101.0
Azeri	1,740	2,298	2,248	2,222	132.1	97.8	98.8	96.7
Armenian	1,152	1,508	1,520	1,547	130.9	100.8	101.8	102.6
Georgian	2,571	2,679	2,989	2,809	104.2	111.6	94.0	104.9
Moldavian	1,121	1,219	1,212	1,223	108.7	99.4	100.9	100.3
Tadjik	643	1,508	1,520	1,084	234.5	100.8	71.3	71.9
Lithuanian	1,876	1,765	1,863	2,014	94.1	105.6	108.1	114.1
Turkmen	513	606	775	875	118.1	127.9	112.9	144.4
Kirghiz	557	734	768	783	131.8	104.6	102.0	106.7
Latvian	929	1,057	1,167	1,247	113.8	110.4	106.9	118.0
Estonian	901	990	1,005	1,072	109.9	101.5	106.7	108.3

Source: *Pechat' SSSR v 1970 godu. Staticheskie materialy* (Moscow, 1971) and the issues for 1975, 1980, and 1984 (Moscow, 1976, 1981, and 1985).

Table 10.5

Journals in Russian and Selected Non-Russian Languages,
1970 to 1984 Press Runs

Language	Copies (in thousands)				Rate of Change			
					1975 as % of 1970	1980 as % of 1975	1984 as % of 1980	1984 as % of 1975
	1970	1975	1980	1984				
Russian	109,600	128,254	140,269	152,629	117.0	109.4	108.8	119.0
Ukrainian	7,162	8,976	8,953	7,368	125.3	99.7	82.3	82.1
Uzbek	2,722	3,701	3,815	3,824	136.0	103.1	100.2	103.3
Belorussian	749	1,007	1,430	1,612	134.4	142.0	112.7	160.1
Kazakh	1,380	1,684	1,844	1,764	122.0	109.5	95.7	104.8
Tatar	533	1,010	637	1,134	189.5	63.1	178.0	112.3
Azeri	866	1,072	1,000	758	123.8	93.3	75.8	70.7
Armenian	510	607	559	600	119.0	92.1	107.3	98.8
Georgian	764	934	990	996	122.3	106.0	100.6	106.6
Moldavian	477	620	608	740	130.0	98.1	121.7	119.4
Tadjik	331	474	433	414	143.2	91.4	95.6	87.3
Lithuanian	1,432	1,696	1,756	1,808	118.4	103.5	103.0	106.6
Turkmen	256	354	414	425	138.3	116.9	102.7	120.1
Kirghiz	326	455	546	575	139.6	120.0	105.3	126.4
Latvian	974	1,286	1,393	1,485	132.0	108.3	106.6	115.5
Estonian	522	611	656	790	117.0	107.4	120.4	129.3

Source: *Pechat' SSR v 1970 godu. Staticheskie materialy* (Moscow, 1971) and the issues for 1975, 1980, and 1984 (Moscow, 1976, 1981, and 1985).

Table 10.6

Average Press Run of *Ukraïna*

Year	Press Run (per issue, in thousands)
1970	300–360
1975	332
1976	332.4
1977	252–332.4
1978	250–270
1979	230–238
1980	144–240
1985	120–124

Source: *Letopis' periodicheskikh i prodolzhaiushchikhsia izdanii SSSR, Chast I. Zhurnaly,* issues for 1966–1970, 1971–75, and 1976–1980. The data for 1985 from figures given in issues of *Ukraïna*. By 1986, the average weekly press run of *Ukraïna* had fallen to 119,000.

Notes

This article was based on a major section ("Media Policies") of a study, "Recent Trends in Soviet Policy Toward Printed Media in the Non-Russian Languages," which appeared in *Radio Liberty Research, Supplement 2/84*, November 7, 1984. It was updated to cover the rules in effect for 1986. The statistical tables were also rearranged and updated in 1986 to include the 1984 data that became available late in 1985.

1. See, e.g., Isabelle T. Kreindler, ed., *Sociolinguistic Perspectives on Soviet National Languages. Their Past, Present and Future* (Berlin, New York, Amsterdam: Mouton de Gruyter, 1985) ("Contributions to the Sociology of Language," ed. Joshua A. Fishman, vol. 40); I. Kreindler, ed., "The Changing Status of Russian in the Soviet Union," *International Journal of the Sociology of Knowledge*, 33 (1982), and Roman Solchanyk, "Russian Language and Soviet Politics," *Soviet Studies* 34, no. 1 (1982): 23–42.

2. M. Zdorenko, "Novyny v kozhnyi dim," *Molod' Ukraïny*, October 29, 1975, p. 3. What preserving the status quo of 1975 meant for some parts of the Ukraine can be seen from the following figures given by Zdorenko: Subscriptions in the Donetsk oblast had already exceeded 200,000 copies for *Pravda* and reached 177,000 for *Izvestiia* and 76,000 for *Trud*, whereas all the newspapers of the Ukrainian Republic ordered in Donetsk oblast amounted to 73,000 copies. In the western regions of Ukraine, the Russian-language press was distributed more widely than the Ukrainian-language press. In 1970—that is, before the policy of restrictions had come into effect—in Lviv, 1,665,000 copies of Moscow (exclusively Russian-language) papers were printed daily from printing plates delivered by plane or transmitted by cable, as compared to 392,000 copies of local papers. *Pravda* printed 160,000 copies and *Komsomol'skaia pravda* 140,000 copies. See M. N. Iablokov, *Gazeta i rasstoianie* (Moscow, 1971), pp. 19, 122, quoted in Roman Szporluk, "West Ukraine and West Belorussia: Historical Tradition, Social Communication, and Linguistic Assimilation," *Soviet Studies* 31, no. 1 (1979): 97. (Reprinted in this volume as chapter 4.)

3. For a history of *Soiuzpechat'* and its predecessors, see B. Frolov, "Tsentral'noe podpisnoe . . . K 30-letiiu so dnia obrazovaniia," *Rasprostranenie pechati* 7 (1985): 5–6.

4. "Vsesoiuznoe soveshchanie," *Rasprostranenie pechati* 9 (1976): 3.

5. Ibid.

6. D. Mangel'din, "Podpiska-77: izvlech' uroki iz proshlogodnei podpisnoi kampanii," *Rasprostranenie pechati* 9 (1976): 2–3.

7. N. Solyanik, "Rabotat' kachestvennee, effektivnee," *Rasprostranenie Pechati* 5 (1976): 10–11. Conforming to the new line, O. K. Melnyk, head of

the Ukraine's *Soiuzpechat'*, admitted in a newspaper interview that for the coming year (1977), the circulation of Ukrainian republic newspapers and magazines would remain on the level of 1976. See "Nash druh—drukovane slovo," *Molod' Ukraïny*, September 26, 1976, p. 3.

8. "Instruktivnoe soveshchanie o provedenii podpiski na 1978," *Rasprostranenie pechati* 10 (1977): 23.

9. "Vazhnaia politicheskaia kampaniia," *Rasprostranenie pechati* 9 (1978): 2–3.

10. M. Shuvaeva, "Doverie opravdaem!," *Rasprostranenie pechati* 10 (1978): 6–7.

11. "Vazhnaia politicheskaia kampaniia," p. 2.

12. See Roman Szporluk, "Recent Trends in Soviet Policy Towards Printed Media in the Non-Russian Languages," *Radio Liberty Research*, Supplement 2/84, November 7, 1984.

13. L. D. Barashenkov, "K novym dostizheniam v trude," *Rasprostranenie pechati* 5 (1979): 18.

14. L. D. Barashenkov, "Podpiska-80," *Rasprostranenie pechati* 9 (1979): 2–3.

15. N. Kosivtsova, "Na pervom plane—voprosy uluchsheniia kachestva podpiski," *Rasprostranenie pechati* 3 (1980): 22–23.

16. L. D. Barashenkov, "Uverennoi postup'iu," *Rasprostranenie pechati* 1 (1979): 2–3.

17. N. Oleinik, "S zadachei spravilis'," *Rasprostranenie pechati* 11 (1978): 13–14.

18. L. Korotchenko, "Iz opyta podpiski na 1981 g. v RSFST," *Rasprostranenie pechati* 7 (1981): 24.

19. Ibid., p. 25. In fact, it should not exceed the level of the preceding year anywhere, not only outside the region of publication. Here Korotchenko appears to have interpreted the rules too narrowly, without any basis in the official Moscow pronouncements for doing so.

20. L. D. Barashenkov, "Vstupaia v 1980 god," *Rasprostranenie pechati* 12 (1979): 2. It is impossible to list here all the articles that tell of triumphs in subscriptions for "central" periodicals. Some examples are *Rasprostranenie pechati* 5 (1979), 7 (1979), 3 (1980), 1 (1982).

21. N. Kosivtsova, "Podpiska proshla organizovanno," *Rasprostranenie pechati* 3 (1979): 2–3.

22. N. Ivanova, "Samyi detskii zhurnal," *Rasprostranenie pechati* 6 (1981): 38.

23. See *Rasprostranenie pechati* 9 (1978), 10 (1978), 3 (1979), 5 (1979), and 9 (1979).

24. D. Mangel'din, "Vazhneishaia politicheskaia zadacha," *Rasprostranenie*

pechati 9 (1982): 1–3. This is a bit puzzling because, according to an official source, all republican periodicals could be subscribed to from any address to be delivered to any other address in the USSR, so long as they were included in the central catalog (see *Spravochnik po uslugam sviazi*, 3d rev. ed. [Moscow: Sviaz', 1977], p. 96). Mangeldin's statement therefore means one of two things: Either the rules of 1977 were tacitly changed and then restored in 1982–83, or the latter rule applied also to those republican periodicals that were not included in the "central catalog." On republican periodicals, the *Spravochnik* was quite clear: They could *not* be sent outside the area in which they were published. It cited the example of *Vecherniaia Moskva*, which could be subscribed to only by "residents of the capital" (ibid.). It should be stressed, however, that beginning in the mid-1950s major periodicals of the Union republics and of the ASSRs have been available by subscription throughout the USSR. In 1971, for instance, 11,000 copies of Ukrainian newspapers and some 700,000 copies of Ukrainian journals were being received by subscribers outside Ukraine but in the USSR. See *Rasprostranenie pechati* 12 (1972): 10.

25. In *Rasprostranenie pechati* 2 (1980): 11, the complaint was voiced that the last such general catalog of union—and autonomous—republican periodicals had been issued in 1965. Barashenkov replied (*Rasprostranenie pechati*, no. 6, [1980]:19) that no new catalog was planned for the foreseeable future. (This type of catalog should not be confused with the single all-Union catalog that contains basic data about periodicals such as name, frequency, price, and the like.)

26. I. Krolik, "Internatsionalizm v deistvii," *Rasprostranenie pechati* 12 (1982): 15. On the question of supplying ethnic newspapers to servicemen and students belonging to Muslim nationalities, see RL 335/82, "Non-Russian Periodical Press to Be Available on Subscription throughout the Soviet Union," August 19, 1982.

27. L. D. Barashenkov, "Podpiska-1985," *Rasprostranenie pechati*, 9 (1984): 1–2.

28. L. D. Barashenkov, "Za dal'neishee sovershenstvovanie raboty Soiuzpechati," *Rasprostranenie pechati* 6 (1984): 2. It is difficult to understand what A. Sal'nikov and V. Karpov have in mind when they say that "as is well-known, at the present time subscription for newspapers and a considerable part of magazines is accepted without restrictions," unless they tacitly assume that only Russian newspapers qualify as newspapers. See their article, "Obozrimye perspektivy Soiuzpechati," *Rasprostranenie pechati* 8 (1984): 22.

29. "Podpiska-86," *Rasprostranenie pechati* 9 (1985): 2.

30. L. Malakhova, "Dobivat'sia bol'shego," *Rasprostranenie pechati* 7 (1985): 13.

31. V. Fedotov, "Tirazhi i podpischiki," *Pravda*, February 11, 1986, p. 2.

32. See Serge Schmemann, "From Purges to Privilege: Lively Debate in Gor-

bachev's Soviet," *New York Times* (national edition), February 22, 1986, p. 2, for a discussion on how the Soviet press has become more lively and informative in recent times. Fedotov (note 31) says that the trade-union paper *Trud* appears in a daily press run of 18.53 million copies, which makes it by far the most popular newspaper not only in the USSR but presumably in the world. (In 1980, *Trud* printed 12.25 million copies.)

33. I did raise such issues in the earlier version of this study noted above.

34. According to *The Ukrainian Herald*, vol. 7–8, *Ethnocide of Ukrainians in the USSR* (Spring 1974, Baltimore: Smoloskyp Publishers, 1976), p. 134, at that time the Politburo of the Ukrainian CP decided to reduce gradually the number of scholarly journals published in Ukrainian.

35. *Letopis periodicheskikh i prodolzhaiushchikhsia izdanii 1976–1980, Chast' I. Zhurnaly* (Moscow, 1985).

36. *Letopis . . . Novye, pereimenovannye i prekrashchennye izdaniem zhurnaly i gazety, 1 aprelia 1982—31 marta 1983* (Moscow, 1983). (The 1985 figures as published in the issues of the paper.)

37. See *Letopis . . . 1976–1980*, and *Letopis . . . 1971–1975*.

38. O. Sytnyk, "Hazeta kyian i dlia kyian," *Zhurnalist Ukraïny* 1 (1986): 36.

39. "Znaiomtesia: zhurnal 'Kyiv'." *Literaturna Ukraïna*, October 21, 1982, p. 2, and "U spiltsi pys'mennykiv Ukraïny," *Literaturna Ukraïny*, October 28, 1982, p. 2. Also, in Belorussia, a concession was made to the cultural intelligentsia in 1983, when a journal devoted to the arts was founded under the name of *Mastatstva Belarusi* (see "Budzem znaiomy: 'Mastatstva Belarusi,' " *Literatura i mastatstva*, January 21, 1983, p. 4).

11 The Strange Politics of Lviv: An Essay in Search of an Explanation

The Election of 1990

The March 1990 election to the Ukrainian Republic's Supreme Soviet produced striking and quite unexpected results. First, the opposition made a very respectable showing in the republic as a whole—even though its main force, Rukh, had been organized formally barely half a year before—and even though opposition candidates were denied registration in many eastern and southern regions. Second, Rukh and its allies won in a landslide in the western areas, in the regions of Lviv, Ivano-Frankivsk, and Ternopil, once known as Austria's Eastern Galicia. The following are rough figures on the affiliation of deputies elected in 1990. (The opposition is grouped in the Narodna Rada, an umbrella organization.)

In the province of Galicia, the core of the ex-Polish West Ukraine, the Narodna Rada won 43 of the 46 seats, which broke down in the following way: In Lviv the Narodna Rada won 24 of 24 seats; in Ivano-Frankivsk, 11 of 12 seats; and in Ternopil, 8 of 10 seats.

In the remaining ex-Polish regions, the northwestern regions of

---

First published in *The Politics of Nationality and the Erosion of the USSR*, 1992.

Rivne and Volhynia, which had been Russian before 1914, the results were: 6 seats out of 9 for the Narodna Rada in Volhynia, and 5 out of 10 seats in Rivne.

These are less overwhelming than the Galician figures but quite noteworthy nonetheless. Adding up these two groups, in the ex-Polish West Ukraine the Narodna Rada won a total of 54 seats out of 65 (or 83 percent).

This result appears to be in striking contrast to what happened in the former Czechoslovak province of Ruthenia (Transcarpathian oblast) or in the ex-Romanian Northern Bukovina (or Chernivtsi oblast). In Transcarpathia the Narodna Rada won only 1 out of 10 seats, and in Chernivtsi it won none of the 8 seats. How is one to explain this puzzling result? If the Polish connection explains the defeat of the party in Lviv, why did the Czechoslovak connection fail to do the same?

Among the eastern (Soviet before 1939) regions, the opposition scored best in the capital and in Kharkiv oblast, whose center is the second largest Ukrainian city. In the city of Kyiv 18 out of 22 deputies belonged to the Narodna Rada, and in Kharkiv 11 out of 28. At the other extreme are the regions where not a single member of the opposition was elected: Luhansk (25 seats), Odessa (23), Mykolaiv (11), and Crimea (22). The opposition scored very low in "core" Ukrainian regions—Kyiv province, Vinnytsia, Poltava, Chernihiv, and so on.

This chapter does not attempt to analyze the Ukrainian election but rather to present information that may help explain the results in Lviv, and by extension in Galicia as a whole. (Perhaps some of our data will also shed light on why the opposition did extremely well in the city of Kyiv, too.)

One year later, in March 1991, returns in the referendum on the future of the Union confirmed the political divisions of Ukraine that had been revealed in March 1990. Ukrainian voters were asked to answer two questions. The first question, formulated in Moscow, asked whether the voter supported a reformed Union of Soviet republics. That question was asked wherever the voting took place (except in Kazakhstan, where it was modified). In Ukraine, a second question was added; it asked whether the voter approved of Ukraine's joining a renewed Union on terms that were compatible with Ukraine's declaration of sovereignty adopted in 1990. (To avoid confusing the reader, we shall not deal with the second referendum question.) Finally, in the three Galician regions there was a third question on the ballot; it asked whether the voter supported full independence of Ukraine—that is, its withdrawal from the Soviet Union, whether a reformed one or not. It is to questions one and three that we shall now turn. Table 11.1 gives the results of the vote on the first question in West Ukraine.

In the Central West region, the results were noticeably more favorable to the Union, as table 11.2 demonstrates.

Kyiv region, however, geographically located in what we call the "Central West," gave only 66.9 percent of votes for "yes," and as many as 31.2 for "no," while the city of Kyiv voted 44.6 percent "yes" and 52.9 percent "no," thus joining Galicia in rejecting Moscow's formula of the Union.

The voting elsewhere in the Ukraine produced "yes" majorities of 75 percent or more in all regions, with Crimea recording as many as 87.6 percent favorable votes (see table 11.3).

Table 11.1

Union Referendum Results, West Ukraine

West Ukraine		Percent Voting	
		Yes	*No*
(Ex-Polish and Ex-Austrian)	Lviv	16.4	80.1
	Ternopil	19.3	76.5
	Ivano-Frankivs'k	19.3	76.5
(Ex-Polish and Ex-Russian)	Volhynia	53.7	42.9
	Rivne	54.3	42.9
(Ex-Czechoslovak)	Transcarpathia	60.2	36.3
(Ex-Romanian)	Chernivtsi-Bukovina	60.8	36.4

Table 11.2

Union Referendum Results, Central West Region

Central West	Percent Voting	
	Yes	*No*
Vinnytsia	81.2	17.7
Zhytomyr	81.8	17.0
Khmel'nytsky	77.7	20.9
Cherkasy	77.3	21.4
Chernihiv	83.4	15.3

Table 11.3
Union Referendum Results

		Percent Voting	
		Yes	No
North	Kharkiv	75.8	22.3
East	Poltava	78.8	19.9
	Sumy	78.8	19.6
South	Odessa	82.2	16.3
	Mykolaiv	84.2	14.4
	Kherson	81.4	17.8
	Crimea	87.6	11.1
	Sevastopol (city)	83.1	15.2
Dnieper	Dnipropetrovsk	77.5	21.1
	Zaporizhia	79.8	18.9
	Kirovohrad	82.4	16.3
Donbas	Donetsk	84.6	14.1
	Luhansk	86.3	12.6

As mentioned earlier, in the three regions of Galicia—and only there—a third question was also on the ballot: "Do you want Ukraine to become an independent state that independently decides all questions of domestic and foreign policy, [and] secures equal rights of citizens regardless of their ethnic or religious affiliation?" Those voting in favor were distributed as follows: In Lviv 90 percent, in Ternopil 85.3 percent, and in Ivano-Frankivsk 89.5 percent.

Demography

Can demography help explain the 1990 and 1991 returns? It would seem that was the case, up to a point: Where the Ukrainian element was stronger, numerically, the opposition got more votes (or there were more negative votes on the "Moscow question").

The Ukrainian republic as a whole shows one clear pattern: The republic is becoming more Russian.

The preliminary returns of the 1989 population census in the USSR appear to confirm what many foreign scholars had been arguing for decades—that the Ukrainian republic is becoming ever more Russian in the language of its population. A vivid illustration of this fact is the revelation that in the intercensal period, 1979 to 1989, the number of Ukrainians in the Ukrainian republic grew by 930,000, while that of Russians grew by an almost equal number—883,980—even though the Ukrainians constituted 77 percent of the republic's population in 1959 while the Russians constituted only 17 percent.[1] Understandably, with such divergent rates of growth, by 1989 the ratio of these two nationalities had changed to 72.7 percent for Ukrainians and 22.1 percent for Russians.

Perhaps even more ominously for the future of the Ukrainians as a distinct ethnic community, only slightly more than one-third of those 930,102 new Ukrainians—to be precise, 331,726 or 35.67 percent—declared Ukrainian to be their native language. Close to 64 percent (591,725) said Russian was their language (63.62 percent), and a much smaller number (6,651) registered some other language as their first.

Even without statistical analysis, it is evident that the number of Russians in Ukraine has been increasing at a rate much higher than the rate of growth of Ukrainians. However, at least one large area, the Lviv region, has over the past 30 years clearly kept moving in a direction opposite to that of Ukraine as a whole (see table 11.4). This disparity becomes evident when the figures are given in percentages (see table 11.5).

In order to locate the Lviv oblast in a wider regional and Ukrainian republic setting, we propose to locate Lviv in the "West," which we view as one of *six* larger regions of Ukraine (see the map in chapter 3).

The West, as we see, is defined by geographical and historical criteria: It consists of those parts of Ukraine that became Soviet in 1939 to

Table 11.4
Lviv Oblast Demographic Profile

	Total Population (in thousands)				Population Change 1959–89
	1959	1970	1979	1989	
Lviv oblast	2,108	2,429	2,569	2,727	619
Ukrainians	1,818	2,134	2,299	2,465	647
Russians	181	200	194	195	14
Jews	30	28	0	14	−16
Poles	59	42	33	27	−32

Table 11.5
Ukrainian Republic and Lviv Oblast, Demographic Profile, Percentage Change

	1959–1970	*1970–1979*	*1979–1989*	*1959–1989*
Ukrainian Republic, total	12.6	5.0	3.7	22.9
Ukrainians	9.7	3.4	2.4	16.2
Russians	28.7	14.7	8.3	59.9
Jews	− 7.5	− 18.4	− 23.0	− 41.9
Poles	− 18.7	− 12.5	− 8.5	− 60.3
Lviv oblast	15.2	5.8	6.2	29.4
Ukrainians	17.4	7.7	7.2	35.6
Russians	10.5	− 3.0	0.5	7.7
Jews	− 6.7	—	—	− 53.3
Poles	− 28.8	− 21.4	− 18.2	− 54.2

1945. (The Izmail area of Odessa oblast, which was annexed in 1940 from Romania, is included in the South.)

Lviv oblast is remarkable enough, but even more striking are the data about the city of Lviv itself (see table 11.6). Lviv is much more than an oblast center; it is arguably the second most important Ukrainian city—and perhaps a more European one than Vilnius or Riga or Tallinn (unlike them, it never was under Russia prior to 1939). It is the center of West Ukraine—which has a population of close to 10 million. Again, the figures speak for themselves, but their translation into percentages (see table 11.7) makes the evidence even more apparent.

Table 11.6
Ethno-demographic Trends in the City of Lviv, 1959 to 1989

	Total Population (in thousands) and Percentage of Total					
	1959	*%*	*1979*	*%*	*1989*	*%*
Total	410,678	100.00	665,065	100.00	786,903	100.00
Ukrainians	246,407	60.04	492,191	74.01	622,701	79.13
Russians	110,883	27.00	128,338	19.30	126,459	16.07
Jews	24,641	6.00	17,592	2.65	12,795	1.63
Poles	16,427	4.00	11,855	1.78	9,730	1.24

Table 11.7
Ethno-demographic Trends in the City of Lviv, 1959 to 1989

| | *Percentage of Change* | | |
	1959–1979	*1979–1989*	*1959–1989*
Total	61.9	18.3	91.6
Ukrainians	99.7	26.5	152.7
Russians	15.7	−1.5	14
Jews	−28.6	−27.3	−48.1
Poles	−27.8	−17.9	−40.8

Many points call for comment here. For example, the gradual but certain decline of the two historic peoples in the city, Poles and Jews, deserves attention. But for a student of the Ukrainian-Russian relationship, the most important trend in these numbers is the more than ten times higher rate of growth of Ukrainians over that of Russians. The Russians have declined from constituting 27 percent of the city's population in 1959 to being only 16 percent in 1989. The absolute figure of 126,000 is by no means an insignificant one and the actual strength of the Russian element in the city certainly exceeds its percentage figure. Yet, we are dealing here with the least Russian city of the European USSR—a city that surpasses in size the capitals of the Baltic states and that of Moldavia, and is less Russified than any of them. This fact of demography, as we shall see, also has a cultural aspect and that, in turn, no doubt also reflects itself in the political sphere.

This may be a proper occasion to make reference, if only in passing, to the quantitative dimension of the current Baltic-Soviet situation in order to appreciate the actual or potential importance of the Ukrainian problem. Most obviously, the Baltic nations are simply small in size: In 1959 and then in 1989, when the total population of the USSR was 208,827,000 and 285,689,000, respectively, the number of Balts in the entire USSR was 4,715,000 (1959) and 5,554,000 (1989).

While Russians in the USSR grew by almost 31,000,000 between 1959 and 1989—from 114,000 to 145,000—Lithuanians grew by 742,000, Latvians by 59,000, and Estonians by a mere 38,000. In their own republics the figures were somewhat different, but most telling is the gain of 350,000 Russians in Latvia—compared with the growth of the Latvian population by 90,000 over the same period—and in Estonia, where Russians increased by 235,000 while Estonians gained by 70,000. In Riga, Latvians constituted less than 40 percent of the total (1979); in Tallinn, Estonians represented just 52 percent in the same year. The situation in 1989 must have been just as bad, if not worse. These facts underscore the striking importance of Lviv.

The demographic situation in Lithuania has been more favorable to the titular nation. Lithuanians increased from 1959 to 1989 by 773,000, while Russians increased by "only" 113,000, and Lithuanians thus retained their share of the total (about 79 percent in 1959 versus a little under 80 percent in 1989).

The demographic situation of the Moldavians closely resembles that of the Lithuanians. There were 2,214,000 Moldavians registered in the 1959 census, and by 1989 their number had risen to 3,355,000, with a net gain of 1,141,000. In their republic Moldavians gained 904,000 and Russians 267,000. (There was also a substantial increase in the Ukrainian population). Overall, Moldavians virtually retained their share of the republic's population, declining from 64.56 percent to 64.42 percent of the total.

In their own republic, Ukrainians gained 5,212,000 but Russians came close with 4,249,000, which increased their share of the republic's population from 17 to 22 percent and correspondingly reduced that of Ukrainians from 77 to 73 percent. In Belorussia analogous figures are a 1,366,000 gain for Belorussians and a 681,000 gain for Russians, and a drop of the Belorussian component from 81 to 78 percent. (Russians grew from 8 to 13 percent.)

Although we do not have any data for the regions of Belorussia, it may be safely hypothesized that Belorussia continues its previous ethno-demographic trends. While West Ukraine was becoming less Russian and more Ukrainian already in 1959 to 1970, nothing comparable happened in the western regions of Belorussia at that time. In fact, the processes of linguistic Russification proceeded in the west faster than in the east of Belorussia. This does not mean that the Belorussian national movement does not have popular support or lacks issues around which to mobilize; quite the contrary is true. It simply means that language as a marker of national identity plays a clearly different role in Belorussia, which evidently differentiates it from the West Ukrainian regions as well as from the Baltic nations. In any case there is no analogy in Belorussia to what the West Ukraine represents in Ukraine, and most certainly the Belorussians do not have a "Lviv" of their own.

Returning to Ukraine and Lviv, it is reasonable to assume that ethnic relations in the entire West Ukraine correspond to the Lviv pattern. (We do not have the detailed statistics of the kind available for Lviv oblast and city.) If this is the case, then West Ukraine, whose population is larger than that of Baltic states combined—close to 10 million in 1989 (that is, about the population size of Hungary)—is becoming more Ukrainian and less Russian. In the meantime, as we have pointed out, the rest of Ukraine—or, to be precise, most of the rest, for Kyiv is also becoming more Ukrainian—is clearly becoming more and more Russian, if not so much in ethnic self-identification then most certainly in declared language choice.

Mass Communications

The special role of West Ukraine, and within it of Galicia and Lviv, is expressed very strongly in the cultural sphere. We shall illustrate this by citing one important kind of evidence, the subscription statistics for select (but important) periodicals.

The Writers' Union weekly, *Literaturna Ukraïna,* published in Kyiv, in 1990 had the number of readers in the west shown in table 11.8.

These figures tell their own story: Lviv oblast, with a bare 5 percent

Table 11.8

Literaturna Ukraïna, 1990 Subscriptions Compared to Total Population Distribution

Region	1990 Subscriptions		1989 Population (in thousands)	
Ukraine	166,420	100.0%	51,704	100.0%
West	106,098	63.8%	9,763	18.9%
Volhynia	10,913	6.6%	2,232	4.3%
Bukovina	2,711	1.6%	938	1.8%
Transcarpathia	3,000	1.8%	1,252	2.4%
Galicia	89,474	53.8%	5,341	10.3%
Lviv oblast	54,355	32.7%	2,748	5.3%

of Ukraine's population, took almost one-third of the Ukrainian literary weekly's subscription total. In 1988, the Kyiv-based monthly *Vsesvit* drew a similarly remarkable large proportion of its subscribers in the west, as table 11.9 shows.

Perhaps less surprisingly, the Lviv-based writers' monthly, *Dzvin*, enjoyed a particular popularity in its home region (see table 11.10).

It should be stressed, however, that *Dzvin* has been, since 1950, a journal with a republic-rank status, not a local publication, and it has always aimed at a republicwide readership. It is evident, however, that its strength lies in a very limited area of Ukraine. Indeed, it is even more

Table 11.9

Vsesvit Subscriptions Compared to Total Population Distribution

Region	1990 Subscriptions		1989 Population (in thousands)	
Ukraine	19,346	100.0%	51,704	100.0%
West	7,629	39.4%	9,763	18.9%
Volhynia	1,735	9.0%	2,232	4.3%
Bukovina	430	2.2%	938	1.8%
Transcarpathia	592	3.1%	1,252	2.4%
Galicia	5,232	27.0%	5,341	10.3%
Lviv oblast	2,726	14.1%	2,748	5.3%

Table 11.10

Dzvin Subscription Distribution Compared to Total Population

Region	1990 Subscriptions		1989 Population (in thousands)	
Ukraine	92,152	100.00%	51,704	100.0%
West	77,463	84.06%	9,763	18.9%
Volhynia	4,434	4.81%	2,232	4.3%
Bukovina	1,007	1.09%	938	1.8%
Transcarpathia	941	1.02%	1,252	2.4%
Galicia	71,081	77.13%	5,341	10.3%
Lviv oblast	48,429	52.55%	2,748	5.3%

concentrated than these figures suggest: We have at our disposal information about numbers of subscribers in individual cities and towns of Lviv region, and some of these figures deserve to be cited (see table 11.11).

These figures show that while Lviv oblast took more than one-half of *Dzvin*'s subscription total, the capital city of the region consumed one-quarter. By any standards, this was a remarkable degree of "saturation" for a journal that is noted for its patriotic fervor. We have here a major *city* that consumes a Ukrainian-language magazine and one that is most explicitly committed to the cause of Ukrainian sovereignty.

We have seen that Ukrainian-language literary journals are popular in Lviv. What about Moscow-based (that is, Russian-language) and Kyiv-based (Ukrainian or Russian) publications that are political, not cultural? Figures have become available regarding subscriptions for leading newspapers and journals in the USSR as a whole, for the Ukrainian republic, and for the Lviv region itself. The figures tell a dramatic and important story.

Let us begin with the USSR-wide statistics for 1991 in comparison with subscriptions for the previous year (table 11.12).

The same data for the Ukrainian republic is in table 11.13. Subscriptions in Ukraine clearly declined more than they did in the rest of the USSR, but the difference is not very striking except perhaps in the case of *Komsomol'skaia pravda*. What is quite dramatic and politically significant is the story of the Lviv oblast. In Lviv, as compared with the rest of Ukraine, the decline of Moscow and Kyiv periodicals and newspapers was precipitous (see table 11.14).

The only exception to this evident decline is *Komsomol'skoe znamia*

Table 11.11
Dzvin Subscription Distribution, Cities and Towns of Lviv Region

Lviv city	24,287
Drohobych	1,705
Stryi	1,598
Chervonohrad	1,212
Boryslav	923
Truskavets	550

Table 11.12

Subscriptions, Leading Newspapers and Journals, USSR, 1990 and 1991

Periodical	1990 (in thousands)	1991 (in thousands)	Change
Argumenty i fakty	32,962	22,773	−30.9%
Trud	20,925	17,335	−17.2%
Komsomol'skaia pravda	21,252	16,317	−23.2%
Izvestiia	9,550	3,665	−61.6%
Ogonek	4,332	1,528	−64.7%
Pravda	6,870	2,080	−69.7%
Literaturnaia gazeta	4,438	1,055	−76.2%

Table 11.13

Subscriptions, Leading Newspapers and Journals, Ukraine and USSR Excluding Ukraine, 1990 and 1991

Periodical	Ukraine			USSR excluding Ukraine		
	1990	1991	Change	1990	1991	Change
Argumenty i fakty	6,094,603	4,065,100	−33.3%	26,867,397	18,707,900	−30.4%
Trud	5,570,870	4,417,700	−20.7%	15,534,130	12,917,300	−16.8%
Komsomol'skaia pravda	4,252,041	2,500,200	−41.2%	16,999,959	13,816,800	−18.7%
Izvestiia	2,340,896	784,200	−66.5%	7,209,104	2,880,800	−60.0%
Ogonek	806,706	276,700	−65.7%	3,525,294	1,251,300	−64.5%
Pravda	1,581,181	428,500	−72.9%	5,288,819	1,651,500	−68.8%
Literaturnaia gazeta	888,710	165,300	−81.4%	889,700	3,549,290	−74.9%

which, on the contrary, has undergone a spectacular rise in its subscriptions, although it is noticeable that its gains were much lower in Lviv than in Ukraine as a whole. The success of *Komsomol'skoe znamia* calls for a separate discussion, which for reasons of space cannot be attempted here. Let us merely note that this Kyiv-based paper appears to have taken away from the Moscow *Komsomol'skaia pravda* those Ukrainian readers who accounted for the latter's loss of 41 percent of subscribers in the Ukraine.

What about the Lviv-based daily—that is, political—papers? Fortunately, we do have some figures for them, as well. *L'vovskaia pravda* and *Vil'na Ukraïna* are party papers. They are clearly and unequivocally

Table 11.14
Subscriptions, Leading Newspapers and Journals, Ukraine
and Lviv Oblast, 1990 and 1991

	Ukraine			Lviv oblast		
Periodical	1990	1991	Change	1990	1991	Change
Trud	5,570,870	4,417,700	−20.7%	142,000	71,000	−50.0%
Komsomol'skaia pravda	4,252,041	2,500,200	−41.2%	143,000	63,000	−55.9%
Izvestiia	2,340,896	784,200	−66.5%	83,000	29,000	−65.1%
Pravda	1,581,181	428,500	−72.9%	53,000	8,900	−83.2%
Komsolmol'skoe znamia	377,825	1,020,554	170.1%	11,000	20,000	81.8%
Molod' Ukraïny	593,438	505,609	−14.8%	54,000	39,000	−27.8%
Pravda Ukraïny	274,378	217,582	−20.7%	2,700	1,500	−44.4%
Radans'ka Ukraïna	243,678	140,602	−42.3%	12,000	3,400	−71.7%
Robitnycha Hazeta	56,057	27,300	−51.3%	14,000	3,900	−72.1%
Sil's'ki visti	2,491,150	2,110,004	−15.3%	154,000	70,000	−54.5%

in opposition to the "democrats" who now are formally in power in
Lviv. *Moloda Halychyna* is a former Komsomol paper (until 1990 called
Lenins'ka Molod') that has been strongly anticommunist in recent years.
Za vil'nu Ukraïnu was founded in July 1990, and is even more anticom-
munist. Table 11.15 gives their figures.

The evident success of *Za vil'nu Ukraïnu* seems thus fully to con-
form to what we noted earlier about the literary papers and journals.
It is the best-selling publication in the Lviv region. What is even more
interesting, its total subscription figure of 443,000 includes 70,100

Table 11.15
Subscriptions, Official and Independent Papers,
Lviv Oblast, 1990 and 1991

	1990	1991	Change
Official papers			
Vil'na Ukraïna	182,000	29,800	−83.6%
L'vovskaia pravda	101,000	58,000	−42.6%
Independent papers			
Moloda Halychyna	166,000	214,000	28.9%
Za vil'nu Ukraïnu	100,000	443,000	343.0%

copies that go to subscribers outside the Lviv region. We may suppose that they live mainly in the other two Galician regions, but it is fair to suppose that a portion of these also live farther east. *Moloda Halychyna* also gained 3400 outside subscriptions, while *L'vovskaia pravda* got 1600 and *Vil'na Ukraïna* 3800.

These figures per se are less important than the underlying fact they reveal: These Lviv papers, whose formal rank is that of regional papers (and which, therefore, are not supposed to be available outside of their own regions) have been de facto, quite informally, elevated to the status of republic-wide publications. Because of the special conditions in the region, and in recognition of a special role of the city of Lviv in Ukrainian politics, Ukraine has thus acquired in Lviv a second media capital, in a sense a rival to Kyiv.

A Very Tentative Conclusion

This discussion has been much stronger on raw material than interpretation or analysis, and the data themselves are not as complete as one would wish. Even with these limitations, however, it is possible to argue that the situation in Ukraine is too complex to draw any general points on the basis of republic averages, whether in the political sphere, demographic trends, or cultural phenomena. The city and oblast of Lviv clearly represent an "anomaly" if a republic average is taken as a norm. Lviv appears to be drawing apart, going in an opposite direction, from the rest of Ukraine. On the other hand, it may be setting the pace and providing a model for the western region, which we defined as consisting of formerly Polish, Czechoslovak, and Romanian areas. Lviv differs from the east in ethno-demographic development as much as it does in its position in politics and in its cultural preferences. It is beyond the scope of this chapter to ask whether the west—and Lviv in particular—is exerting any impact on the eastern regions of Ukraine in any of these spheres. It would be valuable to examine, in this connection, the situation in Kyiv: What were the roots of its vote against the Union (or, earlier, of the overwhelming victory of the democrats in Kyiv in the 1990 election)?

These questions are important and interesting, but they call for a separate treatment. Our concern here was to explore the Lviv case and we conclude that an explanation of Lviv politics is to be found, at least in part, in the region's ethnic composition and in its population's clearly demonstrated preference for Ukrainian culture.[2]

Notes

The author thanks the Center for Russian and East European Studies, University of Michigan, and Paula Powell, his research assistant, for help on this study.

1. The figures mentioned in the text discussion are cited from Oleksandr Laver and Iurii Azhniuk, "Sira tin' asymiliatsiï," *Molod' Ukraïny* (March 6, 1991), p. 2. The article by these two authors is highly emotional in tone even though it is full of various statistical tables; it is a very revealing and dramatic survey of demographic trends in the Ukrainian republic as a whole, and of demographic history of Ukrainians in the USSR between 1959 and 1989. The authors cite certain data from sources that to this writer's knowledge have not been published. They do not consider the ethnic situation in a regional breakdown *within* Ukraine.

2. This essay continues an investigation the author has been conducting over the years, preliminary results of which have been reported in "Russians in Ukraine and Problems of Ukrainian Identity in the USSR," in Peter J. Potichnyj, ed., *Ukraine in the Seventies* (Oakville, Ontario: Mosaic Press, 1975), pp. 195–217 [see chapter 3 of this book]; "West Ukraine and West Belorussia: Historical Tradition, Social Communication, and Linguistic Assimilation," *Soviet Studies* 31, no. 1 (1979) [see chapter 4 of this book]; "Urbanization in Ukraine since the Second World War," in Ivan L. Rudnytsky, ed., *Rethinking Ukrainian History* (Edmonton, Alberta: Canadian Institute of Ukrainian Studies, 1981), pp. 180–202 [see chapter 5]; and "National Awakening: Ukraine and Belorussia," in Uri Ra'anan, ed., *The Soviet Empire: The Challenge of National and Democratic Movements* (Lexington, Mass., and Toronto: D. C. Heath, 1990), pp. 75–93.

Sources to Tables 11.1–11.15

Tables 11.1, 11.2 and 11.3: *Radians'ka Ukraïna*, March 23, 1991.

Tables 11.4–11.7: 1959 and 1970 census returns (see chapter 4, note 21); *Chislennost'i sostav naseleniia SSSR* (Moscow, 1984), table 17; *Vil'na Ukraïna*, April 10, 1990; and *Karta suchasnoho natsional'noho skladu naselennia Ukraïns'koï RSR* (Kyiv, 1966).

Tables 11.8–11.10: *Izvestiia*, April 28, 1990; *Vil'na Ukraïna*, April 10, 1990; *Literaturna Ukraïna*, November 12, 1989; *Vsesvit*, no. 5 (1988); and *Dzvin*, no. 1 (1990).

Table 11.11: *Dzvin*, no. 1 (1990).
Table 11.12: *Komsomol'skaia pravda*, November 24, 1990.
Tables 11.13–11.14: *Komsomol'skaia pravda*, November 24, 1990; *Komsomol-'skoe znamia*, November 23, 1990; and *Za vil'nu Ukraïnu*, December 29, 1990.
Table 11.15: *Za vil'nu Ukraïnu*, December 29, 1990.

12 Nation-Building in Ukraine: Problems and Prospects

Nation-building in contemporary Ukraine is taking place in a setting that was created in 1991 when Ukraine attained its independence and the Soviet Union collapsed. Properly speaking, the events of 1991, and those immediately preceding them, form the initial chapter of the Ukrainian nation-building project. Ukraine's most pressing problems today, domestic and external, are defined by the decisions and solutions adopted at that time. They are the source of Ukraine's strengths, and also of its weaknesses, at the present stage of its history.

The Way to Independence

Ukraine owes its independence to a combination or coalescence of two factors. First, there were external, "objective" conditions on which the Ukrainians depended, but which they influenced only to a limited degree. In 1991 those conditions, or circumstances, included a major political crisis in Moscow; the rise of other non-Russian nations, especially the Balts; and the establishment of formal Russian-Ukrainian relations before the August 1991 crisis. It was very important, too, that at that particular historical juncture democratic nationalists in Russia

First published in *The Successor States to the USSR*, 1995.

were defining the Russian national agenda in opposition to the defenders of the imperial Soviet "center" and also against extreme nationalists of the right. Second, there was the domestic or internal scene; in other words, that "subjective" factor for which the Ukrainians themselves were primarily responsible. As we shall argue below, the Ukrainians seized the arising opportunities, some of which they did not create themselves. They mobilized their forces and built coalitions among former rivals and in the end attained their goal of national independence without having to fight against outside forces, and without civil war or unrest.

The August 1991 coup would not have ended so fast, or it might even have succeeded, had there not emerged, earlier, a conflict between the Russian Federation, led by Boris N. Yeltsin, and the government of the Soviet Union, personified by President Mikhail S. Gorbachev. This conflict reflected the Russian nation's rejection of communism and by extension—or so it looked in 1991—its desire to abandon the idea that Russia had to be an empire. The split between Russia and the USSR— "Russia's secession from the Soviet Union," as some put it—also had a personal dimension, which took the form of a struggle between two leaders for power. Many observers, especially in the West, did not notice that the contenders did not fight for the same job: They represented two different political entities—Russia versus the Soviet Union. Thus it was a triple confrontation: Yeltsin versus Gorbachev; democracy against communism; and the national liberation of Russia against the "center" or empire. There were reasons to believe that the Russians wanted to build their own nation-state, to make Russia a "normal" country, thus breaking once and for all with the old nationalist myth that for the Russian people a multinational empire was the only acceptable home.[1]

The August coup, although an "external" factor for Ukraine, was nonetheless connected to what was going on in Ukraine. The plot had been hatched by diehard Communists as a response to what they saw as a gradual subversion of the Soviet Union that had begun in the late 1980s. In their view, Ukraine played a major part in that subversion of the Soviet state. Indeed, the Ukrainian republic played a role in 1991, when, in June, its parliament decided that Ukraine would not sign the Union treaty on August 20, 1991. The coup organizers rightly viewed the Ukrainian decision for what it was: It amounted to Ukraine's de facto withdrawal from the Union. As some plot leaders have since admitted, Ukraine's June decision was on their minds when they decided to act.

This decision had its antecedents, however. There is no room in this brief summary for an account of those developments in Ukraine prior to 1991, especially in the Gorbachev era, that made Ukraine capable of acting as it did in the closing months of 1991. The Chernobyl nuclear accident created the intellectual and psychological climate in which it would be possible to think about a break with Moscow. The rise of Rukh, in 1989, and the fact that Kyiv party leaders allowed Rukh's founding congress to be held in Kyiv (Rukh's Belorussian counterpart held its first congress in Lithuania) inaugurated the demonopolization of the public discourse. Leonid M. Kravchuk, in his role as party ideology chief, engaged Rukh in public debate, allowing his opponents access to television. That he spoke against Rukh mattered less in the long run than the fact that in so doing he made Rukh a legitimate part of the political scene.

The parliamentary election of March 1990 sent about one hundred noncommunist representatives to Kyiv. Very different people met face to face in the halls of the parliament—including former prisoners and their former persecutors. In local elections, the opposition, led by Rukh, won overwhelmingly in West Ukraine, and something resembling a formal and peaceful transfer of power from communist to national-democratic hands did take place on the provincial level in Lviv and several other western regions.

Following Russia's declaration of sovereignty in June 1990, the Ukrainian parliament adopted its own declaration to the same effect. It envisioned Ukraine's neutrality and spoke about Ukraine's right to have its own military. The declaration publicized the concept of "the people of Ukraine" as an entity embracing all of its citizens, without regard to ethnic or religious affiliation. Early in 1991, the Kyiv parliament in fact sabotaged Gorbachev's referendum regarding the Union by adding a specific "Ukrainian" question about Ukraine's sovereignty. For Ukrainian nation-building, these were significant actions. For the first time in its history, Ukraine had a parliament in which all of its regions were represented, however imperfectly. East met west, Communists sat in one hall with anti-Communists, and nationalist poets learned to talk politics with party officials and plant managers. Ukraine was getting its first lesson in noncommunist politics and was beginning to create rudiments of a tolerant and pluralistic political culture. For the national self-esteem of the newly independent Ukrainians, it was a source of satisfaction that their independence was also a result of their own choices and actions. At the final stage of Ukraine's march to independence, the national-democratic opposition in the parliament managed to reach an accord with important segments of the Soviet Ukrainian establishment on how Ukraine should respond to the events in Moscow on August 19 and after, even though such a decision was not easy to make, considering the Communists' record.

The Ukrainians knew that there was a fundamental difference between the situation in Moscow and that in Kyiv. In Moscow, opponents of the coup could and did raise the national flag of Russia against the communist center. They brought that flag with them as they talked to the troops, appealing to their Russian patriotism. But what worked in Moscow would have created a disaster in Kyiv. Those who criticize Kravchuk, or the Kyiv establishment in general, for their alleged "wait and see" position at the time when Yeltsin actively opposed the coup forget one essential thing. If the Ukrainians in Kyiv had imitated the Russians in Moscow by appealing to the Soviet army in Ukraine in the name of *Ukraine's* freedom, they would have assured the army's prompt and decisive intervention in favor of the coup. It was one thing to ask the army in Moscow to liberate Russia from communism, and quite another to ask it in Kyiv to liberate Ukraine from communism and from Russia. In Ukraine communism and Russia were one and the same thing.

On August 24, 1991, Ukraine's Supreme Soviet, or Rada, adopted a declaration of independence by an overwhelming vote, even though the parliament had a Communist party majority. The forces of national democratic opposition and their Communist opponents proved capable of agreeing on Ukraine's break with Moscow. This called for a willingness to compromise on both sides. One last-minute deal provided that the question of independence would be submitted to a popular vote on December 1. (On December 1 Ukraine also elected its first president in a contested and free election.) The subsequent popular vote was overwhelmingly for independence. By the end of December, the Soviet Union was no more.[2]

Kravchuk and his friends, however, remembered what it was that had forced them to act differently from Yeltsin during the coup. A decision was made, within days after the coup, to establish a Ukrainian armed force. High-ranking officers serving in the Soviet military in

Ukraine agreed to undertake the task of creating a Ukrainian army, navy, and air force. The winning over of the military (and, one may presume, of key elements of the police) after the accord between the opposition and the pro-independence Communists was a landmark step on Ukraine's march to independence.

Setting Priorities

The Ukrainian case offers an interesting perspective on what Barry R. Posen calls "a problem of 'emerging anarchy' " that arises, he argues, after the collapse of empires. Posen writes:

> The longest standing and most useful school of international relations theory—realism—explicitly addresses the consequences of anarchy— the absence of a sovereign—for political relations among states. In areas such as the former Soviet Union and Yugoslavia, sovereigns have disappeared. They leave in their wake a host of groups—ethnic, religious, cultural—of greater or lesser cohesion. These groups must pay attention to the first thing that states have historically addressed—the problem of security—even though many of these groups still lack many of the attributes of statehood.[3]

Posen agrees with the view of "realist theory," according to which "the condition of anarchy makes security the first concern of states. It can be otherwise only if these political organizations do not care about their survival as independent entities. As long as some do care, there will be competition for the key to security—power."[4]

These propositions were understood in Kyiv in 1991. Posen's specific comments, however, require modification with reference to Ukraine. First, new sovereigns in the republics preceded the demise of the "sovereign" in Moscow, and by their very rise they directly contributed to that outcome. Second, Ukraine was a political entity, not something being organized by and for an ethnic group. The concept of a "people of Ukraine" was civic and territorial, not linguistic or ethnic. However, Posen's point that "security" must be "the first concern of states" if they want to survive helps us to appreciate properly the centrality—and propriety—of Kyiv's decision to create its own army at once.

That decision changed Ukrainian politics, which until then had been the domain of poets and professors on the one side, and of party apparatchiks, industrial managers, and bureaucrats on the other. Ukraine's relations with Moscow were transformed as well.

In light of the facts mentioned here it is hard to accept the statement that "Soviet totalitarianism," and with it the USSR, just decayed and collapsed and that Ukraine was practically handed its independence.[5]

There was nothing predetermined in what transpired in Kyiv during or after the collapse. Rather, an unprecedented historical situation did emerge, and within it was contained, among many possible outcomes, the theoretical possibility that Ukraine might become an independent state—provided, that is, that people on the spot, in Ukraine, saw that potentiality and were willing and able to make the potential real. It took more than Soviet collapse, for example, to induce active-duty Soviet generals to organize, in open defiance of their military superiors, a Ukrainian army.[6]

In assessing the contributions to nation-building in Ukraine stemming from the events of 1991 and those preceding, it must be recalled that post-Soviet Ukraine was not an entirely new entity, one based on an ethnic, religious, or cultural group, but a state that claimed to be the legal continuation of the Ukrainian Soviet Republic. As noted above, it defined "the people of Ukraine" in legal and civic terms. Ukraine's withdrawal from the USSR was carried out by constitutional bodies of the Soviet republic, thereby securing acceptance of the new state's independence by Soviet loyalists while preventing the rise of rival claimants to power from among opponents of communism. Thus the actions of political actors of all persuasions made it possible to avoid a civil war between "Sovietists" and nationalists, between ethnic groups, or between regions. There was no war with Russia or "the center."

The Challenge of Nation-Building

Ukraine's independence was a most impressive accomplishment, but it created only the foundation for the task of restructuring and reforming Ukraine's economy, creating a modern state machinery, building democratic institutions, and developing extensive relations with the outside world.

At best, Ukraine was and remains a "protodemocracy."[7] Those who knew how to make Ukraine independent were not best qualified to guide it afterwards. Their strengths—as "insiders" in Soviet politics—became handicaps after the end of the Soviet Union. Ukraine's nation-building requires the emergence of new leaders and activists, especially from among the young.

Neglect, or rather faulty diagnosis and consequent mishandling, of the critical economic issues, besides being destructive economically, may subvert a key element of the Ukrainian nation-building project. Many of those voting for Ukraine's independence in 1991 did so for economic reasons. To retain their loyalty it was imperative to prove they had been right to vote for Ukraine.

It is a gross oversimplification to speak of the Russians or Russian-speaking people in Ukraine as a single ethnic or national bloc. Many Ukrainian patriots, including some major figures in the events of 1991 and after, have been Russian by ethnic identity or Russian-speaking non-Russians. Ukraine's progress in building a culturally plural civil society depends on its retaining the loyalty of the Russian element, and especially in forestalling that element's politicization as an ethnic minority. This would be an especially dangerous development because it might lead to a territorial breakdown of Ukraine along Yugoslavian lines.

This essay argues that Russia played a crucial role in the collapse of the Soviet Union. One might have expected that after August 1991 the relations between the two large Slavic successor states would be, if not harmonious, then at least good. This did not occur. Virtually overnight, within one week of Ukraine's independence declaration, a spokesman for the Russian president raised the possibility of Russian territorial claims on Ukraine and Kazakhstan.[8]

Among the issues of discord, the nuclear weapons question acquired an extraordinary prominence, largely for symbolic reasons, although the consequences of the dispute, and especially of Ukraine's stand in it, have been much worse than merely symbolic. In a period of growing tensions between Moscow and Kyiv, the same author who rather optimistically described Ukraine's "quiet secession" in the summer of 1991 openly worried in March 1992 about "how to keep divorce from leading to war."[9] What went wrong?

Looking for more immediate explanations, one may point to a change in the correlation of forces in Russian politics and the adoption of a nationalist agenda by some democratic politicians. Whether under pressure from the military and other imperially minded circles, or out of their own conviction, many politicians in Moscow appear to have adopted imperial restoration as a goal taking precedence over nation-building within the Russian Federation. In August 1991 it looked as if nation-builders had defeated the empire-savers in the struggle over the definition of Russia.[10] Boris Yeltsin was their leader. Things have changed since then, and the election of December 12, 1993, made Russian politics even more complicated.

Like Ukraine, Russia is led by the old Soviet-descended elites, even though their democratic credentials enjoy more credence in the West. Those elites, especially in the military, are pursuing the goal of empire-restoration. That course is camouflaged in the meantime by politicians and journalists who invoke the rights of "Russian speakers" in the Near Abroad as a justification for Moscow's pressure or even direct intervention. More candid commentators admit that for some people the only way properly to secure the rights of the Russians outside the Russian Federation is to bring those republics back into the empire.[11]

If such views become dominant, this will not bode well for the future of Ukrainian-Russian relations and will be especially dangerous for Ukraine's internal stability. (Crimea is on the current agenda.) What is the Fourteenth Army, now stationed in the so-called Dniester Republic, really for? Is it perhaps preparing to engage in a "peacekeeping" mission somewhere in Ukraine, say Odessa, when an opportune moment comes?[12]

What Is to Be Done?

Obviously Ukraine needs to develop, and then follow resolutely, a comprehensive program of economic, social, cultural, and political development. The country finally may be adopting such a program in the aftermath of the election of Leonid D. Kuchma as president in July 1994. In October, about a hundred days after entering office, Kuchma put forward a radical program of reform that permits private ownership of land. Kuchma's program enjoys the support of the International Monetary Fund. At the G-7 meeting in Winnipeg, Canada, in October 1994, the leading Western democracies pledged support for market-oriented reforms in Ukraine. The meeting was attended by an uninvited participant, Russian foreign minister Andrei Kozyrev, who declared Russia's "solidarity" with Ukraine but also pressed "Russia's case for a role in Ukraine's economic reform."[13]

At home, Kuchma's plan was received very favorably by many of those who had opposed him in the presidential election. Although remaining faithful to his commitment to seek good and close ties with Russia, Kuchma takes great care to declare himself unequivocally an advocate of Ukraine's independence. He has made it clear there would be no return to an unequal relationship between Russia and Ukraine. Although Western commentators at first viewed Kuchma's victory and Kravchuk's defeat as a sign of a deepening polarization of Ukraine along ethnic and linguistic lines, just the opposite seems to have happened. The involvement of areas such as Crimea, Donetsk, and Luhansk in the electoral process not only secured Kuchma's victory, but also legitimized Ukrainian statehood where it had been least popular.

The future of Ukrainian reform, and of the survival of the Ukrainian state itself, will depend heavily on the nature and extent of Western aid. It is especially important for Ukraine's security that the country should develop ties with other nations, especially its Western neighbors. Ukraine's nation-building will be accelerated by such ties. There are signs that some nations, especially Poland, whose role in Ukrainian history is comparable to that of Russia, are disposed favorably toward such ties.[14]

Russia will obviously remain the central issue. Ukraine cannot influence Russia's domestic agenda, but it can work to promote the idea that an independent Ukraine does not need to be perceived as Russia's loss or defeat. The Russians will need to give up, finally, some of their cherished myths about the precise nature of their historic relations with Ukraine. Of these the most misleading and politically dangerous is the idea that Ukraine had been attached to Russia for over three hundred years prior to its "secession" in 1991. This idea is encapsulated in the so-called Pereiaslav myth, which views the year 1654 as the date of Ukraine's incorporation into Russia. Needless to say, this myth is factually wrong. Most of present-day Ukraine has been under Russian control only since the late eighteenth century. Some key areas became Soviet, without ever having been under Russia, during or after World War II. Nevertheless, the Pereiaslav idea serves as a justification of current policies directed against Ukraine's status as a sovereign nation.[15]

Moscow needs to accept the legitimacy of Ukrainian independence. The disintegration of the USSR and the rise of new states has transformed the national identities of their peoples. Russian politicians need to understand that even if it proves within their capacity to restore their dominion over the old Soviet republics, they and the Russian people will pay a heavy price for it.

An independent Ukraine, if it survives, will mark one of the most revolutionary changes on the political map of East Europe, comparable in its impact on the whole region to the restoration of an independent Poland in 1918, or to Poland's partitions in the late eighteenth century, or to Russia's conquest of the northern coast of the Black Sea in the same century. If good relations between Ukraine and Russia are established, they will facilitate democratic nation-building in both countries. There are signs that the younger generation of Russians is more ready to accept the Russian Federation as its country and no longer considers Ukraine to be a part of Russia. If that view prevails, and if Ukrainians do not develop anti-Russian sentiments, prospects for Ukrainian-Russian cooperation will improve.

The prospects for democracy in Russia will also be improved. Since 1991 independent Ukraine has become a normal condition for millions of Ukrainians, especially the young. However critical they may be of their situation or of the politics of their government, they do not wish to "return" to Russia. Educated young people appreciate Ukraine's unprecedented opening to the world at large, which they correctly attribute to Kyiv's transformation into the capital of an independent country. Any attempt by Russia to bring Kyiv, or Ukraine as a whole, back under Moscow's control would meet with fierce resistance; a Russian-Ukrainian war, whatever its outcome, would doom democracy in Russia as well as in Ukraine.[16]

Notes

1. For an analysis of Russian politics during and after the fall of communism, see John B. Dunlop, *The Rise of Russia and the Fall of the Soviet Empire* (Princeton, N.J.: Princeton University Press, 1993).

2. Bohdan Krawchenko, "Ukraine: The Politics of Independence," in *Nations and Politics in the Soviet Successor States*, eds., Ian Bremmer and Ray Taras (Cambridge, Eng.: Cambridge University Press, 1993), pp. 75–98.

3. Barry R. Posen, "The Security Dilemma and Ethnic Conflict," *Survival* 35, 1 (Spring 1993): 27–28.

4. Posen, "Security Dilemma," p. 28.

5. Alexander J. Motyl, *Dilemmas of Independence: Ukraine after Totalitarianism* (New York: Council on Foreign Relations, 1993), pp. 23–24.

6. Bohdan Pyskir, "The Silent Coup: The Building of Ukraine's Military," *European Security* 2, 1 (Spring 1993): 139–61; Valeriy Izmalkov, "Ukraine and Her Armed Forces: The Conditions and Process for Their Creation, Character, Structure and Military Doctrine," *European Security* 2, 2 (Summer 1993): 279–319. See also Bohdan Pyskir, "Mothers for a Fatherland: Ukrainian Statehood, Motherhood, and National Security," *Journal of Slavic Military Studies* 7, 1 (March 1994): 50–66.

7. Timothy J. Colton, "Politics," in *After the Soviet Union: From Empire to Nations*, eds. Timothy J. Colton and Robert Legvold (New York: W. W. Norton, 1992), pp. 17–48.

8. For a close scrutiny of the complexities of Russo-Ukrainian relations under and after communism, see Roman Solchanyk, "Ukraine, The (Former) Center, Russia, and 'Russia,' " *Studies in Comparative Communism* 25, 1 (March 1992): 31–45.

9. Strobe Talbott, "The Quiet Secession of a Large Country," *Time*, July 1, 1991, p. 45; "How to Keep Divorce from Leading to War," *Time*, March 2, 1992, p. 34.

10. For an elucidation of these concepts, see Roman Szporluk, "Dilemmas of Russian Nationalism," *Problems of Communism* 38, 4 (July-August 1989): 15–35. Reprinted in Rachel Denber, ed., *The Soviet Nationality Reader: The Disintegration in Context* (Boulder, Colo.: Westview Press, 1992), pp. 509–43. (Included as chapter 7 in this book.)

11. Leonid Mlechin, "Russkii vopros v rossiiskoi politike 1994 goda," *Izvestiia*, January 4, 1994, p. 4.

12. Karen Dawisha and Bruce Parrott, *Russia and the New States of Eurasia: The Politics of Upheaval* (Cambridge, Eng.: Cambridge University Press, 1994), pp. 42–43, 299–307, and passim; and Daria Fane, "Moldova: Breaking Loose from Moscow," in *Nations and Politics in the Soviet Successor States*, eds., Ian Bremmer and Ray Taras (Cambridge, Eng.: Cambridge University Press, 1993), pp. 121–53.

13. Charles Truehart, "Russia Seeks Role in Ukraine Reform," *Washington Post*, October 28, 1994, p. A35. See also Clyde H. Farnsworth, "Ukraine Wins Pledges of Support at Canadian Finance Meeting," *New York Times*, October 28, 1994, p. A7.

14. Ian J. Brzezinski, "Polish-Ukrainian Relations: Europe's Neglected Strategic Axis," *Survival* 35, 3 (Autumn 1993), 26–37; Stephen R. Burant, "International Relations in a Regional Context: Poland and Its Eastern Neighbours, Lithuania, Belarus, Ukraine," *Europe-Asia Studies* 45, 3 (1993): 395–418; Ilya Prizel, "The Influence of Ethnicity on Foreign Policy: The Case of Ukraine," in *National Identity and Ethnicity in Russia and the New States of Eurasia*, ed. Roman Szporluk (Armonk, N.Y.: M. E. Sharpe, 1994), pp. 103–28.

15. John Morrison, "Pereyaslav and After: The Russian-Ukrainian Relationship," *International Affairs* 69, 4 (October 1993): 677–703. The idea that since Ukraine had been a part of Russia for about 350 years it might "return" to Russia now, after having proved incapable of reforming its own economy, was presented by Eugene B. Rumer, "Eurasia Letter: Will Ukraine Return to Russia?" *Foreign Policy*, no. 96 (Fall 1994): 129–44. In fact, only a small part of Ukraine was ruled by the Russian tsar after 1654, and it was not until after the partitions of Poland in 1793–1795 that a majority of Ukrainians found themselves under Russian rule. For details, see my letter to the editor, *Foreign Policy*, no. 97 (Winter 1994–95): 178–80.

16. For recent assessments of the Ukrainian situation, see Roman Szporluk, "Reflections on Ukraine after 1994: The Dilemmas of Nationhood," *Harriman Review* 7, 7/9 (March-May 1994): 1–10 [see chapter 13 of this book]; Taras Kuzio and Andrew Wilson, *Ukraine: Perestroika to Independence* (Edmonton: Canadian Institute of Ukrainian Studies, 1994); Alexander J. Motyl, "Will Ukraine Survive 1994?" *Harriman Institute Forum* 7, 5 (January 1994): 3–6; Roman Solchanyk, "The Politics of State Building: Centre-Periphery Relations in Post-Soviet Ukraine," *Europe-Asia Studies* 46, 1 (1994): 47–68; Peter van Ham, *Ukraine, Russia, and European Security Implications for Western Policy*, Chaillot paper no. 13 (Paris: Institute for Security Studies, Western European Union, 1994); and Frank Umbach, "Russia and the Problems of Ukraine's Cohesion: Results of a Fact-Finding Mission," *Berichte des Bundesinstituts für ostwissenschaftliche und internationale Studien*, no. 13 (Cologne: Bundesinstitut für ostwissenschaftliche und internationale Studien, 1994).

13   Reflections on Ukraine after 1994: The Dilemmas of Nationhood

In considering the prospects of the Ukrainian state as it approaches its third anniversary, it is essential to remember that the independent Ukraine proclaimed in August 1991 did not define itself as an ethnic state. It was a jurisdiction, a territorial and legal entity—in fact, a successor of the Ukrainian SSR. Its citizens were of different ethnic backgrounds and spoke Ukrainian and Russian to varying degrees, but also other languages. The new state declared that all power in it derives from "the people of Ukraine." The founders of the post-Soviet Ukraine thus adopted and adapted the concept of "the Soviet people," which, the official line had held, consisted of persons of many linguistic and ethnic backgrounds. However, this idea, in a different form, had a genuine Ukrainian pedigree: It had been formulated in the Ukrainian national movement of the 1960s and 70s, when Ukrainian dissidents and human rights activists proclaimed the idea that all persons living in Ukraine were its citizens.

It is important to repeat and elaborate on this theme because attempts are under way now to redefine Ukrainian identity from civic and political to ethnic and linguistic terms. They come from two sources: First, from forces in Ukraine and Russia who define Russianness ethnically and want to subvert Ukraine as a territorial and political entity by

First published in *The Harriman Review*, 1994.

invoking the rights of "Russian-speaking" people, and, second, from those Ukrainians who remain loyal to a linguistic and ethnic Ukrainian identity and for whom, accordingly, Russian-speaking Ukrainians appear to be an anomaly.

The nationality problem in Ukraine also has direct political repercussions for Russia. If the Communists who advocate a reunion of Ukraine or parts of Ukraine with Russia are successful, they will reinforce the anti-Yeltsin and anti-Western camp in Russian domestic politics. Ukraine will become a factor in the struggle about Russia's national identity. Our special concern in this essay is to discuss the interdependence of Ukrainian nation-building and Russian nation-building and the role ethnic identity plays in domestic and external politics in these states.

Independent Ukraine is facing a number of formidable challenges. Everybody knows that it lags behind Russia, not to mention the Baltic states, in economic reforms. There are many reasons that explain the present stagnation. One is a failure of political leadership. Another is the general sense that Ukraine's population is not ready to accept radical reforms and that indeed large segments of it remain attached to Soviet values and institutions. There are indications that there is a split between those ready to accept reforms and those who oppose them and that this split has a territorial and even ethnic dimension.

The elections in March and April of this year [1994] offer some insight into this problem. The citizens of Ukraine cast their ballots for the national parliament according to a rather complicated formula. Contrary to the predictions of pollsters and foreign commentators, who expected that less than 50 percent would vote, the turnout exceeded 70 percent. This suggests that people believe that it matters who will represent them in Kyiv. The politicians who took the trouble to run, even if they came from the eastern regions of Ukraine, clearly indicated that they wanted to be heard in the Ukrainian capital. This is not a behavior typical of secessionists. In the first voting about 10 percent of the seats were filled and the following two votes produced roughly two-thirds of the parliament. Additional voting has been scheduled for May or June. The results have shown a striking pattern. In the eastern regions of Ukraine, which are highly urbanized and industrial, opponents of economic reforms running as Communists achieved an impressive victory. In the western and central Ukrainian regions the Communists fared poorly and the democrats, independents, and moderate nationalists did well. Contrary to the expectations of some observers, the extreme nationalists managed to win no more than five or six seats.

These results reveal that the division in the country is about whether to maintain the state ownership of industry, collective farming, and the social welfare features of the old system, or whether to move away from those Soviet institutions. It so happens that the eastern regions of Ukraine have large Russian populations or areas in which a high proportion of Ukrainians speak Russian as their first language. Western observers, perhaps drawing a facile analogy with the situation in Yugoslavia, feature what they perceive as the emergent breakup of Ukraine along ethno-linguistic lines. They also suggest that the linguistic division coin-

Ukrainian Parliamentary Election Results, 1994

EXTREME NATIONALISTS	
Ukrainian National Assembly	3
Ukrainian Conservative Republican Party	2
MODERATE NATIONALISTS	
Rukh	20
Ukrainian Republican Party	8
Congress of Ukrainian Nationalists	5
Democratic Party of Ukraine	2
CENTRISTS	
Inter-regional Reform Block	4
Ukrainian Democratic Renaissance Party	4
Civil Congress of Ukraine	2
Social Democratic Party of Ukraine	2
Labour Party	4
Christian Democratic Party of Ukraine	1
COMMUNISTS	
Ukrainian Communist Party	86
Peasant Party	18
Ukrainian Socialist Party	14
UNAFFILIATED	163
Total*	338

*112 seats remain unfilled

Sources: Central Election Commission; International Foundation for Electoral Systems; Interfax.
Reprinted from *The Economist* (April 16, 1994).

cides with a division on economic and political issues. They seem to assume that in Ukraine somehow being a Russian-speaker or an ethnic Russian goes together with a sympathetic attitude to communism. But one may ask the question: Why should Russians as Russians favor communism in Ukraine when so many Russians in Russia and especially so many Russians living in urban areas in Russia have voted for democrats in the Russian election? An answer suggests itself. People voted for Communists in Ukraine in those areas where the Communist party apparatus has been especially strong and where social and economic conditions that have no future under a reformed economy prevail (such as a heavy concentration of state-owned industries). One can suppose that those voting for the Communists in East Ukraine included ethnic Ukrainians who chose to vote this way for the same reasons that motivated the ethnic Russians. The real problem Ukraine is facing, therefore, is to establish a national consensus about the question of reform. One might say that Ukraine is facing the same questions Russia is facing, except that instead of a choice between empire and nation-state, Ukraine is faced with the choice of surviving as a political entity or becoming like Bosnia.

The Communists in Ukraine, whether they are in fact Russian or Ukrainian by descent, have now taken up the Russian ethnic cause in Ukraine, while also defending state property and the Soviet political system and, accordingly, opposing privatization and Westernization. There is a danger, therefore, that if they succeed in politicizing Russian ethnicity, not only will an ethnic conflict arise but also it will be reinforced by political and social divisions. Unless a conscious effort is made to counteract this trend, the division between pro-Western and anti-Western forces in Ukraine today may assume the form of an ethnic split. While the Communists speak for the Russians, those who oppose the Communists defend Ukraine's integrity as a multiethnic state.

The implications of the language issue as raised in Ukraine by the Communists go far beyond the threat of secession by some parts of the state. The enemies of Ukrainian statehood, who in Russia also include non-Communists and even anti-Communist forces, are resorting to the language issue in order to force the general body of Ukrainian citizens to define themselves primarily in ethnic terms. If the Kyiv government and the Ukrainian public do accept the narrower definition of Ukrainians as "Ukrainian-speaking people," the principle on which an independent Ukrainian state was built will be subverted and Ukraine will break up in all sorts of ways—-linguistic, regional, confessional, racial, and so forth.

If the Communists succeed in detaching Eastern Ukraine from Russia under their own aegis, they will thereby become a much stronger factor in domestic Russian politics. According to Daniel Yergin and Thane Gustafson, in their book *Russia 2010*, Russia faces a "triple transition": from dictatorship to democracy, from a command economy to a free market, and "from a four-century-old empire to a nation-state." Elsewhere they say that the core of their book is "Russia's struggle to make the transition to democracy, a market economy, and a nation-state."[1] Even though Russia is more advanced than Ukraine in economic reform, the victory of a market economy is not yet definitive, while democracy has been seriously challenged.

The Ukrainian factor will clearly influence the outcome of all three of those transitions and thus will help to determine the shape of post-Soviet Russia. Zbigniew Brzezinski argues in *Foreign Affairs* that "without Ukraine, Russia ceases to be an empire, but with Ukraine suborned and then subordinated, Russia automatically becomes an empire."[2] But if Russia becomes an empire, Brzezinski writes, it cannot be a democracy at the same time. We might add that an imperial Russia will be forced to abandon economic reform in favor of central planning. (In the same issue of *Foreign Affairs*, Yuri Afanasiev, in the article "Russian Reform Is Dead," asserts that Moscow has already chosen central planning.)[3]

The elections in Russia in December 1993 demonstrated the strength of the Communist-nationalist alliance. In the battle over Russia's choice—to be an empire or a "normal" nation—the empire-savers, or more precisely the empire-restorers, at present seem to be defeating the nation-builders. The positions taken by Zhirinovsky support the argument that the enemies of the national independence of non-Russian republics are also enemies of democracy in Russia. Imperial restoration—read: the recovery of Ukraine—under their leadership will mean the end of Russian democracy.

Let us now turn to more specific issues in Russo-Ukrainian relations. One factor is of crucial importance for our understanding of relations between the two states: Increasingly the elites in Russia today do not consider Ukraine to be a legitimate political and cultural entity. In this respect the Communists and extreme nationalists are saying openly what some democrats in Russia are too hesitant to admit. In their reluctance to counter Communist-nationalist propaganda the democrats appear to

have forgotten essential facts about the breakup of the USSR and, especially, about the role of Russia in that outcome.

In his struggle against Mikhail Gorbachev and the USSR, Boris Yel-
tin identified himself with the cause of Russia as well as that of democracy. In November 1990, in his capacity of chairman of the Russian
Parliament, he paid an official visit to Ukraine and signed an agreement
in which Russia and Ukraine recognized each other's territorial integrity.
During the Russian presidential campaign of 1991, it was not unusual
to hear words about Russia's "struggle for independence" from the center or its emancipation from the USSR. Andrei Kozyrev spoke in precisely these words in an interview on the eve of that election: "We suffered our way to independence" [My . . . vystradali svoiu nezavisimost'],
he told the correspondent of *Literaturnaia gazeta*.[4] Ukraine would not
have become an independent state in August 1991 had the government
of Russia not replaced that of the USSR at the center of power in Moscow. In those circumstances the non-Russian republics had no choice
but to become either provinces of the new Russia or her equals as independent states. When they chose the latter, the new Russia accepted that
choice.

It was of critical importance that Russia defined itself within the
borders of the Russian Federation as it existed in Soviet times. It is a
common error to speak about ethnicity as the organizing principle in the
post-Soviet space. The Soviet Union was succeeded by political entities
that were territorial and juridical and not ethnic (the only exception was
in the Caucasus, where Armenia had challenged the inviolability of Soviet territorial arrangements even prior to 1991). There can be no analogy between the breakup of the USSR and that of Yugoslavia. Imagine
that Yugoslavia had broken up under the joint auspices of the presidents
of Serbia and Croatia, who recognized the territorial integrity of each
other's countries. Serbia and Croatia went to war, but Russia and
Ukraine did not. And at least so far neither Crimea nor Donbas has
become a Ukrainian Bosnia.

Indeed, in early December 1991, after the Ukrainian referendum had
ratified Ukraine's declaration of independence, it seemed possible that
the three East Slavic republics would establish some form of loose association, perhaps an East Slavic Commonwealth. With Minsk as the new
entity's prospective center, Kyiv and Moscow would be assured of an
equal standing. If such a possibility did exist, it vanished when the East
Slavic association was replaced by the Commonwealth of Independent

States that also included Central Asia. In such a Commonwealth, Russia would inevitably play a hegemonic role.

Russia's willingness to accept the finality of Soviet borders was not unconditional. As early as August 26, 1991, President Yeltsin's spokesman indicated that Russia might seek territorial revisions in its borders with Ukraine and Kazakhstan if these two states become fully independent. In this way the democratic Russia gave an initial legitimacy to the idea of territorial revisions based on ethnic considerations. Yeltsin and his government disowned that original statement, but as we know the Russian Parliament placed the question of Crimea high on its agenda. The ethnic factor began to play an increasingly significant role in Ukrainian-Russian relations.

Recently, some leading spokesmen of Russian opinion have been less reluctant to raise issues that even the Russian Parliament under Ruslan Khasbulatov had hesitated to discuss openly. Khasbulatov declared the illegality of Ukrainian jurisdiction over Crimea, but Alexander Solzhenitsyn has questioned Ukraine's territorial integrity in much more sweeping terms. Although Solzhenitsyn is not an active politician, he has enjoyed an extraordinary moral authority in Russia and his views on the Ukrainian problem need to be taken very seriously. On several occasions, most recently in an interview with David Remnick, Solzhenitsyn questioned the present borders of Ukraine and explained that "It was Lenin who established these false borders—borders that did not correspond to the ethnic borders."[5]

According to Solzhenitsyn, Ukraine has the right to exist but only in those places where a majority of the population speaks Ukrainian. He does not address the practical implications of such a suggestion, but the net result of his argument is to delegitimize in Russian opinion the presently existing Ukrainian state.

Other Russian intellectuals have recently gone even farther than Solzhenitsyn. For example, Oleg Platonov, doctor of economic sciences, member of the Russian Writers' Union, and author of *Russian Labor* (*Russkii trud)* and *Russian Civilization (Russkaia tsivilizatsiia*), in an interview with Gleb Kuzmin, said:

> The creation of the "states" of Ukraine and Belorussia has an artificial and temporary character. . . . When I speak about the Russian nation . . . I have in mind all its geographical parts, including Ukrainians and Belorussians. . . . Certain linguistic or ethnographic distinctions of

Ukraine and Belorussia are explainable by the special features of their historical development under the many-centuries-long Polish-Lithuanian occupation. The declaration that the Russian people in Ukraine are a distinct nation is the result of subversive action of Austro-German intelligence services (and later on, of Western intelligence services in general) for the purpose of dismemberment and weakening of the single fraternal organism of Russia.[6]

Platonov is no longer just questioning the borders of Ukraine. He is stating that the very essence of Ukraine and Belarus, not only as states but also as cultural entities, is due to the intrigues of foreign enemies of Russia. It is easy to conclude that the actions of foreign intelligence services call for corresponding countermeasures on the part of Russia, whose national integrity is violated by the very existence of a Ukraine and a Belarus. If some Russian "patriot" needed intellectual justification for fighting against Ukraine, he would find more than enough in Dr. Platonov's arguments.

It would be tempting to dismiss such ideas as extremist and therefore not important. Indeed, serious and authoritative voices are still heard advocating a positive Russian policy toward Ukraine and building a Russian-Ukrainian relationship that will be beneficial for both parties. Sergei Karaganov's article titled "Ukraine as an Apple of Discord" is a good example of this approach.[7] In present-day Russia, however, what was extremist only a year ago has become closer to the political mainstream. These kinds of arguments are part of the debate within the country and as such presumably have some influence on forming Russian attitudes toward Ukraine and Belarus. The case of Yugoslavia shows that such "historical" and theoretical reflections prepare the ground for violence, including ethnic cleansing: Long before Yugoslavia fell apart, intellectuals in its constituent republics engaged in polemics of this sort.

In a recent article in *The New York Review of Books*, Michael Ignatieff alerts us to the dangers in the rewriting of history according to ethnic criteria:

What is remarkable is that the true story of Bosnia—an independent country destroyed by an armed insurrection aided by a foreign power—should have been so continuously undermined by false narratives, whose effect was to diffuse and dissipate the buildup of Western outrage. Hence the story that this was a civil war, in which it was foolish to intervene. Hence the story that this was the resurfacing of ancient hatreds, which outsiders could never understand. Both story lines, assiduously propagated by the Serbs as well as by those who opposed intervention on any grounds, successfully sealed Bosnia off into the symbolic exclusion zone of a family quarrel. . . . [8]

Platonov's ideas are most extraordinary because they are being expressed in 1994. Generations of Russian intellectuals and politicians had believed that the Ukrainian national identity was invented by the officials of Austria-Hungary and/or the Poles for the purpose of destroying Russia from within. Nineteenth- and twentieth-century Russian historians viewed Ukraine's and Belorussia's association with Poland as synonymous with Polish and Catholic oppression. In the view of those historians, the partitions of Poland in the late eighteenth century represented the liberation of the Russian people (that is, Ukrainians and Belorussians) by imperial Russia. Even today many Russians seems to be unaware of how questionable that "liberation" was from the Ukrainian point of view, not to mention the Polish perspective. (A Western participant at a Russo-Ukrainian conference held in Moscow several months ago reported in a private conversation that during a difficult moment in the discussion a Russian delegate proposed that in 1995 Russians and Ukrainians celebrate together the two-hundredth anniversary of the third partition of Poland.)

Even such otherwise knowledgeable personalities as Solzhenitsyn are on record expressing views on nineteenth-century Ukrainian history that have long been refuted by serious scholarship. For example, in his book *Rebuilding Russia* (1991), Solzhenitsyn claims that the Ukrainians of the Austrian province of Galicia considered themselves to be Russian during the revolution of 1848. Had he read the works of Polish historians such as Jan Kozik, Solzhenitsyn would have found out that in 1848 the ancestors of today's Ukrainians then living in Galicia had decided not to consider themselves Polish any longer, but had opted for a Ukrainian identity instead. (See John-Paul Himka's article on the question of Solzhenitsyn's ideas about Ukrainians in 1848.[9])

Solzhenitsyn and Platonov are two extreme examples of what appears to be common among the contemporary Russian intelligentsia—a striking ignorance of Ukraine. Who familiar with American universities today has not encountered visitors from Moscow or St. Petersburg who have assured their American hosts, whenever an appropriate (or inappropriate) occasion occurred, that "Ukraine is not serious," or simply that the Ukrainian language is either "a dialect of Russian" or just "a Southern pronunciation of the Russian language"?

It is hard to understand the continuing neglect of Ukrainian studies in today's Russia. On the contrary, on practical or academic grounds one might have expected that the academic world of Russia would not neglect Ukrainian studies. Apart from the importance of Ukraine per se, millions of people of Ukrainian descent, including many who consider themselves Ukrainian, live in the Russian Federation. But no Russian universities offer Ukrainian programs. As of now, students can study Ukrainian in more universities in the United States, not to mention Canada, than in Russia. Even more striking is the contrast between the attitudes prevailing in Poland and those in Russia. According to the Warsaw Ukrainian-language weekly, at least ten Polish universities and colleges offered Ukrainian in 1993–94; they include the universities of Warsaw, Cracow, Poznan, and Szczecin, and both the Catholic and State universities in Lublin. Warsaw alone has over sixty Ukrainian Studies majors.[10] Most of those students are reported to be of ethnic Polish, not minority Ukrainian, background.

Why is it that so many Russians do not take Ukraine's existence seriously when the Poles do? In his new work on nationalism, *Blood and Belonging*, even Michael Ignatieff confesses that when it comes to Ukraine he has problems: "My difficulty in taking Ukraine seriously goes deeper than just my cosmopolitan suspicion of nationalists everywhere. Somewhere inside, I am also what Ukrainians would call a Great Russian, and there is just a trace of old Russian disdain for these little Russians."[11]

There are various ways to explain this attitude on the part of Russians toward Ukraine, but among them, three are very relevant here.

First, many Russians are ignorant of Ukrainian history. They think that Ukrainians regard their historic association with Poland, Austria, and other Central European nations as a period of tragic separation from Russia. But Ukrainians have both good and bad memories of that period and acknowledge that they benefited from ties to the West. Even more important, most Russians are unaware that modern Ukrainian national consciousness first emerged in the eastern parts of Ukraine, those under Russia the longest, and not in Austrian Galicia—contrary to what not only the Russians, but also many Ukrainians, believe. (In the 1820s and 1830s, there was more Ukrainian "nationalism" in Kharkiv than in Lviv.) It is also puzzling that they have overlooked the record of Ukrainian nationalism in the past fifty years. Ignatieff exemplifies this Russian oversight when he makes this odd statement: "For most of the last fifty years, the party was not wrong when it dismissed nationalist feeling here [in Ukraine] as weak, marginal, and easily suppressed."[12] This certainly will be news for people who have studied Ukrainian armed resistance during and after World War II or the dissent of the 1960s and 1970s. Finally, few Russians have appreciated the effect on the Ukrainian nation-building of the unification of Ukrainian ethnic territories previously held by Poland, Czechoslovakia, and Romania with the Soviet Ukraine that took place, under Stalin's aegis, during World War II. As of 1994 a unified Ukraine has existed for fifty years.

Second, as noted earlier, Russians have not paid attention to intellectual and cultural movements in post-Stalinist Ukraine, and the absence of Ukrainian programs at Russian universities illustrates the larger neglect of Ukraine that has long historical roots. (An instructive introduction to the deeper layers of the problematic relationship of these two peoples is provided, from the mainly Ukrainian and Western perspective, by the volume *Ukraine and Russia in Their Historical Encounter*.)[13]

Third, the Russian public and the policymakers have not become aware of what we might call the "psychological consequences" of Ukraine's joining the international community as an independent state. But this is not merely a matter of emotional gratification. There are many people in Ukraine, not only in Kyiv, who are beneficiaries of Ukrainian independence in a more tangible way. Ukrainians now participate in international programs and exchanges, receive fellowships at foreign universities, and host visitors of all kinds from abroad. Most importantly, all of this is done without the control or permission of Moscow. As one Ukrainian academic put it, "I can now go to Vienna or Paris without first changing planes in Moscow." The beneficial effect of independence is not confined to the intelligentsia. The western regions of Ukraine maintain very close relations with their western neighbors; this makes it possible for ordinary citizens to travel to Poland, Hungary, and Slovakia, and farther west. However, these benefits do not extend equally to Ukraine's eastern parts, which are more tied to Russia. An imaginative Ukrainian leadership would try to convince people in all parts of Ukraine that they would benefit from openness to the West. (Odessa appears to be creating its own external links by establishing relations not only with East Central Europe but also with Israel, Greece, and Turkey.)

In general, the post-Soviet republics are building direct relations with non-Soviet parts of the world, and as a result are being drawn apart from one another in the ex-Soviet space as their mental geographies become different. (Those forces in Moscow that imagine they will reconstitute the "Soviet people" in some post-Soviet form by means of the CIS are obviously oblivious to these trends.) This differentiation is reflected especially in the outlook of the younger generation, for whom the pre-Gorbachev, pre-glasnost era of monolithic "Soviet people" is rapidly becoming a distant memory, while the post-1991 conditions, with the newly independent states in place, seem normal.

By ignoring the relevant facts of recent Soviet and current post-Soviet history, including those pertaining to Ukraine—or other post-Soviet states—opinionmakers and policymakers in Russia are adopting unrealistic and therefore dangerous positions. For example, in an open disregard of the actual course of events that led to the demise of the USSR, in which, as we indicated, Russia itself "determined itself" against the Moscow center, Russia now claims to be the sole successor of the USSR. This position is at odds with the view of the other republics. (Another distortion is expressed in the growing tendency to view the Soviet Union as if it had been just another name for Russia.)

The identification of the Russian state with the Soviet Union and the empire is now accompanied by open declarations that the entire space of the former Soviet Union constitutes an area in which Russia is entitled to exercise its supremacy. This area is held to extend to the Baltic region, the Caucasus, and Central Asia, no less than to Ukraine and Belarus and Moldova.

At the same time, in the Russian view, the new states—including Estonia, Latvia, and Lithuania—are obliged to treat their Russian (or Russian-speaking) citizens as a special category of people—in a way, as extraterritorial groups. This amounts to denying the post-Soviet states full nationhood. They are being pressured to define themselves *ethnically*, and the outside world is being manipulated to treat them as such entities within a larger Russian *political* space.

Such a development is directly relevant to the question of Russia's choice between empire and nation. As we know, there has still been no clearly formulated decision in Russia itself about Russian national identity. This issue includes the definition of Russia's national purpose, and it also calls for the definition and delimitation of Russia's physical dimensions and resulting geopolitical position in the international community. Immediately after Russian independence, at the time Yeltsin and Kravchuk agreed to separate amicably, Russia's "Partnership with the

West" (or with the United States) was an appealing idea, because it signified the recognition of Russia's great power status, which the Soviet Union had enjoyed. This in turn had a domestic aspect as well: It strengthened those supporting democracy and a market economy. But this idea of a partnership has not become a reality, and in any case, as we have seen, there are competing models of Russia, including one that defines Russia in opposition to the West.

Those forces within Russia opposed to the West are turning to ethnic Russian nationalism rather than to communism or Sovietism as the distinguishing mark of Russian identity. Communists, of all political currents, had always been most insistent in their opposition to ethnic divisions, and yet in present-day Russia they have taken up positions that make them virtually indistinguishable from extreme nationalists of the traditionally anti-Communist, anti-Western sort. These two currents have found a common cause in the plight of ethnic Russians in the non-Russian republics.

The Russian debates about what is Russia offer insight into the celebrated issue of "the 25 million Russians" in the Near Abroad. (Rather mysteriously, the number of those Russians has recently been raised, according to some Moscow statements, to 30 million—and this despite the much-advertised facts of Russian out-migration from Central Asia and the Caucasus.) The real meaning of the "Russian rights" issue—"the plight of the 25 million Russians"—is to deprive the successor states of the USSR of the right to define themselves in a territorial or civic sense. Instead, it proposes their ethnicization. This position, at the same time as it deprives the Near Abroad of political nationhood, assumes that the Russian state represents not only the citizens of the Russian Federation but also speaks for ethnic Russians abroad—even when these people are not represented in Russia's Parliament and have not authorized the government of Russia to represent them. How can democrats accept the argument that the government in Moscow speaks for 25 million people who played absolutely no role in electing it, and who are not represented in Moscow? Is the Russian Parliament—instead of the Ukrainian Parliament—-the rightful representative of the "12 million Russians" of Ukraine?

Rising ethnicization of politics in Moscow takes us back to Ukraine and the problem we raised at the beginning of this study. There is a crucial need for Ukrainians to uphold the principle that Ukraine really is a multiethnic political nation or, to put it differently, that it is a "jurisdiction" and not an ethno-linguistic entity. It is on this premise that Ukraine should address the pressing problems it faces. These include the problem of regionalism—it would be sensible to recognize the special conditions and needs of individual parts of a country that extends from the Hungarian Plain to the Sea of Azov—and the opening of positions of power and influence to the members of the younger, post-Soviet generation, together with the replacement of the old cadres and, not the least, real action in the economic sphere.

As they respond to the ethnically argued challenges to the integrity of their country, the supporters of Ukrainian statehood will need to resist falling into a nationality trap. They need to remember that throughout modern Ukrainian history Russian-speaking Ukrainian patriots participated very actively in Ukrainian cultural and political endeavors. This is true even more so today. It is common knowledge that persons of Russian descent occupy the most prominent posts in Ukrainian government, academia, and the media today. Anyone who has met exchange scholars and students from Ukraine in Western universities is aware that quite a few of them are not ethnic Ukrainians—which in no way makes them less Ukrainian. There is nothing unusual in all this, and the point would not have been worth mentioning but for the sustained effort to subvert this peaceful situation in the Yugoslav style.

Admittedly, the language question has occupied a prominent place in Ukrainian politics at all times, and in certain historical situations it became the central issue. The explanation of why this was so is not hard to find. There were times when Moscow went so far in its efforts to eliminate the distinct Ukrainian identity as to attempt to remove the Ukrainian language itself from the public sphere. When this happened, and when the political regime was otherwise so restrictive as to deny any other avenue for free expression, the Ukrainian cause came to be identified, in the public arena, with the defense of the language.

Even when this was the case, however, language was not the only or even the key issue. More than twenty years ago, among those in the West who understood the Ukrainian phenomenon correctly was Walker Connor. In what may have been one of the most perceptive assessments of the Ukrainian national movement of the late 1960s and early 1970s, Connor argued, in an article first published in 1972 (and now reprinted in a collection of his articles), that language was the symbol, not the real issue, in the Ukrainian struggle:

The abstract essence of ethnic nationalism is often not perceived by the observer. There is an understandable propensity . . . to perceive the struggle in terms of its most discernible features. Thus, Ukrainian unrest is popularly reported as an attempt to preserve the Ukrainian language against Russian inroads. . . .

In their desire to assert their uniqueness, members of a group are apt to make rallying points of their more tangible and distinguishing institutions. Thus, the Ukrainians, as a method of asserting their non-Russian identity, wage their campaign for national survival largely in terms of their right to employ the Ukrainian, rather than the Russian, tongue in all oral and written matters. But would not the Ukrainian nation (that is, a popular consciousness of being Ukrainian) be likely to persist even if the language were totally replaced by Russian, just as the Irish nation has persisted after the virtual disappearance of Gaelic, despite pre-1920 slogans that described Gaelic and Irish identity as inseparable?[14]

Connor further asked: "Is the language the essential element of the Ukrainian nation or is it merely a minor element which has been elevated to *the symbol* of the nation in its struggle for continued viability?" His answer was that indeed the language is a symbol.

Connor's diagnosis is even more valid today. Ukraine became independent precisely because its leaders rose above a linguistic definition of the nation. They were able to hold together Ukrainian and Russian speakers just as in the area of politics the national-democratic opposition was able to make a deal with the pro-independence elements of the Soviet Ukrainian establishment.

Today the historic compromise of 1991 has to be renegotiated to make room for major reforms, or else the refusal to change will subvert Ukraine's independent statehood. It was fully proper for the Ukrainians to focus their efforts on gaining an independent statehood. The crisis of the Soviet Union in August 1991 represented a historical conjuncture that might not have come again. The way in which Ukraine seceded from the USSR guaranteed a quick transfer of power and prevented the emergence of conflicting claimants to power, but the Ukrainians paid a price for winning independence in this way, although considering the alternatives that were followed elsewhere—in Georgia or Armenia, for example—the price was not excessively high. Ukraine was spared a war, and this made it possible for it to preserve its territorial integrity. This outcome forced ethnic nationalists to remain in the background. No Ukrainian Gamsahurdia or Landsbergis or Karadzic emerged as a leading figure.

The situation in Ukraine today is very complicated, but it won't help to interpret it with false narratives, as has been done with events in Yugoslavia. Ukraine does not have to go the way of Bosnia. It is especially important to resist the temptation to see age-old hatred based on ethnicity wherever people of different languages, cultures, and religions live together. Although it seems to have become an unquestioned truth today that Serbs, Croats, and Muslims have always been enemies, such a view is contradicted by the historical evidence—after all, there also existed a long tradition of their cooperation. The people of Ukraine must not allow themselves to be talked into believing that it is unnatural for them to live together in peace.

Notes

1. Daniel Yergin and Thane Gustafson, *Russia 2010—And What It Means for the World* (New York: Random House, 1993), pp. 4, 6.

2. Zbigniew Brzezinski, "The Premature Partnership," *Foreign Affairs* 73, no. 2 (March-April 1994): 80.

3. Yuri N. Afanasyev, "Russian Reform Is Dead," in *Foreign Affairs* 73, no. 2 (March-April, 1994): 21–26.

4. "My . . . vystradali svoiu nezavisimost'," *Literaturnaia gazeta*, June 12, 1991, pp. 1–2.

5. David Remnick, "The Exile Returns," *New Yorker* 69 (February 14, 1994): 77.

6. "Mir russkoi tsivilizatsii," *Literaturnaia Rossiia*, no. 6, February 11, 1994, p. 7.

7. Sergei Karaganov, "Ukraina kak iabloko razdora," *Moskovskie novosti*, no. 14, April 3–10, 1994, p. 5.

8. Michael Ignatieff, "Homage to Bosnia," *New York Review of Books* 41, no. 8 (April 21, 1994): 3.

9. John-Paul Himka, "Ukrainians, Russians, and Alexander Solzhenitsyn," *Cross Currents: A Yearbook of Central European Culture*, 11 (1992): 193–204.

10. "Mitsniiut' kadry, bil'shaie studenta," *Nasze Słowo*, October 24, 1993, pp. 1, 5.

11. Michael Ignatieff, *Blood and Belonging: Journeys into the New Nationalism* (Toronto, London, and New York: Viking, 1993), p. 81.

12. Ibid., p. 80.

13. *Ukraine and Russia in Their Historical Encounter*, eds., Peter J. Potichnyj et al. (Edmonton: Canadian Institute of Ukrainian Studies, 1992).

14. Walker Connor, *Ethnonationalism, The Quest for Understanding* (Princeton: Princeton University Press, 1994), pp. 43–44.

14   After Empire: What?

For two-thirds of the twentieth century the lands and peoples of the Soviet Union were defined in terms of their common Soviet, or communist, identity. Eastern Europe was similarly defined for almost half a century (although differences within the region were recognized more often). Today, when communism seems to have been defeated, these areas are again viewed in terms of a common, this time postcommunist agenda: Will they establish market economies? Will they be democratic? Will the new elites and societies manage to make a peaceful transition, or will there be violent upheavals?

In addition to asking what will emerge after communism, we must look at another "ism" which existed before communism and has not disappeared along with it. The Soviet Union was in effect a new form of the Russian Empire, and nationalism and nation-building continued in various ways in this region throughout the twentieth century in the shadow of that empire. The intertwined histories of communism and nationalism will largely determine the character of the postempire era.

The continuing relevance of history has not been sufficiently recognized because historical factors have been overshadowed by the communist construct. We need to broaden our thematic and chronological perspective in order to understand why nationalism in these areas is such

First published in *Daedalus*, 1994.

a powerful force today. We also need a better understanding of what "nationalism" means because whatever the successor to communism may be, it will take a national form. The nations emerging from the breakup of the Soviet Union are now redefining themselves, and in some cases a variant of communism may reappear.

This essay focuses on the historical experience of East Central Europe, especially the Habsburg Empire and Poland, and argues that a profound, "organic" link exists between this region and Ukraine and Russia. By studying the fall of communism together with the fall of empire one is alerted to look not only at the domestic affairs of individual countries, but for signs of a new, "postimperial" geopolitical alignment. Zbigniew Brzezinski calls this new phenomenon "geopolitical pluralism": In these new international constellations are we not witnessing the reemergence of precommunist national "neighborhoods" that had been submerged under Sovietism?

After Communism: What?

The twentieth century, according to some commentators, such as Martin Malia and John Lukacs,[1] began in 1914 (when the "long nineteenth century" ended) and ended in 1989. Lukacs sets the twentieth century in a narrow frame between 1914 and 1989, in the course of which the "two main events were the two world wars,"[2] and the end was marked by the collapse of communism. According to Lukacs, prewar Marxist internationalism was a casualty of World War I: "In 1914 Marxism suffered a huge blow from which it never really recovered. . . . There was a Communist revolution in Russia in 1917; but what Lenin achieved was not an international revolution. To the contrary, it was Russia's withdrawal from Europe."[3] Lukacs does not give proper credit to World War I, which was the key factor in communism's rise to power. After 1914 Marxism knew not only defeats but had a series of great triumphs, first of all in Russia. But the history of communism—Marx's own name for his doctrine—goes back to 1848.

Because the collapse of communism also marks the collapse of the last empire in Eastern Europe, it is important to identify which issues on the postcommunist agenda constitute aspects of the *imperial* succession in their own right. The Soviet Union was the first communist state, the self-declared prototype of the future communist world, and at the same time it was a twentieth-century version of the Russian Empire. Communism was commonly perceived as a Russian product in the Soviet Union and in Soviet-controlled Eastern Europe. For non-Russians the communist experience was synonymous with Russian domination.

The premodern, imperial nature of the Soviet Union was evident to the more insightful Western scholars even before its collapse. As Benedict Anderson put it: "The fact that the Soviet Union shares with the United Kingdom of Great Britain and Northern Ireland the rare distinction of refusing nationality in its naming suggests that it is as much the legatee of the prenational dynastic states of the nineteenth century as the precursor of a twenty-first century internationalist order."[4] The Russians themselves are also aware that their Soviet legacy was a Russian imperial legacy. When Daniel Yergin and Thane Gustafson, in *Russia 2010—And What It Means for the World,* argue that Russia faces a "triple transition": from dictatorship to democracy, from a command economy to a free market, and "from a four-century-old empire to a nation-state," they summarize the main dilemmas of postcommunist Russia in a way which many Russians have done.[5]

Nations against Empire, 1848: Nationalism before Communism

Nationalism emerged originally as a critique of premodern supranational empires (or of political entities that were "national" in the premodern understanding of the term). In 1848 the emerging nations in Eastern Europe asked for a reform of the Habsburg monarchy, and later in the century, when they began to lose hope that the empire could be reformed, they turned against it.[6]

In 1948, the centennial of 1848, the British historian Sir Lewis Namier published an article entitled "1848: Seed-Plot of History." Looking at the ideas of 1848 from the perspective of 1948, Namier wrote: "Every idea put forward by the nationalities of the Habsburg Monarchy in 1848 was realized at some juncture, in one form or another."[7] Namier saw that in 1939–1945 the Ruthenes (now better known as West Ukrainians) had disentangled themselves from the Polish bond—a legacy of 1918–19 and of 1848. It seemed to him that after the post-World War II territorial settlement the last of the programs of 1848 had been realized. But as we now know, the dissolution of the "Yugoslavs'" ties to the Italian sphere and the "Ruthenes'" ties to the Polish sphere did not complete the search for national self-determination. It was only moved into new settings and different relationships, and it was further complicated by the infusion of the other great legacy of 1848, communism. In a move nobody could have foreseen a century earlier, when Russia was recognized as the greatest enemy of "revolution," the Russian army drove communism into Central and Eastern Europe. Lukacs is correct, therefore, when he says that when communist states were founded in Eastern Europe after World War II, it was "not because of revolutions or because of the popular appeal of Communism. They were put there because of the national triumph of Russia over Germany, with the result of the Russian occupation of most of Eastern Europe."[8]

Marx and the Nations of Central Europe in 1848

The Communist Manifesto states:

> National differences and antagonisms between peoples are vanishing gradually from day to day, owing to the development of the bourgeoisie, to freedom of commerce, to the world market, to uniformity in the mode of production, and in the conditions of life corresponding thereto.
>
> The supremacy of the proletariat will cause them to vanish still faster. . . . In proportion as the antagonism between classes within the nation vanishes, the hostility of one nation to another will come to an end.[9]

What 1848 means in the history of Marxism is well known. What is remembered less well, however, is that 1848 marked the first major confrontation between communism and nationalism. Marx did not equally oppose all nationalist demands. He supported a revolutionary unification of Germany, and he supported the national causes of the Poles and Hungarians, viewing the Poles as revolutionary Europe's defense against Russian despotism and "barbarism." But he regarded as absolutely reactionary the aspirations to autonomous nationhood put forward by the representatives of the so-called "nonhistoric" nations.[10]

The principal spokesman for the nonhistoric nations was František Palacký, "the father of the Czech nation," who proved that the Czechs *did* have a history, and whom Marx called "a German professor gone mad." According to Marx, the future of the Czechs lay in their incorporation into the German nation; the Slovaks and Croats were to become Hungarian, and the Ruthenes (Ukrainians) of Austria's Galicia were to become Polish. *The Communist Manifesto* envisioned a world without national conflicts and differences; Palacký proposed to increase the number of nations. Delegates from new and old nations met in Prague in 1848 at the Slavonic Congress.[11] The Congress issued a document, a nationalist manifesto, announcing the right of all nationalities, large and small, to live freely in the family of nations.

In 1848 the Ruthenes defined themselves as a distinct nationality, refusing to belong any longer to the "historic" and nonethnic Polish nation. This was not the first time that the Ruthenes came to the attention of the founders of "scientific socialism." That occurred in 1846 in connection with the so-called "Galician massacres," an event that was misleadingly attributed to the Ruthene subjects of the Polish nobility; hundreds of members of the Polish nobility were slaughtered after a group of Polish revolutionary noblemen in Cracow launched an insurrection against Austria. The massacres actually took place in purely Polish parts of *Western* Galicia and were carried out by Polish peasants. However, since the 1840s, it has somehow seemed easier to explain social conflict by pointing to "ethnic" differences, as we are now witnessing in Bosnia. This particular "ethnic" legend has enjoyed a secure life. No Polish historian upholds this narrative, but it is alive and well in textbooks and even in Western academic writing on the Habsburg monarchy today.[12]

One of the main goals of the Ruthene activities in 1848 was to become accepted as a distinct Slavic nationality. Until the revolution of 1848 the Poles generally believed, as did most politically aware Ruthenes, that the Ruthenes were Polish. The peasants in Eastern Galicia spoke a dialect different from that spoken by the peasants of Western Galicia, but nationhood was considered a matter of politics not ethnography. In 1848 the Ruthenes declared that not only were they not Polish but their nationality was not confined to the Austrian Empire: Their conationals, the Ruthene Main Council proclaimed, also lived in the southern part of the Russian Empire, and their homeland extended as far east as the Don River. This meant that while they were not Polish they were also not Russian.

This background note explains what Namier had in mind when he

viewed the inclusion of the Ukrainian parts of the Austrian provinces of
Galicia and Bukovina in the Soviet Union in 1939–1945 as an example
of how the agendas of 1848 were being implemented throughout the
subsequent hundred years. It also helps us see why during the decades
following 1945 the successors of the Ruthenes of 1848 would want to
complete their dissociation from Warsaw with a dissociation from
Moscow.

Soviet Communism: New Civilization or the Old Empire under New Management?

After World War I, two of the three great empires (the Habsburg and the Ottoman) of Eastern and Southeastern Europe ceased to
exist. But, as Ernest Gellner writes, "something quite different happened
in the third empire. It recovered from its military defeat of 1917 and
reemerged by 1920, under entirely new political and ideological management."[13]

It is hard to find a lucid and convincing answer not so much to why
Russia of all places adopted Marxism (in its Russified form) as its official
creed in 1917, but rather why its leaders persuaded themselves that their
country was to be the model for the world. Why did they remain committed to that "international" perspective when Moscow supposedly returned to Russian nationalism in Stalin's time, and even later?

Richard Pipes agrees with those writers, like Paul Miliukov, who
viewed Bolshevism as both international and "genuinely Russian."[14] It
is not essential for our purposes to consider whether Stalin's rule was a
faithful continuation of Lenin's. What concerns us is that in the end the
Soviet model, whatever kind of a combination of communism and empire it may have represented, became "the future that failed," to cite the
title of Johann P. Arnason's book on this subject. Arnason's approach is
especially valuable for our discussion because he explores the connection
between the communist project, the empire, and Russian and other nationalisms:

> Imperial Russia had proved capable of assimilating or initiating mod-
> ernizing processes in various areas, but incapable of moulding them
> into a viable version of modernity. The regime which inherited its frag-
> ments had to develop a new pattern of integration. More specifically,
> its main task was to restructure and unify the economic, political and

cultural patterns of social life; each of the three factors had . . . had its share in the terminal crisis of the imperial order. The result was undeniably a new counterparadigm of modernity, arguably the most important of its kind. But if it brought the imperial order back to life in a new shape, it also—as we now know—reactivated its self-destructive dynamic.[15]

After 1989–1991, if not in 1980, 1968, or 1956, it became obvious that Sovietism had failed to become a viable alternative to the Western model of modernity. It failed to impress Eastern Europe as the promise of a higher civilization. The nations of Eastern Europe had their own tradition of Marxism, which gave them an alternative reading of Marx to that upheld in Moscow. Soviet communism even failed to help solve the problems of Eastern Europe inherited from the past—especially that of the nationalities. Instead of bringing Eastern Europe up to its standards, Soviet expansion into Europe facilitated the exposure of its own society to influences from abroad. In other words, the communist model's failure within the Soviet Union was accelerated by the territorial expansion of the Soviet Union. In a polity that included the Balts and West Ukrainians, it was difficult to sustain the official position that the Russian element was the most advanced.

In the final stage of the decline of Sovietism, Russian nationalism emerged and won wide support by defining Russia as distinct from and opposed to the Soviet communism that won power in Russia in 1917. Russians are facing the dual task of coming to terms with the legacy of the communist "counterparadigm of modernity" and their imperial legacy. These two issues are not easily separated, although the difference is clear enough. The question remains: Will Russia be able to distance itself from the empire?

Communist Heirs of the Romanovs in the Realm of the Habsburgs

The future that the Soviets had in mind for those whom they liberated from Hitler was a future constructed by Moscow designers. East Central Europe in its Leninist-Stalinist version was perceived as a *Russian* product. By 1945 these nations had considerable experience in nation-building and state-building, however imperfect their record may have been. Most of the inhabitants felt that their way of life and their

ideas of a better life were preferable to the Soviet model. Even indigenous communists thought the Soviet model to be inapplicable to the
conditions of Poland, Czechoslovakia, or Hungary. They were proud of
their own revolutionary tradition and experience. Central and Eastern
European socialism before 1917 had produced brilliant thinkers in the
fields of sociology, economics, history, law, and nationalities studies.[16]
Eastern Europe had a rich tradition of labor organization and socialist
politics, and it continued into the period between the two world wars.
Why should the East Europeans have been impressed by Stalin's interpretation of Marxism or the practice of socialism that they saw in 1945?
For them, the notion that Stalinist Russia was the image of their—and
the world's—future appeared preposterous.

As for the future of nations and states, the East Europeans were for
understandable reasons especially reluctant to accept the Soviet Marxist
position on the subject. The idea of "withering away" or the "merger"
of nations did not have many supporters, even among the communists.
The tradition of Austro-Marxism was especially original in this area, as
was the contribution of the main strands of Polish socialism, whether
that was tied to the more nationalistically minded Polish Socialist Party
(PPS) or to the "internationalist" Social Democracy of the Kingdom of
Poland and of Lithuania (SDKPiL), which maintained closer ties with
the Russian revolutionary movement. The Bolsheviks embraced the
most literal interpretation of *The Communist Manifesto* on the future
of nations and languages, even when in practice, as in the 1920s, they
were tolerant of linguistic and ethnic diversity. The Soviets were promoting "the building of socialism" in Eastern Europe as it was understood
in Moscow but they had no special understanding of the conditions prevailing in East Central Europe, and their ideology offered little guidance.

Whether Moscow wanted it or even knew it, as the paramount
power in the region it inherited the mantle of the Habsburgs. The Soviet
Union and its communist friends in the Balkans became involved in issues that were a legacy of the Ottoman-Habsburg struggle. This historical link was noted by the British historian A.J.P. Taylor, a disciple of
Namier. In a book dedicated to Namier, Taylor spoke about post-1945
Czechoslovakia and Yugoslavia as legatees of the Habsburgs:

> Only a Communist Slovakia would preserve the unity of Czechoslova-
> kia; the price would be the ruin of Czechoslovak democracy. Faced
> with unwelcome alternatives, the Czechs used once more the method

of delay which they learnt from the Habsburgs; and hoped that industry and education might in time create in Slovakia a humanistic middle class, which would make Masaryk's Idea a reality.[17]

While Taylor's expectations about the future of Czechoslovakia were not high, and his fears were vindicated in the post-1989 years, he expected Yugoslavia to do much better. He thought that the joint struggle of Serbs and Croats in "the great partisan war" against the Germans "made Yugoslavia, as the Franco-German war of 1870 made Germany." For several reasons, it seemed to Taylor that Tito just might do a better job than the Habsburgs had been able to do:

> "Democratic, federal Yugoslavia" translated into practice the great might-have-been of Habsburg history. Marshal Tito was the last of the Habsburgs: ruling over eight different nations, he offered them "cultural autonomy" and reined in their nationalist hostility. . . . There was no longer a "people of state" [i.e., an officially-designated ruling nation]; the new rulers were men of any nationality who accepted the Communist idea. More fortunate than the Habsburgs, Marshal Tito found an "idea." Only time will show whether social revolution and economic betterment can appease national conflicts and whether Marxism can do better than Counter-Reformation dynasticism in supplying central Europe with a common loyalty.[18]

"Time" did show: Taylor's question was answered forty years later.

According to Namier, in World War II the South Slavs completed their 1848 agenda when the last of the lands they claimed were removed from Italian rule. Likewise, the Ruthenes completed their 1848 agenda when their historic relation to Poland ended. But from the current perspective one might raise a question that Namier did not ask: Might this "Western" extension of a Belgrade-dominated Yugoslavia on the one hand and a Moscow-dominated Soviet Union on the other have weakened Belgrade's (i.e., Serbia's) position versus the Slovenes and Croats in Yugoslavia just as it undermined Russia's traditional relationship with Ukraine? Tito's and Stalin's triumphs of 1945 may have contributed, then, to the process of disintegration that we saw in the 1980s. In both cases the inclusion into the older geographical and political structure of once-Habsburg possessions changed the traditional ethnocultural balance in the older states.

In addition to becoming after 1917 the heir or legatee of the empire of the Romanovs, the Soviet Union became in 1945 a legatee of another prenational dynastic state. At this time, imperial Austria's Eastern Galicia, which had been under Polish rule from 1919 until 1939, northern Bukovina, which had been under Romanian rule from 1918 until 1940, and Czechoslovakia's Ruthenia, which had been a part of Habsburg Hungary until 1918, were brought into the Ukrainian Soviet Socialist Republic. Thus, the Soviet Union also became a successor state of the Habsburgs.

One somehow feels that the dominant position of the Russian element in the Soviet Union, and with it the unity of the state, would have been much more secure without the annexation of Western Ukraine and the reannexation of the Baltic states. In the end, it appears that not only the Yugoslav and the Czech communists but also their Soviet comrades shared the Habsburgs' fate. Gorbachev, not Tito, would prove to be "the last of the Habsburgs."

Domestic Impact of External Expansion: From Little Russia to a Greater Ukraine

Sometime in the 1850s, while living in exile in London, the Russian revolutionary Alexander Herzen wrote that by making Poland a part of the Russian Empire tsarism had opened a gate, extending widely from the Vistula to the Dnieper, for the influx of revolutionary ideas into Russia. With Poland *inside* the empire, said Herzen, there would no longer be a barrier to keep Russia separate from "Europe."

There was truth in Herzen's assessment, but it may well be that the Stalinist annexations of 1939 to 1945 and the introduction of Soviet-style regimes in the formally independent states of East Central Europe, especially Poland, had an even greater impact on the interethnic relations, and domestic situation in general, within the Soviet Union.[19]

The Soviet Union's war-related annexations in Europe were of two kinds: First, the Soviets "recovered" much of what their predecessors had held in 1914, before the war and revolution. And second, they acquired wholly new lands and peoples.

There is no way to prove that the Soviet Union would have been more stable domestically or that the leading role of the Russian element would have been more secure if Stalin had resisted the annexation of those lands. How does one measure the disruptive or subversive role of the Balts? How much tougher to deal with did the Ukrainian problem become after 1939?

Gellner noted an important difference within the Soviet Union:

> In the Soviet Union, generally speaking there is a difference between the so-called seventy-year-old and the forty-year-old areas of Soviet power: there is a perceptible difference between the areas that have been parts of the union ever since the Revolution, and those that were incorporated in it only at the end of the Second World War. The difference between seventy and forty years seems to affect the nature of social memory profoundly: the forty-year-ers have a sharp sense of what the other world is like, and the seventy-year-ers have largely lost it. They know no other.[20]

It needs to be added that the "forty-year-ers" consisted of two different types. In one group were the Balts, the West Belorussians, some of the West Ukrainians, and the population of Bessarabia, now known as Moldova. Although they did not come under Soviet rule until World War II, they or their parents had lived under tsarist Russia long before the Bolsheviks came to power. This tsarist past did not, however, make them more willing to accept the return of the Russians in 1940; their memories of independence between the two world wars were ineradicable. For some Russians, on the other hand, 1940 marked a restoration of normality in the Baltic region. Might this not help explain why so many Russians made Riga their home after 1945, thus turning Latvians into a minority in their own capital?

The second group of "forty-year-ers" was comprised of the once Polish Galicia, the once Romanian Bukovina, and the once Czechoslovak "Carpathian Ruthenia." Their connection to Russia was limited exclusively to the Soviet era. They first got to know Russian rule only in its "advanced" Stalinist form after the Great Terror of the 1930s. Their imperial experience had been under the Habsburgs.[21]

For Galician Ukrainians the central national problem was Poland, which considered all of Galicia Polish. When, in November 1918, the Ukrainians of the Habsburg monarchy proclaimed their independence, their "West Ukrainian People's Republic" found itself at war with Poland.

The West Ukrainian Republic regarded itself as a temporary formation; its goal was the unification of Western Ukraine with the Ukrainian state in Kyiv, which, when the West was fighting the Poles, was engaged in a two-front struggle with both the Red and the White Russians and their respective sympathizers in Ukraine. In January 1919, the two

Ukraines solemnly proclaimed their unification. But this was a declaration only. By the end of 1920, when peace was established in Eastern Europe, Moscow was in charge of Eastern Ukraine, although it legitimated its rule there by creating the "Ukrainian Soviet Socialist Republic."

By the summer of 1919, after a bitter and brutal war, the Poles had won control of Galicia. On June 25, 1919, in Paris, the Supreme Council of the Allied Powers, which was then deciding the future of the peoples of the Habsburg monarchy, authorized the Polish occupation of Eastern Galicia. Namier, who during the war had worked for the British government and was directly involved in the Galician question, commented on the decision:

> They [the Ukrainians] strove hard to be a proper government. But a peasant nation exasperated by centuries of oppression and fighting for its life against landowners—and the foreign domination for which they stand—cannot be expected to show superhuman self-control. My father was always on the Polish side and known to be closely involved with the Polish nobility. The wave of cruel reprisals could hardly bypass him. But the responsibility rests with the Polish jingoes and those Allied statesmen who, lacking adequate energy, bungled. The last decision of the Peace Congress foredooms worse to come. All the massacres in Macedonia will seem as nothing compared with those coming to Eastern Galicia.
>
> For all my personal loss and anxieties I do insist that grievous wrong has been done to the Ukrainians. Left in peace to establish a strongly radical but decent government, they might well have organized themselves. Driven to despair, insidiously pushed forward daily toward bolshevism and into committing atrocious crimes, they know that a Polish military occupation, as foreshadowed in the Foreign Ministers' decision of 25 June, means disaster without end. And I insist that no number of atrocities however horrible can deprive a nation of its right to independence, nor justify its being put under the heel of its worst enemies and persecutors.[22]

In 1923, the Allies recognized Poland's full sovereignty over Eastern Galicia, Warsaw having promised to grant autonomy to the region. For most Ukrainians who had found themselves in Poland against their wishes, the Polish state lacked the legitimacy that they had recognized in Vienna. During World War II, Namier's premonition of things "worse to come" proved to be right to a degree nobody could have imagined in 1919.[23]

When the Soviets invaded Poland in September 1939 and incorpo-rated this region into the Soviet Union, they added to their state a for-merly Habsburg land with a political and cultural experience alien to that of tsarist Russia and the Soviet Union. It is very unlikely that Sta-lin—or his successors—imagined that this territorial gain would prove to be a time bomb. Stalin's actions had three closely related conse-quences that remain politically important today. First, Stalin put an end to the historic relationship between Poland and Ukraine under which Ukraine, or parts of Ukraine, belonged to Poland. In the middle of the seventeenth century virtually all Ukrainians, even those to the east of the Dnieper, lived under the Polish-Lithuanian Commonwealth. Then Poland's retreat began—and Russia started taking Poland's command-ing place. Austrian Galicia had been the first Ukrainian-inhabited area to find itself under Polish kings—uninterruptedly from the middle of the fourteenth century until 1772, and then, after the Habsburg intermis-sion, it remained under Polish rule from 1919 until 1939.

The long-term effects of Poland's withdrawal from its historic entan-glements in the East led to a change in the perception of "the Polish factor" in Ukraine, Belorussia, and Lithuania; their main preoccupation after the war was surviving Russian domination. The Poles, too, saw the new possibilities that the geopolitical change gave them. Despite tradi-tional Lithuanian suspicions of Polish motives, the Polish public gave its wholehearted support to the Lithuanian struggle. It is not an accident that Poland was the first nation to recognize Ukraine's independence—one day after the referendum of December 1, 1991.[24] Namier could not have anticipated the events of the 1980s and 1990s. Poland, Ukraine's "historic enemy," was transformed into, at least potentially, an ally whose support would be especially helpful when facing Russia, now left alone in the role of Ukraine's "constituting other."[25]

Second, by eliminating Poland as one of the powers with which Rus-sia had divided its rule over Ukraine, Stalin laid the foundation for a change in the traditional relationship between Ukrainians and Russians. As the Ukrainian contemporary poet Lina Kostenko put it, by combin-ing in one entity what the Poles called "Little Poland" with what the Russians called "Little Russia," Stalin made a "Greater Ukraine."

Finally, Stalin left the Ukrainians a problem that they are facing still. They could do little about it when the Soviet Union existed but they must address it now. Stalin's successors failed to work out a modus vivendi with a Ukraine enlarged in size and population, and thus qualitatively transformed. Will an independent Ukraine hold together in one nation and one state its disparate regions left over from the Romanovs and the Soviets, from the Habsburgs, and from the Poles, Hungarians, Czechs, and Romanians? If Gorbachev failed in his role as "the last of the Habsburgs," will Ukraine's President Leonid M. Kravchuk escape the fate of being a Ukrainian Gorbachev? Cultural and political movements in Ukraine since Stalin may be understood properly only in terms of a common Ukrainian identity that transcends old imperial borders. It took Eastern and Western Ukraine, acting in accord, to win independence and to avoid internal strife—ethnic, religious, or regional. But questions of national identity and unity remain, and they are inextricably tied to the legacy of communism. This essay began by insisting that when speaking about communism one needs to think about empire and nationalism. It is also necessary to think about communism and Sovietism when discussing the making of nations. Many of the problems Ukraine faces today—economic, legal, moral, social, environmental, or ecological—are legacies of the Soviet system, Soviet institutions, and Soviet values. It is on these issues that Ukrainians are divided today.

In Ukraine, the division between those who are basically for the Soviet system (or for what they think they remember the Soviet system to have been) and those who want to move away from Sovietism toward "Europe" is expressed geographically, with the Eastern industrial regions voting communist. It may even assume an ethnic form (i.e., of a Ukrainian-Russian split) if communists are successful in establishing themselves as spokesmen of the Russians and/or the "Russian-speaking population."[26]

Russia after Communism; Russia after Empire?

Relations between Ukrainians and Russians in Ukraine and interstate relations between Ukraine and Russia will directly influence Russia's political evolution. Zbigniew Brzezinski argues that "without Ukraine, Russia ceases to be an empire, but with Ukraine suborned and then subordinated, Russia automatically becomes an empire." But if Russia becomes an empire, it cannot also be a democracy.[27]

Russian attitudes toward Ukraine will depend on the perception of the Ukrainian situation. Signs suggest that the import of the events summarized here has not penetrated the consciousness of the Russian public or of the policymakers in Moscow. Many continue to view Ukraine in traditionally narrow terms as an internal problem, as the question of "Little Russians" versus "Great Russians," a family dispute. They are quite unaware of the transformation of Ukraine that occurred as a consequence of its changed geopolitical and geocultural location after 1939, and they overlook the fact that many Ukrainians view themselves as European, which places Ukraine, at least in part, outside the traditionally Russian-dominated world.

Communism existed for more than seventy years in Russia and, whether Marx or Russian history played the more important role in shaping the system, communism will forever remain a part of Russian history. For decades, Sovietism was a way of being Russian politically. Russia interacted with the communist Eastern Europe and with Western Europe under the guise of the Soviet Union, and it was as the Soviet Union that Russia was known throughout the world. Today, Russia has a dual agenda: how to deal with communism, and how to deal with empire.

To what extent does Ukraine's departure undermine Russia's claim to leadership in the post-Soviet geopolitical space? What can postcommunist Russia offer the former republics now that they have become sovereign states?

Among those Western observers who never forgot the importance of Ukraine for Russia's imperial status, Hélène Carrère d'Encausse has been one of the most prominent. In her book, *The End of the Soviet Empire: The Triumph of the Nations*, she argued that Ukraine "is little tempted by the union [with Russia] and envisions a future of independence and rapprochement with the countries of Central Europe and even the European Economic Community. The Ukrainians ask: 'Are we, with 50 million citizens, less worthy than Hungary or Czechoslovakia of being considered a large European country?' "[28] Ukraine's independence, she continued, would have profound consequences for Russia's future. Without Ukraine and Belarus to support it, Russia would find it extremely difficult to confront the large (60 million) "Muslim bloc" in the former Soviet Union. This would be difficult for demographic, economic, psychological, and political reasons: "Russia wishes to be European, and the Muslim periphery is rapidly 're-Islamizing' itself, underscoring its distinctiveness from and opposition to Russia. . . . Without the support of the Ukrainians and Belorussians, the encounter between

Russians and Muslims would have the huge drawback for Russia of drawing it into the 'oriental' and even Asiatic destiny that throughout its history it has wished to escape."[29]

This is not quite the case. There has always been a school of thought in Russia which has held that Russia is special in being European and Asian at the same time, in other words, Eurasian. But Eurasianism is definitely a minority opinion in today's Russia. The intelligentsia of Moscow and St. Petersburg certainly favors a European Russia.

The surest way for Russia to be European and democratic is for it to accept the newly independent nations of former Soviet Central Asia as equals, instead of keeping them in a Russian imperial framework. This will remove the need for Ukrainian help in ruling them. Accepting Ukraine's independence will allow Russia to avoid resorting to the violence which would be required for the reconquest of Ukraine. A Russia friendly with both Ukraine and Central Asia would remain a great power with a global presence and at the same time would be able to deal with the problems inherited from the communist era.

Notes

1. Martin Malia, *The Soviet Tragedy: A History of Socialism in Russia, 1917–1991* (New York: Macmillan, 1994), and John Lukacs, *The End of the Twentieth Century and the End of the Modern Age* (New York: Ticknor and Fields, 1993).

2. Lukacs, *The End of the Twentieth Century*, p. 1.

3. Ibid., p. 5.

4. Benedict Anderson, *Imagined Communities: Reflections on the Origin and Spread of Nationalism,* rev. ed. (London and New York: Verso, 1991), p. 2.

5. Daniel Yergin and Thane Gustafson, *Russia 2010—And What It Means for the World* (New York: Random House, 1993), p. 4.

6. The life and career of Thomas G. Masaryk illustrate that transition from belief in empire toward the goal of national independence. Masaryk's road to nationalism is discussed in Roman Szporluk, *The Political Thought of T. G. Masaryk* (Boulder, Colo.: East European Monographs, 1981).

7. Sir Lewis Namier, *Vanished Supremacies* (New York: Harper Torchbooks, 1963), p. 28.

8. Lukacs, *The End of the Twentieth Century*, p. 6.

9. Karl Marx and Friedrich Engels, *The Communist Manifesto*, ed. Samuel H. Beer (New York: Appleton-Century-Crofts, 1955), p. 29.

10. In the language of the time, a nationality without an independent state bearing its name and lacking a traditional elite was a nonhistoric nation. The Poles were recognized as "historic," while the Czechs, the Slovaks, and the Ruthenes were not.

11. Lawrence D. Orton, *The Prague Slav Congress of 1848* (Boulder, Colo.: East European Monographs, 1978). See also Jan Kozik, *The Ukrainian National Movement in Galicia, 1815–1849,* ed. Lawrence D. Orton, trans. Andrew Gorski and Lawrence D. Orton (Edmonton: Canadian Institute of Ukrainian Studies, 1986).

12. For the 1846 legend and a general discussion of Marx and Engels' view on the Ukrainian-Polish relations in Austria, see Roman Rosdolsky, *Engels and the "Nonhistoric" Peoples: The National Question in the Revolution of 1848,* trans. and ed., John-Paul Himka (Glasgow: Critique Books, 1986), pp. 56–78.

13. Ernest Gellner, "Ethnicity and Faith in Eastern Europe," *Daedalus* 119, no. 1 (Winter 1990): 291–92.

14. Richard Pipes, *Russia under the Bolshevik Regime* (New York: Knopf, 1993), p. 503.

15. Johann P. Arnason, *The Future That Failed: Origin and Destinies of the Soviet Model* (London and New York: Routledge, 1993), pp. 87–88.

16. See Leszek Kolakowski, *Main Currents of Marxism. Its Rise, Growth, and Dissolution,* vol. 2 (Oxford: Clarendon Press, 1978).

17. A.J.P. Taylor, *The Habsburg Monarchy, 1809–1918* (Chicago and London: University of Chicago Press, 1976), p. 260.

18. Ibid., pp. 260–61.

19. See Roman Szporluk, ed., *The Influence of Eastern Europe and the Soviet West on the USSR* (New York, Washington, London: Praeger, 1975).

20. Gellner, "Ethnicity and Faith in Eastern Europe," p. 283.

21. "Roman Szporluk, "The Soviet West—Or Far Eastern Europe?," *East European Politics and Societies* 3, no. 3 (Fall 1991): 466–82. [Included as chapter 9 in this book.] The role of the Balts in the subversion and eventual collapse of the Soviet Empire is presented by Anatol Lieven, *The Baltic Revolution: Estonia, Latvia, Lithuania, and the Path to Independence* (New Haven, Conn.: Yale University Press, 1993).

22. Julia Namier, *Lewis Namier: A Biography* (Oxford: Oxford University Press, 1971), p. 144.

23. This tragic subject, which many Ukrainians are reluctant to face fully even today, has been recently treated by the distinguished Warsaw historian Ryszard Torzecki. See Ryszard Torzecki, *Polacy i Ukraińcy: Sprawa ukraińska w czasie II wojny światowej na terenie II Rzeczypospolitej* (Warsaw: Wydawnictwo Naukowe PWN, 1993). Torzecki has dealt with the Ukrainian question in the policies of the Third Reich in Ryszard Torzecki, *Kwestia ukraińska w polityce III Rzeszy, 1933–1945* (Warsaw: Ksiaażka i Wiedza, 1972), and with

Polish-Ukrainian relations in post-1918 Poland in *Kwestia ukraińska w Polsce w latach 1923–1929* (Cracow: Wydawnictwo Literackie, 1989). For a study of the Polish-Ukrainian war of 1918–1919, see Maciej Kozłowski, *Między Sanem a Zbruczem. Walki o Lwów i Galicję Wschodnią, 1918–1919* (Cracow: Znak, 1990).

24. As an illustration of the new cooperative spirit in Polish-Ukrainian relations, let us cite Bohdan Cywiński, noted Polish author and civic activist, who wrote an article describing today's Ukraine as "A Fortress under Siege." Cywiński attended a conference in Kyiv held at the recently restored "Kyiv-Mohyla Academy." The Academy bears the name of Petro Mohyla, a Romanian prince by birth, later a Polish soldier and then an Orthodox monk, whom Ukrainians consider one of their great historical figures. As Metropolitan of Kyiv, in the first half of the seventeenth century, when Kyiv and most of Ukraine was governed from Warsaw, he founded a school which later became a college. It was eventually liquidated by the tsarist government. In the newly independent Ukraine the Academy has been revived as an independent college. Among other things it is a reminder to the Kyivans of their city's past Western ties. Cywiński was especially touched when told that as a visiting professor the next year he would be welcome to lecture in Polish. He summed up his impressions with the words: "It feels good now to be Polish in Kyiv." Bohdan Cywiński, "Oblężona twierdza," *Rzeczpospolita*, 12–13, March 1994. Commemorating the 350th anniversary of its founding (1632), *Harvard Ukrainian Studies* published in June 1984 a special issue entitled "The Kiev Mohyla Academy." For an introduction to Poland's current *Ostpolitik*, see Ian J. Brzezinski, "Polish-Ukrainian Relations: Europe's Neglected Strategic Axis," *Survival* 35, no. 3 (Autumn 1993): 26–37; Stephen R. Burant, "International Relations in a Regional Context: Poland and Its Eastern Neighbours—Lithuania, Belarus, Ukraine," *Europe-Asia Studies* 45, no. 3 (1993): 395–418; and Stephen R. Burant and Voytek Zubek, "Eastern Europe's Old Memories and New Realities: Resurrecting the Polish-Lithuanian Union," *East European Politics and Societies* 7, no. 2 (1993): 370–99.

25. See Iver B. Neumann, "Russia as Central Europe's Constituting Other," *East European Politics and Societies* 7, no. 2 (1993): 349–69.

26. On the connection between communism and ethnicity in Ukraine today, see Roman Szporluk, "Reflections on Ukraine after 1994: The Dilemmas of Nationhood," *Harriman Review*, May 1994. (Included as chapter 13 of this book.)

27. Zbigniew Brzezinski, "The Premature Partnership," *Foreign Affairs* 73, no. 2 (March-April 1994): 80.

28. Hélène Carrère d'Encausse, *The End of the Soviet Empire: The Triumph of the Nations* (New York: Basic Books, 1992), p. 261.

29. Ibid.

15   Ukraine: From an Imperial Periphery to a Sovereign State

Ukraine's present condition and prospects are matters of concern to many who live outside that country's borders. It is, after all, one of the largest states of Europe, geographically comparable to France, with a population only slightly smaller than that of Italy. To understand the country calls for familiarity with a host of problems that stem from the Soviet period but also derive from its much longer pre-Soviet past relations with Poland and Russia. The historic relations between Ukraine and Russia in particular are too little understood, and the most common misperceptions lead to the formulation of all manner of mistaken policies. Thus, for example, one contemporary author, writing for the American quarterly *Foreign Policy*, speaks of Ukraine's future "reintegration into the greater Russian state," imagining that before 1991 Russia had been in possession of Ukraine for "nearly three and a half centuries."[1]

To consider Ukraine's normal condition to be that it is part of Russia is a major misreading of history, one that implies that its present independence is an anomaly. This essay attempts to correct such misreadings by presenting a brief sketch of the formation of the modern Ukrainian nation and state in the wider context of the formation of the modern nations of Poland and Russia. Such an approach reveals an aspect of

First published in *Daedalus*, 1997.

nationalism that is often overlooked—its international perspective and the nationalists' striving for recognition within the world community.

The emergence of a nation from the condition of province or periphery, such as the case of Ukraine in relation to Russia and Poland, may be measured by the extent to which a nation-in-the-making seeks to define itself in a broader international framework extending beyond the confines of the entity from which it is "seceding." The quest for independence is not motivated by a desire to be cut off from the world at large; on the contrary, it is driven by the wish to participate directly in the affairs of the world, not through the capital of another country but by making a capital out of one's own central place. To have standing in the world, even in such matters as sports, music, or science, requires political independence.

The making of modern Ukraine accordingly needs to be viewed in an international context. The first Russian nation-builders wanted the Ukrainians to be Russian; Polish nation-builders wanted "their" Ukrainians to be Polish. The national identity of modern Ukrainians was formulated by those who, in defining Ukraine, rejected both the Russian identity and the Polish identity. But while the Ukrainians made themselves by defining themselves as distinct, and thus "seceding," from Russia and Poland, the Russians and the Poles also formed their own modern identities in a confrontation with, and in relation to, their "Other," the West.[2] Thus, those powers involved in the history of Ukraine—St. Petersburg, Warsaw, Istanbul—confronted the realization that while they commanded a position of supremacy vis-à-vis their respective "Ukraines," they remained in an unequal relationship to the West, to Europe, to "civilization"—which, indeed, viewed *them* as peripheries (or, we may say, "Ukraines").[3] In sum, then, the Ukrainian nation-building project was nothing more nor less than an undertaking to transform the peripheries of several nations, which themselves were civilizational peripheries of the West, into a sovereign entity able to communicate directly with the larger world—with what were seen in the nineteenth century, and even more in the twentieth, to be the centers of modern civilization, in politics, culture and science, and economics.

Basic Facts of Historical Geography

Did Ukraine then become part of Russia three and a half centuries ago? Only a small part. Before 1648, virtually all Ukrainians lived within the Polish-Lithuanian Commonwealth, whose eastern frontier extended to the east of the Dnieper River. Only after 1667 did a part of that vast territory—today's regions of Poltava and Chernihiv with the city of Kyiv—come under rule of the tsar in Moscow. After 1667, Warsaw ruled more Ukrainian territory and more Ukrainians than did Moscow. The land to the west of the Dnieper remained within the Polish-Lithuanian Commonwealth until 1793–1795. The Polish nobility was the dominant group in the area until 1830, if not 1863, and the Poles retained great social and cultural influence until after the Russian revolutions of 1917.[4]

In the nineteenth century, whether Ukrainians lived under the rule of the tsar in St. Petersburg or the emperor in Vienna, the Polish influence remained very substantial. This was true even on the East Bank, where the Poles had lost their dominant position as early as the seventeenth century. It is impossible to understand today's Ukraine if one sees it simply as a province of Russia. The Ukrainian-Polish nexus was critical and remained so until 1939–1945. As Ivan Rudnytsky made very clear some years ago, "The entire course of the Ukrainian national revival in Galicia, from 1848 until World War I and beyond, was determined by the struggle, of ever-increasing intensity, against Polish dominance in the province."[5] Polish landowners remained a dominant presence in Galicia and Volhynia until 1939.

As for southern Ukraine, including the Crimea, conquered by the Russian Empire in the late eighteenth century from the Ottoman Turks, this region showed the continuing influence of centuries of Islamic rule. Very different was the situation in West Ukraine. The region of Transcarpathia was uninterruptedly a part of Hungary from the Middle Ages until 1919, when it was annexed to the new Czechoslovakia. It became Hungarian again from 1939 to 1944, and only after that date—for the first time ever—was it ruled from Moscow.

The Chernivtsi region—the northern part of the former Austrian province of Bukovina—was Romanian from 1918 to 1940 and became Soviet only in 1940, being formally incorporated into the Soviet Union after 1944. As for the present regions of Lviv, Ternopil, and Ivano-Frankivsk, they were part of Poland from the middle of the fourteenth century, were annexed by Austria in 1772, and remained as eastern "Galicia" under the rule of Vienna until 1918. After a brief period of independence as the West Ukrainian People's Republic, in 1918–19, the region fell under the rule of the new Poland, becoming Soviet only when that state was destroyed by the armies of Nazi Germany and Soviet Russia. After Hitler's invasion of the Soviet Union, Galicia came under German occupation, returning to Soviet rule in 1944. It has uninterruptedly been a part of Ukraine since then, under Soviet domination until 1991, part of an independent Ukraine today.

It is obvious that today's Ukraine cannot be viewed simply as a part of a historic Russian or modern Soviet space; Ukraine is intimately linked not only to Russia but also to the countries of Central Europe and the Black Sea region. It was only toward the end of the nineteenth century that the people now known as Ukrainians began to call themselves "Ukrainian" and their homeland "Ukraine." Before that, they were variously known as Ruthenians in Austria, Rusnaks in Hungary, or Little Russians (or Cossacks) in the Russian Empire. The decision to adopt the Ukrainian name for a people living under several different jurisdictions and to consider all the lands where those people lived as one country, Ukraine, had nothing to do with that newly imagined country being a "borderland" of anyplace—a literal meaning of the term "Ukraine," common both in Polish and Russian parlance for centuries. Ukraine came to designate a geographical space extending from the land of the Don Cossacks to the northern counties of Hungary, from the mouth of the Danube to points north of Sumy and Kharkiv. Even a casual glance at the map of Europe will show that such a vast territory could not be the "borderland" or "periphery" of anything. The fact is that for the new and large country they invented—it existed only in their heads—the originators and first promoters of "Ukraine" defiantly adopted the very name that denied them the dignity of a nation. This putting together of all the "Ukraines" was completed by 1945—or by 1954, if we count the time when Ukraine gained one of Ottoman Turkey's former "Ukraines," Crimea. It was then that Ukraine became a single entity, with a center of its own. If these facts are too little known, one other myth about the origin of the nation ought to be mentioned. In the view of many, Ukrainian nationalism was first formulated in Galicia, under Austrian rule, and then spread gradually to the East, to Russian Ukraine. While the Austrian influence was indeed great—giving the Austrian "Ruthenians" a unique exposure to modern government and law, and facilitating their international recognition as belonging to the community of Slavic people—the idea that they were not Ruthenians but part of a larger Ukrainian nation was first formulated in the East, in Russia, and not in Austria. It was to that Ukraine that Austria's Ruthenians decided, after long and careful reflection, that they wished to belong. They never believed that they constituted the core of Ukraine even though, owing to more favorable conditions, they claimed to play a leading role in the national movement in the twentieth century.

Nation Formation: Some General Observations

What Is a Nation?

To understand the problems involved in Ukrainian nation-formation, it helps to draw on theoretical and historical literature on nationalism, beginning with such basic questions as what a "nation" is and how it comes into being. For these purposes, Benedict Anderson's excellent formula is invaluable. Anderson argues that a nation is an "imagined community"—not an imaginary community—that is both inherently "limited and sovereign."[6] Nationalism accomplishes three things: It "nationalizes" a people by separating them from others, by vesting in them the right of national self-determination; it constructs a national history by attributing national ideas to individuals who lived in the prenational age; and it nationalizes territory, designating a certain space as the property of the nation, the boundaries of the homeland. As for typology of nations, Liah Greenfeld has provided a very useful set of definitions in her *Nationalism: Five Roads to Modernity*. Greenfeld argues that modern nations—with the exception of the English, who formed the first modern nation—were all created through confrontation with other nations. For example, modern national consciousness in Russia, she says, was formed as the West impressed itself upon Russian consciousness and on government policies. This happened during and after the reign of Peter the Great. "The West was an integral, indelible part of the Russian *national* consciousness. There simply would be no sense in being a nation if the West did not exist."[7]

Nations, so understood, are a very modern phenomenon. The nation could be defined as a community of people living within a specific territory—this was the prevailing definition of nation in the West—or as a community of language and culture, which became the way of defining nations in Central and Eastern Europe. This modern understanding of nation subordinated class, economic condition, social status, and religion to nationality. Vesting sovereignty in the nation gave nationalism its revolutionary character, subversive toward the old authority of the monarchy, derived from religion. Modern nations were unimaginable without ideas of popular sovereignty. Creating national identities included deciding on the status and future of what in the process of nation-construction would come to be termed subnational identities. What is subnational to one nation or nationalism is, needless to say, national or protonational to others. What is a full-fledged language to one nation's nationalist is a regional dialect to another nation's adherent. Thus, in modern nation-states it is common for only one language to be treated as national (or "standard"), taught in the schools, used in the public sphere.

In the history of modern nation-formation in Europe several ways of treating internal cultural-linguistic-ethnic differences have been followed. In France, for example, there was a tendency to impose one language as official and "national," and accordingly to reduce in status, by coercion if necessary, all the others to the rank of dialects. The leaders of Germany, recognizing how politically fragmented it was when it entered the modern era, could not see their way to imposing such uniformity. Prudently, they tolerated linguistic variations, though only within a broadly defined family of "German" speech, institutions, and traditions. In Britain, yet another strategy was followed. According to Linda Colley, the British nation was created above the existing national identities—English, Scottish, and Welsh. Without denying them their nationhood or eliminating their institutions—England, Scotland, and Wales did not cease to exist—new common bonds were created against a common external "Other."[8]

Periodization

This essay takes a view rather different from that advanced by Miroslav Hroch, another distinguished scholar of nation-formation. Hroch's schema of the formation of the so-called small nations has enjoyed wide international recognition.[9] He treats the formation of a modern nation as an internal process generated by social and economic change, the transition from feudalism to capitalism, in which a given ethnic group or "small nation"—whose existence is assumed as a point of departure—is seen to pass through the academic and the cultural, reaching finally to the political stage of development, as a consequence or reflection of the rise of capitalist society. In the first stage, the main actors are scholars who gather material about the nation's history and give shape to its narrative. This initial stage is followed by the "cultural stage," in which the narrative takes on significance as a means of facilitating growing awareness of a unifying culture; and this in due course is succeeded by the final, political stage, in which the idea of national identity seeks political expression.

In this essay I regard nation-building and nationalism as political *ab initio*—even when those engaged in nationalist activities denied any political intent or meaning, or insisted that their sole object was a scholarly understanding of popular culture, folklore, or local history. Such a view is grounded in an understanding of power as something political not only in the classic formulation (that is, a monopoly on the legitimate use of force); there is also economic power, as well as social and cultural power—power over the production and dissemination of symbols, values, and ideas. Beyond relations of domination or coercion we may also speak meaningfully of relations of production and distribution of material goods, or (by no means unimportantly) relations of information, of communication, and the production and dissemination of symbols, ideas, and values. Thus, "national-awakeners," questioning by virtue of their endeavors established power structures, power relationships, and the values upholding them, are quite obviously engaged in what is at least an inherently political undertaking; the impact of their work is finally to subvert the sphere of ideological domination, in which symbols and values, not identity, are the supreme instruments of social power.[10]

One Nation's Fall Is Another Nation's Rise

Hroch's approach, in the analysis presented here, does not consider that the national revival of what he terms a small nation is also an aspect of the *unmaking* of another, already existing nation. Nation-formation is thus not only an international process in the sense given it by Greenfeld (that is, a process involving sovereign states); it is also an intra-state process, as an old ("large") nation disintegrates and is reconstituted into two (or more) new nations. The epithet "new" then properly applies to the nation that retains the name of the former nation conventionally classified as old, large, or historic; for aside from the continuity of its name, such a nation becomes, in important respects, a new entity, as new as any other nation thus created. Such an approach views the process of the making of Ukraine, Slovakia, or Bohemia as an aspect of the remaking of the Polish and Russian, Hungarian, and German premodern nations respectively. We see, then, that "historic" nations, whose uninterrupted continuity is usually contrasted with the discontinuities in the history of the "small" or "unhistoric" nations, also underwent profound transformations in the modern period of nation-formation.[11] On the one hand, they were transformed by their losses, out of which new nations were formed; on the other, they expanded by integrating into the nation those social groups that had been excluded from the premodern nation.

In the formation of a new nation, a social class with a distinct ethnic-linguistic character, thought to belong to an existing nation and society, becomes transformed into a full-fledged society of all classes. In this process, its ethnic marker becomes the basis of a national language and national culture. Conversely, the process of nation-unmaking often appears at first, and is so diagnosed, as a problem of economic reform or cultural integration: This was the case, for example, when what was for some a Jewish national revival (that is, modern Jewish nation-making) was perceived by others as an "internal" social/religious problem within the Polish nation-remaking process. Theodor Herzl's assertion of the emerging Jewish identity could be voiced by other national writers in countless other cases: "I do not consider the Jewish question to be a social or religious question . . . it is a national problem. We are a nation."[12]

The Making of Ukraine

Little Russia, Great Russia, Russia

The Ukrainian case will provide a concrete example of that dialectical process in which the making, unmaking, and remaking of nations is a simultaneous and concurrent phenomenon. At the historical juncture when the Russian Empire's educated elites began to define themselves as "Russians" in the modern sense, they did so in reaction to "the West" (or "Europe"). Some other subjects of the tsar, viewed as eligible to become Russian, declined the offer of admission to the nation-in-the-making; instead they declared that if they had to define themselves in national terms—which they had not done before—they would do so as members of another nation.

One may find evidence of their reasoning in Semen Divovych's 1762 poem "A Conversation of Great Russia with Little Russia," which we may consider one of the earliest statements of the Ukrainian position. In that work, "Little Russia" patiently explained that while Little Russia and Great Russia both had the same ruler she had her own history and character and was not subordinate to, or a part of, Great Russia. On the contrary, she was the latter's equal.[13]

Here we see why it makes little sense to speak of "Ukraine" becoming part of "Russia" in the seventeenth century; the concept of a Russian state (or nation) as something distinct from the monarch's person and possessions did not then exist. This idea first emerged, as Greenfeld reminds us, only in the time of Peter the Great and was not clearly established until the reign of Catherine II. Yet when the tsar, in addition to being the autocrat of Great Russia, became the sovereign of Little Russia—as the northeastern part of Ukraine came to be called—Little Russia did not thereby become part of Russia in the modern, national sense. This Little Russia, which was a kind of a premodern or historic Ukrainian-Cossack nation, retained its own government, laws, and institutions for at least a century after its acceptance under the scepter of the tsar. The nation-building project of Russia called for the elimination of Little Russia's separate identity: but it was precisely in the final decades of Little Russia's autonomous existence that its rights began to be defended in language revealing a modern conception of nation.

The Russian Project

Before the Ukrainians put forward their national agenda, the nation-and-state-building of Russia was already under way, in ways that had ramifications for those who (in a premodern, prenational sense) we may call the Ukrainian subjects of the Empire. Especially in Catherine II's reign (1762–1796), St. Petersburg held the view that the elimination of Little Russia's traditional institutions was just one element of a larger state- and nation-building project and thus required a variety of measures, the aim of which was to achieve the complete integration of Little Russia into the Russian state and Russian society. Greenfeld notes that, curiously,

> it is possible that as much as 50 percent of this first mass of Russian nationalists were Ukrainians. In itself, this fact would not be signifi-

cant, but in Russia, which was to move steadily toward becoming one of the model *ethnic nations*, the prominence of ethnic non-Russians does indeed add a touch of irony to the story. . . . In St. Petersburg and Moscow, literally in the front ranks of the nascent Russian intelligentsia, the humble youths from Little Russia forged the Great Russian national consciousness.[14]

While Greenfeld's facts are indisputable, one must remember that the nation those Ukrainians were helping to create was at that time not a Russian ethnic nation: The imperial nation-building project did not then define the all-Russian identity simply by reference to its Great Russian ethnic component. It was rather the rise of Ukraine that later contributed to the ethnicization and "downsizing" of Russian identity, which ultimately resulted in making "Russian" a synonym for "Great Russian."

It seemed quite reasonable to the Russian imperial government and society to expect that Little Russia (which, after separating itself from Poland in the middle of the seventeenth century, had been under the tsars for more than a hundred years), as well as the more recent acquisitions of 1793–1795, would join in with the Great Russians in the making of a new, "European" Russia. Many natives of Little Russia (Ukrainians by our contemporary criteria) in fact did participate in the diverse activities we may put under the general umbrella of "nation-building" in Russia, especially in the eighteenth century.

While the same was true in the nineteenth century, it is important to note that Russian nation-building has meant quite different things at different times. In the eighteenth century and into the first half of the nineteenth, the concept of the Russian nation was still relatively open: Russia was not yet understood to mean the country of the Great Russians. Significantly, the construction of a Russian national identity included the construction of a national history, built around the idea of a state distinguished by a thousand-year-long history, which in unbroken procession connected Kyiv with Vladimir, Suzdal, Moscow, and ultimately the St. Petersburg of the tsars. In fact, this construct was first formulated in connection with Ukraine's becoming attached to Russia after 1654; the idea was that modern Russians had possessed a state of their own without interruption from the time of Kyivan Rus to the present. The corollary of this was to disinherit the Ukrainians from any claim to historic statehood and thereby deny them any future claim to independent statehood.

Even if politically expedient, such a reading of history gravely tested credulity. For several centuries prior to the union with Ukraine, official Muscovy had a very dim sense, if indeed any at all, of being the direct heir of Kyiv.[15] It was the newcomers from the South who informed the Muscovites that their state was a direct continuation of the Kyivan state. The idea that they and the Muscovites were really "Russians" performed a significant integrating function in the eighteenth century and afterwards. The Russians further embellished their "national" history by according later to the grand principality of Moscow the claim of sole, legitimate, and direct successor of Kyiv—first by invoking dynastic and religious arguments, and then, in the age of ethnic nationalism, by claiming an ethnic identity between the modern Russian nation (and its empire) and the state of Kyivan Rus, denying any legitimacy as Kyiv's heirs to other polities that functioned in the post-Kyiv space. (This served to make the Lithuanian and Polish presence in those territories illegitimate.) As ethnic nationalism intensified throughout nineteenth-century Europe, this operation was carried one step farther: The Great Russians were declared to be the real Russians, while the Ukrainians and Belorussians were viewed either as a junior branch of the Russian family or as Russians corrupted by foreign influences.

In the early phase of nation-formation the relation of "Little Russians" or of "Great Russians" to "Russians in general" had not yet been resolved. Many "Little Russians," and some "Great Russians" too, thought that what mattered most was that the Russian *narodnost'* was a member of the Slavic family and that the cultural stock of Little Russia, its songs, legends, even historical experiences, could be integrated into a common "pan-Russian" identity—the precise content of which had not yet been defined. If the imperial government promoted the "Official Nationality" idea of the Russian nation, some Russians found in Ukraine's history material with which to promote a more libertarian, anti-tsarist conception of an all-Rus Russian nation (thus the well-known interest of some of the Decembrists in Ukrainian history).

That the imperial version of the Russian nation was defined ideologically—in confrontation with the West—had important domestic implications for the status of Little Russian history and society. The state was promoting a vision of the Russian nation from above, centered on the understanding of Russia as an autocracy; the educated public, the emerging civil society, was not allowed to advance a competing vision. Thus, the Russian nation was forming in an international setting in which comparisons with the West were always made; but the implicit adoption of Western ways went hand in hand with the explicit rejection of some elements of the West.

The Idea of Ukraine

If natives of Little Russia were so prominent in the Russian nation-building project, why did some of them refuse to join what had been crafted, choosing instead to declare themselves Ukrainian? Since the Russian project signified a Europeanization of Russia, was Ukrainianism a reactionary movement, a refusal to accept "Europe"? Or was it the result of a conclusion that the road to Europe being built in St. Petersburg was not the right road for Ukraine?

This essay argues for the latter interpretation. Sensing that both Russia and Poland were themselves peripheral in relation to the West, the early Ukrainian nation-builders believed it better to establish access to "Europe" directly, rather than by way of St. Petersburg—that is to say, without acquiescing in enduring as the periphery of a periphery.

The emergence of modern Ukrainian national consciousness can be dated with relative precision; its beginnings are found in the late eighteenth century. Certain features were common to those who may be characterized as the earliest Ukrainian nationalists: They belonged to what then were upper-strata social groups; they were literate—indeed, well educated; they knew the world beyond the land and people in which they had been born. They already possessed, to a certain degree, a secular outlook, even when they were taken to be religious believers; this outlook extended to understanding the state in terms other than the ones propounded by those who still advocated the divine right of kings. They knew that at least some other nations decided for themselves how they would be governed.

Those few individuals who had a broader view of their own land and of a larger world could see that societies and states were redefining themselves. No longer was it the case that the monarch defined his subjects; increasingly, it was the other way around. But how then was one to know who the "people" were? What were the criteria for defining that collectivity of people entitled to define the government under which they would live, and to whom such a government would be responsible?

The first definition of Ukraine was historical. The Little Russia of the age of Catherine was aware, and took pride in the fact, that it was a child (some said a stepchild) of the Polish-Lithuanian Commonwealth; its defenders asserted their rights against the empire by invoking Little Russia's past ties with the Commonwealth. Such was the view of Hryhorii Poletyka, who "articulated a view of Ukraine ruled as a gentry democracy in the manner of the Polish Commonwealth."[16] In the nineteenth century the populist historian of Ukraine, Aleksander Lazarevsky, criticized the efforts of Ivan Mazepa, a leader of Ukraine's abortive early eighteenth-century quest for independence, for perverting the supposedly open Ukrainian social order. "There is no doubt," Lazarevsky wrote, "that if there had not been the restraining power of the Russian government, then Mazepa would have made out of Little Russia a little Poland, with all its splendour for the *pany* and all its hardships for the *muzhiki*."[17]

However much he disapproved of the social system of old Poland and the ideas of its imitators, Lazarevsky thus acknowledged Ukraine's political ties to the non-Russian world. The construction of a Ukrainian national history that "seceded" from the imperial version of "Russian" history included the declaration of a link, a continuity in political tradition, between Little Russia, itself a direct product of the Cossack association with the Commonwealth on the one hand and Kyivan Rus on the other.

Later, after the historic nation of Little Russia was dissolved for both internal and external reasons, Ukrainians appealed to ethnography for guidance as to who constituted "us" and who was "other." The ethnic argument defined Ukraine territorially as the land where Ukrainian dialects were spoken by the peasantry.

Whether framed in ethnographic, linguistic, or historical terms, declarations of a distinct Ukrainian cultural identity had political significance from the first moment. Their effect was to modify the official definition of the nation in a way that was contrary to the aims and intentions of the empire. If the official ideology held that Russia was an autocracy, then collecting and popularizing folk songs that extolled "freedom" served to question that system.

The Ukraine being constructed was acquiring its existence through the activities of "name givers," classifiers, and conceptualizers; their words created the material entities of national identity. These individuals, members of the Russian-speaking intelligentsia, of Ukrainian, Russian, or mixed Ukrainian-Russian descent, assumed the roles of spokesmen for and leaders of a nation that was overwhelmingly peasant. In many ways these intellectuals were simultaneously Ukrainian and Russian, reflecting the sociological and political realities of Ukraine. The mass constituency of any Ukrainian movement, were it ever to emerge, consisted primarily of serfs and thus remained beyond the pale of social and cultural life in the empire.

The defense of Little Russia was expressed in works of literature, in theater, and in historical, philological, and other researches. At this initial stage in the late eighteenth century, language itself was not regarded as the defining marker of the nation; culture, and especially the politico-historical identity of the nation, was understood as the *sine qua non* of nationhood.

The adoption of the vernacular took place in the part of Ukraine that was the most "Westernized" culturally—the farthest eastern region, in Poltava and Kharkiv. Marc Raeff has written insightfully on this subject, noting the crucial role of educational institutions. Raeff distinguishes between the contribution of those in Kyiv and in Kharkiv. The older intellectual center, Kyiv, had been of central importance during the transition from Muscovite to imperial political culture. Kharkiv, which functioned as Ukraine's cultural center in the early decades of the nineteenth century, on the other hand fostered not only the Russification of the elites but also the reception of idealism and Romanticism, which, according to Raeff, were "the necessary preconditions of modern nationalism."[18]

The new nationalism was not only different in kind from the preceding emphasis on regional and historical identity; it was also subversive of the state and the imperial establishment. The traditional elite of Ukraine, having become largely Russified, was accordingly only marginally involved in this new expression; instead, the first and most energetic propagators of this new sense of national identity were intellectuals, academics who systematically developed its scholarly and philosophical justification. As Raeff notes, "The old regionalism was dead. A new nationalism, based on historicist anthropology, philology, and folk culture (or what was thought to be folk culture) was emerging under the influence of Romanticism, idealistic philosophy, and the government's complete refusal to grant civil society an active role."[19]

Benedict Anderson's argument on the rise of the science of philology helps us to understand the circumstances under which the Ukrainian idea was formulated. Of the revolution in language and the study of languages, which he places in the later eighteenth century, Anderson notes:

> Advances in Semitics undermined the idea that Hebrew was either uniquely ancient or of divine provenance. . . . "Language became less of a continuity between an outside power and the human speaker than an internal field created and accomplished by language users among themselves." Out of these discoveries came philology. . . . From this point on the old sacred languages—Latin, Greek, and Hebrew—were forced to mingle on equal ontological footing with a motley plebeian crowd of vernacular rivals, in a movement which complemented their earlier demotion in the market-place by print-capitalism. If all languages now shared a common (intra-) mundane status, then all were in principle equally worthy of study and admiration. But by who? Logically, since now none belonged to God, by their new owners: each language's native speakers—and readers.[20]

The construction of modern Ukraine also required a different philosophical framework—one no longer theological or monarchical. If one takes into account the dominance of the clergy in the Greek-Catholic (western) parts of Ukraine (which lasted well into the nineteenth century) on the one hand and the formation of a Polish vernacular literature as early as the sixteenth century on the other, it becomes possible to understand both the protracted process of a specifically Ukrainian nation-formation in Galicia and other areas of Austria and the enormous attractiveness of the Polish national project to "Ruthenians"—not evident before 1772, but especially pronounced under Austrian rule. A theological *Weltanschauung* confronted a modern secular outlook. Closely related was the question of power in this society; the clergy, as the masters of a sacred language for divine mediation, did not want to share power with or abdicate power to secular elites. In the 1830s and 1840s, the clergy fought against the vernacular proposed by the young intelligentsia; in 1848 clerics managed to deny admission into the Ukrainian community to members of the landed aristocracy. The Greek-Catholic clergy continued to fight language-power struggles into the final decades of the nineteenth century, not giving up for good until the twentieth.

Ultimately, it was the process leading to the delineation of the territory of modern Ukraine that took the longest to be completed; in a sense, this was completed only after 1917. In the nineteenth century it involved the use of both ethnography and history but also, crucially, had a material, practical aspect: the colonization of the previously Tatar and Turkish South by Ukrainian peasants from the Russian East Ukraine (or Little Russia) and the former Polish, right-bank Ukraine, conquered by the empire in the late eighteenth century.

Geopolitics Rearranges the Stage

We shall never know how the Ukrainian-Russian relationship might have evolved had the Russian Empire remained in its pre-1770 borders. Two major events on the international scene transformed the setting in which the subsequent history of Russian and Ukrainian nation-making took place. First, the partitions of Poland moved the borders of the Russian Empire far to the west—making it possible for Little Russia, a western periphery of the Russian Empire before the partitions, to come into direct contact with former Poland's eastern periphery (or "Ukraine") on the western bank of the Dnieper. In the long run, this resulted in the formation of a new entity—the Ukraine we know today—around a new center, the city of Kyiv, which before the partitions of Poland had been a border town. Second, Russian imperial conquests in the region of the Black Sea made possible a Ukrainian colonization from the Ukrainian peripheries of Russia, and from Poland's former Ukrainian peripheries (annexed by Russia in 1793–1795), to what is now southern Ukraine, which had been peripheral lands of the Ottoman Empire.

With the Russian annexation of what had been Poland's border territories in 1793–1795, an "undoing of 1667" (that is, of the partition of Ukraine between Warsaw and Moscow) took place. For Ukrainians, the Polish partitions rearranged the stage in the midst of their transition from an administrative regional or provincial problem within the empire to an "inter-nationality" and finally an *international* problem. Most obviously, the east and west banks of the Dnieper were now united within one state. Not only were there many more Ukrainians in post-1795 Russia, but for the first time, the Polish question began to play a crucial role in the Russo-Ukrainian relationship.

But the Russian public did not understand that the partitions of Poland had transformed the conditions under which the relations between Great Russia and Little Russia, between the "Ukraine" and the empire, would develop. The critical importance of Poland for the politics and culture of Russia was perceived by few Russians in the nineteenth century. And yet the inclusion of new millions of Roman Catholics and

Uniates, and of several million more Jews, put on the agenda of Russian politics a number of pressing questions. Were these new subjects full-fledged citizens of Russia? Were they *rossiiane* even if they were not *russkie*?[21]

The Russian-Polish Struggle for the "Borderlands"

Andreas Kappeler, in his study *Russia as a Multinational Empire*, rightly argues the importance of the Polish national movement in under-mining the Russian Empire in two ways—through the efforts of Poles themselves and by Polish influence on the Lithuanians, Belorussians, and Ukrainians. "The Poles played this leading role once again in the crisis of the Soviet Empire at the end of the twentieth century."[22]

After 1795, the Russian Empire ruled its former Polish acquisitions in a de facto, and after 1815 a de jure, alliance with the Polish nobility of west-bank Ukraine, Belarus, and Lithuania. This Russo-Polish rela-tionship did not become something formal and lasting, in the manner of the Austro-Hungarian "compromise" after 1866. But it did define the parameters in which the Ukrainians lived for more than a generation: Polish social and cultural dominance, and Russian political, state, and military power.

After 1830, the situation changed dramatically. The Polish insurrec-tion of 1830–31 destroyed this Polish-Russian cohabitation (which was being subverted anyway by imperial violations of the 1815 accord). Each for their own reasons, the Russians and the Ukrainians formed something similar to a common front against the Poles. The Russians were resolved to prove these lands were not Polish, and in this effort they were assisted by the Ukrainians. (It took some time before the Russians realized the Ukrainians were also trying to prove that the lands in ques-tion were not Russian, either.) Thus, the making of a modern Ukraine was taking place not in "Austria" and "Russia," as most textbooks say, but in a social world—the social space—where an overwhelming major-ity of would-be Ukrainians lived under Polish nobles. The modernizers of the Polish nation promised those serfs that they would become free and Polish at the same time.

This new concept of the Polish nation first emerged in the intellec-tual revolution and political reforms—a peaceful revolution from above—of the final decade of the eighteenth century. The Polish nation survived the destruction of the Polish state by Berlin, Vienna, and St.

Petersburg. Poland further survived as a society; the social landscape of the late *Rzeczpospolita* was dominated by the Poles. But the old noble-dominated society was gradually dissolved by industrialization and urbanization and by new ideas of social and political organization. In a real sense the "successor nations" of the Commonwealth—modern Poles, Jews, Lithuanians, Belorussians, and Ukrainians—emerged out of the transformation of its old classes, estates, and religious groups under the impact of modernization.

Ukraine under Russia and Poland: The Nineteenth Century

In the early decades of the nineteenth century, the Russian public did not know Ukraine in any other form except that of Little Russia. As Paul Bushkovitch has noted, the Russians thought of the right bank of the Dnieper as Polish; they knew that the nobility there was Polish. And when the Russians thought about the south—the Steppe region—it was Odessa, the sea, and economic development that came to mind, not the Ukrainians:

> To the Russian writer and reader the Ukraine was Malorossija, the old Hetmanate and the Slobodskaja (later Charkovskaja) *guberniia*. . . . This exclusive concentration on the left bank was in itself the product of several forces. The assumption that the left bank was the entire Ukraine was so powerful that none of the authors of the time explained this identification, but the basic reason was undoubtedly the existence of a gentry society in that area. . . . As most Russian writers of that age came from the gentry, when they turned to the Ukraine, they saw only their counterparts in the so-called Little Russian gentry. Further, these gentry had many personal and family ties with Russian gentry, and many had been and still were prominent in all-Russian politics.[23]

At first glance it might seem that the life of the Ukrainian national poet Taras Shevchenko (1814–1861) supports Hroch's thesis that national awakeners in the so-called small nations are drawn from the lower social strata. Born a serf, Shevchenko technically remained a serf until his freedom was purchased by his friends when he was a man in his twenties, a graduate of the St. Petersburg Academy of Fine Arts. But as Omeljan Pritsak has recently reminded us, Shevchenko did not become a builder of modern Ukrainian consciousness because he was born in the village, because he lived his childhood surrounded by folk culture, or because he spoke the Ukrainian vernacular as his first language. It

was only *after* he had acquired a modern political and cultural awareness—long after he had left his native village and became aware of a
larger world, first in Vilnius and then in St. Petersburg—that Shevchenko began to see the political significance of his native culture and
"nationalized" it by making its language a medium of artistic expression. Pritsak argues that it was the encounter with Yevhen Hrebinka
(1812–1848), "a landowner from Poltava" (among other things), that
opened Shevchenko's eyes to the fact that literary circles had great interest in Ukrainian folk songs and that modern original literature was in
fact being already produced in the language of those folk songs.[24]

The great Russian critic Vissarion Belinsky (1811–1848) understood
instantly what the Ukrainian literati were really up to and knew that
creating a Ukrainian-language literature might—indeed would—lead to
the idea that a Ukrainian society, a nation, to *match* that literature,
should be created next. As George G. Grabowicz has noted, "Belinsky's
consistently negative reaction to Shevchenko was occasioned precisely
by his principled opposition to literary 'separatism' and the political
separatism that it necessarily implied."[25] For their part, however, the
Russians did not understand that Shevchenko represented a qualitatively
new stage in the formation of Ukraine and the decline of Little Russia.
The Ukrainians were operating in the bipolar Russian-Polish world, but
the Russians continued to regard them as their own province. (Interestingly enough, some Poles were gradually accepting the emergence of a
Ukrainian nation and of other nations in formerly Polish lands.)

Indeed, the Russian state responded to this national and religious
diversification of the empire and the coming of the era of nationalism in
Europe by formulating its own definition of Russia: the doctrine of Official Nationality, according to which Orthodoxy, autocracy, and *narodnost'* were the principles on which Russia stood. The nation was the
property of the monarch; serfdom was held to be a national institution.
Peter the Great was extolled to almost divine levels and was routinely
described as the creator of Russia. One tsarist official, Count E. Kankrin
(who incidentally was born in Germany with the surname of Krebs),
even suggested that "Russia should be called *Petrovia*, and we *Petrovi-
ans*; or the empire should be named *Romanovia*, and we *Romanovites*."
A Russian journalist who read this proposal commented: "An unusual
idea, but an essentially correct one!"[26] It is of course significant that
Kankrin's ideas were being aired at precisely the time that an emerging

Ukrainian intelligentsia was defining the Ukrainian people as a nation devoted to liberty.

Before long, the Russians began to understand the connection between the Polish and the Ukrainian questions. They did so in a manner characteristic of a police mentality. Drawing a number of conclusions from the 1863 Polish uprising, which was finally suppressed by the summer of 1864, the government in St. Petersburg modified the terms of the emancipation of 1861 in regions that had been the scene of the Polish uprising; further, it announced a number of anti-Catholic measures. St. Petersburg also concluded that the Ukrainian movement was a product of the Polish plot to dismember the Russian nation.

In 1863 the so-called *Valuev ukaz*, named after the minister of the interior, introduced the first restrictions on the use of the Ukrainian language. The government, which enjoyed the support of a large segment of the public in this respect, concluded that the Ukrainian phenomenon was dangerous—even though the Ukrainians limited their activities to literary and scholarly pursuits, in marked contrast to the Poles. What the Ukrainians were doing, some Russians came to realize, subverted the very unity of the Russian nation, which in the view of educated Russians consisted of three major ethnographic or folkloristic subdivisions—the Great Russians, the Little Russians, and the White or Belo-Russians— yet was one nation, united in its common higher culture and in politics.

The Russian government did not believe that the Ukrainian movement was an expression of any authentic and legitimate aspirations of the population of Little Russia and chose to treat it as a product of foreign (in this case, Polish) "intrigue." This set the tone for how Russia would view Ukrainian nationalism for decades to come: In the future, "Ukrainianism" would be viewed as a product of German, Austrian, or Vatican plots, besides being seen as, in one way or another, an originally Polish invention.

In 1876 the imperial government went even farther in its identification of Ukrainian language and culture with political separatism when, in a secret edict signed by the tsar at Ems, it forbade the publication of Ukrainian writings and the performance of Ukrainian plays and songs. According to Grabowicz, in taking this step the Russian government helped, albeit ironically, to raise Ukrainian literature out of its provincial mode, giving it newfound political import by casting it as something subversive, separatist, or protonationalist: "It goes without saying, of course, that these qualities must already have existed—more or less openly, as in Shevchenko, or *in potentia*."[27]

The model of the Russian nation and society promoted by the tsarist state encountered challenges from two directions. One might say figuratively that there emerged, in approximately the same historical period, two alternative ways, or models, for seceding from the empire. One path of secession amounted to the rejection of, and eventually a challenge to, the fundamental principle on which the empire was built—autocracy. This became the basis of a deep cleavage in Russian identity, as revealed in the title of Nicholas V. Riasanovsky's book *A Parting of Ways*, which examines the relations between the government and Russia's educated elite in the first half of the nineteenth century.[28] The other mode of "secession" was represented by the Ukrainian idea.

Ukraine and the Turkish/Tatar Connection

While the partition of Poland affected the Ukrainians in a way the Russian public failed to notice until long after the event, something similar happened to the Ukrainian perception of, and responses to, the Russian imperial annexation of formerly Turkish and Tatar holdings in the Black Sea region.

From the eighteenth century onward, colonization was carried out in the south and southeast. The newly colonized lands had not in past centuries been inhabited by Ukrainians or other Slavs. Thus, in the Ukrainian case, the nationalization of space was more than a matter of attaching national labels to an already inhabited territory upon which some other nation or nationalist movement had put another designation. Uniquely among the peoples of Europe in the nineteenth century, the Ukrainians were in fact creating what in the age of nationalism would become a major part of their future national space, their *national homeland*. These were new lands of Russia—indeed, the Russians called them "New Russia"—but they were being settled mainly by Ukrainians and in due course would be claimed for Ukraine. The process of settling the south—and expanding the Ukrainian space—was not understood in the national thought as an aspect of Ukrainian nation-building when it was taking place. (Neither the Russian state nor the public attached any special importance to this fact.) The opera *Zaporozhets za Dunaem* ("The Zaporozhian Cossack beyond the Danube") was not written and produced until much later, in the 1860s; and it was only in the late 1870s that Mykhailo Drahomanov clearly set out the reasons why New Russia was included within his definition of Ukraine.

In Russian national consciousness, the conquest of the Black Sea coast and of Crimea is perceived in terms of imperial wars, imperial military grandeur, and the building of Odessa and Sevastopol. By contrast, seen from the perspective of the Ukrainian national epic, the story begins several centuries earlier; moreover, it is a people's history, a story of people's wars and people's settlement. Seeing the matter in this way can help shed light on the psychological background of the current Russo-Ukrainian dispute about the Black Sea fleet. For the Russians, it is a matter of military prestige and national grandeur; from the Ukrainian perspective, it is yet another expression of that brave plebeian insistence upon freedom so typified in Repin's painting "Zaporozhians Writing a Letter to the Sultan of Turkey."

Vienna and the Slavic Question

Only now may we turn to a theme that typically enters accounts of modern Ukraine, though much earlier. We have seen that the formation of modern Ukraine took place as a process of self-definition against both Russia and Poland. Yet there took place a further "culturalization" or "ethnicization" of the nation, beyond that effort of nation-formation that had first been undertaken by a historical elite.

The entry of Vienna directly into Ukrainian history was of enormous long-term significance, although not in a way normally presented by Ukrainian historians. If *esse percipi* is needed to become a nation, Vienna opened a new dimension in the "internationalization" of the Ukrainian phenomenon. The transfer from Polish to Austrian rule also made possible the transition to a different level of life: Serfs became legal subjects with standing in public law, human beings de jure.

What Geoffrey Hawthorn has observed about the impact of the absolutism of the European powers in Africa in the nineteenth century can equally be said about Vienna's impact on "Galicia":

> Absolutist states were, in their absolutism, states. They controlled their territories and the population within them. And even if they did not emerge from an already existing political community, they almost always served to create one. Those who came later to contest them . . . could take that community for granted, or at least could take it that there was a community to be fought for.[29]

Austrian reforms made the rise of a political community possible, but they did not make Ukrainians out of peasants and Greek Catholics. Their first "higher" identity was "Ruthenian," and their first political consciousness was imperial—we may call it, in Tomáš Masaryk's term, "Viennism." The party capable of taking advantage of what the Austrians had set in motion was the Poles; they knew how to benefit from the creation of a single Galicia, i.e., a new entity that consisted of mainly a Ruthenian eastern part, forming the province of "Ruthenia" before 1772, and an overwhelmingly Polish western part. Things would have been quite different had "Ruthenia" been retained as a distinct entity under Vienna. After the Poles had transformed their own identity in the 1790s, it became clear that the Vienna reforms had merely cleared the ground for the subsequent triumphal march of "Polonism." In fact, there was more Polonization in "Ruthenia" after 1795 than there had been in the four centuries between 1370 and 1772.

However slowly, a new social reality was emerging. The ancient, sharply defined barriers and structures were being gradually undermined by "culture"—growing literacy, dissemination of knowledge about the larger world, scientific and secular thought. The meaning of being Polish, as indicated above, was becoming transformed. The new Polish identity was open to these "Ruthenes," to "Greek Catholics," to all who were leaving the peasant stratum—or to those sons of the clergy who did not wish to pursue their father's station in society and hoped to be doctors, engineers, or teachers instead. In the early nineteenth century, the Ruthenes lacked a secular ideology; they did not use their own living language in print, education, or civic affairs. All these spheres were serviced by Polish language and Polish ideas; those individuals who had reached a certain intellectual level and social station had nowhere else to go but to Polonism.

The masses remained Greek Catholic and "imperial" so long as serfdom defined the way of life of the overwhelming majority. In the 1830s—after the Polish Insurrection of 1830–31, and three generations after 1772—some young "Ruthenians" turned seriously to what was going on in Kharkiv, Poltava, and Kyiv. They opened up to Ukrainian culture from the East and discovered in it a force capable of immunizing them to Polonism and at the same time bringing them to a world stage. Thus "Ukraine" entered, as a third party, the great historic contest between Russia and Poland. An observer from the side, the Czech journalist and activist Karel Havlíček (1821–1856), dubbed the polemic (and struggle) between the Russians and the Poles "a fable of two wolves." "If there is a lamb in the picture," he went on, "it is the Ukrainian."[30]

The emergence of a distinct Ukrainian nationality was thus penetrating the consciousness of the world beyond Russian-Polish spheres. The "internationalization" of the Ukrainian phenomenon, begun with the partitions of Poland, was further advanced by the new intellectual climate in Europe associated with the birth of nationality. As the idea of a Slavonic family of nations took hold, and as institutional structures reflecting this emerged—beginning with the establishment of chairs of Slavic studies in Prague and in Vienna—the Ukrainians "arrived" in their own right as a distinct nation, despite lacking political status.

Ukraine—One Nation or Two?

Ukrainian differentiation from Russia and Poland respectively did not necessarily guarantee the unity of those Ukrainians who refused to be Russian with those Ukrainians who refused to be Polish. The Russian Ukrainians needed to defend their identity against the Russians; the Galician Ukrainians—even those in the west bank region, who had lived under Russia from 1793 to 1795—had been traditionally preoccupied with maintaining themselves against the Poles. Some time had to pass before the "Russian" Ukrainians began to think of "Polish" and "Austrian" Ukrainians as a part of one nation, and before the latter took note of the "Russian" Ukrainians as their conationals.

It was the Galicians who first turned their eyes toward "Ukraine." But in dealing with Galicia we need to discern phases in its history. First, there was the partial but critical emancipation from the virtually total social and cultural dependence on the *szlachta*. This was accomplished by Viennese intervention after about 1772. The resulting "Ruthenianism," as soon became evident, was largely helpless in resisting Polonization. Mass Polonization occurred in the second phase, when Polonism came to mean not only the old noble power but also a revolutionary program of emancipation and cultural freedom. Only in the third phase did a turn toward the people and its language come, accelerated by the discovery of, and a receptiveness to, Ukrainian life in the Russian Empire. This third period began only in the 1830s.

But this march was neither simple nor straightforward. There were periods of *moskvofil'stvo*—an orientation toward Russia—before Galicia finally decided it wanted to be a part of Ukraine. Why then did the

Galicians, having decided they would not be Polish and having likewise rejected the Russian option, not want to be a Galician nation? What made them choose instead to be a small part of Ukraine?

Two tentative answers come to mind. First, Ukraine had cultural resources that enabled the culturally impoverished and socially under-privileged Ruthenes of Galicia to compete with Polish culture, society, and politics. Second, by joining Ukraine the Galicians were becoming members of a nation larger than Poland; not by accident did they call it *Velyka Ukraina*, "Greater Ukraine." Without an affiliation with Ukraine, the Galician community was roughly the size of the Slovak or Lithuanian nationalities. Perhaps it was the sense that Ukraine offered them the best hope of survival versus Poland that made it possible for Catholic Galicians to unite with the Orthodox East—against Catholic Poles.

This may be a place to remind oneself of the fact that the period after 1795—indeed, well into the nineteenth century—was, despite Russian political rule, one of Polish cultural hegemony in all the lands of the old republic. This period even saw an expansion of "Polonism" into Kyiv and as far to the east as Kharkiv. (There were Poles involved in the founding of Kharkiv University; moreover, Kharkiv functioned as a link to the West via Warsaw, bypassing the Moscow–St. Petersburg channel, with important ramifications for Ukrainian development.) It was there-fore understandable that the necessity of defining oneself as distinct from Poles was so strongly felt in Galicia. So strong was Ukrainian anti-Po-lonism that when Vienna ceased to be the Ruthenes' protector and made a deal with the Poles (after 1867), some Ruthenes sought their salvation from the Poles even in tsarist Russia.

Little surprise, then, that the question of intra-Ukrainian unity was seen by Ukrainian patriots as a key issue for decades. As late as 1906, Mykhailo Hrushevsky published an article titled "Galicia and Ukraine," in which the historian warned his compatriots that if they did not take care, they might well end up as the Serbs and Croats had—two nations based on one ethnic foundation. Hrushevsky argued that a common ethnicity could not by itself guarantee that one nation would rise on it; the transformation of an ethnic group into a nation required work and the wish to be one. Ethnicity was only a point of departure, a founda-tion. The development of a common Ukrainian literary language re-quired a deliberate policy, a sustained effort, and Hrushevsky appealed to Ukrainians on both sides of the border to step up their efforts.[31]

We can speak confidently of the completion of the Ukrainian nation-building process only when individuals and organizations emerged who thought in terms of a common "pan-Ukrainian" national interest—above western Ukraine's preoccupation with Poland and eastern Ukraine's preoccupation with Russia.

The Ukrainians consciously and energetically worked to create a common language; the Austrian west modeled itself on eastern authors. Even so, the relation between language and nationality is commonly misunderstood. The Ukrainians of Russia and Austria did not become one nation because they spoke the same language; they came to speak the same language because they had first decided to be one nation. They were helped in reaching this conclusion by Hrushevsky's greatest accomplishment—his synthesis of Ukrainian history. Hrushevsky both established the standard and pointed the way toward achieving it; he constructed a conception of Ukrainian history that offered a path toward a common Ukrainian political strategy, toward envisioning the future of the whole nation, not merely its parts. By constructing a historical argument for the unity of the Ukrainian nation, his work especially stressed the crucial importance of links between Kyiv and Lviv at critical junctures of history. Hrushevsky, as John A. Armstrong has argued recently, provided the vindication of the "Ukrainian myth"—and did so in the language of nineteenth-century science.[32]

Just as emphatically (and just as importantly), Hrushevsky argued against the idea of a "thousand-year-old Russian state" and denied that any single "Russian" nation had existed for a millennium. To a contemporary political observer, the so-called Belovezha accords of 1991, in which the leaders of the three East Slavic republics and nations dissolved the Soviet Union, appear to be the implementation in real, political terms of the Hrushevsky schema; the establishment of the independent states of Ukraine, Russia, and Belarus can quite easily be deduced from Hrushevsky's interpretation of the past, as he summarized it in a famous paper of 1904 on the "rational structure" of East Slav history.[33]

Hrushevsky's contemporary Ivan Franko explained at roughly the same time the practical tasks for the present that emerged from the historical constructions of his friend. In "An Open Letter to Young Ukrainians of Galicia," written in 1905, Franko distilled what nationality or nationalism was about:

Before the Ukrainian intelligentsia an enormous practical task [*diiova zadacha*] is opening up now, under freer forms of life in Russia: to create out of the vast ethnic mass of Ukrainian people a Ukrainian nation, a comprehensive cultural organism, capable of an independent cultural and political life, resistant to assimilationist efforts of other nations, whatever their origin, and, at the same time, a nation open to receiving, on the widest possible scale, and at the fastest rate, those universal human cultural achievements without which no nation and no state, however powerful, can survive.[34]

Conclusions

In evaluating the prospects of Ukraine as a nation it may be useful to turn to the ideas of the Russian philosopher and theologian Georgii Fedotov, who as early as the 1920s and 1930s, while living in exile, reflected on the future of Ukrainian-Russian relations after the fall of communism. Fedotov thought the central question involved in the Russo-Ukrainian relationship was the existence of a third party—Poland, "with which it is tied with centuries-long historical links. Objectively, Ukraine will have to make a choice between Poland and Russia, and it depends in part on us that this choice is not made against our old common fatherland."[35]

Equally important to Fedotov for the preservation of the unity of Russia was what he perceived to be the role of Russian culture in giving all of the Empire's peoples "access to world civilization." As he put it: "This was so in the St. Petersburg period of the Empire, and it should remain so [in the post-Soviet future]. If the peoples of Russia will study not in Moscow, not in St. Petersburg, but in Paris and in Berlin, then they will not remain with us."[36]

We do not know what Fedotov would have said about the situation today when Ukraine includes also regions that in his time belonged to Poland, Czechoslovakia, and Romania and were largely Catholic rather than Orthodox. Ukraine does not have to make a "choice" between Russia and Poland; Poland has given up any claims to Ukraine and recognizes Ukraine's independence. Warsaw has thus transformed itself, in the Ukrainian perspective, from a historic enemy into an important ally. And it is not only in Paris, London, and Frankfurt, but also in New York, Boston, Toronto, and Tokyo that non-Russians and Russians themselves are "studying" after the collapse of the Soviet Union.

But Fedotov's general point merits serious attention today. Just as the unity of Russia as he saw it depended on Russia's capacity to be a window to the world for its peoples, so the survival of Ukraine as an independent state (one may reason) will depend to a large extent on how it succeeds in bringing the world to its people—and its people to the world. Success or failure in managing the major "internal" problems of Ukraine today will be affected by the relations it establishes between itself and the world community. The idea of Ukraine as a nation, as argued in this essay, was that its people should have direct access to the centers of civilization rather than being condemned to an inferior status, that they should be communicating with the world at large on their own rather than through intermediaries.

During his visit to Kyiv in May of 1995, President Clinton delivered a speech at Shevchenko University clearly intended to assure ordinary Ukrainians that the United States fully embraced their independence—a message his audience enthusiastically applauded. The crowd at the university roared when Clinton concluded his speech with the Ukrainian phrase *Slava Ukraini*—"Glory to Ukraine."

"He spoke Ukrainian!" came the shout from Oksana Shulga, a sixty-five-year-old retired Aeroflot worker who stood on a stone wall and craned her head over the throng in order to see the American president. Later, spying a clutch of American reporters gathered on the sidewalk to observe the proceedings, she took them under tutelage: "We want to be part of the world, not part of Russia," she explained. Then, approvingly, she added of the president: "And he understands that."[37]

Notes

1. Eugene B. Rumer, "Eurasia Letter: Will Ukraine Return to Russia?" *Foreign Policy* 96 (Fall 1994): 129–44. For comprehensive recent surveys of Ukrainian history see Orest Subtelny, *Ukraine: A History* (Toronto: University of Toronto Press, 1988), and Paul Robert Magocsi, *A History of Ukraine* (Seattle, Wash.: University of Washington Press, 1996). For current debates, see Mark von Hagen, "Does Ukraine Have a History?" and George G. Grabowicz, "Ukrainian Studies: Framing the Contexts," *Slavic Review* 54, no. 3 (1995): 658–73, and 674–90, and the comments by Andreas Kappeler, Iaroslav Isaievych, Serhii M. Plokhy, and Yuri Slezkine, ibid., pp. 691–719.

2. Contrary to common belief, in the early modern period the Poles—despite sharing a religion with the West—viewed themselves as forming a distinct political and cultural entity that was superior to that of the West. They thus sought to define themselves in relation to the West, although they did so in

terms very different from those in which the Russians saw themselves as in opposition to "Europe." See Andrzej Walicki, *Poland Between East and West: The Controversies over Self-Definition and Modernization in Partitioned Poland*, the August Zaleski Lectures, Harvard University, April 18–22, 1994 (Cambridge, Mass.: Ukrainian Research Institute, 1994).

3. Larry Wolff, *Inventing Eastern Europe: The Map of Civilization on the Mind of the Enlightenment* (Stanford, Calif.: Stanford University Press, 1994).

4. Daniel Beauvois, *The Noble, the Serf and the Revizor: The Polish Nobility Between Tsarist Imperialism and the Ukrainian Masses (1831–1863)* (Chur, Switzerland: Harwood Academic Publishers, 1991), translation by Barbara Reising of *Le Noble, le Serf et le Revizor: La noblesse polonaise entre le tsarisme et les masses ukrainiennes (1831–1863)* (Paris: Archives Contemporaines, 1984), and *La Bataille de la terre en Ukraine, 1863–1914: Les Polonais et les conflits socio-ethniques* (Lille: Presses Universitaires de Lille, 1993).

5. Ivan L. Rudnytsky, "Franciszek Duchiński and His Impact on Ukrainian Political Thought," in *Essays in Modern Ukrainian History* (Cambridge, Mass.: Harvard University, Ukrainian Research Institute, 1987), p. 194. For references to recent works on Polish-Ukrainian relations, see Roman Szporluk, "After Empire: What?" *Daedalus* 123, no. 3 (Summer 1994): 21–39. (Reprinted in this book as chapter 14.) See also Ilya Prizel, "The Influence of Ethnicity on Foreign Policy: The Case of Ukraine," in Roman Szporluk, ed., *National Identity and Ethnicity in Russia and the New States of Eurasia* (Armonk, N.Y, and London: M. E. Sharpe, 1994), pp. 103–28. An earlier volume, by Peter J. Potichnyi, ed., *Poland and Ukraine: Past and Present* (Edmonton: Canadian Institute of Ukrainian Studies, 1980), contains useful essays.

6. Benedict Anderson, *Imagined Communities: Reflections on the Origin and Spread of Nationalism* (London and New York: Verso, 1991), p. 6.

7. Liah Greenfeld, *Nationalism: Five Roads to Modernity* (Cambridge, Mass.: Harvard University Press, 1992), p. 254. For a comprehensive treatment of the place of "Europe" in Russian thought and politics, see Iver B. Neumann, *Russia and the Idea of Europe: A Study in Identity and International Relations* (London and New York: Routledge, 1996).

8. Since in the British case the "Other," the defining "negatio," was Catholicism, and in politics, the Catholic France, the Irish did not qualify for admission. See Linda Colley, *Britons: Forging the Nation, 1707-1837* (New Haven, Conn.: Yale University Press, 1992), pp. 5–6. Colley cites, with approval, Peter Sahlins's argument that national identity, "like ethnic or communal identity, is contingent and relational: it is defined by the social or territorial boundaries drawn to distinguish the collective self and its implicit negation, the other." See ibid., pp. 5–6, quoting from Peter Sahlins, *Boundaries: The Making of France and Spain in the Pyrenees* (Berkeley and Los Angeles, Calif.: University of California Press, 1989), p. 271.

9. Miroslav Hroch, *Social Preconditions of National Revival in Europe: A Comparative Analysis of the Social Composition of Patriotic Groups among the Smaller European Nations*, trans. Ben Fowkes (Cambridge, Eng.: Cambridge University Press, 1985). See Ernest Gellner, *Encounters with Nationalism* (Oxford, Eng., and Cambridge, Mass.: Blackwell, 1994), pp. 182–200, for an analysis of Hroch's interpreration of the emergence of nations.

10. According to Prasenjit Duara, *Rescuing History from the Nation: Questioning Narratives of Modern China* (Chicago, Ill., and London: University of Chicago Press, 1995), pp. 65–66, "a[n] incipient nationality is formed when the perception of the boundaries of community are [*sic*] transformed . . . when a group succeeds in imposing a historical narrative of descent and/or dissent on both heterogeneous and related cultural practices. I will . . . coin the word *discent* to suggest the porosity of these two signifiers. . . . The narrative of *discent* is used to define and mobilize a community, often by privileging a particular cultural practice . . . as the constitutive principle of the community—such as language, religion, or common historical experience." At the same time, Duara points out that "[h]istorically, what is unique and new about nationalism is not an epistemological category, such as a type of identity or a mode of consciousness," but "the global *institutional* revolution which . . . produced its own extremely powerful representations of the nation-state." Duara's overall treatment of nationalism is close to that of Greenfeld's (and my own) position: "What is novel about modern nationalism is the world system of nation-states." (Ibid., pp. 8–9.) Although he is not exclusively or primarily concerned with nation-formation, Pierre Bourdieu's *Language and Symbolic Power*, ed., John B. Thompson, trans., Gino Raymond and Matthew Adamson (Cambridge, Mass.: Polity Press, 1991), sheds light on the intellectual effort it involves.

11. For a reminder about this, see for example Jerzy Tomaszewski, *Rzeczpospolita wielu narodów* (Warsaw: Czytelnik, 1985), 38ff. The literature on this question, needless to say, is very large.

12. I discuss the decomposition of the historic Polish nation in relation to the emergence of the Ukrainian nation and, indirectly, of the other successor nations of the Commonwealth in "Polish-Ukrainian Relations in 1918: Notes for Discussion," in Paul Latawski, ed., *The Reconstruction of Poland, 1914–23* (London: Macmillan, 1992), pp. 41–54. My quotation from Herzl is taken from Andrzej Chojnowski, "Problem narodowościowy na ziemiach polskich w początkach XX w. i w II Rzeczypospolitej," in Andrzej Garlicki, ed., *Z dziejów Drugiej Rzeczypospolitej* (Warsaw: Wydawnictwa Szkolne i Pedagogiczne, 1986), p. 180.

13. Zenon E. Kohut, *Russian Centralism and Ukrainian Autonomy: Imperial Absorption of the Hetmanate, 1760s–1830s* (Cambridge, Mass.: Ukrainian Research Institute, 1988; distributed by Harvard University Press), p. 63. An excerpt from the Divovych poem is included in Ralph Lindheim and George S. N.

Luckyj, eds., *Towards an Intellectual History of Ukraine: An Anthology of Ukrainian Thought from 1710 to 1995* (Toronto: University of Toronto Press, 1996), pp. 69–70.

14. Greenfeld, *Nationalism: Five Roads to Modernity*, pp. 238–39; emphasis in original. In a source note to this discussion, Greenfeld comments: "The number of Ukrainians among the non-noble intellectuals . . . is extraordinary; it is beyond doubt that they played a very prominent role in the activities of the eighteenth-century intelligentsia. . . ." (ibid., p. 531, n. 90).

15. Edward L. Keenan argues that Muscovite Russia did not have an awareness of being a continuation of Kyiv: "These people were not even thinking of Kiev." Keenan, "On Certain Mythical Beliefs and Russian Behaviors," in S. Frederick Starr, ed., *The Legacy of History in Russia and the New States of Eurasia* (Armonk, N.Y., and London: M. E. Sharpe, 1994), pp. 19–40, quotation on p. 23. As Keenan sees it, modern scholars, and the general public, have been misled by certain myths regarding early "Russian" history without realizing that they were the product of a much later era, i.e., the time of Russian nation-building. Those misconceptions concern the links between Muscovy and Kyiv ("the Kiev myth" [pp. 21–25]), the nature of the Mongol period ("the Tatar yoke myth" [pp. 25–26]), and the popular myth of an alleged Byzantine or Greek influence, "one of the great mystifications of all of European cultural history. . . ." (p. 27). See also Keenan, "Muscovite Perceptions of Other East Slavs before 1654: An Agenda for Historians," in Peter J. Potichnyj et al., eds., *Ukraine and Russia in Their Historical Encounter* (Edmonton: Canadian Institute of Ukrainian Studies Press, 1992), pp. 20–38.

16. "Poletyka, Hryhorii," entry in Danylo Husar Struk, ed., *Encyclopedia of Ukraine*, vol. 4 (Toronto: University of Toronto Press, 1993), p. 94.

17. David Saunders, *The Ukrainian Impact on Russian Culture, 1750–1850* (Edmonton: Canadian Institute of Ukrainian Studies, University of Alberta, 1985), p. 9, quoting A. M. Lazarevsky, *Zamechaniia na istoricheskie monografii D. P. Millera o malorusskom dvorianstve i o statutovykh sudakh* (Kharkiv: n.p., 1898), p. 15.

18. Marc Raeff, "Ukraine and Imperial Russia: Intellectual and Political Encounters from the Seventeenth to the Nineteenth Century," in Peter J. Potichnyj, Marc Raeff, Jaroslaw Pelenski, and Gleb N. Zekulin, eds., *Ukraine and Russia in Their Historical Encounter* (Edmonton: Canadian Institute of Ukrainian Studies Press, 1992), p. 82.

19. Ibid., p. 80. This case illustrates Bourdieu's thesis that "political subversion presupposes cognitive subversion, a conversion of the vision of the world." Bourdieu, *Language and Symbolic Power*, pp. 127–28.

20. Anderson, *Imagined Communities*, pp. 70–71. The quote within the quote is from Edward Said, *Orientalism* (New York: Pantheon Books, 1978), p. 136.

21. For a review of competing models of the Russian nation in the context of tsarist Russia's and the Soviet Union's politics, see Roman Szporluk, "The Fall of the Tsarist Empire and the USSR: The Russian Question and Imperial Overextension," in Karen Dawisha and Bruce Parrott, eds., *The End of Empire? The Transformation of the USSR in Comparative Perspective* (Armonk, N.Y.: M. E. Sharpe, 1997), pp. 65–93. (Reprinted in this book as chapter 16.)

22. Andreas Kappeler, *Russland als Vielvölkerreich: Entstehung, Geschichte, Zerfall* (Munich: C. H. Beck, 1992), p. 179.

23. Paul Bushkovitch, "The Ukraine in Russian Culture, 1790–1860: The Evidence of the Journals," *Jahrbücher für Geschichte Osteuropas* 39, no. 3 (1991): 343–44. See also D. B. Saunders, "Contemporary Critics of Gogol's *Vechera* and the Debate about Russian *narodnost'* (1831–1832)," *Harvard Ukrainian Studies* 5, no. 1 (March 1981): 66–82.

24. Omeljan Pritsak, "Prorok," *Kyivs'ka starovyna*, no. 2 (1994): 11–12.

25. George G. Grabowicz, "Ukrainian-Russian Literary Relations in the Nineteenth Century: A Formulation of the Problem," in Potichnyj et al., *Ukraine and Russia in Their Historical Encounter*, p. 227.

26. F. Bulgarin, *Vospominaniia* (St. Petersburg: n.p., 1846–49), I, pp. 200–201; cited in Nicholas V. Riasanovsky, *Nicholas I and Official Nationality in Russia, 1825–1855* (Berkeley and Los Angeles, Calif.: University of California Press, 1967), p. 139. Riasanovsky also mentions another author, who slightly later proposed to rename the country "Nikolayevia."

27. Grabowicz, "Ukrainian-Russian Literary Relations in the Nineteenth Century," pp. 226–27.

28. See Nicholas V. Riasanovsky, *A Parting of Ways: Government and the Educated Public in Russia, 1801–1855* (Oxford: Clarendon Press, 1976).

29. Geoffrey Hawthorn, "Sub-Saharan Africa," in David Weld, ed., *Prospects for Democracy: North, South, East, West* (Cambridge, Mass.: Polity Press, 1993), p. 344.

30. Karel Havlíček, *Politické spisy*, ed. Z. Tobolka (Prague: n.p., 1900–1903), I, p. 70; quoted in Barbara K. Reinfeld, *Karel Havlíček (1821–1856): A National Liberation Leader of the Czech Renascence* (Boulder, Colo.: East European Monographs, 1982), p. 25. In his "Slovan a Čech," Havlíček argued that Slavs are not a nation, as shown by the Polish-Russian relationship: "So intense is the hatred between these two peoples that they exclude each other from a Slav brotherhood! The Poles claim the Russians are Mongolians, while the Russians call the Poles Sarmacians. The main bone of contention which has divided every generation of Poles and Russians is the possession of the Ukraine. Both the Poles and the Russians claim this land on the basis of related nationality. The Russians point to the fact that they share the same religion with the Ruthenes; the Poles retort with the formation of the Uniate church. At present the Russians hope to acquire the Ukraine by Russifying the people as the Poles

have been able to Polonize the Lithuanians, by alienating the upper classes from the rest of their own people." Havlíček, *Politické spisy*, I, p. 63, cited by Reinfeld, *Karel Havlíček*, pp. 24–25.

31. Mykhailo Hrushevsky, "Halychyna i Ukraina," *Literaturno-naukovyi vistnyk* 36 (1906): pp. 489–96; cited in Thomas M. Prymak, *Mykhailo Hrushevsky: The Politics of National Culture* (Toronto: University of Toronto Press, 1987), pp. 79–80 n.

32. John A. Armstrong, "Myth and History in the Evolution of Ukrainian Consciousness," in Potichnyj et al., *Ukraine and Russia in Their Historical Encounter*, pp. 125–39. Anthony Smith has noted that ". . . ethnic communities often develop political myths, myths that are constitutive of the political community (or *mythomoteurs*). . . . The main distinction of relevance here is between "dynastic" and "communal" *mythomoteurs*, between political myths attached to sacral kingship or those based on the ideal of the sacred community or people." Anthony D. Smith, "Ethnic Identity and Territorial Nationalism in Comparative Perspective," in Alexander J. Motyl, ed., *Thinking Theoretically about Soviet Nationalities: History and Comparison in the Study of the USSR* (New York: Columbia University Press, 1992), p. 50. As we see it, the Ukrainian "mythomoteur" upheld the idea of a culturally defined people that carried forward ethical and social values and did not depend on the state for its existence. Thus, it was by definition incompatible with the official definition of "nationality" that made autocracy the constitutive element of an imperial Russian identity that also included "Little Russians."

33. Mykhailo Hrushevsky, "Zvychaina skhema 'russkoi' istoriyi i sprava ratsional'noho ukladu istoriï skhidnoho slovianstva" (St. Petersburg: n.p., 1904); reprinted and translated in A. Gregorovich, ed., *The Traditional Scheme of "Russian" History and the Problem of a Rational Organization of the History of the East Slavs* (Winnipeg: Ukrainian Free Academy of Sciences, 1966).

34. Ivan Franko, "Odvertyi lyst do halyts'koï ukraïns'koï molodezhi," *Zibrannia tvoriv u piatdesiaty tomakh* (Kyiv: Naukova dumka, 1976), vol. 45, p. 404, cited in Oksana Zabuzhko, *Filosofiia ukraïns'koï idei ta evropeis'kyi kontekst: Frankivs'kyi period* (Kyiv: Naukova dumka, 1992), p. 61. (The title of Zabuzhko's book reveals its message: "The Philosophy of the Ukrainian Idea and Its European Context: The Period of Franko.")

35. Fedotov, "Budet li sushchestvovat' Rossiia?" in *O Rossii i russkoi filosofskoi kul'ture. Filosofy russkogo posleoktiabr'skogo zarubezh'ia* (Moscow: Nauka, 1990), p. 455.

36. Ibid., p. 461.

37. Ann Devroy and James Rupert, "Clinton Commends Ukrainians for Sticking with Tough Reforms," *Washington Post*, May 13, 1995, p. A20. In 1997, demonstrators in Minsk, at a solidarity rally with Serb and Bulgarian democrats, displayed the slogan, "We want to live in Europe, not in Russia!"

Oleg Moroz, "Kremlevskie politiki izo vsekh sil staraiutsia napugat' tekh, kto nas i tak smertel'no boitsia," *Literaturnaia gazeta*, February 5, 1997, p. 9. The future of Belarus as a state, one may surmise, will depend not on how many people speak Belorussian (rather than Russian) but on the nationalists' ability to convince people that the republic's independence from Moscow means its openness to "the world."

16 The Fall of the Tsarist Empire and the USSR: The Russian Question and Imperial Overextension

Introduction

The Russian state collapsed twice in the twentieth century. In 1917, the Russian Empire disintegrated while it was fighting and losing a foreign war. The Soviet Union broke apart in 1991, in peacetime, several decades after it had won the greatest war in Russia's long history of wars. The first state collapsed before the Communists took power; the second, when it was under communist rule.

Many works have been written—and even more will be written—about causes of the breakup of both the Russian Empire and the USSR.[1] Our task here is much more modest—to focus on certain distinct "factors" ("circumstances," "conditions") which substantially contributed to these events, without claiming, however, that these are sufficient or necessary "causes" of what happened.

Unlike empires of modern times that fell while their former metropoles were gradually being transformed into "normal" nations and nation-states, the tsarist—and then the Soviet—empire fell apart before a modern Russian nation and a Russian nation-state had emerged. A

First published in *The End of Empire?*, 1997.

major factor in the imperial collapse in 1917, and in the Soviet collapse in 1991, proved to be conflict between the imperial state and an emergent Russian nation or "society." In both cases, "Russia" contributed to the fall of "empire." This leads us to the conclusion that both empires failed to solve the "Russian Question"—arguably their most important nationality question.

Another major factor in the fall of both the Russian and Soviet empires was their overextension. They established their hegemony over nations and territories that refused to recognize Russia and/or the USSR as a superior civilization, a higher form of economy and government—qualities an empire must possess if its rule is not to be based on coercion alone. To maintain hegemony over them in the absence of such recognition required a disproportionate reliance on coercion, and this made Russian rule in "Europe" a heavy burden on the Russian people, which in turn further contributed to the alienation of the Russians from "their" state. These were additional obstacles to the formation of a modern Russian nation. Thus, the inclusion of non-Russian peoples under Imperial/Soviet rule negatively affected the conditions under which the Russians lived. Having been called—and coerced—by their rulers, both tsarist and communist, to serve "the great cause" of the empire, the Russians found it very difficult to establish for themselves a political identity distinct from and independent of empire.

Because of this special focus, the historical account of this chapter is highly selective in facts and problems mentioned. We are interested in those elements of the past experience that may be a useful guide for the identification of the future trends, from which one may draw some lessons. Hegel's famous quip that "the only lesson history teaches is that men do not learn any lessons from history" is usually quoted out of context: Hegel did say not that nothing else was to be learned from history; the problem, he said, was that people did not know how to find the deeper meaning behind concrete events.[2]

What do we mean by empire? There are many definitions available and we do not propose to offer a new one here. Instead, we shall help ourselves to some descriptions of empire by others that appear to be helpful in our study. Ghita Ionescu sees "three basic elements" in an empire: (1) "a strong political centre, animated by a historical mission of expansion," (2) "religious or ideological coercion," and (3) "a sense of final purpose" in its elite.[3]

For Dominic Lieven, "an empire has to be a great power," but it must also "play a major role in shaping . . . the values and culture of an historical epoch. To be a great power has implications as regards resources, ideologies, expansionist temptations and cultural styles which, in historical terms, are implicit in the concept of empire."[4]

Finally, Istvan Hont sees an empire as "a kind of territorial state-system within which entire populations or nations (even if they might retain the appearance of being the inhabitants of a distinct and separate territory) are also considered as either superiors or inferiors." Hont agrees with Michael W. Doyle that "Empire . . . is a relationship, formal or informal, in which one state controls the effective political sovereignty of another political society. It can be achieved by force, by political collaboration, by economic, social, or cultural dependence."[5]

Thus, following these authors, we conclude that to qualify as an empire a polity needs to be a great power and to be internationally recognized as such; to extend over a large territory and to include different peoples under different legal and administrative systems; to be endowed with a sense of ideological or religious mission that transcends considerations of power politics; and to act as a leader in the sphere of culture.

The Tsarist Empire

Russia began to call itself an empire only in 1721, but it had in fact become an empire long before Peter I renamed his country. Peter's assumption of a Western title (at that time in Europe there was one other polity in the same class, the "Holy Roman Empire" ruled by the Habsburgs) is rightly associated with his—and Russia's—orientation toward and identification with "Europe."

Empire in the East

Long before these changes in titles, however, Muscovy had already become an empire. A key event in this process took place in the reign of Ivan the Terrible—the so-called "Conquest of Kazan." Andreas Kappeler rightly devotes a chapter titled "Gathering of the Lands of the Golden Horde from the 16th to the 18th Century" in his account of the rise of the Russian Empire.[6]

Subsequently, Muscovite Russians and Volga Tatars and other eastern, mainly Turkic and Islamic, peoples lived under one jurisdiction. The

Muscovite elites worked out a modus vivendi with the elites of the eastern peoples, with whom their ancestors had been acquainted during the so-called Mongol rule over Muscovite Russia. Richard Pipes has noted that the Russians were successful in assimilating those (eastern) nations whose nobility did not enjoy the same privileges their Russian counterparts had, but the Russians were a "complete failure" in the western provinces, where the local nobles had traditionally been better off than they.[7] Under Moscow, the Russian and Tatar elites established a cooperative relationship and Moscow's further expansion to the east was facilitated by this Muscovite-Tatar cohabitation.[8] The Muscovites and the peoples of the Volga and farther east lived together in a polity to which concepts taken from the West European experience did not apply: Moscow's "Eastern Empire" was formed before the age of modern nations and nationalism, and in areas where Western ideas, if known at all, were accessible only via Moscow.

Empire in the West

Things were quite different in Russia's western domains. The Muscovite state also expanded to the West before Peter's time, in the fifteenth and sixteenth centuries, gaining Novgorod and parts of the Grand Duchy of Lithuania, a vast polity that at one time extended over what we know today as Belarus, Ukraine, and western regions of Russia. Those western acquisitions brought areas previously exposed to Western influences into the Muscovite realm, but they were not strong enough to counterbalance the eastern character of the Russian state. The first "Westernization" of Moscow came in the seventeenth century when the tsar established his overlordship in the formerly Polish-ruled parts of Ukraine to the east of the Dnieper, and also over the city of Kyiv. The result was the transformation of Russian culture under the impact of Ukrainian or "West Russian" (including Belorussian) infusions, which prompted some Russian scholars to connect the emergence of a modern Russia to this "Ukrainization" of Muscovy in the seventeenth and eighteenth centuries.[9]

The next major step in the Europeanization of Russia came under Peter the Great. In addition to the many changes in cultural, administrative, and military spheres, Peter gained new territories from Sweden, including the site where St. Petersburg, Russia's new capital, was built and also the Baltic provinces, the present-day Estonia and Latvia. In the partitions of Poland in the late eighteenth century, Catherine II added most of Poland's Ukraine (except Galicia) and all of today's Belarus and Lithuania. Finally, in 1815, under Alexander I, Russia acquired even the central Polish lands, with Warsaw, Lublin, Kielce, and Kalisz, which came to be known as the "Congress Kingdom." A little earlier, in 1809, Russia acquired Finland from Sweden, thus adding a Protestant nation to the mainly Protestant Estonians and Latvians and Baltic Germans who had been under Russia since Peter.

Thus, besides the Orthodox and Muslims (and Russia gained many of the latter in Crimea and other formerly Ottoman possessions), this newly enlarged Russia included millions of Jews, Catholics (including Catholics of the Uniate rite), and Protestants. This kind of imperial expansion into "Europe" had no analogy in the European experience. The West European empires expanded overseas—while Russia, concurrently with eastern conquests, was establishing its rule over regions and peoples who were more "European" than Russia itself. In this respect the Habsburg expansion into the Balkans and parts of Poland (1772, 1795) was different because Vienna was more "Western" than any of its new acquisitions. To be sure, modern Western nations had been built by conquest. Those conquests, however, happened long before the age of nationalism, and this factor in the end made it possible for the Bretons, the Burgundians, and the Provençals to recognize the primacy of Paris and eventually to become "French." As the Russians were soon to learn, it would prove much harder—if at all possible—to convince the new European subjects of St. Petersburg that they should become Russian. However backward the East Europeans may have been in comparison with the British, French, or Germans, they were, or thought themselves to be, more "advanced" than their Russian masters. As new ideas of nationality arose, these new subjects increasingly saw themselves as Poles (in old Poland only nobles were "Polish"), Finns, Ukrainians, Lithuanians, Estonians, and so on. If the Russians were to learn from the experience of the West, they should have sought to forge a new common identity with the Tatars and other peoples ruled by Muscovy, just as England, Wales, and Scotland had combined to produce a common British identity.[10]

Empire in the Age of Nationalism

Instead of working to bring together the peoples and religions it already had, Russia entered the age of nationalism by annexing a nation that would prove to be its relentless and irrepressible enemy.

In his influential book on the rise and fall of "Russia as a Multinational Empire," Andreas Kappeler says:

> The Polish national movement first, and most strongly, undermined the Russian Empire. It challenged not only the government but also a large part of the Russian society, and it influenced the Lithuanians, Belorussians, and Ukrainians, who had been dependent on the Polish nobility for centuries and had been influenced by Polish culture. The Poles played this leading role once again in the crisis of the Soviet Empire at the end of the twentieth century.[11]

Throughout the nineteenth century, Poland represented the most celebrated case of a nation seeking to recover its freedom. There was a series of Polish uprisings directed against Russia, which played the role of Poland's main oppressor. Poland was a proud nation that had been deprived of its state, and the Russian Empire was forced to deal with the Polish question at a time when the fundamental issues of Russian nation-formation had not been solved.

At about the same time East-Central and Eastern Europe became attracted to the ideas, originally formulated in Germany, that nationality was a cultural community based on language, and that nations and languages formed families. Scholars and writers among the Czechs, Serbs, Russians, and others discovered that their languages and thus their nations formed a single "Slavic" family. Some drew from this intellectual discovery an additional political conclusion: The Slavs should unite, there should be "Slavic solidarity," if not a single Slavic state. There were difficulties when it came to implementing the idea, however, as František Graus points out: "The only independent Slav country, Russia, was the most backward region in Europe, where serfdom continued until 1861 and where the non-aristocratic population had no privileges whatsoever." The Czechs felt themselves, rightly, much more advanced than the Russians, to whom being Slavic meant becoming Russian, but "the biggest problem . . . was presented by the Poles," who suffered under their fellow Slavs' oppression.[12]

The Russians felt they had to legitimate their presence in Europe in conformity with the new ideas of nationality then arising in Europe. They began to write the history of the empire and its predecessors as a Russian *national* history. Kappeler argues that in their drive to become—and be accepted as—"European" the Russians constructed their history (and redefined their relationship with the East) by employing concepts derived from the West. Their nineteenth-century historians had taught the Russians to look at the empire as the national state of the Russians—and the new philology and ethnography defined the Russians as a Slavic and Orthodox Christian people. In the works of the great Russian historians of the nineteenth century, "the history of a multinational empire of Russia became Russian history."[13]

This in turn meant relegating the nonethnic Russians—some of whom had lived with the Russians in one state for centuries—as "inorodtsy," or aliens; in short—as Russia's "minorities," if not outright colonial peoples. This approach overlooked a fundamental difference recently noted by Geoffrey Hosking: "Britain *had* an empire, but Russia *was* an empire—and perhaps still is." The British empire, Hosking explains, was distant (Ireland was the exception) and the British people were therefore able to detach themselves from it "without undue distress." On the other hand, the "Russian empire was part of the homeland, and the 'natives' mixed inextricably with the Russians in their own markets, streets, and schools—as indeed they still do."[14]

Clearly, Russia's identification with the Slavs, and the redefinition of the country in European categories, had certain long-term implications for Moscow's relations with the Russian East. It was not immediately obvious to all that moving the capital from Moscow to St. Petersburg, which brought Russia closer to "Europe," also made Russia's domestic "Orient"—Kazan and beyond—more foreign, more distant. The "Slavic idea," which contributed to undermining the dynastic principle in the Habsburg monarchy and helped create a cultural and spiritual barrier between "the Slavs" and the Germanic and Romance peoples, gave the Russians a sense of being the senior and most powerful member of the family of Slavonic nations in Europe; but, on the other hand, if taken seriously, it delegitimized on ethnic grounds Russia's presence in the East, in "Asia."

These implications would become clear only in the twentieth century, however. In the later half of the eighteenth and during much of the nineteenth, the building blocs of Russian national history were assembled. The new history made Muscovite and then St. Petersburg Russia a direct heir of the Byzantine Empire—and through it of ancient Greek culture—and therefore the leader of the Orthodox world.

The Byzantium myth, or popular belief that Byzantine or Greek influence had a formative influence on Russian culture and politics, and thus identity, "is one of the great mystifications of all of European cultural history." According to Edward L. Keenan, "it is difficult to identify a single native Muscovite who knew any significant amount of Greek before the second half of the seventeenth century."[15] But this idea gave historical support to the imperial Russian dream of the "reconquest" of Constantinople, the Tsargrad or "Tsar's City," from Islam.

Another myth linked Muscovy to medieval Kyiv. In fact, Muscovite Russians did not have an awareness of being a continuation of Kyiv until others told them. "These people were not even thinking of Kiev."[16] It was only after Ukraine was attached to Russia in the seventeenth century that Moscow's Kyiv connection was established and projected back into the medieval past. This tie was reaffirmed during the partitions of Poland when most of Ukraine and all of Belarus found themselves within Russia: The Kyiv myth served to counter Polish claims, and was later also invoked to deny Ukrainian demands for recognition as a nation distinct from the Russians.[17]

It should come as no surprise that the Russians reinterpreted their historic experience with the Tatars while they were adding Kyiv and Byzantium to their pedigree. Tatars came to be seen in terms of the "Tatar (or Mongol) Yoke" myth. According to this account, medieval Rus' had suffered under this yoke, and there were numerous wars fought against the Tatars, resulting in, among other things, the conquest of a *Moslem* Kazan by *Christian* Russians.

These ideological constructions of the eighteenth century set the stage for the nineteenth-century controversies so well known to, and so beloved by, intellectual historians of Russia. Of these the most famous has been the Slavophile-Westernizer debate. However deeply their participants may have disagreed on Russia's relations with "Europe," they all thought of Russia in terms they had adopted from that very "Europe." The Slavophile defenders of Russian uniqueness understood their Russia to be Slavic and Orthodox—they did not admit the Tatars to their community. In other words, their understanding of Russia was shaped by the Western theories. Eurasianism, which would argue that Russians and their Eastern peoples belonged to one community, was not invented until after 1917. In the meantime, theory-dependency was a common Russian disorder.[18]

Russian empire-building proceeded in two directions: First, in association with Kazan Moscow undertook a movement eastward; somewhat later, but especially after gaining East Ukraine and Kyiv, it undertook a movement to the west. Russia's eastern drive proved to be more successful—despite religious and cultural barriers, than its drive to the west—despite the religious and cultural affinity between Russians and their immediate neighbors there. Russia's nineteenth-century conquests in the Caucasus and Central Asia, however, were openly colonial, and were of the same kind as European colonial ventures overseas—the French conquest of North Africa, for example. In the nineteenth century the Russians looked at "the East" with European spectacles if not eyes.[19]

The Empire and the Russians

This vast empire, which extended from the Baltic to the Pacific, and, within Europe, included lands and peoples from Finland to Bessarabia and Crimea, faced profound political and social problems in "Russia proper"—problems complicated by the fact that no one knew where "Russia proper" ended and where "empire" began, for, as we have already noted, Russia did not have an empire, it was one.

In a crude summary of its political and social history, we may say that in the course of the nineteenth century the tsarist state was challenged by those Russians who believed in revolution as a means for solving Russian problems and those who preferred reform. The revolutionary tradition included the Decembrist Insurrection of 1825 ("the first Russian revolution"), the activities of Alexander Herzen in exile, the rise of revolutionary movements and political terrorism, which led among other things to the assassination of Alexander II (1881), peasant disturbances, industrial strikes, the emergence of Marxist circles and the formation of the Russian Social Democratic party (1898), its split into the Bolshevik and Menshevik wings and then into separate parties, the revolution of 1905. The revolutionary camp viewed the questions Russia faced at the beginning of the twentieth century as being so fundamental—the abolition of monarchy, liquidation of landlord property, struggle against capitalism—that only revolution could solve them.

There was a parallel "bourgeois," liberal and democratic, constitutional alternative to tsarist autocracy which included people active in regional and local self-government, professional associations, an independent press, and educational and cultural societies. The establishment of the Duma in 1906, and the survival of this representative body until 1917, suggested that the state might gradually evolve toward, if not democracy, then at least liberal constitutionalism. In the meantime, the supporters of the absolute monarchy began to abandon their traditional dynastic legitimism in favor of nationalist or ethnic ideas of identity. In the early twentieth century a Russian nationalist movement emerged, which viewed the empire as a nation-state of the Russians. It treated all others as "aliens" and called for denying them the rights the "real Russians" were to enjoy. During the reigns of Alexander III (1881–1894) and Nicholas II (1894–1917), this chauvinist current won increasing support in the official court circles.

Needless to say, not only ethnic Russians participated in the revolutionary or reformist (or even pro-tsarist) movements: In all camps persons of virtually all ethnic backgrounds were present, which was understandable considering that in the early twentieth century ethnic Russians, or Great Russians as they were then called, formed less than half of the empire's population, with Ukrainians, Poles, Belorussians, Jews, Finns, Armenians, Georgians, and Tatars being among the most numerous "minorities." However, although the more traditionalist elements of the minorities accepted the monarchy as legitimate, its growing identification with Russian nationalism made it difficult for even the most conservative or loyal ethnic to believe in the tsar. Needless to say, the nationalities also had their own ethnic parties and organizations and movements.

Poland was the most serious of all of Russia's nationality problems. The official circles of Russia, and most of its public opinion, considered the Polish question solved by the arrangements adopted at the Congress of Vienna in 1815, and regarded the Polish question an internal matter of the three states in which Poles lived. This was not the point of view of the Poles, as demonstrated by the uprisings of 1830–31 and 1863–64 and the major role played by Russian Poland in the revolution of 1905. In Poland, and in Finland and Latvia especially, as well as in the Caucasus region, 1905 was as much a social as a national revolution.[20]

In 1905 the names of two Poles who would win prominence after 1917—Józef Piłsudski as the founder of an independent Polish state and Feliks Dzierżyński (Dzerzhinsky) as the founder of the Soviet secret police—first became known to a wider public. At the same time the Ukrainian, Lithuanian, and Belorussian national movements, which originally developed within the Russian Empire in a social and cultural confrontation with the Poles, declared themselves in opposition to Russian autocracy. Moreover, the Poles began to see these nationalities as their allies against Russia. The Finns, Estonians, and Latvians also developed an anti-imperial outlook.

From War to Revolution, 1914–1917

We shall never know which way Russia would have gone had war not interfered in 1914. But it did. By 1916 and early 1917 it was clear that Russia was losing the war. Even more than the war with Japan of 1905, the Great War exposed and exacerbated Russia's unsolved issues and problems. A series of crises led to the abdication of the tsar and the fall of the monarchy in March 1917. A new Russia was headed by the Provisional Government drawn from the Duma parties. The Russian people were, or so it seemed, in charge of their state. A general election was to be held to elect the Constituent Assembly that would establish Russia as a democratic and progressive country and solve the most pressing issues, such as land reform and the rights of the nationalities and religious groups; in short, it would complete and ratify the formation of a modern Russian nation along Western lines.

Within months, in November 1917, the Provisional Government was out and the Bolsheviks were in with their own, "Soviet" government. Small wonder that quite a few students and even occasional popular accounts write that "in 1917, the Bolsheviks under Lenin's leadership overthrew the tsar." But the Bolsheviks did not overthrow the tsar. They overthrew Russia's first democratic government.

Again, historians list a variety of "causes" and circumstances, such as the continuation of a highly unpopular war, that made it possible for Lenin and his comrades to seize power, first in Petrograd and Moscow, and then, after a bloody civil war, to establish their rule in most of the old empire.

1917: The Fall of the Empire and the Unmaking of a Nation

Why did a democratic Russia survive only a little over half a year? Why did the Bolsheviks win? All three events in their sequence and connection—the fall of the monarchy, the fall of democracy, and the victory of the Bolsheviks—were proof that the Russian nation-making process had not been completed by 1917.

The population of Russia—here we have in mind the "core" of ethnic Russian people—remained divided along several fault lines. The educated (or "bourgeois") urban society was alienated from the imperial state; a large part of the industrial working class was alienated not only from the state but also from "society"; and, most fundamentally, the masses of the peasantry—that is, a majority of the Russians—were living in a world separated both socially and culturally from the bourgeois society and the urban world. It is well known that the Bolsheviks were able to take advantage of the peasantry in their struggle for power even though their program, as became evident very quickly, had been thoroughly inimical to its interests and aspirations. In 1917, as Pipes explains, "the peasant was revolutionary in one respect only: he did not acknowledge private ownership of land." Even though most of the arable land was in the peasants' possession, they "craved" the land of the landlords, merchants, and noncommunal peasants. Pipes sees in "the prevalence of communal landholding in European Russia . . . along with the legacy of serfdom, a fundamental fact of Russian social history." The collapse of tsarism is explainable by "deep-seated cultural and political flaws that prevented the tsarist regime from adjusting to the economic and cultural growth of the country," and these flaws became fatal under the conditions of war. "We are dealing here with a national tragedy whose causes recede deep into the country's past."[21]

Pipes further elaborates on this point:

> The problem with Russian peasants was not oppression, but isolation. They were isolated from the country's political, economic, and cultural life, and therefore unaffected by the changes that had occurred since the time that Peter the Great had set Russia on the course of Westernization. . . . The peasantry remained steeped in Muscovite culture: culturally it had no more in common with the ruling elite or the intelligentsia than the native population of Britain's African colonies had with Victorian England.[22]

One may remain not fully convinced by Pipes in his assessment of the peasantry's economic condition and yet recognize the force of his argument about the negative consequences of the peasants' cultural and legal isolation from "society." Perhaps that isolation would have been less oppressive if the energy and resources the empire spent (and wasted) on Russifying the non-Russians—and most expensively of all, Poland—had been devoted to "Russifying" the peasants in the Great Russian countryside—by teaching them to read and write, for example. This is just one illustration of how the Polish question profoundly—and fatally—affected Russia's internal development.

Mark R. Beissinger is right that "the national self-assertion of Russia's minorities did not bring down the Tsarist regime," and that "nationalist elites . . . cautiously went about declaring national states in the chaos and confusion that ensued." However, it is hard to agree with him that "the Tsarist system collapsed on its own."[23]

At the time, to those who viewed Russia in light of European history, and they included a majority of educated Russians, the Russian nation or society had emancipated itself from the imperial state in March 1917 and was beginning to establish Russia as a "normal country." Surely they were right to celebrate the fall of the monarchy as the conclusion of a long political struggle, going back to the Decembrists and most immediately to the revolution of 1905, even if the immediate cause of the overthrow was a spontaneous popular demonstration. In this sense the Russian March 1917 was seen by analogy with the revolutions of 1789 and 1848 in "Europe." However, few people then noticed that the bulk of the Russian population, the peasants, had not yet been transformed into nationally conscious Russians, unlike their cousins elsewhere who had by then become French, or German, or, within the Russian Empire, Polish, Finnish, or Lithuanian. The leaders who took power after March did not do enough to "nationalize" the masses—to bring the country people into a larger imagined community of the Russian nation. Indeed, it is arguable that the portion of ethnically Ukrainian peasants (whom official Russia termed "Little Russians") who displayed an awareness of themselves as Ukrainians by nationality was relatively larger than that of ethnic "Great Russian" peasants who thought in terms of a Russian nation and state. If this was the case, perhaps some reconceptualization of the revolution of 1917 is in order. Scholars generally assume that while there was a social revolution in Russia in 1917, there was no *Russian* "national problem" in Russia itself. In conformity with this view, the subject of the Russian revolution belongs to social history, and this social history acquires an additional national coloring, secondary in importance to the real social issue in ethnic borderlands, such as Ukraine—but not in Russia "proper."[24] However, if Pipes is right about the relation of Russia's peasants to the state and the society of "their" country, if class conflict between the rural masses and the urban society in Russia was so deep that it prevailed over any kind of interclass national solidarity—-as confirmed by the events of 1917 and the subsequent civil war—a conclusion about the failure of Russian nation-building is warranted.[25]

The argument that November 1917 constituted the "unmaking of a nation" can be further supported by the program and actual policies of the Bolsheviks, since they viewed Russia, in the words of Pipes, "as a springboard for world revolution."[26] It is highly implausible that the peasants and workers who supported the Bolsheviks also considered world revolution their highest priority. Can such a people be a nation and still succumb to a group of obvious dreamers, if not outright madmen, launching a world socialist republic? The Russian historian Yuri Got'e noted in his diary on January 22, 1918: "What kind of nation is this that allows such experiments to be performed on itself?"[27]

The Soviet Union: Ideology, Geopolitics, and Nations

After it was formally constituted in 1922 to 1924, the Soviet Union was a restored Russian empire in important and self-evident respects. This was acknowledged as early as the 1920s by some Russian exiles who had been bitter enemies of communism but now thought that because the Bolsheviks had saved Russia from breakup they should be supported by "Russian patriots." Such a call for support was a minority view but there was a common recognition that under the Red Flag Russia remained Russia. The Soviet state was also very different, however. Leaving aside the obvious contrast between an essentially conservative tsarism and the revolutionary, "transformationalist" Soviets, the following points are especially relevant in this review.

First, the tsars did not regard their principles suitable for the entire globe and they did not aspire to unify the world under one—their— authority. The Soviet state was not only ideological, but it considered its ideology valid universally and its form of government destined for adoption everywhere. In the words of Ernest Gellner, Soviet communism was "to an extent unusual and perhaps unique in the history of social systems, the implementation of an elaborate, total, all-embracing and deeply messianic theory."[28]

Second, compared with imperial Russia the Soviet state was significantly reduced in size and even more significantly transformed in its population mix. Those nationalities that before 1914 had been the most "Western," the farthest advanced on the road to modern nationhood, did not remain with Russia after the revolution: Finland, Poland, Latvia,

Estonia, and Lithuania emerged as sovereign states. Since these were the nations that by general consensus were the most advanced, and more "European" than the Russians, the Soviet Union was more of a Russian state than tsarist Russia had been. Indeed the census of 1926 recorded a Russian majority in the USSR, whereas before 1914 the Russians had been only a plurality.[29]

Third, although it was so much more "Russian" than its predecessor, the country was called Union of Soviet Socialist Republics and was internally organized according to ethnic or linguistic criteria as a federation of socialist nation-states that reserved for themselves the right, acknowledged in all Soviet constitutions, freely to secede from the Union. This provision was not the result of benevolence on the part of the regime. By 1922, the most "European" dependencies of the empire had seceded. Those who tried but failed to become independent states in 1918 to 1920—Ukraine, Belarus, Armenia, Georgia, and Azerbaijan— received an acknowledgment of their efforts and continuing quest for recognition: As formally equal partners of Russia—that is, the RSFSR— they joined a "new" entity, the USSR. This took place after a dispute between Lenin and Stalin, who had proposed instead to include Ukraine, Belarus, Georgia, Armenia, and Azerbaijan as autonomous republics within the RSFSR.

The establishment of the USSR raised the question of the identity of "Russia proper" and its relation to the USSR. Formally, Russia became a nation-state, a constitutional equal of Ukraine or Belarus. At the same time the RSFSR remained more than that. In 1922 the future Kazakhstan, Uzbekistan, Turkmenia, Krygyzstan, and Tajikistan (under different names) belonged to the Russian Federation, which was thus a Slavic-Turkic and Christian-Moslem entity. Only after 1924, in a major territorial-national reorganization of Central Asia, did these areas leave the RSFSR and join the USSR directly. But even afterward the RSFSR retained a whole panoply of autonomous republics, districts, and regions, each named after an ethnic group, and was thus a smaller replica of the USSR within the USSR.

The Tatar Autonomous SSR was the most important of the republics within the Russian Federation, and as Tatarstan it remains the most important unit within present-day Russia. Stalin refused to grant the Tatars the status of a Union republic on the spurious argument that Tatarstan did not border on a foreign territory and thus would not be able to exercise its constitutional right of secession. But perhaps history rather than geography lay behind Stalin's real motives: Kazan became part of the same state as Moscow long before Tashkent or Baku or even Kyiv had found themselves under Moscow or St. Petersburg. The Russians and Tatars were together first under the khans of the Golden Horde, and then again, uninterruptedly, from Ivan the Terrible to Nicholas II.

From this historical summary it is possible to identify some of the factors that secured the Bolshevik survival in power. On one hand, the Bolsheviks appealed to Russian patriotism when they defended the integrity of what most Russians considered to be their country. Former tsarist generals and officers volunteered their services to Lenin and Trotsky in 1920 during the Polish-Soviet war, which from the Russian nationalist point of view was about saving Kyiv for Russia, and from the Polish point of view was a war first to help the Ukrainians in their struggle for independence and then a war for Poland's survival as a nation (but for Lenin and his comrades it was a means to promote revolution in Europe).[30] On the other hand, because they had started out as resolute opponents of Russian nationalism, the Bolsheviks found support among members of Russia's oppressed nationalities who provided crucial support to the Bolsheviks in the battles of the civil war. These included Poles, Finns, and Latvians, who remained in the USSR after the war because their homelands were "capitalist" countries. The Soviet cause also found some supporters beyond the old Russian empire: For them, as for Lenin, the Polish war was to make the Russian revolution international—and the Polish victory was the world revolution's defeat.

Other, more conventional, geopolitical factors also helped the Soviets. The war against Germany dragged on until November 1918, and the war-exhausted victors were unwilling to intervene in Russia. The Western powers were firmly committed to preserving the territorial integrity of Russia after the expected fall of communism and thus they refused to help the nationalists in the borderlands. (Let us recall that the United States had great problems with recognizing the independence of Finland and the Baltic states—even while refusing to recognize Soviet Russia.)

The Soviet Utopia

After 1917, the Russian nation-building process was interrupted or sidetracked by the communist experiment, in which an empire was restored, or, more precisely, a new empire was founded on an expressly antinational, universalist ideological foundation. The communist state defined itself in global terms—as an alternative to "capitalism" and its political, social, and cultural order. Its aims were much greater than just to be good for Russia and the other Soviet republics. Lenin and his comrades in 1917 had had something different in mind: The USSR was to provide an alternative model of modernity, superior to that represented by the "West."

After 1917, the Bolsheviks persuaded themselves that their system, and therefore their leadership, would extend far beyond such reluctant parts of the old empire as Poland or Finland: They really believed that they represented the prototype of a single global civilization. Even for Stalin, "socialism in one country" was only a beginning.[31] Because the Soviets considered their system superior and suitable for other countries, they imposed it on the states of East Central Europe that they controlled after 1945. But, in the end there was neither socialism nor one country.[32]

Internationalism or Overextension?

This essay argues that practicing internationalism as Moscow understood it—overextension—was the undoing of the Soviet Union just as overextension had been a major factor in the collapse of imperial Russia. The seeds of the eventual collapse of the USSR were planted at the time of its greatest military and political triumph—during and after World War II.

First, in 1939–40, the Soviets annexed the Baltic states and eastern Poland, that is, the western regions of today's Ukraine and Belarus.[33] Then, after 1944, they imposed the Soviet system on those formerly independent states of Central and Eastern Europe that had found themselves under Soviet control at the end of the Second World War.[34] There, too, Sovietism was seen as a form of Russian domination. These nations had a strong sense of being different from Russia and wanted to emulate the West.

Perhaps the decline of the Soviet Union began with the first signs of the breakup of the unity of the communist world. The Stalin-Tito conflict and the expulsion of Yugoslavia was the first breach; the next, and much more important, one was the Sino-Soviet split.

There can be no question that geopolitically nothing could surpass the importance of the Moscow-Beijing break, but Poland posed a challenge to the Soviet communist ideology that it had no way of countering. Starting with the workers' strike in Poznan in June 1956, followed by workers' strikes in Gdansk in 1970, in Radom in 1976, in Gdansk again in 1980, and culminating in the rise of a multimillion Solidarity, Polish workers hit Soviet communism at the heart of its foundation, as a "workers' state." None of this is meant to diminish the role of the workers' strikes in East Germany in 1953, or that of the Hungarian revolution of 1956, or the Prague Spring of 1968. But it was precisely because of the fact that the Polish strikes were organized by workers and led by an electrician whose proletarian credentials were impeccable (and certainly more authentic than those of any of the leaders in Poland or in the USSR), that Poland could delegitimate the Soviet model on its own ground. This feat could not have been achieved by peasants or intellectuals or priests or students. The fact that the workers were both Polish and Catholic added a broader historical perspective to their struggle— making it another act in the centuries-long contest between a Catholic Poland and an Orthodox Russia.

After 1945 the Poles challenged Soviet communism just as their nineteenth- and early twentieth-century predecessors had historically done from the Kosciuszko Insurrection of 1794 to the workers' and students' strikes in Warsaw and Lodz in 1905. The history of Poland after 1945 confirms Kappeler's assessment of the Polish question's role in the decline and fall of the Soviet empire.

In an exercise in counterfactual history, let us imagine that after 1944, the Soviet Union had allowed a "Finlandized" Poland, instead of attempting to Sovietize/Russify it. There would have been no "Polish October" of 1956, and thus no Polish impact in the Bloc, no "Solidarity." (And if they had allowed Estonia, Latvia, and Lithuania to remain formally outside the USSR, the Soviets would have been spared quite a few more troubles at home, such as the attitude reflected in the Baltic slogan: "Moscow insists on treating us like all the other nationalities—so we shall help all them to become like us.") By suggesting a continuity between Kosciuszko and Walesa, we want to underline the fact that in most of Eastern and Central Europe the Soviet system was perceived as a Russian product and a form of Russian domination.

Over thirty years ago, Rupert Emerson described the post-1945 world: "Colonialism was on the way out far more speedily than had seemed at all possible. Only the old Czarist empire remained intact, undergoing the novel rhythms of Communist development, while the European satellites opened up a new dimension of empire."[35] Confirming this assessment of the origins of communist East Europe from the other end, three decades later, another scholar, Raymond Pearson, saw a "momentum of decolonisation" at work in its dissolution.[36]

Why Did the Soviet Empire Fall?

Of course, the Soviet empire in Europe did not fall when it did simply because the East Europeans resented the colonial status of their countries, the workers felt exploited, and the intellectuals made fun of Soviet ideology. The collapse followed the popular realization, which came with the Cold War, that the communist Grand Design had failed. As Pearson put it, "the Cold War strained and distorted the Soviet Empire to a hitherto unrecognised degree, proving as debilitating . . . as were the First and Second World Wars. In its excessive and finally intolerable military, economic and political demands, the Cold War fulfilled the function of a surrogate Third World War." Eric Hobsbawm reached an identical conclusion: "Internationally speaking, the USSR was like a country comprehensively defeated, as after a major war—only without a war."[37] And as factors in this outcome, he continued, Eastern Europe was "the Achilles heel of the Soviet system, and Poland (plus, to a lesser extent, Hungary) its most vulnerable spot."[38]

Why should Eastern Europe have been the "Achilles heel"? Wasn't the whole communist project international in its very essence? In answering this question we need to go beyond the issue of the Cold War.

The Soviet system was based on the idea that while the nation-state was a normal political form for the period of capitalism, socialism by its very nature was international or rather supranational. This international force would compete with and ultimately overtake the capitalist system—which consisted of sovereign nation-states. However, as early as the 1930s, under Stalin, the USSR began to identify itself with the tsarist empire's military traditions and foreign policies and the Russian nation was given the status of "elder brother."

The public and official identification of the Soviet Union with tsarist Russia became even stronger during and after the Second World War. Even as the USSR came to resemble tsarist Russia, however, and to assign a leading position to the Russian language and nation, it did not renounce its claim to represent the prototype of a new socialist civilization that was superior to that of "capitalism," and one that in the end would replace it in the whole world. It was this kind of "international-ism" that the East Europeans had to deal with after 1945.

After Stalin's death, in a changed international situation, Nikita S. Khrushchev renewed the old communist challenge to capitalist powers. The new party program offered a precise schedule of when the USSR would outpace first Western Europe and then the United States in vari-ous economic and social indicators. Soviet leaders were convinced that competing with the West required making the USSR at least equal mili-tarily with the United States, and countering the United States every-where, especially in the Third World. As they said in Moscow in the 1970s, this had to be done because "the United States is intervening in Soviet internal affairs in every part of the globe."

For a time, the Soviets seemed to be winning. Then it became in-creasingly clear that the Soviets would be unable to "produce a social order of both Virtue and Plenty"—indeed not even one of those things. "To add insult to injury," Ernest Gellner wrote, "the Japanese and other East Asians showed that Western capitalism can indeed be overtaken, but that it can be done by a Confucian rather than a Marxist adaptation of the ideas of Adam Smith."[39]

This realization caused a loss of faith—or, where faith had been lacking, produced a firmer determination to oppose communism. The East Europeans could see more easily than Soviet citizens that the West was winning. They would have agreed with Kenneth Minogue and Beryl Williams, who characterized communism as "an abortive form of mod-ernization" and "a mimicry that claim[ed] to be superior to the original performance."[40]

The East Europeans always knew that to see the original perform-ance one had to go west. Besides, they had had their own reasons not to think very highly of anything associated with Russia and to reject Rus-sian claims to superiority. They would agree with Benedict Anderson, who wondered in 1983 if the USSR was not more reminiscent of its nineteenth-century imperial predecessor than a precursor of a twenty-first century organization of humankind. (In a new preface dated Febru-ary 1991, Anderson was more specific, suggesting that "by the opening of the new millennium little will remain of the Union of Soviet Socialist Republics except . . . republics.")[41]

The Empire Breaks Up

From the breakup of the Soviet external empire in Europe we must turn to the fall of the USSR—from the Achilles heel to Achilles.

One can cite many "causes" of that momentous event—we *feel* that events of such enormity deserve nothing less—and the list of candidates is appropriately impressive. It is certainly impossible to ignore and also impossible to precisely weigh the personal factor—Mikhail Gorbachev. The cause that lay behind the East European collapse also helps explain the fall of the USSR—that is, the Soviet defeat in the Cold War. And the fall of Eastern Europe became a contributing cause of the breakup of the USSR. It was an axiom of Western Sovietology that the USSR would never give up its control over Central and Eastern Europe because the loss of East Europe would delegitimize communism within the USSR.[42]

What actually happened closely followed the "script" written by Randall Collins, a Weberian sociologist with no special expertise in the field. Arguing on the basis of a broad comparative survey, Collins concluded that "all major geopolitical processes appear to be working against the continuation of Soviet world power." "If an overextended imperial state," such as the Russian Empire/USSR, "becomes embroiled in ethnic and political conflicts within a distant client state, there is a strong tendency for these foreign instabilities to become gradually incorporated inside the imperial state's own boundaries." Collins therefore thought it "highly likely that, once a first round of serious crises caused the loss of Eastern Europe or other distant territory, there would be set in motion cumulative processes of internal weakening, culminating in the eventual loss of the next tier of ethnically distinct conquest: the Baltic states, the Ukraine, the Caucasus, and the central-Asian Moslem territories."[43]

What an outsider like Collins had so presciently anticipated came as a surprise to experts. Right up to the Soviet Union's fall, it was widely held that the Soviets had succeeded in building an urban and industrial society, indeed, had found a noncapitalist path to modernity, and had carried out a socialist equivalent of nation-building by creating a Soviet people that remained multiethnic and whose members spoke many languages but also had Russian as their common language. This was indeed the intention of the Soviets, except that they did not *call* the Soviet people a nation, *sovetskaia natsiia*, but used the term *sovetskii narod* instead. However, they promoted Soviet patriotism and taught the young the history of "the Great Patriotic War of the Soviet People." There was never any doubt that being a Soviet citizen was an identity overriding ethnicity: "My address is not a house or a street—my address is USSR." Everything in the official characterization of "Soviet people" corresponded to the conventional Western definition of a political or civic nation. Over sixty years ago the émigré scholar N. V. Ustrialov, in an article titled "On the Soviet Nation," noted (approvingly) that the Soviets were turning all peoples of the USSR into a nation defined politically and ideologically, not ethnically.[44]

Western scholarship tacitly, and often openly, understood "Soviet" in this sense. Books and articles were written and conferences held about *Soviet* workers, *Soviet* youth, *Soviet* music, ballet, and sport; lively debates about the political ambitions of a new Soviet middle class took place until virtually the end; and at least one foreign expert, unsolicited, advised Moscow about "inventing the Soviet national interest." People spoke about institutional pluralism in the USSR and they had in mind Soviet institutions. So when glasnost and perestroika came it was natural of them also to expect the emergence of new *Soviet* political parties, movements, and associations.

Little of the sort emerged, however. When the Cold War ended, as Eric Hobsbawm writes, "the international debacle encouraged secessionism in the republics where nationalist sentiment was strong." Hobsbawm is convinced that "the disintegration of the Union was not due to nationalist forces. It was due essentially to the disintegration of central authority, which forced every region or subunit of the country to look after itself. . . ." He argues that "the country moved towards a pluralist electoral politics at the very moment that it subsided into economic anarchy. . . . It was an explosive combination, for it undermined the shallow foundations of the USSR's economic and political unity."[45]

If such was the case, then we must say that a Soviet society did *not* exist. Otherwise an alternative to central authority would have emerged within a Soviet Union framework. Nationalism did not arise because the central state collapsed. The Soviet state collapsed because there was no *Soviet society* to defend it—and no authentic institutions from which a new *Soviet* leadership could emerge. As Anatoly Khazanov put it, the Soviet system was totalitarian, and "a virtual absence of civil society in the multiethnic Soviet state implied that the cooperation was most likely to be achieved by means of ethnic solidarity."[46]

The state did not break up into "regions," but into republics—and of various sizes. The Russian republic extended from the Baltic to the Pacific, with a population of over 150 million. Collins gave us a more persuasive explanation than Hobsbawm, and did so even *before* the event, of why the breakup occurred as it did:

> The formal machinery for the dismemberment of the Soviet Union is already in place. The fifteen largest ethnically distinct areas are officially autonomous states, possessing local machinery of government. . . . In current practice, this autonomy has little effect, as the armed forces, monetary system, and economic planning are controlled by organs of the central government and political control is organized by a single national Communist Party. The importance of the autonomous-ethnic-state structure, rather, is that it both maintains ethnic identities and provides an organizational framework that would allow genuinely separate states to emerge whenever the central government were seriously weakened.[47]

The discourse that replaced Marxism-Leninism in the Soviet Union's final days was the discourse of nation. Moscow did not create modern nations in the Soviet space: They emerged despite the efforts of the Soviet regime to the contrary. This explains why at first national movements were led mainly by writers, poets, artists, and scholars in the fields of humanities: All other spheres of public life had been Soviet. However, when they realized the Soviet ship was sinking, some heretofore Soviet figures decided to become "national" politicians. There were "born again" Uzbeks, Ukrainians, Georgians, and others. With the Moscow center gone, and where the societies and nations were particularly weak, these ex-Communists became masters of their new countries without even pretending to share power with the nationalist intelligentsia. Collins had seen it coming: "The projected disintegration of the Soviet Union would most likely occur under the leadership of dissident communist politicians. Given the current monopoly of communists over political organization in the Soviet Union, it would be difficult for political change to come about in any other way, at least initially."[48]

The Secession of Russia

Even Collins, however, did not predict *Russia's* secession from the empire. Who could have imagined that a former party secretary from the Urals, by defying the Kremlin, would attain the post of president (the first ever) of an independent Russia?

This was exactly what Boris N. Yeltsin did. Historians will argue forever about "objective" and "subjective" factors in the fall of the USSR, but John Barber is right when he says about the events of 1990–91: "The Soviet Union did not simply collapse: It was destroyed by the action of its opponents. . . . The alliance of reform Communists and anti-Communist 'democrats' . . . did not obtain state power in Russia by default."[49] In June 1990 the Russian Republic declared its "sovereignty," and this move was followed by a sequence of actions, including the creation of the office of President of Russia, and these moves "all steadily advanced the Russian republic towards full statehood."[50]

However, as George F. Kennan pointed out, while the Russian declaration of sovereignty simply "ranked the Russian nation with the various other peripheral entities in the former Soviet Union," this action posed "a mortal threat to the Soviet Union itself." The Soviet Union was becoming "an empty shell, without people, without territory, and with no more than a theoretical identity."[51]

Russia's Choices

Under the tsars and under Communists, as we saw, Russia failed to make the transition from an empire to a nation-state. Tension and then open conflict between the imperial state and an emergent Russian nation or "society" was a major factor in the imperial collapse in 1917 and in the Soviet collapse in 1991. In both cases, although in different ways, "Russia" contributed to the fall of "empire." Thus we arrive at a conclusion close, though not identical, to that of Mark R. Beissinger. He points out that "since the emergence of modern state-building within the Tsarist empire, state and empire have proven extremely difficult to separate, profoundly conditioning the collapse of the Russian empire, the demise of the USSR, and the context in which post-Soviet politics is now being played out."[52] In this essay we go further, and argue that the failure in state-building was a result of the more fundamental failure in Russian nation-formation.

In this respect Anatoly Khazanov provides a very illuminating analogy from another case of transition from imperial nationality to nation, one that helps us to understand the present Russian situation. According to Khazanov, the Russians in the Soviet Empire—and we may also suppose their predecessors in imperial Russia—"remained at the Ottoman stage of national identity." This means that they identified their country, Russia, with the Soviet Union much like the Turks used to identify Turkey with the Ottoman Empire. Khazanov argues that the Soviet nationality policy was "detrimental" to the formation of the Russian nation and allowed the rulers "to pass off imperial interests for Russian national interests." He concludes that the formation of a modern Russian nation has not yet been completed. Whether Russia will be a civic or an ethnic nation remains an open question.[53]

Are Russians in the post-Soviet Russian Federation (the country's official name) solving "the Russian question" more successfully than their imperial predecessors?

Let us first take a look at geography. One often hears, in Russia and abroad, that post-1991 Russia is an "artificial" creation because there is no historical precedent for a Russia in its present boundaries. That is true, but the same may be said about a great number of states existing in today's Europe, not to mention Asia or Africa. Before 1990, there was no Germany in its current boundaries. The Poland established in 1945 had never existed before. Turkey, whose shape on the map looks to all—except the Kurds—so natural and "normal," was seen in the 1920s as an "artificial" creation of the post-Ottoman settlement. Yet that new Turkey was even more "unhistorical" than post-Soviet Russia. Needless to say, in all these cases deep and painful reappraisals were necessary before the respective nations could agree on what they accepted Germany, Poland, and Turkey to be. (And very dramatic events had to happen before General de Gaulle could make the French accept that Algeria was not a part of France after all.)

These examples help us to appreciate the identity problems of contemporary Russia. But to understand Russian discomfort with geography one must go back to Russian history. History helps us understand why Kyiv, which was under Moscow "only" from 1667, became the capital of a newly independent country in 1991, while Kazan, under Moscow for more than a hundred years longer than Kyiv, is the capital of a republic *within* Russia.

Russia's relations with Ukraine, and the Russian-"Asian" nexus remain on top of the Russian national agenda today. Many Russians feel that the question of their country's cultural and political "location" (Is

Russia in "Europe" or does it form the core of "Eurasia"?) depends on how one solves these questions.

Ukrainian-Russian relations have received relatively close scrutiny and need not be summarized here except by noting that virtually all political circles in Russia continue to question the very existence of a Ukrainian nationality, even though, for tactical reasons, some prefer not to admit this openly. There is reason to think, however, that behind the controversies about the Black Sea fleet or the status of Crimea lies the refusal to accept Ukraine as a state independent of Russia.[54]

The Russian-"Eastern" connection as an issue in defining the identity of Russia receives less attention even though, as this discussion shows, it is historically tied to Russia's self-definition as a nation and a state. One of the unexpected consequences of the Chechen conflict may be a greater focus on the question of the nationality problem *within* the Russian Federation. An example of how serious these problems are taken to be, by at least some policymakers and scholars, may be found in the account of a symposium held in Moscow in 1995, titled "Russia under the Conditions of Strategic Instability." The following fragment from a statement of N. N. Moiseev reveals what that symposium was about:

> If we think about it profoundly, we shall see that the two millennia of our life with the Tatars and their ancestors have formed similar mentalities in us. And that is why our synthesis with the Islamic world is realistic, provided there is a sufficiently deep mutual respect and understanding. But if we do not attain it, we shall be in trouble [*nam grozit beda*]. I am sure of this.[55]

To this one might predictably respond by saying that all sorts of things, including quite off-the-mark ones, are heard these days in Moscow. Why should it matter what Academician Moiseev says?[56] Indeed, these days policymakers and influential analysts in Moscow do devote much more attention to how to "recover" Minsk, Almaty, and Kyiv than to worrying about how not to "lose Kazan." They think more about restoring an empire—will it call itself the Third Empire?—and less about building a state (the Second Republic?). Perhaps they are being realistic: The first empire lasted several centuries; the second, seventy years—whereas the first republic, the only democracy Russia ever knew until the fall of the USSR, survived a mere eight months.

The restorers of the empire may also be wrong. They may be repeating the fatal mistakes of their tsarist and Soviet predecessors, who, according to Henry Kissinger, suffered from "the Russian mania for new conquests." Only a few "were wise enough to realize that, for Russia, 'the extension of territory was the extension of weakness.' . . . In the end, the communist empire collapsed for essentially the same reasons that the tsars' had."[57]

If a "mania for conquests" links the current elites to the tsarist and Soviet past, so does the neglect of the condition of the Russian people. When Alexander Solzhenitsyn asserts that a Russian nation does not exist today, his words bring to mind the points both Pipes and Got'e made about the 1917 era. Solzhenitsyn deplores "the stratification of Russians as if into two separate nations" and illustrates his meaning as follows: "The immense provincial-village heartland, and an entirely disparate minority in the capital, alien to it in thought and westernized in culture." Solzhenitsyn sees a sign of Russia's national "catastrophe" in "today's amorphous state of Russian national consciousness, in the grey indifference toward one's national affinity and an even greater apathy to compatriots in dire straits." One does not need to share his views or accept his language but he does offer an insight into the condition of Russia that usually escapes the attention of observers—as revealed by their astonishment at how the Russians vote. The real catastrophe of Russia, says Solzhenitsyn, is summed up in these words: "our dying out."[58]

What Solzhenitsyn calls a national "catastrophe," professional demographer V. I. Kozlov describes in only slightly less apocalyptic terms: "The Extinction of the Russians: A Historic-Demographic Crisis or a Catastrophe?"[59] Kozlov says that if the current trends continue, by 2000 the number of Russians in the Russian Federation will decrease by 7 to 9 million compared with 1989, while in "the new abroad" the number of Russians will be down to 20 million (from about 25 million). Kozlov notes with some concern that in 1989 the Russian Federation's net population gain was 289,200 Russians and 287,100 non-Russians. (His concern is understandable, for in 1989 there were 119.9 million Russians in the Russian Federation, where they constituted 81.5 percent of its population.) It is impossible to tell whether the current (as of March 1996) president of Russia and his defense minister have thought of the long-term implications of Chechnya in light of these statistics.[60]

In his account of his mission to Moscow, the former U.S. ambassador to the USSR, Jack F. Matlock, concluded that

Two things do seem as certain as anything in human affairs can be:
1. The Soviet system cannot be rebuilt. . . . 2. The Russian empire cannot be reassembled, even if the Russian people nurse an emotional attachment for an ill-understood past and are periodically victimized by demagogues. Only a healthy Russian economy could bear the cost, but the economy cannot be cured if Russia embarks on an imperialist course.[61]

Matlock reminded his readers that "Russia can no longer afford an empire, however acquired. If the twentieth century taught us anything, it is that empires are costly burdens." He also noted an aspect that is strangely missing in Russian thinking about how to restore the empire: the expected resistance by the former republics. For Russia too, he thought, "internal nation-building is the principal challenge. . . . Russia . . . must, in the long run, reform or fall apart."[62]

History teaches that nations, and their leaders, rarely learn their lessons. There is no guarantee that wise and friendly counsel like that offered by the former ambassador will be taken into account by those who form Russian opinion or those who make decisions for their country.

In 1991, it looked as if Russia would lead the entire post-Soviet space in economic reforms and democratization—just as before Russia had been the driving force of Sovietization. Those Russians who had not accepted the disintegration of the empire but who supported democracy and a market economy had reason to hope that Russia's political and cultural leadership in de-Sovietization would make it possible for the Russian empire to be restored—this time in a liberal or "Western" form.

For this to have a chance to happen, however, economic and political reforms had to be safe in Russia itself. In 1996, this was less obviously the case than it had been five years earlier. Politically, the Communists have been able to gain most from the condition—and mood—that Solzhenitsyn describes. The Communists are also the most determined and best organized promoters of imperial restoration—but their vision of "re-integration" is not that of the democrats or liberals. Today's Russians, like those of an earlier generation, have to choose between different Russias, and not simply between competing parties and leaders. Do they prefer a territorially diminished Russia as it exists now, struggling to build a democracy and a market economy, or a Russia which the Communists promise will bring back to them Kyiv and Tashkent and more, but at the cost of democracy and a free economy?

Notes

1. Among the earliest attempts to set the agenda for such future investigations, see Alexander Dallin, "Causes of the Collapse of the USSR," *Post-Soviet Affairs* 8, no. 4 (October-December 1992): 279–302. For comparative approaches to the study of imperial decline and the rise of nations, see essays by Richard L. Rudolph, Alexander J. Motyl, William O. McCagg, Jr., Miroslav Hroch and John-Paul Himka, in Richard L. Rudolph and David F. Good, eds., *Nationalism and Empire. The Habsburg Empire and the Soviet Union* (New York: St. Martin's Press, 1992), pp. 3–93.

2. For a sound and concise outline of the relevant history, see "The Legacies of History" in Karen Dawisha and Bruce Parrott, *Russia and the New States of Eurasia: The Politics of Upheaval* (Cambridge and New York: Cambridge University Press, 1994), pp. 23–56.

3. Ghita Ionescu, *The Break-up of the Soviet Empire in Eastern Europe* (Baltimore, Md.: Penguin, 1965), p. 7.

4. Dominic Lieven, "The Russian Empire and the Soviet Union as Imperial Polities," *Journal of Contemporary History* 30 (1995): 607–36. Quotation on p. 608.

5. Istvan Hont, "The Permanent Crisis of a Divided Mankind: 'Contemporary Crisis of the Nation State' in Historical Perspective," in John Dunn, ed., *Contemporary Crisis of the Nation State?* (Oxford, Eng., and Cambridge, Mass: Blackwell, 1995), p. 172, quoting from Michael W. Doyle, *Empires* (Ithaca: Cornell University Press, 1986), p. 45.

6. Andreas Kappeler, *Russland als Vielvölkerreich. Entstehung, Geschichte, Zerfall* (Munich: C. H. Beck, 1992), pp. 25–56.

7. Richard Pipes, "Introduction: The Nationality Problem," in Zev Katz, Rosemarie Rogers, and Frederic Harned, eds., *Handbook of Major Soviet Nationalities* (New York: Free Press; London: Collier Macmillan, 1975), p. 2n.

8. Edward L. Keenan, "Muscovy and Kazan: Some Introductory Remarks on the Patterns of Steppe Diplomacy," *Slavic Review* 26, no. 3 (1967): 548–58.

9. Nikolai Sergeevich Trubetskoy, "The Ukrainian Problem," *The Legacy of Genghis Khan and Other Essays on Russia's Identity,* ed. Anatoly Liberman (Ann Arbor, Mich.: Michigan Slavic Publications, 1991); pp. 244–67; originally published as "K ukrainskoi probleme," *Evraziiskii vremennik,* 5 (1927): 165–84.

10. Linda Colley, *Britons: Forging the Nation, 1707–1837* (New Haven: Yale University Press, 1992), p. 6: "Great Britain did not emerge by way of a 'blending' of the different regional or older national cultures contained within

424 Russia, Ukraine, and the Breakup of the Soviet Union

its boundaries. . . . Britishness was superimposed over an array of internal differences in response to contact with the Other, and above all in response to conflict with the Other." Thus, what united the English, Scots, and Welsh was their shared hostility to Catholicism—but this also kept the Irish out of the British nation. We should not assume a priori that in Russia the distance between the Orthodox and the Moslems made it impossible for them to fight together against a common "Other." In fact, on many occasions Russia's Moslems fought together with the Orthodox Russians against Catholic and Protestant powers. But this is something the Russians later chose not to remember. (See note 55.)

11. Kappeler, *Russland als Vielvölkerreich*, p. 179.

12. František Graus, "Slavs and Germans," in Geoffrey Barraclough, ed., *Eastern and Western Europe in the Middle Ages* (New York: Harcourt Brace Jovanovich, 1970), p. 26.

13. Kappeler, *Russland als Vielvölkerreich*, pp. 9–18, especially p. 15.

14. Geoffrey Hosking, "The Freudian Frontier," *Times Literary Supplement*, March 10, 1995, p. 27, review of Susan Layton, *Russian Literature and Empire: The Conquest of the Caucasus from Pushkin to Tolstoy* (Cambridge: Cambridge University Press, 1994). See also Mark Bassin, "Russia between Europe and Asia: The Ideological Construction of Geographical Space," *Slavic Review* 50, no. 1 (Spring 1991): 1–17.

15. Edward L. Keenan, "On Certain Mythical Beliefs and Russian Behaviors," in S. Frederick Starr, ed., *The Legacy of History in Russia and the New States of Eurasia* (Armonk, N.Y., and London: M. E. Sharpe, 1994), p. 27.

16. Keenan, "On Certain Mythical Beliefs," p. 23. See also Keenan, "Muscovite Perceptions of Other East Slavs before 1654—An Agenda for Historians," in Peter J. Potichnyj, Marc Raeff, Jaroslaw Pelenski, and Gleb N. Zekulin, eds., *Ukraine and Russia in Their Historical Encounter* (Edmonton: Canadian Institute of Ukrainian Studies Press, 1992), pp. 20–38.

17. See, for example, David Saunders, *The Ukrainian Impact on Russian Culture, 1750–1850* (Edmonton: Canadian Institute of Ukrainian Studies Press, 1985); Zenon E. Kohut, *Russian Centralism and Ukrainian Autonomy. Imperial Absorption of the Hetmanate, 1760s–1830s* (Cambridge, Mass.: Ukrainian Research Institute, distr. by Harvard University Press, 1988), and Marc Raeff, "Ukraine and Imperial Russia: Intellectual and Political Encounters from the Seventeenth to the Nineteenth Century," in Potichnyj et al., *Ukraine and Russia*, pp. 69–85. For a broader perspective on the nineteenth-century Polish-Ukrainian-Russian triangle, see two strikingly original monographs by Daniel Beauvois: *Le noble, le serf et le revizor: La noblesse polonaise entre le tsarisme et les masses ukrainiennes (1831–1863)* (Paris: Archives contemporaines, 1984), and *La Bataille de la terre en Ukraine, 1863–1914: Les polonais et les conflits socio-ethniques* (Lille: Presses Universitaires de Lille, 1993).

18. Andrzej Walicki, "Russian Social Thought. An Introduction to the Intellectual History of Nineteenth-Century Russia," *Russian Review* 36, no. 1 (January 1977): 1–45.

19. This may be the place to note that, as Alfred J. Rieber has argued, the imperial Russian historical experience included importantly "a struggle on two levels for hegemony over the borderlands"—with the peoples the empire ruled or sought to rule, and with other empires. See Rieber, "Struggle over the Borderlands," in Starr, ed., *The Legacy of History*, pp. 61–89. This aspect of imperial history is not directly related to our argument and cannot be addressed here.

20. Alfred J. Rieber has drawn attention to a very close interconnection between the problem of the non-Russian nationalities and the revolutionary movement in Russia proper. The policies of Russification directed against the minorities generated not only nationalism in response but also facilitated the spread of revolutionary agitation, the ideas of populism, and Marxism, among the Finnish, Jewish, Baltic, and Transcaucasian populations. It was the more assimilated non-Russians who joined the Russian revolutionary movement. "In 1905 the tsarist autocracy reaped the whirlwind of its errant cultural sowing." (Alfred J. Rieber, "Struggle over the Borderlands," p. 81.)

21. Richard Pipes, *Russia under the Bolshevik Regime* (New York: Alfred A. Knopf, 1993), pp. 494, 497.

22. Ibid., p. 493.

23. Mark R. Beissinger, "The Persisting Ambiguity of Empire," *Post-Soviet Affairs* 2, no. 2 (1995): 160.

24. John-Paul Himka, "The National and the Social in the Ukrainian Revolution of 1917–20: The Historiographical Agenda," *Archiv für Sozialgeschichte* 34 (1994): 95–110. Himka writes on p. 110: "As important as the assimilation of the new social history of the Russian revolution is, the history of the Ukrainian revolution . . . had something more to it than the Russian revolution: the national factor."

25. Ronald Grigor Suny, "Ambiguous Categories: States, Empires and Nations," *Post-Soviet Affairs* 11, no. 2 (1995): 192: "Muscovy and Imperial Russia were successful in integrating the core regions of their empire, often referred to as the *vnutrennie guberniya*, into a single nationality, but . . . maintained and intensified differences between the Russian core and the non-Russian peripheries." Interestingly enough, also in his *The Revenge of the Past. Nationalism, Revolution, and the Collapse of the Soviet Union* (Stanford: Stanford University Press, 1993), Suny analyzes all the major nationalities problems in the Russian empire in and after 1917—with one exception, the Russians, as if the revolution and civil war had not been *the* Russian national problem.

26. Pipes, *Russia under the Bolshevik Regime*, p. 497.

27. Iurii Vladimirovich Got'e, *Time of Troubles: The Diary of Iurii Vladimirovich Got'e*, ed. and trans. by Terence Emmons (Princeton: Princeton Uni-

versity Press, 1988), p. 103. Earlier, on November 16, 1917, Got'e wrote: ". . . Russia is betraying and selling out, and the Russian people wreak havoc and raise hell and are absolutely indifferent to their international fate. It is an unprecedented event in world history when a numerous people, which considers itself a great people, a world power despite all kinds of qualifications, has in eight months dug itself a grave with its own hands. It follows that the very idea of a Russian power, a Russian nation, was a mirage, a bluff, that this only seemed to be so and was never a reality." (*Time of Troubles*, pp. 80–81.) The view that "1917"—meaning November 1917—stands for a national catastrophe in Russian history has more recently been stated by many Russians, including those who blame the policies of the tsarist empire for the conditions that made that catastrophe possible. Thus, for example, Ilia Gerasimov, "Rossiiskaia mental'nost' i modernizatsiia," *Obshchestvennye nauki i sovremennost'*, no. 4 (1994): 72, sees in the year 1917 "the failure of the Russian national idea." For an identical evaluation of 1917, see also Boris Zemtsov, "'Otkuda est' poshla . . . rossiiskaia tsivilizatsiia,'" *Obshchestvennye nauki i sovremennost'*, no. 4 (1994): 51–62.

28. Ernest Gellner, "Nationalism in the Vacuum," in Alexander J. Motyl, ed., *Thinking Theoretically about Soviet Nationalities, History and Comparison in the Study of the USSR* (New York: Columbia University Press, 1992), p. 247.

29. Robert J. Kaiser, *The Geography of Nationalism in Russia and the USSR* (Princeton: Princeton University Press, 1994).

30. Piotr S. Wandycz, *Soviet-Polish Relations, 1917–1921* (Cambridge, Mass.: Harvard University Press, 1969), Norman Davies, *White Eagle, Red Star: The Polish-Soviet War, 1919–1920* (London: Macdonald, 1972); and Paul Latawski, ed., *The Reconstruction of Poland, 1914–1923* (London: Macmillan, 1992).

31. For an argument that Soviet "internationalist" outlook should be taken seriously even when the USSR had allegedly been a nationalist power, see Roman Szporluk, "Conflict in Soviet Domestic and Foreign Policy: Universal Ideology and National Tradition," in William Zimmerman and Harold K. Jacobson, eds., *Behavior, Culture, and Conflict in World Politics* (Ann Arbor: University of Michigan Press, 1993), pp. 275–90, in which some of relevant literature is cited.

32. For my earlier attempt to address this question see "After Empire: What?" *Daedalus* 123, no. 3 (Summer 1994): 21–39. (Reprinted as chapter 14 of this book.)

33. There are many good studies of the Baltic states under the Soviets and their struggle for independence, e.g., Anatol Lieven, *The Baltic Revolution: Estonia, Latvia, Lithuania, and the Path to Independence* (New Haven: Yale University Press, 1993). For a brief overview that includes the Balts, as well as West

Ukrainians and West Belorussians and Moldavians, see Roman Szporluk, "The Soviet West—or Far Eastern Europe?" *East European Politics and Societies* 3, no. 3 (Fall 1991): 466–82. (Reprinted as chapter 9 of this book.)

34. Zbigniew Brzezinski, *The Soviet Bloc: Unity and Conflict* (Cambridge, Mass.: Harvard University Press, 1960) is a classic.

35. Rupert Emerson, *From Empire to Nation. The Rise to Self-Assertion of Asian and African Peoples* (Boston: Beacon Press, 1960), p. 36.

36. Raymond Pearson, "The Making of '89: Nationalism and the Dissolution of Communist Eastern Europe," *Nations and Nationalism* 1, no. 1 (1995): 69–79, citation on p. 75.

37. Eric Hobsbawm, *The Age of Extremes: A History of the World, 1914–1991* (New York: Pantheon Books, 1994), p. 491.

38. Ibid., p. 475.

39. Ernest Gellner, "Nationalism in the Vacuum," in Motyl, ed., *Thinking Theoretically*, p. 248.

40. Kenneth Minogue and Beryl Williams, "Ethnic Conflict in the Soviet Union: The Revenge of Particularism," in Motyl, ed., *Thinking Theoretically*, p. 241.

41. Benedict Anderson, *Imagined Communities: Reflections on the Origin and Spread of Nationalism* (London: Verso, 1983), p. 12, and rev. ed. (London and New York: Verso, 1991), p. xi.

42. See, for example, Joseph Rothschild, *Return to Diversity: A Political History of East Central Europe since World War II* (New York and Oxford: Oxford University Press, 1989), pp. 75 and 221; and Ken Jowitt, *New World Disorder: The Leninist Extinction* (Berkeley and Los Angeles: University of California Press, 1992), pp. 217–18.

43. Randall Collins, *Weberian Sociological Theory* (Cambridge and New York: Cambridge University Press, 1986), pp. 203, 208.

44. N. V. Ustrialov, "O sovetskoi natsii," in *Nashe vremia* (Shanghai: n.p., 1934), pp. 38–39, cited in Roman Szporluk, "Nationalities and the Russian Problem in the USSR," *Journal of International Affairs* 27, no. 1 (1973): 40 [reprinted in this book as chapter 1]. For the contrary argument that "the Soviet Union was not conceived or institutionalized as a nation-state," see Rogers Brubaker, "Nationhood and the national question in the Soviet Union and post-Soviet Eurasia: An institutional account," *Theory and Society* 23, no. 1 (February 1994): 50–52. (See also Suny, "Ambiguous Categories," *Post-Soviet Affairs* 11, no. 2 (1995): 190, for this astonishing comment: "There was shockingly little effort to create a 'Soviet nation.' ") I would also qualify the view that the Soviets institutionalized ethnicity at the republic level. This was the case mainly in the cultural sphere. (Ukrainian schools existed only in Ukraine, Latvian only in Latvia, etc.) Soviet propaganda took great pride that most republics were "already" multiethnic and were becoming more so; for this reason it singled out

Kazakhstan, where Kazakhs were a minority, as a model Soviet republic. An interrepublic "exchange of cadres" was an openly proclaimed policy. For an excellent analysis of the Soviet approach to nationality and ethnicity, see Teresa Rakowska-Harmstone, "Chickens Coming Home to Roost: A Perspective on Soviet Ethnic Relations," *Journal of International Affairs* 45, no. 2 (1992): 519–48; and Anatoly M. Khazanov, *After the USSR: Ethnicity, Nationalism, and Politics in the Commonwealth of Independent States* (Madison and London: University of Wisconsin Press, 1995), pp. 3–51.

45. Eric Hobsbawm, *The Age of Extremes: A History of the World, 1914–1991* (New York: Pantheon Books, 1994), first citation, p. 492; second, p. 483.

46. Khazanov, *After the USSR*, p. 28. Cf. ibid., p. 231: "Authoritarian capitalism suppresses civil society but still has to tolerate . . . some forms of societal self-organization. . . . In contrast, totalitarian communism resulted in the utter destruction of civil society." John A. Hall, *Coercion and Consent: Studies on the Modern State* (Cambridge, Mass.: Polity Press, 1994), p. 146, stresses that "one important legacy of communism, namely its destruction of civil society . . . made the liberalization of communist regimes virtually impossible."

47. Collins, *Weberian Sociological Theory*, p. 204.

48. Ibid., p. 207.

49. John Barber, "Russia: A Crisis of Post-imperial Viability," in John Dunn, ed., *Contemporary Crisis of the Nation State*, p. 39. See also John B. Dunlop, *The Rise of Russia and the Fall of the Soviet Empire* (Princeton: Princeton University Press, 1993), and "Russia: Confronting a Loss Of Empire," in Ian Bremmer and Ray Taras, eds., *Nations and Politics in the Soviet Successor States* (Cambridge and New York: Cambridge University Press, 1993), pp. 43–72.

50. Barber, "Russia: A Crisis," p. 40.

51. George F. Kennan, "Witness to the Fall," *New York Review of Books* 42, November 16, 1995, p. 10. (Review of Jack F. Matlock, Jr., *Autopsy on an Empire: The American Ambassador's Account of the Collapse of the Soviet Union*. New York: Random House, 1995.)

52. Mark R. Beissinger, "The Persisting Ambiguity of Empire," p. 158.

53. Khazanov, *After the USSR*, pp. 239–40.

54. Roman Solchanyk, "Russia, Ukraine, and the Imperial legacy," *Post-Soviet Affairs* 9, no. 4 (1993): 337–65, and "Ukraine, The (Former) Center, Russia, and 'Russia,' " *Studies in Comparative Communism* 25, no. 1 (March 1992): 31–45, analyze the current political problem against a historical background.

55. "Rossiia v usloviiakh strategicheskoi nestabil'nosti. (Materialy 'kruglogo stola')," *Voprosy filosofii*, no. 9 (1995): 7. It is ironic that Moiseev also felt the need to tell his elite audience that "few people remember that during the seizure of Kazan all regiments of the Russian army were under command of Tatar princes—not those descended from Genghis-khan but the natives of the Volga

region." (Ibid., p. 4.) (Moiseev also had a strongly negative commentary on the West Ukrainians, whom he thought had been corrupted by the Catholic West and thus had acquired a "mentality" more alien than that of the Tatars.)

56. According to Galina Starovoitova (lecture at Harvard University, March 12, 1996), the establishment of the "Islamic Party of Russia" and its participation in the elections of December 1995 should be seen as one of the repercussions of the Chechnya crisis in Russia's politics. For ethno-political processes among the Tatars and the Chuvash in Russia today, see Victor A. Shnirelman, *Who Gets the Past? Competition for Ancestors among Non-Russian Intellectuals in Russia* (Washington: The Woodrow Wilson Center Press; Baltimore and London: Johns Hopkins University Press, 1996).

57. Henry Kissinger, *Diplomacy* (New York: Simon and Schuster, 1994), p. 176. Kissinger concludes: "The Soviet Union would have been much better off had it stayed within its borders after the Second World War and established relations with what came to be known as the satellite orbit comparable to those it maintained with Finland." (Ibid.) This brings to mind Khazanov's maxim: "Overextension is a common pitfall of empires." (*After the USSR*, p. 10.)

58. See Aleksandr Solzhenitsyn, *"The Russian Question" at the End of the Twentieth Century*, trans. by Yermolai Solzhenitsyn (New York: Farrar, Straus and Giroux, 1995), pp. 104–5.

59. V. I. Kozlov, "Vymiranie russkikh: istoriko-demograficheskii krizis ili katastrofa?" *Vestnik Rossiiskoi Akademii Nauk* 65, no. 9 (September 1995): 771–77. See also Mark G. Field, "The Health Crisis in the Former Soviet Union: A Report from the 'Post-War' Zone," *Social Science and Medicine* 41, no. 11 (1995): 1469–78.

60. See Khazanov, *After the USSR*, pp. 247–71, for important data on ethnic trends in various parts of the former Soviet Union, especially in Central Asia and the Russian Federation.

61. Jack F. Matlock, Jr., *Autopsy of an Empire: The American Ambassador's Account of the Collapse of the Soviet Union* (New York: Random House, 1995), p. 737.

62. Ibid., pp. 738–39. For a discussion of Russian national and state identity in the framework of the Russian Federation today, see Marie Mendras, "La Russie dans les têtes," *Commentaire* 18, no. 71 (Autumn 1995): 501–9.

Index

About the Author

ROMAN SZPORLUK is the Mykhailo Hrushevsky Professor of Ukrainian History and director of the Ukrainian Research Institute at Harvard University. Szporluk received degrees from Lublin State University, Oxford University, and Stanford University. He is a member of the American Association for the Advancement of Slavic Studies.

Szporluk's previous books include *The Political Thought of Thomas G. Masaryk* and *Communism and Nationalism: Karl Marx versus Friedrich List.* He was editor of *Russia in World History, The Influence of East Europe and the Soviet West on the USSR,* and *National Identity and Ethnicity in Russia and the New States of Eurasia.* His interests include nationalism and Marxism in Ukraine, Russia, and Poland.